Abstracts of

Bucks County, Pennsylvania

Wills

1785-1825

Willow Bend Books
Westminster, Maryland
1999

Willow Bend Books

65 East Main Street
Westminster, Maryland 21157-5026
1-800-876-6103

Source books, early maps, CD's—Worldwide

For our listing of thousands of titles offered
by hundreds of publishers
see our website
<www.WillowBend.net>

Visit our retail store

Originally published in 1998

Reprinted in 1999

International Standard Book Number: 1-58549-158-6

Printed in the United States of America

INTRODUCTION

These wills were abstracted under the auspices of the Historical Society of Pennsylvania in the early 1900s. Copies of these abstracts were made available to various libraries in Pennsylvania and microfilm copies made by the Genealogical Society of Utah (LDS). Recently bound photostat copies of the abstracts were offered for sale by the Genealogical Society of Pennsylvania.

We extend our appreciation to the staffs of the Historical Society of Pennsylvania (1300 Locust Street, Philadelphia, PA 19107) and encourage use and support of its facilities and to the Genealogical Society of Pennsylvania whose collections are housed in the Historical Society Library. We also encourage membership in the Genealogical Society of Pennsylvania (1305 Locust Street, Philadelphia, PA 19107-5699).

F. Edward Wright
Westminster, Maryland
1998

Bucks County Townships

Book No. 4

Page 383. William Milnor of Falls, Husbandman. 2-20-1785. Proved 4-7-1785. Wife Rachel and son Jonathan exrs. Sons Jonathan, Stephen and David. Daus. Sarah Martin, Priscilla Merrick, Rebecca Hulme (wife of John), Phebe Crozier and Rachel Milnor -grdau. Marsha Milnor.
Wits: Joseph Gillingham, Michael Wasley, Wheeler Clark.
Land purchased of Michael and Randle Hutchinson, Joseph Kirklinde and Thomas Riche.

Page 385. Joseph Tomlinson of Upper Makfield, yeoman. 4-1-1785. Proved 4-18-1785. William and Joseph Chapman exrs. Son Richard; dau[s]. Elinor Comfort and Mary Atkinson. Gdsn. Joseph Tomlinson son of Joseph. Son John dec'd. left widow Margaret and children John, William, Henry and Hannah. Margaret and Hannah daus. of son Joseph. Farm bought of George Mitchell adj. John Rose and Mary White. Bonds of Richard Worthington, Isaac Kirk and Joseph Martindale.
Wits: John Verity, Hamton Wilson, Joseph Chapman.

Page 388. John Brittian of Plumstead Twp. yeoman. 3-21-1770. Proved 5-2-1785. Sons Nathaniel and Nathan exrs. Wife Elizabeth. Sons William, Nathaniel, Nathan, Joseph and Benjamin. Daus. Elizabeth wife of Edward Morris, Anna wife of William Young, Hannah wife of Peter Cosner, Mary wife of James Lewis and Martha wife of Edward Poe. Lot adj. Peter Cosner and Robert Gibson.
Wits: Joseph Michener and James Erwin.

Page 390. Abraham Black, Gentleman of Bedminster, yeoman. 11-6-1784. Proved 5-4-1785. Bro.-in-law David Culp and Merrick Hoffman exrs. Sons Abraham, Benjamin and Isaac. Dec'd. sons John and Jacob. Dau. Margaret wife of Jacob Wismer and her son Abraham Wismer. Son-in-law John Overholt.
Wits: Abraham Kulp, Jacob Overholt.

Page 392. Jacob Fox of Bedminster Twp. yeoman. 3-31-1783. Proved. 6-14-1785. Michael Teaterly and Peter Stout exrs. Wife Catharine. Sons Jacob, John, George, Dewald and Nicholas.
Wits: Valentine Marsteller and Henry Frets/Fretes.

Page 394. Morris Fell of Richland Twp. yeoman. 11-22-1785. Proved 12-14-1785. William Penrose and John Griffith exrs. Bro. Amos Richardson. 4 bros. and 3 sisters not named. Sarah Kirk dau. of Stephen dec'd.
Wits: Joseph Penrose, Abraham Ball, William Heacock, Jr.

Page 396. Thomas Kelsoe of New Britain, yeoman. 11-8-1785. Proved

12-13-1785. Robert Urir and Samuel Urir exrs. Wife Jeane. Son Hendrey. Daus. Jean, Ann and Margaret.
Wits: Augustius McDaniel, James Snodgrass.

Page 397. Mary Burges of Solebury Twp. 1-31-1783. Proved 11-16-1785. Friends Thomas Smith and William Blackfan exrs. Son Thomas Burges. Daus. Sarah Pitcock and Elizabeth Wilkinson. Goddaus. Sarah dau. of Joseph Burges, Mary dau. of Hugh Burges, Elizabeth, Martha, Ann and Ester daus. of John Smith. Mary, Hannah, Sarah and Ann daus. of Thomas Lee.
Wits: Edward Blackfan and Thomas Smith.

Page 398. Laurence Erbach of Milford Twp., yeoman. 5-14-1785. Proved 11-15-1785. Son Jacob and son-in-law John Streeker exrs. Wife Anna Mary. Daus. Anne Mary wife of Theobald Samsel, Margaret wife of Jacob Rothrock, Barbara wife of John Strecket, Ann wife of John Huber and Catharine dec'd. late wife of David Groff.
Wits: Thos. Beyer, Abrm. Shelly.

Page 400. Christian Swarts of New Britain, yeoman. 11-2-1782. Proved 11-5-1785. Wife Catharine and son Andrew exrs. Sons Christain, Jacob and Andrew.
Wits: Andrew Rush, Henry Wisner.

Page 402. Joseph Wilkinson of Solebury Twp. 10-11-1785. Proved 10-28-1785. Cousin Joseph Chapman and friend John Hillrun exrs. Mother Sarah Wilkinson. Sisters Mary, Zebiah wife of Peter Jenks, Sarah wife of John Price. Joseph Prior son of sister Huldah dec'd. wife of Charles Prior.
Wits: Johannes Van Etter, Thomas Kyle, James Chapman.

Page 404. Tamer Wilkinson of Wrightstown Twp. 4-4-1785. Proved 10-11-1785. Nephew John Chapman exr. Sister Mary Twining. Rachel and Tamer Twining daus. of sister Mary. Mother-in-law Hannah Wilkinson. Bro. Stephen Wilkinson. Half-bro. Elisha Wilkinson. Half-sisters Martha, Ann and Hannah Wilkinson.
Wits: Mahlon Twining, Eleazer Twining, John Terry Jr.

Page 406. John Slack of Lower Makefield, yeoman. 8 mo.-12-1785. Proved 10-1-1785. Sons Cornelius and Philip exrs. Sons Cornelius, Thomas, Joseph, Timothy, Philip, John and Noah.
Wits: Thomas Winder, William Brooks, Jos. Hicks.

Page 407. Samuel Hillborn of Newtown. 8-30-1785. Proved 10-1-1785. Wife Ruth. Son Robert and Friend John Story exrs. Daus. Ann, Ruth, Hannah and Mary Hillborn.
Wits: Robert Hillborn, Thomas Story and David Story.

Page 408. Joseph Dungan of Warwick, yeoman. 6-16-1783. Proved 9-15-1785. Son Joshua exr. Wife Mary. Sons Thomas and Joshua. Daus. Sarah wife of Benjamin Courson and Hannah wife of Benjamin Marpole.
Wits: Mary Yerkes, Harman Yerkes, Jos. Hart.

Page 410. Thomas Richey, Gentleman of Warrington, yeoman. 9-1-1785. Proved 9-14-1785. Sons John and William Craig exrs. Sons, John, Thomas, David and William. Daus. Martha wife of Abraham Hollas, Ann Richey and Agnes wife of son David.
Wits: David Thompson and Robert Thompson.

Page 412. Bathsheba Griffith of Blockley Phila. 5-5-1783. Proved 9-5-1785. Dau. Sarah Griffith exr. Gdch. Joseph Griffith and Abraham, Isaac, Bathsheba, Mary, Jacob and Thomas Heston and Ann Webb.
Wits: Anthony Williams, James Jones Jr.

Page 413. Jeremiah Dungan of Northampton, yeoman. 7-29-1785. Proved 9-3-1785. Sons Thomas and Solomon exrs. Daus. Susanna Van Pelt, Mary, Elizabeth and Martha Dungan. Sons Jeremiah, Thomas, Solomon and Amos. Gdsn. Gilbert son of dau. Mary Dugan. Gdch. Thomas and Mary Vanada.
Wits: David Dungan, Hugh Edams, Gayen Edams.

Page 414. Mary Roberts of Solebury Twp., widow. Aug. 13, 1785. Proved Sept. 1, 1785. Friend Anthony Hartly exr. Daus. Jane and Margery. Sons Richard and William. Gdch. Joseph and Samuel sons of Henry Roberts dec'd. David and Elizabeth Roberts ch. of Thomas dec'd. Joseph, Nathan and Marsa Williams ch. of dau. Mary dec'd.
Wits: Daniel Hough, Henry Bennett, David Forsh.

Page 416. Gilliam Cornell of Northampton, yeoman. July 8, 1785. Proved Aug. 19, 1785. Wife Margaret. Son Abraham and nephew Gilliam Cornell son of Adrian exrs. Sons Gilliam and John when 21. Daus. Phebe, Cornelia, Margaret and Maria Cornell.
Wits: Thomas Wilson, John Cornell.

Page 418. John Smith of Plumstead son and exr. of Thomas Smith dec'd. 7-30-1785 Proved Aug. 17, 1785. Bros. Aaron and Nehemiah exrs. Sister Ann.
Wits: Thos. Ellicott, Rebecka Ellicott.

Page 419. George Suber of Middletown Twp. Feb. 17, 1785. Proved Aug. 13, 1785. Wife Mary and son Joseph exrs. Wife's ch. Jacob Torbert and Elizabeth Brow. Sons Joseph, Benjamin and George. Daus. Mary and Sarah.
Wits: Joseph Moode, Abner Buckman and Jonathan Carlile.

Page 420. Derrick Kroesen of Southampton, Gentleman. May 2, 1783. Proved Jan. 10, 1786. Codicil April 30, 1784. Dau. Else Vanarsdalen and sons Henry and Derrick exrs. Son Derrick's son Derrick.
Wits: Leonard Kroesen, Mathew Light, Garret Kroesen.

Page 423. Thomas Winder of Lower Makefield, yeoman. Dec. 6, 1785. Proved Jan. 12, 1786. Wife Elizabeth. Son Joseph and Bro. Aaron exrs. Daus. Mary and Rebecca. Land adj. Cornelius Vansant lot of Benj. Canby.
Wits: Sarah Campbell, Hannah Brooks, Is. Hicks.

Page 425. Isaac Bennett of Northampton Twp., Farmer. Jan. 14, 1786. Proved Jan. 30, 1786. Wife Mary. Gerardus Wynkoop and Arthur Leffertson exrs. Sons Isaac and William. Daus. Elizabeth and Lena.
Wits: Arthur Bennett and Henry Feastur.

Page 426. Leonard Shaver of Lower Maxfield. Feb. 11, 1786. Proved Feb. 28, 1786. Thomas Jenks Jr. and sons Henry and John Shaver exrs. Sons Joseph and Jacob. Daus. Mary wife of Cornelius Mehan, Ann Shaver, Elizabeth wife of Henry Hile and Annah Shaver.
Wits. John Nield, John Martindell and Jonathan Carlile.

Page 427. Fulkhart Vandegrift Senior of Bensalem Twp., yeoman. April 20, 1774. Proved Nov. 7, 1775. 1st Codicil April 12, 1775; 2nd Aug. 16, 1775. Son Fulkhart exr. Sons Harman, Abraham, Cornelius, John. Daus. Elizabeth Krusen, Alice Larew and Elinor Vandegrift. Gdsn. George Vandegrift.
Wits: Thos. Evens, John Evens. 1st Codicil Bro. Abraham.
Wits: John Evens, Thomas Snodden. 2nd Codicil Aunt Margaret Reynerson, widow and relict of Hendrick Reynerson, yeoman, formerly of Rariton N.J. Said Margaret being now dec'd.
Wits: William McKissack, Jacob Jackson.

Page 431. John Preston of Buckingham, yeoman. Aug. 7, 1767. Proved Jan. 21, 1786. Wife Sarah. Sons William and John exrs. and sole legatees. Land on Durham Road adj. Levi Fell and land late John Bogart's.
Wits: Samuel Fenton, Josiah Fenton, Jas. Irwin.

Page 432. Thomas Bye of Buckingham, yeoman. 6-24-1784. Proved March 21, 1786. Son Thomas exr. Gdsns. Joseph and Benjamin Wilson, sons of dau. Margaret Wilson dec'd. Daus. Martha Longstreth, Elizabeth Hutchinson and Lydia Woolston. Gdsn. Thomas Hutchinson. Gddau. Mary Bye dau. of Thomas.
Wits: John Kinsey, James Simpson, Nathan Doan, Benjamin Doan.

Page 434. Elizabeth Hogeland of Wrightstown. Feb. 15, 1786. Proved

March 27, 1786. Sister Catharine Vansant and Bro.-in-law Jacob
Bennet exrs. Sister Anna Bennett.
Wits: Thomas Warner, John Terry Jr., Thomas Smith.

Page 435. Martha Beal, widow of John Beal of Buckingham. May 16,
1783. Proved March 31, 1786. Son John Beal exr. Dau. Phebe wife of
John Tucker. Gddau. Rebekah Beal.
Wits: John Melone, Watson Welding, Joseph Watson.

Page 436. Mary Purssell, widow of John Purssell of Bristol Twp. 12-18-
1785. Proved April 7, 1786. James Moon of Middletown and Moses
Moon, his son, exrs. Son Mahlon Purssell. Son-in-law Jonathan
Purssell. Dau.-in-law Ann Purssell. Friends John and Elizabeth Nutt.
Bro. John Logan.
Wits: Danl. Wharton Junr., Wm. Wharton.

Page 437. Mary Richardson, widow of Joseph Richardson late of
Middletown, Merchant, dec'd. 3-15-1783. Proved April 7, 1786. Dau.
Ruth Richardson extx. Sons Joshua and William Richardson. Daus.
Rebecca wife of Thos. Jenks Junr. and Mary and Ruth Richardson. Son
Joshua's daus. Martha and Ruth. Son William's dau. Martha
Richardson.
Wits: James Moon, Benjamin Watson, Joseph Hayhurst, Deborah
Hayhurst.

Page 439. Robert Fisher, Buckingham, yeoman. 5-7-1784. Proved June
8, 1784. Daniel Stradling and Bro.-in-law Paul Preston exrs. Bros.
Samuel, Joseph, Barack dec'd. Sisters Sarah Michener, Elizabeth
Lees, Hannah Preston, Deborah Burgess and Katharine Hartley.
Sister-in-law Mary Butler - widow and ch. of Bro. Barack. Nephew
Barak Michener. Niece Deborah Preston.
Wits: Jos. Pickering, John Walton, Jonathan Beans.

Page 441. Robert Lucas of Falls Twp. 4-17-1784. Codicil 5-10-1784.
Proved June 15, 1784. Wife Sarah. Sons-in-law Daniel Lovet and
Benjamin Pitfield exrs. Daus. Hannah Taylor, Sarah Spencer, Grace
Pitfield and Elizabeth Lovet. Gdsons. Benjamin Taylor, Mahlon
Spencer, Robert Pitfield, Mahlon Lovett. Mahlon Linton son of Joshua.
Codicil discharges Daniel Lovet as exr. and makes wife co-exr.
Wits: James Moon and Moses Moon.

Page 446. Mary Bowne of Bristol. 5-24-1777. Proved June 16, 1784.
Mother Grace Bowne and James Moon Junr. exrs. Sister Ann Boutcher
and her ch. Jonathan, Mary and Rebecca Boutcher.
Wits: Em. Williams, Pierson Mitchell, Joseph Church.

Page 447. William Carter of Northampton Twp., Miller. 3-31-1784.

Proved June 25, 1784. Wife Mary and Father-in-law William Hayhurst exrs. Ch. Joseph, William, Rebecca, James and John Carter all minors.
Wits: Jonth. Willet, John Leedom, John Leedom Junr.

Page 451. John Roberts of Warwick Twp. Dec. 19, 1775. Proved July 9, 1784. Son John exr. Son Jonathan. Daus. Lydia Livezey and Elizabeth Hibbs.
Wits: John Craig, Samuel Roberts, William Walker.

Page 452. Henry Hertzel of Rockhill Twp., yeoman. May 17, 1784. Proved Aug. 5, 1784. Sons Michael, Paul and Henry and son-in-law Abraham Stout exrs. Daus. Catharine, Christina, Margaret, Sophia, Magdalena, Elizabeth, Hannah and Susanna. Land in Hilltown adj. Adam Cobe, Ernest Hair, Isaac Derstine and Martin Clemmer. Land purchased of Adam Shriner in Rockhill and Upper Salford Twps. adj. Abraham Gerhart, Samuel Bechtel and Levi Thomas.
Wits: Jacob Hair, John Trumbout, Isaac Dirstine.

Page 455. Mary Roberts of Richland Twp., widow. 1-11-1781. Proved Aug. 14, 1784. Son-in-law Thomas Foulke and Friend Samuel Foulke exrs. Sons Abel, David, Nathan, Everard. Dau.-in-law Margaret Roberts. Daus. Mary and Jane. 3 eldest daus. of dau. Martha, her other ch. viz. Edward, William, John, Martha and Sarah.
Wits: Everard Foulke, Israel Foulke.

Page 457. Joseph Thomas of New Britain Twp, yeoman. June 17, 1784. Proved Sept. 3, 1784. "Aged and weak" wife Elizabeth and son Owen exrs. Getur Evans of Montgomery and Benjamin Thomas Trustees. Sons Thomas, James, Joseph, David and Owen. Daus. Mary Lewis, Johannah Jones, Ann Dungan, Elizabeth Morris. Gddau. Sarah Gelen.
Wits: David Loufbounon, Benjamin Thomas.

Page 461. Margaret Twining of Wrightstown. ---- 1779. Proved Oct. 6, 1784. Dau. Mary Chapman extx. Son Stephen Twining dec'd. Gdch. Stephen and Mary Twining. Nieces Mary Paxson and Elizabeth Hillborn.
Wits: Abrm. Chapman, David Twining, Robert Chapman.

Page 463. Jesse Bryan of Hilltown Twp., yeoman. May 14, 1784. Proved Oct. 19, 1784. Father-in-law William Dorroch and Bro. James Bryan exrs. Wife Rebecca. Son William. "Land I hold by Deed from my Father William Bryan in Northern Liberties." Land in Rockhill adj. John Heany, George Weisel and James Bryan.
Wits: Henry Wismer, Samuel Wallace, Thos. Jones, William Dorroch.

Page 466. William McIntyre of Tinecum Twp., yeoman. Sept. 23, 1784. Proved Oct. 22, 1784. Wife Jane and Thomas Stewart exrs. Cousin

Henry McIntyre, nephew Edward Newton, nephew William McIntyre of Schanactoda. Presbyterian church of Tiencum £50.
Wits. H. McIntyre, Robert Stewart Senr.

Page 468. John Duer of Lower Makefield, yeoman. May 24, 1783. Proved Aug. 25, 1784. Wife --- only son John exr. Dau. Elinor and her ch. Daniel and Jacob Dean.
Wits: Jos. Harvey, Benj. Hickman, Joseph Hicks. The dau. Eleanor was the wife of Joseph Clark as shown by release of Legacy on file with will.

Page 471. Charity Bennett of Northampton Twp., widow. Aug. 28, 1775. Proved Nov. 4, 1784. "Far advanced in years." Sons Isaac, William and John Bennett exrs. Dau. Lena wife of Thomas Craven, Yanaca wife of James Vansant and Iaah (Idah?) wife of Dirck Hogeland. Yanaca Bennett widow of son Richard dec'd. Charity VanPelt only dau. of son Richard dec'd. and her son Richard VanPelt.
Wits: Matthew Bennett, Robert Loller.

Page 473. Stephen Watts of Southampton, yeoman. Jan. 24, 1783. Proved Nov. 23, 1784. Wife Elizabeth. Son Arthur and Thomas Folwell exrs. Dau. Hannah Smith and her ch. James Smith, Hannah Baker, Stephen, John, Elizabeth, Thomas and Fanny Smith. Dau. Sarah Shaw and her ch. Elizabeth Colbert, Mary Fenton, Rachel Shaw, John and Joseph Shaw. Dau. Elizabeth wife of Thomas Folwell and her ch. Nancy, William, Elizabeth and Mary Folwell. Son Stephen Watts. Gddau. Rachel Watts, dau. of John Watts. £5 to Anti Baptist Church at Southampton.
Wits: John Folwell and William Van Horne.

Page 477. Balthazer Weinberger of Lower Milford Twp., weaver. Jan. 13, 1783. Proved Dec. 1, 1784. Wife Anna. Son John and John Stoufer exrs. Sons Balthazer, John and Samuel. Daus. Barbara, wife of Peter Landis and Elizabeth wife of John Landis.
Wits: Abraham Taylor and Samuel Foulke.

Page 479. Conrad Keil of New Britain, miller. May 10, 1779. Proved Nov. 18, 1784. Wife Elizabeth. Ludwick Switzer and Jacob Yoder exrs. Sons John, Jesse and Conrad. Daus. Susanna, Mary Anne and Elizabeth.
Wits: Jacob Schleiffer, Abrm. Stout, Thomas Stalford.

Page 482. Abraham Hibbs of Newtown Twp., yeoman. 10-19-1784. Proved Dec. 6, 1784. Wife Hannah and Valentine Nelson exrs. Son Benjamin. Daus. Mary, Hannah, Susanna, Pheaby and child unborn.
Wits: Robert Comfort, Ann Buckman, John Story.

Page 484. James Briggs of Newtown. 10-9-1784. Proved Dec. 6, 1784. Wife Ann. Sons William and James exrs. Son Moses. Dau. Rachel Heston's 3 ch. Tacy, David and Rachel Heston. Dau. Ann Wilson.
Wits: John Ballance, David Buckman Jr., John Story.

Page 486. Theobald Nase of Rockhill, yeoman. Oct. 27, 1784. Proved Dec. 14, 1784. Wife Barbara. Henry Kettleman and George Adam Kober exrs. Sons John, Nicholas and Henry. Daus. Barbara, Elizabeth and Catharina. Ch. of dau. Magdalena Kornecker dec'd.
Wits: Abraham Johns, Abrm. Stout, Peter Shneider.

Page 488. Abraham Brown. ---- 1784. Proved Dec. 15, 1784. Wife Mary. Bro. Jonathan Brown and David Burson exrs. Land in Middlesex Co. N.J. adj. Wm. Chambers and Ezeblen Brown.
Wits: Isaac Burson, James Medlicott, Charles Posten (?).

Page 489. Sarah Bolton of Southampton Twp., widow. 12-26-1775. Proved Dec. 23, 1784. Daus. Margaret and Rachel Bolton exrs. Dau. Sarah Rigby and Jemima Tomlinson and Margaret and Rachel Bolton. Son Everard Bolton and Joseph Bolton. Gddaus. Ann and Mary Rigby, Sarah Tomlinson, Rebecca Bolton (Daus. of Joseph) and Sarah Bolton (dau. of Everard).
Wits: Daniel Longstreth, John Wynkoop, Joseph Longstreth.

Page 491. Jacob Denzler of Richland Twp., taylor. May 2, 1785. Proved April 10, 1786. Wife Anna Margareta and Stephen Horn, exrs. Jacob Fritz, son of Catharine Fritz. Gddau. Elizabeth Hollerin dau. of Rudolf Denzler. Gddaus. Susanna and Magdalena Burgry.
Wits: Christian Stall, Michael Keller.

Page 493. Stephen Wilkinson of Wrightstown Twp. March 14, 1786. Proved April 11, 1786. Kinsman John Chapman and Friend Joseph Hart, Esq. exrs. Sister Mary Twining (Samuel Kirk and John Thompson Trustees for her) her son Jacob Twining. Half-Bro. Elisha Wilkinson and his 3 sisters, my half-sisters Martha, Ann and Hannah Wilkinson. Land in Forks of Susquehanna River in Northumberland Co. devised by Father. Grist and saw mill in Wrightstown Twp. Grist Mill in New Britain Twp.
Wits: John Scott, Thomas Paltin, John Terry Junr.

Page 497. Thomas Foulke of Richland Twp. Feb. 18, 1786. Proved April 12, 1786. Wife Jane. Son Everard exr. Dau. Susanna Foulke.
Wits: Randal Iden, Evarard Roberts.

Page 499. Henry Harris of New Britain Twp., yeoman. March 27, 1786. Proved April 29, 1786. Wife Martha. David Davis and Thos. Mathew of New Britain Trustees. Sons Samuel and John. Daus. Sarah wife of

Enoch Thomas, Elizabeth wife of William Hines. Gddau. Sarah Harris, dau. of son Thomas. Gdsn. John and Amos Griffith exrs.
Wits: Samuel Weir, David Rees, John Weir.

Page 502. Daniel Cahill of Warwick Twp., yeoman. March 23, 1786. Proved April 25, 1786. Wife Mary and son Edward exrs. Sons Daniel, Edward and John. Dau. Elizabeth. Land in Westmorland Co.
Wits: John Horner, Archibald Darrah, John Kerr.

Page 505. Thomas Ross of Solebury, taylor. 4-12-1784. Proved May 24, 1786. Wife Kezia. Son Thomas and nephew John Chapman exrs. Son Thomas and his son Thomas. Son John and his sons Isaiah and Joseph. Son-in-law Thomas Smith and his ch.
Wits: David Lewis, Rebekah Lewis, Peter D. Cattell.

Page 508. John Hart of Newtown. May 30, 1786. Proved June 16, 1786. Bro. Joseph and Friend Thos. Folwell exrs. Late gdfather John Hart. Housekeeper Elizabeth Kelly. Friend Mathew Banes his wife Sarah and their ch. Daus. Elizabeth Hart, Euphemia Hart. Sons William, Joseph and John. Late wife Rebecca Rees. Father Joseph Hart, Esq., Overseer.
Wits: James Hanna, Samuel Gibbs, Andrew McMinn.

Page 512. Yost Erdman of Milford Twp., yeoman. June 4, 1785. Proved June 26, 1786. Wife Susanna. Sons Jacob and George exrs. Daus. Elizabeth, Eve and Barbara. Gddau. Susanna born of my son Jacob's first wife. Son-in-law Jacob Snider.
Wits: John Edwards, Peter Hackenbergt (a German).

Page 516. Isaac Hough of Warminster Twp., taylor. Jan. 7, 1785. Proved April 17, 1786. Wife Edith and son John exrs. Sons John, Isaac, Thomas, Oliver, Silas, Joseph and William. Daus. Eleanor wife of Thomas Craven and Elizabeth wife of Silas Gilbert. Gddau. Mary Jones dau. of Benj. Jones of Phila., taylor. Gdch. Isaac and Edith Craven, ch. of Thomas, Susanna and William Gilbert ch. of Silas. Joseph Hart and Thomas Folwell Trustees.
Wits: Joseph Dilworth, John Blackwell, Jacob Cadwallader Junr.

Page 521. John Henninger of Rockhill Twp. March 12, 1786. Proved June 21, 1786. Son Leonard exr. Dau. Christina.
Wits: Wm. Sinfras Senr., William Sinfras Junr.

Page 523. Thomas Roberts of Lower Milford, yeoman. May 15, 1786. Proved Aug. 3, 1786. Wife Letitia and son-in-law John Thompson exrs. Eldest son Isaac, son Israel, youngest son Richard. Daus. Abigail Thompson, Alice Foulke, Elizabeth Foulke, Ann Roberts and Letitia Roberts. Bro. Richard.

Wits: Israel Foulke and John Roberts.

Page 526. Tamer Harvey, widow of Thomas Harvey of Upper
Makefield. April 21, 1786. Proved Aug. 8, 1786. Son-in-law Nathaniel
Ellicott exr. Daus. Elizabeth Coryell, Ann Bayly and Letitia Ellicott.
Gddau. Sarah Ellicott.
Wits: Tacy Ellicott and David Forsh.

Page 527. David Muckly of Lower Milford Twp., yeoman. March 2,
1786. Proved Aug. 22, 1786. "Far advanced in age." Wife Anna
Barbara. Son-in-law John George Shitz and Jacob Klein exrs. Dau.
Magdalena wife of George Overback, Margareth wife of Henry
Wambold. Eldest dau. Catharine, wife of John George Shitz. Gdsons.
David Wambold only son of Henry Wambold by my youngest dau.
Margareth. Gdson. John Shitz Junr.
Wits: Abraham Shantz and Christopher Sacks.

Page 533. Richard Margerum of Lower Makefield, yeoman. March 14,
1785. Proved Sept. 12, 1786. Codicil March 23, 1785. Codicil May 30,
1785. Wife Hannah and son Robert exrs. Sons Henry, Edward, John,
Benjamin, William, Robert, Abraham, and Richard. Daus. Mary,
Jenipher, eldest son Henry. Dau. Isabel Phillips. Gdch. by dau. Mary
Clark, Richard, Margaret, Jane, Hannah, Martha and William Clark.
Gdch. by eldest son Richard dec'd. viz. Jinkey and Henry.
Wits: Joshua Anderson, Daniel Anderson, Joseph Gillingham.

Page 539. James Sample of Buckingham Twp. June 28, 1785. Proved
Sept. 14, 1786. "Far advanced in years." Wife Margaret. Robert Smith
of Buckingham exr. Son Robert. Son John's ch. Dau. Mary Johnstone
wife of John Johnstone.
Wits: Timothy Smith and William Aremi.

Page 541. James Green of Richland, yeoman. 6-29-1786. Proved Sept.
25, 1786. Wife Martha. Friend Randal Iden and Bro.-in-law Edward
Foulke exrs. Son Thomas (when 21). Daus. Ann, Elizabeth and
Margaret.
Wits: William Hicks and Israel Foulke.

Page 544. Isaiah Vansant of Lower Makefield. April 15, 1786. Proved
Sept. 28, 1786. Wife Charity. Sons Joshua and Cornelius exrs. Sons
Elijah, Isaiah, Joshua, Peter, Gabriel and Cornelius. Daus. Elizabeth
and gddau. Rachel Merrick. Dau. Rachel's 3 ch. Dau. Charity's 4 ch.
Dau. Sarah's 2 ch. Dau. Mary and her dau. Charity.
Wits: Thos. Stradling, Nathan Brown and John Brown.

Page 547. Nicholas Bock of Springfield, yeoman. Feb. 12, 1785. Proved
Nov. 13, 1786. Wife Elizabeth. Son Leonard and John Smith exrs. Sons

Leonard, Joseph, Jacob, John and Nicholas. Daus. Catharina, Barbara, Elizabeth and Machalina.
Wits: Ludwick Nasfrickle and George Amey.

Page 550. Elizabeth Warder of Lower Makefield, Widow. 10-13-1786. Proved Nov. 14, 1786. James Moon Junr. and Joseph Gillingham exrs. Sister Ellen Mead's ch. William Mead, Ann Mead. Martha Right [Wright]. Niece Elizabeth Potts. Neighbor Nathan Ray.
Wits: Ann Kirkbride, Absalom Howell, Dolly Ray.

Page 553. David Culp of Bedminster Twp., yeoman. Nov. 11, 1786. Proved Dec. 31, 1786. Wife Nancy. Son Jacob, Bro. Tielman and Henry Overholt exrs. Sons Jacob, Abraham, and David. Gdson. Henry Landis. Son Abraham's wife Mary. Son Henry dec'd. six children.
Wits: Jacob Kulp, Jacob Overholt. (Signed by mark - correct spelling probably Kulp. WSE)

BOOK NO. 5

Page 1. Joseph Lovett of Bristol Twp., yeoman. 3-18-1786. Proved May 15, 1786. Wife Ann. Moses Moon and sons Samuel and Jesse Lovett exrs. Eldest son Samuel. Son Jesse. Daus. Hannah Cooper, Susannah and Casey Lovett. Land in Middletown purchased of exrs. of Joseph Wright dec'd. and Joseph son of said Joseph Wright.
Wit: Joshua Blakey, Isaac Watson, Simon Gilliam.

Page 5. Nathan Preston of New Britain, yeoman. 9-12-1776. Proved Feb. 10, 1787. Wife Mary. Dau.. Ellin Preston and Friend Robert Kirkbride exrs. Dau. Mary Preston . Bro. Henry's son Amor. Land adj. Daniel Hough, Richard Reily, John Robinson, Robert Kirkbride and land late of David Worthington.
Wits: Jonathan Shaw, John Carlile, Francis Goode.

Page 7. Peter Alth of Springfield Twp. July 28, 1784. Proved March 13, 1787. 6 stepchildren- David, Michael and Peter Diehl. Peter Heff's son Henry. Philip Thany. Ev. Luth.Ch. Wife Anna Maria and Han Yost exrs.
Wits: Hannah Afflerbach, Valentine Opp, Catharine Oppin.

Page 8. Joseph McIlvaine of Bristol Twp., Gentleman. April 25, 1785. Proved July 23, 1787. Bro. Dr. William McIlvaine and Bro.-in-law Jos. Bloomfield Esq. exrs. Dec'd. Father William McIlvaine, interred at Newtown Pres. Ch. Sister Mary Bloomfield. Natural son Joseph McIlvaine born of Catharine Swan now Catharine Heaton. Col. Augustine Willett. Codicil dated Nov. 23, 1786.
Wits: John Colvin, Fred Kisselman, Augustine Willett, Joshua M. Wallace and John Phillips.

Page 11. William Miller of Warminster, yeoman. Feb. 8, 1786. Proved Feb. 26, 1787. "Far advanced in years." Son Henry and Robert Loller exrs. Sons Henry and Robert. Daus. Mary, Jane wife of Adam Carr and Martha. Gdch. John and Daniel Craig and Isabel Knox, William and Ann Carr. Chas. Enyard, John Kerr.

Page 14. Elizabeth Thomas of New Britain, yeoman. May 6, 1785. Proved Feb. 26, 1787. Son Owen Thomas exr. Dau. Elizabeth Morris. Sons Owen, David and Joseph Thomas. Ann Dungan.
Wits: Peter Evans, Benjamin Thomas. "Son Joseph absent."

Page 16. John Pickering, Solebury Twp., yeoman. 2-26-1785. Proved March 1, 1787. Wife Hannah. Sons John and Jesse exrs. Dau. Hannah Johnson. Land adj. Benj. Eastburn.
Wits: John Watson, Yeamans Gillingham, Benjamin Paxson.

Page 18. Kesiah Ross, Solebury Twp. 1-13-1787. Proved March 2, 1787. William Blackfan of Solebury exr. Son John Ross and his wife Mary, gddau. Kesiah wife of Benjamin Eastburn. Gddau. Patence Ross. Gddaus. Kesiah and Susanna Smith. Gdson. Samuel Smith. Son Thomas Ross. 5 sons of dau. Mary Smith dec'd. viz. Samuel, Joseph, Ezra and Thomas.
Wits: Crispin Blackfan, Thomas Smith.

Page 20. Henry Youngken of Haycock Twp. Jan. 18, 1787. Proved March 13, 1787. Wife Catharine extx. Sons John, Jacob, Frederic, Rudolf and Henry. Daus. Catharine and Elizabeth.
Wits: Jacob Nicholas, Godfrey Boyer.

Page 23. Walter Haddock of Richland, yeoman. Jan. 17, 1787. Proved March 13, 1787. William Penrose exr. Jonathan, William and John Penrose of Richland. Bro. John Haddock and sisters Sarah and Mary Haddock of County Antrim, Ireland. Richard Fossett of Fairfax Co. Va.
Wits: John Walton, Everard Foulke.

Page 24. Jacob Strickler of Southampton Twp. Feb. 28, 1787. Proved March 15, 1787. Sons Shedrick and Isaac exrs. Dau. Elizabeth Strickler. Sons Jacob, Peter, Shedrick, Abraham and Isaac.
Wits: Nicholas Vanartsdalen, Dal. Knight, Henrich Kone.

Page 26. Agnes Dawson of Solebury, yeoman. 2-21-1785. Proved March 26, 1787. Gdsn. John Blackfan and gddau. Rachel Blackfan exrs. Dau. Esther Blackfan's ch. Rachel, John, Hannah, Sarah and Agnes Blackfan. Ch. of dau. Sarah Smith dec'd. viz. Jonathan son of Edmund Smith.
Wits: Samuel Kitchin and David Stackhouse.

Page 28. Hugh Orlton of Springfield Twp. March 27, 1787. Proved April 13, 1787. Only son Hugh and David Burson exrs. Notes in hands of George Rush and Henry Oplibach.
Wits: Chas. Posten, Enoch Morgan and Henry Afflerbach.

Page 30. Catharine Cornish, Falls Twp. Aug. 28, 1786. Proved April 14, 1787. Dau. Elizabeth Palmer, exr. Daus. Mary Vansant, Rebecca Welch, Anna Richardson. Gdson. John Burton. 7 gdch. viz. Mary and Joice Palmer, Elizabeth and Catharine Vansant. Mary and Catharine Margerum and Elizabeth Welch.
Wits: Hannah Linter, Absalom Margerum.

Page 31. Martha Harris, New Britain, widow. Feb. 9, 1787. Proved April 16, 1787. Son Samuel Harris exr. Sons John and Samuel Harris. Daus. Sarah Thomas and Elizabeth Hines.
Wits: David Thomas and Amos Griffith.

Page 34. Philip Trapp of Springfield Twp. July 2, 1786. Proved April 23, 1787. Wife Catarina. Abraham Funk and Ludwick Heller exrs. Son Andreas. Other ch. Philip, Magdalena, Elizabeth, Ma--, Dorothea, Susanna, Catharine and Hannah.
Wits: John Cyphert and John Cyphert Junr.

Page 36. Joseph Large of Buckingham, yeoman. May 10, 1784. Proved June 3, 1787. "Advanced in age." Wife Elizabeth. Sons Joseph and John exrs. Daus. Jane Thomas and Joanna Large.
Wits: John Ely, William Ely, Cynthia Ely.

Page 39. Thomas Litle of Nockamixon. March 13, 1787. Proved April 13, 1787. Wife Sarah and son Robert exrs. Sons Robert, Andrew, Thomas and David. Daus. Jane, Sarah, Margaret and Mary.
Wits: Mary Jamison, Hugh Jamison.

Page 42. Jacob Rohr of New Britain, wheelmaker. May 31, 1778. Proved June 11l, 1787. Friend Jacob Haldeman and Cousin John Wriman, guardians. Wife Anna and Jacob Haldeman exrs. Ch. Chatheren, John, Elizabeth, Susanna and Mary Rohr.
Wits: John Wistler, David Evans, Da. German, Jacob Vyvils (?).

Page 45. John Foulke of Richland, smith. 4-17-1787. Proved June 12, 1787. Codicil May 25, 1787. Kinsman Everard Foulke and son Edward exrs. Sons Edward, Aquillia and Evan. Daus. Ann, Margaret and Lydia. Land purchased of Isaac Lester, Thomas Foulke, John Greasly and Morris Morris, adj. John Button and Richland Mtg. House. Land purchased of George Phillips adj. Thomas McCarty and Abel Roberts.
Wits: John Lester, Geo. Savitz.

Page 48. James Armstrong of Hilltown Twp. May 26, 1787. Proved June 13, 1787. Wife Ruth. Friends Robert Jamison and Thos. Armstrong exrs. Bro. Andrew Armstrong. Sons Abraham, John, William and Andrew. Dau. Sarah wife of Alexander Moon.
Wits: William Armstrong, Fillib Jacobi.

Page 52. Samuel Kirk of Haycock Twp., yeoman. April 2, 1787. Proved July 31, 1787. Wife Margaret extx. Son Frederick.
Wits: Jacob Strawn, Martin Shive Junr.

Page 54. Wheeler Clark of Falls Twp., yeoman. Aug. 1, 1787. Proved Aug. 25, 1787. Wife Franky and son Thomas exrs. Sons John, Thomas and Charles.
Wits: Robert Crozer, Thos. Crozer. Wm. Young.

Page 57. Joseph Milnor of Falls Twp., yeoman. 7-2-1787. Proved Oct. 11, 1787. Wife Catharine. Son Mahlon and Friends Samuel and Moses Moon exrs. Sons Joseph, John and Mahlon. Son John's ch. Joseph, Isaac, Phebe and others. Dau. Sarah, wife of Keirl Rickey and her son Samuel. Dau. Mary Hillegas and Martha Downing. Money due from John Rickey. Land in Trenton bot. [bought] of Samuel Downing.
Wits: Mary Darbyshire, Elizabeth White.

Page 62. Elizabeth Eastburn, of Solebury. 12-9-1785. Proved Oct. 22, 1787. Son Robert Eastburn and dau. Sarah Smith exrs. Son Joseph's ch. Daus. Mary Edwards and Sarah Smith. Gdch. Jonathan White, Rachel Fell and ch. of son Robert.
Wits: James Hambleton, Elizabeth Smith, Jonathan Doan.

Page 63. William Ramsey of Warwick, yeoman. April 27, 1787. Proved Nov. 6, 1787. Wife Eleanor. Son William and John exrs. Son Robert. Daus. Janet Ramsey, Jean Blair. Grdsn. Hugh Ramsey son of Hugh, dec'd.
Wits: Hugh Edams, Gayen Edams. Land adj. John Baird, Saml. Spencer, Jonathan Walton, Robert Bready.

Page 65. Samuel Wilson of Buckingham, yeoman. 2-22-1786. Proved Dec. 31, 1787. "Far advanced in years." Sons Thomas and Stephen and Dau. Sarah exrs. Sons Thomas, Samuel, Oliver, John, Stephen, Isaac and David. Daus. Mary Eastburn, Elizabeth Ely, Rebecca Fell, Rachel Fell, Hannah Kirkbride and Sarah Wilson. Land bought of William Preston, John Hill, Isaac Pennington, Samuel Cooper and James Gillingham. Bro. John Wilson, dec'd.
Wits: John Gillingham, Saml. Gillingham, John Gillingham Jr. Joshua Morris and Sarah his wife late Sarah Wilson renounce.

Page 67. Michael Hoffman of Nockamixon, farmer. Feb. 1, 1786.

Proved Jan. 18, 1788. Wife Mary Elizabeth and son John exrs. Sons John and Anthony. Daus. Elizabeth and Eve Mary. 2 ch. of dau. Eve Wilkelm late of Bethlehem, Hunterdon Co., N.J. viz. Catheren and Eve.
Wits: John Sparvenberg, Lawrence Levinston, and Peter Levinston.

Page 69. Philip Dedesman of Haycock, yeoman. July 28, 1787. Proved Jan. 22, 1788. Wife Catharine. Casper Borger exr. Ch. Philip, John, Jacob, Magdalena and Hannah and gdch. Jacob and Catharine ch. of dau. Catharine dec'd.
Wits: Philip Borgen, Philip Shryer.

Page 71. William Satterthwaite of Lower Makefield, yeoman. 8-30-1786. Proved Feb. 8, 1788. "Far advanced in years." Wife Pleasant. Son William and Samson Cary and Daniel Wharton exrs. Daus. Esther Worstall, Ann Erewagen, Sarah Mitchel and Mary Ball. Gdch. William, Thomas, Robert and Ann Huston ch. of dau. Pleasant dec'd. Son-in-law Robert Huston. Gddau. Ann Buly. Dau. Sarah Mitchell's dau. Hannah. Land where James Worstall lives. Land in Parish of St. Martins London. Land Purchased of Samuel Cary. (Vary?) John Palmer and Daniel West.
Wits: Richard Neeld, Nathaniel Price Junr., William Bayly.

Page 75. Rebecca Winder of Lower Makefield, widow of John. 1-11-1788. Proved Feb. 15, 1788. Son Aaron Winder exr. Sons Moses, John, James and Aaron Winder. Dau. Hannah Brooks, Sarah Whitacre, Rebecca Nuff, Elizabeth Linton and Ann Knight.
Wits: Joseph Taylor, Robert Alexander, John Stapler.

Page 76. Patrick Malone of Buckingham. March 13, 1784. Proved March 12, 1788. Son John exr. Son James. Daus. Elizabeth wife of Henry Stirk, Mary wife of William Kirk, Hannah wife of Benjamin Worthington, Phebe wife of John Tomlinson and Ann Malone. Gdch. Abner and Sarah Worthington ch. of dau. Sarah Worthington dec'd.
Wits: John Beal, Watson Welding, Francis Tomlinson and Joseph Watson.

Page 78. Crispin Blackfan of Solebury, yeoman. 6-18-1787. Proved March 13, 1788. Wife Martha. Son Edward exr. Daus. Rebekah Wilson, Sarah Wilson, Latitia Smith, Hannah Betts, Eleanor, Elizabeth, Martha and Esther Blackfan. Gdsn. Edward Wilson, son of dau. Rebekah. Gdsn. Thomas Smith son of dau. Latitia. Land purchased of Wm. Blackfan, John Wilson and Benj. Canby.
Wits: Robert Smith Junr., Thomas Smith Junr.

Page 82. John Gregg of Middletown, yeoman. March 9, 1787. Proved April 4, 1788. Wife Elizabeth. Bros. James and Francis exrs. Bros.

Michael and William Gregg.
Wits: Daniel Martin, Henry Shaver, Mathew Weaver.

Page 85. Jeremiah Vastine of New Britain, yeoman. March 5, 1788.
Proved April 21, 1788. Wife Elizabeth and Isaac Van Horn exrs. Father
Jeremiah Vastine dec'd. Mother Deborah Vastine. Jeremiah Vastine
son of Jonathan. Mary and Rebecca Van Horn, daus. of Isaac and
Rebecca Van Horn. Ch. of John and Martha Louder. Baptist Church of
Hilltown. Ch. of Samuel and Hannah Graham.
Wits: John Davis, Edward Mathew, John Davis Junr.

Page 88. Thomas Janney of Newtown, yeoman. 12-26-1787. Proved
April 24, 1788. Jacob Janney and Jonathan Carlile exrs. Gdsn. Jacob
Janney. Daus. Mary Janney, Alice Daws and Martha Warner. Gdch.
Ann Buckman and Daniel Richardson. John Brock.
Wits: John Palmer, John Roney, Joseph Suber.

Page 91. Harman Youngkin of Neckamixon, Blacksmith. Feb. 28, 1788.
Proved March 26, 1788. Wife Eve, her first husband George Shill,
dec'd. Son John and son-in-law Henry Houpt, exrs. Sons Abraham,
Gillion, John, Daniel, George and Harman. Ch. of son-in-law Henry
Houpt and Catharine his wife. viz. John and Magdalena Houpt.
Wits: Nicholas McClarty, Michael Streby, John Barclay.

Page 94. William Pearson of Buckingham, yeoman. 2-8-1783. Proved
May 10, 1788. Wife Elizabeth and dau. Margaret and her husband
Samuel Cary, exrs. 3 ch. of dau. Elizabeth Jenks, dec'd., viz.
Margaret, William and Elizabeth Jenks.
Wits: John Thornton, Joseph Worstall, Jos. Thornton Jr.

Page 94. Leonard Vandegrift of Bensalem, yeoman. April 20, 1785.
Proved May 20, 1788. Wife Charity and son Leonard exrs. Sons
Abraham, Thomas, Josiah, Leonard, Amos, Aaron and Joseph. Daus.
Rebecca.
Wits: Jacob Vandegrift, John Harrison.

Page 98. William Carr of Warminster, yeoman. April 20, 1788. Proved
June 5, 1788. Wife Mary. Bro. Adam Kerr and friend John Kerr,
overseers. Sons Peter, William and Adam exrs. Ch. Peter, Jean,
William, Adam, Mary, Elizabeth, Joseph, John and Lot Carr.
Wits: Elijah Shrison and John Kerr.

Page 99. Joseph Hart of Warminster, Esq. Feb. 21, 1788. Proved June
11, 1788. Sons Josiah, Silas and Joseph exrs. Ch. of son John, dec'd.
viz. William, Joseph, Elizabeth, Euphemia and John. Land purchased of
Joseph Longstreth adj. John Kroesen, Isaac Banes, Jonathan Walton
and Samuel Spencer.

Wits: Henry Wynkoop, Saml. Spencer, James Banes Jr.

Page 100. Anna Ledterman of Plumstead Twp. March 29, 1788. Proved
Sept. 9, 1788. Bros. Johannes Ledterman and Bro.-in-law Jacob Hoch
of Hilltown exrs. Mother Magdalena Ledterman, widow. Sister
Catharine Ledterman and Magdalena wife of Jacob Hoch.
Wits: Abrm. Shout (Stout?), Jacob Gross, Rudolph Landis. Translated
from German.

Page 103. Thomas Lewis of Solebury Twp., yeoman. July 6, 1788.
Proved July 26, 1788. Wife Lydia. Son Jonathan and Friend Aaron
Phillips exrs. 5 sons, Jonathan, Nathaniel, Zachariah, Samuel and
William. Daus. Mercy Cooper, Grace Johnston, and Elizabeth ---. Sons
Thomas and Nathan.
Wits: Timothy Scott, Phebe Scott.

Page 104. Martha Baxter of Plumstead Twp., widow. Aug. 18, 1787.
Proved Aug. 22, 1788. Joseph Brittain and William McCalla, exrs. Sons
George and John Cook. Daus. Ann Howard, Mary Fetherby, Mary
Comble. Gdsns. John Howard and William Cook. Gddaus. Martha
Howard and Mary Dunn.
Wits: Jesse Britton, Smith Price.

Page 105. Henry Krewsen of Southampton Twp. Aug. 15, 1788. Proved
Sept. 27, 1788. Wife Letitia and Henry Wynkoop Esq. and Enoch
Edwards of Phila. Co. exrs. Sons Henry, Isaac, Absalom. Half-Bro.
Peter Huft. Bro.-in-law Andrew Reeder. Henry son of John Blake.
Wits: Joshua Praul, John Blake.

Page 107. Leonard Thomas of Milford Twp., Blacksmith. Aug. 24, 1788.
Proved Sept. 27, 178-. Wife Lydia and son George exrs. Ch. Robert,
Margaret, George, Mary, Lydia, John, David, William and Leonard
Thomas and Elizabeth wife of Henry Smith.
Wits: Jacob Huber, Joseph Phillips, George Myer.

Page 108. James Dungan of Northampton Twp. Sept. 22, 1788. Proved
Oct. 4, 1788. Wife Sarah. Bro. Elias and Friend Samuel Erwin of
Moreland exr. Son Samuel and dau. Jane Dungan. "Goods that were
their dec'd. mothers." Their gdfather Samuel John dec'd. Wife's
sister Phebe Dungan. Niece Elizabeth Dungan, dau. of Bro. Clement
dec'd. Bros. Jeremiah and Elias.
Wits: Garret Dungan, Joshua Dungan, Hugh Edams.

Page 110. Michael Dowd, Lower Dublin Twp., Phila. Co., yeoman. Oct.
6, 1788. Proved Oct. 30, 1788. Dr. Hugh Tomb, Joseph Fenton, James
How exrs. Daniel Dollachn [?] of County Down, Ireland sole legatee.
Wits: John Keen, Strickland Foster.

18

Page 111. Abraham Harrye of Upper Makefield, yeoman. 10-14-1784. Proved Nov. 22, 1788. Sons Abraham and Moses exrs. Son-in-law John Brown Junr. and Martha his wife "my dau." Dau. Elizabeth.
Wits: William Lownes, Benjamin Canby.

Page 112. Ann Jones of Upper Makefield. 10-30-1788. Proved Dec. 10, 1788. Kinsman John Brown of Oxford Twp. and William Wood of Makefield exrs. Niece Martha Brown, Cousins Mary and Moses Harvye, niece Elizabeth Paxson dau. of Moses Brown and wife of Abraham Paxson. Cousin Elizabeth Harvye. Eldest dau. of Abraham and Martha Harvye. Kisnwoman Ann Brown dau. of John Brown. Nephew Thomas Brown son of Thomas. Beulah Porter dau. of William and Margaret Porter. Kinswoman Martha Harvye, dau. of cousins Abraham and Jane Harvye. Nephew Mark Brown son of Bro. Thomas. extx. of dec'd. husband.
Wits: Joseph Taylor, John Stapler.

Page 113. John Weidner of Lower Milford, yeoman. Nov. 12, 1787. Proved Dec. 10, 1788. Wife Elizabeth and son Jacob exrs. Sons John, Jacob, Leonard and Daniel. Daus. Mary Johnson, Magdalena Undercufler, Platina Gruber, Elizabeth Weikel, Hannah Weiser and Catharine Hertzel.
Wits: Hameolis Trimbour, Peter Hackenburg.

Page 115. Mathew Banes of Southampton Twp. Sept. 9, 1788. Proved Dec. 9, 1788. Wife Sarah. Sons Joseph and Evan exrs. Son Erwin, a minor. Daus. Euphemia Leedom and Letitia Foster. Bro. James Trustee.
Wits: Arthur Watts, Safety Meghie, Derrick Hogeland.

Page 117. Robert Gibson of Plumstead Twp., yeoman. April 24, 1788. Proved Aug. 22, 1788. Wife Elizabeth. Joseph Britton and William McCalla exrs. Sons Thomas, James, Moses, John and Robert. Daus. Elizabeth Armstrong, Mary Britton and Jean Gibson. Gdsns. Robert Armstrong and John Gibson.
Wits: Nathaniel Britton, John Rees.

Page 119. Peter Taylor of Newtown, yeoman. Feb. 1, 1783. Proved Jan. 26, 1789. "Far advanced in years." Sons-in-law John Knowles and Jacob Buckman exrs. Gdsns. William, Peter, Banner and Joseph Taylor. Gddaus. Hannah and Mercy Taylor and their mother Hannah Taylor. Gdch. Jemima and Mercy [or Mary] Taylor and John and Sarah Taylor, Hester Martindell and Sarah Smith.
Wits: Bernard Taylor, David Buckman Junr., Rachel White.

Page 120. John Eberhart of Lower Milford Twp. Batchelor. Jan. 20, 1789. Proved Feb. 5, 1789. Bro.-in-law Valentine Beidleman exr. Elder

Bro. Michael. Sister Margaret widow of Peter Wetzel late of Md. dec'd. Sisters Anna wife of John Jacoby and Elizabeth wife of Valentine Beidleman.
Wits: George Erdman, Thomas Boyer.

Page 123. Samuel Stewart of New Britain, yeoman. March 8, 1774. Proved Feb. 10, 1789. Wife Ann and son Thomas exrs. Dau. Mary McHenry.
Wits: Robert Stewart, Samuel Wigton.

Page 124. Benjamin Suber of Middletown. Jan. 18, 1789. Proved Jan. 28, 1789. Mother Mary Suber extx. Dec'd. father George Suber. Bros. George and Joseph. Sisters Mary and Sarah Suber.
Wits: Thomas Jenks Junr., Abner Buckman, John Roney.

Page 124. Brakey Roberts of Northampton Twp. Jan. 21, 1789. Proved Feb. 19, 1789. Husband John Roberts exr. Mother Else Cornell. Bros. and sisters John and Gilliam Cornell, Cornelia Craven, Margaret Corson and Elizabeth Vansant.
Wits: John Linton, John Hall.

Page 125. William Hibbs Junr. of Northampton Twp. 9-12-1785. Proved March 4, 1789. Wife ---. Son Benjamin exr. Son Nehemiah's ch. Benjamin, William, Isaac and Hester. Sons James and William. Daus. Anna Worshall, Abigail Parsons and Ann Smith.
Wits: Jonathan Kirkbride, Mary Dougherty and Edmund Plumly.

Page 126. Effe Pownal of Solebury Twp. July 4, 1789 (?). Proved March 11, 1789. Robert Eastburn and son George Pownal exrs. Sons Reuben, John , Elisha, Benjamin and George Pownal. Daus. Jane Brotherton, Rachel Peters, Grace Carlin and Hannah Lee. Gddau. Effe Carlin.
Wits: Oliver Hampton, Ebenezer Large, Moses Pownal.

Page 127. Christian Overholt of Plumstead Twp. Oct. 19, 1784. Proved March 24, 1789. Wife Sarah. Bro.-in-law Martin Didwiler and Jacob Meyer exrs. Bros. Jacob, Abraham, and Samuel. Sister Catharine, wife of George Frederic; Mary wife of Christian Souder. Ch. of Bros. John and Henry (both dec'd.). John Funk, Mathias Finckman and Jacob Yodder Trustees for Mennonity Mtg. at Bedminster. Land adj. Christian Gehman, Jacob Gross, John Obybach and John Didwiler.
Wits: John Bradshaw, David Evans, Jacob Holdeman.

Page 129. Cornelius Vansant. Wrightstown Twp. Feb. 8, 1788. Proved March 26, 1789. "Far advanced in years." Wife Mary. Nephew David Dungan and Joseph Carver exrs. Cornelius Brittain son of nephew Joseph Brittain. Cornelius Dungan, son of nephew David Dungan and

Cornelius Carver, son of nephew Joseph Carver.
Wits: Robert Ware, Hannah Lee, John Terry Junr.

Page 130. Elizabeth Johnson, Warminster Twp., Widow. March 20, 1775. Proved April 13, 1789. Sons Benjamin and John exrs. Daus. Catharine, Elizabeth, Mary and Ann. Son William. Mother ---. Money due from Joseph Miller.
Wits: Stephen Burrows, Joseph Dilworth, Joseph Miller.

Page 131. Henry Krewsen, Southampton, yeoman. May 7, 1788. Proved May 12, 1789. Wife Ann. Friends John Hoagland and Simon Vanarsdalen exrs. Dau. Alice Hoagland. 4 gdch., ch. of dau. Else, Simon Vanarsdalen, Alice Lefferson, Jane Krewson and Jacob
Wits: Nicholas Vanarsdalen, Henry Krewisen Jr., Simon Vanarsdalen.

Page 132. Gabriel Vanhorn of Middletown, yeoman. March 9, 1789. Proved May 23, 1789. Wife Martha. Sons Jacob and John exrs. Daus. Rebecca Cabe, Elizabeth Palmer, Martha Mitchel, Charity Moode. Gddaus. Hannah Burley and Rebecca Rue. Henry Mitchel and Joseph Moode Trustees. Sons Peter, Gabriel, Israel, Jacob and John.
Wits: Joshua Vanhorn, John Sotcher.

Page 134. Ann Hayhurst of Harford Co., Md. May 6, 1789. Proved May 24, 1789. "Being indisposed in Northampton Twp., Bucks Co." Sons James and David Hayhurst exrs. Daus. Hannah Hayhurst and Sarah Newberry. Gddaus. Ann Hannaway and Ann Newberry. Land sold to William Lee.
Wits: Hugh Edams, Thomas Spencer, James Spencer.

Page 135. John Ball of Richland Twp., yeoman. Feb. 23, 1789. Proved May 25, 1789. Wife Rebecca. Sons Abraham and Aaron exrs. Sons Nathan and Joseph. Daus. Sarah Phillips, Diana Walker and Katharine Ball. Land bot. [sic] of Heirs of Diana Hewlings.
Wits: Robert Penrose, John Roberts.

Page 136. John Mitchell of Middletown Twp., yeoman. 3-4-1789. Proved May 26, 1789. Sons Richard, Henry, Samuel and Pearson exrs. Daus. Sarah Wilson and Margaret Wilson. Gdsns. John, Joshua and Amos and gddau. Margaret Mitchel ch. of son John, dec'd. Monthly Meeting of Friends at Middletown "of which I am a member." Thomas Wilson of Bristol Twp. and William Richardson of Middletown Trustees. Land adj. Richard Milchel, Henry Huddleston, Jonathan Woolston, William Huddleston, Isaac Stackhouse and William Hayhurst.
Wits: Benj. Buckman, William Linton, Joseph Hayhurst.

Page 139. Thomas Hartley of Solebury, yeoman. 1-27-1787. Proved May 31, 1789. Sons Anthony and William exrs. Sons Benjamin, Joseph,

Mahlon. Daus. Sarah Beans, Elizabeth Fell, Rachel Smith and Martha -
--. 5 ch. of dau. Martha by Luke Williams. 2 daus. of Dau. Ann Hill.
Wits: Robert Eastburn, John Balderston, Joseph Wilkinson, James
Hambleton. Land adj. David Forst, William Roberts, Jacob Beans,
George Bradshaw, Isaac Pickering, Jane Scarborough and William
Hambleton.

Page 141. Isaac Rinker of Lower Milford Twp., yeoman. Oct. 11, 1788.
Proved June 9, 1789. Wife Catharine. John Clymer and Abraham
Taylor exrs. Ch. not named.
Wits: Jacob Stover, John Leech.

Page 142. Johannes Ledrach of Hilltown, yeoman. April 13, 1788.
Proved June 9, 1789. Wife Mary. Abraham Stout and Abraham Taylor
exrs. 3 daus. of Bro. Jacob. Jacob son of Bro. Christian dec'd. 2 daus.
of Bro. Christian. 10 ch. of Bro.-in-law John Triechler by his dec'd.
wife Elizabeth.
Wits: Jacob Hunsicker, David Funk.

Page 143. John Bailey, Falls Twp., yeoman. 4-23-1789. Proved June 30,
1789. Wife Edith and William Satterhwaite exrs. Son Marriott at
Niagara. Sons Amos and John.
Wits: James Moon, Yeamans Gillingham.

Page 144. Garret Vansant of Middletown, yeoman. July 7, 1789. Proved
Aug. 7, 1789. Sons John and Garret Jr. exrs. Son George. Dau.-in-law
Mary Vastine, once wife of Jacob. Daus. Rachel Harrison, Kesiah
Sweetman, Vashti Vansant and Sarah Hise. Son -in-law James Rue.
Gdsn. James Vansant.
Wits: John Praul, John Hellings, John Sotcher.

Page 145. John Taylor of Newtown. May 1, 1789. Proved Aug. 8, 1789.
Cousin Joseph Taylor and Friends Moses Smith exrs. Aunt Hannah
Taylor and her ch., viz. Barnard and Joseph Taylor, Hannah Buckman
and Mercy Taylor. Bros. and sisters, viz. William Taylor, Jemima Scott,
Mary, Peter and Sarah Taylor.
Wits: Benjamin Tomlinson, Bernard Taylor.

Page 146. Joseph Cooper of Bensalem Twp., Farmer. May 23, 1788.
Proved Sept. 29, 1789. Wife Elizabeth and son Benjamin exrs. Eldest
son Joseph. Daus. Catharine Searl, Mary Booz, Rebecca Urinner
(Winner?), Charity Wright, Ann and Letitia Cooper.
Wits: Samuel Benezet, Daniel Severns.

Page 147. William Walker, Warrington Twp. July 14, 1789. Proved
Sept. 29, 1789. Wife Olimpias. Friend John Weir and Bro.-in-law Peter
Jodon exrs. Ch. John and Mary Walker. Land in Northumberland Co.

22

Wits: Thomas Griffith, Nathaniel Strahone, Nathaniel Irwin.

Page 148. Isaac Hunsberger of Rockhill, yeoman. Dec. 13, 1785. Proved
Oct. 20, 1789. Wife Catharine and sons-in-law Adam Kern and Andrew
Schlichter, exrs. Dau. Christiana Gerhart. Son Abraham. Daus.
Susanna, Catharine, Elizabeth, Mary and Margaret and gddaus.
Elizabeth Bernt and Hannah Hunsberger.
Wits: John Landis, Abraham Stout.

Page 150. Tilman Kulp, Bedminster Twp., Wheelwright. Oct. 14, 1789.
Proved Oct. 26, 1789. Friends Henry Overholt and Jacob Kulp Senr.
exrs. Sons Henry and Jacob. Dau. Elizabeth wife of Henry
Rosenberger.
Wits: Jacob Overholt, Abraham Kulp.

Page 151. Barnard Taylor, Newtown Twp. 10-17-1789. Proved Nov. 21,
1789. Son Benjamin exr. Son Mahlon. Nephew Bernard Taylor. Son of
Bro. Timothy. Gddau. Mary Taylor. Land where Widow Harvey lives.
Do. where Joseph Vernon lives.
Wits: John Story, David Barton, Letitia Taylor.

Page 152. John McFarren of Upper Makefield Twp. April 4, 1787.
Proved Nov. 30, 1789. Dau. Jannett Grimes and gdsn. Archibald
Grimes exrs. Sons William and John. Daus. Margaret McFarren and
Jannet Grimes.
Wits: Hugh Edams, Sarah Church.

Page 152. John Nase of Rockhill Twp,. yeoman. Oct. 14, 1786. Proved
Dec. 7, 1789. Codicil Oct. 8, 1789. Wife Susanna and George Adam
Kober exrs. Sons Henry, Theobald, John and Mathias. Daus. Cathrina
and Magdalena.
Wits: Jacob Snyder, Abraham Stout, Jacob Smith.
Wits. to Codicil: Johannes Loh, Peter Shneider, George Shneider.

Page 155. Henry Mitchell of Middletown Twp. 8-10-1789. Proved Dec.
7, 1789. Wife Hannah extx. and sole legatte. Unsettled acct. against
dec'd. Father's estate referred to David Twining, Isaac Watson and
Benjamin Buckman. "Note" nephew Henry Mitchell.
Wits: Samuel Mitchell, Jonathan Kirkbride, John Mitchell.

Page 155. Catharine Hughes of Warwick Twp. Aug. 1, 1789. Proved
Jan. 6, 1790. Friend John Ely of Buckingham exr. Sisters Charity Price
and Martha Matthews. Ch. of sister Charity Price and her husband
Thomas Price, Catharine, Elizabeth, and Stephen Price. Ch. of sister
Martha, Catharine and Tacy Mathews.
Wits: John Lovett, Margret Coate, Thomas Hambleton.

Page 157. Elenor Dungan of Northampton Twp. Dec. 31, 1785. Proved Jan. 15, 1790. Sons Jeremiah, James and Elias exrs. Husband Clement Dungan dec'd. Grddaus. Ann Marpole and Elizabeth Dungan. Gddau. Jean Dungan dau. of son James.
Wits: Hugh Edams and Abraham Black.

Page 158. William Moche of Rockhill, yeoman. March 24, 1786. Proved Jan. 27, 1790. John Jamison and Jacob Shipe exrs. 2 ch. by 1st wife, fiz. Catharine Lamahe and Sananah Rise. 6 ch. Jacob, George, David Moche, Catharine Shipe, Mabath Crose and Margaret Moche.
Wits: Richard Roberts, Jeremiah Heacock, Johannes Polt.

Page 158. Jonathan Walton of Warminster, yeoman. 2-7-1789. Proved Jan. 29, 1790. Son of Joshua dec'd. Samuel Erwin, Abraham Lukens of Horsham and Samuel Gourley of Moreland, Thomas Spencer of Warwick and Joshua Walton son of Jacob Walton dec'd. exrs. Nephew Jesse, eldest son of Job Walton late of Hatfield Twp. dec'd. Jesse, Jonathan and William, sons of Bro. Albertson. Samuel, Josiah, Joshua, Elizabeth and Ann ch. of Bro. Joshua, dec'd. Jonathan and John Vandegrift ch. of sister Ann, now Ann Fetters. John, Enoch and Jonathan, ch. of Samuel Walton, late of Richland. Jonathan Thomas son of niece Martha Thomas. Elijah Walton. Joseph Roberts, William Walton son of Benjamin. Thomas Walmisley and Thomas Knight members of Byberry Meeting. Jonathan Jarret, David Parry and Seneca Lukens of Horsham Meeting and James Walton, Samuel Nixon and Joseph Kesber of Richland Meeting 1/3 of est. for education of poor ch.
Wits: Thomas and Jona. Lloyd, Thomas Lloyd Jr. and Mordecai Thomas.

Page 161. Patrick Doyl of Middletown Twp. Feb. 1, 1790. Proved Feb. 13, 1790. Abner Buckman exr. Son James known by name of James Cammel had by Catharine More. Debts against Daniel Martin, John Jenks and Mark Hapenny. James Learl. Robert Carr. John Bennett. Joseph Worstall.
Wits: John Roney, Samuel Johnson, Robert Cunningham.

Page 163. Philip Fluck, Bedminster Twp. Feb. 13, 1790. Proved Feb. 23, 1790. Wife ---. Conrad Jacobs and John Fluck exrs. Son Samuel.
Wits: Andrew Allgert and Henry Hoover.

Page 164. John Buckman, Lower Makefield. 3-2-1789. Proved March 6, 1790. Wife Elenor. Sons John, David, Jonathan, Samuel and Abdon exrs. Daus. Ruth Buckman and Margaret Lee. Land bought of Robert Grant.
Wits: John Story, Phinehas Buckman, Deborah White.

Page 168. Daniel Groce of Hilltown, Weaver. March 20, 1790. Proved April 2, 1790. Wife Sarah. Friends Amos Bright and Bro.-in-law Jacob Landis exrs. Ch. not named.
Wits: Henry Wisme, Samuel Meyer.

Page 169. James McMullan, Plumstead Twp. Dec. 5, 1789. Proved April 10, 1790. Son James exr. Eldest son John. Dau. Elizabeth wife of John Vanfassen. Land in Plumstead Patented March 29, 1774.
Wits Alex Hughes, George Geddes.

Page 165. Margaret Thornton, widow of Joseph, Newtown Twp. 1-16-1790. Proved March 12, 1790. Son Joseph and son-in-law William Bidgood exrs. Gdch. Joseph, John, Jesse, Margaret and Sarah Thornton ch. of son John dec'd. Gdch. Joseph and Mary Paxson, Margaret, Hannah and Rachel Knowles ch. of dau. Hannah Knowles, wife of John Knowles. Gdch. Joseph, Isaac, Samuel, John, James, Henry, Lucy, Margaret, Elizabeth and Sarah Thornton, ch. of son James dec'd. Gddau. Mary Griffith. Gdch. Samuel and Joseph Yardley, sons of dau. Lucy Yardley dec'd. Daus. Margaret Strickland, Elizabeth wife of William Bidgood. Son Joseph.
Wits: William Richardson, Robert Drake, Moses Moon.

Page 167. Margaret Henderson of Warrington, married woman. Jan. 29, 1790. Proved March 15, 1790. Col. Joseph Hart of Warwick, miller and Nathaniel Irwin of Warrington, clerk, exrs. Nephew Earls Barnes, now or late of City of Phila. Niece Mary Shay of Horsham. Nephew John Barnes of Whitpain. Nephew William Barnes and Thomas Barnes of Warminster. Niece Isabel Bright of Warminster. Nephew Jesse Barnes of Moreland. Nephew William Vanhorn. Nephews Barnet Vanhorn Junr. and Isaac Vanhorn and niece Rachel Vanhorn of Upper Makefield. Niece Mary wife of Thomas Hart. Margaret dau. of John Barnes. Margaret dau. of Isabel Wright. Thomas Bright son of Isabel by her late husband --- Bright.
Wits: John Carr, John Homer, George Harkeshimer.

Page 170. John Cremor of Hilltown Twp., yeoman. Feb. 20, 1790. Proved April 10, 1790. Wife Christiana. Samuel Myers and Henry Eagle exrs. Sons George, Andrew, Henry, John, Paul and Daniel. Daus. Christiana wife of Nicholas Frantz. Land adj. Samuel Dean, John Mathias, Michael Frantz, Martin Fretz, Henry Hendricks and Peter Sellers.
Wits: Michael Snyder, Ephraim Thomas, John Mathew.

Page 172. Daniel Piper, Lower Milford, "Singleman." Dec. 22, 1789. Proved April 16, 1790. Ludwig Dersham exr. Michael, Henry, Jacob and Polly ch. of Bro. Michael, dec'd. George Engel son of Sister Christiana. Sister Susanna Sitzman. Luth. Church called Shipe's

Church.
Wits: David Spinner, Abraham Dillon.

Page 173. David Hamton of Solebury Twp., yeoman. 11-15-1789.
Proved April 22, 1790. Wife Rebekah. Bro. Joseph and Friend Aaron
Paxson exrs. Sons Aaron and Joseph. Daus. Mary and Mercy Hamton.
Bro.-in-law Thomas Phillips.
Wits: Oliver Paxson, John Hillborn, James Paxson.

Page 174. John Ashburn of Newtown Oct. 18, 1788. Proved April 23,
1790. Son-in-law Samuel Beekers and Isaac Hicks Esq. exrs. Bro.
Jacob. Daus. Mary wife of Joseph Dyer, Agnes Cary, Buley, Sarah and
Hannah.
Wits: Samson Cary, Jesse Buckman.

Page 175. John Burger of Richland Twp. Nov. 14, 1788. Proved May
11, 1790. Wife Catharine and son George exrs. Son John. Daus.
Magdalena, Elizabeth and Catharine.
Wits: Solomon Gruber, John Smith.

Page 176. Deborah Free[s]tone, Solebury Twp. Jan. 11, 1790. Proved
May 29, 1790. Benjamin Paxson of Solebury exr. Mother Elizabeth
Freestone. Bro. Hezekiah Freetone [sic] and sister Elizabeth Freestone
(minors).
Wits: Hezekiah Linton, Mahlon Paxson.

Page 177. Simon Kallender of New Britain, yeoman. Sept. 24, 1787.
Proved June 7, 1790. Son John exr. Dau. Mary Goode.
Wits: Richard Wilgus, Josiah Jones, David Evans.

Page 178. Nathaniel Griffith, Hilltown, yeoman. July 2, 1776. Proved
June 22, 1790. Wife Elizabeth. Son Benjamin exr. Eldest son Daniel.
Daus. Ann Morris and Sarah Heaton. Abraham Cone, overseer.
Wits: John Seller, Amos Thomas, Abraham Stout. Land adj. John
Bean, Levi Thomas, Abraham Cope, George Cressman, Charles Leidy.

Page 179. Barbara Shaffer of Springfield, Twp., Widow of George
Shaffer. Jan. 31, 1789. Proved June 26, 1790. John Cyphert of
Springfield Twp. exr. Anthony Nichouse. Elizabeth his wife and their
son George. George Shively, son of George Shively, now living in
Northampton Co. Minister and Vestry of Lutheran Church.
Wits: Mathias Shneider, Michael Ernst, Michael Sloyer.

Page 181. John Terry of Wrightstown. "Aged man." Dec. 9, 1788.
Proved July 10, 1790. Wife Sarah. Son John exr. "Teaspoons marked
R.T. which were his mother's." Gdch. Charles, Rachel, John, Mary
and William ---. Nephew Joseph Terry.

No witnesses.

Page 183. James Crose, of Upper Makefield, yeoman. Aug. 13, 1765. Proved Aug. 4, 1790. Wife Margaret and son-in-law William Reader exrs. Son-in-law Joseph Roberts. Dau.-in-law Sarah Good.
Wits: Richard Tomlinson, Robert Flack, Joseph Thornton. Letters to Francis Good, Margaret being dec'd. and William Reeder, removed out of state.

Page 183. Margaret Cross of Plumstead Twp. 2-13-1787. Proved Aug. 10, 1790. Son-in-law Francis Goode exr. Son William Reeder, carried dec'd. husband's will to Va. with him and refused to deliver same or have it proved. Dau. Sarah Goode.
Wits: John Carlile, William Mitchener, Mahlon Michener.

Page 184. Joseph Chapman of Wrightstown, yeoman. 6-2-1781. Codicil 8-23-1786. Proved Sept. 6, 1790. Wife Ann. Bros. Abraham and William and sons Edward and Isaac exrs. Gdsns. Edward, Isaac, Abraham, Thomas, Joseph, Benjamin, John, Jonathan and Samuel. Daus. Ann and Sarah Chapman. Codicil make sons Edward, Isaac and Abraham exrs. Bros. Abraham, William and Dr. John Chapman and William Linton to divide Lands between sons.
Wits: John Verity, Jane Fell. Land purchased of John Chapman and Mercy his wife. Also of Ichabod Wilkinson and Sarah his wife. Nephew Benjamin Chapman. John Morton.

Page 188. Hezekiah Bye of Solebury Twp. May 6, 1788. Proved Sept. 13, 1790. Wife Mary. Son Jonathan exr. Sons Samuel, John, Hezekiah and Enoch. Gdsn. Jesse Betts.
Wits: Yeomans Gillingham, Mathias Hutchinson and Martha Hutchinson.

Page 189. Sarah Paxson of Wrightstown Twp. July 13, 1790. Proved Sept. 25, 1790. William Thomas exr. Sons William and James Paxson. Daus. Jane Thorn and her daus. Mary and Letitia Thorn. Dau. Elizabeth Jice. Gddau. Sarah Paxson.
Wits: Thomas Warner and Ruth Warner.

Page 190. Jacob Cadwallader of Warrington, yeoman. 9-16-1790. Proved Oct. 20, 1790. Wife Phebe, son Cyrus and son-in-law Oliver Hough exrs. Sons Cyrus, Jacob and John Cadwallader. Daus. Rebecca Jarrett and Phebe Hough.
Wits: Samuel Gummere, Jonathan Jarrett, John Johnson.

Page 191. Michael Shelly, Lower Milford, yeoman. March 13, 1790. Proved Oct. 24, 1790. Wife Elizabeth. Abraham Yoder of Upper Saucon and Jacob Nold of Milford exrs. Only dau. Barbara Shelly. Step-Bro.

Jacob Nold. Step-sister Eve Musselman. Barbara, Anna and Joseph
Landis ch. of sister Elizabeth Landis.
Wits: Johannes Young and Abraham Cope.

Page 192. Sarah Feffery of Newtown Twp. Oct. 9, 1789. Proved Oct.
30, 1790. Thomas Story exr. Daus. Sarah and Flora.
Wits: David Story, Benjamin Taylor.

Page 194. Samuel Wilson ---. Oct. 15, 1790. Proved Nov. 3, 1790. Wife
Mary and Robert Stewart Junr. exrs,. Sons David, Samuel and John.
Daus. Jane, Martha, Rebecca, Mary Ann and Mary.
Wits: Thomas Stewart Senr., Thomas Stewart Jr., Francis Wilson.

Page 194. Elizabeth Fell of Buckingham, widow of Titus Fell. 7-27-
1778. Proved Nov. 15, 1790. Son Ganas Fell exr. Daus. Rachel Perry
and Joyce Fell. Gdch. Elizabeth, Joice and Mercy Perry.
Wits: Jonathan Fell, Ann Preston.

Page 195. John Thomas of Hilltown Twp., Minister. May 31, 1788.
Proved Nov. 15, 1790. Codicil Oct. 24, 1789. Wife Sarah and gdsns.
John Brittin and John Pugh, exrs. Daus. Ann, widow of Nathan Brittin
dec'd.; Rebecca wife of Daniel Pugh; Leah wife of Samuel Jones and
Sarah wife of John Blackwell. Gdch. John Brittin, Samuel Jones.
Thomas Rowland, son of Stephen. Mark Hardy. Land adj. Amos
Thomas, Abraham Miller, Peter Boder, James Shannon. Thomas
Morris. Thomas and John Biggle. Josiah Lunn.
Wits: Benjamin Morris, Joseph Thomas, Thomas Jones Junr.

Page 199. Martin Sheive of Haycock Two., yeoman. July 27, 1790.
Proved Nov. 19, 1790. "Far advanced in years." Wife Margaret
(marriage contract dated Jan. 25, 1774). Bro. George Sheive and son
Martin Sheive exrs. Sons George, Peter, Martin, John and Jacob. Daus.
Catharine Hetrick, Elizabeth wife of Frederick Waak. Ch. of dau. Mary
dec'd. Gdsn. George Waak. Gddau. Mary Althouse. Land adj. George
Swenker, Thomas Kan, Frederick Premoner, Casper Thorn and Jacob
Strahan. Land in Manchester Twp., York Co. bequeathed to son Jacob
and dau. Catharine Hetrick.
Wits: George Swenker, Jacob Allum, Thomas Gruver.

Page 202. Stephen Lahy. Nuncumpative. Declared a few hours previous
to his death which happened Nov. 6, 1790. Dated Nov. 12, 1790 [sic].
Proved Nov. 12, 1790. Wife Hannah and Father-in-law Richard
Tomlinson. Ch. not named. Died at house of James Tomlinson, near his
own house, from fall from horse.
Wits: Richard Tomlinson, Benjamin Buckman, Isaac Huddleston.

Page 204. Robert Whiteacre Sen., Upper Makefield, yeoman. 4-4-1786.

Proved Dec. 27, 1790. Son-in-law David Johnson. Gdsn. Robert Merrick
and William Atkinson exrs. Son Robert and gdsn. John Whitacre son of
son Joseph dec'd. Daus. Martha Merrick, Mary Simmons, Jane
Stockdale, Sarah Large and Mercy Johnson. Gdsn. John Hutchinson.
Wits: Henry Cooper, John Tomlinson, Jonathan Kinsey.

Page 205. Thomas Blackledge, Lower Milford Twp., Tanner. Feb. 11,
1790. Proved Jan. 3, 1791. Son Robert and Gdsn. Jeremiah Williams
exrs. Gdsns. Thomas and Robert, sons of son Robert. William
Blackledge and Mary Williams ch. of son Thomas. Gch. Thomas and
Ann Hoge ch. of Elizabeth. Dau. Elizabeth Hoge. Dau.-in-law Ann
Blackledge. Son-in-law John Clymer. Gddaus. Elizabeth Burson and
Rachel Roberts. Land Patented to Thomas Banks Oct. 16, 1742.
Wits: John Strahr, Abraham Taylor, Joseph Lester.

Page 207. Jacob Ruff, Nockamixon Twp,. yeoman. April 19, 1788.
Proved Jan 4, 1791. Wife Elizabeth and son Frederick exrs. Sons
Jacob, Henry, Christian, George and Frederick. Only dau. Sophia, wife
of George Folmer.
Wits: Frederick Everhart, Michael Krauss and John Spankenberg.

Page 208. Ann Brown of Plumstead Twp. Jan. 1, 1791. Proved Jan. 21,
1791. Son Abram and gdsn. Abram Brown exrs. Sons Joseph, Isaac,
Abram and Dawson Brown. Gdsn. Abram son of son Abram. Ch. of
dec'd. daus. Ann Rich and Leah Ellicott. Gddau. Hannah Brown, dau.
of Abram.
Wits: Joseph Walton, John Young.

Page 209. James Paul of Warrington Twp. 6-18-1790. Proved Jan. 22,
1791. Sons Joseph and James exrs. Sons John, Jonathan, Thomas and
Caleb. Dau. Hannah wife of George Bewley.
Wits: Thomas Austin, Joseph Longstreth.

Page 210. John Woolston of Middletown Twp. 3-8-1787. Proved Jan.
31, 1791. Wife Elizabeth extx. Sons Jonathan and Joshua. Daus. Sarah
Watson, Mary Smith, Elizabeth Knight and Mary Bye.
Wits: William Blakey Junr., Samuel Blakey, Joshua Blakey Jr.

Page 211. Peter Walter of Rockhill Twp. Nov. 20, 1787. Proved June 9,
1787 [sic] Wife Catharine Elizabeth. Sons Peter and Philip exrs., Ch.
Peter, Magdalen Reiner, Philip, Abraham and Jacob.
Wits: Philip Shetz, Henry Fetter, Philip Allum.

Page 212. Sarah Day, Relict of Christopher Day, late of Plumstead.
Aug. 23, 1788. Proved May 12, 1789. Thomas Wright exr. Son
Benjamin Day. Daus. Sarah Michener, Ursula Poulton and Adith
Bradshaw.

Wits: Francis Goode, Thomas Goode and Elizabeth Hill.

Page 212. Joseph Kohll, Nockamixon Twp., yeoman. Jan. 13, 1789. Proved Feb. 17, 1789. Wife Margaret. Jacob Kohll of Nockamixon and Nicholas McCarty Jr. of Haycock exrs. Sons John, Jacob, George, Joseph and Nicholas.
Wits: George Kohll and Nicholas McCarty.

Page 215. Thomas Walmsley of Southampton Twp. 2-14-1788. Caveat filed March 12, 1788. Proved Sept. 20, 1788. Gddau. Mary Reed and Friend Daniel Livezey exrs. Sons Henry and Ralph. Daus. Margaret Parsons. Gddaus. Esther and Sarah Reed, daus. of dau. Mary Reed. No witnesses.

Wills Proved before Isaac Hicks and omitted to be Registered.
Page 216. William Bennett of Northampton Twp., Blacksmith. 1766. Proved March 28, 1775. Wife Charity and sons Isaac and William exrs. Ch. Isaac, William, John, Leanna wife of Thomas Craven, Yanaea wife of James Vansant and Idah Bennett. Gddau. Charity Bennet dau. of son Richard dec'd.
Wits: John Hart, Joseph Hart.

Page 217. Job Noble of Warminster Twp., Blacksmith. Dec. 19, 1773. Proved May 12, 1775. Wife Rachel. Samuel Shoemaker and Jacob Tompkins exrs. Daus. Rebecca Gilbert and Hannah Moland wife of William Moland. Land adj. Jacob Rush, Clement Dungan, Isaac Hough, Jacob Fry and Harman Yerkers.
Wits: Jacob Rush, Barnard Vanduren, Samuel Gourley.

Page 219. Miles Harrison of Nockamixon Twp. Nov. 3, 1774. Proved May 19, 1775. Wife Sarah and son-in-law Henry Richey exrs. Dau. Ann Richey and her ch.
Wits: Nicholas Custard, Geo. Mickleroy.

Page 219. Sarah Bills of Buckingham Twp. 5-14-1775. Proved Jan. 12, 1775 [sic] Bro. Jonathan Paxson and Joseph Preston exrs. Sisters Harriet, Rebeckah and Rachel. Bro. Daniel's 4 eldest ch. William, Gersham, Hannah and Elizabeth.
Wits: John Cutler, Thomas Fell.

Page 220. Eunophronough Groover, widow of Nicholas Groover. Jan.14, 1775. Proved June 12, 1775. Tinicum Twp. Ludwick Long exr. Sons Simon, Ludwick and Henry. Henry Haas. Dau. Catharine Massmor. Son-in-law Harman Shiman, Tinicum Twp. Jacob Beidleman and Nicholas Groove exrs. of husband's will.
Wits: Edward Murphy, Nicholas Vickers, Arnold Shuman.

Page 221. John Hampton of Wrightstown Twp. 3-24-1773. Proved Oct. 3, 1775. Wife Ann and son Joseph exrs. Sons Jonathan, David and John. Daus. Asenath Comly, Sarah Smith and Ann Hampton.
Wits: James Briggs, Abra. Chapman, John Wilkinson.

Page 223. Katharine Wilmington, Lower Makefield. Oct. 16, 1769. Proved Nov. 25, 1775. Sister Ann Rickey and Alexander Rickey exrs. Kinswoman Sarah Hutchinson. Nieces Katharine Hutchinson, Ann Kirkbride and Mary Derbyshire.
Wits: Hugh McGlaughlan, Mahlon Kirklande Jr.

Page 224. Ann Ray of Bristol Twp. Oct. 23, 1775. Proved Nov. 23, 1775. George Stockham and Laurance Johnson exrs. Daus. Elizabeth Sanders, Ann Worrell and Sarah Johnson. Joseph Worrell.
Wits: Thomas Guy, Elizabeth Stockham.

Page 225. Thomas Abbott of Solebury, Woolcomber. April 16, 1774. Nov. 28, 1775. John Watson of Wrightstown exr. Niece Mary wife of Bosham Fisher and her 4 ch. Nephew Thomas Ashton. Mary wife of Jacob Walton and their 10 ch. Martha Bye. Sarah Fell. Susanna wife of Jacob Vanduren and their 6 ch. Sarah Wilson. Amos White. Joseph son of Daniel White.
Wits: Joseph Watson, Frances Watson, Achsah Hill.

Page 226. Thomas Gill of Buckingham, yeoman. Feb. 5, 1765. Proved Dec. 12, 1775. Daus. Agnes and Uree Gill exrs. Dau. Grace widow of William Beal. Gdch. Sarah, Thomas, Joseph & William Beal, ch. of dau. Grace. Gdch. Isaac, Thomas Meral and Gill Pennington ch. of dau. Mary dec'd. Gdsn. Isaac Pennington son of dau. Hannah dec'd.
Wits: Thomas Watson, Joseph Watson, John Watson.

Page 227. John Geddes of Plumstead, yeoman. June 3, 1775. Proved March 4, 1776. Wife Jane and son George exrs. Sons William, John, George and Henry. Dau. Elizabeth Taylor, now of Sherman's Valley, Cumberland Co., Pa. Dau. Mary Geddes.
Wits: Robert Mitchell, Joseph Braden, Edward Murphy.

Page 228. Anthony Pattison of Warwick Twp., yeoman. Dec. 4, 1772. Proved March 12, 1776. "Far advanced in years." Daus. Jane and Elizabeth Pattison extxs. Gdsn. John Bann. Gddau. Margaret Mathers. Daus. Jane and Elizabeth Pattison and Mary wife of Thomas Mathers of near Shippensburg, Cumberland Co., Pa. Margaret wife of Benjamin Griffith of near Shippensburg, Cumberland Co., Pa.
Wits: Thomas Lusk, Jno. Shannon, John Mathers.

Page 229. Alexander Brown Junr. of Buckingham, yeoman. 1-23-1776. Proved March 19, 1776. Wife Elizabeth. Jonathan Shaw and Robert

Kirkbride exrs. Daus. Lavinia, Sarah and Elizabeth Brown.
Wits: Christopher Day, Jonathan Worthington, Thomas Goode Jr.

Page 230. Joseph Warder, Lower Makefield Twp., yeoman. March 9,
1774. Proved March 26, 1776. Wife Elizabeth and John Larzelere exrs.
Bro. Willibe Warder. Nephews Charles, Joseph and Wheeler Clark,
sons of sister Rachel.
Wits: John White, Henry Hough, William White.

Page 231. William Ridge of Bensalem Twp. 11-13-1775. Proved June 1,
1776. Wife Mary and sons Thomas and Henry exrs. Son William. Daus.
Grace Cooper and Mary Praul. Gddau. Mary Ridge, dau. of son Henry.
Land bought of John Naylor in Southampton.
Wits: Thomas Walmsley, James Thornton, Joseph Thornton.

Page 232. Susanna Vanhorn of Newtown Twp. April 18, 1776. Proved
June 22, 1776. Sons-in-law John Johnson and Euclider Longshore and
daus. Jane Johnson and Susannah Longshore exrs. Son Henry
Vanhorn. Gddau. Susanna Johnson.
Wits: Henry Wynkoop, Gerardus Wynkoop.

Page 233. Jacob Walton of Buckingham Twp., yeoman. 7-31-1776.
Proved Nov. 31, 1776. Wife Mary. Son Jacob and Friend Paul Preston
exrs. Sons Jacob, John, Jesse, Isaac. Daus. Mary, Ann and Rachel. Sons
William and Amos.
Wits: John Gillingham and John Parry.

Page 234. Andrew Crozer of Falls Twp. June 7, 1776. Proved Nov. 8,
1776. Wife Mary and son Robert exrs. Sons Robert, John, Joseph,
Thomas and William. Daus. Mary and Jane Croshier. [sic] Son-in-law
Hugh Morton. Gdsn. Andrew Morton.
Wits: Joseph Richardson, Thomas Nugent, Daniel Ellis.

Proved by John Hart and omitted to be Registered.

Page 236. Jane Collison of Middletown Twp., Widow. 10-25-1782.
Proved May 14, 1784. Bro.-in-law Philip Perry and cousin Isaac
Cadwallader exrs. Sister Rachel wife of Philip Perry and their dau.
Hannah. Bro. Samuel Harker's son James. Sister Mary Lloyd's sons
John and Thomas. Sister Martha Michener's daus. Sarah, Tyson and
Elizabeth Cadwallader. Sister Grace. Simon Gillam. Hannah Wildman.
Jane Brown, Middletown Monthly Meeting.
Wits: Joshua Blakey, William Paxson, Moses Moon.

Page 237. Ann Huber of Lower Milford Twp., Widow. June 2, 1782.
Proved May 24, 1784. Son John Hauser and son-in-law Jost Reling
exrs. Dau. Catharine wife of Jost Reling. Heirs of son Jacob and dau.

Ann, both dec'd.
Wits: Christian Willauer (Willaner?), Peter Hackenberg.

Page 238. Elizabeth Fell of Buckingham, widow. 10-30-1777. Proved
May 24, 1784. Son Thomas exr. Gdsn. Zenas Fell. Daus. Sarah Church
and Rachel Kirk.. Gddaus. Rachel Fell and Cynthia Ely.
Wits: John Bradfield and Jesse Fell.

Page 239. Francis Titus of Middletown, yeoman. Dated June 30, 1783.
Codicil Sept. 15, 1783. Proved May 14, 1784. Sons Francis and Timothy
exrs. Ch. Francis, Martha Slack, Elizabeth Hellings, John, Timothy and
Samuel. Gdch. Archibald, Martha, Mary, Elizabeth and Tunis Titus, ch.
of son Tunis dec'd. Land adj. Jonathan Hibbs for public Burying
Ground.
Wits: John Hellings, John Sotcher.

Page 241. Ralph Wilson of Nockamixon Twp. Jan. 16, 1764. Proved
April 19, 1776. Wife Mary Ann and son David exrs. Ch. David, John,
Samuel, Martha, Robert, Andrew, Francis, William and Judith. David's
son and dau. John's dau. Mary.
Wits: James Steel, Robert Ramsey, John Howey.

Page 242. Hannah Hartshorne of Bristol Boro. 9-3-1781. Proved June
14, 1785. Late husband Hugh Hartshorne. Sons Paterson and Richard
Hartshorne exrs. Daus. Elizabeth Gregg, Sarah and Rachel Hartshorne.
Lands in or near Alexandria Va.., purchased since death of husband,
with money of his estate and of Large and Hartshorne of this place.
Wits: Samuel Kinsey, John Deverell.

Page 244. Isaac Gale of Bristol Twp. Dec. 9, 1788. Codicil Dec. 13,
1788. Proved May 21, 1790. Sons John and Isaac exrs. Daus. Sarah
Stackhouse wife of Benjamin, Margaret wife of Jacob Gosline and
Elizabeth Gale.
Wits: Samuel Wright, Amos Gregg.

Page 243. John Gray of Warwick Twp. April 12, 1759. Exhorted May
14, 1785. Wife Hannah and dau. Jane ("if they return from captivity")
sister Mary extx. Lands on Juniata River in Tuscarora Valley adj. lands
of Bros. James Gray. Nephew John Gray son of Bro. James. Mother
Margaret Gray. Sister Jean McDonal.
Wits: Andrew Long and Daniel McLeone. Exhibited by Enoch Williams.

Page 246. Valentine Nelson, Northampton Twp. April 17, 1773. Proved
July 8, 1790. David Twining and Thomas Jenks exrs. Mother Phebe
Kinsey and her ch. Joseph Smith, John and George Kinsey. Naomi
Wilson. Land devised by Thomas Nelson.
Wits: Benjamin Hibbs, Susanna Hibbs. (Susanna Worshall at proof of

Will)

Page 248. John Ratcliff (no residence given). Jan. 12, 1788. Proved
Feb. 21, 1791. Sons James and Jonathan exrs. Legatees James Radcliff,
Phoebe Cadwallader, Jonathan Radcliff, Isaiah Radcliff, Rebecca
Hough, Rachel Nelans, and Joseph Radcliff.
Wits: James Rankin, Charles Dean, John Rankin.

Page 248. John Winner of Lower Makefield Twp., Weaver. 1-3-1791.
Proved Feb. 23, 1791. Sons Samuel and John exrs. Ch. Rachel wife of
Jacob Watson, Didwell wife of John Smith, Samuel, John, David,
Joshua, and David Winner. Gdsns. Levi and John Terry sons of Joshua
Terry.
Wits: James Moon, Richard Neeld, Peter Vanhorn.

Page 249. William Allen of Bensalem Twp., yeoman. 1-26-1791. Proved
Feb. 24, 1791. Wife Mary. Sons William and Joseph and son-in-law
Samuel Wright, sons Joseph, Samuel and William. Richard, Nicholas,
Samuel, Mary and Margaret, ch. of son Samuel. Daus. Jane, Mary,
Abigail and Margaret.
Wits: Joseph Baldwin, William Mannington, Samuel Allen.

Page 251. Philip Stein of Bedminster Twp., yeoman. Jan. 9, 1791.
Proved March 9, 1791. Wife Maria Catharina. Son Christian and
George Fulmer exrs. Eleven ch. 2 sons Philip and ---.
Wits: Philip Harple and Jacob Allum.

Page 252. John Lancaster of Richland Twp., yeoman. 2-19-1791. Proved
March 11, 1791. Wife Elizabeth and son Israel exrs. Daus. Abigail and
Ann.
Wits: John Engle, Phebe Walton.

Page 253. William Frake of County of Bucks. 3-29-1788. Proved March
14, 1791. Wife --- and Anthony Burton Jr. exrs. Son Samuel and dau.
Mary Winner. "Estate in England and America."
Wits: John Burton, Samuel Danford and Joseph Hutchinson. Letters
granted to Samuel Frake and John Winner. (wife dec'd. Burton
renounced)

Page 253. Ann Michener of Solebury Twp., Widow. 5-18-1790. Proved
March 16, 1791. Sons Samuel and Jonathan Schofield exrs. Dau. Jane
Smith and her ch. Gddau. Ann Schofield. Wife and dau. of son David.
Ch. John, Thomas, Samuel, David and Jonathan Schofield and Phebe
Speakman.
Wits: Jonathan Doan, Benjamin Schofield, Edith Schofield.

Page 254. John Baird of Warwick Twp., yeoman. May 24, 1785. Proved

March 25, 1791. Wife Elizabeth. Son Francis and son-in-law Alexander Boid exrs. Daus. Jennett wife of Alexander Boid, Ann Baird, Elizabeth wife of William Richards, Sarah wife of Andrew Boid and Mary Baird.
Wits: Hugh Edams and Robert Bready.

Page 256. Abraham Landes of Bedminster Twp. Feb. 18, 1791. Proved April 4, 1791. Wife Magdalen. Sons Jacob and Samuel exrs. Ch. Abraham, Sarah, Barbara, Mary wife of Ulrich Basler, Jacob, Henry, Magdalen, Samuel, Daniel, Joseph and Benjamin.
Wits: Jacob Gottscalk, Rudolph Landes. (Translated from German).

Page 257. John Fry of Springfield Twp., yeoman. Feb. 14, 1791. Proved April 4, 1791. Sons Solomon and Joseph exrs. Land adj. David Rees and Samuel Myers. Eldest son Solomon.
Wits: Daniel Cooper, Samuel Myers, David Sliver.

Page 258. Anthony Scout of Warminster Twp. April 10, 1789. Proved April 9, 1791. Son-in-law Abraham Sutfan and Neighbor Daniel Longstreth exrs. Ch. James, Adrian, Anthony, William, Elinor and Mary. Gddau. Rachel, dau. of son Andrew dec'd. Gddau. Mary dau. of son Thomas, dec'd.
Wits: Giles Craven, Harman Vansant, Elcie Vansant.

Page 258. David Buckman of Newtown Twp., yeoman. 4-18-1788. Proved April 25, 1791. Bro. John Story and Friends Isaac Wiggins and Joseph Chapman exrs. Sister Elizabeth Heston. Nephews David Zebulon, William, John and Joshua Heston. Nephews David and Samuel Story. Cousins Isaac and Abraham Buckman sons of Isaac dec'd. William and James Buckman sons of cousin William dec'd. Jesse and Thomas sons of cousin Thomas Buckman dec'd. David son of cousin John Buckman. Joseph son of cousin Joseph Buckman. Late father William Buckman. Nieces Agnes and Elizabeth Buckman, daus. of Bro. Thomas Buckman, dec'd. Phebe, wife of Isaac Wiggins. Mary wife of Joseph Hampton. Phebe late wife of Timothy Scott. Ann wife of John Osmond. Isaac Wiggins of Northampton, David Buckman and James Briggs of Newtown and Joseph Hampton and Isaac Chapman of Wrightstown, Trustees for Free school at Wrightstown Meeting House.
Wits: Daniel Hunt, Edward Chapman, Amos Briggs.

Page 260. Jacob Roth of Rockhill Twp., yeoman. June 15, 1789. Proved May 2, 1791. "Aged and infirm." Wife Charlotte. Sons Jacob and Henry exrs. Sons John, Jacob, Peter and Henry. Daus. Charlotte, Elizabeth and Catharine.
Wits: Jacob Hartzell, Johannes Groff, Abraham Stout.

Page 262. Matthew Beans of Buckingham, yeoman. June 15, 1787. Proved May 3, 1791. Wife Elizabeth. Bro.-in-law Henry Paxson and son

Jonathan and Friend William Preston exrs. Sons Jonathan, David, Aaron and Moses. Daus. Ann White and Elizabeth Beans. Gddau. Margery White.
Wits: Francis Goode, Jacob Walton, James Price.

Page 263. William White of Solebury Twp., yeoman. Sept. 8, 1789. Proved May 4, 1791. "Advanced in age." Son-in-law Abraham Bennett and Friend Jacob Beans exrs. Sons David, William (if living). Daus. Mary Hartley (if living), Martha Bennett, Elizabeth Bennett, Sarah Morton and Rachel Sebring.
Wits: William Roberts, Benjamin Hartley, Joseph Skelton.

Page 265. Hannah Wilkinson of Wrightstown Twp. April 23, 1791. Proved May 4, 1791. Cousin Thomas Ross exr. Son Elisha Wilkinson. Daus. Hannah, Martha and Ann Wilkinson. Dau.-in-law Mary wife of Stephen Twinning.
Wits: Joseph Worthington, Silas Twinning, Isaac Chapman.

Page 265. Elizabeth Warner of Wrightstown Twp. 10-24-1790. Proved May 4, 1791. Benjamin Wiggins and Thomas Warner exrs. Sons John, David, Isaiah, Jonathan, Simeon and Amos Warner. Daus. Rachel Weber and Elizabeth Flood.
Wits: Ruth and Mary Warner.

Page 266. Davold Brouchler of Milford Twp. Jan. 6, 1781. Proved May 9, 1791. Wife Mary and son-in-law Stophel Sax exrs. Sons Michael and Adam. Daus. Elizabeth wife of Martin Sax, Mary wife of Stophel Sax. Madlanah wife of Daniel Kline.
Wits: Benjamin Seigel and Martin Sax.

Page 267. Hugh Ely of Buckingham Twp., yeoman. 2-22-1791. Proved May 25, 1791. "Advanced in age." Wife Elizabeth. Son Hugh exr. 2 elder sons John and William. Sons Jesse and Joseph. Dau. Elizabeth Smith. John Kinsey.
Wits: William Blacfan, Thomas Bye and Nathaniel Ellicott.

Page 269. Abraham Reasor of Springfield Twp.,yeoman. May 14, 1790. Proved May 27, 1791. Wife Mary. Son Abraham and Friend William Bryan exrs. Daus. Susanna and Anna (married.) Christine Snider to live with wife.
Wits: Robert Ashton, Peter Ashton, James Chapman.

Page 270. Ludwick Benner of Rockhill Twp., yeoman. Jan. 19, 1791. Proved June 14, 1791. Wife Catharine and son Ludwick exrs. Sons John, Ludwick, George and Henry. Daus. Christina, Elizabeth and Magdalena.
Wits: Mathias Hartman, John Heany, Abraham Stout.

36

Page 271. James Rose of Solebury Twp. 1-22-1786. Proved July 2, 1791. Wife Eleanor. Son Thomas and Friend Thomas Smith exrs. Ch. Thomas, John, Alice Hollingshead, Priscilla Reeder, Richard, Joseph and Susanna. Bro. Thomas late of Germantown, dec'd.
Wits: William Magill, Aaron Philips.

Page 272. Anna Margaretha Rese of Springfield, widow of Jost Rese. Sept. 9, 1790. Proved Aug. 4, 1791. "Antient and infirm." Son Henry exr. Elizabeth, Susanna, Joseph and Henry. Ch. of son Henry Rese. Dau. Elizabeth, wife of Michael Herring. Other ch.
Wits: Jacob Scough, William Diehl.

Page 257[sic]. Margaret Williams of New Britain Twp., widow. Nov. 19, 1784. Proved Aug. 4, 1791. Gdsn. Joshua Jones and Friend David Evans exrs. Son Isaac. Daus. Hannah Jones and Mary Edars. Gdch. Rachel Jones, Margaret McCarty (by dau. Casandra), Elizabeth Wells by dau. Elizabeth Wells, dec'd. Ch. of Dau. Ann Cornell, dec'd. Gdsn. Levy Barton.
Wits: Joseph Barton, Daniel Evans.
Codicil May 10, 1790.
Wits: James and Isaac Evans.

Page 274. John Twining of Warwick Twp. May 21, 1791. Proved Aug. 8, 1791. Wife Sarah and Silas Twining exrs. Son Joseph. Daus. Elizabeth Briggs, Mary Tomlinson and Rachel Balderston. Gddau. Elizabeth Tomlinson. William and Thomas Tomlinson.
Wits: Stephen Twining, Jacob Twining, Hannah Twining.

Page 275. John Addis of Northampton Twp., yeoman. Jan. 15, 1790. Proved Sept. 6, 1791. Wife Elizabeth. Sons John and Enoch exrs. Daus. Martha Carver, Mary Duffield, Elizabeth Duffield. Gdch. Elizabeth Duffield and Henry Harding. "To be buried at Trinity Ch. Oxford."
Wits: Isaac Edwards, Joseph Strickland, Silas Watts.

Page 276. Michael Wasley of Middletown, yeoman. Feb. 7, 1777. Proved Oct.10, 1791. Dau. Barbara and Jonathan Carlile exrs. Sons Peter and Michael Daus. Elizabeth's ch.
Wits: Hannah Cutler, Mary Carlile, David Carlile.

Page 277. Isaiah Walton of Bensalem Twp. 4-16-1791. Proved Oct. 28, 1791. Wife Sarah. William Walmsley and Daniel Knight exrs. Son Isaac. Daus. Mary, Agnes and Jane. Sons Isaiah and Nicholas.
Wits: David Parry, Daniel Knight, and Jonathan Knight.

Page 278. Ludwick Fluck of Richland Twp. Oct. 10, 1791. Proved Nov. 28, 1791. Wife Barbara, son John and George Smith exrs. Dau. Elizabeth (eldest). Dau. Catharine wife of George Smith.

Wits: Christian Kern, Thomas Armstrong.

Page 279. John Trego of Upper Makefield, husbandman. Aug. 14, 1784. Proved Nov. 29, 1791. Wife Hannah. Sons Jacob and William exrs. Daus. Sarah Wiggins and Rachel Trego.
Wits: William Smith, Anna Smith and William Atkinson.

Page 280. David Twining of Newtown Twp. 10 mo.-25-1791. Codicil 11 mo-12-1791. Codicil 11 mo-25-1791. Proved Dec. 10, 1791. Wife Elizabeth. Bro. Jacob and son-in-law Jesse Leedom exrs. Daus. Beulah Torbert, Sarah, wife of Thomas Hutchinson, Elizabeth Hopkins, Mary Leedom. Gdson Thomas Twining Hutchinson. Gdson David Leedom. Couzen David Twining son of Bro. Eleazer. Couzen David Twining son of Bro. Jacob. Son-in-law William Hopkins. Bro. Eleazer Twining. Friend Thomas Story. William Levinga. Land purchased of William Hibbs, Owon Hagerman, Shff. Jacob Bennett, Robert Thomas, Richard Leedom, George Wood and Jonathan Schofield and Anthony Tate. Ch. of Eleazer, Jacob, and Stephen Twining. Stephen Twining's son Jacob.

Wits: John Story, William Buckman, James Briggs, John Cavender, Joseph Worshall. Lands in Westmoreland Co., Northern Liberties and Northampton Twp., Bucks Co.

Page 284. Joseph Mitchell of Tredeffrynn, Chester Co. March 24, 1788. Proved Dec. 12, 1791. Thomas Watts, Isaac Warner of Blockley. John Bartholomew exrs. Wife ---. Son William. Ch. of Joseph Mitchell and Jane his wife late of Charlins in Summerset Co., viz. Sarah, Joan, Jane and Richard. Daus. Ruth and Mary. Ann Coffin dau. of William and Abigail. Nathaniel Blake of Padnoller.
Wits: John Davis and John Kugler.

Page 286. Joseph Phillips of Lower Milford Twp., Blacksmith. Feb. 23, 1785. Proved Dec. 19, 1791. Wife Mercy and son Jonathan exrs. Bro.-in-law Nathan Walton Trustee. Ch. Lydia, Mary, Joseph, Alice, Susanna, Jonathan, Martha, Mercy, Nathan, Edmund and Jane. Dau. Mary wife of James Miller. Land adj. David Phillips and Rebecca Walton.
Wits: Nathan Ball, Aaron Ball.

Page 287. Elizabeth Hibbs of Middletown, spinster. Aug. 30, 1791. Proved Dec. 19, 1791. Sister Mary Hibbs, extx. Bro. Jonathan Hibbs. Sisters Sarah Lovett, Amelia and Mary Hibbs. Sister Mary Hibbs; dau. Elizabeth Hibbs.
Wits: John Lotcher, Lewis Rue.

Page 287. John Kidd of Bensalem Twp. Nov. 14, 1791. Proved Dec. 22, 1791. John Swift, the elder of Bensalem. John Maxwell Nesbitt of

Phila. merchant, and Samuel Benezet Esq. of Bensalem exrs. Mary
Roberts niece of late wife. Sisters Theodosia Kidd, spinster and
Margaret wife of Thomas Braithwaite. Mary Young "my
Housekeeper." William Green "Who lives with me." John Faulder of
Wnthank (?), Cumberland Co., Farmer, "my 1st cousin" "and such of
his brothers and sisters of the whole blood then living."
Wits: Elizabeth Foulke, John D. Coxe.

Page 296. James Burson of Springfield Twp., yeoman. Jan. 30, 1785.
Proved April 26, 1792. Wife Sarah. Sons David and Joseph exrs. 8 ch.
David, Joseph, Isaac, Mary Roberts, Ann Posty, Sarah Brown, James
and Edward Burson. Gdch. Lewis and Joseph Lewis ch. of dau. Mary
Roberts. Land bought of Isaac Kidd and John Lester.
Wits: John Greasley, James Chapman, Rebecca Chapman.

Page 302. John Carey, Plumstead Twp., yeoman. 9-4-1760. Proved Aug.
9, 1792. Wife Elizabeth and son Thomas exrs. Ch. John, Thomas,
Elizabeth, Ann, Mary, Hannah, Elias and Samuel Carey.
Wits: Luke Severne, John Smith, Samuel Armitage.

Page 303. Edward McCarty of Nockamixon Twp. Oct. 7, 1783. Proved
Aug. 21, 1792. Nicholas Hoogey of Northampton Co. and gdsn. Thomas
McCarty, Blacksmith (son of John dec'd.) exrs. Son Thomas of Va..
Dau. Margaret Doran, living in Baltimore Co., Md. Catharine and Mary
McCarty, daus. of John. Son Nicholas and his dau. Catharine. Gdsn.
Patrick McCarty, son of Patrick, dec'd.
Wits: Edward Murphy, Catharine Murphy, Neol McDuffee.

Page 289. John Fenton, Northampton Twp. Jan. 19, 1792. Proved Feb.
14, 1792. Wife Sarah and Father-in-law Richard Leedom exrs. Ch.
Joseph, John, Benjamin, Richard, Jesse, Sarah and Mary.
Wits: John Cornell, Jacob Vanhorn.

Page 289. Isaac Stackhouse, Middletown Twp. 3-16-1789. Proved Feb.
17, 1792. Sons Jonathan, John and Isaac exrs. Son Thomas. Daus.
Mary Heston, Ann Gilbert, and Martha Gilbert.
Wits: Jonathan Kirkbride, Jeremiah Croasdale, Robert Croasdale.

Page 290. Jane Philpot of Newtown Twp., Widow of William. May 31,
1784. Proved Feb. 18, 1792. Dau. Jane Philpot extx. and sole legatee.
Wits: James and John A. Hanna. Codicil May 16, 1785. Dau. Phebe,
wife of John Huston. Seven ch. of late dau. Mary Torbert , dec'd.
Wits: Henry W. Blackly.

Page 291. James Bartley of Warrington Twp. Feb. 12, 1792. Proved
Feb. 24, 1792. Wife Margaret. Sons John and Hugh exrs. Son John of
Springfield Twp. Son James of Warwick Twp. Sons Hugh and Richard.

Daus. Mary Barr of Kentuckey, Sarah Hufty of Springfield, gdch.
Margaret Hufty. James Barr and James Barclay son of John. Bond of
Daniel Roymer.
Wits: Thomas Craig, James McGuown(?).

Page 292. John White of Falls Twp. "aged and infirm." June 6, 1789.
Codicil Oct. 23, 1791. Proved Feb. 29, 1792. Son John and Friend
Joshua Anderson exrs. Sons Joseph, George, John and William. Daus.
Elizabeth and Martha, son-in-law Joseph Vanhorn.
Wits: Joseph Gillingham, John Derbyshire.

Page 293. Alexander Wilson of Plumstead, yeoman. March 26, 1791.
Proved April 4, 1792. Bro. James Fairis and George Geddes exrs. Gdch.
William, James, Alexander and Elizabeth Wilson. Eleanor Hixon.
Wits: John Closson Senr., Amos Shaw, Adam Devison.

Page 294. Benjamin Dyre of Northampton Twp. 1-11-1791. Proved
April 10, 1792. Son Henry exr., Daus. Charity Dyre, Mary Lesly and
Jane Morrison.
Wits: David Vanhorn, Alexander Miller, Jacob Harding.

Page 298. Benjamin Swain of Bristol Twp., yeoman. 3-31-1791. Proved
April 23, 1792. Son David and gdsn. Benjamin Swain exrs. Dau.
Catharine Silvers, wife of James. Gdch. Benjamin, Samuel, David,
Jonathan, Abraham, Elizabeth and Hannah Swain ch. of Abraham,
dec'd. Jonathan Woolston of Middletown, Blacksmith Guardian.
Wits: Isaac Watson, Thomas Watson, Is. Hicks.

Page 298. James Rankin of Warminster Twp., yeoman. July 25, 1791.
Proved May 3, 1792, "Aged." Wife Catharine. Sons William and John
exrs. Ch. John, William and Elizabeth. Mary McKinney, dau. of Mary
McKinney dec'd.
Wits: Samuel Erwin, Mahlon Van Booskirk.

Page 299. David Dungan Jr. of Northampton Twp. May 5, 1792. Proved
May 9, 1792. Wife ---. Son David and Bro. Garret Dungan exrs. Son
Garret, "Dish marked with his grfather Nevel's name." Son David
"his gdfather David Dungan." Sons Cornelius, Mahlon and Levi. Dau.
Mary Dungan. Son Joseph. Peter Hoks. £7, 10 s. "by his gdfather
David Dungan's orders." Father.
Wits: Benjamin Eastburn, David Dungan, Hugh Edams.

Page 300. Martha Biles, widow of Samuel, late of Northampton. 2-26-
1792. Proved May 24, 1792. Sons Charles, Langhorne, and Samuel
Biles exrs. Children Charles Biles, Mary Willet, Doughty Biles,
Langhorne Biles and Samuel Biles.
Wits: Joseph Thornton, Phineas Paxson and William Bailey.

Page 300. Frederick Kyler, the elder, Durham Twp. May 28, 1792. June 12, 1792. "Old and infirm." Charles Jehline and Andrew Barnet exrs. Children, Mary wife of George Wagoner, Michael Conrad and Frederick Koyler and Margaret wife of Philip Gresler.
Wits: Richard Backhouse, Thomas Black.

Page 301. Hannah Balderston of Solebury Twp., widow. 5-1-1791. Proved June 25, 1792. Sons John and Jonathan Balderston, exrs. Sons Jacob and Bartholomew. Dau. Hannah Beans, Sarah Ely, Lydia Quinby. Son Bartholomew's dau. Hannah and son John. Sons Timothy, Isaiah and Mordecai Balderston.
Wits: William Lee, John Atkinson and William Atkinson.

Page 302. John Carey. Plumstead Twp., yeoman. 9-4-1760. Proved Aug. 9, 1792. Wife Elizabeth and son Thomas exrs. Children, John, Thomas, Elizabeth, Ann, Mary, Hannah, Elias and Samuel Carey.
Wits: Luke Severne, John Smith, Saml. Armitage.

Page 303. Edward McCarty of Nockamixon Twp. Oct. 7, 1783. Proved Aug. 21, 1792. Nicholas Hoogey of Northampton Co. and gdsn. Thomas McCarty, Blacksmith (son of John dec'd.). Exrs. Son Thomas of VA. Dau. Margaret Doran, living in Baltimore Co., Maryland. Catharine and Mary McCarty, daus. of John. Son Nicholas and his dau. Catharine. Gdsn. Patrick McCarty, son of Patrick dec'd.
Wits: Edward Murphy, Catharine Murphy, Neol McDuffee.

Page 305. Mathew Grier, Plumstead, yeoman. Aug. 11, 1792. Proved Sept. 15, 1792. Wife Jane. Sons John and Mathew exrs. Son John. Dau. Agnes, late wife of William Kennedy, dec'd. but now wife of Cephas Child and her seven ch., 5 by Kennedy and 2 by Child. Dau. Susanna, wife of Joseph Grier.
Wits: Isaac Hall, Abraham Hill, Thomas Jones.

Page 307. Henry Somp of Solebury. March 5, 1789. Proved Nov. 5, 1792. Wife ---, son and dau. John and Mary Parker exrs. Son-in-law John Mires res. in Va. Gddau. Elizabeth Royly.
Wits: Jonathan Ingham Junr., Jesse Pickering.

Page 306. Sarah Watson, Buckingham. 5-3-1792. Proved Oct. 1, 1792. Daus. Elizabeth and Sarah Watson, exrs. Mother ---. Son Thomas Watson. Bro. Jonathan Woolston's dau. Sarah. Friend Ann Hamton, widow.
Wits: Watson Fell, John Beale, Hannah Knight.

Page 308. Thomas Riche of Falls Twp. Feb. 18, 1792. Proved Nov. 10, 1792. 3 sons-in-law, Charles Swift Esq., John D. Coxe Esq., and Dr. Thomas Rodman and Relative Col. Augustine Willet, exrs. Dau. Lydia

Riche. Late dau. Mary, wife of Charles Swift. Dau. Sarah wife of Dr. Thomas Rodman. Gdch. Thomas Riche Swift, Charles Swift, Sarah and Magdalena Swift. Nephew Thomas Joseph and Philip Riche and niece Ann Riche, ch. of Bro. Philip Riche. Sister Ann, wife of Peter Toolman. Catharine Carey, widow. George, son of late George Gillespie. Horatio Gates Willet, Sarah, Margaret and Euphemia Willet, ch. of Augustine and Elizabeth Willet.
Wits: John Abraham Denormandie, Reading Beatty, William Bailey.

Page 313. Joseph Ball of Richland Twp. Jan. 23, 1790. Proved Nov. 16, 1792. Son John and Everard Foulke exrs. Son Isaac. Wife Sarah. Dau. Elizabeth. Land formerly Joseph Burr's now Casper Crosis, Joseph Penrose, Jonathan and John Griffith.
Wits: Hugh Foulke, Theoth. Foulke.

Page 314. John Ernest Herr, Rockhill Twp., yeoman. Aug. 29, 1792. Proved Nov. 19, 1792. Wife Gertrude. Sons Jacob and David Herr, exrs. Daus. Catharine and Christine. Son John. Land adj. Adam Cope, Henry Hertzell, Samuel Bechtel, Paul Bean, Isaac Derstine and Heirs of Michael Hertzell dec'd.
Wits: Henry Hertzel, Paul Bihn.

Page 316. Abraham Gehman, Rockhill Twp. April 18, 1792. Proved Nov. 19, 1792. Wife Elizabeth. Son Samuel and Isaac Barkay exrs. Sons Samuel, John and Abraham. Dau. Mary.
Wits: Isaac Bergy Junr., John Barkey Senr.

Page 317. Barnard Vanhorn of Upper Makefield Twp. Nov. 3, 1792. Proved Dec. 31, 1792. Sons Barnard and William exrs. Ch. William, Barnard, Isaac, Margaret Barnes, Edith Barnes, Isabel Hagerman, Rachel Temple, Mary Hart. John and Catharine Vanhorn, ch. of son Abraham dec'd. Ch. of Dau. Martha Hagerman, dec'd.
Wits: John Knowles Junr., Robert Knowles.

Page 318. Robert Thorn. Proved Jan. 16, 1793. George Wall, George Geddes, and Elias Carey, exrs. Ch. Isaac Thorn son of Ann Seboun. Joseph Thorn son of Ann Fetherby. Nephew John Thorn. William Sellers and wife.
Wits: William McPeake, Ann McPeake, George Rife.

Page 319. John Margerum of Bucks Co. Jan. 13, 1793. Proved Jan. 22, 1793. Friends Henry Margerum and William Satterthwaite exrs. Ch. John, Thomas, Mary, Katharine and Richard Margerum.
Wits: Edward Worstall, George Jobes, Samuel Winder.

Page 320. Rebecca Bye of Buckingham Twp. 3 mo.-4-1786. Proved Feb. 8, 1793. Nephew John Ely exr. Seneca, Elizabeth and Letitia Ely, ch. of

John and Hannah Ely. Sister Elizabeth wife of Hugh Ely.
Wits: Nathl. Ellicott, John Large, William Ely.

Page 326. John Clark Esq., Fairview, Bristol Twp. June 23, 1788.
Proved Feb. 22, 1793. Wife Margaret Extx. Rev. James Boyd and his
dau. Margaret Clark Boyd. Cornelia Bridges "my Goddaughter." Capt.
William Smith, nephew of late major Barnsley. Wife's cousin Margaret
Cross "who lives with me." Friend, William Dobel Esq.
Wits: Robert Patterson, John Gosline.

Page 323. John Lapp of New Britain Twp., yeoman. April 14, 1791.
Proved March 21, 1793. "Advanced in years." Wife Mary. Son John
exr. Ch. John, Isaac, Abraham, Mary, Barbara and Christiana.
Wits: George Sheip, Henry Hiestand, Evan Jones.

Page 325. John Forman of New Britain Twp. 8-23-1788. Proved April 1,
1793. Son Alexander and son-in-law Joseph Ambler exrs. Son Robert
Dau. Elizabeth Ambler. Grch. John Evans Senr. and Thomas
Shoemaker Trustees.
Wits: Mordc. Moore, Richard Moore, Henry Moore.

Page 325. John Praul Esq., Middletown, yeoman. July 7, 1790. Proved
April 3, 1793. Wife Catharine, son John and Bro.-in-law John
Vandegrift exrs. Daus. Sarah, Mary and Elizabeth Praul. Gdsn. John
Hise.
Wits: John Sotcher, John Hellings, Barnard Vandegrift.

Page 327. Philip Gressler of Nockamixon Twp., yeoman. Sept. 1, 1792.
Proved April 3, 1793. Andrew Barnet and Conrad Kyler exrs. 6 ch.
Michael, Killion, George , Philip, Eve and Margaret. Ch. of Dau. Eve by
George Shill.
Wits: Henry Barnet, Frederick Kylor.

Page 327. Martha Simpson of Warwick Twp., widow. May 3, 1790.
Proved April 4, 1793. Nephews Joseph Johnson and Samuel Carpenter
exrs. Sister Elizabeth Whitton. Niece Mary wife of Joseph Ledrw.
Step-daus. Elizabeth and Anna and Brita Simpson. Nieces Christian
Bane and Elizabeth wife of James Sutter, Martha Carpenter dau. of
Samuel. Nancy Johnson, Elizabeth Carpenter, Margaret Bane and
Mary Bane.
Wits: Thomas Barr, John Dunlap.

Page 328. Henry Lymbacker, Northampton Twp. March 2, 1793.
Proved April 16, 1793. Wife Elizabeth and Friend and neighbor
Gerardus Wynkoop exrs. Wife's Brother's son Henry Hillbrandt and
his Bro. John and sisters Elizabeth, Mary and Diana. Henry Lymbacker
Roberts. Land adj. John Bennett, William Cooper, Paul Blaker, Richard

Leedom and Achilles Blaker.
Wits: Henry Wynkoop, Henry DuBois.

Page 329. Catharine Clemens, widow of John of Buckingham. Aug. 22, 1787. April 29, 1793. George Kern and Deborah his wife of New Britain exrs. Margaret Fry, Elizabeth Shuler, Catharine Breneman dau. of Henry Breneman. Catharine Kern dau. of George. George Marklee.
Wits: Hugh Meredith, William Stephens, Joseph Dungan.

Page 330. Robert Hillborn of Newtown Twp. 3 mo.-8-1793. Proved May 14, 1793. Wife Jane. Son Amos exr. Sons Thomas, Robert and John. Daus. Rachel Beans, Elizabeth Taylor, Fanny and Mercy Hillborn.
Wits: John Story, Thomas Story, Aaron Cahoon.

Page 332. Jonathan Mason, New Britain, Clothier. Feb. 17, 1790. Proved May 14, 1793. Son Samuel exr. Son John. Dau. Rachel Mason, Lucretia McIntosh, wife of Alexander, Mary wife of Benjamin Morris, Jemima wife of Isaac James and Christiana Mason. Gddau. Mary Mason, dau. of John.
Wits: Benjamin Mathews, John Bray, David Evans.

Page 334. Mary Thomas of Hilltown, widow. June 22, 1781. Proved May 21, 1793. Dau. Anna Thomas extx. Sons Amos, Abel and Asa Thomas, Margaret wife of Abel. Daus. Sarah wife of Patrick Mettlin, Elizabeth wife of Isaac Williams, Catharine wife of Charles Miller. Gddau. Ruth Thomas and Mary Thomas. Gddau. Elizabeth Godshalk.
Wits: John Mathias, Thomas Jones, and a German.

Page 335. Joseph Reasoner of Nockamixon, yeoman. April 24, 1778. Proved June 21, 1793. Wife Catharine and Anthony Greason exrs. Son John and Dau. Barbara.
Wits: John George Kohl, Nicholas McCarty.

Page 336. Hugh Tomb, Bensalem, practitioner in Physic. May 26, 1793. Proved June 27, 1793. Wife Jane. Son Hugh and son-in-law William Pickens exrs. Sons John, Hugh and David. Dau. Margaret.
Wits: Joseph Baldwin, John Hawke, James Browne.

Page 338. John Merrick of Fallsington, Falls Twp. 2-8-1793. Proved July 9, 1793. Wife Phebe. 3 sons-in-law, Jesse Hough, Mahlon Milnor and Thomas Pearson exrs. Daus. Mercy wife of Jesse Hough, Ann wife of Jesse Rosco, Phoebe wife of Mahlon Milnor and Letitia wife of Thomas Pearson. Nephew John Field. Land adj. Daniel Burgess.
Wits: William Dean, Charles Clark, Samuel Moon.

Page 341. Abraham Zeby, Milford Twp., yeoman. April 7, 1787. Proved Sept. 16, 1793. Wife Anna and eldest son Peter exrs. Youngest son

Christian, 4 daus., Elizabeth wife of Henry Barem, Anna wife of
Christian Clemmer, Catharine wife of Abraham Shneider and youngest
dau. Hanna.
Wits: Christian Clemmer, Johannes Landes, and Abraham Yollr (?).

Page 344. Peter Hedrick of Richland Twp. Feb. 23, 1791. Proved Sept.
16, 1793. Wife Catharine. Son John and John Penner of Hilltown exrs.
Sons Philip, John and Peter. Sons-in-law Philip Shitz and Frederick
Shitz. Daus. Mollena wife of Philip Shitz, and Catharine wife of
Frederick Shitz.
Wits: Hugh and Everard Foulke.

Page 346. John Shelly of Lower Milford Twp. Aug. 14, 1781. Proved
Sept. 16, 1793. Uncle Joseph Shelly exr. Only Bro. Michael Shelly.
Sister Elizabeth. John and Barbara Hiestand ch. of sister Anna dec'd.
Barbar Shelly "keeping house for one."
Wits: Abraham Shelly, Jacob Shelly, Michael Musselman.

Page 347. James Fulton of New Britain, yeoman. Aug. 5, 1793. Proved
Sept. 18, 1793. Wife Mary and David Evans, exrs. Sons John and
Benjamin. Daus. Elizabeth, Anna and Ann Fulton.
Wits: Ashbel Jones, James Craig, Vallentine Toman.

Page 349. Elizabeth Shelly, Lower Milford, Widow. Feb. 28, 1791.
Proved Sept. 16, 1793. Abraham Yoder and Jacob Nold, exrs. Dau.
Barbara Shelly. Bros. and sisters.
Wits: Abraham Taylor, Michael Musselman.

Page 351. William Cooper, "the elder," Northampton Twp. Nov. 3,
1788. Proved Oct. 7, 1793. "Far advanced in years." Richard Leedom
and Jacob Twining exrs. Bro. Henry Cooper. Bro. Jacob Strawen.
Cousins John Cooper, Miles Strickland, Sarah wife of George Cammell,
Mary wife of John Atkinson. Friend Elizabeth wife of Jonathan
Williard.
Wits: John Fenton, Isaac Harding.

Page 352. Jane Scarbrough, of Solebury, Widow. 9-12-1793. Proved
Oct. 19, 1793. Samuel Armitage and Aaron Paxson of Solebury, exrs.
Aaron Paxson and wife Latitia and ch. Latitia, Ezra, Eliada and Aaron.
Ebenezer Doan, wife Ann and their ch. Jonathan Pearson's son [or
Jonathan Pearson], Crispin Pearson. Martha and Elizabeth dau. of
nephew Abraham Harvey dec'd. Several ch. of nephew Henry Harvey.
Ch. of niece Mary Armitage dec'd. Ch. of niece Jane Brown dec'd.
Wits: Oliver Paxson, Hugh Ely, John Watson.

Page 353. Sebastian Steer, Rockhill Twp. Sept. 21, 1793. Proved Oct.
29, 1793. Wife Eve. Sons Andrew and Nicholas exrs. Daus. Christina

and Margaret.
Wits: Peter Walker and Thomas Armstrong.

Page 355. Samuel Brod, Rockhill Twp., Tanner. April 6, 1788. Proved
Oct. 28, 1793. Wife Salome. Son Samuel and Friend Henry Hirtzell,
exrs. Dau. Sharlott
Wits: Jacob Smith, Michael Shoemaker.

Page 357. William Webb of Island of Dominica. Nov. 5, 1793. Proved
Nov. 15, 1793. "Now residing in Boro. of Bristol." Dr. Joseph P.
Minnich and William Allen exrs. Estate to be transmitted to Island of
Dominica to Thomas Court, William Ogden and William Atkinson to be
distributed in accordance with directors of Power of Atty. to them by
me.
Wits: George Merrick, John Gosline.

Page 359. William Long, Warrington Twp., Miller. Sept. 24, 1793.
Proved Dec. 10, 1793. Wife Elizabeth. Sons William and Hugh exrs.
Sons Andrew and Alexander of Fayette Co. Sons William, Hugh and
John. Dau. Isabel, wife of Alexander Crawford of Plymouth Twp.
Wits: Andrew Long, Thomas Griffith and William Long.

Page 363. Christian Miller of New Britain Twp., yeoman. Sept. 3, 1793.
Proved Dec. 18, 1793. Sons John and Jacob exrs. Son Henry. Ch. of
son Christian dec'd. Dau. Elizabeth wife of Conrad Keely. Esther
Miller, widow of son Christian.
Wits: James Haltiman, Samuel Garner, John Barclay.

Page 366. Joseph Pickering of Buckingham, yeoman. 1-1-1792. Proved
Dec. 30, 1793. Wife Jane. Son Isaac and James Hambleton exrs. Dau.
Anne Carver and Sarah Michener. Gdsn. Joseph Pickering. Gddaus.
Jane and Sarah Carver. Step-mother Sidney, widow of my father Isaac
Pickering.
Wits: Aaron Beans, Benjamin Paxson Junr., John Yillingham Junr.

Page 370. Stephen Townsend, Solebury, yeoman. 6-24-1793. Proved
Dec. 30, 1793. Thomas Carey Senr. and John Armitage exrs. Wife's
sister Ann Price. Sons Joseph and Jonathan.
Wits: John Hutchinson, Joshua Ely Junr., John Balderston.

Page 371. William Hough, Solebury. 4-16-1793. Proved Dec. 31, 1793.
Bro. Richard Hough and his son William exrs. Bro. Richard's dau.
Mary Hough.
Wits: John Skelton, Thomas Carey, Robert Walker.

Page 373. Grace Beal, New Britain Twp. 8 mo-16-1790. Proved Feb. 4,
1794. Joseph Beal and William Beal, sons exrs. Son Thomas Beal, dau.

Sarah Thompson. Jane Thompson.

Page 374. William Rodman, Bensalem. Dec. 1, 1789. Proved Feb. 5, 1794. Bro.-in-law Peter Reeve, of Phila., merchant, and sons Gilbert and William exrs. Gddau. Mary Howard. Gdsn. Lewis Howard, children of dau. Hannah. Gddau. Mary Ann McIlvaine, gddau. Rachel McIlvaine, ch. of dau. Margaret, cousin Euphame Gibbs. Housekeeper Mary Rees. Land in Bensalem in tenure of William Kindell surveyed by Paul Preston. Land in Warwick purchased of John Ewer dec'd.; tenants Serick Titus, Alexander Harvey, John Mason and John DeCoursey. Land in Kingwood twp., Hunterdon, N.J. in occupation of John , Joseph and Samuel Cowdrick, and Philip Forker; Land at Palinskill, Sussex Co., N.J. Demands against Roholand Robinson and Nathan Gardner in the gov't. of R.I.
Wits: John Miller, Henry Birkbeck, John Miller Jr., John Gallagher. Codicil, Dec. 25, 1793, freeing slaves. Wits: John Miller, John Gallagher, Pierson Tomlinson, Samuel Johnson.

Page 380. Daniel Burges, Falls Twp., yeoman. 8 mo.-5-1793. Proved March 17, 1794. Wife Sarah. Ch. Joseph, Elizabeth, Sarah, Amos, Daniel, (a minor) Hannah, Edith, Rebekah and Phebe. Wife Sarah and son Joseph and bro.-in-law Samuel Moon, exrs.
Wits: Cadwallader Foulke and Joseph Knowles.

Page 382. Ezra Croasdale, Southampton, weaver. Jan. 27, 1790. Proved March 25, 1794. Codicil dated Sept. 23, 1793. Proved Sept. 13, 1841. Wife Mary and two sons Joseph and Benjamin exrs. Dau. Anna Knight, son Joseph, dau. Mary Simpson, son Benjamin, dau. Hannah Croasdale, son-in-law Jonathan Croasdale, son Ezra, 3 youngest daus. Grace, Sarah and Achsah. Legacy due son Benjamin from myself by virtue of will of his gdmother Jane Scott. Land adj. Ruth Richardson.
Wits. to will: Joseph Thornton, William Bailey and Robert Comfort.

Page 386. Mary Lapp, New Britain Twp., Widow. Feb. 20, 1794. Proved April 1, 1794. Bro. Ulrick Hockman, exr. Friend Jacob Grose of Bedminster, Susanna dau. of Jacob Lapp, Barbara Rood, niece Elizabeth Beller, wife of David Beller bro. Jacob Hockman's ch., viz: Christian, Elizabeth, Mary Jacob, Anne, Abraham and Barbara; bro. Henry's ch. Elizabeth; bro. Ulrick Hockman's ch., viz: Jacob, Christian, Elizabeth, Henry, Barbara, Abaraham, Ulry and Anna.
Wits: Andrew Swarts, Johannes Lapp.

Page 387. Ludwick Wooldunger, Bedminster Twp., yeoman. Feb. 8, 1793. Proved April 28, 1794. Magdalene Algart and Philip Weymore of Haycock, exrs. 5 ch. of Bro. Mathias Wooldunger, dec'd. 5 ch. of Andrew Algart late of Bedminster Twp. dec'd. "My two brothers" aforesaid." Magdalene Algart widow of said Andrew. Dutch

Presbyterian Congregation of Bedminster.
Wits: Jacob Showalter, Adam Pysher, Isaac Burson.

Page 389. Susannah Stokes, "What she said on her death bed 2 mo.-
19th-1794." Sons James Stokes and his ch.
Wits: David Buckman, and John Scott. Letters c.t.a. to James Stokes.
Proved April 19, 1794.

Page 389. Richard Roberts of Rockhill Twp., yeoman. Jan. 22, 1789.
Proved May 1, 1794. Exrs. Matthew Fitzwater of Abington, Miller, and
Elizabeth Tyson, wife Rosamond, insane. Friend "Elizabth Tyson and
three of her ch. to wit. Mary, Alice and one unborn. Jesse Roberts "a
minor born in my house."
Wits: Amos Richardson, John Stull and Jacob Stull.

Page 391. Joan Rowland, New Britain Twp., widow. Jan. 25, 1781.
Proved May 28, 1794. Dau. Elizabeth Rowland extx. Dau. Elinor Mills.
Wits: Daniel Evans and David Evans.

Page 392. Joseph Gillingham, now of Buckingham, but late of Solebury,
blacksmith. 4 mo.- 6-1794. Proved June 10, 1794. Wife Phebe. Father
John Gillingham, exr. Dau. Mary.
Wits: James Price and Jesse Ely.

Page 393. William Simpson, Buckingham Twp. Jan. 3, 1794. Proved
June 12, 1794. Wife Jane. Son Thomas and John Wilson exrs. Son
John and 4 daus., Isabel, Mary, Elizabeth and Sarah. Money in James
Loughry's hands.
Wits: James Bonner, Abram Pugh and John Heanely.

Page 395. Joanna Longshore of Middletown. 4 mo.-22-1792. Proved
June 14, 1794. Exrs. James Wildman Junr. and Andrew Hunter. Sister
Jane McLear. 3 ch., Euclydes Longshore. Elizabeth Hunter and
Margaret Wiley; gdch. Jane and Amos Longshore and ch. of son Cyrus
Longshore.
Wits: Robert Drake and Martin Wildman and John Wildman.

Page 396. Bezaleel Wiggins of Upper Makefield Twp., yeoman. April 2,
1794. Proved July 24, 1794. Exrs. son Benjamin and son-in-law John
Eastburn. Ch. Benjamin Wiggins, Elizabeth Eastburn, Mary Hayhurst,
Isaac Wiggins; gdsn. Cuthbert Wiggins; Benajah Hayhurst. Lands adj.
Joseph Smith, John Stockdale, Timothy Balderston and Heston's
tract.
Wits: Zebulon Heston, Titus Heston and Joseph Atkinson.

Page 398. John Frick, Milford Twp., yeoman. "Advanced in years."
Oct. 15, 1785. Proved 8/6/1794. Wife Salome. Abraham Stout of

Rockhill and Jacob Rotrock of Springfield exrs. German Baptist congregations (vulgarly called Dunkers) of Germantown. Widow Eve Demuth; widow Elizabeth Krieling, Henry Kuhn of Springfield; ch. of bro. Jacob Frick.
Wits: David Shelly and a German.

Page 400. Hubert Cassell, Hilltown Twp. July 17, 1794. Proved Aug. 20, 1794. Wife Susanna and Leonard Eberhard, exrs. Son Isaac. Daus. Barbara and Elizabeth.
Wits: Thomas Armstrong, Christian Flin.

Page 402. Jane Jones, Northampton Twp. "Far advanced in age." Aug. 12, 1794. Proved Aug. 21, 1794. Isaac Chapman exr. Ch. Mary Ann Courson, William Jones, Benjamin Jones; Jane Jones dau. of son Benjamin, gdsn. John Jones; son-in-law Cornelius Courson.
Wits: Isaac Edwards, Kuerthe Jones, Isaac Chapman.

Page 403. Peter Johnson, Bensalem Twp., Farmer. "Advanced in age." July 15, 1788. Proved Sept. 6, 1794. Son Nicholas exr. Son John.
Wits: Adam Weaver, Isaac Johnson, David Woodman.

Page 404. Solomon Headley, Middletown Twp., yeoman. 4 mo.-16-1789. Proved Sept. 10, 1794. Ch. of Bro. John Headly. Kinsman John Bunting. Kinsman William Moad and Joseph Headly, exrs. Sisters Lydia Bunting, Hannah Moad and Christian Bunting, Bros. David and Joshua.
Wits: William Brelsford, Sarah Brelsford, Hannah Sotcher.

Page 406. Paulser Keeler, Tinicum Twp., yeoman. April 7, 1794. Proved Sept. 15, 1794. Wife Mary. Sons George and William, exrs. Dau. Magdalene wife of John Swope, and Mary wife of Philip Trauger, and Catharine wife of Elias Shull.
Wits: William Cooper, George Mash, and Aron Vanderbelt.

Page 408. Charles Stewart, Upper Makefield Twp. May 12, 1787. Proved Oct. 30, 1794, wife Sarah. Daus. Hannah Harris and Mary Hunter and James Hanna and Robert Thompson exrs. Son Robert. Sister Ann Hunter. Real Estate in County called Kentuckee, State of Virginia.
Wits: Henry W. Blackly, Andrew McMinn, Isaiah Van Horne.

Page 411. John Mourer, Nockamixon Twp,. weaver. Sept. 29, 1793. Proved Oct. 20, 1794. Wife Margarith. Son Peter, and George Rufe, exrs. Ch. Peter, John, Charity, Margaritta. Gddau. Margaritta Adams.
Wits: Philip Rapp, Peter Ulmer.

Page 412. Jane Patton, Lower Makefield. Dec. 29, 1791. Proved Nov. 1,

1794. Kinsman William Stackhouse exr. Cousin Joseph Johnson. Bond against William Biles to Rebekah, wife of William Stackhouse.
Wits: Joseph Gillingham, Peter Girton.

Page 413. Valentine Noll, Lower Milford Twp., yeoman. Jan. 2, 1794. Proved Nov. 3, 1794. Wife Barbara. Abraham Yoder, bro.-in-law,, exr. Son Jacob. Dau. Eve Musselman.
Wits: Jacob Clymer, Peter Bickler.

Page 414. Benjamin McCarty, Richland Twp. ?, yeoman. Sept. 25, 1794. Proved Nov. 5, 1794. Wife Margaret and Bro.-in-law Daniel Walton and son Benjamin McCarty exrs. Sons ---. Dau. Mary wife of Peter Ashton, and Sarah Mitchell, Mira, dau. of dau. Sarah.
Wits: Samuel Folke, Randall Iden, Casper Johnson.

Page 415. James Gray, Warwick Twp., Schoolmaster. Oct. 20, 1794. Proved Nov. 22, 1794. William Long son of Andrew Long, exr. Mary Long widow of Hugh Long, and Isabel, widow of James Wallace. Debts and Funeral expenses of dec'd. mother to be paid.
Wits: Andrew Long, John Kerr.

Page 416. Peter White, Middletown Twp., yeoman. Nov. 21, 1785. Proved Dec. 18, 1794. Wife Elizabeth and 2 sons Francis and Joseph White exrs. Daus. Jane Sisem and Ruth Rue. Land adj. William Gosline, Peter Van Horne.
Wits: John Bodine, John Sotcher.

Page 418. James Brooks, Tinicum Twp., yeoman. Nov. 13, 1777. Proved Dec. 22, 1794. Wife ---. Sons Joseph and Benjamin exrs. Sons David, John and Thomas. Daus. Mary Melalin, Margaret Momullin and Sarah ---. Gdch. James Sirlock and Jane Henderson.
Wits: James Carrell and Moses Kelly. Joseph and Benjamin Brooks the exrs. report that the little Personal Estate their father left was possessed by their mother during her life and then with her own Personal Estate was given away to them, Dec. 22, 1794.

Page 419. Elizabeth Carey, Plumstead Twp., widow of John Carey, late dec'd. Son Elias Carey and Abel Knight, exrs. Son Thomas. Daus. Mary Skelton and Hannah Wilson.
Wits: Joseph Watkins, Nehemiah Smith. 2 mo.-3-1793. Proved Dec. 23, 1794.

Page 420. John Carey, Plumstead Twp. 11 mo.-6-1794. Proved Dec. 23, 1794. Wife Ellen. Bro. Elias Carey and Friend Joseph Strodling, exrs. Israel Luvenner, "the young man that lives with me." Enos Halsey. Bros. and sisters, namely, Thomas Carey, Elizabeth Banghat, Ann Fisher, Mary Skelton, Hannah Walton, and Samuel Carey.

Wits: Ann Preston, Paul Preston, Junr.

Page 421. Mary Ramsey, Tinicum Twp. Aug. 13, 1793. Proved Jan. 15, 1795. Sons Robert and Samuel exrs. Five sons, William and David Ramsey, living in N.C., Robert living on my estate in Bucks Co. Thomas Ramsey living in Northumberland, Pa. and Samuel Ramsey living in Sussex Co., N.J. Gdch. William, John and Mary Ramsey, ch. of son Robert, Mary and Jane Ramsey, ch. of son Thomas. Mary wife of son Robert, and Ann wife of son Samuel.
Wits: John Neeve, Jacob Weaver, George Wall.

Page 423. Thomas Kennedy, Tinicum Twp. Aug. 22, 1794. Proved Feb. 2, 1795. Wife Jane sole extx. Nephew Thomas Kennedy, son to James. William Poulson, son to Pheby McConaughy. Land adj. John Bergstresser, Rebecca Erwin.
Wits: William Erwine, and a German name.

Page 424. Daniel Fratz, Bedminster Twp. Oct. 23, 1794. Proved Feb. 3, 1795. Wife Mary. Son Daniel and Friend Jacob Krout, exrs. Five ch., Christian, Elizabeth, Eve, Daniel and Jacob.
Wits: Jacob Crout, Alex. Hughes.

Page 426. Daniel Larrew, Middletown Twp. March 10, 1786. Proved Feb. 16, 1795. Sons Daniel and Moses exrs. Sons Abraham, Peter. Dau. Mary wife of Richard Stillwell. Dau.-in-law Apama, widow of son David and her son unborn.
Wits: Thomas Wilson and John Larzelere.

Page 427. Jane Philpot, single woman, Newtown. Sept. 9, 1794. Proved Feb. 21, 1795. Niece Mary Torbert exttx. Sister Mary Torbert's ch., viz.: John Torbert, Jane Burrows, Ann Burrows, William Torbert, Samuel Torbert and Phebe McNair. Sister Phebe Huston and her two daus. Elizabeth Spear and Jane Huston.
Wits: Samuel Torbert, Is. Huddleson.

Page 429. James Thackray, "Far advanced in age." 6 mo. (June) 14, 1794. Proved March 14, 1795. Son Amos exr. Sons Phineas and Joshua.
Wits: Jonathan Carlile, Jonathan Carlile, Junr., Benjamin Carlile.

Page 430. Daniel Church, Upper Makefield Twp., Taylor. Feb. 22, 1795. Proved March 20, 1795. Mother, estate bequeathed by my gdfather Joseph Church; "Own Bros." and sisters. Bro. John Church; Charles Reeder. Thomas Story and William Lownes exrs.
Wits: John Dungan, Josiah Yerkes, David Reeder.

Page 431. Gabriel Bevikiser (signed by mark), Bedminster Twp. "Far advanced in years." July 28, 1791. Proved April 6, 1795. Christian

Atherholt and Daniel Atherholt exrs. Gabriel Atherholt, youngest son of Frederick Atherholt, dec'd. Niece, Ester Atherholt, and her ch., to wit., Daniel, Mary, Abraham, Christian, Frederick, David, Joseph, Samuel, Hester, Anne and Gabriel.
Wits: Jacob Ott, Alex. Hughes.

Page 431. Conrad Jacobi, Bedminster Twp. Feb. 10, 1795. Proved April 6, 1795. Wife Hanna. Sons John and Benjamin exrs. Sons Philip, Peter. Dau. Margaret, Catharine, Elizabeth. Gdch. Sarah Woolslayer and Samuel Fluck.
Wits: John Bevikisor, Thomas Armstrong.

Page 433. John Starr, Lower Milford Twp., yeoman. June 20, 1786. Proved April 6, 1795. Wife Susanna and John Newcomer, Senr. of Upper Saucon exrs. Sons Conrad and John. Dau. Elizabeth and other children. Land adj. Peter Zuck and Christian Fry.
Wits: Robert Blackledge and Abraham Taylor.

Page 434. George Hughes, Buckingham Twp. Feb. 15, 1793. Proved April 11, 1795. John Ely and John Large, exrs. Jennet Austin. Natural son Amos Austin Hughes. Bro. Elias Hughes dau. Sarah Hughes. Bros.'s son Mathew Hughes.
Wits: William Bennett, Lewis Palmer, and David Forst.

Page 435. Moses Larrew, Falls Twp. Feb. 9, 1795. Proved April 16, 1795. Son Jesse and Bro.-in-law Richard Stillwell exrs. Sons Daniel, John, Moses, Aaron, Nicholas. Bro. Daniel. Dec'd. Father Daniel.
Wits: John Brown Junr., Charles Brown, Benjamin Watson Junr.

Page 437. Elizabeth Kinsey, Buckingham Twp. 1792. Proved May 5, 1795. Son John Kinsey exr. Sons Thomas, Samuel, Edmund, David, and Benjamin Kinsey. Daus. Sarah Fell and Elizabeth Fell, Mary Scott and Abigail Bye. Son Jonathan. Gddau. Elizabeth Kinsey, dau. of John.
Wits: Samuel Johnson and William Ely.

Page 438. Elizabeth Linton, Wrightstown Twp. 3 mo.-8--1794. Proved May 12, 1795. Son William Linton exr. Dau. Rebecca Linton, Dau.-in-law Mary Linton, Son-in-law Charles Chapman and Elizabeth his wife. Daughter-in-law Sarah Linton, ch. of my son Isaiah Linton, to wit, Laura, Thomas, James, William and Sarah; ch. of son William Linton, to wit, John and Elizabeth; children of Charles and Elizabeth Chapman, to wit. Susanna, Isaiah, Rebecca, Stephen, Elizabeth, Marcy, Mary, Charles, Letitia and Joseph. Gddau. Elizabeth Buckman.
Wits: Eber Heston, Ann Heston, and Daniel Linton.

Page 439. Mary Stats, Bensalem Twp. Jan. 27, 1785. Proved June 1, 1795. Son James Stats, exr. Sons Isaac, Andrew. Daus. Mary Schlock,

Martha Wright, Jemima Shaw. Gddau. Mary Shaw, son Peter Stats ch.
Wits: Henry Tomlinson, Ezra Townsend and Jesse Tomlinson.

Page 440. Leonard Vandegrift, Bensalem Twp., Cordwainer. Sept. 5,
1793. Proved June 16, 1795. Wife Rachel extx. Apprentice Henry
Vandegrift.
Wits: Abraham Vandegrift, R. Whitehead.

Page 441. John Rodman, Bensalem Twp., yeoman. 4 mo.-16-1798. Wife
Mary, son Joseph and Joseph Baldwin and Joseph Paxson exrs. Codicil
makes dau. Sarah Paxson extx. in place of her dec'd. husband. Dau.
Charity Lovett, Dau. Margaret Baldwin. Land where Widow McMinn
live. Do. adj. Isaac Johnson, Samuel Allen and William Rodman, Joseph
Rodman, John Johnson, Henry Tomlinson, Giles Knight and Adam
Weaver. Surveyed by Silas Watts Oct. 21, 1768.
Wits. to will Henry Tomlinson, Benjamin Tomlinson, James Street. To
codicil, Samuel Allen.

Page 443. Ann Carter, Buckingham Twp. April 12, 1793. Proved July 2,
1795. Son Benjamin Woods, exr. Dau. Elizabeth Skinner, Lydia Woods,
dau.-in-law Sarah Woods. Dau. Fanny Carter. Elen Carter. Gddau.
Nancy Woods.
Wits: Jacob Heston.

Page 444. Alexander Edwards, Bensalem Twp. May 16, 1795. Proved
July 7, 1795. Wife Ann. Dau. Esther, extx.
Wits: David Parry, Isabel Parry, John Hawke.

Page 445. Charles Garrison, Warminster Twp. "Advanced in years."
March 20, 1793. Proved July 20, 1795. Wife Elizabeth and Charles
Vanzant exrs. Nephew Abraham Egbert, son of my sister Elizabeth
Egbert. Son and dau. of Nephew Charles Garrison dec'd. - who was
son of my bro. Daniel. Two surviving sons of Bro. Daniel. Charles
Vanzant, son of James Vanzant of Northampton Twp. Trustees of
Presbyterian Church of Warminster Twp.
Wits: Arthur Watts, John Hallowell, Nathaniel Erwin.

Page 446. Thomas West, Warwick Twp., yeoman. Sept. 1, 1792. Proved
Aug. 25, 1795. Codicil May 16, 1795. Wife Britta, Gdsns. Jesse and
Elias Anderson and Joseph Barton, exrs. Dau. Charity, wife of Adam
Barr, dau. Mary wife of John Dunlap. Gdsns. Joseph Barton, Job
Barton, Elias Anderson, Jesse Anderson. Gdch. Pleasant Barton, Silas
Barton, Britta Barton, John Barton, John Simpson, Elizabeth Simpson,
Ann Simpson, Britta Simpson, Martha Dunlap and Mary Dunlap.
Wits. to will: Benjamin Jones, Elizabeth Jones and Thomas Jones Junr.
To codicil John Blankinhorn and John Kerr.

Page 449. Richard Betts, Solebury Twp. 8 mo.-24-1795. Proved Sept. 12, 1795. Dau. Susanna Betts extx. and sole legatee.
Wits: Stephen Betts and Samuel Betts.

Page 450. Jonathan Thomas, Warminster Twp., Carpenter. Aug. 11, 1795. Proved Sept. 3, 1795. Mother Martha Thomas. Exrs. Martha Thomas and Joshua Walton, John Ramsey, John Kerr.

Page 451. Jenepher Harvey, Falls Twp., widow. July 9, 1795. Proved Sept. 16, 1795. Exrs. Mary Borden and John Hulme, Esq., sister Mary Borden, sister Rebecca Bilis, sister-in-law Elizabeth Guillingham, niece Elizabeth Harvey, niece Elizabeth Borden, niece Ann Pennington, cousin Lidea Bunting, son John.
Wits: William Dean, Rebecca Hulme, Mary Brown.

Page 452. William Hayhurst, Northampton Twp., yeoman. Sept. 7, 1795. Proved Oct. 15, 1795. Wife Rebeckah. Exrs. son John Hayhurst and cousin Joseph Hayhurst. Dau. Mary Leedom, gdsn. Lewsia Leedom, son Custhbert, Rebeckah, Spineer. Gdch. Joseph Carter, William Carter, dau. Rebeckah Carter and James Carter.
Wits: Joseph Thornton and Joseph Crossdale.

Page 454. Richard Gibbs, Bensalem Twp., yeoman. Nov. 4, 1790. Proved Oct. 17, 1795. Exrs. son Samuel Gibbs, dau. Mary Carey, Sarah Rodman, Elizabeth Gibbs, Hannah Gibbs and Gilbert Rodman, and John Ruan. Dec'd. Bro. John Gibbs of City of London by codicil dated Oct. 3, 1772 devised annuity of £50 to Margaret Hubbard for life then Principal to me, I devise same to niece Bridget Lowther, wife of Richard Lowther, now or late of Earl St. London, Laceman. Niece Mary Cullam, wife of Thomas Cullam of Charing Cross, London, Sword Cutler. Cousin Mary Partridge and her sister --- Bowell of Bristol, England. 350 acres of land in Baltimore Co., Md. bought of Thomas Harrison called "Ashman's Hope." Other Lands in Baltimore and Anne Arundel Co., Md. bought of Benjamin Wells. Gdch. Margaret Carey, Mary, Margery and Gibbs Rodman. Land in Newtown, Bucks Co. bought of Daniel Martin. Lot in Bensalem adj. Patrick Griffin bought of Joshua Vandegrift. Son Samuel, son-in-law Albert Rodman and his Bro. William Rodman, Guardians and Trustees. Birckwood Pratt & Co. and Richard Lowther aforesaid Trustee &c. in Great Britain.
Wits: Hannah Jackson, Jesse Jackson, Elenor Jackson and John Jackson.

Page 459. Folkard Vandegrift, Bensalem Twp. July 18, 1795. Proved Oct. 20, 1795. Wife Elizabeth. Sons Jacob and Benjamin exrs. Dau. Anne. Gddau. Mary Vandegrift. Land adj. Leonard Vandegrift, and "Captain Josiah." Do sold to Isaac Johnson, bought of Daniel Knight.

Wits: Jacob Jackson, Barnit Van Kirk.

Page 460. Morris Morris, Nockamixon Twp. Farmer. Oct. 2, 1795.
Proved Nov. 3, 1795. Nephew John Morris, exr. William Morris, son of
John. Land Adj. Widow Webber, Peter Taough, Lawrence Pearson,
Michael Streep.
Wits: Peter Tough, Christian Troser.

Page 462. John Fell, Buckingham Twp. 9 mo.-22-1795. Proved Nov. 3,
1795. Wife Elizabeth. Cousin Jonathan Fell and son John Fell exr. Sons
Jonas, George and John. Dau. Miriam, Hannah and Rachel. Sons
Jonathan, Seneca and Mahlon. Land purchased of Jonathan Marin. Do.
devised by father, agreeable to contract with Nicholas Waln exr. of
Jacob Shoemaker.
Wits: John Bradshaw, John Watson, John ---. Codicil dated 10 mo.-7-
1795. Dau. Rachel Paxson.

Page 464. Henry Pile, Nockamixon Twp. "Aged and infirm." Jan. 21,
1795. Proved Nov. 4, 1795. Wife Caharena: John Fulmore of
Springfield and George Fulmore, the elder of Haycock, exrs. Son John
"absent several years." Dau. Elizabeth wife of Jacob Moyer alias
Henry Kelmore.
Wits: Henry Miller, Anthony Lamping, George Vogel.

Page 466. Benjamin Carrel, Northampton Twp. Oct. 11, 1795. Proved
Nov. 14, 1796. Bro. Jacob Carel exr. Friend [sic] Benjamin Carel.
Wits: Thomas Dungan, Joseph Dungan, Hugh Edams.

Page 467. Robert Caldwell, Montgomery Co. of Montgomery, Laborer.
Oct. 21, 1791. Proved Nov. 30, 1795. Maj. Samuel Hines exr. Half-bro.
Andrew Crearey. Matthew Hines son of Samuel. Mary Hines, Margaret
and Elizabeth Hines, dau. of Samuel Hines.
Wits: John Harry and John Donely.

Page 468. Richard Neild, Lower Makefield Twp., yeoman. Sept. 27,
1795. Proved Dec. 1, 1795. Son John and Neighbor William
Satterthwaite exrs. Dau. Hannah wife of James Johnson. Housekeeper
Mary Bateman.
Wits: Eli Neild, Jacob Watson, Moses Neild, James Hicks.

Page 469. Samuel Smith, Rockhill Twp. April 6, 1795. Proved Dec. 14,
1795. Wife Martha. Son Robert Smith and James Bryan exrs. Sons
James, Samuel, Robert and Jesse. Daus. Mary, Martha, Jane. Land in
Westmoreland Co.
Wits: Henry Hofford, Michael Keller, Alexander Hughes.

Page 471. Conrad Mitman, Senr., Bedminster Twp., yeoman. April 15,

1795. Proved Dec. 14, 1795. Wife Barbara. Son Conrad and son-in-law
Henry Bernd, exrs. Dau. Elizabeth wife of Henry Bernd.
Wits: Jacob Landis, Casper Shoen.

Page 474. Ludwick Long, Tinicum Twp. March 24, 1794. Proved Dec. 4,
1795. Wife Elizabeth and eldest son Peter, exrs. Other sons not named.
Dau. Margaret, wife of Philip Gover.
Wits: William Kealer, Elias Shull Jr. and Elias Shull.

Page 475. Robert McNeely, Bedminstter Twp. Nov. --, 1795. Proved
Dec. 14, 1795. Wife Rebecca. Friend Alexander Hughes and son William
exrs. Sons John, Robert and Andrew; 4 (?) youngest ch. William,
Joseph and Margaret.
Wits: John Lutz and John McKinney.

Page 476. Richard Jopson, Solebury Twp., yeoman. Oct. 10, 1785.
Proved Dec. 22, 1795. Codicils March 8, 1786. Wife Rebecca and son
Joseph exrs. Codicil adds Isaac Van Horne, Esq. Daus. Ursula Jopson,
Jane Cummins, Judith Jopson, Rebecca Jopson, Mo. Mtg. of
Wrightstown. Thomas Ross Jr. overseer of Will.
Wits. to Will: John Vanhorn and Isaac Vanhorne. Same to codicils.

Page 479. Phebe Gillingham, Buckingham Twp., widow. 10 mo.-16-
1795. Proved Jan. 5, 1796. Father-in-law John Gillingham exr. Dau.
Mary Gillingham. Sarah Gillinham (sic) Junr., Esther Gillingham,
Samuel Gillinham (sic), John Gillingham Junr., Benjamin Gillingham,
Amos Gillinham (sic) and David Gillingham (no relation mentioned).
Bro. Levi Brown and sister Letitia Parry. Dec'd. husband Joseph
Gillingham.
Wits: Jacob Walton, Philip Parry.

Page 480. Jacob Hystrand, Lower Milford Twp., yeoman. Jan. 13, 1795.
Proved Feb. 29, 1796. Wife Elizabeth. Christian Beidler and Abraham
Schontz, of Upper Milford exrs. Bro. John's eldest dau. Mary wife of
Michael Hottle. "All my Bretheren and sisters and their children."
Wits: Jacob ---, John Leigter.

Page 481. Mary Bateman, Lower Makefield Twp., Housekeepr. Oct. 21,
1795. Proved March 25, 1796. Ely Nield and John Nield, son of Richard
Nield, both of Twp. afsd. exrs.
Wits: Phin. Thackeray, Moses Nield and Joseph Walton.

Page 484. Richard Durden, Falls Twp. Feb. 1, 1788. Proved May 25,
1793. Codicil dated April 24, 1793. Wife Frances, extx. and Guardian.
Son Alexander Henry Durden and such other children that may be
born &c.
Wits. to Will: William McIlvaine, William Dobels, Samuel Torbert.

Wits. to Codicil: Thomas Nixon, Robert Dougherty, Mary Dougherty.

Page 484. Andrew Seagafooss, Springfield Twp. Feb. 16, 1796. Proved
April 4, 1796. Wife ---. Sons Peter, Jacob and Michael exrs. Ten ch.,
Andrew, Elizabeth, George, Barbary, Caty, Mary, Jacob, Margrit,
Peter, Michael.
Wits: Andrew Overpeek, Isaac Burson, George ---.

Page 485. Daniel Stradling, Plumstead Twp. 3-12-1794. Proved April 6,
1796. Wife Sarah. Son Joseph exr. Dau. Sarah Mitchener.
Wits: Thomas Carey, Samuel Shaw.

Page 487. James Moon, Junr., Lower Makefield Twp. 11 mo.-12-1789.
Proved April 9, 1796. Wife Sarah and Father James, bro. Moses and
son James exrs. Dau. Mary Thornton. Gdch. Sarah, James Thornton.
Wits: Jonathan Kirkbride, Thomas Barnes, Hannah Barnes.

Page 489. Sarah Suber, dau. of George Suber, late of Middletown,
yeoman, dec'd. Feb. 28, 1796. Proved May 2, 1796. Mother Mary
Suber and bro. Joseph Suber exrs. Late death of Bro. George. Son
William Suber. Anne dau. of bro. Joseph. Sister Mary.
Wits: Charity Moode, Magdalena Suber, Is. Hicks.

Page 490. James Moon, Middletown Twp. 5 mo.-5-1783. Proved June
18, 1796. Wife Ann. Sons James and Moses and son-in-law Yeamans
Gillingham exrs. Dau. Bridget Gillingham. Gdch. Moses Gillingham and
Mary Moon. Land bought of Joseph Gillingham, Robert Lucas, William
Satterthwaite, and Daniel Creely.
Wits: William Satterthwaite Jr., John Brown Jr., William Paxson.

Page 492. Daniel Livezey, Southampton Twp., Farmer. 7 mo.-14-1795.
Proved Aug. 2, 1796. Wife Margery and Bro. Thomas Livezey and Bro.-
in-law Jaremiah Croasdale, exrs. 8 ch., Robert, Jonathan, Sarah, Isaac,
Deborah, Thomas, Ezra and Samuel.
Wits: Benjamin Croasdale, Jonathan Croasdale.

Page 494. Michael Wisell, Bedminster Twp. June 3, 1796. Proved Aug.
2, 1796. Widow ---. Sons Michael and Henry exrs. Sons Michael, Henry
and George, "and all the rest of my children."
Wits: Thomas Armstrong, Jacob Twartley.

Page 495. John Paxson, Solebury Twp., weaver. 7-12-1796. Proved
Aug. 3, 1796. Wife Rachel. Bro.-in-law George Fell exr. Dau. Marian
under ten years of age. Lot purchased of Thomas Carey, Jr.
Wits: Samuel Paxson and Edmund Smith.

Page 496. Rudolph Shivler, Nockamixon Twp., Farmer. June 10, 1796.

Proved Aug. 27, 1796. Wife Mary Margaret and John Adams, the younger, exrs. Ch. Mary Magdalene, Susanna, Sarah, Abraham, John and Elizabeth Shivler. Bro. Henry Shivler.
Wits: Michael Dise, Henry Riegel, Jacob Schribler.

Page 498. William Foulke, Richland, weaver. 2 mo.-9-1791. Proved Sept. 5, 1796. Wife Priscilla. Eldest son Asher and Bro.-in-law John Lester, exrs. Sons Asher, Issachar and Jesse and Dau. Mary Foulke.
Wits: John Greasley, Samuel Nixon, William Nixon. Proved by John Greasley, Samuel Foulke, Esq., and Israel Lancaster.

Page 500. Jacob Buckman, Newtown Twp. 8 mo.-14-1794. Proved Sept. 20, 1796. Son-in-law William Matindell [sic] and cousin William Buckman exrs. John Buckman, Joseph Buckman, Junr. and Thomas Story, Trustees. Daus. Ester Martindell and Sarah Smith.
Wits: Samson Cary, Moses Kelly.

Page 502. Hugh Mearns, Warwick Twp., Miller. Nov. 15, 1788. Proved Sept. 27, 1796. Codicil Sept. 22, 1796. Wife Rachel. Sons Robert and William exrs. Dau. Sarah, wife of Robert Jamison.
Wits: William Ramsey, Robert Bready and Nathaniel Irwin. Bond due to John Wharton by son Robert.

Page 504. William Blackfan, Solesbury Twp., yeoman. June 3, 1796. Proved Sept. 29, 1796. Wife Hester. Sons John and Thomas exrs. Son Jesse. Daus. Elizabeth Fell, Rachel Chapman, Hannah Smith, Sarah and Agnes Blackfan. Bond of Thomas Molloy and William Betts, conditioned for procuring one Patents from the state of N.C. for 3200 acres of land in the county of Tenese [Tennessee], on or near the Cumberland River.
Wits: Isaac Chapman, Joseph Chapman, Benjamin Thomas.

Page 507. Nicholas Fisher, Rockhill Twp., yeoman. Jan. 13, 1796. Proved Oct. 13, 1796. Son John and Theobald Nase exrs. Daus. Elizabeth and Eve. House where Jacob Hendrick lives.
Wits: Benjamin Soladay and Abraham Stout.

Page 508. Joseph Watson, Buckingham. Aug. 2, 1790. Proved Oct. 24, 1796. Wife Frances. Nephew Jonathan Fell, exr. Son John Watson. Gdsons. Joseph and John Watson. Gddaus. Alice, Frances, Ann and Rachel Watson. Wife's Bro. Joseph Hillborn. Bonds of John Shaw and Christian Dorrick. Land devised by Father John Watson.
Wits: John Melone, Watson Welding, Robert Smith Junr.

Page 510. Christian Bechler, Lower Milford Twp., yeoman. Feb. 24, 1794. Proved Oct. 20, 1796. Wife Magdalena. Christian Hunsberger, Abraham Shneider and son-in-law Peter Zety, exrs. Eldest son Peter

Bickler, David, Christian, Samuel Jacob and John. Daus. Elizabeth wife of Abraham Shelly, Susanna wife of Peter Zety, Magdalena, Barbara, Anna and Catharine. Deed from Robert Morris dated June 1, 1773. Wits: Jacob Clymer, Jacob Holtz.

Page 517. Conrad Krouse, Nockamixon Twp., "Halder". Oct. 13, 1796. Proved Nov. 7, 1796. Wife Elizabeth and Bro. Frederick Krouse exrs. Son Michael and two daus. Wits: Jacob Krouse, Phillip Rapp.

Page 514. John Green, Bristol Twp. May 28, 1796, codicil Sept. 22, 1796. Proved Oct. 26, 1796. Wife Alice, son John and sons-in-law Walter Sims, Dr. Joseph P. Minnick and William Hewson exrs. Son Robert Morris Green and dau. Magdalen Hollock Green, minors. Wits: Newberry Field, David Osmond, Daniel Benezet.

Page 518. Benjamin Watson, Falls Twp., Tanner, "infirm of Body." 6 mo.-23-1796. Proved Nov. 8, 1796. Wife Phebe, son Benjamin , Friend John Brown Junr. and son-in-law William Blakey exrs. Sons Mahlon, Charles, Joseph. Daus. Hannah, Elizabeth, Grace, Lucy and Mercy. Gdsn. Benjamin Burton. New Bible bought of Isaac Collins. Wits: Isaac Watson and Benjamin Buckman.

Page 519. Henry Weirbacker, Springfield Twp. May 6, 1796. Proved Nov. 8, 1796. Wife Barbara and Friend Henry Erhard exrs. Ch. Margareth, Anthony, Susanna and Henery. Wits: John Green, Jacob Clymer.

Page 521. Nathaniel Ellicott, Buckingham. Sept. 9, 1784. Proved Nov. 7, 1796. Caveat filed July 1, 1796. Letters pendente lite to Benjamin Ellicott Aug. 1, 1796. Letters Testamentary to same Nov. 7, 1796. Wife Letitia and nephew Benjamin Ellicott exrs. Bond with Bro. Joseph to Thomas Hicks, to be paid out of my estate and no charge made to "Joseph's Estate." Sarah Ellicott wife of Jonathan, Letitua Harvey, Half-sister Mary Dixon, Mother, nephew Nathaniel Ellicott, nephew Benjamin Ellicott, son of Andrew. Wits: Thomas Bye, William Ely, John Kinsey, Hugh Ely Junr.

Page 523. Anthony Himble, Buckingham Twp. "Advanced in age." Oct. 15, 1791. Codicil dated April 13, 1793 and Oct. 5, 1796. Proved Nov. 10, 1796. Wife Sarah. Sons-in-law Jesse Pickering to John Skelton, exrs. Sons Christopher, Anthony and John. Sons-in-law Henry Paxson and Joseph Paxson. Daus. Matilda Paxson, Sarah Skelton, Ann Pickering, Mary Paxson, Elizabeth Carver, Pheby Bailey, Rachel Worthington, Ester Worthington, Cynthia and Tabitha. Deeds from William Brown, Hugh Miller, Richard Murray, Eleazer Doan, Benjamin Chapman. Wits: William Carver, Joseph Carver Junr., John Terry, Isaac

Chapman.

Page 529. Uree Bradfield, Buckingham Twp. 1 mo.-27-1795. Proved
Nov. 19, 1796. Husband John Bradfield exr. Merab Wood, Agnes
Vankirk, Gill Pennington, Mary Pennington, dau. of Thomas
Pennington, Uree Cadwallader, dau. of Benjamin Cadwallader and
Sarah Hartley, dau. of Thomas Hartley. Land devised by Father
Thomas Gill, dec'd.
Wits: Joseph Burgess, Jonathan Shephard, John Watson.

Page 530. Daniel Ryan, Upper Makefield Twp. March 11, 1795. Proved
Nov. 21, 1796. Wife Elizabeth and sons Isaac and Daniel, exrs. Son
William. Daus. Margaret Williams, Sarah Van Pelt, Tesey Harry. Gdsn.
Modake Ryan and his sister.
Wits: William Smith, Thomas Smith, Isaac Chapman.

Page 531. Adam Frank, Rockhill Twp., wheelwright, "Aged." July 22,
1793. Proved Nov. 22, 1796. Wife Margaret. Son Peter Frank and son-
in-law Henry Nase, exrs. Sons Peter and John. Daus. Wilhelmina,
Magdalena, Catharine and Mary.
Wits: George Snyder, Henry Neice.

Page 533. Phillip Barron, Springfield Twp., yeoman. "Old and infirm."
Dec. 28, 1789, codicil same date. Proved Nov. 23, 1796. Wife Margaret.
Michael Fackenthall and Frederick Everhart exrs. Sons Jacob, George,
Philip. Dau. Elizabeth. Dau. Juliana wife of Philip Lambauch. Son
John.
Wits: Henry Applebaugh, Mary Applebaugh.

Page 536. Robert Skelton, Buckingham Twp., yeoman. Aug. 12, 1796.
Nov. 23, 1796 [proved]. Joseph Stradling of Plumstead and Samuel
Gillingham of Buckingham exrs. Daus. Ellener Rice and Mary Shreigly.
Bro. William Skelton. Gdsn. John Skelton and his son Robert. Gddau.
Ann Rice.
Wits: Thomas Wood, John Gillinham Jr., Isaac Pickering Jr.

Page 538. Benjamin Scott, the Elder, Buckingham Twp. Nov. 29, 1796.
Proved Dec. 15, 1796. Samuel Gillingham and Joseph Stradling, exrs.
and Guardians. Bro. John. Nephew Benjamin Scott. Ch. and gdch. viz;
John, Moses, Elizabeth, Job and Mary Scott and Thomas Wood Jr. Ann
Wood mother of said Thomas Wood Jr.
Wits: Samuel Hanin, John Gillingham Jr., John Skelton Jr.

Page 540. Stephen Smith, Wrightstown. Feb. 14, 1794. Proved Jan. 9,

1797. Wife Phebe. Benjamin Schofield and nephew Thomas Smith exrs. Sons Stephen, Marshall, Cyrus. Six ch. Stephen, Rebecca, Ann, Phebe, Marshall and Cyrus. Land bought of John Smith. Deed to be made to Joseph Roberts.
Wits: Moses Kelly, Thomas Gaine, William Kelly.

Page 542. Jonathan Wilcoxe, Bristol Twp., Cordwainer. Dec. 24, 1796. Proved 1 mo.-26-1796.[*sic*] William Mode of Middletown and Elizabeth Orrisson, exrs. Son John, dau. Sarah.
Wits: George Mitchell, John Edgar.

Page 543. Henry Lewis, Hilltown Twp., yeoman. Oct. 23, 1792. Proved Feb. 4, 1797. Wife Margaret. Son William,. son-in-law James Thomas, son-in-law Philip Miller, exrs. Daus. Rachel Jones, Rebecca Congle, Mary Thomas, Margaret Miller, sons William Isaac and James. Gddau. Margaret Jones. Land where Jacob Fence lives.
Wits: Asa Thomas, Henry Core, Amor Griffith.

Page 545. Joseph Rawlings, Richland Twp. 11-25-1796. Proved Feb. 7, 1797. Wife Ann. William Penrose and Kinsman Amos Richardson, exrs. 4 ch., Margaret, Thomas, Ann and Jane. Step-dau. Ann Pugh. Kinsman Samuel Rawlings.
Wits: Edward Roberts, Everard Foulke, Israel Roberts.

Page 548. Samuel Foulke, Richland Twp., yeoman. "Advanced in Age." Oct. 8, 1796. Proved Feb. 7, 1797. Wife Ann. Son Israel and nephew Everard exrs. Sons John, Judah, Cadwallader. Daus. Eleanor wife of Randal Iden, Amelia wife of Joseph Custer, Hannah wife of George Iden. Gdsn. Samuel Iden. Servant Abner Dalby.
Wits: Thomas Lester, John Lester.

Page 550. John Roberts Senr., Lower Milford Twp., yeoman. Dec. 1, 1791. Proved Feb. 7, 1797. Wife Mary. Son Edward, son-in-law John Penrose exrs. Sons Edward, John and William. Daus. Anne Penrose, Mary Penrose, Jane Green, Martha Worrall and Sarah Foulke. Gdsn. John Penrose.
Wits: Abraham Bace, Nathan Ball, David Roberts.

Page 553. William Dobel of Boston, Province of Mass. Bay, now res. in New Found Land. March 20, 1783. Proved Feb. 25, 1797. Wife Rachel and Bro.-in-law, John Benger and Thomas Benger exrs. Sister-in-law Mary Benger. Sons William John Benger Dobel and Peter Dobel. Daus. Elizabeth, Sarah and Ruth Dobel. Sister Mrs. Abigail Billings, wife of Joseph Billings.
Wits: William Carter, Robert Carter, James McCulley. Proved on testimony of Dr. Samuel Torbert and Isaac Hicks.

End of Will Book No. 5

Will Book No. 6

Page 1. Philip Johnson, Bensalem Twp., Farmer. Jan. 7, 1796. Proved
Feb. 8, 1797, codicil same date. Wife Sarah and sons Richard and
Samuel exrs. Son Henry defective in sense, his sons George and
William. Daus. Mary Severns, Sarah Yearkes and Elizabeth Hibbs.
Gdch. Elizabeth and Jesse Johnson.
Wits: Isaac Johnson, Samuel Allen.

Page 4. Barned Smiter, Tinicum Twp. July 4, 1790. Proved March 13,
1797. Wife Eve. Jacob Beitelman exr. 8 ch., Peter, John, George,
Daniel, Anna Mary, Margaret, Eve and Rosina. Wits: Abrm Beidelman,
Frederick Woolfinger.

Page 6. John Fluke, Middletown Twp. Oct. 29, 1796. Proved March 18,
1797. Wife ---. John Milner exr. Wife's dau. Mary Fitzjerel, wife of
James Fitzgerel.
Wirs: David Roney, Alx. Moore, Samuel Twining.

Page 8. Charlotte Strickland wife of Amos Strickland, of Morrisville.
Feb. 13, 1797. Proved March 29, 1797. Husband Amos, exr. Sarah wife
of Isaac Pennington, Mary Borden widow, Rebecca and Nancy Bile.
Wits: Mr. Hapenny, Joseph Bailey, Jacob Risler.

Page 9. Michael Deemer, Durham Twp., yeoman. Aug. 11, 1795. Proved
March 30, 1797. Wife Elizabeth. Son Henry and Solomon Mills exrs.
Sons John, Jacob, Solomon, George, Frederick and Barnet. Daus.
Merelles, Catharine, Madelina, Sarah and Margaret.
Wits: Thomas McKean, Elizabeth McKean.

Page 13. Israel Doan, Plumstead, husbandman. Dec. 25, 1787. Proved
April 11, 1797. Philip Krotz, exr. Sons Joseph and Mahlon. Gdch.
Abraham, Israel, Thomas, Elizabeth, Mary, Rachel and Leih ch. of
dec'd. son Israel Doan. Gdsn. Samuel Doan son of son Elijah, dec'd.
Daus. Elizabeth Lewis, Mary Wharton, Rachel Lepper, and Martha
Mitchener.
Wits: Benjamin Scott, William Preston, Elizabeth Preston.

Page 15. John Edgar, Bristol Twp., Carpenter. April 3, 1797. Proved
May 3, 1797. Wife Mary. Dr. Joseph P. Minnick and Robert Patterson
exrs. Nieces Sarah Drummond Junr. and Mary Drummond.
Wits: David Guyant, Joseph Guy. Tenant Charles Bessonet.

Page 17. Valentine Opp, Sr., Springfield Twp., yeoman. May 7, 1793.
Proved May 4, 1797. Caveat Filed Nov. 10, 1796. Letters Pendente Lite

Feb. 7, 1797. Valentine Opp one of Executors, the other having renounced. Wife Anna Catharina, and son Valentine exrs. Ch. Valentine, Catharine and Christina. Dau. Maria Eva, wife of Daniel Beidelman. Land adj. Andrew Dewig, Jacob Landes, Bought of Philip Deily, Gratius Lerch and Abraham Monich. Do. adj. Peter Erhart, Meyer, and Sterner.
Wits: Valentine Marstellar, Joseph Smith, George Jamison.

Page 21. William Coates of Kingwood, County of Hunterdon, N.J. May 30, 1775. Proved May 5, 1797. Son Joseph and son-in-law John McFarson, exrs. Sons Joseph, William and Walter. Daus. Sarah, Mary, Hannah.
Wits: Martin Cogart, Levi Katcham, John Vankirk.

Page 23. Samuel Spencer, the Elder, Northampton Twp., yeoman. July 12, 1794, codicil dated May 5, 1797. Proved May 23, 1797. Sons Samuel and John, exrs. Daus. Elizabeth Powers, Margaret Spencer and Ann Walton. Step-dau. Sarah Jones.
Wits: John Ramsey, John Kerr, Thomas Spencer.

Page 26. Amos Strickland, Fallsington. May 15, 1797. Proved May 24, 1797. Bro.-in-law Mark Hapenny, exr. Dau. Mary Rogers Strickland. Nephews John, Amos, Anthony and James De Normandie, sons of sister Elizabeth De Normandie. Amos, Fanny and James Hapenny, ch. of Mark and Rachel Hapenny.
Wits: John Elton, Joseph McIlvaine, John Smith Gardiner.

Page 28. Christopher Rutenaner, Lower Miller Twp., yeoman. Oct. 6, 1796. Proved May 27, 1797. Wife Ann Mary and son John exrs. 6 sons, Christopher, John, Henry, Samuel, John Adam and George. Oldest son Christian. Son Henry supposed to have been killed in a battle with the Indians. Daus. Catharine now widow of Peter Kutar, Anna Mary wife of Conrad Everland, Eva, Elizabeth and Susannah.
Wits: Adam Schnider, Christian Miller.

Page 30. Ezra Evans, Hilltown Twp., Farmer. Dec. 22, 1796. Proved May 30, 1797. Wife Mary and Jeakin Evans and Joseph Dungan, exrs. 6 ch., Eleanor, Rachel, Joel, Robert, Givenna, and Ezra. Niece Elizabeth dau. of Bro. Nathan Evans.
Wits: Thomas Memminger, Charles Humphrey, David Thomas.

Page 33. Sarah Church, Bristol Boro. Jan. 29, 1795. Codicil May 10, 1797. Proved May 30, 1797. Sons William and Samuel Church exrs. Dau. Sarah Church, in codicil wife of Thomas Hall. Money due from Phineas and Thomas Buckley. Land adj. Sarah Marriott, John Ellwood, Society of Friends, John Hutchinson and William Davis and Joseph Clunn.

Wits. For Will John Boose, Amos Gregg. Codicil John Hutchinson Jr.

Page 36. Mary Chapman, Wrightstown. 6 mo.-20-1786. Proved June 26, 1797. Son James Chapman and nephew John Hillborn, exrs. Daus. Elizabeth Black, Sarah Chapman, Susanna Chapman. Sons James, Robert, Abraham and Charles Chapman. Gddaus. Mary and Margaret Ashton, Agnes and Elizabeth Vance.
Wits: Mary Vansant, Hannah Lee, John Hillborn.

Page 38. Peter Larrew, now of Borough of Bristol. July 29, 1797. Proved Aug. 9, 1797. Nephew Daniel Larrew, son of Bro. Moses and Dr. Amos Gregg, exrs. Nephews, Daniel, John, Moses and Nicholas Larrew. Nieces, Ann Larzelere, dau. of bro. Abraham Larrew, dec'd., and Mary Larrew dau of Bro. David Larrew, dec'd. "To be buried in the Grave Yard on Nicholas Larzelere's Plantation."
Wits: Joseph Clunn, Jason Merrick.

Page 41. Francis Clark, Lower Makefield Twp., widow. May 21, 1779. Proved Aug. 14, 1797. Sons Thomas and Charles, exrs. Son John Clark.
Wits: Joseph Gillingham, Richard Green.

Page 42. Michael Shick, Nockamixon Twp., weaver. June 12, 1797. Proved Sept. 7, 1797. Wife Margaeate. Sons Lawrence and Jacob, exrs. "All children to share alike except 3 sons, Michael, John and Frederick, and five daus. which are not married."
Wits: Philip Rapp and --- Lerrnt.

Page 44. Jane Kerr, widow of Adam Kerr, late of Warwick Twp. dec'd., Innholder. March 28, 1796. Proved Sept. 27, 1797. Son Adam Kerr, and Nathaniel Irwin of Warrington, Clerk, exrs. Eldest dau. Anne "excluded on account of her distance," other ch., Mary, Jane, Esther, Adam, Isabel, William, Lydia. Dau. Mary wife of Andrew Long and her son Adam Kerr Long. Her support to be recovered from her husband Andrew Long.
Wits: Gideon Prior, Joseph Carr.

Page 45. Jonathan Paxson, Upper Makefield. 7 mo.-23-1797. Proved Oct. 12, 1797. Wife Rachel, William Lownes and Joseph Taylor, exrs. Ch., Rebekah, Jane, Sarah, Rachel, Deborah, Betsy, Leatitia, Esther and Jonathan.
Wits: Benjamin Taylor, Moses Smith.

Page 47. William John Benger Dobel of Phila., Physician. July 7, 1797, codicil dated Aug. 17, 1797. Proved Oct. 31, 1797. Wife Lucy Dobel. No exr. named, wife recommended to employ William Waln as Agent to settle estate. Letters c.t.a. granted to Lucy Dobel "Sisters, Sarah and Ruth and Peter Dobel." Thomas Hewson of Phila., Physician. Thomas

64

Benger of Bucks, Co. Mary Benger.
Wits: C. Haight. Proved by William Waln and William Billings.

Page 48. Jonathan Penrose, Richland Twp. April 27, 1795. Proved Nov.
7, 1797. Wife ---. Bro. William and son Isaiah, exrs. Sons Isaiah, David
and Robert. Daus. Mary, Phebe, Martha and Sarah. Son-in-law John
Walton. Gddau. Alice Richards.
Wits: Everard Foulke, George Shaw.

Page 51. John Dennis, Rockhill Twp. 12 mo.-14-1792. Proved Nov. 7,
1797. "Aged and infirm." Wife Keziah, William Penrose and Amos
Richardson exrs. Sons Joseph, Ezekiel and John. Daus. Catharine
Speakman, Sarah Dennis, Tamar Thomas and Keziah Strawn. Amos
Richardson "whom I have raised." Friends Joseph Penrose, Samuel
Nixon, John Penrose and Everard Foulke.
Wits: Hugh Foulke, Jesse Ball, Everard Foulke.

Page 55. Thomas Jenks, Middletown, "Being nearly ninety five years
old." 11 mo.-17-1794. Proved May 12, 1797. Sons Thomas and Joseph
and ch. of dec'd. son John. Daus. Elizabeth Richardson, Ann Watson
and Mary, wife of Samuel Twining. Gdsn. Joseph Jenks, son Thomas
and son-in-law Isaac Watson exrs. Tenant John Miller.
Wits: Jonathan Woolston, Mahlon Grigg, Is. Hicks.

Page 57. Joseph Carver, Senr., Buckingham Twp., yeoman. 12 mo.-29-
1790. Proved Nov. 9, 1797. Sons William and Joseph exrs. Son John.
Daus., Ruth wife of John Terry, Martha Price, Rachel Tomlinson, son
Joel. Gdsns. John and Joseph Worthington, and Jacob Carver, natural
son of Dau. Ruth.
Wits: Robert Smith, Junr., Jacob Heston, Elizabeth Heston.

Page 61. Jacob Smith, Richland Twp., yeoman. Feb. 26, 1790. Proved
Nov. 14, 1797. Wife Elizabeth and Abraham Taylor of Richland, exrs.
Ch. Jacob, George, Michael, Ann, Elizabeth, Katharine and Margaret.
Dau. Barbara Benner.
Wits: Michael Bliler, Edward Roberts, Jacob Rruuar.

Page 62. William Nelson, Richland Twp., weaver. June 12, 1795.
Proved Nov.8, 1797. Wife Mary extx. Dau. Sarah.
Wits: William Hicks, Israel Lancaster.

Page 64. Robert Darroth, Senr., Bedminster Twp. "Aged and weak."
Oct. 7, 1793. Proved Nov. 15, 1797. Son Robert, exr. Son Thomas "if
living." Dau. Ann, wife of Thomas Bates. Gddau. Mary Bates. Land in
possession of Henry McGill.
Wits: James Jones, Benjamin Jones, Thomas Jones Senr.

Page 66. John Brown, Buckingham Twp, yeoman, "Far advanced in age." 9 mo.-4-1797. Proved Dec. 8, 1797. Wife Rachel. Cousin Mathias Hutchinson, and Bro.-in-law David Bradshaw, exrs. Sons George, Jonathan, John and Amos and gdch. Daniel and Jane Brown, ch. of son Mathias dec'd. Daus. Sarah Ellicott and Jane Beaumont.
Wits: Robert Kirkbride, Hannah Kirkbride, Bernard Hellyer.

Page 68. Margaret Johnson, Middletown Twp. Dated 10 mo.-25-1797. Proved Jan. 30, 1798. Son Samuel Johnson exr. Son Samuel's son Joseph. Margaret Bratt, dau. of Samuel Bratt. Gddau. Margaret Johnson.
Wits: Jonathan Carlile, Jonathan Carlile, Junr., John Knight.

Page 70. William Newlands, (nuncupative). Dec. 25, 1797. Wits: John Winner and John Sands. Another declaration made to Peter Williamson, Dec. 28, 1797. Proved Jan. 25, 1798. Indebtedness to John Hulmes to be paid; Residue to William Belford. In this Proof of Will it is Brelsford. Letters Pendente Lite to John Hulme Jan. 3, 1798. Will proved Jan. 25, 1798 on testimony of above witnesses and Isabel Wright, and Letters of Administration with will annexed granted to John Hulme.

Page 72. James Vansant, Northampton Twp., Joyner. July 7, 1795. Proved Feb. 9, 1798. Son Harman and dau. Charity Courson, exrs. Sons William, John, James, Adrian or Aren. "Son Isaac, dec'd., his sons William and Wilhalmus." Son Richard. Daus. Charity Courson, Elshe Kroeson, Elizabeth Kroeson, Lenah Brown and her dau. Elizabeth Vansant, alias Dickson. Dau. Mary Vansant to be educated; son Charles.
Wits: James Lefferts, Gasper Kizer, John Knight.

Page 75. Martha Dean, Solebury Twp. 11 mo.-11-1797. Proved Feb. 20, 1797. Sons Jesse and Joseph Dean exrs. Sons Hezekiah, Jacob, Joseph, Jesse, Benjamin. Daus. Mary Duer, Martha Pettet, and Sarah Bye. Dau.-in-law Hannah Dean. Gdch. Martha Dean dau. of Jesse.
Wits: Hannah Dean, Jesse Betts.

Page 76. George Ramson, Middletown Twp. Feb. 3, 1798. Proved March 1, 1798. Wife Mary, extx. Daus. Mary Richardson and Sarah Ramson. Son Jacob Ramson. Other ch.
Wits: Jesse Johnson, John Hibbs, Isaiah Mitchell, John Cronin.

Page 78. Joseph Buckman, Newtown Twp. 12 mo.-12-1794. Proved March 12, 1798. Son Joseph exr. Daus. Ester Cooper, Mary Carver, Agnes Blaker, Latitia Briggs, Sarah Blaker, Elizabeth Pownall and Asenath Warner. Gdch. Martha Briggs, Joseph Pownall, Son-in-law John Carver.

Wits: William Buckman, Abner Buckman, Elizabeth Buckman.

Page 79. Amos Thackeray, Lower Makefield Twp. 2 mo.-27-1798.
Proved March 17, 1798. Wife Sarah and Jonathan Carlile exrs. Ch. not
named.
Wits: Abraham Watson, Moses Neeld, Joshua Knight.

Page 81. Joseph Sackett, Wrightstown Twp., yeoman, "far advanced in
age." Oct. 21, 1793. Codicil Nov. 1, 1794. Proved March 27, 1798. Wife
Sarah. Son Joseph, son-in-law Simon Bennitt and son-in-law Joshua
Dungan, son of Joseph, exrs. Sons Simon and Joseph. Daus., Clauche,
Rachel, Sarah, Elizabeth, Rebecca. Gddau. Mary Kinsey, "Goods lent to
Dau. Patience, and in possession of her father John Kinsey." Land
purchased of Joseph Wilkinson and John Watson. Do. adj. Garret
Vansant and Samuel Kirk.
Wits: Isaac Chapman, Thomas Chapman, Sarah Chapman.

Page 84. John Dungan, Northampton Twp. March 26, 1798. Proved
April 16, 1798. Wife Mary and Bro. Benjamin Dungan exrs. Sons Uriah
and Jonathan. Daus. Ester and Elizabeth Dungan.
Wits: John Bennitt, John Corson.

Page 86. William Worthington, son of Richard Worthington of
Buckingham, yeoman. April 16, 1798. Proved May 3, 1798. Wife Mary.
Bros. Mahlon and Joseph Worthington exrs. Daus. Jane and Ann
Worthington.
Wits: Andrew Collins Junr., Samuel Richardson.

Page 88. John Dannehouer, Hilltown Twp. Oct. 19, 1797. Proved May
8, 1798. Wife Elizabeth. George Shnyder and John Pugh, exrs. 7 ch. 4
sons. Dau. Catharine, dec'd. late wife of John Yhost.
Wits: Michael Rittenhouse, Monia Frantz, John Pugh.

Page 90. George Riegel, Nockamixon Twp., Farmer, "Aged." May 2,
1798. Proved May 23, 1798. Wife Elizabeth. Peter Rapart, exr. Son
Peter's ch. Sons George, Jacob, Michael, Henry, Daniel, John. Daus.,
Elizabeth and Margaret. Son Nicholas 8 ch.
Wits: William Williams, Valentine Hager, John Amey.

Page 92. Timothy Smith, Buckingham. 1-28-1795. Proved May 28, 1798.
Wife Sarah. Son Joseph exr. Son Robert. Daus. Sarah Atkinson, Mary
Beans and Jane ---.
Wits: Thomas Smith Junr., David Smith, Jonathan Wilkinson.
Pot House in possession of Loran Thorn.

Page 93. Thomas Worthington, Southampton, "Well advanced in
years." May 3, 1796. Proved June 9, 1796. Wife Hannah. Son John and

nephew William, son of Bro. William Worthington, exrs. Six sons, William, Joseph, Isaac, Benjamin, Thomas and Amos. Dau. Mary Thomas. Dau. Rebecca, wife of James Swinney. Sons John and Nathan. Wits: Jesse Worthington, Benjamin Worthington, Hiram Worthington and Joseph Worthington.

Page 96. Alexander Hughes, Esq., Bedminster Twp. April 21, 1798. Proved June 15, 1798. Wife Margaret. Bros.-in-law Samuel Wigton and Griffith Owen, exrs. Ch., James, Mary, Elizabeth, Samuel, Alexander, Rebekah and Thomas.
Wits: William McNeeley, Jacob Kulp.

Page 98. Robert Smith, Wrightstown, yeoman. 6 mo.-9-1788. Codicils 5-28-1792 and Sept. 9, 1795. Proved July 19, 1798. Wife Bridget. Sons John and Abram exrs. Daus. Phebe, Ann and Rachel. Gdsn. Jonathan Heaton. "His father Dr. Heaton." Thomas and Joseph Smith exrs. of my bro. Joseph dec'd. Land purchased by John Hurst. Do. of heirs of Jacob Rush in Hartford [sic] Co., Md. Do. of William Newburn.
Wits. to Will: William Trego, Thomas Trego, Mahlon Trego. To codicil John Trego.

Page 101. Arnst Klinker, Haycock Twp., yeoman. Jan. 10, 1795. Proved July 5, 1798. Wife Catharina. Son John Klinker, exr. Sons Abraham, John, Jacob. Daus. Christina, Catharine, Elizabeth, Mary Elizabeth, 4 ch. of late dau. Madlin dec'd. Land adj. John Mills and Joseph Fulmer. Codicil June 10, 1798.
Wits: Daniel Fulmer, Nicholas McCarty, John Fulmer.

Page 104. Hugh Smith, Buckingham Twp. Jan. 22, 1791. Proved Aug. 2, 1798. Wife Barbara. Sons Samuel and Thomas exrs. Daus. Barbara McDowell, Margery Gregg, Margaret ---. Gdsns. Hugh Johnston and Hugh McDowell. Money in hands of William McCalla.
Wits: John Wilson, Robert Sample, William Simpson.

Page 106. Henry Friedt, Rockhill Twp., widower. July 23, 1798. Proved Aug. 7, 1798. Son-in-law John Fellman Junr. Exr. Ch., Elizabeth Graver, John Friedt, Agnes Fellman, Mary Frederick and Henry Friedt.
Wits: Mattin Zegafoose, Everard Foulke, George Zegafoose.

Page 107. Hugh Thompson, Newtown, Schoolmaster. Aug. 8, 1795. Proved Aug. 17, 1798. Wife Sarah, son John and Cousin William Neeley, exrs. Dau. Elizabeth wife of Abraham Johnson. Gdch. Robert Thompson, Hugh Johnson, Hannah Thompson Pitner,
Wits: Joseph Worstall, Susanna Worstall.

Page 109. George Overpeck, Nockamixon Twp., yeoman. Sept. 14,

1791. Proved Sept. 15, 1798. Wife Magdalena. Jacob Young and
Lawrence Messer, exrs. 7 ch. by wife Margaret, dec'd., Andrew, Anna,
Magdalena, Sarah, Rebecca, Catharine, George and John. Three by 2nd
wife, Magdalen, viz., Anna Maria, Henry and Conrad. Land adj. Henry
Frankenfield, John McCammon, Jonathan Gregory, John Youngken,
Jacob Sheup, Michael Thick.
Wits: George Kohll, Jacob Kohll.

Page 111. John Bradfield, Buckingham Twp. 8 mo.-19-1798. Proved
Sept. 6, 1798. Bro.Jonathan and Bro.-in-law Benjamin Cadwallader,
exrs. Bros. Abner, James, Benjamin and Jonathan. Thomas Price who
lived with one. Housekeeper Sarah Hartley. Nephews, John Bradfield,
John Hough Junr. John Hough's ch. issue of sister Jane Hough.
Sister[s] Hannah Cadwallader, Rachel Burchall and Elizabeth Heed.
Wits: Daniel Carlile, Samuel Gillingham.

Page 113. William Griffith of City of Phila., but now of Buckingham,
"Stationor." Aug. 27, 1798. Proved Sept. 10, 1798. Rev. William
Stoughton of Bordentown, and William Maxwell Esq. of N.Y., exrs. Bro.
John Griffiths, now in Wales, sole legatee.
Wits: Phebe Dickerson and Jonathan Kelly.

Page 114. Giles Craven, late of Warminster, now of Southampton Twp.,
yeoman. March 16, 1798. Proved Sept. 11, 1798. Harman Vansant, exr.
Sister Ester Gilbert of Warwick Twp. her son Elias Gilbert.
Presbyterian church of Warwick, Nathaniel Irwin, Present Pastor.
Harman Vansant, son of my nephew James Vansant. Nephews,
William, James, Giles, Isaac and Thomas Craven Jr. sons of Bro.
Thomas Craven. Jane eldest dau. of Harman Vansant. James,
"youngest and only surviving son of said Vansant." Bro. James Craven
of Va., his sons Giles and John.
Wits: Joseph Hunt, William Ramsey Junr.

Page 117. Joshua Mitchell, Northern District, Phila. Co. 9 mo.-18-1798.
Proved Oct. 4, 1798. Kinsman Pierson Mitchell exr. "Only child Joshua
Mitchell." Bros. and sisters. William and Anna Merrick, ch. of Bro.-in-
law Robert Merrick. Bro.-in-law, Jason Merrick.
Wits: John Hutchinson Jr., Amos Gregg.

Page 119. Thomas Lee Shippen, City of Phila. March 4, 1795. Codicil
dated Jan. 24, 1797, at Williamsburg. Proved Sept. 25, 1798. Wife
Elizabeth Carter Shippen. Father Edward Shippen and Edward Burd
Esq. Kinsman, exrs. and Guardians. Sons William and Thomas Lee
Shippen. Sister Anne Home Livingston. Niece Margaret Buckman
Livingston. Estate in Antiqua and N.C., devised by Francis Farley Esq.
To his gddau. Elizabeth Carter Farley.
Wits. to will: John Brown Cutting and George Howell. To codicil R.

Dawson, B. Barnard. Proved by John Brown Cutting and Joseph Erwin of Bucks Co.

Page 121. Henry Briggs, Mittletown Twp. 9-29-1798. Proved Oct. 12, 1798. Bro. Josiah Briggs exr. Bros. Josiah, Amos and John Briggs. Sisters Mary Chapman and Francis ---. Friends Preparative Mtg. of Middletown.
Wits: Mahlon Gregg, Amos Bailey, Henry Atherton.

Page 122. Robert Kirkbride, New Britain Twp., yeoman. 9 mo.-26-1798. Proved Oct. 24, 1798. Wife Hannah. Sons-in-law, Samuel Eastburn and John Longstreth exrs. Sons Robert and David. Daus. Mary, Esther, Hannah, Sarah, Letitia and Ann. Benjamin Kirkbride, son of Dau. Mary.
Wits: John Bierley, Matthew Gill, Jonathan Fell.

Page 125. Charles Clark, Senr., Fallsington, in the Falls Twp. 10 mo. (Oct.) 13, 1798. Proved Oct. 29, 1798. Wife Ann Clark. Son William and John Hulme exrs. Son Richard. Daus. Jane Barber, Hannah Brown, Martha Thawman, Margaret Plummer. Gdch. Charles Clark Plummer, and Theodoshe Clarke and Benjamin Brown ch. of Hannah Brown.
Wits: Charles Hutchin, Naylor Child, Gainer Hutchin. Deed to be made to Charles Stackhouse for Land in Makefield Twp.

Page 127. Thomas Smith, Solebury Twp., Lumber Merchant, "Advanced in age." 8 mo.-18-1797. Proved Nov. 6, 1798. Sons Thomas and John exrs. Sons William, Stephen, Isaac, Joseph, John and Thomas. William's 7 ch., William, Jacob, Amos, Sarah, Mary, Esther and Rebekah. Daus. Sarah wife of John Smith, Mary wife of Edward Blackfan and Rebeckah (single) "Room in House in Solebury, (called Mary Burgesses)."
Wits: Robert Smith, Robert Smith Junr., Isaac Vanhorn.

Page 130. Philip Heager, (signed by mark), Lower Milford Twp., yeoman. ---- 1795. Proved Nov. 14, 1798. Sons Valentine and Peter exrs. Eldest son John, "By first wife." Sons Valentine, Christian, Philip, Emanuel and Peter. Daus. Christina wife of John Derr, Margaret wife of William Hoffman and Elizabeth wife of John Getmann.
Wits: Philip Mumbower and George Shitz.

Page 132. Margaret Lewis, Hilltown Twp., Widow. Nov. 5, 1798. Proved Nov. 15, 1798. Philip Miller and John Pugh exrs. Sons Isaac, James and William Lewis. Daus. Rachel wife of Edward Jones, Rebekah wife of George Congle, Mary wife of James Thomas, and Margaret wife of Philip Miller. Gdch. Margaret, Henry and John Jones; Henry and Margaret Congle; Margaret Lewis, dau. of James; Henry Lewis son of

Isaac; Margaret Thomas; Margaret, Henry L. and Tirzah Miller. Margaret, dau. of John and Mary Fry. Rev. James McLaughlin, Pastor of Hilltown church. Rev. James White, Pastor of New Britain or Montgomery churches.
Wits: Griffith Owen, Henry Cope, John Pugh.

Page 135. Henry Huber, Lower Milford Twp., wheelwright. Feb. 15, 1791. Proved Nov. 19, 1798. Son-in-law Frederick Hillegas and son Henry exrs. Sons Henry and Jacob. Daus. Catharin Brodsmen, Anna Hillegas, Anna Mary Hartzel and Adelhit Widner.
Wits: David Spinner, George Mitchel.

Page 137. Mark Overholts (signed by mark), Rockhill Twp. Oct. 23, 1798. Proved Dec. 18, 1798. Wife Catharine. Son Abraham and Abraham Silfuse [Tilfuse?], exrs. Ch. Abraham, Elizabeth, Mary Susanna and Ann.
Wits: Robert Smith, John Shloter, Henry Selfoose [sic].

Page 139. Mary Elizabeth Hoafman (signed by mark), Widow of Michael Hoafman, late of Nockamixon Twp., dec'd. Oct. 7, 1795. Proved Dec. 28, 1798. Christopher Trougher of Nockamixon, Exr. Son Anthony Hoafman. Dau. Elizabeth wife of Sol. Melone, Catharine and Ave Wilhelm, ch. of dau. Ave, dec'd., who intermarried with Henry Wilhelm.
Wits: Nicholas Carty, Elizabeth McCarty. (in Probate both McCarty).

Page 140. Isaac Pickering, Solebury Twp., Blacksmith, "Far advanced in age." 2 mo.-21-1795. Proved Jan. 8, 1799. Wife Sidney. Son Jonathan exr. Daus. Sarah Butler, Mercy Roberts, Rachel Wright. Son-in-law Solomon Wright. Gdsn. Isaac Pickering, son of Joseph dec'd.
Wits: Aaron Phillips, John Gillingham, Samuel Johnson.

Page 143. Christian Frey, Springfield Twp., yeoman, "very much advanced in years." Dec. 23, 1795. Proved Jan. 9, 1799. Gdsns. Joseph Frey and Joseph Minchinger, Exrs. Son-in-law Michael Rothrock, who mar. dau. Catharine, now dec'd.., their ch. John, Mary and Barbara. Gdsns. Solomon and Joseph Frey, sons of son John dec'd. Gdsn. Joseph Frey, son of son Joseph dec'd. Gdsns. John Dreichler and Joseph Minchinger. Gddau. Ann, wife of Henry Nuspickle and her ch. Ggdau. Ann Gehry, dau. of Jacob Gehry Junr. of Upper Hanover Twp., Montgomery Co.
Wits: Jesse Hicks, John Bechtel.

Page 146. Isaac Hill, Plumstead Twp., yeoman. Oct. 6, 1798. Proved Jan. 11, 1799. Wife Elizabeth. Sons Isaac and William Hill exrs. Sons Richard, Isaac, Thomas, Abraham and William. Daus. Mary wife of Benjamin Day, Elizabeth wife of Nathan Reiley, Margaret, Sarah,

Rebecca and Liddia.
Wits: Henry Wimer, Lewis Lunn.

Page 148. John Booz, Bristol Twp. Aug. 16, 1787. Proved Jan. 14, 1799.
Wife Barbara, sons John and Peter exrs. and sole legatees. Land in
Pigeon Swamp adj. Michael Allen.
Wits: Charles Bessonett, Samuel Torbert, Samuel Benezet.

Page 149. John Davis, New Britain Twp. Jan. 3, 1799. Proved Feb. 5,
1799. Son John exr. Daus. Sarah, Susanna, Catherine and Rachel.
Land adj. John Delph, Elizabeth Vastine, Philip Miller, Benjamin
Butler, Abiah Butler, Henry Root, "Late" Hugh Edmond, late George
Reife, and Michael Redlion.
Wits: David Thomas, Philip Miller, John Pugh.

Page 152. Thomas Ellicott, Solesbury twp., wheelwright. 12 mo.-28-
1797. Codicil dated 1 mo.-19-1799. Proved Feb. 5, 1799. Wife Jane.
John Balderston and Jonathan Pickering exrs. Wife's Bro. James
Kinsey. Sons Joseph, George, Thomas. Daus. Letitia, Hannah and
Rachiel Ellicott, Ruth Warner, Ann Crook, Pamela Ingham. 7 daus.
Contract with Thomas Lowrey for building mills to be carried out.
Wits: Thomas Carey, Able Knight, Ann Knight, Joseph Knight, Thomas
Carey Jr.

Page 155. Henry Margerum, Bucks Co. Jan. 6, 1798. Proved Feb. 5,
1799. Wife Judith. Friends Robert Margerum and William
Satterthwaite exrs. Bro. Edward Margerum. Nephew Henry
Margerum. Sister Isabella Phillips.
Wits: Jonathan Vanhorn, Obijah Reed, John Wood.

Page 157. William Wilkinson, Upper Makefield Twp., Husbandman. 2
mo.-1-1788. Proved Feb. 8, 1799. Zachariah Betts exr. Mother
Elizabeth Wilkinson. Bro. Jonathan Wilkinson.
Wits: William Lowner, William Lownes, Junr.

Page 159. George Bauman, Springfield Twp., yeoman. Nov. 29, 1798.
Proved Feb. 13, 1799. Wife Margaret. Sons Jacob and George Bauman
exrs. Ch. Jacob, George, Catharine, Peter, Nicholas and Philip.
Wits: Valentine Marstellar, Adam Switzer.

Page 160. Jonathan Ingham, Senr., Solebury Twp., "Far advanced in
age." 1 mo.-9-1794, codicil dated 8 mo. 1795. Proved March 1, 1791.
Benjamin Paxson and Aaron Paxson, both of Solebury, exrs. Son Jonas
and his sons Joseph, Jonas and John. Gdch. Jonas, Ingham, Charles
and Deborah Kinsey. Nine ch. of son Jonathan dec'd. His widow Anna
Ingham, land in N.J. devised to her by her gdmother Hannah
Bickerdite. Buckingham and Wrightstown Monthly Meetings.

Wits. to will: Robert Smith Junr., Jonathan Pickering, Mahlon Paxson. To codicil same.

Page 164. John Sisom, Bristol Borough. 12 mo.-26-1797. Proved Feb. 27, 1799. Wife Mary. Sons William and Joseph exrs. Dau. Martha Sisom. Gddau. Jane Sisom, dau. of Joseph. Land purchased of Pearson Mitchell, Peter White and "Marriotts."
Wits: Jonathan Purssell, John Hutchinson.

Page 166. Jones Metzger, Springfield Twp. April 1, 1792. March 25, 1799. Wife Susana. John Smith exr. Sons Andrew, John and Casper. Daus. (Christina-Catarina), (Mary-Elizabeth), Anna and Maria. Note. In the original there is no punctuation between names, and the testator names them as "five daus." The clerk divides them as above, making only four.
Wits: Joseph Smith, Philip Hearing.

Page 168. John Johnson, Newtown. Feb. 26, 1799. Proved March 30, 1799. Wife Jane, son John and Friend William Buckman exrs. Son Abraham's ch., Sarah, Mary, Hugh, John and Robert. Sons John and Joseph. Daus. Sarah, Susanna (her son John McConkey), Mary wife of William Parker, Margaret, Jane and her ch. Rebecah and her ch.
Wits: William Albertson Junr., Jesse Leedom.

Page 171. John Watson, Middletown Twp. 2 mo.-14-1799. Proved April 1, 1799. Wife Rachel. Son John exr. Dau. Hannah. Gdsns. Joseph and Watson Newbold.
Wits: William Blakey Junr., Samuel Blakey, John Blakey. Lot adj. William Richardson "where Henry Atherton lives."

Page 173. John O'Connor, Warwick Twp., "Native of Doublin, Ireland, but residing for past 20 years in N. America." Feb. 19, 1799. Proved April 6, 1799. Gen. Stephen Moylan of Phila. exr. Bro. Patrick O'Conor of Cork, his present wife Elizabeth Kerr. Aunt Martha Byrne of Duther "cozens" Joseph Silby, of Madem, and Kitty Lilly, now Lyons. Sister Eleanor O'Conor. Nephew John Rochfort, son of sister Elizabeth. Niece Elizabeth Rochfort. Debts due to Peter Thillusson of London, William Palmer of London, Dowell O'Reilly formerly of Dublin. No Witnesses. Handwriting proved by Bartholomew Geohghegan, who "resided with testator," and Richard German of Phila.
Note dated 29-6-1964. John O'Connor was the brother of Lee (?) Patrick O'Conor of Cork whose present wife was Elizabeth Therry (?) (not Kerr) ward and 1st cousin once removed of Rt. Wm. Edomond Burke (1729-1797).

Page 175. Dinah Mathews, Warwick Twp. March 30, 1793. Proved May

6, 1799. Kinsman Edward Mathews exr. Sons Benjamin and Joseph Mathews; 4 daus., Margaret Young, Rachel Meredith, Ann Doyle and Mary Barton. Gdch. Joseph, John and Azael Thomas.
Wits: Ezl. Hill and John Meredith.

Page 176. Sarah Lucas, widow of Robert Lucas dec'd., Falls Twp. Jan. 15, 1789. Proved May 7, 1799. Codicil dated 5 mo.-23-1794. Dau. Hannah Linton and John Brown, Jr. exrs. Son Joseph Hutchinson. Gdsns. Benjamin, Mahlon and Joshua Linton. Money in hands of Joseph Gillingham.
Wits: William Satterthwaite, Michael Vanhart, Michael Satterthwaite. To codicil, William Wharton Junr. and Esther Alexander.

Page 179. Joseph Shaw, Plumstead Two., yeoman. 4 mo.-8-1791. Proved May 10, 1799. A partly executed Will dated March 2, 1799 was offered for probate, but was set aside. Uriah Hughes of Tinicum and Jonathan Shaw of Plumstead exrs. Sons Thomas, Moses, and Amos. Daus. Martha Dunken and Phebe Hughes. Gdch. John and Mary Hennard.
Wits: Joseph White, Sarah Shaw, Joseph Brooks and Mary Brooks. "Uriah Hughes removed to a distance." Letters with will annexed, to James Shaw and John Lewis.

Page 181. Philip Nice, Nockamixon Twp. April 22, 1799. Proved May 21, 1799. Wife Elizabeth and John Fluck of Bedminster exrs. 7 ch., viz.: Catharina, Elizabeth, John, Magdalena, Philip, Barbara and Margaret.
Wits: Anthony Greaser, Henry Strouse, Michael Ott.

Page 183. Thomas Jenks, Middletown Twp., Fuller. July 12, 1798. Proved June 20, 1799. Wife Rebecca. Sons Joseph and Thomas and son-in-law Thomas Story, exrs. Sons Thomas, Joseph Richardson, and Phineas Jenks. Daus. Rachel wife of Thomas Story, Mercy wife of Abraham Carlisle, Rebecca, Mary, and Ruth Jenks. Isaac Chapman, Abraham Chapman and William Linton, "to run the lines of Land devised." Land bought of Israel Jacobs, William Paxson and Thomas Carey. Do. "late of" John Cawley and Patrick Gregg. Do. adj. James Wildman, Bro. Joseph Jenks, Joseph Suber, John Dean and Jonathan Carlisle.
Wits: James Wildman, Nathaniel Price.

Page 188. Hugh Ferguson Sr., Plumstead Twp., yeoman. Jan. 21, 1791. Proved July 8, 1799. Sons John and James exrs. Matthew Grier of Hilltown, Thomas Stewart of New Britain and Alexander Hughes of Bedminster, overseers. Sons John and Hugh, each 500 acres they live on in Pipe Creek Hundred, Md., Frederick Co. Son Josiah, do. Son Hugh indebted to exrs. of Mary Bogart, dec'd. Son James. Two daus. Agnes wife of John Shaw and Mary wife of James Grier. Gdch. Mary

Grier, Mary Shaw, Margaret dau. of son John. Hugh son of son James.
Rev. Francis Ceppard. Rev. Nathan Grier of Brandywine Manor. Pres.
congregation of Deep Run. Debt due William Norris, dec'd.
Wits: Joseph Grier, John Grier.

Page 191. Thomas Craven, Warmister Twp., "Being Aged." May 7,
1797. Proved Aug. 5, 1799. Wife Kelena and sons James and Isaac exrs.
Sons William Giles, James, Isaac, Thomas. Daus. Ann, Catrin, Helena,
Edath and Christiana. Father Jacobus Craven. Bro. Giles Craven. Land
bought of Robert Noble and John Brooks.
Wits: Anthony Scout, Abraham Sutphin, Jonathan Delaney.

Page 194. Giles Knight, Bensalem Twp. 6 mo.-24-1799. Proved Aug. 5,
1799. Wife Phebe. Sons Joseph, Israel and son-in-law James Paul exrs.
Sons Evan T. and Jesse Paul. Daus. Susanna Paul, Abigail Walmsley,
Rebecca Parry, Mary wife of William Satterthwaite, Phebe Walmsley
and Rachel Paul. Gdsns. Townsend, Giles and Joseph Knight. Ch. of
son Giles dec'd. Land bought of Beales Heirs.
Wits: Evan and Ezra Townsend, John Comly.

Page 198. Nicholas Larzelere, Makefield Twp., Farmer. Aug. 2, 1791.
Proved Aug. 5, 1799. Wife Sarah. Sons Nicholas and John exrs. 9 ch.
Nicholas and John. Daus. Catharine Lerue, Hester Mitchell, Anne
Vansant, Elizabeth Cope, Margaret Johnson, Hannah Burley and ch. of
dau. Mary by George Applegate of Bordentown.
Wits: Lewis Howard, Rebecca Patterson, Stephen Cronin.

Page 199. Thomas Dyer, Plumstead Twp. June 27, 1799. Proved Aug.
5, 1799. Nephew John Dyer Junr. Dau. Jane Dyer and son Jesse Dyer
exrs.
Wits: Joseph Burgess, George Burgess.

Page 200. James Rose, Newtown Twp. 8 mo.-3-1799. Proved Aug. 12,
1799. Friend William Buckman exr. Bros. John and Thomas Rose.
Sisters Alse Hollingshead and Priscilla Reeder.
Wits: Abner Buckman, Elizabeth Buckman.

Page 202. John Knowles, Upper Makefield Twp. 10 mo. 17-1798.
Proved Aug. 13, 1799. Bro. Robert exr. Bro. Jacob.
Wits: William Lownes, Mary Duer.

Page 202. Henry Paxson, Solebury Twp., "Somewhat advanced in
age." 8 mo.-12-1790. Proved Aug. 16, 1799. Wife Elizabeth. Sons
Mahlon and Isaac exrs. Sons Henry, Joseph and John. Daus. Elizabeth
Hambleton, Ann Scarborough, Sarah Wilkinson, Anne Worthington,
Rahel, Mary and Mercy Paxson.
Wits: Robert Eastburn, Oliver Hamton, Aaron Eastburn.

Page 205. Thomas Darroch, Senr., Bedminster Twp. Dated 24, 1799. Proved Aug. 23, 1799. Wife Agnes. Eldest son Thomas Darroch and son-in-law James Ferguson exrs. Sons Thomas and Mark. Daus. Nancy Ferguson, Martha Dana, Susannah Darroch, Rebecca Fair and Elizabeth Darroch.
Wits: Uriah Du Bois, Robert Darroch.

Page 207. Thomas Jones, Buckingham Twp., Farmer. Aug. 22, 1798. Proved Aug. 24, 1799. Wife Hannah. Sons Joshua and John exrs. Ch. Joshua, John, Rachel (wife of Richard Yardley), Martha, Margaret, Mary and Anna.
Wits: Elias Anderson, Richard Yardley, Thomas Memminger.

Page 209. Jacob Lederach, Richland Twp., yeoman. Feb. 13, 1792. Proved Aug. 26, 1799. Sons-in-law Jacob Hackman and Michael Deal exrs. Daus. Catharine, Anne and Mary (married).
Wits: Peter Nargang, Abraham Overholt.

Page 211. John Thompson, Northampton Twp., yeoman, "far advanced in years." June 14, 1798. Proved Sept. 24, 1799. Wife Mary. Sons Hugh, Robert and John exrs. and Guardians. 6 sons, Hugh, Robert, John, Thomas, James and William. Gdsn. Charles McClellen.
Wits: John Wilson, Moses Kelly, William Neeley.

Page 213. Henry Magill, Bedminster Twp. Nov. 14, 1797. Proved Sept. 25, 1799. Wife Dority. Jacob Ott and William McNeely, exrs. Son Henry. Dau. Latitia.
Wits: John McKinney, James McNeely.

Page 214. James Worstall, Upper Makefield Twp. 2 mo.-18-1798. Proved Oct. 8, 1799. Sons Samuel, John and Edward exrs. Son William. Dau. Pleasant, wife of Gideon Shaw. Gdsns. James and Hugh Worstall, sons of Samuel. Samuel Worstall, son John, Richard Worstall, son of William and John Worstall, son of Edward and Joseph Shaw, son of Gideon.
Wits: Joseph Johnson, Rachel Wildman, James Wildman.

Page 215. Joseph Knight, Middletown Twp. 9 mo.-20-1799. Proved Oct. 12, 1799. Wife Elizabeth. Sons-in-law William Hulme and Samuel Hulme exrs. Son Joseph (an invalid). Daus. Sarah Knight, Elizabeth Brown, Rachel Hulme, Mary Hulme and Susanna Knight. Land adj. John Hulme and William Letchworth.
Wits: John Hulme, Mahlon Gregg, Amos Gregg.

Page 218. Amos Shaw, Plumstead Twp. April 18, 1799. Proved Nov. 2, 1799. Wife Sarah. John Lewis of Plumstead, exr. Nephew Samuel Shaw, "son of my uncle James Shaw."

Wits: Henry Black, George Rice.

Page 219. Mathias Wisner, Lower Makefield Twp. Oct. 11, 1799.
Proved Nov. 2, 1799. Wife Deborah extx. Nephews Isaac and George
Wisner.
Wits: William Hollingshead, William H. Duer, John Duer.

Page 220. George Shade, Warrington Twp., yeoman. Dec. 28, 1797.
Proved Nov. 4, 1799. Codicil dated Oct. 7, 1799. Wife Ann Maria. Son
Jacob and son-in-law Jacob Rapp exrs. Codicil substitutes John Barclay
of Warwick Twp. for son Jacob. Dau. Mary wife of Peter Shearer. Ch.
of son George dec'd. Son Jacob. Dau. Elizabeth wife of Jacob Rapp.
Son William and dau. Rebecca. John Barclay, Guardian. Of 4 ch. of son
George.
Wits: John Barclay, James Barclay. Codicil unproved.

Page 223. Jacob Barnet, Tinicum Twp. June 27, 1799. Proved Nov. 4,
1799. Wife Mary. Son Peter and John Keller exrs. Ch. Jacob, Peter,
Michael, Philip, John and Tobias Barnet. Dau. Margaret wife of John
Keller and dau. Elizabeth wife of Philip Stone ("has left her").
Wits: Gilliam Kressler, John Hellebort, John Bergstresser.

Page 224. Valentine Housewerts, Tinicum Twp. May 11, 1799. Proved
Nov. 5, 1799. Wife ---. Son Jacob and George Ruff, exrs. Nine ch.,
Jacob, Abraham, Isaac, Solomon, Molly, Salomy, Elizabeth, Nancy and
Sarah.
Wits: William Erwin, Jacob Housewert.

Page 226. William Kitchin, Solebury Twp. May 10, 1796. Proved Nov.
12, 1799. Wife Sarah. Sons David and William exrs. Jonathan, John
and Ely, and Sarah Kitchin, ch. of son John dec'd. Dau. Rebecca
Eastburn.
Wits: John Watson, Oliver Hamton, Hanna Hamton.

Page 227. George Weicher, Senr., Lower Milford, Esq. March 4, 1794.
Codicil dated July 21, 1799. Proved Nov. 15, 1799. Wife Magdalena and
son George exrs. Sons George and Jacob. Daus. Elizabeth wife of
Henry Shellesark, Catharina wife of Jacob Barnes, Magdalena, Hannah
wife of Abraham Samsell, and Sally. 3 ch. of Dau. Barbara, dec'd., late
wife of Peter Shull.
Wits: Jacob Baker, Jacob Sheetse, Paul Samsell, Jacob Shuck, Jacob
Bruner.

Page 230. John Woolfanger, Nockamixon Twp. Nov. 4, 1799. Proved
Dec. 12, 1799. Sons Solomon and Frederick exrs. Ch. Solomon,
Frederick, Jacob, John, Elizabeth wife of John Hoffman, Catharine
wife of Nicholas Grover, and Sarah Woolfanger.

Wits: John Adams, Jacob Freely, Jacob Shoop, Hugh Jameson.

Page 233. Jane Hughes, New Britain Twp., widow, "aged." May 15, 1799. Proved Dec. 14, 1799. Son-in-law Samuel Wigdon exr. Son Thomas. Gdsn. James and other ch., of son Alexander dec'd. Daus. Mary wife of William Wilson, Jane wife of Griffith Owen, Susanna wife of James Sulliman, Elizabeth wife of Samuel Wigdon. Gddau. Jane Wigdon.
Wits: Ellis Pugh, John Mettlen, David Ewing.

Page 234. Jacob Yearling, Tinicum Twp. Aug. 26, 1794. Proved Jan. 10, 1800. Wife Magdalena. Jacob Bidleman, Nockamixon; Philip Groover of Tinicum exrs. Daus. Barbara wife of Peter Reppard and Susanna. Step-ch. Conrad Shemell, Cartrout Bidleman.
Wits: Jacob Bidleman Junr., John Bidleman.

Page 236. Jane Grier, widow. May 19, 1797. Proved Jan. 15, 1800. Son Matthew Grier exr. Eldest son John Grier. Daus. Agnes wife of Cephas Child., Susanna wife of Joseph Greer, Mary wife of Josiah Ferguson.
Wits: Benjamin Jones, Elizabeth Brittin, Thomas Jones Senr.

Page 238. Joseph Hair, Senr., New Britain Twp., yeoman, "advanced in years." April 27, 1798. Proved Jan. 20, 1800. Wife Isabel. Sons William and Joseph Hair exrs. Son Joseph "now or late of Northumberland Town." George, Elizabeth, Robert and William Hair, ch. of dec'd. son George. Daus. Mary widow of Edward Poole dec'd., Sarah wife of William Stevens, Elizabeth wife of John Steel, and ch. of late dau. Margaret wife of James Watson.
Wits: Benjamin Snodgrass, David Johnson, Nathaniel Irwin.

Page 241. Adam Cape (probably Cope), Hilltown Twp., yeoman. Aug. 4, 1794. Proved Jan. 21, 1800. Wife Margaret and son Henry and Henry Hertzel exrs. Sons Jacob and Abraham Cope. Sons Henry, John and Paul Cope. Land adj. Benjamin Griffiths, do. Bought of Levi Thomas.
Wits: Frederick Fluke, Henry Hartzel Junr., Abrm. Stout.

Page 244. Isaac Derstine, Rockhill Twp., yeoman. May 11, 1797. Proved Jan. 21, 1800. Wife Catharine. Sons George and Isaac exrs. and Guardians. Father Michael Derstine dec'd. Sons Abraham, Henry and Samuel Derstine. Daus. Catharine, Hannah and Magdalena. Land purchased of Jacob Hornecker, Isaac Savecool and Henry Seller and Paul Bean and Jacob Leister.
Wits: Henry Cope, Andrew Schlichter, Abraham Stout.

Page 247. Sarah Larzelere, wife of Nicholas Larzelere, Lower Makefield Twp. Feb. 6, 1791. Proved Jan. 22, 1800. No exrs. Letters with will annexed granted to William Aspy. Will of her father, dec'd.,

devised money, (now in hands of Abraham Cocherun, by virtue of
Articles of Agreement dated May 25, 17 67). Devises to "my ch.,"
John Depuy's ch., John, Mary and Joseph, their father's. share.
"Now to John's ch., Nicholas Depuy, Jacob Depuy, Abraham Depuy
and Joanna Brerly."
Wits: John Strickland, William Aspy.

Page 248. William Brown (unsigned), no date. Proved Oct. 23, 1799 by
George Merrick, who wrote it, and Christian Merrick; Affirmed by
Supreme Court Jan. 24, 1800. Benjamin Larzelere, Adm. Pendente
Lite. Letters granted to Thomas Brown as exr. Uncles and aunts on his
father's side, John Brown of Phila., Mary Thompson and Chritina
Merrick of Bristol Borough. On his mother's side James Higgs of
Horsham, Mary Wooster of Newtown and Jane Hall of Schoolkill.
Sister Sarah Larzelere's ch. Ann and Joseph Larzelere. Exrs. George
Merrick and Thomas Brown of Phila. No Wits.

Page 250. Adam Vanhart, Bucks Co. Jan .20, 1797. Proved Jan. 27,
1800. Wife Elizabeth and son Jacob Vanhart exrs. Son James. Mary
Benjamin, dau. of dau. Jane Vanhart.
Wits: John Watson, Jesse Smith, Samuel Davis.

Page 251. Henry Resch, Bedminster Twp. Jan. 23, 1800. Proved Jan.
31, 1800. Wife Christina Resch. Bro.-in-law Conrad Mitman exr. Ch.
John, Jacob, Peter, Nicholas and Polly.
Wits: John Keller, Abraham Black.

Page 252. John Burley, Upper Makefield Twp. Sept. 17, 1799. Proved
Feb. 5, 1800. Wife Jane. John Wilson Esq. of Buckingham and Moses
Kelly of Newtown, exrs. Sons David, John and Joshua. 8 daus. Alice
Johnson, Elizabeth Vanhorn, Hanah, Pheby, Sarah, Rachel and Polly
Burley.
Wits: James Torbert Senr., James Boyd.

Page 254. John Chapman, Upper Makefield Two., "Practioner of
Medicine." Jan. 16, 1800. Proved Feb. 5, 1800. Wife Margery. Sons
John and Seth exrs. Sons John, Seth and Josiah. Daus. Sarah Ross,
Jane and Mary/Mercy Chapman. Nephew Isaac Chapman. Dau.-in-law
Rebecca. Land adj. John Randle. Gdch. Sarah and John Chapman.
Wits: Aaron Chapman, Martha Palmer, Isaac Chapman.

Pgae 256. Elizabeth Woolston, widow of John Woolston, late of
Middletown dec'd. 9 mo.-1-1796. Proved Feb. 18, 1800. Son Joshua
exr. Ch. Joanthan and Joshua Woolston, Mary Smith, Elizabeth Knight
and Mercy Bye. Gdch. Elizabeth Woolston, dau. of Joshua. Sarah
Woolston, dau. of Jonathan. Sarah Jenks, Mary Knight and Susanna
Knight. Sarah Knight dau. of Joseph Knight.

Wits: Jonathan Kirkbride, Thomas Blakey.

Page 258. John Fluke, Springfield Twp. Nov. 30, 1799. Proved Feb. 25, 1800. Wife Elizabeth. Bro. Jacob Fluke and George Olerdine exrs.
Wits: Jacob Rotdrick, Benjamin Rosenberger.

Page 259. Francis Jodon, Warwick Twp. May 5, 1791. Proved March 13, 1800. Wife ---. Son Peter Jodon exr. Son Francis. Daus. Olympas ---, Martha Madders. Gddaus. Hannah and Martha Guy.
Wits: John Rickey, Thomas Bready, Charles Doane.

Page 261. Mathias Creamor, Springfield Twp. May 11, 1799, codicil dated Sept. 5, 1799. Proved March 28 , 1800. Wife Mary and son-in-law Leoanrd Bucks exrs. Dau. Mary and other ch.
Wits: Peter Piper and Peter Seigler.

Page 263. John Watson, Nottingham, County of Burlington, N.J. July 16, 1795. Proved March 31, 1800. Wife Bisha and son John at present in Norfolk, Va. and Robert Wright of Nottingham exrs. Ch. John, Joseph,Mary, Samuel, Ann, Naomi, Ruth and Elizabeth.
Wits: Thomas Ashmoor, William Douglass, Peter Hunt.

Page 264. Henry Silveues, Rockhill Twp. Aug. 24, 1799. Proved April 8, 1800. Wife Mary and son John Silveuse [sic] exrs. "All ch." Son Henry and dau. Elizabeth, mar.
Wits: John Armstrong, Thomas Armstrong.

Page 266. John Verity, Wrightstown Twp., "advanced in age." Feb. 16, 1795. Proved April 8, 1800. Isaac Chapman and Isaac Wilson exrs. Ellonor, Elizabeth and Jesse Verity, ch. of Bro. Jacob Verity. John, Ann and Sarah, ch. of Joseph Chapman.
Wits: Ann Chapman, Edward Chapman.

Page 268. William Atkinson, Upper Makefield Twp., yeoman. 5 mo.-7-1778. Proved April 19, 1800. Wife Mary. Son John and newphew Thomas Atkinson exrs. Sons Isaac, William and Joseph. Daus. Mary Rose, Sarah Lee, Eleanor Lee and Phebe Atkinson.
Wits: Crispin Blackfan, Edmond Smith, Deborah Smith.

Page 269. Jacob Gieste, Nockamixon Twp. Dec. 19, 1789. Proved May 5, 1800. Wife Eve Catharine and her bro. Nicholas Strouse exrs. Estate to all his ch. and wife's dau. Mary Catharine, wife of Jacob Fair.
Wits: Philip Item, Andrew Campbell.

Page 271. Charles Sellner, Bedminster Twp., Taylor. Feb. 5, 1800. Proved May 5, 1800. Wife Mary and son Charles exrs. 8 ch., sons, Daniel, John and Charles. Daus. Susan and Madlin.

Wits: Henry Wismer, Abrm. Winner.

Page 273. William Heacock, Rockhill Twp., yeoman. Feb. 2, 1797, codicil dated Jan. 5, 1800. Proved May 8, 1800. Kinsman William Penrose and son Jesse exrs. Sons William, Jonathan and Jesse. Daus. Ann wife of Joseph Rawlings, Alice wife of Josiah Dennis, Jane wife of Amos Dennis. Gdch. Jane, Ann and Tacy Wilson. Dau.-in-law Sarah Heacock, widow of son Jeremiah dec'd. and their ch. Son-in-law Thomas Strawhen, gdsn. Thomas Strawhen Jr. Land adj. Michael Blyler, Philip Dosh. William and John Penrose, Edward Roberts and Everard Foulke, Appraisers.
Wits: Everard Foulke, Hugh Foulke, Josiah Penrose, Aquiala Jones, James Chapman, Surveyor.

Page 276. Henry Huber, Milford Twp., wheelwright. (Translated from German) April 10, 1800. Proved May 9, 1800. George Adam Ewalt and Christian Miller, exrs. Mother Ann Huber. Bros. Jacob and John, sister Adelhite Ott and Catharine Brouchler, Elizabeth Brouchler, daus. of Michael Brouchler and sister Ann Brouchler. Catharine and John and Peter Huber, ch. of Bro. John.
Wits: Adam Shnider, Daniel Miller, Henry Huber.

Page 278. Henry Tomlinson, Bensalem Twp. "Far advanced in years." 9 mo.-10-1796. Proved May 12, 1800. Wife Jemima and son Jesse and Joshua Comly exrs. Daus. Sarah and Jemima. Land that was Bro. Thomas's, bought of Thomas Jenks and William Craig. Do. bought of Lawrence Growdon. Bond against John Townsend. Land adj. Thomas Walmsley and Harman Titus.
Wits: Silas Walmsley, William Walmsley, Jesse Walmsley.

Page 280. Jacob Vandegrift, Bensalem Twp. Jan. 1, 1800. Proved May 22, 1800. Wife Sarah. Sons Jacob, David and William exrs. Daus. Mary Bennett and Elizabeth Larrew. Gddau. Elizabeth Bennett. Land adj. Bro. John, Jesse Jackson, Jacob Jackson, Abraham Vandegrift, "where Henry Brouse lives."
Wits: Abraham Larrew Junr., Isaac Prawl, Abraham Vandegrift.

Page 281. Rachel Watson, Middletown Twp., widow. 5 mo.-29-1799. Proved May 24, 1800. Son John Watson exr. Dau. Hannah Newbold. Hannameel Canby.
Wits: Oliver Paxson, Benjamin Parry.

Page 282. Mary Blackshaw, Falls Twp. April 30, 1772. Proved July 24, 1800. Son-in-law Daniel Wharton and his son Daniel exrs. Dau. Rebecca Wharton. Gdch. Daniel, Phebe and Nehemiah Wharton and Sarah Welch. Gddau.-in-law Mary Wharton.
Wits: Anthony Burton, Elizabeth Winder.

Page 284. Henry Bucher, Nockamixon Twp. May 1, 1800. Proved May 31, 1800. Wife Hanah and son Georath exrs. Ch. Henry, Hanah, Andrew, Jacob, Barbara and Anna. Gddau. Sara Bucher.
Wits: Jacob Mill, Phillip Rapp.

Page 285. Jacob Crout, Bedminster Twp., Miller. March 10, 1796. Proved July 9, 1800. Wife Anne. Sons Henry and Jacob Crout and son-in-law Christian Letherman exrs. Daus. Ann wife of Christian Letherman, Elizabeth wife of Christian Rasenberg, Ester, Susanna, and Mary.
Wits: --- Loux, Andrew Loux, Samuel Landes.

Page 287. Robert Means, Sr., Warwick Twp., yeoman. May 7, 1800. Proved May 7, 1800. Nephews Robert and William Mearns exrs. Sons of Bro. Hugh Mearns dec'd. Father Robert Mearns dec'd. Half-bro. Thomas Hustin of Cumberland Co. Hugh Jamison, son of nece [sic] Sarah, wife of Robert Jamison. Rachel Jamison, dau. of said Sarah Jamison. 3 ch. of said Robert Mearns, Jr., Rachel, Maria and Sally.
Wits: William Ramsey, Robert Bready.

Page 289. Mahlon Rickey, Fallsington, Falls Twp. 6 mo.-18-1800. Proved July 1, 1800. Mahlon Milnor, John Rickey and Allen Lippencut exrs. John Rickey. Bro., sole legatee.
Wits: Samuel Alexander, Benjamin Palmer Junr., William Hoper.

Page 293. Joseph Howel, Upper Makefield Twp., yeoman. June 12, 1800. Proved July 23, 1800. Wife Jemima and son David exrs. Sons Samuel, Timothy and David. Daus. Mary Jemima, Phebe and Susanna (Burroughs).
Wits: Garret Johnson, Archibald Graham and Oliver Hough.

Page 295. John Townsend, Bensalem Twp. 8 mo.-7-1799. Proved Aug. 6, 1800. Wife Grace. Son Ezra exr. Gdch. ---, Byberry Preparative Meeting.
Wits: Jesse James, John Conley, Susanna Tery.

Page 296. Mary Barton, New Britain Twp., widow. Sept. 3, 1799. Proved Aug. 5, 1800. Dau. Elizabeth James extx. Sons Joseph, John, Kimber and Eli Barton son Levi Barton. Daus. Sarah Payl, Pathany Stewart, and Deborah Stewart, dec'd. Dau. Elizabeth James, widow.
Wits: Lewis Bitting, David Evans.

Page 298. James Jolly, Lower Makefield Twp. "Far advanced in years." 8 mo.-1-1793. Proved Sept. 15, 1800. Nephew James Longshore exr. Nephew James Longshore, son of sister Ursula Longshore, his sons Jolly and James Longshore. Sarah Benner, dau. of Bro. Benjamin Jolly. Nephew Jolly Longshore. Hannah Beaks, dau. of sister Juliann

Ashburn. Cousins Beula Cary, dau. of neace [sic] Agnes Cary; and cousin John Paste, son of John Paste, Jolly Paste, son of do. Bro. Benjamin Jolly. Sister Ursula Longshore. Sister Perthena Hutchinson. Sister Martha Stackhouse, "debt he owes." Niece Phebe Smith, wife of Joseph Smith. Cousin Richard Boulby Longshore and Robert Longshore, sons of nephew Jolly Longshore. Nephews Robert Jolly and David Griffith.
Wits: Joseph Taylor, Cornelius Slack.

Page 300. John Farrens, Warrington Twp. Nov.17, 1798. Proved Nov. 3, 1800. John Barcley, Esq. exr. Ch. Hugh, Mary, John and Elizabeth Farrens and Jean Farrens (now Ratcliff).
Wits: James Dunn, William Jackson, Charles Dean.

Page 301. Abraham Beidler, Lower Milford Twp. Aug. 30, 1800. Proved Nov. 2, 1800. Wife Frone. Peter Zetty and Abraham Gehman of Lower Milford Exrs. Son-in-law John Star. Dau. Mary.
Wits: Two Germans.

Page 303. Mary White, Wrightstown Twp. "Far advanced in age." Oct. 24, 1794. Proved Nov. 26, 1800. Sons John and Joseph White exrs. Daus. Ann White and Mary Clark.
Wits: Edward Chapman, Isaac Chapman.

Page 305. Lawrence Johnson, Falls Twp. Oct. 28, 1800. Proved Dec. 9, 1800. "Relations" Susanna Wosley, John Pitner and Abner Pitner exrs. Dau. Pricilla Reeder and Sarah Thackery.
Wits: John Johnson, John Lotcher.

Page 306. Francis Titus, Bristol Twp., Farmer. Dec. 22, 1798. Proved Dec. 20, 1800. Wife Jane K. (or H.) Titus. John Hillings, Sen. and son Francis Titus exrs. Daus. Rebecca Vanarsdalen, Mary Vansant and Margaret Wilcoxe.
Wits: Samuel Richardson, Clement Richardson.

Page 307. Joshua Richardson, Middletown Twp. 10-14-1800. Proved Dec. 22, 1800. Son Joseph and "nephew by marriage," Thomas Story exrs. Ch. Joseph, Sarah wife of William Allen, Martha wife of Seth Chapman Esq. Jane and Ruth Richardson. Four gdch. by dau. Mary, late wife of Joshua Woolston, viz: Sarah, Rachel and Ann Woolston. Exrs. and Joshua Woolston Guardians. Land bought of Isaac Watson, William Paxson, late Jonas Preston's, adj. Bro. William, sisters Mary and Ruth, Jonathan Stackhouse and James Wildman "Late John Paxson's."
Wits: Joseph Hayhurst, Benjamin Buckman, Mahlon Gregg.

Page 310. Richard Mitchel, Lower Makefield Twp., Mason. July 7,

1800. Proved Dec. 22, 1800. Wife Esther and William Aspy, of Lower Makefield, exrs. Ch. John, Elizabeth, Carlile, Mahlon, Mary Mitchel, Sarah Mitchel, Esther Mitchel and Daniel Mitchel.
Wits: Joseph Vanhorn, David Vanhorn, Alexander Derbyshire.

Page 311. Benjamin Eastburn, Northampton Twp., caprenter. Dec. 8, 1800. Proved Jan. 22, 1801. Sons Joseph and Benjamin exrs. 5 daus. Elizabeth, Sarah, Ann, Margrate and Mary.
Wits: George Newell, Abraham Hardin.

Page 313. Jacob Heany, Tinicum Twp., yeoman. Nov. 19, 1798. Proved Jan. 29, 1801. Wife Catharine. Sons Simon and Michael Heany exrs. Sons Anthony, Simon, Michael, Jacob, John and Joseph. Daus. Eve, Abigail, Catharine, Elizabeth and Mary. Abigail's dau. Margeret.
Wits: William Williams, Jacob Lipecap, Frederick George. Land adj. Frederick George and John Heany.

Page 315. Francis White, Middletown Twp. Dec. 10, 1800. Proved Feb. 9, 1801. Wife Sarah and Bro.-in-law Jesse Johnson exrs. Son Francis. Daus. Martha, Christina and Ruth White.
Wits: William Vansant, Mathew Rue, William Sisom.

Page 317. Amos Vickers, Baltimore, State of Md. March 22, 1800. Proved at Baltimore Sept. 3, 1800. Bucks Co. Feb. 25, 1801. Joseph Skelton Senr. of Bucks Co. and Charles Stow of Phila. exrs. Sisters Susannah and Ann Vickers. Lot in Solebury Bucks Co. where my Parents Peter and Ann Vickers now live. Nephews William Jones Dutton and Benjamin Vickers Dutton.
Wits: Hanna Dutton, Benjamin Brown.

Page 320. Daniel Bevikison, Bedminster Twp., "Aged and infirm." Feb. 12, 1797. Proved Feb. 17, 1801. Wife Mary, Henry Overholtzer and Joseph Fratz exrs. Son Abraham and his ch. Dau. Hester Overholt.
Wits: Alexander Hughs, Henry Kulp.

Page 322. Michael Sholl, Rockhill Twp. Aged and infirm. Nov. 13, 1798. Proved March 23, 1801. Friend Peter Sholl and Jacob Kerber exrs. Wife Elizabeth. Powder horn to Andrew Fritz.
Wits: Johannes Gettman, George Gettman.

Page 323. Philip Dosh, Rockhill Twp., yeoman. Sept. 26, 1800. Proved March 11, 1801. Henry Hartzel exr. Mary Hennericks. Philip Dosh. Mary Dosh, Junr. Hanna Hendricks.
Wits: Jacob Lowr, Michael Blyler. Hartzel renounces. Letters granted to Abraham Dosh.

Page 324. Daniel Martin, Middletown Twp. March 26, 1801. Proved

April 10, 1801. Wife Agnes. Peter Sharps of Greenwich Twp. Sussex Co. N.J. exr. 7 ch. Mary, Frances, Agnes, Thomas, William, Murray, Daniel and Charles Alexander.
Wits: Mahlon Gregg, William Blakey Junr.

Page 325. Christian Kearn, Hilltown Twp. April 5, 1800. Proved April 27, 1801. Wife Mary, son Adam and son-in-law Henry Hober, exrs. Daus. Catharine wife of Henry Hober, Margaret wife of George Shive. 3 Gdch. by son Philip Kearn, "late dec'd."
Wits: Samuel Armstrong, Thomas Armstrong.

Page 326. John Carl, Bedminster Twp., yeoman. March 4, 1801. Proved May 5, 1801. Wife Ketrin and Abraham Wesmore Junr. exrs. Estate coming from Father when dec'd., to children.
Wits: Henry Wismer, Samuel Zollner[?]

Page 328. Andrew Drieweg, Senr., Springfield Twp., yeoman. June 1, 1799. Proved May 5, 1801. Wife Margaret. Son Philip exr. Sons Philip and John Yost Driewig.
Wits: --- Germans.

Page 329. Samuel Armitage, Senr., Solebury Twp., yeoman. 11 mo.-1798. Proved May 11, 1801. Sons James and John exrs. Daus. Jane McAdams, Sarah Kinsey and Mary Perry. Sons Amos and Samuel.
Wits: Moses Paxson, Joshua Ely Junr., Joseph Townsend.

Page 330. Jacob Clymer, Lower Milford Twp., yeoman. Dec. 8, 1800. Proved June 2, 1801. Wife Ester. Son-in-law Isaac Kolb and son Henry Clymer exrs. 3 ch. Sons Christian and Henry.
Wits: Jacob Clymer and Christian Bieler.

Page 331. Sarah Fell, Plumstead Twp. 7 mo.-7-1799. Proved June 9, 1801. Cousin John Kinsey of Solebury and nephew David Fell, son of Bro. Joseph, exrs. Sister Martha wife of Edward Bice; her dau. Mary Bice. Nephews Jonathan Bice and John Fell and David Fell, sons of Joseph Fell, Jonathan Fell, son of Joseph. Bro. David Fell and his ch. Land adj. Philip Hinkel, John Shitenger, Charles Dyer and Abraham Shitenger and Peter Loucks.
Wits: Thomas Carey, Amos Mitchener and Abel Knight.

Page 333. James Shaw, Plumstead Twp. 8 mo.-13-1798. Proved June 17, 1801. Wife Sarah. Sons James and Samuel exrs. Daus. Mary Bradshaw and Susannah Walker. Sons Josiah and Ephraim.
Wits: Joseph Brooks, George Fell.

Page 334. Anthony Burton, Bristol Twp., yeoman. Feb. 17, 1798. Proved July 25, 1801. Wife Mary and John, Anthony and Jonathan

Burton exrs. Sons John, Anthony and Jonathan Burton. Dau. Martha Minster and her 4 ch., Mary, John, Anthony and William Minster. John Cornish, son of Rebekah Welch, late Cornish House where Hannah Cooper dwells. Lands bought of Paxson Lovet and Richard Stillwell. Land adj. Thomas Rees, Joseph Richardson, John Brown and Samuel Rhoads.
Wits: Peter Williamson, Mahlon Williamson, John Sotcher.

Page 338. Eleazer Twining, Warwick Twp., yeoman. July 8, 1798. Codicil dated March 25, 1800. Proved July 27, 1801. Son Silas Twining and son-in-law Abraham Wilkinson exrs. Son David. Daus. Hannah McDole, Ann Twining and Mary Wilkinson. Gdch. William, Mary, Ann and Sarah McDole; Ruth, William and Hannah Twining. Land bought by Father of William Shippen and Swift and Coleman; do. adj. Joseph Briggs and David Cummings. Bought of Jonathan Barrington. Bonds against Isaac Ryan and Francis Tomlinson.
Wits: Jacob Twining, Stephen Twining, Mary Briggs.

Page 343. Joseph Warner, Falls Twp. Jan. 21, 1801. Proved Aug. 6, 1801. Wife Mary and Father-in-law James Cooper, the Elder, exrs. Ch. ---.
Wits: William Milnor, --- Palmer.

Page 344. Hannah Headley, Bristol Twp., widow. 2 mo.-2-1797. Proved Aug. 6, 1801. Son-in-law Daniel Wharton and dau. Sarah White exrs. Son John Headly. Daus. Sarah White, Lucy Mitchell, Abigail Wharton and Nancy Bastow. John Bastow. Dau. Hannah Carter's ch., Zebdee, Daniel and John Brelsford and Rebecca Carter. Gdch. Elizabeth Brelsford, Joseph White and Hannah Mitchell. Bond against James Denormandy.
Wits: William Vansant, Amos Brelsford.

Page 346. Jonathan Worthington, New Britain Twp. March 7, 1801. Proved Sept. 15, 1801. Wife Mary. Son James Worthington and Bro-in-law Cephas Child exrs. 11 ch., sons James, Jonathan, David, Benjamin, Israel, Zenas, Cephas and William; daus. Phebe, Jane and Macre.
Wits: Moses Dunlap, John Price.

Page 348. John Nutt, Falls Twp., "about 88 years of age." 11 mo.-20-1795. Codicil dated Nov. 5, 1796. Proved Sept. 15, 1801. John Hulme and Daniel Wharton Junr. exrs. "No children." Housekeeper Elizabeth Baker. James Townsend, gdsn. of sister Hannah. Nephews Jonathan, Joseph and Edmond Nutt.
Wits: Elizabeth Baker, Is. Hicks, William Wharton, Junr.

Page 349. Isaac Moyer, Plumstead Twp. May 22, 1801. Proved Aug. 1, 1801. Wife Madelena. Bros. Henry and John Moyer and Bro.-in-law

Jacob Overholt exrs. Sons Jacob , Henry, Isaac and John. Daus.
Elizabeth, Barbara and Ester.
Wits: James McMullen, Henry Black.

Page 351. John Lester, Richland Twp. Dec. 30, 1798. Proved Aug. 3,
1801. Wife Jane. Sons Thomas and John exrs. James Chapman to
assist them. Son Shipley Lester. Daus. Sarah wife of Hugh Foulke,
Hannah widow of Theophilus Foulke dec'd. and Jane wife of Moses
Wilson. Land adj. Samuel Thomas and John Greasley, bought of
Cadwallader Foulke.
Wits: William Green, James Chapman.

Page 355. Elizabeth Paxson, widow, Solebury Twp. 10 m.-28-1799.
Proved Sept. 6, 1801. Son-in-law Joseph Wilkinson exr. Daus. Rachel
Paxson, Elizabeth Hambleton, Sarah Wilkinson, Mary Paxson, Ann
Scarborough, Mary Paxson and Amy Worthington.
Wits: Oliver Paxson, Aaron Paxson.

Page 356. Samuel Schofield, Solebury Twp. 6-12-1801. Proved Sept. 26,
1801. Sons John and Benjamin Schofield exrs. Sons Samuel and
Jonathan Schofield. Daus. Ann Taylor, Phebe and Rebecca Schofield.
Wits: Phebe Heston, Anna Armitage.

Page 357. Everard Roberts, Richland Twp., yeoman. 7 mo.-28-1801.
Proved Sept. 28, 1801. Wife Ann. Son John and Israel Lancaster exrs.
Ch. John, Susanna, Ann, Edward, Rebecca, Rachel and Everard. Land
adj. Casper Johnson and Michael Deal.
Wits: Moses Shaw, Benjamin Johnson.

Page 360. John Rice, Buckingham Twp., yeoman. Oct. 1, 1800. Proved
Oct. 4, 1801. Wife Rachel. John Kerr and son-in-law Thomas Kirk exrs.
Ch. Mary Kirk, Edward Rice, Elizabeth Stirke, John, James, Hannah,
and Nancy Rice.
Wits: Thomas Carver, Joseph Paxson.

Page 361. Alice Larew, Bensalem Twp., widow. 9-18-1801. Proved Oct.
6, 1801. Son Abraham Larew exr. Daus. Elizabeth Vansant, Eleanor
Lackett, and Ann Larzelere.
Wits: Thomas Groom, Ezra Townsend.

Page 363. Garret Vanhorn, Springfield Twp., yeoman. Sept. 13, 1801.
Proved Oct. 14, 1801. Wife Ann. William Bryan and James Chapman
exrs. Dau. Jemima "to live with her step-mother" Son John. 4 ch. of
son Barnet Vanhorn dec'd. Daus. Mary Green widow of Joseph Green
dec'd., Sophia wife of Benjamin Walker, Rachel Walton widow of
Ezekiel Walton dec'd., Charity wife of Thomas Loyd, and Jemima.
Gddau. Mary dau. of dau. Ann dec'd. Gdsn. James Swartz, son of dau.

Jannakey dec'd. Land adj. Peter Groom and Robert Ashton.
Wits: Peter Ashton, David Loyd. So spelled in origin.

Page 365. Daniel Benner, Rockhill Twp., yeoman. Aug. 29, 1801.
Proved Oct. 20, 1801. Wife Barbara.. John Heany and John Benner
exrs. Ch. Daniel, Ludwick, John, Jacob, Salome, Magdalena and
Elizabeth.
Wits: George Gettman, Samuel Gettman.

Page 367. Ellin Harvye, Wrightstown Twp. 9 mo.-13-1793. Proved Oct.
24, 1801. Bro. Mathias Harvye and Thomas Story exrs. Cousins
Rebecca and Elenor Broadhurst, daus. of Henry Broadhurst and their
sisters. Land bought of Barnard Vanhorn.
Wits: Abraham Reeder, David Reeder.

Page 368. Timothy Titus, Bristol Twp. Feb. 21, 1801. Proved Nov. 12,
1801. Wife Martha. Son-in-law James Vanhart and Friend Amos Gregg
exrs. Daus. Edith Bergen wife of George Bergen (her son Charles
Titus), Sarah wife of James Vanhart. Rachel, Martha and Sarah
Stackhouse, ch. of dau. Mary Stackhouse dec'd. Ira Titus. Codicil
dated Sept. 13, 1801, wife then dec'd.
Wits. to will Joseph Clunn, John Larew. To cidicil Joshua Headly Jr.,
Ebenezer Headly.

Page 372. George Madera, Warrington Twp. Nov. 21, 1801. Proved
Dec. 8, 1801. Wife Barbara. John Barclay. Esq. of Warwick and William
Long of Warrington, Miller, exrs. "All my ch."
Wits: Justus Rubenkam, George Summers.

Page 374. George Cumings, Warwick Twp., yeoman. Dec. 16, 1801.
Proved Dec. 1, 1801 [sic]. Wife Jean. Son Robert exr. Sons James
Cumings. Daus. Margret and Grizel Cumings. Dau. Ann Collins. Gdch.
James Cumings son of Robert, James Ashton, Robert Collins.
Wits: Hugh and James Edams. Note: The name of this Testator is
James.

Page 375. John Brown, Bristol Twp., "Aged seventy-seven years."
Dec. 30, 1801. Proved Jan. 6, 1802. Wife dec'd. Sons John and Joseph
exrs. Sons Samuel, Benjamin, Charles, John and Joseph. Daus.
Elizabeth Yardley, her son John Yardley. Gdch. Ann, Samuel, John,
David and Benjamin Allen, ch. of dau. Sarah Allen dec'd. John Brown,
son of Samuel, John Brown, son of Joseph.
Wits: William Vansant, John Stackhouse, Reading Beatty.

Page 377. William Linton, Newtown, "Esq.." April 8, 1799. Proved
Feb. 2, 1802. Wife Letitia. Son John exr. Dau. Elizabeth Buckman.
Land bought of John Martin.

88

Wits: Nicholas Wynkoop, Ann Murray.

Page 379. Hannah Paxson, widow of Thomas Paxson of Solebury twp.
6 mo.-19-1798. Proved Feb. 23, 1802. Nephew Edward Blackfan exr. 4
ch. of dec'd. husband, viz. Abraham, Aaron and Moses Paxson; and
Anne Kitchin. Hannah Paxson, dau. of Abraham Paxson, Hannah
Paxson, dau. of Moses and Letitia Paxson dau. of Aaron Paxson.
Edward Wilson, son of Isaac Wilson of London Grove, Chester Co.
Nieces Hannah Smith, Hannah Betts and Hannah Norris. Watson Fell.
Widows of two Bros., viz., Martha Blackfan and Hester Blackfan. Mary
wife of nephew Edward Blackfan. Sister Sarah Wood. 23 ch. of Bros.
and sisters. Hannah Smith, gddau. of dec'd. sister Elixabeth Ely.
Hannah Blackfan, dau. of Edward Blackfan. Ch. of nephew James
Wood. Friend John Watson dec'd., his sister Sarah, widow of Thomas
Lewis of Plumstead.
Wits: Thomas Ross Senr., Daniel Swallow.

Page 381. Manassah Thomas, Hilltown Twp., yeoman. Dec. 17, 1796.
Proved March 2, 1802. Son Eber Thomas exr. Father William Thomas
dec'd. Dau. Emma wife of Elisha Lunn. Gdsn. Ely Thomas. Land adj.
Edward Jones, Philip High, Ann Lewis, John Lewis, Henry Hartzel,
Thomas Thomas, Michael Hartzel, Michael Mire and Job Thomas. Do.
bought of John Custard.
Wits: George Leiday, Elias Thomas, John Pugh.

Page 385. Mary Johnson, Wrightstown Twp., "advanced in age." Dec.
19, 1801. Proved Feb. 3, 1802. Robert Smith of Buckingham, surveyor,
exr. Sons John and Robert Johnson. Dau. Margaret, wife of Thomas
Lee. Dau. Agnes Johnson.
Wits: Joseph Roberts, Benjamin Smith.

Page 385. Richard Jennings, Falls Twp. Oct. 25, 1801. Proved March 9,
1802. Moses Moon and Joseph Burges, exrs. Sister Rose Lux's son
John Lux. Rebecca Burges. Benjamin Vanhorne of Phila. Friends Free
School of Phila. "For education of Blacks."
Wits: Timothy Moon, Daniel Burges.

Page 386. William Magill, Solebury Twp., yeoman. "Advanced in age."
10 mo.-4-1790. Proved March 13, 1802. Son John exr. Son William.
Daus. Sarah wife of George Ely, Elizabeth wife of Elnathan Pettit.
Gddau. Sarah Dean. Sarah Magill dau. of son William.
Wits: Aaron Paxson, Lititia Paxson.

Page 388. John Strawsyder (?), Springfield Twp., yeoman. March 10,
1802. Proved April 23, 1802. Son John and Jacob Fulmer exrs.
Housekeeper Hannah Bugher and her dau. Catharina. Dau. Catharine
wife of Henry Ziegenfuss. Dec'd. daus. Elizabeth and Margaret, their

ch.
Wits: William Gamel, James Smith.

Page 391. Samuel Bechtel, Rockhill Twp., yeoman. March 12, 1796. Proved May 2, 1802. Wife Mary. Gdsn. Samuel Gehman and Michael Shoemaker exrs. 4 gdch., Samuel, John and Abraham Gehman and Mary wife of John Yoder.
Wits: Jacob Cressman and --- , a German name.

Pae 394. Leonard Kiser [Kaiser?] (signed by his mark), Wrightstown Twp. March 5, 1802. Proved May 5, 1802. Wife Margaret. Isaac Chapman and Thomas Atkinson, exrs. Sons Michael, Philip and Joseph. Dau. Mary Barron.
Wits: Thomas Gain, Sarah Gain.

Page 395. Ann Wier, Warrington Twp. "Single woman." March 19, 1800. Proved May 10, 1802. Bro. John Weir exr. Bro. Robert Wier, his wife Mary. Sisters Jane Kelso, and Mary wife of Robert Flack. Ann and Thomas Wier Flack, ch. of sister Mary Flack. Hannah Jones "living with me." Land adj. Henry Wierman and Bro. Robert.
Wits: John Jones Junr., Henry Wierman, Nathaniel Irwin.

Page 397. Rudolph Landes, Bedminster Twp., yeoman. Nov. 30, 1801. Proved May 25, 1802. Wife Sara. Sons Jacob and Abraham Landes exrs. Sons Jacob, Abraham and Joseph. Daus. Magdalena, wife of Philip High, Elizabeth wife of Isaac Moyer, Mary wife of Christian Moyer of Montgomery Co., Barbara wife of Chistropher Moyer of Springfield Twp. Bucks Co. Land adj. Jacob Overholt, Henry Leatherman, Andrew Soux, Abraham Leatherman, Henry Krout, Jacob Krout dec'd., Henry Overholt and Abraham Overholt.
Wits: Christian Leatherman and Henry Leatherman.

Page 400. Eleanor Thomas, New Britain Twp., widow. March 12, 1802. Proved June 4, 1802. Sons Elias and Ephraim Thomas exrs. Sons Enoch and Joseph. Daus. Margaret wife of Richard Lewis, Eleanor wife of Edward Mathew, ch. of dau. Dinah dec'd. Gddau. Elizabeth wife of Thomas Lunn.
Wits: Moses Aaron, Griffith Owen, Benjamin James.

Page 402. William Silvius, Rockhill Twp., "advanced in years." Dec. 26, 1800. Proved June 4, 1802. Wife Catharine. Sons Abraham and Jacob exrs. Ch. John, Joseph, William, Abraham, Jacob and Isaac. Ch. of dec'd. son Henry. Daus. Barbara wife of Frederick Huth, Mary wife of David Tresler.
Wits: Daniel Schaefer and Capser Schaen.

Page 404. Jacob Fry, Bedminster Twp. Feb. 10, 1802. Proved May 28,

1802. Wife Mary. Neighbor Joseph Hart and Joseph Puff exrs. Mary wife of Henry Puff and her ch. John Griffith, son of Thomas Griffith dec'd. Jacob Waterman, son Humphrey Waterman. Jacob Griffith son of John Griffith. Elizabeth McLean, wife of Joseph McLean and her ch.
Wits: Isaac Longstreth, John Spencer, Joseph Longstreth, Junr.

Page 406. Jacob Fluck, Richland Twp., Weaver. May 17, 1802. Proved June 4, 1802. Wife Elizabeth. John Heany and Robert Smith, Esq. exrs. Ch. Samuel Fluck and Hannah Fluck.
Wits: John Neisler, George Ort.

Page 407. Hannah Ely, "consort of Abner Ely," Solebury Twp. May 20, 1793. Proved May 6, 1802. Isaac Vanhorn, Esq. exr. Husband Abner Ely. Son Barnet Pitcock. Dau. Sarah Ely.
Wits: Isaac Vanhorn, Thomas Paxson, Hezik. Linton.

Page 409. Johannes Carl, Bedminster Twp., cordwainer. April 8, 1801. Proved Aug. 10, 1802. Wife Cuniande. Son Jacob and Dau. Ketrin and Mary exrs. Ch. of son John dec'd. "if living."
Wits: Johannes Loux, Abraham Wismer.

Page 412. George Jobes, Lower Makefield Twp. 10-25-1801. Proved Dec. 26, 1801. Wife Jenniser, and Bro.-in-law Robert Margrum exrs. Son George. Daus. Clarrisey, Mary, Juliana and Hannah Jobs. [sic]
Wits: Abraham Margerum, Mahlon Paxson, Thomas Marshall.

Page 413. James Flack, Buckingham Twp., Husbandman, "Being Anchiant." Aug. 3, 1793. Proved Sept. 11, 1802. Wife Ann. Sons Joseph and John exrs. Ch. Joseph, Sarah McMullen, Robert, William, Samuel, John and Benjamin Flack. Benjamin dec'd. leaving 3 ch., Edith, John and Ann Flack.
Wits: Robert McKinstry, Joseph Paxson, Henry Paxson.

Page 415. John Hough, Upper Makefield Twp. 1 mo.-27-1802. Proved Sept. 6, 1802. Wife Hannah and son William exrs. Ch. Joseph, John, Jonathan, William, Moses, Hannah and Samuel. Lease of Moses Harvey for Fishery, near Taylor's Ferry.
Wits: David Howell, Timothy Howell, Oliver Hough.

Page 417. William Hewson, Bristol Twp. May 11, 1802. Proved Sept. 8, 1802. Wife Alce, Bro. Thomas Tickell Hewson and Bro-in-law David Caldwell exrs. and Trustees. Property in England and United States to ch. at death of wife.
Wits: Alce Green, Magdalen K. Green.

Page 418. Catharine Heston, Bristol Borough. July 22, 1802. Proved Sept. 9, 1802. Son Charles Heston and Kinsman Robert Petterson exrs.

Son William Adair, son William Heston and Charles Heston. Daus.
Mary, Sarah, Rebecca, gdsn. William Sanderson. Legacy to David
Queen.
Wits: Thomas Watson, John Wright.

Page 419. George Wisel, Richland Twp. Nov. 6, 1798. Proved Sept. 20,
1802. Son Peter Wisel and Friend Jacob Cressman exrs. Sons Peter
and Joseph and Jacob. Daus. Mary and Sarah Wisel. Other ch. not
named.
Wits: Jacob Selsor, Jacob Nestler.

Page 420. Abraham Slack, Lower Makefield Twp. Nov. 6, 1798. Proved
Sept. 7, 1802. Wife Martha. Sons Cornelius and James exrs. Son
Abraham and dau. Sarah Kelley.
Wits: Cornelius Slack, Anthony Torbert.

Page 422. John Edwards, Lower Makefield Twp., yeoman. Oct. 16,
1802. Proved Nov. 3, 1802. Wife Jane and son Aaron exrs. Son John.
Daus. Jane, Margaret Wever, Mary and Martha.
Wits: Abraham Gayman, Joseph Thomas.

Page 423. Casper Fryling, Tinnecum Twp., Farmer. Feb. 23, 1801.
Proved Nov. 13, 1802. Wife Barbara. Sons John Adam and Harman
Fryling exrs. Ch. Elizabeth, Henry, John, George, Mary, John Adam,
Harman, Peggy, Abraham, Cattrout and Jacob.
Wits: Philip Harpel, Peter Rebbart, Johannes High.

Page 424. Martha Blackfan, Solebury Twp. 7 mo.-25-1797. Proved Dec.
23, 1802. Son-in-law Thomas Smith exr. Son Edward. Daus. Rebekah
Wilson, Sarah Wilson, Letitia Smith, Hannah Betts, Elenor Smith,
Elizabeth Simpson, Martha Tyson and Esther Lloyd. Gddau. Martha
Wilson dau. of Stephen and Sarah Wilson. Other gddaus. Martha
Wilson, Martha Betts, Letitia Smith, Esther Lloyd.
Wits: William Lee, John Atkinson.

Page 426. Mary Mearns, Warwick Twp., single woman. Oct. 10, 1801.
Dec. 4, 1802. Robert Mearns and William Mearns exrs. Sister Mary
Thompson. Niece Mary Christy, dau. of niece Mary Williams. Nephew
Dr. William Smith. Nephews Robert and William Mearns, sons of bro.
Hugh Mearns. Father Robert Mearns dec'd.
Wits: William Ramsey, Sarah Dungan.

Page 427. John Smith, Plumstead Twp., yeoman. 3 mo.-11-1801.
Proved Dec. 30, 1802. Son William and dau. Esther Smith exrs. Daus.
Elizabeth Shaw, Martha Cooper, Ann Fell and Esther and Mercy
Smith.
Wits: Josiah Brown, Joseph Stradling, Joseph White.

Page 429. Philip Harpel, Bedminster Twp., yeoman. Dec. 24, 1802. Proved Jan. 5, 1803. Wife Anna Maria; sons Philip and Conrad, exrs. Daus. Elizabeth, Magdalen and Margaret.
Wits: David White, Jacob Wilthonger.

Page 432. Jost Fulmer, Haycock, yeoman. April 7, 1798. Proved Jan. 4, 1803. Wife Magdalena. Friends John Fulmer and George Fulmer, exrs. (See scrap paper in file D, "Bros.") Ch. Jacob, Jost Daniel, George, Magdalena, Catharine, Elizabeth, Maria and Susanna.
Wits: John Green, G. Felix Lynn.

Page 435. William Biles, Falls Twp. June 20, 1802. Proved Jan. 7, 1803. Wife Sarah and William and John Mott and George Thorn exrs. Sister Susanna Thorn, widow of Thomas Thorn of Burlington Co., N.J. Their ch. and gdch., viz. Joseph, Benjamin, John, Enoch and William Thorn (dec'd.) and Ann Taylor. Two ch. of William Thorn. Sarah Taylor, wife of Lewis Taylor. William, John, Mary and Margaret Mott, ch. of Asher and Ann Mott. Martha Stanbury, wife of Abraham Ogier Stanbury of City of New York.
Wits: Huldah Mott, William Crozer, William Warner.

Page 438. Elizabeth Morrison, New Britain Twp. Nov. 4, 1800. Proved Feb. 7, 1803. Isaac Morris exr. "Nephew Elizabeth Ferguson, by maiden name, since married, husband's name unknown to me, and now a widow" her dau. name unknown. "Nephew" Ann Ferguson. Martha Childs. Nephew Nathaniel Parker. Pastor James McLaughlin. Arthur Thomas and Sarah his wife. Elizabeth Harding.
Wits: Thomas Mathias, Enoch Mathias.

Page 440. Abigail Weaver, alias Pearson, widow of James Pearson, Pennsbury Manor. Dec. 15, 1802. Proved Jan. 13, 1803. Joseph Ashton Junr. and Joseph Knowles exrs. Daus. Susan Pearson and Mary Pearson alias Ashton.
Wits: Rachel Scott, Robert Scott Jr., Mary Linton.

Page 441. William Goforth, Bensalem Twp., Cordwainer. Dec. 22, 1802. Proved Jan. 26, 1803. Wife Elizabeth and Gilbert Rodman exrs. Sons Thomas and John. Daus. Elizabeth and Nancy.
Wits: Joseph Jackson, Robert Wood, William Hane.

Page 444. Michael Itterly, signed by mark, Rockhill Twp., yeoman. Jan. 16, 1799. Proved March 3, 1803. Everard Foulke exr. Ch. Maricha, Wrchila, Christina, Rosanna and Chaterine.
Wits: George Beringer, ---.

Page 446. Joseph Allen, Bensalem Twp. March 16, 1802. Proved March 14, 1803. Wife Sarah. Son William exr. Sons John, Israel, Joseph and

William. Daus. Mary and Sarah Allen. Land adj. bro. Samuel Allen, bro. William and widow Shippen.
Wits: Jonathan Paul, Samuel Allen.

Page 448. Lawrance Pearson, Senr., Nockamixon Twp., yeoman. "Far advanced in life." Sept. 5, 1801. Proved April 12, 1803. Jacob Saucerman and Jacob Woolfanger exrs. Sons Henry, Philip, Christian, Lawrance and Peter. Daus. Mary wife of John Cole, Catharine wife of Jacob Sauceman, Susanna wife of John Easterling. Gddau. Catharine Saucerman. [sic] Wife Elizabeth.
Wits: Michael Streby, Philip Leidigh.

Page 451. Christina Merrick, wife of George Merrick, Bristol Boro. 2 mo.-25-1803. Proved May 3, 1803. Pearson Mitchell exr. Thomas, son of bro. John Brown. Thomas Brown, son of bro. Clark Brown. Christian Thompson. Eleazer Lundy. Nieces. Christian Thomson and dau. of sister Rachel.
Wits: Samuel Allen, Amos Gregg.

Page 452. Owen Swarts, New Britain Twp., yeoman. April 7, 1801. Proved May 5, 1803. Bros. Jacob and Christian Swarts, exrs. Sons John, Henry and David Swarts.
Wits: Jacob Clemens, Joseph Swarts.

Page 454. Harman V. Kinsey, Bristol Boro. July 8, 1801. Proved May 6, 1803. Wife Ann. Amos Gregg exr. Bro. Joseph. Sisters Sarah Stackhouse, Mary, Rebecca and Elizabeth Kinsey.
Wits: Jacob Vanhart, Amos Gregg, Jr.

Page 456. Isaac Brelsford, Lower Makefield Twp., "far advanced in life." 3 mo.-30-1801. Proved May 9, 1803. Four sons-in-law, Nehemiah Wharton, Jesse Palmer, Joseph Wharton and Thomas Stradling, exrs. Sons Joshua, Isaac and Abraham. Ch. of sons David and Timothy. Daus. Elizabeth, Joyce, Rachel, Susanna and Rosamond. Land adj. Daniel Wharton, Benjamin Palmer, Daniel Lovett and William Satterthwaite. Due from Abrham Winer. (Uriner?).
Wits: John W. Balderston, Daniel Wharton, William Wharton.

Page 460. Amos Dennis, Richland Twp., wheelwright. 6 mo-6-1801. Proved March 3, 1803. Wife Jane and bro. Josiah Dennis exrs. Ch. Dinah and Charles Dennis.
Wits: Israel Foulke, Jesse Iden.

Page 462. George Wall, Solebury Twp. May 1, 1801. Codicil Feb. 10, 1803. Proved June 11, 1803. Wife Sarah. Dr. John Wilson and Joshua Beans exrs. Codicil adds son Thomas as exr. Sons Thomas and John. Daus. Sarah Clauson, Elizabeth Thomas, Martha, Ann and Euphemia

Wall.
Wits: Thomas Hambleton, David Michener, Michael Keller, John Goucher and Mahlon Cooper.

Page 466. George Smith, New Britain Twp., yeoman. April 29, 1803. Proved June 11, 1803. Philip Miller exr. Benjamin Butler and his son George Butler. Rachel, Margaret, Sarah and Mary Thomas, daus. of James Thomas. Land in Mt. Bethel Twp., Northampton Co.
Wits: James Thomas, David Thomas.

Page 468. William Hambleton, Solebury Twp. July 31, 1795. Proved June 19, 1803. Wife Martha. Sons Joseph and William exrs. Amy and Benjamin Hambleton, ch. of Benjamin. William Hambleton, son of Thomas. Daus. Hannah Dean, Mary, Sarah, Elizabeth and Martha Hambleton. Land adj. Stephen Hambleton and --- Hartley.
Wits: Benjamin Paxson, John Watson, James Hambleton.

Page 471. Peter Heft, Haycock Twp., yeoman. April 7, 1803. Proved June 8, 1803. Son Henry Heft and son-in-law George Shive, exrs. Eldest son Philip Heft, William Heft, Henry Heft. Dau. Margaret Heft, ---. Appraisers John Stokes, John Smith, Henry Eagle, William Bryan and Daniel Strawn. Land adj. Philip Herring, John Mann and others.
Wits: Josiah Dennis, William Stokes.

Page 474. Martin Sacks, Milford Twp., Blacksmith. Feb. 10, 1803. Proved July 25, 1803. Wife Elizabeth. Bro.-in-law Adam Broughlar exr. Sons Martin and Adam Sacks. Dau. Catharine, wife of Jacob Shelly.
Wits: David Spinner, George Horlacker.

Page 476. Elizabeth Vastine, widow, New Britain Twp. April 8, 1803. Proved July 28, 1803. Nephew Edward Mathew of New Britain exr. Isaac Vanhorn Trustee. Nephew Thomas Mathew. Elizabeth Mathew, dau. of Thomas and Elce Mathew. Abel, son of Edward and Elenor Mathew. Rebecca, Simon and John Mathew. Mary and Rebecca Vanhorn, daus. of Isaac and Rebecca Vanhorn. Nieces Jane and Mary Evans, daus. of Jenkin and Jane Evans. Ch. of Jacob and Lavina Wells. Elizabeth Gray, dau. of George and Mary Gray. Jeremiah Gray.
Wits: John Davis, George Siegfried, Sarah Siegfried.

Page 480. Sarah Stockton, Lower Makefield Twp. July 7, 1803. Proved Aug. 6, 1803. Son John Stockton and Abner Buckman exrs. Ch. Sarah Sevin, Ann Oppey, Rachel Skillman, John Stockton, Hellenor Stockton and Elizabeth ---.
Wits: Joseph Watson, Mark Watson.

Page 481. Thomas Wilson, Bristol Twp., yeoman. 7-21-1803. Proved

Aug. 6, 1803. Wife Margaret. Sons Joseph, Thomas and David exrs.
Sons John and Benjamin. Joseph, Martha and Agnes, ch. of son
Benjamin. Dau. Rebecca Johnson. Bond of John Minster. Land adj.
Daniel Larrew.
Wits: Samuel Lovett, Moses Moon.

Page 484. Hester Dyer. April 5, 1784. Prove July 4, 1803. Five daus.,
Phebe's two oldest daus., Rachel's oldest son, Mary's dau. Mary.
Son Josiah Dyer. John Dyer exr.
Wits: Benjamin Rich Junr. Proved by testimony of Elizabeth Poeton
[Polton?] and Esther Bradshaw.

Page 485. Andrew McMickin, Warwick Twp., yeoman. April 26, 1800.
Proved May 11, 1803. Nathaniel Irwin exr. John Crawford Junr. of
Warwick guardian. James McMickin, son of bro. David McMickin
dec'd. Andrew, Elizabeth, Naomi McMickin, and Charles McMickin
Junr., ch. of bro. Charles McMickin of Warwick Twp.
Wits: Joseph Flack, John Flack, John Connard.

Page 487. Margaret Dumont, Northampton Twp., "advanced in years."
March 9, 1801. Proved Sept. 16, 1803. Sons Gilliam Cornell and John
Cornell exrs. Son Abraham Cornell. Daus. Phebe wife of Cornelius
Cornell, Cornelia wife of William Bennett, and Mary Cornell.
Wits: Elias Dungan, Elizabeth Dungan, Rachel Dungan.

Page 487. Catharine Wireman, Buckingham Twp., widow. March 31,
1803. Proved Sept. 20, 1803. Son John Wireman and Friend John Kerr
exrs. Daus. Nancy Roar, Mary Ruth and Catharine Fritzinger.
Wits: Abraham Geil, Samuel Godshalk. Letters to Ann Road, exrs.
renounced.

Page 500. William Carver, Buckingham Twp., "advanced in age." Sept.
17, 1803. Proved Oct. 15, 1803. Wife Sarah. Sons William and Joseph
Carver exrs. Daus. Elizabeth wife of David Bradshaw and Mary wife of
John Kirk.
Wits: John Malone, Jonathan Worthington and John Terry. Land
bought of William Chapman.

Page 502. William Simpson, Horsham Twp., Montgomery Co.,
Schoolmaster. Aug. 24, 1803. Proved Oct. 27, 1803. Bro.-in-law
Benjamin Hugh exr. Bro. John Simpson. Sisters Anne Smith wife of
Jonathan Smith and Hannah Hough.
Wist: Thomas Craig, William McEwen.

Page 504. Samuel Harrold, Buckingham Twp. 5 mo.-6-1803. Proved
Nov. 10, 1803. Wife Rachel. Jonathan Fell, John Ely and son David
Harrold exrs. Sons William, David, James, Samuel, Joseph and John

(removed to Niagara). Daus. Elizabeth wife of James Dungan and Rebecca wife of Joseph Gillingham. Samuel, David, Henry, James and Elizabeth Carver, ch. of dau. Sarah Carver dec'd. Gdch. Samuel Harrold son of Joseph, Samuel Harrold son of William. William Harrold son of John, Samuel Harrold Dungan son of James and Elizabeth and Elizabeth Harrold, dau. of Samuel and Hannah Harrold. Benjamin Warner, Jesse Ely, David Bradshaw and John Watson (Farmer), Guardians. Land purchased of Jonathan Pickering and Thomas Gilbert in Buckingham. Do. in Lycoming Co. purchased of John Heap, in partnership with Joseph and Samuel Carpenter. Do. in Harrison and Randolph Co., Va. purchased of Christian Wireman and Joseph Pryor. Note of James Rice. Haertshorne and Large, and John Field, Merchants of Phila.
Wits: John Melone, John Watson, John Watson Jr.

Page 512. Elizabeth Gillingham, wife of Joseph Gillinham [sic], Makefield Twp. 6 mo.-17-1803. Proved Nov. 9, 1803. Thomas Yardley exr. Eight ch., Thomas Gillingham, Mary Moon, Ann Breally, Elizabeth Swain, John, William, Harvey and Joseph Gillingham. Bro. William Harvey. Bro. John Harvey dec'd. Husband Joseph Gillingham.
Wits: Jonathan Swain, Amos Gregg.

Page 514. Mark Watson, Falls Twp., Blacksmith. 3 mo-16-1799 & 4 mo-27-1799. Proved Nov. 12, 1803. Wife Mary. Son Abner exr. Six ch., Abner, Deborah, Rebecca, Mary, Ann and Tace.
Wits: John Brown Junr., Moses Comfort.

Page 517. Peter Rodenbush, Springfield Tpw., Hatter. Aug. 7, 1803. Proved Nov. 24, 1803. Wife Sarah. Bro.-in-law Conrad Harpel exr. Father-in-law Joseph Himmelwright, Guardian of "only child" William.
Wits: Nicholas Roudenbush [sic], John Smith.

Page 519. Sarah Smith, widow of Benjamin Smith, late of Buckingham Twp, "Aged." Dated 3 mo.-22-1802. Proved Nov. 23, 1803. Robert Smith, Surveyor, exr. 4 ch. Benjamin, Samuel, Elizabeth Heston and Phebe Smith.
Wits: Rebecca Smith, Mary Canby.

Page 520. John Bennett, Northampton Twp., yeoman. Feb. 27, 1802. Proved Dec. 7, 1803. Son Lot, John MacNear and John Corson exrs. Ch. Isaac, Benjamin, Lot, Elizabeth, Joshua, Mary and John Bennet and Catharine Miles.
Wits: Joshua Praul, Joseph Johnson and Simon Vanartsdalen.

Page 523. Kezia Penrose, wife of Abel Penrose, of Richland Twp., and dau. of Joseph Speakman, late of Upper Canada, dec'd. Nov.8, 1803. Proved Nov. 28, 1803. Husband Abel Penrose exr. and sole legatee.

Legacy under will of Uncle William Speakman, late of Great Britain.
Wits: Cadwallader Foulke, John Foulke.

Page 524. Daniel Longstreth, Warminster Twp., - mo.-4-1799. Proved
Dec. 7, 1803. Wife Martha. Sons John and Joseph exrs. Sons Isaac and
Jonathan. Son-in-law Thomas Ross, dau. Martha Michener. Gdch.
Rachel Ross, Daniel Michener and Daniel Longstreth. Land adj. Arthur
Watts, --- Cornell, John Hough and Amos Watson.
Wits: Mathias Hutchinson, Robert Lewis, Martha Bye.

Page 530. James Howe, Bensalem Twp., "Far advanced in years." May
6, 1800. Proved Dec. 6, 1803. Son William exr. Sons William and John.
Wife's gddau. Christener Mornington.
Wits: Lawrance Johnson, Samuel Allen.

Page 531. Mary Finley, New Britain Twp., single woman. Aug. 16,
1803. Proved Dec. 29, 1803. Codicil dated Nov. 1, 1803. Bro. James
Finley of New Britain exr. Mo. Sisters Martha wife of William Demun
of N.J. and Sarah wife of William Long of Warrington, Miller. William
Alexander Long, son of sister Sarah.
Wits: Samuel Wier, Nathaniel Irwin.

Page 533. Mary Miller, Warminster Twp., Spinster. July 16, 1803.
Proved Jan. 3, 1804. Dau. Margaret, and friend Robert Loller of
Moreland Twp., Surveyor, exrs. Dau. Margaret Miller sole legatee.
Wits: John Barns, Mary Barns.

Page 536. Michael Stoneback, Richland Twp., Potter. Oct. 12, 1803.
Proved Dec. 8, 1803. Wife Mary and uncle Christopher Keller, exrs. 4
"living ch." one unborn.
Wits: Henry Keller, John Green.

Page 539. Christian Rhoar, New Britain Twp. Aug. 15, 1803. Proved
Jan. 19, 1804. Wife Barbara and son Jacob exrs. David Ruth Overseer.
5 ch. Jacob, Christian, Barbary and Freaney and Ann and dec'd. dau.
Elizabeth.
Wits: Jane Davis, Jacob Moyer, John Davis.

Page 541. Oliver Hough, Upper Makefield Twp. -- 29, 1803. Proved
Feb. 3, 1804. Wife Phebe and bro.-in-law Cyrus Cadwallader and John
Stapler exrs. "Ch. born and unborn."
Wits: Joseph Knowles, William Taylor.

Page 543. Jacob Ort, Richland Twp., yeoman. Jan. 21, 1804. Proved
Feb. 3, 1804. Wife Margaret. Sons George and John exrs. 3 daus.,
Mary, Elizabeth and ---. Land adj. John Keiper.
Wirs: Henry Beringer, George Sterner.

Page 546. Sarah Smith, Plumstead Twp. 8-14-1800. Proved Jan. 15, 1804. Robert Smith of Buckingham exr. Dau. Mary Smith, "sons and daus."
Wits: John Kinsey, Thomas Carey Jurn., Abel Kisney.

Page 548. Richard Raile, New Britain Twp., yeoman. 6 mo.-4-1790. Proved Feb. 8, 1804. Wife Mary. Son John exr. Sons Joshua and Nathan.
Wits: Robert Kirkbride, David Worthington, Thomas Brain. Land in Cheltenham in possesesion of William Letham.

Page 550. Sarah Price, City of Phila. Dec. 13, 1791. Proved Feb. 9, 1804. Son James Price exr. Daus. Permela Kiser and Rebecca Weaver.
Wits: Henry Huddleston, Isaac Huddleston.

Page 551. George Kinsey, Buckingham. Jan. 16, 1804. Proved Feb. 9, 1804. Friend Edward Blackfan and cousin Joseph Smith Junr. exrs. Sons John and George. Daus. Ann and Sarah Kinsey. Gdch. George and Eliza, ch. of son John. 2 ch. of son George. Amos Kirk, son of Thomas and Asee Kirk.
Wits: Edmund Smith, Samuel Paxson.

Page 553. George Kern, New Britain Twp., yeoman. Jan. 17, 1804. Filed Feb. 10, 1804. Wife Deborah. Sons John and George and son-in-law James Evans exrs. Son Jacob. Daus. Margaret wife of James Evans, Catharine wife of Philip Brunner, Elizabeth, Deborah, Susanna and Ann Kern.
Wits: John Riale, Isaac Hill, David Evans. No probate recorded.

Pae 555. Sarah Betts, Buckingham Twp. "Advanced in years." Aug. 16, 1800. Proved Feb. 14, 1804. Sons Stephen and Isaac Betts exrs. Sons John, William, Isaac, Stephen and Zachariah. Gdsn. Thomas Betts, son of Thomas. Daus. Ann Sample, Mary --- and Susanna. Dau. Sarah's ch. Dau. Rebecca's ch. Thomas and Sarah and others.
Wits: Jacob Heston, Elizabeth Heston.

Page 557. Elias Dungan, Northampton Twp. Nov. 23, 1802. Proved Feb. 27, 1804. Wife ---, son James Exr. Daus. Ellen Lefferts, Ann Wilkinson, Rachel Dungan and Rebecca Shelmire.
Wits: Cornelius Cornell, John Thompson, Thomas M. Thompson. Land adj. Garret Dungan and Robert Thompson.

Page 559. Thomas Buckman, Newtown, Farmer, "Now upwards of seventy." July 5, 1799. Codicil dated June 19,1802. Proved April 9, 1804. Abraham Chapman (attorney at law), Benjamin Chapman (miller) and Archibald McCorkle (shoemaker) exrs. Codicil adds son Thomas. "But three ch. and they all born out of wedlock of Mary Wisener."

Thomas, Mary and Stacy Buckman. Mary mar. before date of codicil. Wife Elizabeth. Land adj. Patrick Hunter and Archibald McCorkle. Wits: Aaron Philips, Levi Bond, Is. Hicks. Codicil William Kelly.

End of Book 6.

Book 7.

Page 1. Christian Tranger/Trauger?, Nockamixon Twp. April 2, 1804. Proved April 14, 1804. Wife ---, Frederick Krause and Frederick Ruff exrs. Ch. not named. Mother and her husband.
Wits: Henry Miller and John Cauffman.

Page 2. James Carrell Senr., Tinicum Twp., yeoman. June 19, 1799. Proved April 21, 1804. Eldest son Daniel and Joseph Nash exrs. Eldest dau. Rachel Wiker, dau. Ann Carrell, son James Carrell.
Wits: Elizabeth Nash, Abraham Nash, Joseph Brooks.

Page 3. Hugh Ely, Solebury Twp., Cordwainer. 6 mo.-3-1803. Proved May 5, 1804. Wife Elizabeth. Son John exr. Daus. Sarah Smith and Hannah Harrold.
Wits: Aaron Paxson, Letitia Paxson Jur., Ezra Paxson, Father's will dated 9 mo.-4-1766.

Page 4. Anthony Scout, Warminster Twp., "advanced in years." March 8, 1803. Proved May 8, 1804. John McDowell and Jonathan Delaney exrs. and sole legattes.
Wits: John Hunter, Abraham McDowell and Harman Vansant.

Page 5. Ruth Warner, Wrightstown, "Advanced in age." 9 mo.-7-1803. Proved May 10, 1803. Bro. Thomas Warner exr. Bro. Croasdale Warner. Sisters Mary Wildman, Sarah Wiggins. Amos Warner, John Warner and Mary Warner, ch. of Croasdale Warner. Niece Ruth Warner, dau. of Isaac Warner, her sisters Mary and Martha. Nieces Rachel, Agnes and Sarah Wiggins, ch. of sister Sarah. Niece Rachel Weaver and her son Jonathan Weaver. Niece Hannah Ely, dau. of Croasdale Warner. Sarah Morton. Elizabeth Flood. Joseph Miller and his son Mahlon Miller.
Wits: Mahlon Worthington, Jona Smith, John Terry.

Page 6. Joseph Shelly, Milford Twp., yeoman. April 10, 1804. Proved May 21, 1804. Wife Mary. Sons Michael and Joseph exrs. Ch. David, Michael, Joseph, Elizabeth, Jacob and Isaac. Land adj. Henry Ackerman, Henry Ott. Do. bought of William Roberts and Valentine Beidelman.
Wits: Joseph Shelly, Francis Shelly.

Page 8. Derick Kroesen, Northampton Twp., Shoemaker. May 6, 1804. Proved May 28, 1804. Thomas Dungan and Bro.-in--law James Cantley exrs. Sister Hester Cantley.
Wits: Jesse Dungan, Sarah Dugnan.

Page 9. Robert Lotcher, Upper Makefield Twp. April 28, 1804. Proved June 8, 1804. Robert Knowles Miller, Miller, exr. and sole legatee. [sic]
Wits: Joseph Thornton, Jesse Doan.

Page 9. Hannah Stackhouse, Falls Twp., "Old." May 15, 1803. Proved June 12, 1804. Nephew Mahlon Gregg and Moses Comfort exrs. Sons Moses and Job Stackhouse. Daus. Deborah Sirrell, Mary Merrick wife of Joseph and Hannah ---. Gddau. Mary wife of Charles Clark. Gddau. Deborah Johnson and her dau. Hannah. Nephew David Watson and his daus. Mary and Alice, his dec'd. bro. Jacob and Jacob's daus. Deborah and Martha. Niece Hannah Gregg. Nephew Dr. Mahlon Gregg. Deborah Barton, dau. of Anthony.
Wits: William Cox, William Blakey Jr.

Page 10. Euclides Longshore, Middletown Twp. April 28, 1804. Proved June 22, 1804. Wife Sarah. Simon Gillam and James Wildman exrs. 12 ch. Abner, Anna Vanhorn, Alce Cremer, Abi Scout, Euclides, Margaret, Abraham, Joseph, Grace, Rachel, Thomas and James Longshore.
Wits: John Blakey, William Gillam.

Page 12. Joseph Foster, Bensalem Twp., yeoman. Nov. 11, 1795. Proved March 14, 1804. Wife Rebecca and son John exrs. Ch. John Foster, Jane Spencer, Christine Dyer, Rebecca Strickler, Ann Edwards.
Wits: Neal Vansant, Stephen Cobley, Joseph Banes.

Page 12. Elizabeth Lymbacker, Northampton Twp., widow of Henry Lymbacker. Sept. 26, 1796. Proved Aug. 6, 1804. Gerardus Wynkoop and Leffert Lefferts exrs. Low Dutch Ref. Ch. of Southampton and Northampton.
Wits: Henry Wynkoop, David Taggart.

Page 13. Casper Grose, Richland Twp., yeoman. May 23, 1804. Proved Aug. 7, 1804. Wife Anna Mary. Sons-in-law Adam Bartholomew and Rudolph Shock exrs. Dau. Susanna Toman and her ch. Son-in-law George Sterner. Land bought of Joseph Burr and Elizabeth his wife, and of exrs. of George Weiker.
Wits: Eliza Chapman, Abigail Chapman, James Chapman.

Page 15. John Kelly, Bensalem Twp. Dec. 5, 1800. Proved Aug. 20, 1804. Wife Grace, Jesse James and Ezra Townsend exrs. Daus. Elizabeth, Grace and Rachel.
Wits: Samuel James, Thomas James.

Page 15. Benjamin Snodgrass, Warwick Twp., yeoman. "Advanced in Year." Dated July 13, 1803. Proved Aug. 22, 1804. Wife Mary and son James exrs. Gdch. Benjamin Snodgrass, son of James, Benjamin Snodgrass Mann, James Snodgrass Mann, Mary Mann, Martha Mann and Eliza Mann, ch. of dec'd. dau. Mary and John Mann. Land adj. John Mann and Christian Clemens.
Wits: James Watson, Josiah Y. Shaw.

Page 17. Seneca Fell, Buckingham Twp. 7 mo.-31-1804. Proved Sept. 1, 1804. Wife Grace and son Ely Fell exrs. Sons Stacy, Seneca and Jesse Fell. Daus. Sarah, Martha, Rachel and Grace Fell.
Wits: Meshack Michener Jr., George Fell.

Page 18. Charles Reeder, Upper Makefield Twp., yeoman. June 16, 1800. Proved Sept 8, 1804. Dr. Isaac Chapman exr. Sons Joseph, Merrick, Abraham, David, Jesse, Benjamin, John. Dau. Eleanor Reeder. Gdsn. Richard Hovenden.
Wits: Joseph Tomlinson Jr., John Rose.

Page 20. Abraham Ball, Richland Twp., yeoman. May 8, 1796. Proved Sept. 19, 1804. Son Thomas and son-in-law Jesse Hicks exrs. Ch. Mary Hicks, Rebecca Shaw, Thomas Ball, Nathan Ball, Hannah Shaw and Abraham Ball. Gddau. Anne Hicks.
Wits: Nathan Ball, Christian Smith.

Page 20. Abraham Cornell, Northampton Twp. Aug. 7, 1804. Proved Sept. 28, 1804. Wife Agnes. Bro.-in-law William Bennett and John McNair Esq. exrs. Sons Gilliam and Abraham Cornell. Daus. Margaret, Cornelia and Maria Cornell. Land adj. John Cornell.
Wits: Thomas Folwell, Joseph Dungan, Joshua Jones.

Page 22. William Walker, Warrington Twp. Sept. 19, 1804. Proved Sept. 29, 1804. Wife Rebecca. Sons Robert and Richard exrs. Daus. Margaret wife of Michael Kain, Mary Ann wife of Henry Irwin, Sarah wife of John Holland, Rebecca, Rachel and Jane Walker.
Wits: John Sorver, Benjamin Hough.

Page 23. Thomas Jones, Senr., Hilltown Twp., yeoman. May 13, 1804. Proved Oct. 2, 1804. Sons Thomas, James, Benjamin and Amos and Nephew Thomas Mathias, Merchant, exrs. Daus. Mary wife of David Thomas, Elizabeth wife of Abel Mathew, and Jane Jones. Gdsn. Jesse Jones. Re. James McLaughlin. Land bought of Cadwallader Evans and Thomas Jones of New Britain; adj. George Siple, John Shaw Esq., Isaac Morris, Isaac Williams and John Mathias dec'd. Andrew Bryson. Nephew Thomas Leedom (removed West).
Wits: Benjamin Williams, Abraham Godshalk, John McKinney.

Page 29. Jacob Twining, Wrightstown Twp., "advanced in years."
Sept. 11, 1804. Proved Oct. 15, 1804. Wife Sarah. Thomas Story and
Isaac Chapman exrs. Sons John, Jacob, David and Henry. Daus.
Elizabeth, Sarah, Susanna and Rachel.
Wits: Benjamin Chapman, Elias Twining. Land adj. Henry Cooper, Joel
Carver.

Page 30. Anna Suber, widow of Jacob Suber, yeoman of Middletown
Twp., dec'd. 8 mo.-12-1799. Codicil Jan. 4, 1802. Proved Oct. 19, 1804.
Gdsn. William Paxson and Friend William Buckman exrs. Son Amos
Suber. Dau. Mary Paxson. Gdch. Annah Tomlinson, Samuel and Amos
Paxson. Cousin Jacob Larrew.
Wits: Isaac Watson, Gabnill Mitchell, Benjamin Buckman, Jacob
Vanarsdale, John McCoy.

Page 32. Jane Price, Solebury Twp., "advanced in age." Sept. 10,
1803. Proved Oct. 22, 1804. Aaron Paxson exr. Bro. John Price. Sisters
Eleanor and Ann Price. Nephew Joseph Townsend. Niece Ann Ellicott
wife of Thomas Ellicott. Niece Jane wife of Leonard Wright. Abraham
Price, son of Joseph Price dec'd. His mother Annie Price.
Wits: Joseph Eastburn, Samuel Mathews, Merrick Reeder Jr.

Page 33. Derrick Kroesen, Northampton Twp., yeoman. Feb. 18, 1789.
Proved Nov. 2, 1804. Sons Jacob and Derrick exrs. Sons Jacob,
Derrick, John, Isaac and Nicholas. Daus. Elizabeth Corson and
Margaret Black. Farm bought of Solomon Dungan.
Wits: Gawn Edams, Hugh Edams, Samuel Henderson, Carswell
Gardener.

Page 34. Michael Myers, Richland Twp., yeoman. June 4, 1804. Proved
Nov. 3, 1804. Wife Margaret. Son Samuel exr. Sons Samuel, George,
Michael. Daus. Sarah wife of John Roberts, Catharina wife of Enoch
Edwards and Hannah.
Wits: Eliza and James Chapman.

Page 36. Isabel Phillips, Lower Makefield Twp. Oct. 20, 1804. Proved
Nov. 8, 1804. Daniel Richardson exr. Brothers Edward and Benjamin
Margerum. Nephews Samuel and Richard, sons of Benjamin Margerum.
Jane Richardson. Letitia Mitchell. Marty Margerum, dau. of Benjamin.
Hannah Wetherill. Margaret Plummer.
Wits: Mahlon Kirkbride, John Kirkbride.

Page 37. Benjamin Scott, Buckingham Twp. 8 mo.-12-1802. Proved
Nov. 26, 1804 John Gillingham Jr. and Joseph Stradling exrs. Sons
Moses and Job. Daus. Ann Wood, Jane McAdams, Elizabeth Hughes
and Mary Scott.
Wits: John Skelton, Daniel Stradling.

Page 38. Robert Thompson, Solebury Twp., Miller. "Far advanced in age.." Oct. 26, 1804. Proved Nov. 29, 1804. Gdsn. Robert T. Neeley exr. Dau. Elizabeth wife of William Neely. Step-gdsn. John Cauthron. Step-gt. gdsn Robert Simpson, son of John Simpson Jr. Gddau. Jane wife of John Poor. Dec'd. Bro. Hugh Thompson's son Robert.
Wits: John Wilson, Samuel Caffey.

Page 39. Henry McKinstry, Buckingham Twp. Nov. 25, 1804. Proved Dec. 3, 1804. Wife Anne and Bro.-in-law Giles Craven exrs. Ch. Hellena Spencer, Mary Snodgrass, Christiana, Thomas and Anna McKinstry Jr.
Wits: Robert McKinstry, Henry Breece.

Page 40. Mary Roberts, Bristol Twp. April 3, 1793. Proved Dec, 18, 1804. Bro. James Roberts exrs. Bros. Edward, William and John Roberts.
Wits: William Coxe, Andrew Allen.

Page 41. George Jacobs, Warrington Twp., Labourer. Dec. 12, 1804. Proved Dec. 19, 1804. Joshua Paul exr. and sole legatee.
Wits: Thomas Craig, Samuel Polk.

Page 42. Peter Reppard, New Britain Twp., yeoman. Jan. 7, 1803. Proved Dec. 22, 1804. Wife Margaret. Sons-in-law Conrad Shamel and Jacob Swartz exrs. Sons Peter, Frederick, Jacob. Daus. Molly wife of Conrad Shamel, Margaret wife of Jacob Swartz, Christiana wife of Jacob Frees, Catharine wife of Henry Solliday, and Mary Reppard.
Wits: Jacob Yother, George Kern, Jacob Kern, Robert Shewell.

Page 43. Robert Comfort, Upper Makefield Twp. Dec. 6, 1804. Proved Dec. 27, 1804. Wife Ellenor and Abraham Buckman and Benjamin Carrel exrs. Daus. Mary Church, Sarah Dungan, Phebe Harden, Ellenor Buckman, Rachel Harden, Hannah Comfort and Marcey Carrel.
Wits: John Keith, John Tomlinson, John Atkison.

Page 44. John Story, Newtown Twp., "Far advanced in years." 3 mo.-3-1801. Proved Jan. 19, 1805. Sons Thomas and David Story exrs. Sons John, Thomas, David and Samuel Story. Dau. Mary wife of Edmund Smith, and her ch. Amos, Phineas, Thomas, James and David Briggs, Elizabeth Ashton (formerly Briggs), Ann, Mary and Rachel Briggs. Land adj. John Thompson, Hampton Wilson, James Briggs, Jacob Twining, Francis Murray, Aaron Phillips, Joseph Worstall, Abraham Chapman, John Torbert, Bro. David Buckman, Jacob Buckman.
Wits: Hamton Wilson, Ann Wilson, Phineas Jenks.

Page 47. Abraham Harvye, Upper Makefield Twp. Dec. 3, 1803. Proved Jan. 26, 1805. Wife Jean and Bro.-in-law John Brown exrs. Six ch., unnamed.

104

Wits: Cornelius Slack and William Gregg.

Page 47. Ursula Werner, Durham Twp., widow of Michael Werner, late of Springfield. Dec. 20, 1803. Proved Sept. 14, 1804. Son-in-law Peter Seigler exr. Ch. of Dau. Catharina Seigler.
Wits: Michael Fackenthall, Peter Long.

Page 48. John Pursley, Nockamixon Twp., yeoman. Dec. 24, 1793. Proved Feb. 5, 1805. Wife ---. Signed by Ann Pursley together with testator, both by mark. Sons John and Thomas exrs. Sons John, Thomas, Brice and Dennis. Daus. Ruth, Elizabeth, Ann, Margaret and Jane.
Wits: Benjamin Williams, James Templeton.

Page 50. Isaac Walton, Warminster Twp. 4 mo.-24-1802. Proved Feb. 11, 1805. Wife Susanna and son Jonathan exrs. Daus. Mary and Agnes.
Wits: Joseph Longstreth Jr., Daniel Michener, Benjamin Michener.

Page 51. David Dungan, Northampton Twp., yeoman. May 24, 1804. Proved Feb. 25, 1805. Wife Mary. Son Garret and Friend Joshua Dungan Sr. exrs. Daus. Elizabeth Fisher and Mary Bennett. Gddaus. Rachel Richardson, Mary Dungan and Rachel Osmond. Male heirs of dec'd. son David Dungan. Land adj. Robert Thompson and Jacob Kroesen.
Wits: George Cummings, Thomas Dungan.

Page 53. John Fretz, Warwick Twp., yeoman. Sept. 3, 1803. Proved Jan. 10, 1805. Wife Anna. Bro. Joseph Fretz of Haycock and son Christian Fretz exrs. Son John. Daus. Rachel, Barbara, Elizabeth and Mary. Ch. unborn. Land bought of Richard and Willet Smith and exrs. of John O'Connor, in possession of Lawrence Emmery and John Johnson.
Wits: Nathaniel Irwin, Isaac Fretz.

Page 57. Peter Gruber, Senr., Springfield Twp., yeoman. Feb. 13, 1802. Proved March 11, 1805, by Register's Court. Wife Margaret. Son Peter exr. Sons Peter and Tobias.
Wits: Valentine Marsteller, Jost Smith, Henry Frankenfield.

Page 59. Joseph Winner, Bristol Twp. Sept. 11, 1801. Proved March 18, 1805. Step-father. Thomas Barton of Bristol Twp. exr. Mother Rebecca Barton.
Wits: Amos Gregg Junr., Amos Gregg.

Page 59. Samson Cary, Newtown Twp., yeoman. July 31, 1799. Codicil dated June 22, 1801. Proved March 11, 1805. Wife Margaret. Sons Samuel, Joseph, Silus and Joshua Carey exrs. Dau. Sarah wife of

Solomon Wildman. William Buckman, Thomas Story and Moses Smith, to make Partition of Real Estate.
Wits: A. Chapman, Eliza Chapman.

Page 61. Thomas Wilson, Southampton Twp., yeoman. "Growing old and infirm." 6 mo.-4-1799. Proved March 20, 1805. Sons Joseph and Jesse exrs. Son Amos and his two ch. Thomas and Rachel. Sons John, Joseph and Jesse, the latter a cripple. Daus. Elizabeth and Rachel.
Wits: Jeremiah Croasdale and Nathan Baker.

Page 63. Helena Dubois, Northampton Twp. March 6, 1804. Proved March 25, 1805. Son Henry Dubois and son-in-law Leffert Lefferts exrs. Dec'd. husband Jonathan Dubois. Sons Henry, Nicholas, Abram (dec'd.). Daus. Sarah Dubois, Ann Lefferts, Helena Taggart and Susanna Dubois. Simon Vanarsdale, David Knight, David Wynkoop, John Courson, Rem Cornell, Jonathan Wynkoop, Aaron Feaster, John Wynkoop and John Lefferts to make Partition of Estate.
Wits: Christopher Vanartsdalen [sic]. Henry Wynkoop.

Page 64. John Thompson, Tinicum Twp., yeoman, "Old and weak." Dec. 9, 1803. Proved April 15, 1805. Wife Agness and William Long of Durham exrs. John Thompson Carothers. Elizabeth wife of Robert Galloway of Northampton Co., Pa. James Little of Phila. and his dau. Agnes Little. Mariah Ledlie. Trustees of Tinicum Pres. Church.
Wits: Jacob Weaver, Michael Ott.

Page 65. Edward Bayley, Lower Makefield Twp., yeoman. "Now eighty-six years of age." 1 mo.-7-1798. Codicil dated 10 mo.-22, 1803. Proved April 15, 1805. Wife Ann, son Samuel and sons-in-law John Roberts and David Watson exrs. Son Thomas. Daus. Mary Johnson, Martha Johnson, Letitia Roberts, Elizabeth Buckman, Hannah Yardley, Tamar Watson and Mercy Bayley. Son-in-law Abner Buckman. Gdsn. Edward Buckman. Land adj. John Brown, Jesse Palmer.
Wits: William Linton, John Linton, Is. Hicks, Thomas Ross.

Page 67. Ann White, Wrightstown Twp. 3 mo.-5-1802. Proved April 16, 1805. Isaac Chapman exr. Bro. Joseph White. Sister Mary Clark. Nieces Ann Clark and Sarah Feaster.
Wits: John Rose, Ann Chapman.

Page 68. Aaron Wright, Bristol Twp. Aug. 23, 1803. Proved April 27, 1805. Wife Amy and sons Andrew, Aaron and Moses Wright exrs. Daus. Ann Wright, Mary Brodnax, Rachel Walker.
Wits: William Vansant, Amaziah White, Jesse Brelsford.

Page 69. Johan Hubrick Lear, Tinicum Twp., yeoman. Feb. 2, 1797. Proved April 29, 1805. Ralph Stover Esq. and nephew Joseph Lear

exrs. Son Anthony and daus. Eve and Mary. Gdsns. George and Jacob Bysleish, son's of dau. Elisabeth dec'd., and Gddau. Catharine Lear.
Wits: Philip Groover, George Long.

Page 70. John Vandegrift, Bensalem Twp. Sept. 27, 1804. Proved May 3, 1805. Son Jacob exr. Sons John and Bernard. Dau. Jane Johnson. Father Jacob Vandegrift. Bro. Jacob. Land adj. John Bavington.
Wits: David Vandegrift, William Vandegrift.

Page 72. John Stokes, Burlington Co., N.J. certified from Burlington Co., "yeoman." 10 mo.-8-1743. Proved Sept. 11, 1749. Wife Elizabeth and Revel Elton exrs. Son John . Daus. Mary Mullen and Sarah Rogers.
Wits: Thomas Green, Samuel Woolman, John Woolman. Gdch. Elizabeth and William Blackham.

Page 73. John Stokes, Wellingborough, Burlington Co., N.J., yeoman. 3 mo.-7-1786. Codicil dated Aug. 20, 1791. Proved Aug. 30, 1798. Wife Hannah and sons John, David and Jervas Stokes exrs. Wife dec'd. before Probate. Daus. Mary Newton, Hannah and Elizabeth Stokes and Rachel Hackney.
Wits: Thomas Buzby, Samuel Kelle, Daniel Smith. To Codicil Jonah Woolman, Edith Peddle, Mary Stokes. Land purchased of Exrs. of Thomas Green, Vincent Leeds, Revel Elton, adj. Jonathan Borden, bought of Exrs. of John Stockton. Do. in Haycock Twp., Bucks Co., where son John lives. Aaron Wiles.

Page 77. William Williams, Nockamixon Twp. April 17, 1805. Proved May 6, 1805. Wife Barbara extx. Mother Elizabeth Williams. Sisters Ester, Rachel and Christina. "Daus. of my mother."
Wits: Michael Heaney, Simon Heaney, Henry O'Daniel.

Page 78. Henry Ott, Bedminster Twp. March 9, 1805. Proved May 6, 1805. Wife Barbara. Sons John and Henry Ott exrs. Ch. John, Henry, Christian, Peter, Daniel , Elizabeth, Magdalena, and Barbara.
Wits: Johannes Fluck, Henry Miller.

Page 80. Ann Roberts, Richland Twp. 10 mo.-31-1804. Proved May 13, 1805. Shipley Lester of Richland exr. Sons Edward, Everard and John Roberts. Daus. Rebecka wife of Aquila Foulke, Rachel wife of John Carr Jr., Susanna and Ann Roberts. Gdsns. Everard Foulke, Daniel Roberts. Gddaus. Ann and Jemima Foulke, Ann Roberts, dau. of John Roberts.
Wits: Israel Foulke, Thomas Foulke.

Page 82. Thomas Merrick, Bucks Co. May 2, 1805. Proved May 25, 1805. Isaac Chapman exr. Sisters Mary Cooper, Mercy Sturky, and

Martha Martindell. Nephew Thomas Starky.
Wits: Thomas Chapman, Hannah Merrick.

Page 83. Joshua Ely, Senr. of the Twp. of Solebury, yeoman. 7 mo.-25-1802. Proved May 27, 1805. Sons Joshua and Jonathan exrs. Son Abner. Land purchased of Oliver Hamton, 50 acres. Son Jonathan Plantation confirmed by Deed from Father. Daus. Elizabeth Tucker and Hannah Hampton.
Wits: Joshua Vansant, Cephas Ross, Seneca Ely.

Page 85. Sarah Hall, Bristol Boro. 7-12-1802. Proved May 29, 1802. Nephews Alexander Hall and Joseph Hall exrs. Letters C.T.A. granted to Thomas Hall of Burlington, N.J. Exrs. named being dec'd. 4 nephews John, Alexander, Joseph and Thomas Hall. Niece Sarah Biles. Nieces Hannah and Nancy Biles.
Wits: Sims Betts, William Allen.

Page 86. Jacob Parry, Warminster Twp. 11-10-1802. Proved June 22, 1805. Wife Sarah and sons Isaac and Thomas Parry exrs. Letters to Isaac and Thomas only.
Wits: David Jarrett, Rebecca Jarrett.

Page 87. Samuel Cary, Buckingham Twp, yeoman. 9-21-1801. Proved July 6, 1805. Wife Margaret. Son-in-law Joseph Thornton, Friend Samuel Gillingham, of Buckingham, and Nephew William Blakey of Middleton exrs. Dau. Mary wife of Joseph Thornton. Bros. Asa and Phineas Cary. Phineas son Asa and dau. Elizabeth.
Wits: Samuel Johnson, Thomas Hutchinson, Ann C. Hutchinson.

Page 89. Henry Harvye, Lower Makefield Twp. Oct. 3, 1803. Proved July 27, 1805. Son Henry and Friend Joshua Vansant exrs. Son Henry Harvye, 152 1/2 acres off South end of Plantation, adj. Delaware River and John Duer's land, being Lots No. 1 and No. 2, laid down by Robert Smith 6 mo.-16-1790. He to provide home &c. for my dau. Sarah Whitacre during life or widowhood. Sons Jonathan and George, balance of Real Estate being Lot. No. 3. Daus. Elizabeth Wolston, Susannah Brown, Mary Warner, Anna Smith and Jane Vansant each One Dollar. Son Henry "Island oposite my land."
Wits: William Duer, Jain Harvye.

Page 91. Jonathan Willett, Middletown. 10-8-1804. Proved July 25, 1805. Wife Deborah. Son-in-law Samuel Mitchell exr. Residue to 8 ch., Obadiah, John and Samuel Willett, Ann Mitchell, Elizabeth Kirkbride, Sarah Mitchell, Mary Paxson and Helena Carter. "If son Jonathan, who is now absent should return" to have an equal share. Son Walter Willett "Has had a large portion of my estate" no demand to be made for it. All negroes, "in whom I have any lawful right to be free at my

decease." Dinah, the mother of 5 Blacks to be maintained.
Wits: Pierson Mitchell, John Mitchell.

Page 93. Sarah DuBois (no residence given). July 22, 1805. Proved Sept. 2, 1805. Bro.-in-law Leffert Lefferts and Bro. Henry DuBois exrs. Sisters Helena Taggart, Ann Lefferts and Susannah DuBois. Bros. Henry and Nicholas and representatives of Bro. Abram DuBois dec'd. Nieces Sarah Ann, and Catharine DuBois, goods devised by will of Mother Helena DuBois.
Wits: David Wynkoop, Henry Wynkoop.

Page 94. Barnard Carrell, Warminster Twp. June 30, 1787. Proved Sept. 2, 1805. Wife Lucretia. Sons Isaac and Cornelius Carrell exrs. Son James. Daus. Rachel and Hannah, minors.
Wits: Elijah Stinson, Nathaniel Erwin.

Page 95. Thomas Cooper, Solesbury, "being advanced in years." 6 mo.-23-1803. Proved Sept. 2, 1805. Son Thomas Cooper exr. Dau. Mary wife of Benjamin Cooper. Gdch. Phebe Hagerman, Thomas, Evan, Mary and John Groom, ch. of dau. Phebe Groom dec'd. Joseph, Samuel, Thomas and William Cooper, sons of son Thomas Cooper.
Wits: Robert Smith, David Smith, John Smith.

Page 97. Sims Betts, Bristol Boro. Nov. 25, 1803. Proved Sept. 17, 1805. Wife Rachel. Isaac Morris and Jonathan Pursell exrs. Amos Gregg, guardian. Charles and Bethany Bessonett and their sons James and Charles Bessonett. All estates to wife for life, then to James Bessonett, if he die to his bro. Charles.
Wits: Benjamin Swain, Isaac Wilson.

Page 99. Peter Brodder, New Britain Twp. Nov. 25, 1801. Proved Sept. 18, 1805. Wife Rachel. Son Jacob Bodder exr. Wife all estate for life; then Plantation to be sold, proceeds to sons Jacob and John and Daus., Sophia wife of Abraham Sellers (for life) and Catharine wife of Samuel Sellers.
Wits: William Snare, Enoch Fowler and John Pugh.

Page 101. Jacob Letherman, Bedminster Twp., yeoman. March 22, 1805. Proved Sept. 26, 1805. Wife Ester. Sons Jacob and Christian exrs. Daus. Elizabeth, Mary and Anne.
Wits: Ralph Stover, Henry Letherman.

Page 103. David Roberts, Richland Twp., yeoman. 6-22-1805. Proved Sept. 27, 1805. Codicil dated 7-27-1805. Son David and Son-in-law Israel Foulke exrs. Son Nathan Plantation he lives on adj. Evan Foulke, John Griffith, and John Roberts, also Lot bought of John Lancaster, adj. Abel Roberts, William Shaw, 100 acres. Son David balance of Plantation. Son Evan. Daus. Elizabeth, wife [of] Israel Foulke; Jane wife of Samuel Ashton, and

Abigail wife of Benjamin Johnson.
Wits: Hugh Foulke, Cadwd. Foulke.

Page 106. Jeremiah Routenbush, Rockhill Twp., yeoman. April 13, 1797. Proved March 25, 1805. Wife Margaret. Son George Routenbush and son-in-law Henry Leidy exrs. Son Peter two pieces of Planation I live on, 43 acres, 99 P. and 5 acres adj. Peter Rhoads, David Sorver, Paul Bean and North branch of Perkiomey Creek, and Samuel Bechtel's. Son George balance of Plantation, 130 acres. Dau. Catharine 40£, in lieu of what was heretofore given to other daus. Daus. Barbara, Charlotte, Margaret and Catharine.
Wits: Samuel Gehman, Henry Hartzel, Abraham Stout.

Page 110. Isaac Wireback, Springfield Twp. Feb. 20, 1805. Proved April 13, 1805. Wife Anna. Sons Jacob and Henry exrs. Son Henry Plantation. Sons Peter, Jacob and Isaac. Daus. Elizabeth wife of Michael Smell and Margaret Herpts. [sic]
Wits: Abraham Ryer, James Chapman.

Page 113. Samuel Yardley, Newtown Twp., yeoman. July 29, 1801. Proved Oct. 14, 1805. Son Samuel T. Yardley exr. Plantation whereon I live 272 acres adj. Benjamin Taylor and others. Son Joseph Yardley 150 acres where on Benjamin Wharton lives adj. David Buckman & others. Also 1 acre in Newtown in Tenure of John Smock on Ground Rent. Gdsn. Samuel Yardley Gold watch.
Wits: Aaron Phillips, Abraham Chapman.

Page 114. George Heinlein, Durham Twp., yeoman. July 5, 1804. Proved Oct. 9, 1805. Wife Sarah, son William and William Long of Durham exrs. Wife 5 Acres of the land purchased of Jacob Bucher, balance of land to be sold, notice to be given in "Easton English and German Newspapers." Proceeds to Dau. Margaret, wife of Nicholas Prutzman, 1/13 part. Dau. Eleaner wife of John Bucher, 1/13 part. Son Lawrence Heinlein 1/13th part. Dau. Sarah wife of Abraham Bucher 1/13th part. Son James 1/13th part. Son George 1/13th part. Dau. Catharine 1/13th. Son William 1/13th part. Son Reading 1/13th part. Dau. Ann 1/13th son John 1/13th part. Wife 2/13th parts to keep son John as long as she lives.
Wits: John Boyar, Margid Stam.

Page 117. Susanna Terry, Upper Makefield Twp. Oct. 24, 1805. Proved Nov. 6, 1805. Bro. Jasper Terry and Friend Isaac Chapman exrs. Nephews and Nieces, viz.: Susannah and Jane, daus. of Bro. Benjamin Terry. Jane dau. Bro. David. Grace and John ch. of Bro. David Terry. David and Elizabeth, ch. of bro. Thomas Terry. Joseph, Ralph and Esther, ch. of bro. Daniel Terry and Rachel dau. of bro. David Terry. Sister-in-law Lucy Terry, her dau. Martha. Bro. David's wife. Bro. Daniel's wife. Bro. Thomas's widow. "Guinea that Grace Townsend gave me." Bro. Jasper

Terry and his son-in-law Ezra Wharton.
Wits: David Reeder, Mary Tomlinson..

Page 119. Nicholas Vanortsdalen, Southampton Twp., yeoman. April 27, 1802. Proved Nov. 6, 1805. Sons Christopher and James exrs. Wife use of Plantation for life. Son James to Rent it. Son Simon and his present wife Rebecca. Son John. Daus. Anna Stevens, Jane Kroesen.
Wits: Henry DuBois, Silas Vansant, Thomas Fenton.

Page 123. Henry Cooper, Northampton Twp. June 10, 1805. Proved Nov. 25, 1805. Wife Martha. Isaac Chapman exrs. Son Phineas and dau. Sarah.
Wits: Thomas Chapman, John Cooper.

Page 125. Samuel Watson, Middletown Twp. 6-1-1805. Proved Dec. 7, 1805. Sons David and Abraham and William Blakey Junr. exrs. Son David Land in Falls Twp., also Grist Mill &c. Dau.-in-law Mary Watson, widow of son Jacob, her eldest son Henry, and daus. Deborah and Martha. Gddau. Beulah Hough and Tacey Stradling. Son Abraham £500.
Wits: William Cox, Charles Watson.

Page 127. Jacob Bidleman, Nockamixon Twp., yeoman. Nov. 12, 1805. Proved Dec. 7, 1805. Wife Elizabeth Margaret. Sons Jacob and John and Bro.-in-law Hanus Yost exrs. Sons Abraham, Jacob and John. Daus. Elizabeth, Catharine, Margaret, Mary and Sarah, and ch. of dau. Rosina, dec'd.
Wits: Ralph Stover, Frederick Wolfinger.

Page 129. John Thomas, Richland Twp., yeoman. 7 mo.-12-1804. Proved Dec. 20, 1805. Kinsman Amos Chilcott and James Chapman exrs. Amos Chilcott and Ann his wife. Land conveyed by Bro. Thomas Thomas dec'd., Dec. 20, 1762. Bro. William Thomas and his four sons, Absalom, Daniel, Thomas, Edward, and the said Daniel's son John Thomas £40. Nephews John and Elijah Lester £25. Eman Pettit $30. Niece Catharena Lester $20. Mary Wagle £5. Niece Mariann Heacock $20. Surviving ch. of nephew Joseph Green £30. Surviving ch. of nephew Thomas Green, dec'd. £15. Amos Chilcott's 3 eldest daus. Martha, Penana and Mary $50. Nephew Isaac Lester £5. Niece Jane Miller, dau. of bro. William Thomas. Niece Ann Heston dau. of said bro. William Thomas £5.
Wits: Evan Green, Thomas Green.

Page 132. Abraham Black, Hilltown Twp., yeoman. Oct. 10, 1805. Proved Jan. 13, 1806. Son John Black of Phila. Co. and son Elias of Bucks Co. exrs. Ch. Mary wife of Jasper Fleat, Bethinie wife of Edward Danely, John, Rebekah Brown widow, Elias and Elizabeth.
Wits: Elias Thomas, Griffith Owen.

Page 134. John Barndt, Rockhill Twp. (written (Bant) signed in German

Barnd). Probated as "Bandt." Aug. 15, 1803. Proved Jan. 15, 1806. Wife Catharine. Sons Ludwig and Peter exrs. Son George £10. Son Peter Plantation on which he lives, partly in Rockhill and partly in Talford Twp., Montgomery Co. 97 acres. Sons John, Henry, Philip, Ludwig, Peter and George. Daus. Margaret, Catharine, Elizabeth, Christina, Susanna and Mary.
Wits: Abraham Cressman, Henry Deets and Abraham Stout.

Page 136. John Sliff, Nockhamixon Twp., "Aged and weak." Sept. 11, 1805. Proved Jan. 24, 1806. Friend George Wyker and son-in-law Solomon Housewert exrs. Sons John, James, Samuel and Joseph all Lands &c. Ch. of son Benjamin dec'd. £150. Daus. Martha, Sarah, Lidia, Mary and Margaret. Youngest dau. Margaret yet single, to receive as much as the others received "as an out set" when they were mar.
Wits: Michael Frankenfield, George Wyker, Jacob Frankenfield.

Page 138: Richard Rue, Bensalem Twp. July 28, 1796. Proved Feb. 7, 1806. Wife Rebecca and nephew James Roberts exrs. Nephews Joshua Rue, son of Bro. Samuel; Israel and James Rue sons of Bro. Joseph; Bro. Mathew, who has been maintained by me for many years to be maintained by nephew James Roberts, son of Timothy Roberts dec'd., to whom I devise all my lands and residue of Estate.
Wits: Samuel Cox, Joseph Thompson, Nicholas Larzelere.

Page 140. Thomas Cooper, "County of Bucks." July 4, 1804. Proved Feb. 11, 1806 by Samuel Allen and Benja. Albertson, as will of "Thomas Cooper of Falls Twp., Esq." Wife Jane extx. all estate for life or widowhood. "Miner children" Sarah, James, Thomas, William and Joseph.

Page 142. Michael Raught, Junr., Springfield Twp., Miller. Jan. 24, 1806. Proved Feb. 19, 1806. Jacob Kooker and John Brock exrs. Father Michael Raught, Bro. John and sister Catharine Raught.
Wits: George Cyphert, Jonas Kirk.

Page 143. James Peller, Solebury Twp. 1-2-1806. Proved Feb. 24, 1806. John Pickering and Edward Blackfan exrs. Plantation adj. land lately sold to Isaac Betts to James P. Moore. William Ely to act as his Guardian. Maria Bewley, dau. of Katharine Bewley £5.
Wits: Benjamin Paxson, John Watson, William Pickering.

Page 144. Michael Crouse, Nockamixon Twp., Farmer. July 23, 1797. Proved Jan. 9, 1806. Wife Barbara. Sons Ludwick and Jacob exrs. Dau. Anna Barbara. Son Conrath's ch. to have their father's share.
Wits: Ann Krouse, Philip Rapp, Ann Krouse's affidavit made before James Smith a Justice of the Peace in Nockamixon.

Page 146. Sarah Stackhouse, Middletown Twp. 5-4-1801. Proved Feb. 21, 1806. Joseph Croasdale exr. All money Bonds and Notes to Ann Stevenson and Rachel, wife of Joseph Croasdale. Sarah Croasdale dau. of Joseph, Bed &c. Ann Bunting wearing apparel.
Wits: Jeremiah Corasdale and Nathan Baker.

Page 148. Archibald McElroy, Bristol Borough, Feb. 14, 1806. Proved March 31, 1806. Wife Sarah, dau. Sarah McElroy and son John McElroy exrs. Wife all Estate for life. Then to be sold and proceeds to five ch. John McElroy, Ann Little late McElroy, Archibald McElroy Junr., Sarah McElroy Jur. and Scuyler McElroy.
Wits: Amos Gregg, Henry Disborough.

Page 149. John Headly, Bristol Twp. 1-6-1806. Proved April 15, 1806. Wife Catharine and William Vansant exrs. Wife use and profits of Plantation he lives on and one where on Joshua Bunting lives till son John comes of age. Part of former tract, (described) to be sold and proceeds to 4 daus. Rebecca, Hannah, Phebe and Sarah Headly; balance to son Solomon Headly. Tract on which Bunting lives to son John, adj. lands of Amaziah White, John Booz and George Walker. Former adj. Thomas Barton and Joshua Headly. John to still his own liquor without molestation from Solomon.
Wits: Daniel Brelsford, Joshua Bunting.

Page 152. James Flowers, Middletown Twp. Feb. 10, 1806. Proved April 16, 1806. Wife Rachel all Personalty for bringing up and schooling two youngest ch. George and Charles McKaine Flowers. James Linton of Middletown exr. All estate to wife and two ch. above named.
Wits: Joseph Houghton, Jonathan Carlile Junr.

Page 153. Robert Dunlap, Newbritain Twp. Feb. 14, 1806. Proved April 19, 1806. Bro. Moses and James Dunlap exrs. Bro. Andrew, Moses and James. Bro. Moses and his wife Agnes to be compensated for care of me in present illness. Bro. James use of £100 until death of Father and Stepmother, they to be supported. Sister Mary Magill, gold watch; nephew Robert Dunlap son of Bro. Andrew, desk after death of Father, Sisters-in-law Phebe, Agnes and Julia Dunlap, "complete set of mourning." Niece Jane Hughes.
Wits: Daniel Stradling, George Burgess.

Page 155. Thomas Smith, Buckingham Twp., yeoman. 11-25-1805. Proved April 21, 1806. Having already provided for six of my children to wit., Edmund, Thomas, Elizabeth, Sarah, Elinor and Martha, in goods or Real Property," each £5. Son David all Estate and Lands, being part of 213 acres in Buckingham and Solebury devised by will of Father, and makes him exr.
Wits: Robert Smith, Edward Blackfan.

Page 157. Casper Johnson, Richland Twp., yeoman. March 18, 1800. Proved April 21, 1806. Wife Mary. Sons Henry and Benjamin exrs. Son Casper 50 acres where his buildings now stand, adj. Everard Roberts and Joseph Himmelwright. Son Joseph 109 acres in Skippack, Montgomery Co. where he lives. Son Benjamin, Balance of Plantation whereon I live (less Casper's). Son Henry £393 also £207 given him when her purchased Plantation whereon he lives. Dau. Christina, wife of Edward Burk. Dau. Elizabeth, widow of Charles Hinkle. Dau. Mary, wife of Philip Hinkle.
Wits: Everard Foulke, John Beidler.

Page 159. Joseph Fretz, Haycock Twp., Fuller. Dec. 17, 1805. Proved April 22, 1806. Wife Mary. Bros. Henry and Martin Fretz exrs. Son John. Daus. Barbara, Anne, Susanna, Agnes, Rachel and Sarah. Lot in Bedminster whereon Barbara Crout lives to be sold, if she will move off therefrom, otherwise Deed to be made to her therefor on payment of the money paid by me. Woodland purchased of Jacob Beidelman. Exrs. to purchase Lot for use of wife and ch.
Wits: Ralph Stover, Isaac Fretz.

Page 162. James Nelson, Falls Twp. 9-15-1805. Proved April 26, 1806. Wife Mary and Anthony Burton exrs. All estate for life to wife, then to daus. Mary and Margareth.
Wits: William Bunting, Joseph Howell.

Page 163. Elizabeth Twining, Newtown Twp., widow. June 12, 1805. Proved April 28, 1806. Dau. Beaulah E. Twining extx. Dau. or daus. of my dau. Sarah Hutchinson. Dau. or daus. of daus. Elizabeth Hopkins. Dau. or daus. of dau. Mary Leedom.
Wits: A. Chapman, William Kroesen.

Page 164. Stephen Hambleton, Solebury Twp. 4-4-1804. Proved May 31, 1806. Wife Hannah. Nephew John Armitage and Friend Aaron Paxson exrs. Sons Aaron, James, John, William, Jonas, and Moses Hambleton. Daus. Jane Webster, Rachel Kester, Margaret Kinsey and Mary Coate. Gddau. Latitia Hambelton. Land adj. Joseph Hambleton, William Hambleton, Robert Eastburn, John Armitage, and the Suggin Road.
Wits: Abraham Paxson, John Watson, Moses Paxson.

Page 167. John Detweiler, Hilltown Twp., Farmer. Jan. 28, 1806. Proved June 2, 1806. Son-in-law David Rosenberger of Hatfield Twp., Montgomery Co. and son Samuel Detweiler of Hilltown Twp exrs. Ch. Samuel, Abraham, Henry, Barbara Rosenberger, Ann Heckler, Susana, Froney and Margred. Plantation of 156 acres in Hilltown to sons Samuel and Abraham. Son Henry £80 when 21 years of age.
Wits: Andrew Levy, John Funk, Jacob Clemens.

Page 168. Mary Richardson, Middletown Twp. Jan. 5, 1803. Proved June

16, 1806. Nephew (by Mar.) Thomas Story and niece Rachel Story, his wife, exrs. Thomas Story and Rachel, his wife, (Dau. of my sister Rebecca Jenks) Lands &c. devised by will of my late Father Joseph Richardson, dated Sept. 20, 1770, now in tenure of Joshua Paxson. Sister Rebecca Jenks £100. Sister Ruth Dixon do. Nieces Mercy Carlile, dau. of Rebecca Jenks, Mary and Ruth Jenks, Jane Richardson, Rebecca Fell Jr., Martha Chapman and Sarah Allen. Ann Stephenson, dau. of Edward Stephenson, dec'd. Cousin Joshua Paxson, son of Uncle William Paxson. Ann Johnson, wife of Armstrong Johnson, and her 3 ch., namely Fender Carter, Pennington and Ann Johnson. Friends' Mtg. at Middletown, School Fund.
Wits: Benja. Buckman, A. Chapman.

Page 171. Leonard Kroesen, Southampton Twp., Weaver. Jan. 5, 1804. Proved June 20, 1806. Son John exr. Dau. Elizabeth wife of Daniel Vanpelt. Ch. of son Francis Kroesen, dec'd.
Wits: John McNair, Abraham Stevens.

Page 173. Garret Vansant, Wrightstown Twp., April 7, 1796. Proved June 30, 1806. Wife Rebekah, son-in-law Joseph Carver and Friend Isaac Chapman, exrs. Friends Isaac Chapman and Hugh Thompson Southwest part of Plantation adj. Cornelius Vansant dec'd., my bro. Joseph Sackett in trust for use of dau. Elizabeth Addis for life then to her 3 duas. Mary Vansant, Rebekah McClellan and Elizabeth Vansant. Dau. Mary Carver, N.E. part of Plantation; for life and then to gdsn. Garret Carver. Land for Burying Ground.
Wits: Joseph Roberts, William Wetherill.

Page 176. Sarah Forst, widow of David Forst, late of Solebury Twp., dec'd. June 21, 1806. Proved July 5, 1806. Samuel Johnson Esq. exr. Philip Forker $50. for services. Wearing apparel to sister Ann Hart and friends Martha Longstreth and Martha Johnson. Residue of Estate to be "put to interest until my youngest child comes of age" and interest applied to bringing up and educating younger ch.; then to be equally divided between ch. (not named).
Wits: John Balderston, M. Hutchinson, Thomas Hutchinson.

Page 177. Anna Switzer, New Britain Twp., widow. June 6, 1806. Proved July 19, 1806. Son Valentine Switzer and son-in-law Jacob Funk exrs. Wearing apparel to dau. Barbara Switzer. Wagon, plow and harrow to son Simon Switzer. Balance of Personalty sold for payment of debts. Dwelling house and land to be on Rent until Simon comes of age then to be sold. Son Conrad Switzer £50. Son Simon £100. Dau. Barbara £50. Residue to sons Valentine, Lewis, Conrad, Henry and Simon Switzer and daus. Anna wife of Jacob Funk, Mary wife of Christian Clemens, Elizabeth wife of Simon Haupt and Barbara Switzer.
Wits: Abraham Hill, Jacob Swartzlander, David Evans.

Page 179. Michael Schneider, Hilltown Twp., Carpenter. June 1, 1806. Proved Aug. 9, 1806. Wife Mary. Sons Jacob and Conrad Shneider [sic] exrs. Son Conrad 136 1/2 acres I live on, his mother to live with him. He paying £13 per acre therefor. Tract of land bought of George Frantz to be sold, and proceeds together with amounts advanced to ch., and what Conrad is to pay for farm divided between ch. Jacob, Michael, Conrad, Christian, Rebecka, Catharine and Hannah.
Wits: Nicholas Frantz, Paul Frantz, John Pugh.

Page 181. James Long (Falls Twp.) Nov. 5, 1802. Proved Aug. 18, 1806. Wife Lavinah. Nephew James Johnson exr. Wife all land (5 Acres) for life; if son James return then to him, if not, to dau. Hannah Bray.
Wits: Mary Wismer, John Lotcher.

Page 182. Richard Worthington, Buckingham Twp., "An Aged man." March 21, 1803. Proved Aug. 26, 1806. Sons Mahlon and Joseph exrs. Devises them Plantation he lives on bought of John Wilson. Son Thomas £200. Son John 28 acres, part of Tract he lives on bought of Thomas Lacey, on South side of Carver's Millrace. Son Isaac, part of same tract, adj. land I live on, Andrew Collons , William Kirk and Joseph Lacey. Remainder of said tract to be sold. Proceeds to Gdsns. Richard son of son John, Richard Plumby son of dau. Elizabeth and William Wetherell. Gddaus. Jane and Ann Worthington, ch. of dec'd. son William. Thomas Atkinson of Wrightstown and Benjamin Smith of Buckingham Guradians of said minors. Dau. Sarah Wetherell £100 and goods brought home at dec. of her late husband. Dau. Mary Wood £100. Dau. Elizabeth Plumly £100. Dau. Tamar Lacey £100. Dau. Hannah Flood £100. Dau. Letitia Collons £100. Residue to ch. Mahlon, Joseph, John, Isaac, Mary, Sarah, Elizabeth, Tamar, Hannah and Latitia.
Wits: Joseph Lacey, Isaac Lacey, John Terry.

Page 185. John Bidleman, Nockamixon Twp. Feb. 25, 1806. Proved Sept. 1, 1806. Codicil July 29, 1806. Wife Sarah to live with three ch. Conrad Harpel of Bedminster Twp and John Kicklin of Rockhill Twp. exrs.
Wits: Jacob Buck, Henry Miller.

Page 187. Thomas Mathias, Hilltown Twp. June 11, 1806. Proved Sept. 1, 1806. Wife Giner Lot of land whereon Michael Buzzard lives, purchased of Thomas Lunn and Elizabeth his wife in 1798, for life then to son Ashbel also 100 acres purchased of Daniel Griffith and Ann his wife in 1796 and 5 acres in Bedminster Twp. conveyed by William Hill and Hannah his wife May 24, 1806, Dwelling House already arranged for with Jonathan Jones, carpenter, to be built for use of Ashbel, when 21. Son Abel, Plantation I live on, when 21 (105 acres). Abel and Ashbel jointly land in Newbritain, on which Christian Slaughter lives subject to Dower of widow Elizabeth Jones. Bros. Abel and Joseph Mathias. Bro. Joseph Mathias exr.

116

Wits: Mickel Buzzard, Griffith Jones, John Pugh.

Page 192. Jane Smith, Upper Makefield Twp. 7-12-1801. Proved Sept. 3, 1806. Nephew Timothy Smith exr. Sarah Ely dau. of Bro. Robert Smith and wife of George Ely, £25 and a bed, her sister Rebekah Smith Do. Mary Atkinson, dau. of Sarah Atkinson do. Her sister Sarah Atkinson Junr. do. Sarah Beans dau. of sister Mary Beans and her sisters Rachel and Elizabeth Beans each £25. Cousin Alice Kinsey, dau. of Uncle Benjamin Kinsey dec'd.
Wits: Benj. Smith, Robert Smith Junr.

Page 193. Paul Hartzel, Rockhill Twp., yeoman. July 19, 1806. Proved Sept. 15, 1806. Wife Catharine 25£, Household Goods and use of Plantation until son Henry comes of age, he to work for her, be obedient &c. then to said Henry, said land being partly in Rockhill Twp. and partly in Upper Salford, Montgomery Co. adj. Samuel Detweiler, Henry Bernard, Frederick Barnard, Theobold Nase, George Nase and Philip Hartzel, 200 acres, and 12 acres purchased of George Ashton. Son-in-law Andrew Reed, Tan Yard and 18 acres. Gdch. Samuel and Sarah Berndt. Daus. Catharine, Magdalena and Susanna. Bro. Henry Hartzel and Friend John Bernard the Blacksmith exrs.
Wits: David Sorver, John Truckenmiller, and ---.

Page 196. John Crawford, Warwick Twp. "Esq." "being advanced in years" July 1, 1806. Proved Sept. 18, 1806. Wife Jane. James Barclay Esq. (late the husband of dau. Jane dec'd.), Nathaniel Irwin, David Dowlin and Samuel Mann exrs. Wife to have use of Rooms during life and widowhood, "shall not go to reside with nor permit to reside with her Henry Wilson, his wife, or any of their ch." Ch. of dau. Margaret wife of Paul Dowlin and Elizabeth Dowlin dec'd. late wife of David Dowlin, both of Twp. of Horsham. Son William Crawford of Fayette County and his surviving ch. either by first or second wife; his son William Crawford Junr. Gdsn. John Crawford, Carpenter, son of son William and Hannah his wife, dec'd. Having purchased in partnership with son William 390 acres in Fayette Co. of John Wrigton, and 300 acres in "the then County of Westmoreland" of Andrew Douglas &c. Son John Crawford of Warwick 1/2 interest in last tract. Dau. Mary Crawford, widow of Samuel Crawford, dec'd., late of Kentucky, her ch. Moses, John, Mary, Samuel, William and Isabell. Dau. Margaret Dowlin 200 acres Donation Lands in Westmoreland Co., her ch. John and Josiah Dowlin. Paul, Mary, Jane, Hannah, Eliza and Esther Dowlin, ch. of late dau. Elizabeth Dowlin, like quantity of said donation lands. Nathaniel Irwin and David Dowlin, husband of dau. Elizabeth dec'd., Guardians of said ch. of Elizabeth. Samuel Mann of Horsham and Nathaniel Irwin guardian of Margaret's ch. Son John and gdsn. John Crawford, Carpenter, Guardian of William and other ch. of son William of Fayette Co. Son John has rec'd. "his child's share and released for it."

Wits: Archibald McCorkle and Pricilla McKinstry.
*Added note: James Barclay is incorrect, should be <u>John</u> husband of Jane, dec'd. Mrs. Warren S. Ely.

Page 202. John Shick, Nockamixon Twp., Farmer. Dec. 21, 1798. Proved Sept. 20, 1806. Son Jacob Shick and Philip Rapp exrs. Jacob to have the place as long as my wife liveth, "to give her yearly 8 bushels of Rye, 2 of wheat, 50 lbs. of bork [sic] and 50 lbs. of Beef and fire woot." &c. as long as she live. Then place to be sold and proceeds to four ch. viz. "Mary and Markeretha and Jacob and Elizabeth." Dau. Elizabeth shall not have her share while her husband liveth.
Wits: Fredeick [sic] Stone, Jacob Wolfinger.

Page 203. Bridget Smith of Plumstead. 4-30-1805. Proved Sept. 23, 1806. John Townsend and Jonathan Fell exrs. Bro. Thomas Dillon. Sisters Esther Doan and Elizabeth Townsend. Nieces Mary Doan and Rachel Vickers, dau. of my sister Rebekah Vickers each £20. £10 each to the following persons "vizt; Elizabeth Doan (dau. of sister Esther Doan), Moses Dillon, Rachel Baker (dau. of Moses Dillon), John Townsend, Mary Fell, Esther Michener dau. of sister Rebekah Vickers, Mary Mendenhall, Mercy Heaton, Amos White, Sarah Vickers (dau. of Abraham Vickers), Robert Smith (son of John Smith) and Martha Hilbern and Margery White. "Elizabeth Fell dau. of Jonathan Fell pewterpot." John Townsend "large bible." Elizabeth Templeton pewter dish and plates. Martha Hillbern dau. of Bro. Thomas Dillon, Margery White dua. of Amos White, wearing apparel.
Wits: Daniel Carlile, William Robinson.

Page 205. Henry Richey, Senr., Nockamixon Twp., yeoman. (Signed in German) March 2, 1804. Proved Sept. 26, 1806. Wife Ann, son Henry and son-in-law John Racener exrs. Ch. Jacob, Isaac, Henry, Moses, Margaret, Ann Mary, Elizabeth and Hannah. Jeremiah Clirk mar. to dau. Margaret.
Wits: Jacob Tumstone (Sumstone?), William Long.

Page 207. Samuel Polk, Warrington Twp., yeoman. Sept. 24, 1806. Proved Oct. 6, 1806. Bro. James Polk of Warwick Twp. and John Carr exrs. Wife Margaret and four sons, James, Robert, John and Samuel, to live together and cultivate estate as long as they think expedient, for benefit of all the ch. Sons $200 a piece, "as I suppose equal to advance made to dau. Rebecca James." Bro.-in-law John Carr, Guardian of son John, and Bro. James Polk Guardian of son Samuel. Exrs. to sell Messuage and 136 Acres adj. Jonathan Jones, Joshua Paul and others in Warrington.
Wits: Hannah Paul Junr., William Long.

Page 209. Thomas Fell, Buckingham Twp. 4-3-1806. Proved Oct. 21, 1806. Wife Jane. Two ch. Samuel and Sarah Fell exrs. 4 ch. Jesse, Samuel, Sarah and Amos. Gddaus,. Jane and Deborah Fell, and ch. of Aby

118

Meredith. "Statement made by Joseph Fell that his bro. Jesse was indebted to him." if it prove so said amount to be deducted from Jesse's shair [sic].
Wits: Jonathan Fell Senr., Hugh Fell.

Page 211. Sarah Twining, Warwick Twp. 4-2-1805. Prove Oct. 25, 1806. Friends Mahlon Trego and Silas Twining exrs. Son Joseph Twining. Daus. Elizabeth Briggs, Mary Tomlinson and Rachel Balderston.
Wits: Ephraim Addis, Jacob Twining, John Fenton.

Page 212. Eleazer Fenton, Buckingham Twp., yeoman. April 18, 1806. Proved Nov. 11, 1806. Wife Margaret. Uncle David Evans and cousin Ephraim Fenton of Montgomery Co., Pa. exrs. Wife use of House and Plantation and 1/2 of Rent of Tavern house occupied by James Dunlap, until son Ephraim arrives of age. Son Ephraim Plantation and Tavern House. He and dau. Mary Fenton 100 Acres in Buckingham adj. Street Road and lands of John Jones, Randle Fenton and Robert Michener.
Wits: George Burgess, Daniel Stradling, Robert Michener.

Page 214. Zachariah Tethro, New Britain Twp., "well stricken in years." Oct. 1, 1806. Proved Nov. 17, 1806. Wife Catharine and John Sheipe of New Britain exrs. Deed made April 25, 1800 to son-in-law Jacob Bodder for Plantation on which I live, in consideration of his providing for wife Catharine for life. Agreement with said Bodder Sept. 9, 1806, to be carried out unless wife re-marrys. Residue of Personal Estate to ch. of dau. Elizabeth.
Wits: Wendle Fisher, Joseph Waggoner, John Pugh.

Page 216. James McMasters, Upper Makefield Twp. "Advance age (about seventy)." Oct. -, 1806. Proved Nov. 28, 1806. Wife Mary. Sons John and James exrs. 3 mar. daus., Hannah, Margaret and Sarah. Other dau. Mary. Gdsn. James (son of John) and James (son of James). (Draft of land as devised to sons of record with will.)
Wits: James McNair, Is. Hicks.

Page 218. Jesse Lovett, Middletown Twp., yeoman. July 25, 1803. Proved Dec. 4, 1806. Samuel Lovett, John Booze Junr., Daniel Lovett and Abraham Chapman exrs. Wife Sarah Lovett house and Lot where we live which was her fa's. Jonathan Hibbs, dec'd. "No child or ch." Mother Ann Lovett and Bro. Samuel Lovett Money at interest. Plantation in Middletown (formerly Joseph Wright's) to be sold 1/3 of proceeds to Bro. Samuel, 1/3 to ch. of sister Hannah Cooper, dec'd. 1/3 to ch. of sister Kosia Boozer. Nephew Jesse Hibbs $40.
Nephew Jesse Booze $80.
Wits: P. Hunter, Is. Hicks.

Page 220. John Burroughs, Upper Makefield Twp., "Far advanced in old

age, being near Eighty-two." May 9, 1800. Proved Dec. 8, 1806. Codicil dated Jan. 15, 1804. Eight Ch., "Eldest son Samuel by imprudent conduct has cost me more than his proportion, and youngest Henry by industry and frugality has considerable on hand." Samuel $1. His son John £100. Daus. Hannah Thomton, Margaret Harvey, Elizabeth Taylor, Rachel Beatty, Sarah Buckman and Esther Fell. Exrs. son Henry and son-in-law Benjamin Taylor to sell Plantation of 140 acres where Amos Martindell lives. Plantation of 200 acres where we live to son Henry.
Wits: Barnet Hageman, Pleasant Smith, Letitia Mathews, Peter Hoddle.

Page 222. Moses Aaron, New Britain Twp. June 20, 1804. Proved Dec. 26, 1806. Ephraim Thomas and John Riale of New Britain, yeoman exrs. Real and Personal Estate to be sold and proceeds invested until son Benjamin attains age of six years. Ch. Ann Aaron, Elizabeth wife of James Pool, Catharine, Margaret, Moses, Erasmus, Obed, Mary, Samuel and Benjamin Aaron, all estate equally.
Wits: Simon James, Elias Black, David Evans.

Page 223. Nathan Roberts, Richland Twp., yeoman. 7-10-1803. Proved Dec. 26, 1806. Nephew Everard Foulke and Friend James Chapman exrs. Niece Martha wife of Isaiah Worrell. Sister Elizabeth wife of Israel Foulke. Nephews David and Abel Roberts, sons of Bro. John, dec'd., Enoch Edwards, son of Thomas and Hannah; Evan and Nathan Roberts, sons of Bro. David; Edward and Everard Roberts, sons of Bro. Everard dec'd. William Roberts. Edward Roberts, son of sister Martha dec'd. Evan Foulke, son of Sister Mary Aquilla Foulke. Nieces 4 daus. of late bro. Everard. 3 daus. of bro. David. Martha wife of Isaiah Wornell. Abigail wife of Edward Roberts. Lydia Edwards wife of Nathan and Susanna wife of Israel Penrose. 4 sons of John Penrose and their lunatic bro. Joseph and Martha Foulke, ch. of Hugh Foulke. Jane Green, wife of Bejamin, niece Martha Walton's 3 ch. by James Green. Clara wife of Abel Dolby. Rachel, wife of Thomas Penrose. Martha wife of Benjamin Foulke. Mary wife of William Penrose. Hannah Green dau. of Benjamin Green. Amos Roberts. Ann wife of John Penrose.
Wits: William Green, John Lester. Draft of Land devised on record with will.

Page 224. Esther Blackfan, Solebury Twp. 6-16-1804. Proved Jan. 3, 1807. Son John Blackfan exr. Sons John, Thomas and Jesse Blackfan. Dau. Elizabeth Fell and her ch. Frances, Charles, John, George, Esther, Sarah and Elias. Dau. Rachel Chapman's ch. Jesse, Martha, Charles, Amos and Ann. Dau. Hannah Smith and her dau. Esther and Jane Smith. Dau. Agnes Scofield's daus. Esther and Agnes Scofield. Gdsn. John Blackfan.
Wits: Aaron Paxson, Moses Eastburn.

Page 230. Henry Simmons, Bensalem Twp., "Advanced by years." 9-9-1806. Proved Jan. 6, 1807. Wife Sarah, son William Simmons and Samuel

Allen exrs. Son John £50. Son Thomas £50. Dau. Ann Walker £15. Son Henry £40. "My aforesaid 4 ch. by my first wife, having rec'd. their mother's legacy, with what I have already given them I consider the just portion of my estate." Dau. Elizabeth Middleton £10. Dau. Mary Shin £10. Dau. Anna Middleton £10. Dau. Sarah Simmons 120£, when 18. Son Joseph 40 acres of Land purchased of John Swift. Two sons, William and Mordecai, 160 acres whereon I dwell paying £20 per year to their mother during life.
Wits: Mahlon Gregg, Samuel Doan.

Page 233. Josiah James, Senr., New Britain Twp. Dec. 6, 1806. Proved Jan. 15, 1807. Wife Elizabeth and son Evan exrs. Wife use of Plantation of 108 acres and tract of 16 acres purchased of Simon Callender, during life or widowhood, then to sons Evan, Josiah and John. Dau. Elenor wife of Benjamin Williams £5. Other daus. Huldah, Elizabeth and Rhoda. Son Josiah, Wheelwright Tools.
Wits: John Davis, Simon and Jesse Callender.

Page 235. Thomas Hill, Buckingham Twp. 11-9-1806. Proved Jan. 9, 1807. Son William Hill and gdsn. Thomas Hill exrs. Son William Dwelling and 24 perches of Land. Gdsn. Thomas Hill bal. 5 acres 28 perches. Gddau. Deborah Hill, Case of Drawers.
Wits: Josiah Shaw, Jono. Watson Jr., William Pickering.

Page 236. John Thomas, Buckingham Twp., yeoman. May 27, 1804. Proved Jan. 16, 1807. Bro. Evan Thomas and his son John Thomas exrs. Bro. Evan Farm "which by law descended to me by the death of my Uncle Lewis Thomas" for life then to his son Evan. Bro. Evan "My moiety or half part of Farm where I now dwell (which dec'd,. to me from my Father)" for life, then to his son John. If nephews die without issue, to said bro. three daus. Susanna, Mary and Rebekah Thomas. Sister Susannah Stewkesbury, £50.
Wits: Joseph Worthington, John Kerr.

Page 237. George Hillegas, Lower Milford Twp., wheelwright. July 12, 1803. Proved Jan. 16, 1807. Wife Elizabeth. Ch. Eve wife of Anthony Slisenbaum, George, John, Adam, Michael, ---, Henry, Eilzabeth and Jacob.
Wits: David Spinner, George Shull.

Page 241. Peter Stout, Rockhill Twp. Feb. 15, 1806. Proved Jan. 23, 1807. Wife Catharine and dau. Mary Catharine, Farm on which I dwell. Sons Peter and Jacob exrs. Sons John, Peter, Jacob and Daniel. Daus. Sarah, Magdalen, Elizabeth wife of John Gares. Jacob, Mary, John, Daniel and Polly Ness, ch. of dau. Eve, late the wife of Jacob Ness.
Wits: John Heany, John Kachline.

Page 243. Joseph Custard, Richland Twp. 12-29-1806. Proved Jan. 26, 1807. Wife Amelia, 1/3 of estate forever and use of whole until son George comes of age. Daus. Ann and Mary. Nephew Samuel Iden and Friend Jesse Foulke exrs. Money bequeathed by Jonathan Watson for use of Poor ch.
Wits: William Shaw, Israel Foulke.

Page 245. Mathias Zeiginfuss, Richland Twp,. yeoman. Oct. 22, 1806. Proved Jan. 26, 1807. Wife Margaret. Sons Adam and Henry exrs. Ch. George John, Adam, Henry, Peter, Abraham, Elizabeth, Catharine, Mary and Christina. Son-in-law Martin Althouse. Friends Everard, Hugh and Benjamin Foulke to fix compensation to son Henry for care of me in my weak state.
Wits: J. Shimer, Everard Foulke.

Page 247. Joseph Adgerson. March 28, 1797. Proved Jan. 23, 1807. Wife Sufvina extx. and sole Legatee.
Wits: Matthew Cunnignham, Thomas Cunningham, John Smith.

Page 248. William Thompson, Warrington Twp., yeoman. Jan. 28, 1803. Proved Feb. 2, 1807. Wife Margaret. Nathaniel Irwin and Nephew Robert Thompson exrs. Sister Elizabeth Clemens, now or late of Kentucky. Her son Rodger and other ch. Margaret, Widow of Bro. David Thompson, dec'd. Ann Fratt "now living with me." Sister Ann blind aged woman now living with me.
Wits: John Richey, William Whittingham, William Picker.

Page 250. Elizabeth Hockman, Bedminster Twp., widow, "advanced in years." July 29, 1797. Proved Jan. 6, 1807. Ulrich Stover exr. Two sons and two daus., namely, George Beck, Jacob Hockman, Elizabeth wife of Rudolph Youngken and Eve wife of John Bissey.
Wits: Michael Strauss, Benjamin Jacoby, Casper Schoen.

Page 252. Joseph Watson, Lower Makefield. 12-3-1805. Wife Deborah. Sons David and Mark Watson exrs. Ch. David, Mark, Levi, William, Rachel and Rebecca.
Wits: Esther Mitchell, Moses Moon.

Page 253. Jonathan Wilson, Northampton Twp. 10-28-1806. Proved Jan. 23, 1807. Wife ---. Sons Jacob, David, Thomas, Joshua. Daus. Hannah, Sarah and Rachel. Son Asa.
Wits: Abraham Buckman, Thomas South.

Page 254. Joseph Erwin, Bucks Co. Dec. 2, 1803. Proved March 2, 1807. Bros. William and Hugh exrs. Will made "During my illness in Phila. in the winter of 1803." Maj. Gen. Thomas Craig, Mr. John Bohlen, Benjamin R. Morgan, William Moore Smith Esq. and Dr. C. Wistar (?), $50. each.

Dr. William McGill $200. Dr. Hugh Scott of Pittsburgh $200. Anna Price, my housekeeper $80. (signed)
(Nov. 5, 1804. Much valued Friend Pressly Nevile $50.) (Above entered on margin). Friend James Chapman $50 and Proud's Hist. of Penna. Sister Sarah wife of John Mulhallon £60 a year for life, should she survive her husband. (Note on margin under date of Nov. 5, 1804, makes annuity for life unconditional). Bro. Hugh Erwin Bond of £1000 he owes, Plantation where I reside bought of Edward Pennington, Housewarts exrs. et al and Stock &c. for life, also Land on River bank in Nockamixon Twp. In default of issue to Bro. William Erwin (signed). Last mentioned land in tenure of Belteshazer Smith. Bro. William 416 acres in tenure of Thomas Silverthorn and William Thompson, and woodland (222 acres) in tenure of Dinnis O'Daniel and Jacob Garey, Bro. William "part of eleven tracts at Tioga Point in County of Luzerne, part of Estate of my late Father Arthur Erwin Esq. Also 80 acres in Plumstead, also rights in two Townships of Land in Steuben Co., N.Y. known by name of "Cannaster Towns" conveyed by Nathaniel Gorham and Oliver Phillips to Arthur Erwin, Joel Thomas, Uriah Stevens and Solomon Bennet, containing 23,040 acres each.
To Bro. William "My books worth about $800." Note on margin dated Jan. 1806, "Thomas McBurney, Esq. of Steuben Co., N.Y. $600 for assistance in securing property there."
Gold watch and seals which were my late Uncle Hugh Scott's, to Nephew Scott E. Erwin. (Note on margin dated Nov. 5, 1804.)
Wits: John Wilson, Benjamin Evans, Lewis A. Prevost.
Evidently declared and witnessed at later date as declaration in presence of wits. includes Marginal additions.

Page 258. Benjamin Stephens, New Britain Twp., yeoman. Dated June 18, 1803. Proved March 10, 1807. Sons David and John exrs. Ch. viz: Thomas, Isaac and the ch. of my son Joseph dec'd., David, Robert, John, Mary (the wife of Jonathan Doyle) and Elizabeth (the wife of Isaac Hull).
Wits: Jeremiah Dungan, Robert Shewell.

Page 259. Henry Clymer, Lower Milford Twp., yeoman. May 5, 1806. Proved March 31, 1806. Wife Barbara. Son Jacob and son-in-law Joseph Shelly exrs. Daus. Elizabeth Shelly and Molly Hoddle.
Wits: Christian Zetty, Jacob Clymer.

Page 260. Margaret Jones, (widow), Hilltown Twp., "Aged and weak." Sept. 17, 1800. Proved May 1, 1807. Son-in-law Nathaniel Jones exr. Daus. Catharine wife of Owen Owens, Sarah wife of Ebenezer Owens, Elizabeth wife of Nathaniel Jones. Son Jonathan Jones. Gdch. Margaret Costner, Mary wife of Robert Heaton, Elizabeth wife of John Pugh Esq., Rachel, Margaret and Catharine Owens, Bety Owens, Aaron Jones and his bros. and sister (by said mother), Margaret Lewis, Elizabeth wife of Nathan Jones, Griffith and Jonathan Jones, sons of Nathaniel and

Elizabeth, Margaret Jones, Catharine Beaulick, Rachel (dau. of son Jonathan), --- Trustees of Baptist church at Kelly's in Hilltown.
Wits: Benjamin Jones, Dorothy Ewer, Thomas Jones.

Page 262. Joseph Williams, Warwick Twp., yeoman. March 19, 1807. Proved May 4, 1807. Wife Mary. George Shelmire, the Elder and Hiram McNeile, both of Moorland, exrs. Son William £50 Specie if he marry Elizabeth, dau. of Paul Dowlin of Horsham. Ch. Jane, John, William, David, Joseph, Mary, Ann, Rachel, Sarah and Susanna.
Wits: Benjamin Hough, Andrew Bisbing.

Page 264. Thomas Wishart, Late of City of Phila., now of Bristol Borough. 1-8-1807. Proved May 6, 1807. Kinsman Amos Gregg and William Maris exrs. Kinswoman Margaret Evans, late Maris, Brick House on Pewter Platter Alley, Phila. adj. Ellis Yardnell's lot. Kinswoman Ann Gregg, all estate bequeathed me by Will of my sister Ann Wishart, dec'd. , being moiety or half part of her Real Estate in Phila. fronting on Second St, adj. Ground late of my bro. William Wishart and others known as the "Buck Tavern" also all property in her or her husband's possession. Residue to Kinsman William Maris.
Wits: William Patterson, Mahlon Gregg.

Page 265. Evan Johnson, Upper Makefield Twp. Dec. 19, 1806. Proved May 6, 1807. Jacob Strickler, House and Lot in Southampton and all other Estate and makes him exr.
Wits: William Tomlinson, Absalom Dubre.

Page 266. Valentine Cramer, Hilltown Twp., Farmer. March 28, 1806. Proved May 12, 1807. Wife Mary and son John exrs. Daus. Elizabeth wife of John Fretz (her dau. Mary), Magdalen, Hannah, Catharine wife of James Nunnemaker. Son George interest of £400 for his support. Ch. Hannah, Ann, Elizabeth, Lawrence, John, Jacob, Barbara and Margaret May. Land whereon John Mitchell lives.
Wits: Jacob Cramer, Mason and John Kolb.

Page 268. Isaac Stackhouse (son of Jonathan Stackhouse), Middletown Twp. "Having a mind to travel." Oct. 1, 1806. Proved May 30, 1807. Two Uncles John Stackhouse and Isaac Stackhouse, exrs. Sisters Marcy and Grace Stackhouse. Mother Grace Stackhouse profits of land adj. Dr. Mahlon Gregg, for life, then to bro. Jonathan Stackhouse. Elizabeth Hawke 100£, Mary Bankson £100.
Wits: Phebe Buckman, Benjamin Buckman.

Page 269. Melchor Hevener, Bedminster Twp., yeoman. April 14, 1803. Proved June 2, 1807. Wife Barbara. Son Abraham and friend Jacob Kulp exrs. Sons John, Jacob and Abraham. Daus. Elizabeth, Margaret and Mary. Sale of Land and Mills in Tinicum and Plumstead Twps. to Jacob

Stover, of Bedminster, miller, to be completed by exrs.
Wits: Abraham Kulp, Ralph Stover.

Page 270. Benjamin Chapman, Wrightstown Twp., Miller. April 12, 1807.
Proved June 4, 1807. Wife Mary. Bro. George Chapman, Friend David
Story and son Owen Chapman exrs. Wife and three sons to carry on
Milling business until dec. of Father. Son George, Mills &c. and 15 acres
of land. Balance of land to sons Owen and Abbit. George Chapman, David
Story, Thomas Story and Isaac Chapman to divide same. Daus. Martha,
Susannah and Elizabeth $500 each.
Wits: Sarah Gillam, Susan Willard, Isaac Chapman.

Page 272. Joseph Miller, Warminster Twp. March 12, 1807. Proved June
8, 1807. Henry Puff and Isaac Retherford exrs. Only dau. Mary wife of
Henry Puff, all estate for life, at her death proceeds of Land to her ch.
£150 each to John, Joseph and Mary Retherford, ch. of Isaac Retherford.
Tombstones to be erected "for me and my first wife."
Wits: Jesse Banes, Cornelius Carrell. Codicil, same date, verbal, Elizabeth
Retherford, 2 Beds and Bedsteads &c.

Page 273. John Adams, Nockamixon Twp. March 21, 1807. Proved June
8, 1807. Wife Mary all estate for life or widowhood. Son George exr.
Gddau. who from infancy has lived with me. Sons George, Henry, John
and Jacob. Daus. Elizabeth and Margaret, and two gdch. of my dau. Mary
dec'd.
Wits: George Wyler, Jacob Rymond.

Page 275. Thomas Hellings, Northampton Twp., yeoman. May 3, 1805.
Proved June 10, 1807. Wife Elizabeth in Codicil, Rebecca in will. Original
not on file. Son John exr. Daus. Elizabeth Randall and Hannah Everett.
Wits: Joshua Comly, Joseph Thornton, John Hellings.

Page. 276. Lawrence Johnson, Bensalem Twp. Jan. 10, 1807. Proved June
30, 1807. Wife Sarah and sons Lawrence and James exrs. Sons Abraham
and Clark. Daus. Mary Cooper, Deborah Hibbs, Elizabeth Vankirk.
Gddaus. Ann Cooper and Ann Hibbs.
Wits: Hasell Benezett, John Goforth.

Page 278. John Ruth, New Britain Twp., weaver. Oct. 28, 1805. Proved
Aug. 1, 1807. Gdsn. Henry Ruth of Twp. and Co. on [sic] Montgomery
exr. 100 acres I live on to Ann Ruth, widow of son Henry dec'd. and her
ch. by him. Dau. Magdalena Delp.
Wits: David Ruth, Jacob Swarts, Abraham Swarts.

Page 279. George Kressler, Durham Twp., yeoman. April 8, 1807. Proved
Aug. 5, 1807. Wife Modelena. Son Henry and William Long of Durham
exrs. Sons John, George and Henry. Daus. Mary wife of Daniel Bostian,

Susy wife of Leonard Roup, Sarah wife of John Eichline, Margaret wife of Michael Zigafoos, Elizabeth, Catharine, Ann and Rachel Kressler.
Wits: John Kohl, Philip Hager.

Page 281. Alice Thomas, Richland Twp., widow. July 1, 1800. Proved Aug. 28, 1807. Codicil July 8, 1801. James Chapman and Benjamin Green exrs. Daus. Margaret, Mariam possibly Mariann Heacock, Mary and Martha.
Wits: Eliza Chapman, Mary Black, Abigail Chapman.

Page 282. Amos Huddleston, Middletown Twp. April 17, 1807. Proved Sept. 1, 1807. William Tomlinson exr. Mother Sarah Huddleson [sic]. Bros. Lewis, Mahlon and John Huddleson [sic].
Wits: Charles Goheen, Benja. Buckman.

Page 283. William Duncan, Bensalem Twp. 11-23-1805. Proved Sept. 10, 1807. Bro.-in-law John Praul and nephew William Ridge and Nephew William Giles exrs. Ethan Briggs, Blacksmith Tools. Nephew William Ridge share in Byberry Library. Niece Rachel Duncan. George Ridge son of Mahlon Ridge. Sisters Rachel Ridge and Esther Praul. Nieces Ester Briggs, Abigail Giles and Phebe Rich.
Wits: John Comly, Henry Ridge, Amos Ridge.

Page 284. Valentine Nicholas, Haycock Twp., yeoman, "advanced in age." March 15, 1798. Proved Sept. 26, 1807. Son Christian exr. "Have several years ago confirmed lands to sons Christian and George." Ch. Valentine, Jacob, Catharine wife of Frederick Premauer, John, Henry, Daniel, Christian and George.
Wits: Casper Boroyer, Casper Schoen, Henry Apple. "Have my dwelling with son Christian and mean to continue to my end."

Page 285. John Clymer, Lower Milford Twp., yeoman. April 29, 1807. Proved Oct. 5, 1807. Wife Elizabeth and son Jacob Clymer exrs. Son Jacob 177 Acres whereon I live. Son-in-law John Fink, Mill and 26 Acres in Upper Milford Twp., Northampton Co. adj. George Ness, Henry Leeperts and others.
Wits: Christian Zetty, Moses Wilson.

Page 287. Jacob Most, Nockamixon Twp. Sept. 16, 1807. Proved Oct. 12, 1807. George Maust and Stophel Trauger exrs. Sons Jacob, John George and Frederick Most. Daus. Magdalen wife of Stophel Trauger, Mary wife of William Keeler, Elizabeth wife of Jacob Wooldonger. Gdch., ch. of dau. Kathren wife of Michael Young dec'd.
Wits: Hugh Jamison, Frederick Trauger.

Page 287. Elizabeth Jones, New Britain, Widow. April 24, 1807. Proved Oct. 13, 1807. Son Ashbel Jones exr. and Guardian of Gdsn. Benjamin Fulton. Dau. Mary wife of Isaac Worthington. Gddau. Elizabeth Craig wife

of James Craig; her dau. Mary Craig. Gddaus. Anna wife of Enoch Mathias and Ann wife of John Richards. Gdsns. John and Benjamin Fulton, Ashbel and Abel Mathias (by dau. Anna Mathias dec'd.), Abner, Thomas, Asbel [sic] and John Jones (by son Ashbel Jones). Gddaus. Elizabeth, Catharine and Mary Jones by said son Ashbel.
Wits: Jacob Sleiffer, David Evans.

Page 289. Stephen Kniseler, Haycock Twp., yeoman. March 17, 1807. Proved Oct. 16, 1807. Wife --- and Everard Foulke exrs. Estate to all ch. alike, not named.
Wits: George Swinker, Jacob Funk.

Page 290. Johannes Funk, Hilltown Twp. "My Trade a Smith." Aug. 13, 1807. Cert. of Translation Oct. 7, 1807. Son-in-law Johannes Kolb and Martin Fretz exrs. Ch. Anna, Abraham (dec'd.), Isaac, David, Maria and Barbara. Land to Johannes Kolb.
Wits: Joseph Meyer, Johannes Kolb.

Page 291. John Goodwin, Bucks Co. Aug. 24, 1807. Proved Oct. 19, 1807. Wife Susannah extx. all estate except wearing apparel, that to Bros. Joseph, Jonathan, William and George Goodwin.
Wits: Nicholas McCarty, Jacob Meyer.

Page 292. Paul Rymond, Nockmaxion Twp,. "Aged." Nov. 1, 1803. Proved Oct. 22, 1807. Wife Anna Margaretta. George Roof and son Jacob Rymond exrs. Sons John, Jacob and Michael, £15 in advance of what daus. Margarette, Elizabeth (dec'd.) and Catharina were advanced at time of their mar. 4 ch. of dau. Elizabeth dec'd.
Wits: George Wyker, Henry Wyker.

Page 293. Thomas Watson, Buckingham. 11-9-1806. Proved Nov. 4, 1807. Wife Mary extx. £1000 and income of Real Estate until son Thomas comes of age; she paying annuity to the widow of her late uncle Isaac Chapman dec'd., now wife of Benjamin Olden being her interest in land we conveyed to Noah Lambert in Wrightstown. She also to support my six ch. Anna, Mary, Sarah, Thomas, Elizabeth and Robert. Cousin Jonathan Fell, Bro.-in-law James Verree, and Relative Dr. Isaac Chapman, Guardians of ch.; they with John Terry to divide lands devised. Son Robert 187 Acres adj. John Lewis and John Beal. Son Thomas 25 Acres of Woodland called the Forest adj. John Melone and Isaiah Jones, and 245 acres with Mansion House where I dwell. 151 acres adj. John Melone and Isaiah Jones and John Beal to be sold.
Wits: Elisha Wilkinson, Sarah Woolston and John Terry.

Page 298. John Moore and Ann Moore his wife of Nockamixon Twp. Son William and son-in-law John Williams exrs. Farm in Alexander Twp., Hunterdon Co., N.J. to be secured for the use of ch. that are minors. 6-

16-1807. Proved Nov. 9, 1807. Codicil Oct. 6, mentions nephew John Buffaloe Moore and son John Moore Junr.
Wits: John Moore Junr. and Jacob Moore.

Page 300. Ann Lee, Solebury Twp. 9-13-1807. Proved Nov. 9, 1807. Aaron Paxson exr. Sister Mary Pownall, her daus. Mary Mattison and Elizabeth Pownall. Sister Sarah Kitchin, nieces Mary and Rachel Kitchin, sister Hannah Lee. Bro. Thomas Lee.
Wits: Thomas Phillips, Charles Morrow.

Page 301. John Cronin, Bristol Twp. April 3, 1806. Proved Nov. 9, 1807. Joseph Bailey exr. Joseph Bailey and Lydia his wife and their sons Daniel and Joel Bailey.
Wits: Daniel Mitchell, Charles Bessonett Jr.

Page 302. Job Walton, Warwick Twp., yeoman. May 7, 1796, Codicil Nov. 17, 1804. Proved Nov. 11, 1807. Wife Margaret. Son John exr. Son Job, 5 s. having lately conveyed to him 92 acres of land. Son Isaac 5 s. having lately conveyed to him 93 acres of land. Son John Plantation 105 acres I live on, adj. John Kerr, John Jamison, Isaac and Job Walton.
Wits: Robert Loller, Mary Loller, Mary Marple. To codicil, James Barclay, John Barclay.

Page 305. John Knizely, Richland Twp., yeoman. Aug. 18, 1806. Proved Nov. 20, 1807. Wife Catharine. Everard Foulke and Henry Messimer exrs. Maricha wife of Stephen Winner, Catharine and Henry Hause and Jesse Hinkle each £25. Ch. of Bros. Stephen, Jacob and Henry. Ch. of sisters Elizabeth wife of Conrad Lams and Catharine wife of Peter Zeigenfuss.
Wits: Peter Narragong, Henry Heft.

Page 306. John Getman, Lower Milford Twp., yeoman, "advanced in years." Aug. 6, 1807. Proved Nov. 20, 1807. Wife Elizabeth and Bro. George Getman exrs. Wife use of Plantation until youngest ch. comes of age. Ch. George, John, Sarah and Elizabeth.
Wits: Philip Hinkle, William Getman.

Page 308. Jacob Beans, Solebury twp., yeoman. 7-20-1807. Proved Nov. 24, 1807. Wife Hannah. Moses Paxson and John Armitage (Miller) exrs. Sons Mahlon, Joseph and Benjamin. Daus. Ann Beans, Tamar wife of David Newburn, Asenath widow of Robert Walker. Benjamin's dau. Elizabeth.
Wits: Benjamin Paxson, Thomas Paxson, Jno. Ruckman.

Page 310. David Rees, New Britain Twp., "Aged and weak." Feb. 1, 1799. Proved Nov. 25, 1807. Wife Mary extx. all estate unless she mar., then to her ch. by her first husband. Her gdsn. John Doke.
Wits: John Harris, Samuel Garner, Amos Griffith.

Page 311. Sarah Dennis, Rockhill Twp., Spinster. 10-8-1807. Proved Dec. 9, 1807. Amos Richardson exr. Cousin Catharin Ball. Martha Richardson. Son Bela Gouznel. Niece Esther Speakman. Rebekah, Jane, Hezekiah, Ann, Sarah and John Richardson. Sarah Richardson dau. of Amos Richardson.
Wits: Nathan Penrose, Enoch Penrose, Everard Foulke.

Page 313. Catharine Blaker, Northampton Twp. Sept. 28, 1807. Proved Dec. 10, 1807. Neighbors Joel Carver and Jesse Leedom exrs. "But one ch. a dau. Sarah,. ten years of age the second of this instant." "Friend Joshua Vanhorn, who has lived with me for several years." Dau. all estate and land; if she die, to Bros. Jason and John Blaker.
Wits: Abraham Longshore, Is. Hicks.

Page 314. Garret Vanhorn, Middletown Twp., yeoman. Jan. 26, 1799. Proved Dec. 12, 1807. Sons Joshua and John Vanhorn, and William Moore exrs. Dau. Eleanor Davis's four ch. Son Peter. Dau. Elizabeth Doble's two ch. John and Mary Doble. Dau. Mary Vanhorn's dau., called Rachel Vansant. Two youngest sons Joshua and John Vanhorn.
Wits: William Vansant, William Sisom, Daniel Brown.

Page 316. Bartle White, Bedminster Twp., yeoman. March 11, 1803. Proved Dec. 29, 1807. Wife Elizabeth. Sons David and George exrs. Eldest son David, Plantation on which I live; son George, Plantation in Nockamixon Twp. "where on is a House of Entertainment kept." also Plantation in Bedminster whereon he lives. Daus. Mary and Elizabeth.
Wits: Conrad Harpel, Jacob Wildonger.

Page 318. Ann Goforth, Bensalem Twp. Nov. 4, 1807. Proved Dec. 29, 1807. Bro. Thomas Goforth, late of Bensalem and Joseph Jackson of Lower Dublin Twp. exrs. Mother Isabel Goforth, sister Elizabeth.
Wits: William How, John Goforth.

Page 319. Abraham Black, Plumstead Twp. Jan. 28, 1806. Proved Jan. 7, 1808. Wife Elizabeth. Sons Andrew and George Black exrs. Son Abraham to have the place I live on, pay out to sons Henry and George. Dau. Mary's ch. Joseph Fried's wife. Wooldrich Stover. Gddau. Elizabeth wife of Philip Kratz. Gddau. Barbara Stover and her bros. and sisters. Land adj. George Fox and Andrew Black, in Plumstead.
Wits: Abraham Leatherman, Philip Leatherman.

Page 321. William Hartley, Solebury Twp. 4-10-1805. Proved Jan .11, 1808. Wife ---. Gdsn. William Rice and Elias Paxson exrs. Son-in-law Joseph Rice, has lately purchased land "late of bro. Benjamin Hartley." Dau. Letitia wife of Joseph Rice. Gddau. Catharine Paxson and Letitia Rice. Gdsns. Joseph Rice Jr. and William Rice.
Wits: John Armitage, Oliver Hampton, Israel Child.

Page 322. Jacob Angeny, Bedminster Twp., Miller. Dec. 22, 1803. Proved Jan. 12, 1808. Wife Elizabeth. Son Jacob and sons-in-law Abraham Moyers, Jacob Overholt and Joseph Moyers exrs. Son Jacob Plantation and Mill, paying out to daus.; Elizabeth and Barbery Moyers and Mary Overholt, Abraham Moyers and Elizabeth his wife, Jacob Overholt and Mary his wife, Joseph Moyers and Barbery his wife.
Wits: Abraham Overholt, Isaac Gross.

Page 324. Isaac Buckman, Newtown Twp. 1807. Proved Feb. 3, 1808. Wife Joyce and David Story exrs. Wife and ch. to carry on the farming until son Zenas comes of age. Lands to sons Zenas and Isaac, when of age, Jacob Janney and Jesse Buckman and Isaac Chapman to divide same. Daus. Hannah, Elizabeth and Rachel Buckman.
Wits: Benjamin Smith, John Perry.

Page 326. James McNair, Upper Makefield Twp., yeoman. Aug. 16, 1805. Proved Jan. 19, 1808. Wife ---. Sons Solomon and David exrs. All lands, Isaac Hicks, Esq., John McNair and Garret Johnson, to divide it. Son Samuel what he owes. Daus. Margaret, Ann, Elizabeth, Martha and Rachel.
Wits: John McNair, George Randal.

Page 327. William Penrose, Richland Twp,. yeoman. 1-1-1808. Proved Feb. 15, 1808. Wife Mary, son-in-law Evan Roberts and Bro.-in-law John Roberts exrs. Wife Legacy left her by her Uncle Nathan Roberts. Daus. Abigail Roberts, Margaret and Sarah Penrose. Land purchased of Leonard Hinkle, adj. land of John Martin and Michael Brown.
Wits: Jesse Foulke, Isaac Morgan, George Hicks.

Page 330. William Kirkpatrick, Morrisville Borough. Jan .27, 1807. Proved Feb. 16, 1808. Reading Beatty of Falls Twp. exr. Abijah Reed sole legatee.
Wits: Thomas Clark, Edmund Nutt.

Page 330. Thomas Lancaster, Falls Twp., yeoman. 1-18-1807. Proved Feb. 25, 1808. Wife Martha extx. Isaac Barns of Falls and Joshua Woolston of Middletown, Trustees. Son Thomas Lancaster of White Marsh. Daus. Jane Woolston and Martha Lancaster (a minor).
Wits: William Warner, Joseph Warner, Corn's. C. Blatchly.

Page 331. John Tucker, Warwick Twp., yeoman. July 12, 1805. Proved Feb. 27, 1808. Codicil Nov. 18, 1805. Wife Phebe. Son John and son-in-law Jacob Twining exrs. Sons John, Septimus, Joseph, Isaac, David and Thomas Tucker. daus. Sarah Lovett, Martha Twining, Phebe Twining and Mary Twining.
Wits: Mathew C. Jamison, Abraham DeCoursey, Robert Jamison.

Page 333. Abel Roberts, Richland Twp., yeoman. 1-13-1801. Codicil dated

12-25-1806. Proved March 1, 1808. Gdsns. Shipley Lester and Israel Lancaster exrs. Codicil revokes appointments of Israel Lancaster and puts son-in-law Samuel Penrose in his place. Daus. Sarah Penrose and Susanna Edwards. Gdsns. William, Abel and Samuel Nixon, sons of Susanna Edwards. Abel, William and Everard Penrose and Shipley Lester., Codicil, Abel Nixon absent many years, if does not return in 14 years his share to go to his sisters. Son-in-law Samuel Penrose land where Abel Dolby lives, adj. John Penrose and John Foulke.
Wits: Eliza Chapman, Abigail Chapman, James Chapman. To Codicil John Lester, James Chapman.

Page 337. Samuel Miller, Upper Makefield Twp. Sept. 29, 1794. Proved March 1, 1808. John Keith exr. Bros. Robert, Isaac and Joseph. Sister Rachel.
Wits: John Keith, Anthony Torbert.

Page 338. Mary Vansant, Southampton Twp., "Old and infirm." Aug. 15, 1804. Proved March 12, 1808. Late husband Nicholas Vansant. Son Nathaniel Vansant exr. Dau. Rebecca Boileau.
Wits: Abraham La Rue, William Ridge, John Sickle.

Page 339. Zachariah Betts, Upper Makefield Twp. 7-8-1807. Proved March 15, 1808. Wife Mary and sons Jesse and Thomas exrs. Ch. Jesse, Mariann Lownes, Samuel, Mary Hampton, Zachariah, Thomas, Joseph, Esther, Mercy, Rachel and Susanna.
Wits: William Lownes, Susanna Betts, Joseph Taylor.

Page 340. Elizabeth Beringer, Hilltown Twp., widow. "Aged and infirm." --- 15, 1798. Proved April 1, 1808. Son John Beringer exr. Sons John, Henry and George. Daus. Elizabeth and Mary. Gdch. John and Elizabeth Miner.
Wits: Jacob Stout, Abraham Stout.

Page 341. John McDowell, Warminster Twp., weaver. Nov. 22, 1806. Proved April 1, 1808. Wife Mary and son Abraham exrs. Ch. Hannah, Samuel, Ann, John and Sutphin.
Wits: Ann Boileau, Nathaniel B. Boileau (Boilean?).

Page 342. John Scott, Warwick Twp., "Advanced in age." Oct. 1, 1807. Proved April 27, 1808. Sons Andrew, John and Archibald exrs. Son James; Gdch. Mary Scott dau. of son William dec'd., John Scott son [of] Andrew, John Scott son of Archibald, Mary Scott dau. of Andrew and Mary Scott dau. of Archibald.
Wits: John Welding, Watson Welding, Amos Welding.

Page 344. Rebekah Jenks, Middletown Twp., widow of Thomas Jenks, late of same place. 5-8-1807. Proved April 27, 1808. Son Phineas Jenks and

son-in-law Thomas Story exrs. Daus. Rachel Story, Mercy Carlile, Rebekah Fell, Mary and Ruth Jenks. Sons Joseph R. Jenks, Thomas Jenks and Phineas Jenks.
Wits: Joseph Worstall Jr., A. Chapman.

Page 345. Adam Keiper, Lower Milford Twp., mason. May 12, 1808. Proved May 19, 1808. Wife Anna Mary. Sons Peter and John exrs. Wife all estate coming from Estate of her father Michael Idderly dec'd. Dau. Catharine wife of John Rosenberger. Gddau. Molly Rinker. Land (60 acres) to John and Peter.
Wits: Henry Strunk, John Drissel.

Page 347. William Hutchinson, Buckingham Twp. May 14, 1808. Proved May 20, 1808. Wife Isabel extx. All estate for life or widowhood, then to sons. N.B. requests that she ask Geremiah Hutchinson to assist as Exr.
Wits: Joseph Harrold, John Connard, John Connard Sr., Robert Kennedy (?). Letters to Isabel only.

Page 348. Isaac Williams, Hilltown Twp., yeoman. March 20, 1805. Proved May 26, 1808. Thomas Williams and William Williams exrs. "Son Benjamin rec'd. £200 in Real Estate, beside other benefits." "My dau. Ann now wife of Benjamin James, rec'd. several benefits. I alow her £50 more." "My son Thomas Williams rec'd. £200 in Real Estate besides several other benefits." "My son William Williams, Rec'd. £200 in Learning, and going through the Medical line, besides other benefits." "My dau. Elizabeth Williams £150 in money, besides £50 for her setting off, and £9 yearly from the death of her Mother; which did commence the 20th day of March 1803, during the time she remains my housekeeper." "My dau. Rebekah now wife of William Tennis Rec'd. several benefits I alow her £150 more." Son Joseph Williams, 130 acres of land whereon I live at £8 per acre "allowing him £200 he not having rec'd. any Tread or sufficient learning, and to have the farm rent free during the life time of his Uncle John Williams."
Wits: John Anglemoyer, Joseph Anglemoyer, William Godshalk.

Page 349. Nicholas Wyker, Tinicum Twp., yeoman. Aug. 17, 1797. Proved June 20, 1808. Sons Henry and Antony exrs. Sons Antony and Abraham, Plantation, they paying each £500 to my other six ch., Henry, George, Catharina, Elizabeth, Mary and Dina and wife Susannah. Elizabeth's ch. Abraham and Mary Youngken.
Wits: Christopher Drauger, Peter Laubenstein.

Page 349. Sarah Carey, Newtown. 1-19-1796. Proved June 18, 1808. Son-in-law Samuel Johnston and Gdsn. William Blakey exrs. Daus. Sarah Blakey, Hephzibah Johnston, Beulah Woolston, Hannameel Gilbert. Sons Samson, Phineas, Samuel and Asa Carey. Gddau. Sarah wife of Thomas Paxson.

Wits: Thomas Blakey, Joshua Blakey Jr., John Blakey.

Page 352. Henry Blyler Jr., Lower Milford Twp., yeoman. April 29, 1808. Proved July 28, 1808. Elizabeth [wife?]. Son Peter and son-in-law Henry Trumbauer exrs. Wife use of Plantation where Jacob Bartholomew lives for life. Son Peter Plantation "whereon I live" 195 Acres. Dau. Catharine, wife of Henry Trumbauer. Dau. Hannah Blyler.
Wits: David Spinner, Daniel Blyler.

Page 354. Mary Dungan, Northampton Twp. May 23, 1807. Proved Aug. 15, 1808. Lot Bennett, son of my sister Ann Bennett, exr. Garret Dungan, son of my late husband, David Dungan.
Wits: Jacob Thomas, John Corson.

Page 355. Joseph Richardson, Mansfield, Burlington Co., N.J. Oct. 6, 1806. Proved Aug. 23, 1808. Son David and Mahlon Milnor exrs. Wife's son Samuel Richardson. Sons Malachi, Clement, Jeremiah, David and Joseph Richardson. Dau. Mary Vastine £250 for life free from any claim of her husband, her ch. John and Ann Vastine and other ch. Dau. Ann Craven and daus. Mary and Bersheba Richardson.
Wits: William Milnor Jr., William Bunting.

Page 357. Mary Vansant, Wrightstown Twp., "Far advanced in years." April 30, 1804. Proved Sept. 1, 1808. Thomas Atkinson and Isaac Chapman exrs. Nieces Mary Pownal, Sarah Kitchin, Hannah and Ann Lee, daus. of Bro. Thomas Lee. Sarah wife of John Scott. Hannah Atkinson, "John's wife."
Wits: Jonathan, Sarah and Mary Atkinson.

Page 358. Michael Swartz, Plumstead Twp., yeoman. June 5, 1808. Proved Sept. 5, 1808. Wife Sophia, house and lot bounded by Tohickon Creek, River Delaware, and Hickory Run, where homemakers live. At her death said lot with the Run so far below as shall be necessary for bulding or keeping a Mill, to son Thomas. Sons Nicholas and Jacob exrs. To said 3 sons Fishery at mouth of Tohickon. Ferry Lot and Fishery in N.J. and right in Cave Bank Fishery to be sold. Proceeds to sons Andrew, Michael and Thomas, Daus. Catharine and Susanna and Gddau. Elizabeth Long. "Plantation I now live on" to sons Nicholas and Jacob, they to suport their bro. Joseph during life.
Wits: Henry Wismer, John Lewis.

Page 360. Julius Rosenberger, Rockhill Twp., yeoman. Sept. 12, 1808. Proved Oct. 3, 1808. Son Penjamen [sic] Rosenberger exr. To him Plantation and 144 Acres where I live, adj. Andrew Sclichter Esq., Abraham Stout, John Wambold and Frederick Shaffer. Son Henry. Dau. Anna wife of Joseph Naragang £1000. Dau. Heliekk. wife of Jacob Bachtel, Land in Springfield Twp. where John Bissey lives.

Wits: Daniel Cooper, David Bachman, Joseph Geisinger.

Page 362. Samuel Detweiler, Rockhill Twp., yeoman. March 6, 1807. Proved Oct. 7, 1808. Sons John, Jacob and Leonard exrs. Dau. Anne (unm.) household Goods, Money &c. and rooms in House. Son Jacob Plantation, 150 Acres where I dwell adj. Christian Clemmer, Isaac Derstine, Land devised to son John, [adj.?]Abraham Gerhart and North branch of Perkimey Creek; also 42 ½ acres ½ of Tract bought of Henry Berkey. Son John Plantation purchased of Ph. Henry Seller 135 acres and remaining half part of tract bought of Henry Berkey. Son Samuel, Grist and Oyl Mill and 76 ¾ Acres bought of George Meyer, partly in Montgomery Co. Son Leonard Plantation purchased of John Treichler, in Hilltown 170 ¼ Acres.
Wits: Abraham Stout, Jacob Kinsey, George Clemens.

End of Book No. 7.

Will Book No. 8.

Page 1. David Feaster, Northampton Twp. Feb. 4, 1808. Codicil Sept. 23, 1808. Proved Oct. 11, 1808. Wife Elizabeth. Son Aaron and sons-in-law Adrian Cornell and Lambert Cornell exrs. Plantation on which I live and stock to son Aaron. Daus. Jane Stewart, Mary Cornell and Rachell Cornell. Dau. Mary Cornell, 9 acres purchased of Abraham Harding part of Logan's Tract. Son and 3 daus. land purchased of Jonathan Thomas, part of Logan's Tract, to be divided by David and Jonathan Wynkoop. Isaac Vanhorn, Safety Maghee and Joshua Praul; (Draft thereof and cert. of above parties on record with will) 309 ½ Acres in Catyissey Twp., Northumberland Co. to be sold. 211 acres in Noeltown Twp., Sussex Co., N.J. in tenure of Jacob Brant, to be sold after dec. of sister Dorothy, wife of said Jacob Brant and the some of £222.7.7 to be paid to heirs of said Dorothy, including £100 bequeathed to her by will of father John Feaster, dec'd. and her share as residuary legatee.
Wits: David Taggart, Henry Wynkoop, Jona. Wynkoop, Thomas Chapman.

Page 4. Michal Musselman, Lower Milford Twp., yeoman. Aug. 18, 1791. Proved Oct. 17, 1808. Son Jacob and son-in-law Abraham Gehman exrs. Gddau. Barbara Shelly 5 s. Son Samuel 124 ½ Acres on which I live, adj. John Stouffer, Benedict Gehman, Jacob Frick, Jacob Shelly, William Roberts and son Jacob, he paying £350. Sons Henry, Michael and David and dau. Verona £400. Residue to sons Jacob, Samuel, Henry Michael and David and dau. Verona.
Wits: Abraham Taylor, Peter Zetty, Jacob Kolb.

Page 6. Abraham Ditlow, Lower Milford Twp. Aug. 30, 1805. Proved Oct. 31, 1808. Wife Hannah use of Plantation during life. Wife Hannah and son David Ditlow exrs. Estate to "all my ch. at dec. of wife."

Wits: David Spinner, Philip Mumbower.

Page 7. Thomas Carey, Solebury Twp., yeoman. 12-24-1806. Proved Dec. 6, 1808. Son Thomas exr. "All my Lands" and all estate, paying my daus. Elizabeth Pickering and Hannah Carver £200 each and step-daus. Mary White and Sarah Stradling and Sarah White, dau. of Step-dau. Martha White dec'd.
Wits: Jesse Ely, Jonathan White.

Page 9. William Hollingshead, (no residence given). May 29, 1808. Proved Dec. 12, 1808. Wife Elizabeth all estate except 1 s. each to son William, daus. Jane and Hester and son Peter. Son-in-law John Duer exr.
Wits: Joseph Richardson, William H. Duer.

Page 10. Barbara Fluke, the Elder, widow, Richland Twp. Sept. 28, 1808. Proved Dec. 21, 1808. Son-in-law George Smith exr. Sons Ludwick and Henry. Gdch. Samuel Fluke and Hannah, --- ch. of son Jacob dec'd. Mary Smith and two ch. of son Philip dec'd. Daus. Catharine and Elizabeth. Elizabeth to be paid for services for time she has lived with me.
Wits: Everard Foulke and Samuel Myers. Codicil dated Dec. 6, 1808.

Page 13. Nathan Brelsford, Middletown Twp. April 22, 1805. Proved Dec. 25, 1808. Wife Margaret and son Nathan exrs. Son Nathan all Estate, paying legacies to sons Amos and Asa Brelsford, daus. Letitia Watson, Martha Harrison, Sarah Brodnax and Rachel Hellings, and gddau. Jamimah Brelsford.
Wits: William Vansant, Joseph White, William Jones.

Page 15. John Pennington, New Britain Twp. Nov. 10, 1808. Proved Dec. 31, 1808. Wife Margaret. Daniel Carlile and George Burgess exrs. and guardians of ch. Son John Plantation whereon I live, 150 acres and Lot of 11 acres in Plumstead purchased of James Ferguson when 21. Daus. Mary and Martha Pennington, part of Plantation in Warwick purchased of Lewis Lewis on S.E. side of New Road to Doylestown, when 21. Balance of Warwick land to be sold.
Wits: James Ferguson, Joseph Overholt.

Page 18. Benjamin Buckman, Middletown Twp. 12-23-1808. Proved Jan. 8, 1809. Wife Ann interest of ½ of residue of estate. Bro.-in-law Jacob Janney and Henry Atherton exrs. Ch. Mary Gillingham, Richard Buckman, Phebe Buckman, Jesse Buckman and Benjamin Buckman.
Wits: Joseph Hayhurst, David Landis.

Page 20. Thomas Cabe, Bristol Twp. 4-7-1808. Proved Jan. 14, 1809. Wife Rebekah. Sons Elias and Elisha Cabe exrs. Dau. Sarah Johnson 5£, residue to sons Elias and Elisha.
Wits: William Vansant, William Lisom, Samuel Stackhouse.

Page 21. Michael Crowman, Richland Twp., weaver. Aug. 8, 1806. Proved Jan. 30, 1809. Wife Eve. Son Michael and Friend Adam Dimick exrs. Sons Conrad and George all lands. Dau. Barbara wife of Jacob Diehl. Ch. Catharine, Michael, Elizabeth, Barbara, Susanna, Margaret, Maria, Conrad and George. Dau. Maria's son John Gross.
Wits: Philip Wimmer, Adam Hinkle.

Page 25. Henry Meyer, Springfield Twp., Farmer. May 29, 1804. Proved Feb. 15, 1809. Son Peter exr. Dau. Barbara £6 per yr. for keeping house since death of wife. Ch. Catharine, Christel, Peter, William, Anna, Babara and Mary.
Wits: John Smith, Frederick Atherholtz.

Page 26. Mary Meredith, widow of William Meredith, late of Plumstead Twp. dec'd. March 22, 1808. Proved Feb. 18, 1808. Letter of Attorney to Joseph Thomas and Asher Foulke of Plumstead, to collect her share of her husband's estate and in case of her death as exrs. to distribute same to her ch., Rebekah Swager, dau. of her son John Stiver dec'd. to be considered one of her legal heirs and rec. said John Stiver's share.
Wits: Philip Kratz, Abraham Overholtz, Josiah Brown, Henrich Morgan.
Ack. before Ralph Stover, J.P.

Page 28. Gayen Edams, Northampton Twp., yeoman. Feb. 28, 1803. Proved March 1, 1809. James and Gayen Edams, sons of Bro. Hugh, dec'd., exrs. and sole legatees paying interest of ½ of estate to their mother Jane Edams during her life.
Wits: Jno. McMasters, Nathaniel Iwin.

Page 29. Gilliam Cornell, Northampton Twp., "Advanced in age." Jan. 7, 1808. Proved March 13, 1809. Sons James, John and Gilliam Cornell exrs. Son Adrian £50 "having settled him on a Farm purchased of William Thompson." Son Lambert, Negro boy, having settled him on west end of Homestead Farm, to have 103 acres purchased of Barnet Vanhorn. Son James 56 acres which was my Father's, released to me by my bro. Rem Cornell. Son John 100 acres bought of Henry Dyer. Son John 100 acres bought of Henry Dyer. Son Gilliam 103 acres East End of Homestead Farm. Dau. Abigail Du Bois, £480. Dau. Mattie Feaster 30 acres part of lot purchased of Jonathan Thomas. Dau. Jean Vanartsdalen balance of said Tract adj. John Finney and Newtown Road.
Wits: John Finney, Rem Cornell, Simon Vanartsdalen.

Page 31. Nicholas Strouse, Bedminster Twp., yeoman. Dec. 12, 1808. Proved March 14, 1809. Wife Christiana. Conrad Harple and Peter Ott exrs. Ch. Michael, Christopher, John, George, Leonard, Henry, Jacob and Rosina, wife of Michael Lambert.
Wits: Ralph Stover, Abraham Fretz.

Page 33. Benjamin Doan, Upper Makefield Twp. 11-1-1808. Proved March 18, 1809. Codicils 11-7-1808 and 11-11-1808. Son Amos, son-in-law John Tomlinson and cousin Thomas Story exrs. Son Amos Plantation whereon I live, adj. Benjamin Wiggins, Abraham Smith and others, provided my son Ephraim lives with him as he now does. Plantation bought of Isaiah Keith to be sold, proceeds to son Ephraim and daus. Patience Kirk, Cynthia Tomlinson and Mercy Wilson and gdsn. Hugh Worstall, son of dau. Jemimah Worstall. Jonathan Kinsey and Mary Doan "ch. of my dec'd. wife" £150. Residue of Personal Estate to Gdsns. Benjamin Wilson son of dau. Mercy Wilson and Benjamin Doan.
Wits: Edmund Smith, Abram Smith, Ezra Smith, Nathan Bewley.

Page 36. Michael Blyler, Richland Twp., yeoman. Jan. 3, 1809. Proved March 20, 1809. Codicils Jan. 11 & Feb. 27, 1809. Dau. Catharine use of Plantation during life, then to be sold, proceeds to son Michael, dau. Susanna wife of Peter Hager and gdch. Abraham, Susanna and Elizabeth Housekeeper, whom I have brought up from childhood, they to pay the interest to dau. Elizabeth during her life of her husband George Frederick, if she outlive him, then to have principal. Son-in-law Peter Hager and George Haist Exrs.
Wits: Everard and Benjamin Foulke and Amos Richardson.

Page 39. Mary Williams, Buckingham Twp., "of advanced age." Feb. 7, 1797. Proved March 22, 1809. Bro. Benjamin Williams exr. Bro. Benjamin's ch. Frederick, Benjamin, William, Samuel and Anne Williams. Cousins Elizabeth Skinner, wife of Rulin Skinner; Lydia Wood dau. of Fortunatus Wood, Benjamin Wood, son of Fortunatus; Frances Carter, wife of Ebenezer Carter; Mary, wife of Thomas Turner; Lydia, wife of David Burson. Dau. Lydia Burson.
Wits: John Parry, Philip Parry, Benjamin Williams of Nockamixon renounced executorship on account of age and infirmity and they were granted to his gdsn. John Williams.

Page 41. James Snodgrass, New Britain Twp., yeoman. No date. Proved April 1, 1809. Wife Ann Plantation whereon I live and two wood lots during life. Son James and son-in-law John Todd exrs. Ch. Jane Todd, Mary Rich, Ann Harrow, Rebecca Pool and Sarah Grier. Ch. of dau. Margaret Armstrong and David Evans son of dau. Sarah Grier. Son James Plantation after death of wife.
Wits: John Mann, Charles Meredith, Robert Shewell.

Page 43. John Hutchinson, Bristol Boro. 4-17-1800. Proved April 5, 1809. Codicil dated 7-21-1808. Wife Ann and son John exrs. Wife two rooms in house we live in next Charles Bessonetts. Five ch., Rebecca, John, Joseph, Mary and Edward Church.
Wits: Hugh Tombs, Samuel Wright, the latter dec'd. before probate, to co. Isaac Morris, Jona Pursell.

Page 46. Bernardus Kepler, Plumstead Twp., yeoman. June 1, 1807. Proved April 22, 1809. Wife Eve Catharine: sons John and Jacob (exrs.). 104 ¾ acres whereon I live. Dau. Elizabeth. Ch. of dec'd. son Christopher and of dec'd. dau. Susanna.
Wits: Abraham Shatinger, Ralph Stover, Abr'm. F. Stover.

Page 48. John Folwell, Southampton Twp., yeoman. July 5, 1803. Proved Sept. 21, 1808 and April 26, 1809. Wife Ruth extx. who renounced. Nephew Safety Maghee 200 acres in Westmoreland Co. Donation Lands. Nephew John Folwell do. First wife's 3 sisters, Ann Folwell, Sarah Wilson and Rachel Barns. Nieces Frances Dean, Amy White and Mary Stone. Nephew William Watts and Nat. L. Boileau exrs. Dau. Mary.
Wits: William Mitchell.

Page 51. Jonathan Griffith, Richland Twp. 1-13-1809. Proved May 1, 1809. Wife Sarah. Bro. John Griffith and Everard Foulke exrs. Plantation whereon I live, purchased of Joseph R. Jenks, to sons James and Joseph, Joseph a minor.
Wits: Benja. Foulke, Samuel Foulke.

Page 54. Benjamin Palmer, Lower Makefield Twp. March 23, 1801. Proved May 2, 1809. Sons William and Robert exrs. Sons Benjamin, Richard, John, Thomas, William and Robert. Daus. Charlotte Brown, Ann Burrows, Alice Harvey and Pamelia Tomlinson.
Wits: Jame Gilkyson, Thomas Stradling, Phin Thackray.

Page 55. Isaachar Heacock, Bedminster Twp., yeoman. April 11, 1809. Proved May 8, 1809. Wife Susannah. Uncle Jesse Heacock exr. and Guardian of ch. Sons John, Henry (hired to Isaac Cassel), Isaac (hired to Peter Shive).
Wits: Daniel Magul, Everard Foulke.

Page 56. Joseph Wildman, Middletown Twp., "seventy-seven on second of next month."1-22-1807. Proved May 8, 1809. Five sons and two daus. Son Solomon Tract of land where he lives, bought of Daniel Martin. Sons Martin and Joseph Land on easterly side of Newtown and Bristol Road. Daus. Abigail and Rachel £300 a piece. Sons William and Thomas land we live on on westerly side of said Road. Gddau. Elizabeth, dau. of son Solomon. Solomon and William exrs.
Wits: John Warner, John Wildman, Is. Hicks.

Page 58. Benjam Williams, Nockamixon Twp., yeoman. 3-16-1809. Proved May 30, 1809. Sons William and Samuel exrs. Nine ch. of John Iliff, by my dau. Margaret, his late wife, dec'd. £400. Dau. Lydia, wife of David Burson, £400. Dau. Ann wife of Jacob Ritter £500. Son Jeremiah £100. Residue to sons William, Benjamin and Samuel Williams. Bonds given by sons when land was confirmed to them in 1803/4 to be part of Estate.

Wits: Brice Pursell, Charles Williams.

Page 60. Peter Heist, Upper Hanover Twp., Montgomery Co., wheelwright. Jan. 3, 1801. Proved (P.S.?) March 31, 1802. Codicil Feb. 3, 1807. Proved June 2, 1809. Wife Catharine. Son Frederick Heist and son-in-law George Heist exrs. Plantation intended to be conveyed to son Frederick. Four ch., sons Frederick and George, and Daus. Elizabeth Heist and Susannah Hillegas.
Wits: Abr'm. Schultz, George Moch, --- (German).

Page 63. Peter Erhart, Springfield Twp., yeoman. May 4, 1809. Proved June 5, 1809. Wife Cathrina. Peter Lloyd Junr. and Henry Erhart exrs. Ch. Catharina, Magdalena, Susanna, Elizabeth, Christina, Lydia and Maria - residue of estate at 21.
Wits: Valentine App (Opp?), Jacob Hembt, Philip Frankenfield.

Page 65. Margaret Wilson, Falls Twp., "advanced in age." 1st mo., 1808. Proved June 23, 1809. John Brown exr. Step-Dau. Rebekah, wife of Joel Johnson. George Wardell, son of Nephew Daniel Wardell. Margaret Wilson, dau. of Step-son John Wilson. Thomas Wilson, son of Step-son David Wilson.
Wits: William Bunting, Allen Lippincott.

Page 66. David Watson, Falls Twp. 10-20-1808. Proved July 26, 1809. Wife Rachel and cousin John W. Balderston Exrs. Wife 1/3 of Estate. 1/3 of Personal Estate to be put at interest until son David comes of age for education and support of ch. Mary, Betsy, Rachel and David. Estate to said four ch. when of age.
Wits: Tacy Palmer, Hannah Balderston.

Page 69. Esther Kitchin, Solebury Twp. July 8, 1809. Proved Aug. 3, 1809. Oliver Hamton exr. Mother Rebecca Kitchin. Wearing apparel to Elizabeth Reader, Letitia, Sarah, Hannah and Mary Eastburn dau. of Joseph Eastburn and Hannah Dubre. John Kitchin son of John Kitchin dec'd. Bees and Beehives. Charles Kitchin son of David $8. Eleanor Price, little desk and what is contained therein. Residue to David Kitchin, Senr., (with whom I live), Rebecca Eastburn, and Amelia Kitchin.
Wits: Oliver Hamton, Hannah Hamton, Sarah Paxson.

Page 70. George Nase, Rockhill Twp., Blacksmith. Oct. 2, 1801. Proved Aug. 8, 1809. Wife Catharine. Son Michael and son-in-law Jacob Cressman exrs. Sons Jacob, John, Michael and Henry. Daus. Mary, Elizabeth and Margaret.
Wits: Jacob Stout, Abraham Stout, Johannes Fullmer (?).

Page 72. Margaret Shive, Springfield Twp. May 27, 1802. Proved Aug. 14, 1809. Henry Frankenfield exr. Son Lawrence Messer, £100 in continental

money "as he paid his mother in continental money, so he must recieve his share or portion in the same kind of Money." Dau. Maria Fronig, wife of John Foltz, "unto their children Michael and Margaret" £25 "Lett on interest to John Foltz in the year 1774." Adam Frankenfield's ch. by his first wife, John Shopps ch. and Jacob Uhler's ch. remainder of Personal Estate, "if any of gdch., dec'd. having left ch., those ch. to receive parent's share."
Wits: Abraham Frankenfield, Joseph Hess.

Page 74. Peter Henry, Rockhill Twp. May 9, 1800. Proved Aug. 18, 1809. Wife Margaret, ½ of all estate and ½ to Heirs of Bro. Casper Henry dec'd.; viz., Margaret wife of John Swise, Mary wife of Daniel Miller, Sarah wife of Philip Allom and Casper Henry. Wife Margaret and Bro.-in-law John Ratzel exrs.
Wits: Robert Smith, Thomas Armstrong.

Page 75. Christian Fluke, Hilltown Twp., yeoman. Aug. 18, 1809. Proved Sept. 21, 1809. Wife Hannah. Son Philip and son-in-law Daniel Housekeeper exrs. Son Philip Plantation bounded by lands of Christian Eckart, College Land, Leonard Eckart, Michael Kramer, Isaac Cassell, Henry H. Stout and late Valentine Kramer, paying £2400 therefor. Plantation purchased of Henry Drumbore to be sold, Proceeds to sons Philip, Christian and Abraham and daus. Elizabeth, Catharine, Magdalena, Hannah, Barbara and Susanna.
Wits: Isaac Cassel, Christian Eckart, Abraham Stout.

Page 79. Bernd Heller, Senr., Richland Twp. April 6, 1808. Proved Oct. 18, 1809. Wife Arshel. Sons John and Henry exrs. Son Henry Plantation, he to provide for wife and son Michael during life. 2d dau. 2 cows and 2 sheep. 3d dau. do.
Wits: John Hoot, Adam Shearer.

Page 80. Mary Bevihouse, Bedminster Twp., widow. April 6, 1801. Proved Oct. 28, 1809. Martin Fretz of Hilltown Twp. and Isaac Fretz of Tinicum Twp. exrs. Barbara and Mary and other ch. of son Abraham Bevihouse, all estate.
Wits: Christian Hockman (dec'd. before proof) and Abraham Landers.

Page 81. Joseph Large, Buckingham Twp. Oct. 20, 1779. Codicil dated June 21, 1805. Proved Oct. 30, 1809. Wife Milicent. Son Joseph exr. Only son Joseph Plantation of 100 acres and all estate except £500 to dau. Rebekah Large when 21 or mar.
Wits: John Ely, Samuel Fell, Isaiah Jones.

Page 84. Jeremiah Dungan, Northampton Twp., "Far advanced in years." Dec. 8, 1808. Proved Nov. 15, 1809. Son Joshua and sons-in-law Abel Marple, Edward Dyer and Cornelius Dungan exrs. Son Joshua Plantation

on which I dwell; paying £500 to my daus. Elizabeth Dyer, Elenor Marple, Mary Kirk and Nancy Dungan. Gddau. Nancy Cummings 5 acre lot where her father lately lived and proceeds of Goods I gave her mother, son-in-law Edward Dyer to be her guardian during minority. Wearing apparel to son-in-law Cornelius Dungan.
Wits: Garret Dungan, Cornelius Cornell.

Page 86. Sarah Bunting, Falls Twp., late of Bristol. Jan. 25, 1809. Proved Nov. 18, 1809. Son William Bunting exr. Five ch. Ann Pearson, Israel Bunting, Ester Lundy, William Bunting and Sarah Fleming. Gddaus. Sarah Bunting dau. of Israel and Elizabeth and Sarah Bunting dau. of William and Mary.
Wits: Joel Johnson, John Birkey.

Page 87. John Hough, Warwick Twp., yeoman. April 22, 1809. Proved Nov. 30, 1809. Son-in-law John Meredith exr. and trustee for son John Hough and dau. Mary wife of Robert Walker, to hold Real Estate devised to them in trust. Dau. Charlotte wife of John Meredith. Sons Joseph and Thomas already provided for. Gddau. Mary Walker dau. of dau. Mary. Real Estate devised in trust for use of John Hough to go to his ch. by present wife.
Wits: Jacob Shade, Simon Meredith, David Evans.

Page 90. John Guyon, Senr., Bensalem Twp., Farmer. June 15, 1808. Codicil dated July 13, 1808. Proved Dec. 2, 1809. Wife Jane and John McElroy Esq. exrs. Wife all estate for life, then to son John Guyon for life, then to his ch.
Wits: Tyrringham Palmer, Ann Palmer, George Harrison.

Page 93. Margaret Thompson, Moorland Twp., Montgomery Co., widow. Aug. 2, 1809. Proved Dec. 2, 1809. Hiram McNeil of Moorland exr. Tombstones to be procured for graves of late husband William Thompson and for her own. Rebeka wife of Charles Johnson of Moorland. Elizabeth wife of James Vansant of Horsham Twp. Elizabeth, wife of Isaac Ruth of Moorland. Margaret Weir, dau. of Robert Wier, late of Warrington Twp., Bucks Co. Mary wife of William Long of Warminster Twp. Phebe Jones of Moorland. Mary wife of Robert Uers of --- Twp., Bucks Co. Residue to Hiram McNeil for purpose of Repairing School House near County Line in Warrington Twp.
Wits: James Carrell, John Slifer.

Page 95. Henry Wismer, Hilltown Twp., Weaver. Oct. 6, 1806. Proved Dec. 4, 1809. Wife Barbara. Son Abraham of Bedminster Twp. and son-in-law John Funk of Hilltown exrs. "Eleven Heirs" to share equally except son Samuel who has his share, and £20 of dau. Nancy's share to go to her to ch. by her first husband, James and Henry Rute, £10 each.
Wits: Jacob Wismer and Jacob Landes.

Page 97. John Wright, Falls Twp. Dec. 9, 1803. Proved Dec. 16 ,1809. Wife Jane. Sons Samuel, Benjamin, Stephen, and Amos Wright exrs. and sole legatees, they providing for the Widow.
Wits: Reading and Christina Beatty.

Page 98. Giles Craven, Northampton Twp. Dec. 8, 1809. Proved Dec. 29, 1809. Wife Ann. Bro. Thomas Craven and Bro.-in-law John McNair exrs. Sons Samuel, Thomas, John, James and Charles. Dau. Ann Craven.
Wits: Isaac Edwards, George Edwards.

Page 100. William Buckman, (unsigned but acknowledged and accepted by the heirs as a valid instrument). --, ---,1809. Proved Jan. 13, 1810. Wife Hannah. Ch. Abner, Dilworth and William Buckman, Elizabeth wife of John W. Balderston; Lydia wife of John Warner; Sarah and Martha Buckman. Proved by Joseph Taylor, Mary his wife and Mahlon Taylor their son. Jacob Janney and Benjamin Field witnesses to Agreement of heirs.

Page 103. Walter Brewer, Falls Twp., yeoman. 5-3-1806. Proved July 15, 1810. Wife Hannah, "Goods she brought upon her mar. as mentioned in Schedule and Memorandum heretofore made 1-14-1788 and signed by one 2-26-1799 in presence of Isaac Hicks." John Burton and Anthony Burton exr. Estate to Daus. Mary Bunting and Elizabeth Williamson and gddau. Elizabeth Wildman and her ch., after death of wife.
Wits: Joseph Burgess, Stephen Woolston.

Page 105. John Harvey, Bordentown, Burlington Co., N.J. July 3, 1809. Proved Jan. 15, 1810. Wife Harriet and Azariah Hunt of Lamberton exrs. Ch. William and Mary (minors), Kinswoman Elizabeth Wistar wife of John Wistar of Phila. and her ch. Kinsman Thomas Harvey.
Wits: Anthony Taylor, John Sager, Joshua Carman.

Page 107. Elce Vanartsdalen, (widow of Simon Vanartsdalen), Southampton Twp., "of advanced age." Son-in-law Thomas Fenton exr. Daus. Margaret Lefferts, Elizabeth Fenton, Mary Fenton, Cornelia Vandegrift and Jane Praul. Sons Simon, Derrick, Jacob and John Vanartsdalen.
Wits: Daniel Hogeland, Derick K. Hogeland, John McNair.

Page 109. Valentine Huber, Senr., Lower Milford Twp., yeoman. Nov. 7, 1809. Proved Feb. 17, 1810. Sons Valentine and Henry exrs. Sons Valentine, Christian, Peter, John and Henry. Dau. Catharine Shitz. Dau.-in-law Magdalena.
Wits: George Scholl, George Mumbower.

Page 111. William Hicks, Rickland Twp., yeoman. 10-9-1809. Proved Feb. 26, 1810. Son George and son-in-law Nathan Penrose exrs. Sons Jesse,

142

Samuel, George, William and John. Daus. Mary Reimer, Abigail Walton, Margaret Jamison wife of Isaah Jamison and Hannah Penrose. Ch. of dau. Abigail by former husband Nathan Dolby, dec'd. and of dau. Margaret by former husband Aaron Ball, dec'd.
Wits: Everard Foulke and John Smith.

Page 112. Phebe Cadwallader, Upper Makefield. 7-30-1805. Proved Feb. 27, 1810. Sons Cyrus and Jacob Cadwallader exrs. Ch. Rebecca Jarrett, Cyrus, Jacob, Phebe Hough and John Cadwallader. Cyrus' son Jacob, when 21.
Wits: John Stapler, Samuel Austin.

Page 113. Thomas Long, Durham Twp., Esq. Feb. 16, 1810. Proved March 7, 1810. Wife Rachel. Sons William and Morgan and son-in-law Thomas McKeen Esq. exr[s]. Ch. Elizabeth wife of Thomas McKeen Esq. William Long, Eleanor wife of William Stokes, Morgan Long, Rachel wife of John Kelly, Jane wife of Stephen Bennett, Sarah and Mary Long.
Wits: John Reily, Mahlon Welch.

Page 117. Joseph Dungan, Northampton Twp., "advanced in years." Dated May 16, 1809. Proved March 17, 1810. Bro. Jesse Dungan and Nephew Daniel Dungan exrs. Sister-in-law Deborah Dungan. Mahlon and Lewis Dungan and Elizabeth Ryneal, ch. of dec'd. bro. John Dungan. James, Daniel and Sarah Dungan, ch. of dec'd. bro. Thomas Dungan; Nephew Isaac Dungan.
Wits: Benjamin Corson, John Corson, John Corson Jr.

Page 119. Jonathan Roberts, "far advanced in years." Oct. 29, 1809. Proved March 19, 1810. Son Jonathan (exr.) all real Estate. Daus. Hannah wife of Morgan Meredith, Elizabeth wife of Rodman Lovett, Gdch. Nacy [sic] and Jonathan Lovett and Nancy Meredith. Wife Ann.
Wits: William C. Rogers, John Roberts.

Page 120. Arthur Watts, Southampton Twp. Oct. 19, 1809. Proved March 20, 1810. Wife Elizabeth. Son William exr. Wife has separate estate secured by Mar. Contract. Dau. Ann Hart, 35 acres of Farm I live on adj. Charles Vansant and Warminster line; and 15 acres in Warminster adj. Robert Lewis. Son William, Residue of Estate.
Wits: Joshua Jones, Samuel Miles.

Page 122. John Roberts, Village of Newport, Bristol Twp., Miller. Dec. 29, 1809. Proved March 23, 1810. Dau. Mary Roberts extx.
All estate except what came to me from Sister Mary Roberts dec'd. at Duck Creek, that to ch. Sarah, William, Mary and Lydia.
Wits: Henry Mitchell, William Roberts.

Page 123. Rachel Fell, Plumstead Twp. 6-6-1807. Codicil 12-18-1809.

Proved March 23, 1810. Son John exr. Sons John, David and Jonathan. Daus. Martha Schofield and Rachel Speakman. Son Joseph. Ann Fell dau. of son John.
Wits: Jonathan Fell, Rebekah Fell, John Shroger.

Page 125. Samuel Baker, Junr., Upper Makefield Twp. 2-22-1810. Proved March 24, 1810. Thomas Norton exr. Bro. Thomas Savery, interest of all estate for use of Father and Mother, during their lives. At their death to Bro,. John H. Scottergood, Henry Baker Junr., Elizabeth wife of John Brooks and Margaret H. Baker. Sister Margaret H. Baker stock utensils &c. John Hedley $50.00. James Headley, minor, a batteau (n?). Patence Johnson $10 for services during late illness.
Wits: Thomas K. Biles, Robert Beatty, Jolly Longshore.

Page 126. Thomas Stapler, Lower Makefield Twp., Blacksmith. 2-16-1806. Proved March 29, 1810. Sons John, Stephen and Thomas exrs. Son Stephen all estate for life, daus. Esther and Sarah to live with him. At his death to ch. William, John, Thomas, Esther and Sarah. Charles son of son John when 21. Falls Meeting $26. for use of Poor ch.
Wits: Alexander Derbyshire, John Miller, Martin Wildman.

Page 128. Abraham Sutphin, Warminster Twp., yeoman. June 14, 1804. Proved March 31, 1810. Wife Leanah. John McDowell and Jonathan Delaney exrs. Dau. Mary McDowell Lot of land where she lives in Warminster adj. James and Anthony Scout and Charles Vansant. Dau. Ann Delaney land on which I live adj. Harman Vansant and Anthony Scout. Dau. Elizabeth Craven land adj. above.
Wits: Nathaniel Boileau, John Hunter.

Page 132. John Connor, Labourer, Bristol Boro. Nov. 25, 1809. Proved April 10, 1810. Wife Mary sole legatee, she and Joseph Clunn Esq. of Bristol Exrs.
Wits: Job Stackhouse, Hugh Tombs, William Kinsey.

Page 133. Elizabeth Baner. Feb. 11, 1803. Proved April 25, 1810. Joseph Croasdale exr. George Randal £25. Five ch. of Thomas Paxson, Phineas, Sarah, Israel, John and William, £25. Sarah Wynkoop 25£, Son John 10£, 3 daus. Sarah Wynkoop, Esther Leman and Mary Mashall. Residue to George and John Randall, Sarah Wynkoop, Joseph Banes, Ester Leman, James Banes, Mary Marshall and five ch. of Thomas Paxson.
Wits: John Hayhurst, John Gregg.

Page 134. Jacob Beidler, Lower Milfrod Twp., yeoman. May 22, 1801. Proved May 12, 1810. Wife Anna. Son John and son-in-law John Newcomer exrs. Have recently conveyed lands to son Christian. Daus. Anna wife of Henry Overholtzer, Barbara wife of John Newcomer, Elizabeth wife of Christian Swartz, Ch. of dec'd. sons Abraham and

Jacob.
Wits: Jacob Musselman and Francis Shelly.

Page 136. George Adam Kober, Rockhill Twp., yeoman. "Aged and infirm." Dec. 29, 1807. Proved May 15, 1810. Wife Elizabeth. Son Abraham and son-in-law Abraham Keeffer exrs. Son Abraham 115 acres where I live purchased of Emanuel Waner and George Boone and Anthony Cressman. Dau. Christina Nicholas land in Haycock purchased of Jacob Stout. Daus. Barbara and Elizabeth.
Wits: Jacob Creesman, Philip Hetzel, Henry Kerr.

Page 139. Samuel Flack, Buckingham Twp., Carpenter and Joiner. April 14, 1810. Proved May 21, 1810. Wife Mary. Son Samuel exr. if he die John Hough Miller to succeed him. Dau. Sarah wife of John Rodman. Nephew James Anderson, son of sister Sarah. Son Samuel Moiety which belongs to me in 99 ½ acres in Buckinham [sic] adj. Joseph Flack, Ebenezer Conrad and others and residue of estate.
Wits: Robert Flack, Robert Kennedy.

Page 141. Joseph Stradling, Newtown Twp. March 8, 1805. Proved May 21, 1810. Nephews Moses Smith and Joseph Stradling, son of bro. Daniel dec'd. exrs. Sister Sarah Stradling. Nephew Thomas Stradling son of bro. Thomas, dec'd. Niece Sarah Mitchener wife of Robert Mitchener.
Wits: Benjamin Taylor, Thomas Story, Robert Harvey.

Page 143. Joseph Shelly, Lower Milford Twp., Turner. Oct. 31, 1809. Proved May 23, 1810. Wife Elizabeth. Bro. Michael Shelly and Bro.-in-law Jacob Clymer exrs. Real estate to be sold when youngest son comes of age, ch. Henry, Molly and John.
Wits: Francis Shelly, Jacob Shelly.

Page 144. Stephen Twining, Newtown Twp., "far advanced in years." July, -- 1807. Codicil dated May 19, 1808. Do. April 19, 1809. Proved May 28, 1810. Son Elias, part of Plantation "whereon I live" remainder to son Jacob. Dau. Rachel Watson (died before date of second codicil leaving four ch.). Dau. Tamar Palmer (died before date of 1st codicil leaving five ch.), Elias and Jacob exrs. Land in Newtown twp. adj. Jesse Leedom and Beulah Palmer to be sold.
Wits: Thomas Chapman, Isaac Chapman, Ann Chapman.

Page 147. Patrick Hunter, Township and Town of Newtown, late Jailer 75 years of age. April 19, 1810. Proved June 4, 1810. Bro. Andrew Hunter and Enos Morris exrs. 2 Messuages and Lot of Land on which I live adj. Newtown common, Lands of Archibald McCorkle and Thomas Buckman to Daus. Margaret and Sarah. Residue of Estate in six shares, one to dau. Agnes who mar. Aaron Sutfan, deducting advancements. 1/6 to John and Margaret Hunter ch. of son James. 1/6 to dau. Margaret. 1/6

to Catharine Johnson and James Sterling, ch. of dau. Nancy retaining advancement to their mother and father Levi Sterling. 1/6 to dau. Pamela Vanhart deducting account against her husband Michael Vanhart. 1/6 to dau. Sarah. "Make no provision for son William he having gone and left no legal issue in this part of the World."
Wits: Archibald McCorkel, James Raquet.

Page 149. Ebenezer Robinson, late of City of Phila. now of Bristol Borough, Brass maer, advanced in years. 7-7-1809. Proved June 5, 1810. Wife Mary. Phineas Buckley of Bristol and Joshua R. Smith of Burlington Exrs. Wife use of Tenement and Lot on N.W. cor. 5th and Cherry Sts. Phila. Dau. Sarah Lownsbury and ch. of dec'd. dau. Elizabeth Stackhouse.
Wits: Isaac Morris, Jonathan Pursell.

Page 153. Abraham Bennett, Solebury Twp. April 5, 1810. Proved July 26, 1810. Wife ---. Nephew Jonathan Ely exr. Nephews Abraham and Jehu Bennett, sons of Bro. Henry, Abraham and Isaac Bennett sons of bro. Rich-- Jonathan Ely and Courtland Morton. Nieces Martha Morton and Euphemia --- dau. of bro. Richard.
Wits: Oliver Hamton, John Lewis, Joseph Skelton Junr.

Page 155. William Stackhouse, Lower Makefield Twp., yeoman. 4-3-1810. Proved July 26, 1810. Wife Rebecca and Mahlon Kirkbride exrs. Ch. Daniel, Charles, Sarah, Rebecca, Thomas and Letitia. Gdsn. Samuel Stackhouse, £10. Benjamin Price £10.
Wits: John Kirkbride, Joseph Kirkbride.

Page 156. William Hart, late of Newtown, now of Warrington. Aug. 6, 1810. Proved Sept. 13, 1810. Bro. John Hart and Uncle Joseph Hart exrs. Sister Elizabeth wife of Dr. Silas Hough. Apparel of dec'd. wife to be disposed of by friend Nathaniel Irwin. Friends Dr. Wilson and Dr. John Moore, Brooks, &c. 120 acres in Warminster adj. Silas Hart, Joseph Longstreth and others to be sold, proceeds and other estate to sister Elizabeth aforesaid, Sister Euphemia wife of Thomas Humphries and Bro. John Hart. Right in land in Clearfield to same.
Wits: William Hard, Jane Hunt.

Page 157. Rachel Bolton, Southampton Twp. 9-19-1792. Proved June 18, 1810. Sister Margaret Bolton extx. Sister Jemima Tomlinson.
Wits: Jacob Jeanes, Leah Jeanes, Isaiah Jeanes.

Page 157. Daniel Thomas, Plumstead Twp., yeoman. June 19, 1810. Proved Sept. 29, 1810. Wife Sarah. Son-in-law John More and Abraham Chapman Esq. exrs. Daus. Charlotte, wife of John More and Levina Thomas. Gdch. Daniel, Thomas More and Violet More. Land purchased of Jame Ferguson.

146

Wits: George Burges, Samuel Pownall, David Evans.

Page 159. Abigail Wildman, Miccletown. 12-15-1809. Proved Oct. 9, 1810. Bros. William and Thomas Wildman exrs. Niece Ann Wildman, dau. of bro. Solomon Wildman. Ch. of Bros. Martin and Joseph Wildman. Cousin John Simmons. Daniel Saxton.
Wits: Samuel Harvey, Jacob Willard, Henry Atherton Jr.

Page 160. Leonard Hinkle, Richland Twp., yeoman. May 6, 1806. Proved Oct. 20, 1810. Codicil Feb. 13, 1809 and June 6, 1810. Sons John and George exrs. 2d codicil removes John and substitutes son-in-law Joihn Heany as exr. Personal Estate in 12 parts, 1/12 to son John, 1/12 to son Adam, 1/12 to son George, 1/12 to dau. Elizabeth wife of John Solady, 1/12 to dau. Polly wife of John Heany, 1/2 to dau. Christina wife of Leonard Weidener, 1/2 to ch. of dau. Susanna, dec'd., late wife of Henry Trough, 1/12 to dau. Mobelina wife of Joseph Huber, 1/12 to dau. Sarah wife of Jacob Trumbower, 1/12 to dau. Hannah wife of John Weinholt, 1/12 to exrs. for use of dau. Margaret wife of Christian Haus and 1/12 for use of dau. Catharine wife of John Knizely. Son George, Plantation at death of wife ---.
Wits: --- (?), Everard Foulke, Hugh Foulke.

Page 163. Nicholas Vansant, Southampton Twp., yeoman, "Aged and infirm." May 16, 1800. Proved by Common Pleas Court. Verdict May 31, 1800. Confirmed Sept. Term, 1810. Letters Testamentary Nov. 16, 1810 to Nathaniel B. Boileau and Jacob Rhoads. Caveat filed May 4, 1801 by Nathaniel Vansant and Letters pendentelite granted to Exrs. above named June 22, 1801. Wife Mary, use of whole estate for life, then Land and Goods to be sold. Son Nathaniel Vansant £350. Dau. Rebecca Boileau (n?) £450. Abington Pres. Congregation £20. Residue to all Gdch. Nathaniel Boileau, son of Isaac Boileau, and Jacob Rhoads, exrs.
Wits: Thomas Ridge, Joseph Foster, Jacob Lightwood.

Page 164. William Bennett, Northampton Twp., Farmer. "Far advanced in years." Sept. 21, 1791. Proved Nov. 20, 1810. Wife --- and son Barnet and bro. John Bennett exrs. All est. to Barnet after death or mar. of wife.
Wits: John Bennett, William Bennett Junr. Letters to John and Barnet, only.

Page 165. John Conrad, Buckingham Twp. Jan. 2, 1810. Proved Nov. 27, 1810. Wife Martha. Sons John and Ebenezer exrs. Wife and son Joseph to be supported during life. Dau. Ann Bodine $12 per year during life. Residue to ch. Jacob, William, John and Ebenezer Conrad, Mary Doan and Martha Gordon.
Wits: Robert McDowell, William McDowell, John Watson.

Page 166. John Rose, Wrightstown Twp. Nov. 3, 1810. Proved Dec. 3,

1810. Wife Mary. Sons Atkinson and Thomas Rose exrs. Sons Atkinson, Thomas and Jonathan. Daus. Mary, Deborah, Sarah and Phebe. Gdch. John, Thomas, Deborah and Rebecca, ch. of son John. Jonathan Rose Lamb son of dau. Hannah.
Wits: James Closson, Isaac Chapman.

Page 167. Matthew Hughes, Plumstead Twp., yeoman. April 12, 1804. Caveat filed Dec. 13, 1810. Proved Dec. 20, 1810. Son Mathew (caveator) 1/5 of Estate for life then to his ch. 1/5 to ch., of dau. Elizabeth Humphreys, viz. Mary Hughes, Samuel and Matthew Humphries when 21. 1/5 to son Hezekiah Hughes. 1/5 to son Samuel Hughes. Dau. Jane Hughes. Wife Jane. Sons Hezekiah and Samuel exrs.
Wits: Mahlon Carver, Ephraim Shaw, Edward Updegrave.

Page 169. John Connard, Buckingham Twp. Jan . 22, 1810. Proved Nov. 27, 1810 (same as on page 165, being twice recorded). Same is true of John Rose.

Page 170. Rebekah Linton, Newtown Twp. --- 30, 1807. Proved Dec. 6, 1810. Nephews Thomas and James Linton exrs. Sister Elizabeth Chapman. Nephews Thomas, James and William Linton and Niece Sarah Linton ch. of Isaiah Linton. Niece Laura Linton. Sister-in-law Sarah Linton.
Wits: Thomas Chapman, Isaac Chapman.

Page 171. Jacob Gross, Bedminster Twp., Minister of the Gospel at Deep Run. Nov. 26, 1810. Proved Jan. 2, 1811. Wife Mary. Sons Isaac and Christian, exrs. Plantation to be sold and proceeds to all ch. alike.
Wits: Abraham Atherholt, Henry Landis, William Godshalk.

Page 173. Thomas Wildman, Middletown. 12-1-1810. Proved Jan. 22, 1811. Cousin Joshua Knight exr. 1/3 of Estate to wife Mary. 2/3 to sons John and Thomas, when of age.
Wits: John Watson, John Blakey.

Page 173. Christian Trauger, Nockamixon Twp., yeoman. Jan. 31, 1807. Proved Feb. 5, 1811. Wife Barbary. Sons Stophel and Frederick exrs. 6 ch. Frederick, Barbary wife of Peter Lowdenstone, Caty wife of Peter Jacoby, Mary wife of Peter Trough, Stophel and Christian.
Wits: Isaac Burson, Jacob Fulmer, William Burson.

Page 175. John Cornell, Northampton Twp., yeoman. Jan. 23, 1810. Proved Feb. 8, 1811. Sons Gilliam and John exrs. Wife Cornelia. Five sons, Gilliam, John, Wilhelm, Jacob and Isaac. Gilliam 70 acres whereon he lives in Southampton Twp. John 60 acres of Tract I live on, willed me by my father, adj. Daniel Hogeland and others. Wilhelm 60 acres in Southampton, bounded by lands of my bro. Gilliam Cornell, Garret

Krewsen and others. Younger sons Jacob and Isaac, balance of land in Northampton, adj. Rem Cornell, Abraham Harding and others. 2 daus. Elizabeth Feaster and Cornelia Cornell $400.
Wits: John McNair, Leffert Lefferts.

Page 176. Michael Blank, Rockhill Twp. July 29, 1810. Proved March 6, 1811. Wife Elizabeth. Son John and Friend Benjamin Foulke exrs. Ch. John, Catharine, Henry, Motlena, Maricha and Elizabeth. Last four minors. Amos Richardson Guardian.
Wits: John Zeigenfus, Evarard Foulke.

Page 179. Robert Drake, Middletown. 12-27-1810. Proved March 12, 1811. Wife Rachel. Simon Gillam and Thomas Blakey. Apparel to bros. Jacob and John. Daus. Elizabeth (mar.), Ann and Mary.
Wits: John Watson, John Blakey.

Page 179. William Chapman, Wrightstown Twp. -- day of 1803. Codicil Dec. 20, 1804. Proved March 16, 1811. Sons Benjamin and George, exrs. Son Benjamin, Grist & Saw Mills and Eighty acres of Plantation I live on purchased of Robert Kimmens. George balance of Real Estate (in Northampton Twp.), son William £520 he owes and £100 payable to his ch. Jane, David and Aaron. Son David £515(?) he owes; £100 for his ch. Dau. Susanna Buckman £140.
Wits: Joseph Roberts, Isaac Chapman.

Page 181. Catharine Swarts, widow, New Britain Twp., "Far advanced in years." Jan. 31, 1810. Proved April 6, 1811. Sons Andrew and Jacob Swarts exrs. "Whereas I have given my son Abraham Swarts £50 in his lifetime." Son Jacob's dau. Catharine Swarts. Mary, wife of Christian Swarts, son of my son Andrew.. Gdch. Henry and David Swarts son of son Owen. Catharine Zegalor, Jacob, Emanuel, Anna, Elizabeth, Andrew and John Swarts "ears" of son Christian Swarts.
Wits: Valentine Clymer, Christian Swarts.

Page 182. Samuel Weir, New Britain Twp., yeoman. "Advanced in years." Aug. 13, 1803, codicil July 29, 1807. Proved April 22, 1811. Friend and Minister Nathaniel Irwin exr., in case of his death James Findly of New Britain exr. Dau. Mary McKinstry, living with me, her youngest ch. James McKinstry. Son John Weir of New Britain. Son James now living with me. Mary, Samuel, Hannah and Sarah Simpson, ch. of dau. Rebecca Simpson, dec'd. Gdsn. Samuel Weir, son of John.
Wits: William Hines, William Darrah, Priscilla McKinstry, Israel Mullen.

Page 183. Henry Crout, Bedminster Twp. Jan. 29, 1811. Proved April 30, 1811. Son Joseph Crout and Henry Kinsey exrs. Wife Mary, 100 acres of Plantation with stock utensils &c. Eldest son Henry, dau. Catty. Son Joseph, weaver's loom. Other ch.

Wits: John Myer, William Kealer.

Page 184. Joseph Hart, Warminster Twp., yeoman. Dec. 5, 1810. Proved May 2, 1811. Wife Ann, son John and Bro.-in-law William Purdy exrs. William Watts Esq. Guardian of minor ch. Have surveyed Land devised by father and divided into 3 parts for three sons, Thomas, John and Lewis when 21. Daus. Eliza Ann and Clarissa Maria. Land late the property of Dr. William Hart.
Wits: William Hart, John Scott, Silas Hough.

Page 186. Susanna Starr, of Lower Milford Twp., widow of John Starr, dec'd. "Advanced in years." Nov. 13, 1806. Proved Ma-- [May?] 2, 1811. Sons Jacob and Samuel exrs. 2 tracts of land, one in Milford Twp. adj. Peter Funk, John Dreichler, Abraham Taylor and others, 60 acres; the other in Springfield Twp., 25 acres to said sons Jacob and Samuel Five ch., Conrad, John, Anna, Susanna and Hannah $1 each. Daus. Elizabeth and Mary pewter &c.
Wits: David Spinner, John Zuck.

Page 187. Ann Hunt, Wrightstown Twp. April 10, 1811. Proved May 3, 1811. Isaac Chapman exr. Sisters Elizabeth Hunt and Mary Kinsey and Bro. John Hunt.
Wits: Elizabeth Addis, William Atkinson.

Page 188. Thomas Spencer, Northampton Twp., yeoman. 1-31-1811. Proved May 7, 1811. Wife Mary. Sons William, Thomas and Amos Spencer exrs. Thomas, Tenement where I live and 3 tracts of land 63 3/4 acres, adj. Griffith Miles and John Ramsey, 12 acres adj. Bready's and Adams land. Son William, Tenement and tract where he lives adj. Garret Kroesen 75 acres. Son Amos residue of Land &c. Daus. Sarah Hallowell and Mary Walton.
Wits: Griffith Miles, Samuel Hart.

Page 189. Anthony Hartley, "now living in Buckingham Twp." 6-5-1810. Proved May 7, 1811. Stephen Betts and son-in-law John Ely Junr. exrs. Son Thomas Hartley's widow Elizabeth Monagan and his four ch. Amos Hartley, Parmelia, Sarah and Ann. Son Samuel. Son Jonathan's widow Elizabeth and his six ch.Martha, David, Jesse, Jonathan, Aaron and Sarah. "My Children, Samuel H., Mary Rice, Sarah Howard, Elizabeth Blackledge, Rachel Ely, Jane Randolph, Hannah Walker and Amy Hartley."
Wits: Aaron Paxson, Joseph Eastburn, Moses Eastburn.

Page 190. Joseph Townsend, Bedminster Twp., yeoman. Oct. 7, 1810. Proved May 21, 1811. Wife Elizabeth. Son John and Friend Jacob Loux exrs. Son John all estate, he maintaining his mother, and paying Dau. Mary £500.

Wits: John Moyer, Isaac Fretz.

Page 191. John Bebighouse, Bendminster Twp., yeoman. Nov. 30, 1807. Proved May 27, 1811. Son Henry exr. all estate, paying legacies to three dau's. ch., Magdalena's, Maria's and ---. Son Henry and John Heany exrs.
Wits: John Eckle, John Green.

Page 192. Jeremiah Dungan, New Britain Twp. Aug. 5, 1809. Proved June 1, 1811 By Court of Common Pleas. Son Jeremiah Dungan Jr. exr. Dau. Martha Monro.
Wits: Abel Maris, Robert Shewell.

Page 193. William Beans, Buckingham Twp., yeoman. July 17, 1805. Proved June 4, 1811. "Advanced in age." Son Joshua exr. Gddau. Eleanor Beans, her gdmother's chest and six silver teaspoons marked W.S.B. Gdsns. Joseph Beans, Silas Hough Beans and William Beans £50 each. Residue to son Joshua.
Wits: Samuel Fell, Isaiah Jones.

Page 194. Jane Campbell, Nockamixon Twp., widow. June 23, 1808. Proved Feb. 14, 1811. James Smith Esq. and Dau. Margaret Campbell alias Margaret Wallace, Exrs. "Good Friend Francis McHenry, for life, Land leased to him April first last" Frances Gordon, wife of Joseph Gordon to her ch., land in occupancy of said Frances Gordon. Residue to dau. Margaret, aforesaid.
Wits: Jno. Kaufman, Margaret Campbell alias Wallace and Francis McHenry.

Page 195. Henry Johnson, Richland Twp., Nuncupative, Declared May 22, 1811, committed to writing May 24, 1811, "which was two days after his death" by James Green and Benjamin Green. Proved June 18, 1811. Wife Hannah and son Benjamin exrs. Estate to be divided equally among all ch. except son William "having paid a great deal for his studies and he is better off than the rest of the ch."

Page 195. Benjamin Hampton, Wrightstown Twp. 9-6-1807. Proved May 25, 1811. Sons Benjamin and Oliver exrs. Dau. Elizabeth Coleman. Gdsn. John Watson, surveying instruments in his possession. Gdsn. Moses Hampton. Gddau. Sarah Watson.
Wits: Issachar Morris, John Lacey, Jesse Burroughs.

Page 196. Mathew Grier, Plumstead Twp. June 12, 1811. Proved July 6, 1811. Wife Sarah. Bro.-in-law Joseph Greer and Neighbor James Ferguson exrs. Joseph Harris who now lives with me $30. Sister Mary Ferguson silver buckles. Residue to four ch. John, Jane, Jefferson, and Ann, as they arrive at 21 years of age.

Wits: Andrew Dunlap, Joseph Pool.

Page 197. Michael Rapp, Warminster, "considerably advanced in years." 4-22-1806. Proved July 20, 1811. Codicil May 10, 1807. Wife Elizabeth. Seneca Lukens and Isaac Parry of Warminster exrs. Four sons Jacob, George, Samuel and Michael. Son John Land bought of Charles Ingard and Silas Gilbert. Daus. Susannah Rapp, Mary Carr and Elizabeth Carr. Gddau. Sarah Rapp, dau. of Dau. Susannah.
Wits: Jesse Banes, Isaac Shoemaker, Ann Howley. Codicil, Gdsns. William and Joseph Carr.

Page 199. John Ely, Solebury, Nuncupative. 7 mo.-6-1811. Proved July 25, 1811. Son Asher and Nephew Jonathan Ely exrs. Wife ---, Daus. Sarah and Merab. Son Samuel "other five ch." Asher, Phineas, Hugh, Mary and Elizabeth. Gdsn. Phineas Elys.
Wits: Oliver Hampton, Mercy Philips (d. 7 mo. 6th, 1811).

Page 200. Joseph Hutchinson, Bristol Boro., Farmer. March 8, 1811. Proved July 25, 1811. Bro. John Hutchinson exr. Mother Ann Hutchinson all estate for life, then to niece Ann Kraft, dau. of Michael Kraft and only sister Mary Kraft, Jonathan Pursell to be her guardian.
Wits: Phineas Buckley, Isaac Morris, John Reed.

Page 200. John Wilson, Buckingham Twp. May 9, 1811. Proved Aug. 14, 1811. Wife Mary. Sons-in-law Robert Thompson, John Thompson and Thomas Thompson exrs. Daus. Jane, Betsy, Polly and Sally.
Wits: Thomas Smith, John Simpson.

Page 201. Henry Blyler, Milford Twp., yeoman. June 10, 1808. Proved Aug. 26, 1811. Wife Susan. Sons Daniel and Lazarus exrs. Ch. Peter, dec'd. (his ch. to have their fa's. share), Daniel, Abraham, Jacob, David dec'd. (his ch.), Henry, John, Hannah, Lazarus and Anna Mary wife of George Wise.
Wits: David Spinner, Peter Blyler.

Page 203. Abraham Larue, Bensalem Twp. 8-1-1811. Proved Aug. 30, 1811. Wife Elizabeth. Son Joshua Larue and Ezra Townsend exrs. Dau. Rebecca Green, interest of $100 during life of her husband, principal thereof at his death. Son Emanuel $4 if he return and demand it, his sons Emanuel and Isaac $10 each at 21. Ch. of dec'd. dau. Rachel Ridge. Son Jacob, Dwelling House and land in Muney Twp., Lycoming Co., purchased of John Burrowes, and six acres of land in Bensalem Twp. adj. Mahlon Hutchinson. Residue to son Joshua.
Wits: Jesse James, Robert Searl, Gace Praul.

Page 204. Lambert Vandyke, Warminster Twp., yeoman. Aug. 18, 1810. Proved Sept. 20, 1811. Son Joseph Vandyke exr. Plantation adj. Joshua

Walton, Gideon Prior, Charles Terry, Harman Yerkes, Nathan Beans and Joseph Hart, and all Personal Estate, paying son Jonathan 300£, and dau. Sarah wife of James Carroll £200.
Wits: Joseph Hart, Mary Hart, Thomas Coughlin.

Page 205. Robert Jamison, "Upper Side of Warwick Twp., yeoman. Sept. 29, 1807. Proved Oct. 3, 1811. Wife Hannah. Sons John and James exrs. "Sons Robert and William sons-in-law Daniel Craig and James Means, already provided for". All estate to sons John and James, paying wife annuity &c.
Wits: John Kerr, Andrew Long, William Lee.

Page 205. William Kendall, Springfield Twp. May 7, 1811. Proved Oct. 11, 1811. Wife Catharine and son John exrs. Seven ch. John, Catharine, Susanna, Jacob, Peter, Elizabeth and Joseph.
Wits: William Gruber, Conrad Groman.

Page 206. Barbara High, Hilltown Twp. June 24, 1811. Proved Oct. 26, 1811. Martin Fretz Exr. "Husband David High, to be full heir of legusees [sic] from first husband Daniel Bechtel, rec'd., and yet remaining in hands of Christian Beery." Bro.-in-law Joseph Bechtel £180. Bro. Valentine Kratz, £100.
Wits: Abraham Moyer, John Fretz.

Page 206. Benjamin Courson, Wrightstown Twp. Sept. ---, 1811. Proved Oct. 11, 1811. Sons Richard and Amos and Son-in-law Issachar Morris, exrs. Plantation of 159 acres "Whereon I live" in Wrightstown and Upper Makefield to be sold. Proceeds to ch. Benjamin, Joseph, Thomas, Richard, Mary, Sarah, Rachel, and Elizabeth, £100 each. Joshua £150. Jane and Amos £300.
Wits: Isaac Chapman, Benjamin Hamton.

Page 207. Peter Smith, Springfield Twp., yeoman. Aug. 1, 1811. Proved Oct. 13, 1811. Wife Catharine. House and Lot of 7 acres and Personal Estate for life. Then to 7 ch. John, Catharine, Susanna, Jacob, Peter, Elizabeth and Joseph. Wife and son John exrs.
Wits: William Gruber, Conrad Groman.

Page 209. Zachariah Lewis, Warrington Twp., yeoman. June 4, 1809. Proved by C. P. Court May 31, 1811. Issue from Register's Court Nov. 1809. Wife Sarah £18 per year cow &c. Son Thomas Lewis and James Scout exrs. Dau. Rachel Heaton's ch. £100. Dau. Sarah Kelly's ch. £130. Dau. Fanny Scout's ch. £100. Anna Thompson's ch. £100. Dau. Rebecca Roberts ch. £130. Son Thomas 100 acres I live on for life then to his ch.
Wits: Robert Shewell and Eliza Carrie, (Robert Thompson Caveator).

Page 210. Daniel Hunt, Northampton Twp. 11-1-1811. Proved Nov. 13,

1811. Wife Meribah and James Dungan exrs. Wife 3/4 of Estate, son John 1/4.
Wits: Thomas Story, Thomas Briggs.

Page 211. James Stokes, Wrightstown Twp. "far advanced in age." 10-24-1811. Proved Nov. 21, 1811. Son-in-law Elias Twining and Friend Edward Buckman exrs. Dau. Phebe, wife of John Atkinson 5 acres of Plantation in Catawysse Twp., Northumberland Co. Balance of 90 acres adj. Samuel Shakespeare, Edward Barrel, William P. Brady and others and lot of land where I live adj. Isaac Wilson, Jno. Chapman and Noah Lambert to be sold. Son John "all he owes." Gddaus. Ann and Sarah Twining £5 each. Gddau. Hannah Stokes bureau that was dau. Sarah's. Residue to dau. Jane Stokes.
Wits: Isaac Wilson, John Chapman.

Page 212. Isaac Gale, Bristol Twp. Nov. 5, 1811. Proved Dec. 2, 1811. Wife Abigail, Personal Estate for life then to her ch. Aso [s] use of House and Lands for life, then to be sold by son William Gale, proceeds to "sons and daus." Kinsman John Gosline of Bristol exr.
Wits: William Howell, Amos Gregg.

Page 212. Ulrich Stover, Haycock Twp., Miller. Oct. 30, 1811. Proved Dec. 3, 1811. Wife Barbara "New House erected on Premises where I live" £48 per year &c. for life. Sons Henry and Jacob exrs. Son Henry 214 acres in Bedminister Twp. whereon he lives at valuation of £2140 he retaining £800. Son Jacob 155 acres with Mill thereon where I now live in Haycock Twp. and Bedminster aforesaid and wood Lots for 2500£, retaining £800. Residue to sons Henry and Jacob, ch. of dau. Mary dec'd. and ch. of son Joseph dec'd. Henry and Jacob exrs.
Wits: Michael Young and Joseph Fretz.

Page 214. Mary Clymer, Lower Milford Twp., widow of Christian Clymer, dec'd. Son-in-law Henry Beitteler, exr. Ch. Jacob, Ester wife of Adam Shitz. Ch. of son Christian Clymer dec'd. Isaac, Anna wife of Henry Louder, Gerhard Clymer, Mally wife of Henry Beitteler, John, David and Samuel Clymer.
Wits: David Musselman, Daniel Cooper.

Page 215. James Oliver, Warrington Twp. Jan. 3, 1811. Proved Dec. 6, 1811. Wife Mary and dau. Mary Oliver extx. Dau. Isabel and her husband[,] 3 younger daus. Ann, Mary and Rachel.
Wits: Samuel Weir, William Whittingham.

Page 216. Isaac Burson, Springfield Twp. Nov. 13, 1811. Proved Dec. 6, 1811. Wife Elizabeth. Sons John and James exrs. Ch. James, William, Rachel Meredith, John, Jane and Eliza Burson.
Wits: John W. Burson, Joseph Afflerbach.

154

Page 217. Ralph Stover, Bedminster Twp. Oct. 18, 1811. Proved Dec. 9, 1811. Wife Catharine. Son Abraham and neighbor John Meyer of Tinicum exrs. "Legacy devised wife by her father at death of her mother." Son Abraham 151 acres in Bedminster and Tinicum and 13 Acres in Haycock. Son William 127 Acres and 16 Acres purchased of Francis Erwin, when of age. Five ch. Abraham, Mary wife of Christian Fretz, Elizabeth wife of Philip Fretz, Ann and William.
Wits: George Burgess, Abraham Fretz.

Page 220. Julianna Dunlap, wife of James Dunlap, of Buckingham Twp. Nuncupative. Declared in presence of Nathaniel Shewell and Andrew Dunlap, Nov. 2, 1811. Proved Dec. 13, 1811. "Her share of Painswick Plantation, bequeathed by her gdfather Walter Shewell "in New Britain Twp. now in tenure of Robert Shewell, Esq., to be enjoyed by her husband James Dunlap, during his life for the purpose of bringing up her ch."

Page 220. Joseph Thomas, Hilltown Twp. Sept. 23, 1808. Proved Dec. 16, 1811. Wife Sarah and son Nathan, Nurseries of Fruit Trees now on Plantation. Sons Ephraim and Nathan exrs. Plantation to Ephraim, Nathan and Abner. Dau. Eleanor Williams and Gddau. Sarah Williams. Dau. Sarah when 18.
Wits: John Beringer, John Mathias, John Pugh, John Pugh Esq. Guardian of dau. Sarah.

Page 223. Amos Austin Hughes, Buckingham Twp. Oct. 21, 1811. Proved Dec. 21, 1811. Samuel Gillingham, Samuel Ely and Thomas Ely exrs. "All my Real Estate shall remain forever for use of a free school." Friends John Ely, Nicholas Austin, John Watson Junr., William Ely, Thomas Bye, John Wilson M.D., Samuel Johnson, Joseph Shaw, Isaiah Jones, Joshua Anderson, Joseph Watson and Stephen Wilson to apply to Legislature for incorporation Charter establishing them and their successors as "The Trustees and Directors of the Hughesian Free School" to establish a school for education of "Poor ch. or other persons residing in Buckingham." Housekeeper Mary Paxson use and profits of Real Estate for life. Hannah wife of John Ely $2000. Nicholas Austin $2000. Elizabeth wife of William Harrold interest of $2000. Sarah wife of Isaac Bennett $500. Samuel Ely $800., his bro. Thoams $400. Amos son of Isaac Bennett $300, his sister Lucretia Bennett $200. Samuel and George Hughes each $50. Amos Hughes Large, Amos Hughes Dean and Amos Hughes Roberts each $30. Joseph Broadhurst wearing apparel. His sister Rachel Broadhurst Furniture &c. Residue to Free School. Plantation lately sold to Conrad Carpenter and Casper Heft of Germantown to be conveyed to them by exrs.
Wits: Cornelius Vanhorn, John Watson Junr., Martha Hambleton Junr.

Page 226. Joseph Thomas Esq., Plumstead Twp., yeoman. Declard Dec.

2, 1811, and written by David Evans, but testator d. the 4th instant without signing. Son John G. Thomas exr. Dau. Martha wife of John Kerr, yeoman, interest of $2000. Son John G. Plantation "whereon I live." Tract in Northampton and Luzerne Cos. to son John G. Thomas and Dau. Ann wife of William Bryan. Ack. by John Kerr, Martha Kerr, William and Ann Chapman.

Page 227. George Bennett, Tinicum Twp., yeoman. May 13, 1811. Proved Jan. 2, 1812. Wife Charity. Sons Stephen and George exrs. Deed to son Isaac for land in Westmoreland Co. to be delivered to him. Sons Gershom, John, Isaac, Stephen and George. Daus. Mary, Elizabeth, Anne, Sarah, Mercy and Hannah.
Wits: Joseph Nash, Henry Overholt, Merrick Reeder.

Page 228. Isaac Thackray, Middletown, "Pretty far advanced in years." 9-4-1802. Codicil 2-23-1811. Proved Jan. 6, 1812. Benjamin Buckman and William Blakey exrs. Former dec'd. before date of codicil. Sarah Thackray, widow of nephew Amos Thackray and her 3 ch. Isaac, Rebecca and Ruth Thackray. Nephews Joshua and Phineas Thackray. Bro. Ezer and sister Ruth Thackray. Bro. Joseph dec'd. Codicil "Ezer and several others dec'd. since date of will." Preparative Meeting of Middletown.
Wits: Joseph Hayhurst, Henry Atherton Junr., Amos Bailey, Robert Croasdale.

Page 229. John Hayhurst, Upper Makefield Twp. 5-29-1804. Codicil 11-12-1805. Do. 6-21-1810. Proved Jan. 6, 1812. Wife Mary. Son Benajah exr. Sons Benajah and Bazaleel. Daus. Rachel Smith, Marjory Smith, Elizabeth Knowles, and Ruth Hayhurst.
Wits: Benjamin Wiggins, Joseph Wiggins, John Tomlinson.
1st Codicil: Gdsns. John and Ely Smith, sons of Joseph Smith. Thomas Story one of exrs. 2d. Cod.
Wits: Edmund Smith and Benjamin Smith.

Page 232. Magdalena Wenig, widow of Henry Wenig, Milford Twp. May 1, 1808. Proved Jan. 6, 1812. David Spinner Esq. exr. Dau. Gertrude Wenig debt owing by John Bechtel. Son-in-law Jacob Wenig. Daus. Magdalena Wenig, Christiana, wife of Thomas Boyer. Gdsns. John and Henry Walman. Henry, Eve and Jacob, ch. of dau. Anna Mary dec'd. Dau. Susan wife of John Fricke's ch. Mary, Henry, Gertrude and George.
Wits: Isaac Shelly, John Eckerman.

Page 232. William Lee, Upper Makefield Twp. 4-8-1801. Proved Jan. 6, 1812. Wife Hannah. Friend Edward Smith exr. Sons Ralph and William. Dau.-in-law Mary Lee. Dau. Esther Twining's dau. Esther Harvey. William Twining son of dau. Mary Twining. Gdsns. Lee Collins and Lee Barcroft. Daus. Hannah, Sarah, Elizabeth, Lydia and Rebekah.
Wits: James Briggs, Benjamin Smith.

Page 233. Elizabeth Feaster, Northampton Twp. Jan. 4, 1810. Proved Jan. 13, 1812. Adrian Cornell exr. Son Aaron Linton. Gddaus. Sarah Martin, Elizabeth Martin and Mary Belford. Ch. of Gdsn. Mordecai Martin.
Wits: Aaron Feaster, James Cornell.

Page 234. Adam Weaver, Bensalem Twp., "Advanced in years." Jan. 12, 1802. Proved Jan. 13, 1812. Wife Christiana and 3 sons-in-law John Vandegrift, Matthew Rue and Lewis Rue exrs. Wife all estate for life except Smith tools and iron. Dau. Anna Vandegrift land bought of Joseph Allen 20 acres bounded by lands of Richard Rue, Joseph Leverns and Samuel Doan. To Adam, Richard, Lewis, Barsheba, Elizabeth, Christiana, Elijah and Jacob Rue, ch. of dec'd. dau. Mary Rue, 40 acres bounded by lands of Joshua Headley and land of their father Martha Rue to be under care of my son-in-law, the aforesaid Matthew Rue. Dau. Elizabeth Rue, "Land I live on" 38 acres, bounded by lands of Giles Knight, Sarah Paxson and Nicholas Johnson. Money put into my hands by bro. Peter Weaver for use of ch. of bro. Michael's ch. to be paid to his 3 ch., David, John and Elizabeth.
Wits: Jonathan Paul, Jno. Paxson, Samuel Allen.

Page 235. John Simpson, Union Twp., Miami Co., Ohio. 4-18-1811. Proved in Ohio Sept. 16, 1811. Wife --- extx. Sons David and John exrs. Wife all estate in Ohio. "My affairs in Bucks Co. must be changed." Sons David and John to settle them. Daus. Hannah Shinn and Ruth Hilburn to have 50 acres of land in "Salisbury" Twp., between John Simpsons and William Neeley's land. Son James Simpson.
Wits: David Mote, Francis Jones.

Page 236. Esther Smith, Plumstead Twp. 11-7-1806. Proved Jan. 23, 1812. Bro. William Smith exr. Sister Elizabeth Shaw £100. Half-sister Mercy McCalla and her dau. Eliza McCalla.
Wits: James Davison, Joseph Stradling.

Page 237. Gane [sic Jane?] Burley, Upper Makefield Twp., widow. Nov. 18, 1809. Proved Jan. 28, 1812. Dau. Phebe Burley and son-in-law John Slack exrs. Sons John, Joshua and David. Daus. Hannah, Elizabeth, Rachel, Jane, Phebe, Sarah and Mary. Dau. Hannah's son Absalom Burley.
Wits: Sarah C. Linton, Is. Hicks.

Page 238. Thomas Paxson, Solebury Twp. 9-14-1811. Proved Feb. 17, 1812. Son George Paxson, son-in-law William Hough and Friend John Armitage exrs. Sons George, James, Stacy and Thomas. Daus. Amy Hough, Mary Paxson, Jane Broadhurst. Gdch. Thomas Paxson Broadhurst, Mary Ely and Thomas and Ahaz Paxson, sons of son James.
Wits: Elias Paxson, Henry Armitage, John Armitage.

Page 238. Christian Atherholt, New Britain Twp., yeoman. Feb. 1, 1806. Proved Feb. 25, 1812. Son Christian exr. Son Frederick's widow and ten ch., each one English shilling. Daus. Willimina, Lovey and Catharine. Wits: David Ruth, Andrew Trewig.

Page 239. Philip Muth, Bedminster Twp., yeoman, "Aged." June 1, 1808. Proved Jan. 15, 1812. Wife Barbara. Son John Muth and son-in-law Jacob Shepherd exrs. Sons Philip, John and Andrew. Daus. Elizabeth, Margaret, Molly, Magdalena, Catharine and Susanna. Philip's share to be held for his use by wife during her life, then by son John and John Fluke. Wits: Connard Mitman, John Fluck, Philip Fluck.

Page 241. Martha Heacock, Richland Twp. Nov. 10, 1807. Proved March 2, 1812. Bro. Nathan Heacock and Benjamin Foulke. Mother Sarah Heacock. Dau. Edith, a minor. Sisters Rosemond, Mary, Hannah and Jane. Sarah, Mary and Tacey Heacock, daus. of bro. Issachar, dec'd. Wits: Jesse Heacock, Everard Foulke.

Page 241. Henry Funk, Springfield Twp., Miller. Feb. 7, 1812. Proved March 2, 1812. Wife Barbary. Son Ralph and John W. Burson of Springfield exrs. Land to be divided between four sons, Abraham, Ralph, Henry and Cauffman Funk. Daus. Elizabeth, Mary and Sarah, Land partly in Lower Laueon Twp., Northampton County, adj. Jacob Kooker, Jacob Rose, Jacob Funk, Jacob Rensimer, Conrad Shoemaker, Andrew Overpeck and Kook's Creek. Plantation he lives on and grist mill to son Henry. Wits: Jacob Kooker and William Long.

Page 244. Cato Adams, Bristol Twp. 12-16-1810. Proved March 5, 1812. Anthony Burton exr. Daus. Margaret Cummings and Esther Matlock. Gdsn. Adam Matlock. Son Adam Adams, "all my First day Clothes." £5 to Friends Mtg. at Middletown for keeping in repair Burial ground appropriated to interments of black people. Wits: John Burton Jr., Reading Beatty.

Page 245. John Lutz, Bedminster Twp., Taylor, "Old and weakly." June 10, 1811. Proved March 4, 1812. Wife Magdalina. Son-in-law Andrew Crowthamel exr. Son Frederick, Plantation 130 acres. Wits: William McNeeley, Henry Bebighaus.

Page 246. Nathaniel Irwin, Bucks Co., Clerk. March 1, 1812. Proved March 12, 1812. Wife Priscilla, Bank and Insurance stock that was hers before mar. Samuel Mann of Horsham and Samuel Hart of Warwick exrs. Dau. Mary Hart dec'd. Son Henry's dau. Mary Irwin. "Other ch. of first wife, I leave my blessing and nothing more." Sister Jane, wife of John McEacham, now or late of Spencertown, N.Y. 4 shares of Bank of Penna. to be held by Trustees of Pres. Church of Warwick for her use. Niece Mary Park, formerly Clingan, wife of James

Park. Apprentices Thomas Richards, George Grant, Mary Day and Mary Foster. Schedule of son Henry's debts to be paid, viz., John Bradshaw, Thomas Lunn. Mary Rees, Isabella Wallace, John Carr, David Dougherty, Hugh McGooden, William Garges, Martha Brady and Dr. John Jones. William Mearns, Esq. of Warwick Guardian of minor legatees, John Harvey Junr. to succeed him in case of death.
Wtis: John Long, Jesse Rubinkam.

Page 250. Issachar Morris, Wrightstown Twp. Aug. 24, 1810. Proved March 24, 1812. Wife Hannah. Son Issachar and Isaac Chapman exrs. Son Issachar 125 Acres whereon I live, bought of Joseph Hamton. Son Joseph 38 acres purchased of Benjamin and George Chapman. Plantation on which son-in-law John Trego lives to be sold. Daus. Elizabeth Wharton, Mary Trego and Hannah Morris. Gdsns. Seth, David and Morris Davis.
Wits: Thomas Warner and Letitia Briggs.

Page 251. Elizabeth Fell, widow of John Fell, late of Bucks Co. 10-4-1796. Proved March 30, 1812. Son Jonathan Fell, exr. Ch. Jonathan and John Fell, Ann widow of Joseph Chapman, Jane wife of Moses Quinby, Alice wife of Ezra Comfort, Elizabeth wife of John Wilson and Watson Fell. David and John Wilson sons of dau. Sarah dec'd. Elizabeth dau. of son Thomas Fell. Elizabeth dau. of Alice Comfort. Sarah and Ann Chapman, daus. of dau. Elizabeth.
Wits: John Watson, Thomas Watson, Mary Watson. Codicil 8-2-1799, Warwick Twp.
Wits: Hannah Kirkbride, Ezra Fell. Dau. Jane Quinby's share to go to her surviving ch.

Page 253. John Bergstresser, Tinicum Twp. Dec. 1, 1811. Proved April 3, 1812. Wife Anna. Son George and George Wyker exrs. Sons Jacob, John, Philip, Frederick, George, Henry, Samuel and Joseph. Daus. Susanna, Catharine, Elizabeth and Anne. "Several of older ch. mar." Land adj. John Root and Jacob Fulmer.
Wits: Joseph Heany, John Ruth.

Page 254. John Carr, Warwick Twp., yeoman. March 25, 1812. Proved April 11, 1812. Wife Jane. Son William and Samuel Hart, Surveyor, exrs. Son Joseph ½ of Plantation whereon I dwell, adj. Robert Ramsey and Francis Baird's subject to payment of $20 annually to widow. Son William balance of Plantation. Daus. Isabella, Elizabeth, Maria, Jane and Pricilla. Francis Baird, Guardian.
Wits: Josiah Hart, James Hart.

Page 256. Gaun McGraudy, Warwick Twp. April 13, 1812. Proved May 1, 1812. Wife Mary. Sons Robert and Thomas exrs. Son Samuel. Daus. Margaret wife of Andrew Mearns and Isabell a wife of John Opdyke.
Wits: John Magrady and Samuel Hart.

Page 257. Jacob Overholt, Bedminster Twp., yeoman. June 8, 1805. Proved May 2, 1812. Son Jacob Jr. and Nephew Abraham Culp, son of David Culp, dec'd., exrs. Son Jacob 152 Acres I live on, he paying out to daus. Barbara, Magdalena, Ester and Elziabeth.
Wit: Joseph Landes.

Page 258. Anthony Wyker, Tinicum. April 11, 1812. Proved May 7, 1812. Bros. George and Abraham Wyker exrs. Mother Susanna Wyker. Dec'd. father Nicholas Wyker. Bros. Henry, George and Abraham.
Wits: Jesse Dungan, George Kealer.

Page 259. Jesse Johnson, Bristol Twp. May 18, 1812. Wife Catharine and Nephew Jesse Johnson Jr., son of bro. Isaac, exrs. and sole legatees.
Wits: Henry Tomlinson and Caleb Butcher.

Page 260. John Gillingham, Buckingham Twp., yeoman, "Advanced in age." 9-17-1804. Proved May 19, 1812. Son Samuel exr. Sons Samuel, John and Benjamin. Daus. Mary wife of George Kinsey; Sarah Rich widow of Benjamin Rich and Esther Gillingham. Gddau. Mary Gillingham, dau. of son Joseph dec'd. Bible printed by Isaac Collins.
Wits: Robert Smith, Jonathan Paste.

Page 261. Jesse Walton, Warminster Twp., yeoman. April 25, 1812. Proved May 13, 1812. John Spencer of Warminster, yeoman, exr. Sons Abraham and Isaac, all estate.
Wits: Stephen Murray, Thomas Coughlin.

Page 261. Jacob Gayman, Springfield Twp. May 16, 1811. Proved May 19, 1812. Wife Eve, sons Jacob and Abraham and son-in-law Jacob Angeny exrs. Son Jacob 140 acres whereon he lives adj. Peter Rute and John Garis, and 12 acres in Northampton Co. adj. Andrew Stahlnecker and John Rodrock. Son Abraham 150 acres adj. John Lester, Andrew Trewig and Christian and Jacob Gross. Estate to ch. Jacob, Abraham, Benjamin, Anna and Barbara. Shares of Anna and Benjamin to be held in trust during their lives by Jacob Sleiffer, Abraham Yoder, Abraham Myer, Elders of Springfield Menonist Society. Anna to live with her mother.
Wits: Abraham Funk, Henry Funk.

Page 265. Sarah Smith, widow of Timothy Smith, dec'd., Buckingham Twp. 6 mo.-3-1799. Proved May 19, 1812. Son Robert Smith exr. Sons Robert and Joseph Smith. Daus. Phebe, Sarah Atkinson, Mary Beans and Jane Smith.
Wits: Rebecca Smith (now R. Ely), Mary Canby alias Smith.

Page 266. Jacob Vansant, Southampton Twp., yeoman. May 1, 1807. Proved May 24, 1812. Son-in-law Jacob Rhoads and Samuel Dickson exrs. Dau. Elizabeth Vansant 90 acres of Plantation devised me by Will of my

father Jacob Vansant. Gdsn. Samuel Dickson, son of dau. Jane late wife of Samuel Dickson Sr. balance thereof 93 Acres. Dau. Margaret wife of Jacob Rhoads 52 acres in Byberry, bought of estate of Thomas Groom and £400.
Wits: Jospeh R. Dickson, Michael Stevens.

Page 267. John Kratz, Hilltown Twp., yeoman, Aged. May 3, 1801. Codicil May 8, 1808. Proved June 1, 1812. Wife Anne. Son Jacob Kratz and "My son John Hoch (alias High)" exrs. Son Jacob 150 acres I live on, bounded by lands of Samuel Mayer, George Seibel, John Funk, Jacob Lederach and others. Sons Christian, Valentine and Jacob. Daus. Anne, Barbara and Magdalena. Barbara d. before Testator without issue.
Wits: Martin Fretz, Joseph Moyer.

Page 269. John Benner, Hilltown Twp., Miller. Nov. 23, 1811. Proved June 3, 1812. Wife Mary Magdalena. Sons John and Adam Benner exrs. Lands and Grist Mill in Rockhill and Hilltown Twp. to be sold. Wife ⅓ proceeds. Gddau. Eleanor Appenzeller £50. Residue to all ch. equally, except $75 of Dau. Elizabeth's share to go to her dau. Eleanor Appenzeller, and son Conrad's share to be held by exrs. during his life and paid to his ch.
Wits: Jacob Stout, Abr'm. Stout Jr.

Page 271. William Smith, Solebury Twp. Aug. 19, 1810. Proved May 11, 1812. Codicil dated Nov. 8, 1811. Wife Sarah. Son William and Isaac Chapman exrs. Wife has Plantation given her by her father My 140 Acres on which I live to be sold, proceeds to Graddau. Mary Smith Watts and ch. William, Sarah, Esther, Jacob, Amos, Rebekah, Jane and John.
Wits: Thomas Cooper, David Thomas, John Vandycke.

Page 272. Peter Zuck, Lower Milford Twp., yeoman. Nov. 10, 1809. Proved June 15, 1812. Wife Margaret. Son John and Friend Abraham Taylor exrs. Daus. Mary, Elizabeth and Susan.
Wits: Samuel Harwick and George Walter.

Page 273. Edward Dyer, Northampton Twp. (wife Charity all estate for life). Dec. 7, 1805. Codicil Jan. 8, 1807. Do. June 2, 1811. Proved June 20, 1812. Joseph Hayhurst of Middletown and Joseph Dyer of Montgomery Co. exrs. 1st codicil removes Joseph Dyer and substitutes son Edward Dyer; 2nd codicil substitutes David Knight for Joseph Hayhurst as exr. Son Edward and gdch. Edward, Joseph, Deborah, and Mary Dyer.
Wits: Jonathan Wynkoop, John Lefferts, Henry Wynkoop, Derick Kroesen, John Vandegrift.

Page 274. Sidney Pickering, Solebury Twp., widow. 6-10-1800. Proved June 24, 1812. Son Solomon Wright exr. Sons John, James, Edward and Nathan Wright. Daus. Ruth Fenton and Mary Adams. Gddaus. Sidney and

Sarah Wright daus. of son Solomon Wright. Dau.-in-law Rachel Wright.
Wits: John Pickering and William Doan. William Doan had "left this part
of the Country," before proof of will.

Page 275. John Kroesen, Northampton Twp. Nov. 1, 1806. Codicil Aug.
14, 1809. Proved June 29, 1812. Wife Jean. Son Garret and son-in-law
James Craven exrs. Ch. Garret, David, Derick, John, Margaret,
Areyantye, Sarah and Elizabeth. Sons-in-law Thomas Dungan and James
Craven. Land adj. Nathan Beans and Garret Vanartsdalen. Elizabeth
Vansant, dau. of dau. Elizabeth.
Wits: Elizabeth Beans, Evan Beans, Joseph Hart.

Page 278. Gerardus Wynkoop, Northampton Twp. March 26, 1811.
Proved June 30, 1812. Sons Isaac and David exrs. Sons Isaac, John,
Garret, Matthew, David and William. Daus. Susanna wife of David Wiley
and Elizabeth wife of Stephen Rose. Son Garrett, dec'd. Son James'
wife Catharine.
Wits: Leffert Lefferts and John Courson.

Page 280. Abraham Stout, Rockhill Twp., yeoman, "Aged." May 14, 1812.
Proved July 11, 1812. Sons Jacob and Abraham exrs. Dau. Hannah
Worman, a widow. Son Henry H. Stout 214 Acres in Brush Valley
formerly in Northumberland Co. now Centre Co. bounded by lands of
Henry Bolanger and Andrew Moore. Son Abraham 80 acres of Plantation
I live on adj. John Groff, John Landes, Jacob Stout, Benjamin
Rosenberger and Henry Groff and 20 acres adj. John Landes, Adam Kern,
John Hoot, John Zearfoss and the College land. Son Jacob balance of
Plantation adj. Henri Nunnemaker, Adam Kern, Abraham Stoffer and
Philip Reeser. 120 acres and 28 acres adj. Abraham Wanholt, Henry Gross
and College land. Daus. Anne, Margaret, Hannah and Magdalena. As
surviving Trustee of Union School House, I appoint my son Jacob as
Trustee. Son Abraham share in Richland Library.
Wits: Samuel Sellers, Henry Schlichter.

Page 283. Thomas Bulger, New Town, "advanced to age of eighty five
years." May 17, 1811. Proved July 11, 1812. John Roney of New Town
exr. Benjamin Butler, son of "My old Friend and long acquaintance John
Butler, dc'd." sole legatee.
Wits: N. Burrows and Isaac Hicks.

Page 283. Henry Guettleman, Rockhill Twp., yeoman, "Aged." April 6,
1808. Proved July 27, 1812. Wife Barbara. Son George Guettleman and
son-in-law Jacob Herring exrs. Ch. of son Theobald dec'd. Sons John,
Henry and George. Daus. Magdalena, Barbara, Elizabeth and Catharine.
Wits: Jacob Lowe and Peter Barndt.

Page 285. Sebastian Horn, Richland Twp., yeoman. June 16, 1810. Proved

July 21, 1812. Son Daniel exr. Sons Sebastian and Daniel. Daus. Elizabeth Bartholomew, Sevill Crowman, Mary Horn and Barbara Prong. Ch. of Dau. Catharine Charles.
Wits: George Snyder, James Chapman.

Page 286. Phebe Campbell, Northampton Twp. 2-10-1812. Proved July 30, 1812. Bro.-in-law Garret Dungan exr. Ch. Elizabeth, Tacey, Nancy, Sarah and Joseph Campbell.
Wits: Joshua Dungan Junr. and Cornelius Cornell

Page 287. Isaac Paxson, Solebury, yeoman. 2-20-1812. Proved Aug. 3, 1812. Bro. John Paxson and Moses Eastburn exrs. "Four of my sisters, Rachel, Mary and Mercy Paxson and Amy Worthington" all Personal Estate. Bro. John Plantation devised by will of Father dated 1-12-1790 and Land which Watson Fell as atty. for Thomas Blackfan conveyed to me, and share in I had Fishery at Oliver Paxson's, paying 4 sisters £600 &c.
Wits: Aaron Paxson, Asher Paxson, Mordecai Pearson.

Page 288. Abraham Overholt, Plumstead Twp., Farmer. Oct. 23, 1802. Proved Aug. 18, 1812. Wife Madlin. Sons Abraham and Isaac exrs. Sons Abraham, Isaac, Jacob and Henry and son-in-law William Moyer.
Wits: Henry Wismer and Jacob Landes.

Page 290. John Vansant, Middletown Twp. 8-5-1811. Proved Aug. 11, 1812. Wife Letitia. John Praul and Thomas Blakey of Middletown exrs. Wife, Hose now occupied by Israel Doan. Natural dau. Rachel. Son John and daus. Ann Leah and Amelia.
Wits: Jona. Woolston, John Blakey.

Page 300. Mathias Sandham, New Britain Twp., yeoman. Nov. 9, 1811. Proved Aug. 13, 1812. Mother Rebecca Sandham and Thomas Morris exrs. Sister Anna wife of Barton Stewart.
Wits: James Evans, John Gibson and David Evans.

Page 301. Hannah Dyer, Northampton Twp., "advanced in age." June 13, 1812. Proved Aug. 27, 1812. Andrew Bouzer and Phineas Jenks exrs. Hannah, wife of Caleb Oliver and dau. of Joshua Dyer, House and 15 acres adj. Gilliam Cornell and Negro Garret. Hannah wife of Samuel Caster, Furniture &c. Balance of Real Estate, where I live to Andrew Bouzer, his dau. Sarah Dyer and Dr. Phineas Jenks. Cousin Joseph Dyer son of Uncle James. John, Joseph and James Dyer $4 each. Mary, wife of Andrew Bouzer. Exrs. to wall in place where Father and Mother are buried, and where I desire to be interred.
Wits: Jonathan Scott and Isaac Hicks.

Page 301. Michael Redline, New Britain Twp., yeoman. July 21, 1812.

Proved Sept. 2, 1812. Wife Elizabeth. Philip Miller exr. Wife ½ of Estate including 4 Bonds given to Christian Swartz April 1, 1812, to will to whom she pleases if she outlives my son Christian, and interest of the other half for life. Son Christian £25 and so much more as is necessary to support him. Sarah Forker £10 if she live with my wife until 18. Bros. John and Jacob Redline, and wife's bros. and sisters.
Wits: John Miller and Levy Markley.

Page 302. Margaret Englishback, Rockhill Twp., Spinster. Nov. 7, 1808. Proved Sept. 14, 1812. "Far advanced in years." Friend Adam Richard, exr. Six acres in Rockhill Twp. John Richard a cow. Elizabeth and Margaret Richard, Bedding &c.
Wits: Morgan Custard, Jacob Low, George Breish.

Page 303. William Roberts, Solebury Twp., yeoman, "Advanced in years." April 6, 1810. Proved Sept. 17, 1812. Wife Grace. Aaron Beans exr. Son John Land bought of Thomas Hartley where said son has built. Sons Benjamin, Joseph, Henry, Jonathan, William and John. Daus. Elizabeth, Sarah and Mary. Gddau. Mariah Doert.
Wits: Isaac Pickering, Jonathan Beans Jr., John Farale.

Page 304. Edward Good, Plumstead Twp., "advanced in age." 1-9-1812. Wife Eleanor. Sons John and Edward exrs. 10 ch. Daus. Ganor Hutchins, Hannah Quinby, Margaret ---, Mary, Eleanor and Jane. Gddau. Eleanor Good, dau. of son Jonathan.
Wits: Alexander Rich, Jonathan Rich, James S. Rich.

Page 305. George Fox, Tinicum Twp., yeoman. May 1, 1807. Proved Oct. 7, 1812. Sons John and Jacob exrs. Wife Elizabeth. Sons John and Daniel Plantation where I live at £1700. Son George, 100 acres in Bedminster Twp. at £900. Son Abraham £550. Son Barnard £350. Daus. Mary and Susanna each £200. Residue to all ch. equally.
Wits: Ralph Stover, Arnold Lear.

Page 307. Elizabeth Lewis, Upper Makefield Twp., widow. April 7, 1802. Proved Oct. 13, 1812. Dau. Elizabeth and her husband Joseph Thornton exrs. Daus. Susannah Bender, Rachel Carey and Rebekah D. Catell. Gdsn. William Thornton, son of Joseph and Elizabeth.
Wits: Robert Knowles and Thomas Smith.

Page 308. Samuel Wigton, New Britain Twp., yeoman. June 13, 1812. Proved Oct. 14, 1812. Son Samuel exr. Wife Elizabeth £32 annually. Sons Christopher and Samuel. Daus. Jane Morgan, Isabella Kennedy, Mary, Elizabeth, Margaret and Nancy Wigton.
Wits: Jacob Haldeman, Ellis Pugh and Griffith Owen.

Page 308. Jacob Shelly, Lower Milford Twp., yeoman. Nov. 27, 1804.

Proved Nov. 2, 1812. Son Daniel and Bro.-in-law John Landis exrs. Wife Barbara, "One full child's share of the ch. I got by her." Francis Shelly one of sons by first wife. Eldest son Abraham's ch. Dau. Elizabeth dec'd., was mar. to one Isaac Kolb and left a dau. Elizabeth Kolb. Wife and her ch. provided for in agreement with son John.
Wits: David Spinner, Joseph Shelly.

Page 310. Aaron Vanderbelt, Tinicum Twp. Feb. 17, 1804. Proved Nov. 14, 1812. Sons Jacob and Peter exrs. Wife Egnes £10 per year use of House and goods. Dau. Cherity [sic], wife of John Eaton £222 she now has and £127. Residue including Land to sons Jacob and Peter Vanderbelt.
Wits: William Kealer, James Cooper.

Page 311. Mary Dickerson, Falls Twp. Nov. 17, 1812. Proved Nov. 23, 1812. Friend John Carter exr. Bro. John Smith my English silver watch. Mother Mary Smith residue for life, then to my dau. Elizabeth Smith.
Wits: Richard Stephenson and John Carter.

Page 311. Jane Cummings, Warwick Twp., widow. July 24, 1812. Proved Nov. 23, 1812. Son and dau., John and Catharine Marshall exrs. Sons William and John Marshall. Daus. Jane wife of Robert Cummings, Rebekah Hare, widow, and Catharine Marshall.
Wits: John Matthew and William Mearns.

Page 312. Andrew Long, Senr., Warrington Twp., yeoman. Oct. 7, 1807. Son William exr. Wife Mary £25 per year. Room in House and Goods. Ch. John, Andrew and William Long, Isabella wife of Solomon Hart, Mary wife of Barnet Vanhorn, Margaret wife of Harman Yerkes and Letitia wife of William Yerkes. Gdsns. Andrew son of John Long, Andrew son of Isabella Hart, Andrew son of William Long, Andrew son of Mary Vanhorn, Andrew son of Margaret Yerkes, Andrew son of Letitia Yerkes. Gddau. Mary Hart.
Wits: Andrew Long and William Long.

Page 313. Amos Griffith, New Britain Twp. Oct. 11, 1803. Proved Nov. 26, 1812. Wife Sarah and Nephew Amos Griffith exrs. Jesse Humphrey and Abel Mathias, Guardians of minor legatees. Wife Real Estate for life and Personal Estate absolutely. Niece Ann wife of Jesse Humphreys and her dau. Sarah Humphreys. Nephew Amos Griffith son of Bro. Abel and his son Amos. Niece Sarah wife of Abel Mathias and her son Amos Mathias. William White, Pastor of Baptist Church of Montgomery. Land bought of William Thomas.
Wits: John Harris, Thomas Harris, Henry Harris.

Page 314. Michael Dieterly, Haycock Twp., yeoman. Dec. 22, 1806. Proved Nov. 4, 1812. Son Michael and son-in-law Philip Wierner exrs. Ch. Michael, Henry, John, Elizabeth, Catharine, Barbara, Margaret, Mary,

Magdalena, Susanna and Eve. Margaret's son Jacob to have nothing.
Wits: John Green and John Whisler. (Green dec'd. before probate.)

Page 315. Hannah Hambleton, Solebury Twp., "far advanced in years."
1-3-1810. Proved Dec. 18, 1812. Friends John Armitage and Aron Paxson
exrs. Sons James, John, William, Jonas, Moses and Aron Hambleton.
Daus. Mary Coates, Jane Webster, Rachel Kester, Margaret Kinsey.
Gddaus. Hannah Wiggins and Hannah Sharp.
Wits: Joshua Ely, John Armitage Jr., Samuel Armitage.

Page 315. Adam Litzenberger, Haycock Twp. May 11, 1812. Proved Jan.
1, 1813. Sons Peter and Solomon Litzenberger exrs. Wife Anna Mary all
estate for life. Dau. Juliana and her dau. Mayri. Dau. Willimina dec'd.
was mar. to William Singe, and left 5 ch. Caty, John, Juliana, Ann Mary
and Solomon; if dau. Juliana mar. her dau. Mayri to have £20. Dau.-in-law
Henry Apple.
Wits: John Keller and John Borgen.

Page 316. John Miller, Haycock Twp,. yeoman. Feb. 9, 1807. Proved Jan.
5, 1813. Wife Susanna and William Stokes of Haycock exrs. Wife all estate
for life, then to son-in-law Abel Dalby and Clarah his wife.
Wits: William Stokes and Abr'm. Kachline.

Page 316. Jacob Hunsicker, Hilltown Twp., "Far advanced in years." Oct.
17, 1808. Proved Dec. 28, 1812. Sons Jacob and Isaac exrs. Wife Elizabeth
400£, use of House newly built &c. Son Isaac 130 Acres of Plantation I
live on, balanace to be sold. Nine ch. Jacob, Isaac, Elizabeth wife of Jacob
Detweiler, Catharine wife of John Bierly, Sarah wife of Abraham Kolb,
Barbara wife of John Bechtel, Anna wife of Henry Kolb, Mary, single
woman, Esther wife of Isaac Hunsberger.
Wits: Jacob Fretz and John Kolb. Henry Hunsicker wrote Will.

Page 317. Edward Eaton, Warminster Twp., Chairmaker. Aug. 3, 1808.
Proved Jan. 22, 1813. Son Joseph and Charles Terry exrs. Wife Esther
Interest of £200 for life, residue to ch. Martha McAllister, John and
Joseph Heaton [sic], Elizabeth Knight, Edward and Esther Heaton [sic].
Signed Eaton.
Wits: Isaac Carrell and Samuel Hart. Certificate filed with will signed by
Joseph Eaton, Esther Eaton, Edward Eaton, Jonathan and Elizabeth
Knight, sets forth that Edward Eaton, late of Warminster, lately died,
leaving widow Esther and six chidren, viz. Martha wife of Hugh
McAllister, John, Joseph, Elizabeth wife of Jonathan Knight, Edward and
Esther. That Martha and John are now supposed to reside in the
nortwestern [sic] part of the state of N.Y., and that one of the Witnesses
declines to come forward. Will proved on testimony of Isaac Carrell and
letters granted to Joseph Eaton.

Page 318. Hugh Morton, Falls Twp. Jan. 14, 1800. Proved Jan. 30, 1813. Wife (Ann) (name not given in Will or probate) and sons William and Hugh exrs. Wife House and Lot bought of John Doble for life, then to be sold. Mansion House at Tyburn and all other property to be sold. Proceeds to Sons William, Hugh and John as they arrive at age of 21. Dau. Theodosia Johnson £10.
Wits: M. Milnor, Reading Beatty, Moses Comfort. Widow Ann, filed Sett. Dec. 1816 as "surviving extx." Letters c.t.a. to John Morton May 1822. Invty [inventory] "House and Lot, late the reidence [sic] of Ann Morton."

Page 319. Samuel Brelsford, Bristol Twp. Dec. 19, 1812. Proved Feb. 3, 1813. William Sisom Junr. and Abner Johnson exrs. Bro. William Brelsford. Sister Priscilla Merrick bedding that was her mo's. Niece Mary Serl. Nephew Samuel Merrick.
Wits: Samuel Stockham and Levy Johnson.

Page 320. George B. Kelly, Buckingham Twp. Feb. 11, 1813. Proved Feb. 13, 1813. John Ruckman and Thomas Hutchinsn exrs. Wife Elizabeth and two ch. William Tomlinson Kelly and George Pearson Kelly, under 5 years of age.
Wits: Matthias Hutchinson, Charles Sheave and Phineas Kelly.

Page 320. Margaret Ely, Solebury Twp., 8-6-1811. Proved Feb. 24, 1813. Dau. Sarah Ely extx. and sole legatee.
Wits: Aron Paxson, Thomas Phillips.

Page 321. Rebekah Sandham, Doylestown. Feb. 8, 1813. Proved May 9, 1813. Asher Miner, Printer of Doylestown exr. Son-in-law Barton Stewart, gdsn. Sandham Stewart, a minor. Christiana Durling $10. in remembrance of kindness to my deceased dau. Anna Stewart. Residue of Estate of dec'd. son, to Mary Stewart, as mark of recollection of kindness to dec'd. dau.
Wits: Thomas N. Meredith and Mary Meredith.

Page 321. Samuel Smith, Upper Makefield Twp. 3-9-1807. Proved March 10, 1813. Son Thomas and Gdsn. Henry Smith exrs. Wife Jane, Household Goods use of House, Money that came from Samuel Schofield and £30 per year. Sons William, Thomas and Samuel. Daus. Elizabeth Carlile and Edith Fell. Gdch. Samuel and Joseph Heston ch. of dau. Phebe dec'd. Gddau. Jane Heston.
Wits: Jesse Heston, John Atkinson Jr., Samuel Atkinson. Codicil 3-21-1809 gddau. Phebe Right [sic] dec'd., her 2 ch. Joseph and Joel Right. [sic]

Page 323. Robert Paxson, Solebury Twp., "late of Cincinati, Ohio, Merchant." 1-5-1813. Proved March 1, 1813. Bro. Charles Paxson exr.

Father Moses Paxson. Mother Mary Paxson. Bros. and sisters, Charles Paxson, Ann Heston, Hannah Livezey, Thomas Paxson, Mary Paxson and Moses Paxson. Nephew Stephen S. Paxson, son of Charles.
Wits: Elias Paxson and Robert Livezey.

Page 324. John Ramsey, Warwick Twp., yeoman. July 29, 1811. Proved March 1, 1813. Son Robert and Elijah Stinson exrs. Son Robert 50 acres in Warwick whereon he lives, and part of Farm in Warminster. Son John Balance of Warminster Farm for life, then to his son John. Dau. Elizabeth £400 and privileges in house "I now occupy." William and Maria Ramsey ch. of son William, shares in Bank of North America.
Wits: Josiah Hart and Samuel Hart.

Page 325. Margaret Carey, Newtown. 8-12-1812. Proved March 3, 1813. Sons Joseph and Joshua Carey exrs. Sons Samuel and Silas Carey. Dau. Sarah Wildman and Gddau. Margaret Wildman.
Wits: William Blake Junr. and John Price.

Page 325. Simon Meredith, Warwick Twp., yeoman. Nov. 13, 1810. Proved April 6, 1813. Sons James and Joseph exrs. Samuel Gillingham of Buckingham and John Riale of New Britain Overseers. Wife Hannah. Sons James, Joseph, Morgan, Hugh and Simon. Dau. Mary wife of John Burson. Gddau. Letitia Meredith by son James 100 acres in Ravensdale, Luzerne Co., part of 400 acres. Gdch. Joseph, Silas, William and Eleanor Beans, ch. of dau. Elizabeth, dec;'d., balance of said 400 Acres. Wife Hannah 37 acres purchased of John Hough for life, then to sons.
Wits: James Evans, Margaret Evans and Morgan Thomas.

Page 327. Mary Fry, Warminster Twp., widow. July 9, 1807. Proved April 10, 1813. Codicil Feb. 11, 1811. Jon Griffith (son of bro. Thomas Griffith) and James Craven exrs. Nieces Elizabeth McClean, Elizabeth Funk, Mary Kyser and Rachel Readheffer. Jacob Fry McClean. Mary McClean dau. of niece Elizabeth McClean. Jacob Griffith son of nephew John Griffith.
Wits: Nath. B. Boileau, Ann Boileau.

Page 327. Elizabeth Vandegrift, Bensalem Twp. Relict of Folkert Vandegrift, dec'd., late of same place. March 9, 1811. Proved April 17, 1813. Dau. Ann Walton, relict of Joseph Walton dec'd,. extx. All Dowery due me from son Jacob and son Benjamin's Estate agreeable to will of late husband.
Wits: Daniel Knight, Jonathan Knight, Abraham Vansant.

Page 328. Mary Drake, Middletown Twp. 1-9-1813. Proved April 27, 1813. Cousin Joshua Knight exr. Sisters Elizabeth Carey and Ann Drake. Aunts Elizabeth Drake and Ann Hayhurst. Ann Nelson.
Wits: Joseph Hayhurst and John Blakey.

Page 328. Margaret Hoffman, Nockamixon Twp., widow of George Hoffman, dec'd. Aug. 23, 1812. Proved May 1, 1813. Michael Diemer Exr. Best Friend Catharine Zellefont, all estate for services, paying nephews of said George Hoffman, expenses incurred by them.
Wits: Jno. Cauffman and Peter Kuckart.

Page 329. John Vandyke, Warrington Twp., Cooper, "advanced in years." Dec. 8, 1807. Proved May 4, 1813. John Barclay Esq. late of Warwick Twp., but now of Phila. and William Whittingham of Warrington Twp. exrs. Dau. Elizabeth wife of Hugh McGookin, goods in her possession that were her Gdmother Mary Erwin's and Samuel Erwin's, dec'd. and $60 per year until death of Rebecca Erwin, widow of said Samuel. William Walker, natural son of dau. Elizabeth McGookin. Gdch. John Vandyke son of son Abraham; John Erwin Barclay son of dau. Mary Barclay. Dau. Mary wife of Hugh Barclay. Son Abraham and his wife Mary.
Wits: Thomas Griffith and George Arnel.

Page 331. James Tate, Middletown Twp. Jan. 12, 1808. Proved May 4, 1813. Bro.-in-law James Ewing and his son Charles Ewing of Trenton, N.J. exrs. Wife Jane all goods she brought to me and $300 per year, out of profits of Real Estate for life. Nieces Margaret Elizabeth and Sarah Boyd, daus. of sister Jane Boyd dec'd. £200 each. Residue to dau. Elizabeth when 21 years of age. If she die to above nieces, Sisters Sarah Moore, Elizabeth Ewing and Margaretta Tate and Nephew Alexander T. Moore.
Wits: Andrew Gilkeson, Th. G. Kennedy, Thomas Bond.

Page 332. Cornelius Venastin, Middletown Twp., Miller. April 26, 1813. Proved May 8, 1813. Wife Zilpha and John Praul exrs. Dau. Rachel Vanostin. [sic]
Wits: John S. Mitchell, George Murray and George Hulme.

Page 333. Thomas Craig, Warrington Twp., yeoman. "Far advanced in years." Feb. 29, 1812. Proved May 8, 1813. William C. Rogers of Bucks Co. and Hiram McNeal of Mungomery [sic] Co. exrs. Son Daniel Craig and his son Thomas. Daus. Mary Reed and Margaret Miller. Gdsns. Thomas Craig Reed and Thomas Craig Miller. Son-in-law William Miller.
Wits: John Sorver and Benjamin Hough.

Page 334. Jacob Cope, Hilltown Twp., yeoman, "Aged." Oct. 20, 1812. Proved May 28, 1813. Sons John and David exrs. Wife Salome 80 acres where I live for life, then to son David. Sons John, Isaac, David, George and Jacob. Daus. Polly, Hannah, Rebecca, Catharine, Salome and Elizabeth. Elizabeth's son Joseph Swarts.
Wits: Abraham Jacoby and Jacob Detweiler

Page 336. Rachel Paxson, Solebury Twp. 11-5-1813. Proved May 31, 1813.

Moses Eastburn exr. Bros. Henry and Joseph. Sisters Elizabeth Hambleton, Amy Worthington, Mary and Mercy Paxton. Niece Rachel Hambleton.
Wits: Aron Paxton, Letitia Paxton, Ann Paxton (so recorded, but original is signed Paxson, both testatrix and witnesses.)

Page 337. John Pringle, Durham Twp. May 30, 1813. Proved May 31, 1813. Mother Elizabeth Pringle extx. Dec'd. father John Pringle.
Wits: Elizabeth James and William Long.

Page 337. John Bower, Richland Twp., "Missen." May 5, 1811. Proved May 31, 1813. Son Stoffel Bower and son-in-law Jost Wever exrs. Wife Elizabeth. Dau. Elizabeth wife of Jost Wever.
Wits: John Bechtel, John Duchler and Daniel Cooper.

Page 338. George Singmaster, Milford Twp., Wheelwright. Dec. 2, 1809. Proved May 31, 1813. Son Philip and Jacob Smith exrs. Wife Christina. Sons Jacob, Philip, Adam and Daniel. Daus. Elizabeth, Molly and Christina.
Wits: John Heller, Abraham Smith.

Page 339. Isaac Vanhorn, Solebury Twp., yeoman. May 5, 1813. Proved June 1, 1813. Bro. Cornelius Vanhorn exr. Barnet Vanhorn, son of bro. Cornelius, Amasa Vanhorn natural son of sister Sarah Campbell. Joseph Campbell, son of sister Alice Campbell. Land in State of Ohio to be sold.
Wits: Robert Smith and Elias H. Smith.

Page 340. John Fellman, Rockhill Twp., yeoman. May 20, 1812. Proved June 1, 1813. Sons John and Henry exrs. Wife Matlina. Son Jacob use of Plantation where on I live during life of wife, paying rent to Trustees of Academy at Phila. Son Henry Book called "Rise and Sufferings of People called Menonists."
Wits: Abraham Keil and Everard Foulke.

Page 341. Sarah Dungan, Northampton Twp. April 25, 1807. June 4, 1813. Step-son Dr. Samuel Dungan and William Folwell exrs. Sister Catrin Roughcorn. Step-dau. Jane Folwell. Sarah Folwell dau. of William Folwell. "Elizabeth near my sisters dau. Phebey Dungan."
Wits: Joshua Dungan, Sarah Hart and James Dungan.

Page 342. George Wendle Moyer, Lower Milford Twp., Wheelwright. June 5, 1813. Proved June 12, 1813. Bro.-in-law Philip Mumbower exrs. Wife "Mary Moyer." Son "Abraham Moyer" and other ch.
Wits: T. N. Newton, Daniel Broughler and Henry Roeder.

Page 342. Jacob Stover, Haycock Twp., yeoman. June 4, 1813. Proved Aug. 9, 1813. Bro. Henry Stover and Bro.-in-law John Fretz of

Nockamixon exrs. Wife Susannah, and ch. John Henry and Lidy Stover, estate equally. Ch. "to be taut and scooled at discreation of executors." Wits: Michael Yost, Jacob Kohl and Nicholas McCart.

Page 343. Isaac Carrell, Northampton Twp., Carpenter. May 21, 1813. Proved July 30, 1813. Bro. Joseph Carrell exr. Bro Jesse and Sister Elizabeth Carrell all estate, Real and Personal Estate in "Township of Ovid, County of Siniky, New York." Wits: Daniel Dungan and John Corson.

Page 344. John Stokes, Haycock Twp., yeoman. 3-30-1809. Proved Aug. 14, 1813. Sons William, John, Samuel and Stogdell exrs. Wife Susanna. Gdsn. Peter Lester son of dau. Mary dec'd. Daus. Hannah Praul, Rachel Smith, Elizabeth Roberts and Susanna Stokes. Codicil dated 6-4-1811. Wits: John Smith, James Chapman.

Page 346. Jane Vanartsdalen, Southampton Twp., widow. Aug. 20, 1808. Proved Aug. 14, 1813. Sons-in-law John Kroeson [Karveson?] and Garret Stephens exrs. Daus. Ann Stephens, J. Kroeson and Margaret Wilard. Gddau. Jane Stephens. Wits: Christopher Vanarsdalen [sic], Phebe Vanarsdalen [sic].

Page 347. Elizabeth Harwick, Richland Twp. June 14, 1813. Proved Aug. 30, 1813. Bros. John and Samuel Harwick exrs. Bro. Samuel Harwick's ch. Nephew Samuel Harwick's ch. John Bidler, Mason's ch. Sister Hester's ch. John Wineberger's ch. Nieces Elizabeth Musselman, Elizabeth Taylor and Mary Bidler. Sisters Barbara and Mary. Nephew Jacob Climer. Michael Huddle. John Bidler and daus. Elizabeth and Abigail. Wits: Benjamin Johnson and Casper Johnson.

Page 348. Frederick Everhard, Nockmixon Twp., weaver. Nov. 16, 1804. Proved Aug. 30, 1813. Michael Fackenthall Esq. of Durham Twp. exr. Wife Elizabeth, use of Plantation for life, then to be sold. £100 to Sister's ch. "now in Urope." Residue to wife's Gdch. Wife's son Christophex [sic] Trauger, and her gdsn. Frederick Trauger. Jacob Sumstone, tenant. Wits: William Long, Philip Overpeck.

Page 349. Thomas Cunningham, Lower Makefield Twp., "Advanced in years." June 17, 1813. Proved Sept. 2, 1813. Son Thomas and Thomas Yardly exrs. Sons Thomas and Matthew. Daus. Martha Irving, Margaret Vanhorn, Ann Irving and Sarah Moon. Wits: Mahlon Yardley, William Yardley, John Yardley.

Page 349. William Richardson, Middletown Twp. 11-9-1812. Proved Sept. 18, 1813. Sons William and Joseph exrs. Sons William, Joseph and Thomas. Daus. Mercy wife of Jacob Shoemaker, Rachel wife of David

Story, Ann Richardson, Elizabeth wife of Josiah Reeve and Mary Watson. Gdch. Jonathan and Thomas Shoemaker, Susannah M. Watson, money received as Exr. of the will of her father Marmaduke Watson. Land adj. Abraham Longshore, William and Joshua Blakey, Peter Rice, William Jenks, Joshua and Jonathan Woolston.
Wits: Simon Gillam and Joseph Richardson.

Page 352. Thomas Smith, Riverside, Upper Makefield Twp. April 21, 1812. Proved Sept. 23, 1813. Sons Thomas and Moses exrs. Wife Latitia, interest of £1000 for life. 200 acres I live on, and land in Northampton Co. to be sold. Ch. Thomas, Moses, Letitia, Edward, Oliver, Mary, Job, Eliza and Septimus.
Wits: Stephen Betts and David Fell.

Page 354. John Matthias, Hilltown Twp., yeoman. Aug. 28, 1812. Proved Sept. 23, 1813. Son Enoch and son-in-law William H. Rowland exrs. Son Morgan and dau. Elizabeth part of Plantation conveyed to me by John Mathew and Rachel his wife March 18, 1788, adj. George Cramer, Benjamin Morris, Philip Jacoby, Jacob Coupt and Ashbel Mathias, they to maintain my dau. Margaret during life and give decent burial. Daus. Gainor wife of Abel H. James, Mary wife of Griffith Jones, Sarah wife of William H. Rowland and Alice yet single. Gdch. Rowland and Mary Mathias ch. of son Thomas, dec'd. (minors).
Wits: Michael Buzzard, Elisha Lunn and Joseph Mathias.

Page 356. Daniel Pugh, Hilltown Twp. 1806. Proved Sept. 25, 1813. Son John Pugh exr. Wife Rebecca Plantation for life, then to be sold, proceeds to two ch. John and Sarah.
Wits: George Leidy, saddler; Isac [sic] Swart and William H. Rowland.

Page 358. Lanah Sutphin, Warminster Twp,. widow. April 27, 1812. Proved Oct. 9, 1813. Abraham McDowell exr. Daus. Mary McDowell and Ann Delaney. Gch. Eliza and Helena Delaney ch. of Jonathan and Ann.
Wits: William Delaney and Eliza Delaney.

Page 359. John H. Marcellus, Wrightstown Twp. Sept. 22, 1813. Proved Oct. 9, 1813. Son-in-law Samuel Johnson and Isaac Worthington exrs. Wife Joice. Ch. Sarah, Mary, John, David, Joseph, William, Beulah Ann and Christiann (youngest under 10 years of age).
Wits: Benjamin Field, Samuel Roberts Junr., William Stockdale.

Page 360. John Matts, Richland Twp., Tanner. Aug. 24, 1813. Proved Oct. 15, 1813. Son John exr. Wife Barbara use of Rooms, $60 per year, etc. Son John Tan yard 718 acres, paying my dau. Sarah wife of Jacob Anthony £250.
Wits: Stephen Horn and William Stokes.

Page 361. Benjamin Summers, Tinicum Twp. July 24, 1813. Proved Oct. 16, 1813. Son Lewis Summers exr. Wife Catharine, Son David to live with her and have interest of £450. Son Lewis, ch. of son Peter, dec'd., and 4 daus.
Wits: John Myer and Henry Bissey.

Page 362. Catharine Loux, widow, Bedminster Twp. Feb. 9, 1810. Proved Oct. 18, 1813. George Ratzel exr. Petr [sic] Ott's oldest sons by his second wife, Frederick and Daniel Ott [Att?], my small plantation of 28 acres, on which I live, adj. Abraham Black, Peter Ott and Thrand Hammels. They to provide for my dau. Juliana.
Wits: Jacob Godshalk and Peter Solladay.

Page 364. Charles Swift, Esq. of City of Phila. Feb. 3, 1803. Codicils Aug. 24, 1811, Sept. 4, 1810 and one without date. Proved Oct. 19, 1813. Will names Alexandria James Dallas as exr. Codicil revokes it, "because of the multitude of business he is engaged in and distance he lives from my family." 1st codicil makes son Robert E. G. Swift exr. when of age. Last codicil names son Robert Eaglesfield Griffith Swift, John and Samuel Hulme as exrs. Present wife Mary, furniture, plate &c. for life, then to ch., "by any marriage." Land purchased that was his Fa's. 10,000 acres purchased in company with Dallas, Ingersoll and Chew, partly in Hunterdon Co.
Wits: Joseph S. Lewis and Pearson Hunt. To Codicil John Gallagher and Rebecca Keen.

Page 365. Thomas Folwell, Southampton Twp., yeoman. --- 1809. Proved Nov. 1, 1813. Son William W. Folwell and 3 sons-in-law Joseph Hart Esq., William Purdy and Joshua Jones. Wife Elizabeth use of House and Plantation devised to son William, if son William return from state of N.Y. where he is at present settled, said wife to admit him at moderate rent in preference to any other tenant. Dau. Ann Hart land adj. Nathaniel B. Boileau, William Purdy and Samuel Miles and lot bought of Joseph Longstreth in Warminster. Dau. Elizabeth wife of Joshua Jones. Dau. Mary Purdy wife of William Purdy. Dau. Rachel Reader; her dau. Elizabeth W. Hemphill.
Wits: George S. Shelmire and William Miles.

Page 369. James Torbert, the elder, Upper Makefield Twp. Sept. 18, 1813. Proved Nov. 8, 1813. Sons James and Anthony Torbert exrs. Son Abner, Plantation on which I live. Sons Samuel, James, Anthony and Lamb Torbert each £90. Dau. Alice wife of James Slack. Five ch. of son-in-law Abraham Slack. Dau. Ann's ch. (late the wife of John Hare). Ch. of son-in-law Christopher Search by his last wife. Nine gdch. James Torbert, son of Samuel; James Slack son of Abraham; James Slack son of James; James Torbert son of Anthony; James Torbert son of Lamb; James Torbert Search son of Christopher; James Hare son of John;

James Torbert son of James and James Torbert son of Abner, each £10. James, Robert and Elizabeth, ch. of son Abner.
Wits: William Taylor, John Slack.

Page 370. Catharine Pownall, Solebury Twp. 9-2-1813. Proved Nov. 8, 1813. Bro. Moses Pownall exr. Sisters Ann Balance, Mary Paxson and Margaret Hampton $300. Catharine Balance and Hannah Hampton now living with me each $400. Bros. Simeon and Moses Pownall.
Wits: John Ely and Joseph Doan.

Page 370. John Scarborough, Solebury Twp. Dec. 20, 1810. Proved Nov. 8, 1813. Thomas Hutchinson of Buckingham exr. Daus. Rachel Osman, Elizabeth Hartly and Charity Hartly, sums payable to them from sons Isaac and Joseph as per Bonds held in trust by Matthias Hutchinson. Sons Robert and John.
Wits: George Grubum, Charles Shaw and Charles Paxson.

Page 371. Thomas Wood, Solebury twp., "Now living at Watson Fells." Nov. 1, 1813. Proved Nov. 29, 1813. Watson Fell, exr., if he die his son Charles Fell. Sister Rebecca Randall and her sons Thomas and William Randall. Sister Mary Barbin and her ch. Thomas, Mary, Amos and Elizabeth Barbin.
Wits: William Mitchell and Francis Fell.

Page 372. Henry Trumbower, Richland Twp., yeoman. Oct. 18, 1813. Proved Nov. 30, 1813. Wife Elizabeth interest of £500 for life. Sons John and Jacob exrs. Plantation to be sold. Ch. Henry, John, George, Jacob, Joseph, Philip, Michael, Elizabeth and Mary.
Wits: Benjamin Johnson, Joseph Mininser and Abraham Taylor.

Page 373. Thomas Smith, Upper Makefield Twp. 3-22-1806. Proved Dec. 2, 1813. Sons Joseph and Ezra Smith exrs. Son John's ch. "when of age." Daus. Keziah, Margaret and Susanna.
Wits: Thomas Smith and Joseph Smith.

Page 374. Patrick Hines, Haycock Twp., yeoman. Nov. 10, 1813. Proved Dec. 2, 1813. Jacob Fulmer, Senr. of Springfield and Nicholas McCarty of Haycock exrs. Housekeeper Elizabeth Adams, 150 acres and all estate for life, then to Nicholas McCarty, Senr.
Wits: Charles McEntee and Nicholas McCarty Jr.

Page 374. William Rankin, Warminster Twp., yeoman. March 11, 1809. Proved Dec. 11, 1813. Wife Mary and John Harvey Jr. of Warminster exrs. Bro. John. Nephew Jonathan Knight and his son Charles wearing apparel. Plantation devised by father James Rankin to wife for life, then it with all other estate to Trustees of General Asembly [sic] of Pres. Church of U.S.

Wits: Cornelius Carrell and Amos Dungan.

Page 375. Martha McNair, Upper Makefield Twp., widow, "advanced in age." Sept. 8, 1808. Codicil Dec. 25, 1813. Proved Jan. 7, 1814. Son Solomon McNair and son-in-law James Torbert, exrs. Sons David and Samuel. Five daus. Margaret Torbert, Ann Wynkoop, Elizabeth McNair, Martha Vanhorn and Rachel Robinson.
Wits: Samuel and Margaret Mann, Enos Merrick.

Page 376. John Stockdale, Upper Makefield Twp., yeoman, "Far advanced in age." June 22, 1803. Jan. 11, 1814. Isaac Chapman and Thomas Smith, Samuel's son, exrs. Wife Ann, Household Goods, use of House and lot where Thomas Leonard lives, during widowhood. Son John wearing apparel. Ch. of son Joseph, viz. Sarah, Elizabeth and Mary. Dau. Marcy Stockdale. Gdch. Luke and Susannah Gillum. Ch. of dau. Sarah by her late husband David Whitson. Dau. Mary Whitson. Dau. Rachel Scarborough, Plantation to be sold, procceds to son John, Dau. Elizabeth Harvey, Marcy Stockdale, ch. of dau. Mary Whitson, ch. of dau. Hannah, ch. of dau. Rachel.
Wits: Edward Chapman, Rachel Chapman and Sarah Moley. Rachel Chapman dec'd. and Sarah Moley left neighborhood, before probate.

Page 378. Philip Louderbough, New Britain Twp. Dec. 212, 1813. Proved Jan. 12, 1814. William Godshalk and Samuel Detweiler exrs. Niece Anna Kern, now wife of Peter Abel. Ch. of Niece Polly Kern, now wife of James Taylor. Sickly dau. of Henry Yellers of Haycock. £200 to be held in trust by her Uncle Benjamin Johnson. Catharine Moyer dau. of Christian Moyer of Bedminster bond on Joseph Shelly and Samuel Landis for £90 Menonist [sic] Church near Doylestown £50. Abraham Krotz son of Abraham Krotz of New Britain, £50. Abraham Wismer of Bedmisnter £15. Isaac and Susanna Godshalk, ch. of William Godshalk. Sister Catharine wife of Anthony Kern. Bucks Co. Almshouse wearing apparel.
Wits: Henry Fretz, Isaac Godshalk and William Godshalk.

Page 379. Azaliah Schooley. 11-21-1813. Proved Jan. 14, 1814. John Comfort exr. Sister Ezeby Devauld's dau. Edith $60. Bro's. son Azaliah Schooley $50. Azaliah Scott, apparel. Ann Comfort. Mary wife of Stephen Comfort and Barclay Irvins, chest etc. to all my bros. and sisters ch.
Wits: Isaac and Barclay Irvins.

Page 379. Cornelius Vanhorn, Buckingham Twp. Feb. 10, 1814. Proved Feb. 16, 1814. Dr. John Wilson and Samuel Gillingham of Buckingham Twp. exrs. Wife Mary. 4 ch. Juliann, William Bennet Vanhorn, Catharine and Mary Vanhorn.
Wits: Samuel Gillingham and Moses Beans.

Page 380. William Ramsey, Warwick Twp., yeoman. Jan. 15, 1814. Proved

March 1, 1814. Nephews Robert Ramsey, son of bro. John and William Blair, exrs. Wife Ann. Nephew William Blair, part of Plantation n.w. of old Road passing my house and Bready's, 70 acres. Sister Jane Blair. Nieces Nancy Beans, Agnes Blair and Elizabeth Ramsey, dau. of bro. John. Robert son of Bro. John Ramsey. Nephew William Ramsey son of bro. Robert, balance of land about 150 acres for life. Bro. Robert and his ch. Wits: William Mearns and Isaac Chapman.

Page 381. Michael Stoneback, Hilltown Twp., yeoman. "Aged." Aug. 12, 1813. Proved March 16, 1814. Henry Keller of Haycock and Andrew Star of New Britain, exrs. Wife Barbara, all estate for life. Son Christopher interest of £1000 for life. Gddau. Juliann Gier £500 when of age. Gddau. Susanna Stoneback. Gdch., ch. of ch. Christopher, Catharine, Samuel, Mary, Joseph, Susanna and Lidia. Ch. of dec'd. dau. Elizabeth Gier, viz. Elizabeth, John, Mary Ellis and Juliann Gier.
Wits: Abraham Fretz, Frederick Croner and Griffith Owen.

Page 382. Daniel Bergey, Lower Milford Twp. (unsigned), died while will was being drawn, Feb. 26, 1814. Proved March 3, 1814. (Carpenter). Wife Catharine land bought of John Cooper, house to be built for her. Ch. Charles and Maria, minors. Bro.-in-law Joseph Weaver exr. Will drawn by Andrew Reed Esq. and proven by Jacob Bergey father of Testator.

Page 384. Martha Blair, Lower Makefield Twp. Jan. 30, 1814. Proved March 19, 1814. John Stockton exr. Dau. Elizabeth Blair sole legatee. Wits: Joshua Lovett, Samuel Paxson, Aaron Cox and John Stewart.

Page 384. William Wildman, Falls Twp. 3-8-1813. Proved April 1, 1814. Father-in-law John Miller and Relation Moses Comfort exrs. Wife --- all estate for life, then to sons Elias and John.
Wits: James Simpson and John Miller Jr.

Page 385. Benjamin Paxson, Solebury Twp., yeoman, "In the decline of life." 2-4-1814. Proved April 2, 1814. Sons Thomas and Charles exrs. Wife Mary, all she brought with her at mar., gold watch and $400. Sons Timothy and Benjamin each $1866. Daus. Hannah Betts, Deborah Bye and Rachel Paxson. Sons Timothy and Benjamin 1000 acres of Land in Harrison Co., Va. Son Thomas, farm I live on and land bought of Samuel Wilson in Manor of Highlands. Son Charles 100 acres in Buckingham whereon he lives purchased of John Parry subject to Dower of Rachel Parry exrs. to complete sale of Land adjudged to me as my Bro. Isaiah Paxson's to John Thompson.
Wits: Robert Smith, Joseph Worthington and Jesse Johnson.

Page 386. John Magill, Solebury Twp. 10-31-1812. Proved April 2, 1814. Codicil dated 2-11-1814. Sons Jacob and William exrs. Wife Amy. Son Jacob farm he lives on. Son William land he lives on, devised me by my

176

father; paying son John $300. Son David part of Land bought of Samuel Jones on N.E. side of Lugan Road and Wood Lot bought of Abner Ely adj. Samuel Kinsey, Benjamin Parry and others. Daus. Jane and Rachel land lying between Lugan and York Roads at junction thereof bounded by land of David Kitchen.
Wits: Oliver Hampton, Samuel Kinsey and David Heston Jr.

Page 388. George Horlacher, Lower Milford Twp., yeoman, "Advanced in years." April 19, 1813. Proved April 6, 1814. Sons-in-law Adam Levy and Jonathan Trexler, exrs. Wife Eve, Lot wheron we reside, Chattels and Furniture and £600. Calvinist Congregation of Great Swamp £5. Ch. Catharine late wife of David Spinner, dec'd.; Eve wife of Adam Levy; Elizabeth wife of Jonathan Trexler.
Wits: Philip Reed and Adam Snyder.

Page 389. Jacob Jackson, Bensalem Twp., yeoman. July 18, 1812. Proved April 7, 1814. Bro. Jesse Jackson exr. Dau. Eleanor Vandegrift and her dau. Catharine Vandegrift all estate.
Wits: Joseph Thompson and Saml. Gibbs.

Page 390. Margaret Fenton, Plumstead Twp,. nuncupative, declared May 10, 1814. Proved May 19, 1814 before John Haas and her sister Catharine Morris. Daniel Brown and Ephraim Fenton exrs. Daniel and Jane Brown. Ephraim and Mary Fenton legatees.

Page 391. Elizabeth Wright, Falls Twp. 12-18-1813. Proved May 30, 1814. Stephen Woolston exr. Ch. Seth Wright, Amy Shure and Mary Harvey.
Wits: William Crozer and Moses Burges.

Page 391. Jacob Rothrock, Springfield Twp., yeoman. May 17, 1814. Proved May 30, 1814. Sons John and Abraham exrs. Wife Margareth, son John Land where I live on Road from Quakertown to Bethlehem. Son Jacob Land bought of the two Penns John the elder and John the younger. Son Abraham balance of Land 83 acres. Daus. Catharine wife of Michael Woolbach and Susanna wife of Peter Dichard.
Wits: Daniel Cooper and John Bechtel.

Page 392. Abraham Watson, Lower Makefield Twp. May 18, 1814. Proved May 31, 1814. Henry Watson and James Linton exrs. Wife Letitia. Son Jonathan £150. Daus. Hannah White, Parmelia Watson, Martha Moore and Letitia Watson. Lands to son Samuel.
Wits: Moses Neeld, James Linton, Henry Watson.

Page 393. Sarah McHenry, New Britain Twp. May 2, 1814. Proved June 1, 1814. Thomas Stewart exr. Sisters Elizabeth wife of Evan Jones; Ann wife of Benjamin Coles and Rebecca wife of Isaac Michener. Bro. William McHenry. Uncle Charles McHenry dec'd. Mother Mary McHenry.

Wits: William Godshalk and Thomas Stewart.

Page 394. Elizabeth Beans, widow of Mathew Beans of Buckingham Twp. 4-4-1814. Proved June 2, 1814. Friend James Rice and Gdsn. William Rice, son of Joseph exrs. Ch. "now living" Edward Rice, George Rice, Mary Kinsey, Joseph Rice, Thomas Rice, William Rice, Aaron and Moses Beans. Ch. of son John Rice dec'd.
Wits: John Watson, Joseph Hambleton.

Page 394. Elizabeth Garrison, widow of Charles Garrison, dec'd., Warminster Twp. Jan. 1, 1810. Proved June 9, 1814. Nephew Harman Vansant exr. Harman Vansant son of Bro. James, dec'd. Charles Garrison Vansant son of bro. Charles. Elizabeth Adams dau. of bro. Harman Vansant. Elizabeth Reed and Cornelia Hogeland daus. of bro. William Vansant dec'd.
Wits: Thomas Craven and Hamilton Roney.

Page 395. John Grier, Warwick Twp., yeoman. March 18, 1814. Proved June 23, 1814. Son John S. Grier exr. Wife Jane, use of Farm during life or widowhood. Son John S. said Farm, 220 acres at wife's death. Daus. Martha Mann and Jane Grier.
Wits: William Hart, Robert Kennedy and John Carr.

Page 396. Elias Thomas, Hilltown Twp. May 8, 1812. Proved June 12, 1814. Sons Ephraim and Issachar Thomas exrs. Wife Elizabeth £100 Goods &c. Ch. Walter, John, Nathan, Ephraim, Issachar and Sarah Thomas. Land devised to each, described in Will and draught annexxed. Ephraim and Issachar, Tan Yard and 55 Acres.
Wits: Abel Miller, Ephraim Thomas, George Leidy, Satler, and Nathan Thomas. Land adj. Heirs of Eben Thomas, Martha Shannon, Daniel Pugh, George Frantz and swamp Road.

Page 401. Ann Schleiffer, New Britain Twp. April 26, 1814. Proved July 9, 1814. "Confidential Cousin Jacob Stout" exr. £50 to pay debt bro. Abraham Scleifer [sic] owes Henry Lisey. Sisters Barbara wife of John Fulton, and Elizabeth Donahaver. Bros. Jacob, John and Isaac Scleifer [sic]. Nieces Ann Fulton, Salome dau. of bro. John; Ann Scleifer, dau. of bro. Abraham; cousins Catharine Swartzlander and Margaret Huntsberry. Nephew Jacob Donahaver.
Wits: George Burgess and Susanna Fritz.

Page 402. Elias Lewis, Richland Twp., yeoman. Oct. 26, 1801. Proved Feb. 25, 1814. Wife Margaret and James Chapman exrs. Nephew Lewis Lewis' son Ellis Lewis, all lands, if he die under age then to Trustees of Richland Meeting for use of School on lot given by Thomas Thomas for use of a school. William and Evan Green, sons of Benjamin, to sell same and pay proceeds to Trustees.

Wits: Frederick Deal and Cadwallader Foulke.

Page 403. John Randle, Upper Makefield Twp. Nov. 13, 1809. Proved July 28, 1814. Son William and Thomas Smith Pr. [sic] exrs. Wife Rebecca all Estate for life. Sons John, Joseph, William and Thomas. Daus. Elizabeth, Sarah and Margaret.
Wits: Robert Neeley and David Fell.

Page 403. John Godshalk, New Britain Twp. April 29, 1814. Proved Aug. 1, 1814. Jacob and John Godshalk exrs. Son John Plantation, 103 acres, paying to all my ch. their proportionate shares therein.
Wits: Henry Fretz and William Godshalk.

Page 404. John Moyer, Bedminster Twp., "advanced in Age." June 22, 1814. Proved Aug. 5, 1814. Wife Judah, Goods, use of Lands &c. Ch. Rebekah Detweiler, Henry, Barbary, Catharine, John, Abraham, Christian, William, Dorothy, Samuel and Isaac Moyer. Henry, Abraham and John exrs. Minor ch. to be educated &c.
Wits: George Burgess, Samuel Moyer, Christian Myers.

Page 406. George Stockham, Junr., Fells Twp., yeoman. Aug. 5, 1814. Proved Aug. 19, 1814. "In too low a state to write his name." Bro. Thomas Stockham and George Hulme of Milford exrs. Wife Elizabeth formerly Elizabeth Mulhaun. Sons John and George and child unborn. Son Joseph, by Mary Belford.
Wits: M. R. Calbraith and Charles Ettel.

Page 407. J. Daniel Kerns, at Falls Twp., Pennsbury Manor, Aug. 20, 1814. Proved Aug. 26, 1814. To be interred at German Lutheran Church, Phila. John Gier, Mayor of Phila. and Adolph Aaronhoes, exrs. Jacob Lut $100 Anne Jean Newman, $500. "Everything here and in the South to be divided equally between my heirs in Europe and America." Blacks in Carolinas to choose their masters, under their Guardian Reuben Flanagan. "Back Lands to be settled with I. F. Kerin." Watch at Balie's watch store on 2d St., Phila., to namesake John D. Kerr at Charlestown.
Wits: Thomas Crozer and Alex. Quinton. (Heirs in Europe were Theodore Lazzani, in right of his wife and Dorothea Maria Cattarina Lagan). Letters to John Geyer and Adolph Ehrinhaus.

Page 407 & 416. John Duer, Lower Makefield Twp., yeoman. June 21, 1807. Codicil dated April 28, 1814. Proved Aug. 22, 1814. Wife Jane and sons William, James and John exrs. Son Josiah, a minor. Dau. Thomasine wife of Joseph Richardson. Sister Ellen Clark, (annuity under will of father John Duer). Indentured servants Patience Jones, Joseph Slack, Samuel and Hannah Mathews, Still, Still House Fisheries, Boats, Lands &c.
Wits: William and Joseph Slack, Joseph Taylor and Joseph Davis.

Page 416. Silas Hart, Junr., "at his Father's House in Warminster Twp." Nuncupative, declared in presence of Thomas B. Montanye, John Hart, James Travers, William Lee and others, Aug. 9, 1814. "Griffith Miles and John Hart, Storekeeper, to settle my affairs. "Estate equally to my three sisters present." Proved Aug. 26, 1814. "Said three sisters are Mary, Sarah and Mira Hart, there being none other present."

Page 417. William Heacock, Richland Twp., yeoman. Dec. 10, 1813. Proved Aug. 29, 1814. Son Edward Heacock, exr. Wife Miriam, all estate for support of helpless dau. Mira. Dau. Margaret $8. Son James, wearing apparel.
Wits: Everard Foulke and George Custard.

Page 418. Christian Hunsberger, Lower Milford Twp., yeoman. July 26, 1814. Proved Aug. 29, 1814. Wife Modlina Hunsberry, all estate for life. At her death Plantation, 100 acres, to be sold. Bros. Peter, Abraham, and John Hunsberry. Sister Maria Richard's ch. "names not known." Sister Susanna Overholt. Sister's ch. Christian and David Bealer. Bro. Peter's son Christian. Relations Jacob and Joseph Wisemer. Jacob Clymer and Peter Strunk.
Wits: Henry Clymer and Henry Strunk.

Page 420. Ann Lovett, Bristol Twp., widow. 3-20-1814. Proved Aug. 31, 1814. Son Samuel Lovett and son-in-law John Booz exrs. Dau. Cassandra Booz. Gdch. Martha Shippey, Cassandra Stackhouse, William Cooper and Elizabeth Cooper, ch. of dau. Hannah Cooper, dec'd. Jesse Hibbs, Sarah, Samuel and Jonathan Hibbs, ch. of dau. Susanna Hibbs dec'd. Gddau. Ann Booz.
Wits: Anthony Burton and Joseph Brown.

Page 421. Sarah Dungan, Northampton Twp. June 6, 1814. Proved Aug. 31, 1814. John McNair Esq. and Bro. Daniel Dungan exrs. Mother. Bros. James, Isaac and Daniel Dungan. Cousins William, Deborah and Mary Done. Aunt Mary Done.
Wits: John McNair and Samuel Young.

Page 422. Mary Snyder, Bucks Co. June 4, 1814. Proved Sept. 3, 1814. Son Henry Snyder and Henry Ridge exrs. Sons Peter, William and Henry Snyder and dau. Barbara Hillpot. Ann wife of son Henry. Ann Snyder widow of son George. Elizabeth wife of son William. Late husband Peter Snyder. Mother Barbara Adams. Niece Mary Magdalen Adams dau. of bro. Henry Adams. Gdch. Mary Madalen Snyder, Catharine. Ch. of dau. Barbara Hillpot, viz. Leah and Zipporah Ann. Mary, Sarah and Lily, ch. of son Peter. "Son William now a soldier in the Army of the United States should he survive the War."
Wits: Scott R. Erwin, John Ruth, John Weaver.

Page 423. Sarah Griffith, New Britain Twp., widow. Oct. 20, 1813. Proved Oct. 1, 1814. David Evans and Nephew Abel Mathias exrs. Niece Ann wife of Jesse Humphrey and her daus. Maria and Sarah; and her 3 other ch. Niece Elizabeth Griffith and her only dau. Niece Sarah G. wife of Abel Mathias and her 6 ch. Nine ch. of nephew Amos Griffith. Late husband Amos Griffith.
Wits: Richard Wilgus, Abraham Lapp, Elizabeth Foreman.

Page 424. William Twining, Northampton Twp. Feb. 18, 1794. Proved Oct. 10, 1814. Silas Twining and Elias Twining exrs. Bro. John Twining and ch., viz. Elizabeth Briggs, Mary Tomlinson, Joseph Twining and Rachel Balderston. Bro. David Twining's ch. Sarah Hutchinson, Elizabeth Hopkins, Mary Leedom and Beulah E. Torbert. Bros. Eleazer, Jacob and Stephen Twining, Wrightstown Monthly Meeting of Friends £5 for use of a Free School.
Wits: Joseph Buckman Junr. and Jesse Buchman.

Page 425. John Trissel, Senr., Tinicum Twp. July 24, 1814. Proved Oct. 3, 1814. Bro. Joseph Trissel exr. and sole legatee.
Wits: William Kealer, Peter Shuman.

Page 426. Jacob Shleiffer, Springfield Twp., widower. June 5, 1805. Proved Oct. 23, 1814. Youngest son Henry and son-in-law Samuel Kauffman exrs. Second son Jacob land adj. Adam Frankenfield, Peter Gruber and Jacob German. Eldest son Abraham. Dau. Elizabeth wife of Samuel Kauffman. Eve Meyer wife of John Kauffman who I brought up.
Wits: Jacob Fry, Christian Mann and Jacob Gehman.

Page 430. Christina Kremer, Loer [sic] Salford Twp., Montgomery Co., Pa., widow. April 16, 1811. Proved Nov. 5, 1814. Son Daniel and Benjamin Reiff, Esq. exrs. Dec'd. husband John Kremer. Sons Andrew, Henry, John, Daniel, George and Paul. Dau. Christiana wife of Nicholas Frantz. Son Andrew's dau. Madaline.
Wits: John Shekel and Jacob Ely.

Page 431. Stacy Buckman, Newtown Twp. Dec. 7, 1812. Proved Nov. 22, 1814. Bro. Major Thomas Buckman and Enos Morris exrs. Sister Mary and her ch. Stacy, Sarah, Mary and Elizabeth Flanagan £50 each. Residue to bro. Thomas.
Wits: Archibald McConkle, William R. Hanna and E. Morris.

Page 432. William Lownes, Upper Makefield Twp. 11-17-1814. Proved Nov. 29, 1814. Son-in-law Robert Knowles and Thomas Betts exrs. Dau. Mary wife of Robert Knowles, 30 acres of land bought of William Jackson and 27 acres off Plantation, island and ⅔ interest in Fisheries thereon, $600 etc. Son Joseph $1300. Son David $50 and Samuel Pancoast Jr. to hold House on 4th St. near Race in Phila. bot. [sic] of George Chambers

in trust for use of said son, his wife and children. Son William $20 and Joshua C. Canby and Joseph Hulme to hold 77 Acres of land in trust for use of him, his wife and ch. Son James $20 and Thomas Betts and Dr. Thomas Chapman, to hold 75 acres of land in trust for use of him, his wife and ch. Exrs. to convey interest in Land in Salem Co., N.J.
Wits: William Taylor and John Stapler.

Page 435. Andrew Singley, Bensalem Twp. Sept. 25, 1811. Codicil Nov. 24, 1814. Proved Nov. 30, 1814. Sons-in-law John Hill and Joseph Rees exrs. Wife Agnes, Household Goods and £80 per year. Son John 44 acres of land where he lives adj. Francis Ingram. Son Joseph 55 acres whereon he lives purchased of John Kidd, Esq. adj. above. Dau. Catharine Hill, House and 5 Acres on Bristol Road. Son-in-law Joseph Rees, balance of Plantation, he paying out to my dau. Jemima Singley, son Andrew, and two sons of dau. Mary dec'd. Daus. Elizabeth Ozman and Phebe Erwin.
Wits: Asa Walmsley, Joshua Canby and Jona. Thomas.

Page 437. Michael Ott, Bedminster Twp,. Farmer. Aug. 5, 1814. Proved Dec. 1, 1814. Sons Michael and Abraham exrs. Wife Elizabeth, Household Goods and ⅓ of Estate for life. Son Abraham part of Plantation adj. his own land balance to be sold. Ch. John, Michael, Henry, Abraham, Hannah, Madalena, Caty and Sarah. £30 of Caty's share to Gdsn. Joel Heller.
Wits: Peter Ott and Joseph Ott.

Page 438. Robert Flack, New Britain Twp. May 4, 1814. Proved Dec. 10, 1814. Codicil dated June 30, 1814. Wife Mary $250 and Plantation whereon I live for life. Sons James, Henry, Thomas Wier, Robert and William Flack. Daus. Ann wife of Dr. Beans, Sarah wife of Jacob Picker, and Mary Flack. Heirs of dec'd. dau. Jane late wife of Andrew McEwen. Sons James, Henry and Robert exrs. Nephew James Flack of Warrington Guardian of ch. of Andrew McEwen dec'd.
Wits: William Hines, John Wier.

Page 440. Andrew Overpeck, Springfield Twp., yeoman. Sept. 26, 1814. Proved Dec. 19, 1814. Son Jacob exr. Family to live together for 1 year. Sons Jacob and Andrew to furnish support. Wife Anne. Ch. Jacob, Mary, Sarah and Andrew.
Wits: Jacob Funk and Philip Overpeck.

Page 442. Adam Kerr, Warrington Twp., yeoman. Nov. 11, 1814. Proved Dec. 20, 1814. Sister Mary Long exr. "with whom I live." Sisters Ann McLacheran, Hester Kerr and Lydia McClean.
Wits: William Long and John Kerr.

Page 443. Joseph Richardson, Middletown Twp. 11-23-1814. Proved Dec. 24, 1814. Wife, Bro. William Richardson and John Watson exrs. Land

lately purchased in Northampton Twp. and stock in Tan yard to be sold. Son William 70 acres given me by my father, and Tan Yard, when 21. Son Clayton Farm I live on and 16 Acres purchased of John Watson. Daus. Mary, Elizabeth, Susanna, Hannah and Rebecca $2000 each. Bro.-in-law William Newbold.
Wits: William Jenks, Mahlon Gregg and William Newbold.

Page 446. Eve Kepler, Plumstead Twp. June 4, 1814. Proved Dec. 26, 1814. Ch. Elizabeth Luse, John Kepler and Jacob Kepler.
Wits: George Rice and Robert Gibson. Sons John and Jacob Kepler exrs.

Page 447. John Yoder, Rockhill Twp., yeoman. May 6, 1814. Proved Jan. 16, 1815. Son Abraham and Isaac Berkey exrs. Wife Mary. Sons Abraham and Samuel Plantation and 120 Acres adj. Isaac Berkey, David Sorver and others. Ch. Abraham, Samuel, John, David, Henry and Barbara.
Wits: Michael Shoemaker and Peter Roudenbush.

Page 449. Robert Allcorn, Solebury Twp. Oct. 18, 1813. Proved Jan. 16, 1815. Wife Ailsie and Enos Scarborough exrs. Wife all estate for life; at her death to Elizabeth Hill's present ch., Mary, Patty and others. Rebecca Kelly's present ch.
Wits: Robert Paste and Thomas Sands.

Page 450. Joshua Blakey, Middletown. 1-1-1813. Proved Jan. 24, 1815. Son William exr. Wife ---. Sons William, Samuel and Joshua. Daus. Esther Linton, Sarah Walker.
Wits: William Cox, David Watson, Giles Satterthwaite.

Page 452. Michael Fabian, Springfield Twp., yeoman. Dec. 13, 1814. Proved Jan. 24, 1815. Son Michael Fabian and Nicholas McCarty Sr. of Haycock exrs. Wife Sarah. Son Michael, Plantation. Dau. Barbara Snyder. Gddau. Modlena Fullmer.
Wits: Fredk. Fosbenner and Jacob Starner Jr.

End of Will Book No. 8

Will Book No. 9

Page 1. Sarah Baldwin, Bristol Twp. 6-17-1814. Proved Jan. 24, 1815. Samuel Hulme exr. Bro. John Baldwin. Sisters Rachel McElroy, Elizabeth Hutchinson, Margaret Swain, Elenor Kirkbride, Rebecca and Tamala Baldwin. Niece Martha Baldwin. Nephews Baldwin and Archibald McElroy, and Joseph B. Howard. Cousin Mary Roberts.
Wits: William Allen and Andrew Crozen.

Page 2. Martha Willet, Southampton Twp. Dec. 15, 1814. Proved Jan. 25, 1815. John McNair and Langhorn Biles exrs. Ch. Caroline Paxson,

Thomas Willett, Ann Walton, Phineas Willet, Walter Willet, Martha Dyer. Ch. of late dau. Rachel Baldwin. Gdsn. George Willet, natural son of Gilbert Willet, dec'd. Gddau. Martha Baldwin.
Wits: John McNair, Jesse Randal, Hannah Croasdale.

Page 3. George Ely, Newtown Twp., yeoman. 1-23-1808. Proved Jan. 26, 1815. Wife Sarah and son Joseph exrs. Wife Sarah 24 Acres bought of William Magill, adj. David Heston and David Simpson in fee. All personal estate and use of Rooms in present dwelling for life. Son Joseph 100 acres he lives on. Son Amos 100 acres he lives on. Son George 90 acres he lives on, part of tract I bought of Hampton Wilson on Newtown Rd. adj. Philip Heizer. Son Aaron Land bought of Oliver Paxson and 14 acres off tract devised to Amos. Son Mark land bought of Jesse Ely, adj. Joseph Eastburn, and 10 acres adj. Son Matthias land bought of Jonathan Ozmand and 15 Acres balance of tract given to wife Sarah. Son Amasa, 50 acres, residue of tract bought of Hampton Wilson.
Wits: Thomas Story, Amos Briggs and Thomas Briggs. Dau. Jane, wife of Benjamin Paxson.

Page 4. Catharine Thomas, Hilltown Twp., Spinster. March 30, 1795. Proved Feb. 11, 1815. Son-in-law Thomas Russell exr. Natural dau. Jemima, wife of Thomas Russell.
Wits: Samuel Wigton and Alex. Hughes. Both dec'd. Signatures proved by Samuel Wigton and Thomas Stewart.

Page 6. Abraham Roberts, Milford Twp., yeoman. 2-1-1808. Proved Feb. 7, 1815. Sons Levi and Judah exrs. Wife Penninah interest of £100. Son Levi 100 Acres whereon I live. Ch. Judah, Isaiah, Thomas, Miriam, Eleanor, Catharine and Abigail. Ch. of Dau. Pricilla Field, dec'd.
Wits: John Foulke, Abel Penrose and Everard Foulke.

Page 9. Arthur Thomas, Bristol Boro., "Advanced in age." Nov. 12, 1812. Codicil dated Dec. 12, 1814. Proved Feb. 27, 1815. Step-Gdsn. Benjamin Coobs [sic] and Dorcas Brown exrs. Bro. Isaac Thomas. "My boy John Thomas Brown." (Gdsn.) Hannah Herbert, bed in place of one her Aunt Martha got that was hers by her Aunt Morrison's will. Step-Gddau. Martha Coombs. Nephew Isaac Ryan. Son John Thomas. Housekeeper Dorcas Brown "who has lived with me upwards of 30 years" at request of my wife on her death bed I devise her Lot on Pond St. adj. Samuel Church and Samuel Leves. Gdsn. John Drinker Thomas and his wife Mary Ann. Stepdau. Ann Ferguson. Step-gddau. Elizabeth Manington and her ch. Hannah and George. Step-gdsn. Benjamin Coombs.
Wits: Jona Pursel, Abraham Warner.

Page 12. Hannah Eastburn, Solebury Twp. 1-8-1815. Proved March 1, 1815. Sisters Letitia, Sarah and Mary. Cousin Moses Eastburn exr. Cousin Dr. Ely Kitchin. Nephews David K. and Joseph Eastburn Reeder.

Wits: Oliver Hampton, John Kitchin and Hannah Hampton.

Page 13. George Miller, Nockamixon Twp., weaver. Oct. 27, 1797. Proved March 10, 1815. Jacob Rymond exr. Wife Catharine. Ch., Minors.
Wits: Philip Rapp and Peter Uhlmer. "Philip Rap old and feeble, did not appear."

Page 14. John Ziegenfus, Rockhill Twp., Blacksmith. Feb. 14, 1815. Proved March 10, 1815. Bro. Peter Ziegenfus exr. Wife Catharine. Ch. Abraham, Enos, John, Hannah and Catharine, all minors. Jacob Stout Guardian.
Wits: Everard Foulke and John Blank.

Page 17. Jason Blaker, Northampton Twp. 2-22-1815. Proved March 16, 1815. Wife Mary and dau. Martha and Sarah, minors. "Farmer, John Blaker" and Paul Blaker exrs.
Wits: John Blaker and John Blaker, Mason.

Page 18. John Mann, Senr., Springfield Twp. April 27, 1811. Codicil dated May 2, 1814. Proved May 4, 1815. Sons John, George, Jacob and Abraham exrs. Sons John, Jacob, Abraham, John George, Philip, Christian and Henry. Daus. Catharine (died before date of codicil), Margret, Elizabeth wife of Henry Hess. Son-in-law George Ruth or Ruht, and his ch. Land, 364 Acres to Jacob and Abraham. Son Philip, absent, his dau. Catharine, whom I have raised.
Wits: Paul Apple and John Apple.

Page 24. John Smith, Esq., Springfield Twp. Nov. 2, 1811. Proved Feb. 6, 1815. Son Joseph Smith and son-in-law Nicholas Mensch exrs. Wife Berndina, interest of £500 . Ch. Joseph, Maria wife of Nicholas Mensch and Jacob. Gdsn. John Smith, son of son John, dec'd. and his mother Nancy, now wife of Henry Zeagenfuse. Gddau. Mary, dau. of son Joseph. Deed to be made to Jacob Wierback for land sold to him 1810.
Wits: Michael Heft and Henry Wyreback. Agreement of heirs reocorded with will shows that Mary Smith the gddau. had married John Apple.

Page 26. John W. Burson, Springfield Twp. March 9, 1815. Proved April 16, 1815. Edward Burson of Stroudsburg and Isaac Burson of Springfield Twp. exrs. Wife Mary, Household Goods and $2000 for life. Dau. Evelina and Hannah Burson.
Wits: Jacob Funk and Jacob Teichler. Signed John W. Burson.

Page 27. Mary Hambleton, Solebury Twp. 2-21-1815. Proved April 8, 1815. Abraham Paxson exr. Sister Sarah Hambleton £100. Bro. Thomas Hambleton's 3 daus., Sarah, Margaret and Elizabeth. Bro. Benjamin's dau. Amy Hambleton. Nieces Martha, Eunice and Mary Dean. Bro. Joseph Hambleton; his daus. Elizabeth, Mary, Sarah and Margaret.

Wits: Aaron Paxson and Elias Paxson.

Page 29. Benjamin Wiggins, Upper Makefield Twp., "far advanced in years." 1-21-1807. Proved April 13, 1815. Sons Joseph and Benjamin exrs. Son Joseph 152 Acres devised me by father, where Joseph now lives. Son Benjamin balance of lands, 263 Acres. Daus. Rachel Lacey, Agnes Simpson and Sarah Wiggins.
Wits: Thomas Chapman and Isaac Chapman.

Page 30. Isaac Pickering, Solebury Twp., Innholder. March 31, 1815. Proved April 26, 1815. Bro.-in-law Mahlon Carver and sons Isaac, Thomas and John exrs. Wife Elizabeth. Part of Real Estate in Buckingham, Tavern, House and Store and 20 acres of Land adj. Isaiah Michener to be sold. Residue of land in Buckingham Twp. to sons Thomas and John; paying out to sons Joseph, Isaac, James, Stephen, Mahlon and Carey.
Wits: Elias Carey, Joseph Carver, Henry Carver.

Page 33. John Heacock, Bedminster Twp. March 7, 1815. Proved April 26, 1815. Jacob Kramer Junr. of Bedminster exr. Wife Mary. Ch. Mary Ann and Joseph. John Kramer Junr. their Guardian.
Wits: William McNeeley and Isaac Heacock.

Page 34. Joshua Anderson, Lower Makefield. 9-27-1811. Proved April 27, 1815. Wife Elizabeth. Daus. Catharine Jone, Mary Clossin, Rachel Henderson, Charlotte Duer, Ann Anderson, Abigail White and Rebecca Stombock. Son-in-law William Clossin. Sons Daniel, James and David. Dr. Reading Beatty exr.
Wits: Cyrus Cadwallader, John Stewart and John Kinsey.

Page 35. Francis Wilson, Tinicum Twp. March 20, 1815. Proved May 2, 1815. Sons Andrew, John and Francis A. Wilson exrs. Wife Mary, interest of $1300. Son Francis A. the Homestead 100 Acres in Tinicum. Residue of Land to sons William and James. Sons Andrew and John and dau. Mary Ann each $800. Daus. Mary and Juliann each $600. Gdsn. Francis A., son of Andrew.
Wits: George Neice and Henry Ridge.

Page 39. Nicholas Mumbower, Lower Milford Twp., yeoman. April 1, 1809. Proved May 30, 1815. Eldest son Philip exr. Sons Philip, Henry, John, Conrad and George. Daus. Anna Mary wife of Wendel Moyer, Catharine wife of Deval Poff. Son Philip's wife Magdalena and his ch. Philip and Magdalena.
Wit: David Spinner and Philip Kuntz.

Page 40. Matthias Cowell, Solebury Twp. Jan. 3, 1812. Proved June 21, 1815. Son Joseph Cowell and Ebenezer Large of Solebury exrs. and ch. Elizabeth Bennett, Ann Opdyke, Catharine Hambleton, Mary Rice,

Margaret Kiple, Rebecca Heed and Joseph Cowell. Legacy left to sister Ann Search by her father.
Wits: Thomas Wall and David McCray.

Page 41. Joshua Headly, Bristol Twp. 2-20-1815. Proved June 21, 1815. Sons Joseph, Joshua and Ebenezer exrs. Son Joseph 176 Acres purchased of William Smith in Falls Twp. Adj. Mary Swift, now in tenure of Benjamin White and 7 1/2 Acres purchased of Jacob Shull, 13 Acres in Bristol Twp. purchased of Amos Burgess, 17 Acres in Middletown, part of estate of late bro. Solomon Headly, 2 Brick Messuages and lots in Bristol Twp. purchased of Jacob Vanhart and Amos Palmer, and 1/2 of Orchard purchased of James Martin adj. George Stockham, and place where I live, with right of way to Saw Mill, by cartway and by water. Son Daniel, 120 Acres he lives on Bristol Twp. purchased of Mary McIlvaine now Mary Bloomfield, son William 210 Acres he lives on in Bristol Twp. on which I last resided and 9 Acres adj. purchased of Benjamin Swain. Son Joshua 175 Acres he lives on. Fisheries thereon to sons Joseph, Joshua and Ebenezer. Son Ebenezer 120 Acres he lives on in Falls. Daus. Sarah White and Christiana Bower.
Wits: William Crawford and Amos Gregg.

Page 47. James Stringer, Bristol Twp., "Far advanced in years." May 5, 1815. Proved June 21, 1815. Son Charles Stringer exr. Daus. Elizabeth, Rachel, Sarah, Ann, Hannah, Edith and Phebe.
Wits: Joseph Headley and Amos Burgess.

Page 48. Killiam Kresler, Tinicum Twp. March 28, 1815. Proved June 28, 1815. William Kealer, Senr. exr. Step-son John Hillapot all real estate. Stepch. Margaret wife of George Snider, John, George and Barnet Hillapot, Elizabeth wife of Peter Barnet, Henry and Frederick Hillapot and Molly wife of John Snider.
Wits: George Kealer and Abraham Worman.

Page 49. Joseph Moyer, Hilltown Twp. June 19, 1815 (?). Proved July 7, 1815. Martin Fretz and Jacob Overholt exrs. Wife Barbara and ch. to live together on Plantation until youngest child is 21. Sons Jacob, Samuel, Joseph, William and Henry. Daus. Elizabeth and Mary.
Wits: Abraham Kratz and Joseph Matthias.

Page 51. Hugh Meredith, M.D. of village of Doylestown. Dec. 9, 1812. Codicil dated March 8, 1815. Sons Charles and Thomas and son-in-law Abraham Chapman Esq. exrs. Wife Mary 150 Acres of land in Warwick Twp. in tenure of George Rapp, in fee simple. Gdch. Wilhelmina and Henry Chapman, ch. of dau. Elizabeth, dec'd.
Wits: Asher Miner, Timothy Price, Enoch Harvey, Charles L. Armstrong.

Page 53. David Jarrett, Warminster Twp., yeoman. 5-9-1815. Proved May

30, 1815. Nephew Anthony Williams exr. Wife Rebecca, interest of whole proceeds of sale of Plantation during widowhood, if she marry £800. Sister-in-law Phebe Hough £500. Sister-in-law Rachel Jarret, widow of Joseph Jarret, interest of £500. Bro.-in-law John Cadwallader, do. Niece Hannah wife of Ezekiel Harland, do. Bro. Jesse Grant do. Niece Elizabeth widow of David Parry interest of £100 for life then to her son David. James Watson £100. Richard Jarret £50. Ann wife of Henry Meloy interest of £75. Cyrus Cadwallader, Jacob Cadwallader. Rebecca wife of William Follis. Niece Tacey wife of Michael Trump. (Jona. Iredell, William Lukens and Gove Mitchell members of Horsham Meeting) for use of Free School £300.
Wits: Thomas Stackhouse, Isaac Parry.

Page 57. Jesse Clatter, Buckingham Twp. June 1, 1815. Proved June 6, 1815. Isaac Kirk Senr. exr. Personal Estate to John Melone Junr.'s three sons Charles, Scinica and Benjamin Melone. Land in Buckingham, adj. William Kirk to Isaac Kirk Senr.
Wits: Amos Kirk and Samuel McDowell.

Page 57. John Melone, Buckingham Twp. 4-10-1813. Proved June 15, 1815. Son John exr. Gddaus. Margaret, Rebecca, Alice and Mary Walton, daus. of Job Walton, $40 "which would have been their mother's share if living." Daus. Hannah Walton ($160) and Alice Melone, Phebe Kirk and Rachel Wood. Son John 117 Acres on which I live, 47 Acres 156 P. purchased of Aaron Phillips and ½ part of Wood lot purchased of John Longstreth. Son James 84 Acres on which he lives, bought of William Corbet, ½ of wood lot aforesaid on York Rd. adj. Everard Roberts. Sons to provide for Alice while single.
Wits: John Watson, John Watson Junr. and Rebecca Walton.

Page 59. William Albertson, Newtown Twp., yeoman. June 13, 1815. William Grant of Abington and Thomas G. Kennedy of Newtown exrs. 126 Acres bounded by lands of Jesse Leedom, Beulah E. Twining and Neshaming Creek, to sister Ann Severns, for life, then to be sold and proceeds to William, son of cousin Benjamin Albertson of Falls Twp. ½ share. ¼ of the other ½ to Elizabeth wife of George Logan, of Northampton Twp. and ¼ to Elizabeth wife of Joshua Wiser of New Castle Co. Del. The other ¼ of proceeds in 10 shares, 1 to William, son of Bernard Vandegrift of Northampton Twp. 1 to William, son of John Titus of Lamberton N.J. 1 to Sarah wife of said John Titus and her heirs. 1 to all the sons of Uncle Jacob Albertson, late of Egg Harbor, dec'd. 1 to sons of Uncle Josiah Albertson, late of Egg Harbor dec'd. 1 to Elizabeth wife of Robert Bond of Newtown. 1 to Sarah Wiser, dau. of Joshua, before mentioned. 1 to Joseph Willard and Sarah his wife of Newtown. 1 to ch. of Jonathan Phelps and Rachel his wife and George Campbell and Hannah his wife. The other to Trustees of Newtown Pres. Church ½ and trustees of Bensalem Pres. Church ½.

Wits: Jesse Leedom and Thomas Jenks.

Page 63. Jane Bartram, Newtown, widow. 11-13-1813. Proved Aug. 15, 1815. David Story and Joseph Richardson (Turner) exrs. Estate to be divided into 5 parts. 1 to Alexander James Bartram, son of Ann Bartram, late Ann Nicholson, Phila. 1 to William and Ann Martin, ch. of Nephew Dr. William Martin. 1 to Nephew John Martin, son of Bro. John Martin dec'd. 1 to Niece Sarah Martin dau. of said John. 1 to ch. of Niece Deborah wife of David Davis.
Wits: William Watts and Thomas G. Kennedy.

Page 64. Cephas Child, Plumstead Twp., "advanced in age." April 26, 1815. Proved Aug. 19, 1815. Son Richard exr. Son Joseph $30. 5 ch. of dau. Mary Worthington, dec'd., $6 each. 3 ch. of son Cephas, dec'd., $10 each. Sons William and Naylor Child and dau. Priscilla Pennington $30 each. Son Cadwallader Child $485. Phebe Carman, table &c. Son Richard Child Plantation 80 Acres where I reside and residue of estate, paying debts and above legacies.
Wits: Jonas Fry and George Burgess.

Page 65. Stephen Akerman, Haycock Twp., yeoman. May 22, 1812. Proved Aug. 17, 1815. Sons Stephen and John Akerman exrs. Wife Barbara. Son Michael 9 Acres where he lives. Son Stephen 35 Acres in Richland where he lives. Son John 63 Acres of Plantation whereon I live. Son George balance of Plantation 33 Acres. Ch. Catharine Akerman, Susanna wife of Jacob Zingmaster, Barbara wife of Lewis Alcort, Modlena Akerman, Mary wife of Jacob Horn, Lydda, Michael, Stephen, John, George and Sarah Akerman and gddau. Elizabeth Wireback.
Wits: John Damuth and James Bryan.

Page 68. Mary Backhouse, Bucks Co. March 30, 1815. Proved Aug. 21, 1815. Friend Dr. Ely Kitchin, exr. Son John Backhouse £100 in hands of Jacob Fulmer. Son Allen Backhouse Lot I live on. Daus. Margaret Clymer and Isabella Lewis.
Wits: Jacob Burgy and James Ruckman.

Page 69. Sarah Brodnax, widow of William Brodnax, late of Bristol Twp. Nov. 7, 1814. Proved Sept. 21, 1815. Son William Brodnax and dau. Amelia Mendenhall exrs. Son Robert Brodnax. Gdsn. Richard Brodnax. Dau. Sarah Corder. Dower in hands of Dr. Amos Gregg in estate of Leopold Chotnagle. Money in hands of William Crawford and Jonathan Burrell.
Wits: Joseph Clunn and Hugh Tombe.

Page 70. James McMasters, Bensalem Twp. 6-23-1814. Proved Aug. 26, 1815. Wife Catharine and Michael Trump exrs. Son John McMasters, Lands and residue of estate when 21. Son-in-law Morris Hortwick and

dau.-in-law Margaret Hortwick, each $200.
Wits: Bertrand Laforgue, John Vandegrift and Michael Trump.

Page 71. James Banes, Southampton Twp., yeoman. Sept. 10, 1814.
Proved Aug. 29, 1815. Sons Josiah D., Mahlon, Lemmes (?) and Valerius
Banes exrs. Wife Ann, daus. Elizabeth Anderson and Tacey McDowell.
Gddau. Juliann Banes Anderson.
Wits: John McNair and Christopher Search.

Page 72. Joseph Mitchell, late of Moreland Twp., Montgomery Co., now
of Falls Twp., "far advanced in years." March 29, 1811. Proved Aug. 29,
1815. Neighbors Joshua Comley and Jonathan Comley of Moorland Twp.,
Phila. Co., exrs. Ch. Thomas Mitchell, Sarah Miller, Mary Stapler,
Elizabeth Comfort, Hannah Harmer and Ann Waterhouse. Gdch. Joseph
Mitchell son of Thomas, Joseph Stapler, Joseph Mitchell Harmer, Mary
Miller, Mary Harmer, Mary Elliott, Thomas, John and Joseph Butler.
Wits: Elisha Thomas and Samuel W. Comly. [sic]

Page 73. Thomas Ross, late of Newtown, now of New Hope, Bucks Co.,
Esq. Aug. 29, 1814. Proved Sept. 20, 1815, in Northampton Co., Pa. Bro.
John Ross of Easton, Northampton Co., exr. and sole legatee "including
estate now settled on my wife during her lifetime."
Wits: Daniel Waggoner, Robert James and George Ihrie.

*Note dated 25 Nov. 1947 from Lewis D. Cook, to Miss McMahon reads:
The attached abstract (below) of Will of Benjamin Hibbs was omitted, I
find, from the Society's books of BUCKS COUNTY WILLS. This will
serve as valuable complement, may I suggest, if it can be inserted now in
the proper place . . .*

Page 77. Benjamin Hibbs of Northampton Twp. 5-9 mo.-1815. Proved 23
Oct. 1815. Desires wife, three sons and dau. Mary to live together and
have the farm until son William comes of age, "Which will be one year
from the 24th of third month next", when wife shall have choice of one
room in the house where we now live, and use of kitchen and family fire,
during widowhood, also choice of furniture and $100 a year during lifetime
paid by sons Benjamin and James $40 each and William $20; rest of
personal estate divided between sons. Devises to four mar. daus. Ann
Roberts, Elizabeth Cooper, Sarah Mitchell, and Susan Heston, £100 each,
with interest annually, during life times, and afterward the principal to
their respective ch., to be paid by said 3 sons. Devises to dau. Mary Hibbs
200£, to be paid within year after his dec.; to sons Benjamin, James, and
William Hibbs all lands and residue of estate, Benjamin to have the
homestead of 55 acres, bought of Thomas Hutchinson and valued at
$4350.00 exclusive of Twining's mortgage. James to have 50 acres tract
bought of Jonathan Schofield and valued at $3500.00, and William the 35
¾ acres bought of John Baylor and valued at $1950.00, all subject to their

190

payment of above bequests. Appoints wife Sarah Hibbs and son Benjamin Hibbs exrs.
Wits: Joseph Worstall and Edward Hicks.

Page 74. George Sheip, New Britain Twp. Dec. 30, 1804. Proved Sept. 25, 1815. Son John and son-in-law George Weisel exrs. Son George Trustee. Wife Elizabeth. Ch. John, Margaret, Elizabeth, Catharine and George.
Wits: Morgan Thomas, Joseph Ratzal and John Pugh.

Page 78. Harman Vansant, Bensalem Twp. "Far advanced in years." May 6, 1802. Codicil dated July 11, 1815. Proved Nov. 20, 1815. Son Garret exr. Wife Eleanor. Ch. of son Jacob, dec'd., viz. Joseph, Harman and Garret. Son Joseph. Daus. Mary Vanhorn, Eleanor Wood, Catharine Johnson, Sarah Cox and Ann Pleamas. Gdch. Mary Kinsy and Jacob Ramson.
Wits: Joseph Headley, Benjamin Swaine, Samuel Allen and William Simmons.

Page 80. James Harrison, Bristol Boro. Cooper. Sept. 5, 1815. Proved Nov. 27, 1815. Son Joseph exr. Wife Martha. Son William. Dau. Rachel Harrison, when 18. Son James when 21. Gddau. Rachel Harrison, when 18.
Wits: Gilbert Tomlinson, John White.

Page 82. Lewis Stagner, Warwick Twp. July 31, 1813. Proved Nov. 27, 1815. Signed "Ludwick Stegner." Sons Christian and Henry exrs. Wife Louise. Land to sons Christian and Henry Stegner. Ch. of son Lewis, dec'd., viz. Elias, Lewis and Mary.
Wits: Jacob Cassel and Benjamin Hough.

Page 83. Jane Smith, Upper Makefield Twp., widow of Samuel Smith, dec'd. 8-30-1812. Proved Nov. 29, 1815. Ezra Smith exr. Four daus. Sons Thomas, William and Samuel; gddau. Hannah Fell. Gdsn. Henry Smith.
Wits: Samuel Paxson and William Atkinson.

Page 84. Susanna Rush, Hilltown Twp., "Far advanced in years." [no date] Proved Dec. 8, 1815. Son Abraham Harman exr. Ch. David and Abraham Harman, Catharine Eastong, Elizabeth Fretz and Mary Kline. Dau.-in-law Margaret Harman. Friend John Kephard.
Wits: Andrew Trewig and Isaac Morris.
Signed Susanna X. Harman (alias Ruth).

Page 85. Robert McGraudy, Warwick Twp. Nov. 23, 1815. Proved Dec. 27, 1815. Bro. Thomas McGraudy and Samuel Hart exrs. Mother 1/2 income of Real Estate. Bros. Thomas and Samuel. Sisters Margaret and Jane. William son of sister Isabella and Robert son of bro. John.
Wits: Amos Stirke and John McGraudy.

Page 86. John Goforth, Bensalem Twp. 12-24-1815. Proved Jan. 23, 1816. Wife Elizabeth and John Paxson exrs. Land devised by Father's will to wife for life, then Dwelling House where I live and land on South side of Newport Road to son William, (adj. Samuel Allen, John Paxson and Samuel Hibbs). Balance of land to son Jacob Hibbs Goforth.
Wits: Joshua Barker and Daniel Neall.

Page 87. Martha Slack, Lower Makefield Twp. March 28, 1813. Proved Jan. 26, 1816. Tunis Hellings and Samuel Hellings exrs. Bro. Samuel Titus £50. Bro. John Titus's son John and Abraham each £15. Bro. Francis Titus's ch. Francis Titus, Rebekah Vanarsdalen and Margaret Wilcox, do. Bro. Tunis Tisus's ch. Archible and Tunis Titus, Mary Bennet and Elizabeth Vanhorn. Sister Elizabeth Hellings's ch. John, Tunis, Samuel, Jesse and Jacob Hellings, Mary Everett and Martha Rodman. Aron Everett £5. Martha White, dau. of Tunis Hellings £5. Sarah, wife of Moses Celly (?) £10. Cornelius Slack's daus., Ann and Sarah Slack. Martha Titus, dau. of Archible. ¼ of apparel to Edith Burgin. Balance to sister Elizabeth Hellings and her daus.
Wits: William and Aaron Vanhorn.

Page 88. Jonathan Purssell, Bristol Boro., Shopkeeper and Trader. 11-2-1809. Proved Feb. 7, 1816. Wife Lydia extx. and sole legatee.
Wits: Isaac Morris and Ebenezer Headley.

Page 89. Serick Titus, Buckingham Twp., yeoman. Jan. 18, 1816. Proved Feb. 27, 1816. Edmund Smith of Upper Makefield and Thomas G. Smith of Buckingham exrs. (Thomas resigned in 1821, "having removed to a distant state.") Wife Jane ½ of clear estate for life. Eldest son, a minor, other ch. not named.
Wits: Thomas Smith and Robert Smith.

Page 90. Joel Carver, Northampton Twp., yeoman. Jan. 27, 1816. Proved March 7, 1816. Wife Ann and sons Robert and Joel exrs. Daus. Rachel, Martha and Hannah Carver. Land bought of Ephraim Thomas.
Wits: Owen and Geroge Chapman.

Page 92. David Howell, Upper Makefield Twp., yeoman. 7-29-1815. Proved March 11, 1816. Sons Samuel and Charles exrs. Plantation 218 acres subject to privileges granted to my mother by my father's will. 4 younger ch. Elizabeth, Moore, Phebe and Joseph, all minors.
Wits: Garret Johnson and William Taylor.

Page 94. David Vanhorn, Bristol Boro. April 3, 1812. Codicil Nov. 11, 1815. Proved March 15, 1816. Adrian Cornell exr. Son Abraham. Ch. of dec'd. dau. Mary Margerum. Son William's wife Mary and ch. Robert Vanhorn heir to son David, dec'd.. Gdch. Hetty and William Williard; their father Isaac Williard. "If son Abraham do not return" his share to William.

Wits: James and Adrian Cornell. Gddau. Ann Larzelere.

Page 96. George Rogers, Plumstead Twp. Nov. 12, 1815. Proved March 21, 1816. Son-in-law Robert Kirkbride and Mary his wife exrs. Wife Mary all estate for life, then to ch. Hezekiah Rogers, Mary Kirkbride, Elizabeth Walton and Ann Gary.
Wits: John Leer, Nicholas Swartz.

Page 97. Abner Thomas, Hilltown Twp. Jan. 1, 1816. Proved March 23, 1816. Josiah Lunn exr. and Guardian. 33 acres of Land to be sold, proceeds to nephews Joseph and Ephraim Thomas, when 21. Bro. Nathan Thomas; sisters Eleanor Williams and Sarah Thomas.
Wits: Amos Thomas, Jacob Leidy and Stephen Rowland.

Page 98. Abraham Wilkinson, Warwick Twp., yeoman. March 8, 1816. Proved March 23, 1816. Bro.-in-law Robert McDole and cousin Isaac Chapman exrs. Wife Mary. Mother Jane Wilkinson. Son Samuel T. [?] spoons marked "S.W.P." left to bro. John by gdfather John Wilkinson Esq. 5 ch. Jane, John C., Abraham, Samuel T. [?] and Eleanor Wilkinson. Thomas Story, John Buckman, Silas Twining, William Worthington, Abner Worthington and Amos Briggs to divide 172 acres I live on between said ch.
Wits: Thomas Chapman, Watson Welding Jr. and Silas Twining.

Page 99. Elnathan Pettit, Warwick Twp. Aug. 25, 1814. Proved March 27, 1816. Codicil dated Oct. 26, 1815. Col. William Hart and Nephew Benjamin Pettit exrs. Nephew Elnathan Pettit. Bros. Daniel and Samuel Pettit. Sisters Charity wife of Jonathan Dean, Sarah Burson, Elizabeth Cottral. Ch. of bro. John, viz. Lydia, Margaret and Sarah. Ch. of sister Mary Powell, (3 daus). Charity, Elizabeth, Martha and Alydia Dean, daus. of Charity. William, Jacob, Daniel and Andrew, sons of bro. William. Elizabeth wife of Jacob Paxson. Sarah wife of William Burson. Her son Pettit and dau. Elizabeth. Letitia McCleas, Jane Hughs, Heirs of Thomas Rose, heirs of Benjamin Paxson, Deborah dau. of Jona. Ingham, Joseph Forsythe who lives with Col. John Crawford, William and John sons of bro. Samuel.

Page 101. Cornelius Vansant, Lower Makefield Twp. Nov. 19, 1813. Codicil dated March 2, 1816. Proved March 28, 1816. John Linton exr. Housekeeper, Jemima Tomlinson, her ch. Ann, Susanna, William and Cornelius Tomlinson, all minors. Sons Nicholas, Abner and Nathan Vansant.
Wits: Thomas K. Biles, Jacob Jenny, Thomas Potts and John Linton.

Page 103. Jane Weber, Nockamixon Twp. Jan. 22, 1812. Proved March 29, 1816. Nephew John Morris exr. Cousin Morris Morris.
Wits: John Raisner and Michael Cole.

Page 104. Michael Deihl, Richland Twp. Jan. 26, 1816. Proved April 1, 1816. Wife Ann and son Jacob Deihl exrs. Land to be sold. 1/5 of estate to son Jacob. 1/5 to ch. of dau. Elizabeth dec'd., late wife of Daniel Horne. 1/5 to dau. Susanna wife of Jacob Moyer. 1/5 to son Henry, a minor (bro.-in-law William Moyer of Springfield and William Moyer, Taylor, Guardians). 1/5 to Abraham Moyer of Springfield; my son-in-law Jacob Moyer, (son of said Abraham) and Nephew David Deihl, in trust for use of son Michael "weak in mental faculties."
Wits: Henry Fried and Frederick Deihl.

Page 106. Robert Eastburn, Solebury Twp. 5-8-1813. Proved April 3, 1816. Sons Moses and Aaron exrs. Daus. Sarah Phillips, Ann Comfort and Latitia Eastburn. Son Moses Plantation whereon he lives and woodland adj. York Road nearest Mitchell's Ferry. Son Samuel, tract on which I live. Gdsn. Robert Eastburn tract lying on river Delaware, purchased of Joseph Paxson, 100 acres. Son Aaron residue of lands.
Wits: Abraham Paxson, Robert Livezey and Sarah Livezey.

Page 107. Owen Rowland, Hilltown Twp. March 26, 1816. Proved April 9, 1816. Bro. William H. Rowland exr. Sons Milton, Adison, Horatio and Arkmus (minors), Eleazer Bitting, John D. Rowland and Stephen Rowland, guardians. Wife Mary. Land adj. Abraham Miller; Eleazer Bitting, George Leidy and others.
Wits: Eleazer Bitting, Jacob Leidy and William H. Rowland.

Page 109. Bartel Knechel, Springfield Twp., yeoman. March 28, 1812. Proved April 11, 1816. Jacob Rufe and William Knechel exrs. Wife Barbara Catharine. Ch. William, Elizabeth, John, Anna Maria and George.
Wits: Christian Gross and Abraham Frankenfield.

Page 110. Jonathan Ring, Hulmeville, Middletown Twp. June 27, 1815. Proved April 15, 1816. Wife Elizabeth all estate in trust, until son Jacob Ring is 21, to carry on the coopering business "as at present." Stepch. Jonathan, Jacob and Jesse Randal, Ann Rampson wife of George Rampson, Eliza and Mary Randal. 4 ch. Rebecca, Jacob, Grace and Sarah. Joseph Hulme, Merchant, and John Mitchell, Physician, both of Hulmeville exrs. Land bought of Ann Kimble in Bensalem.
Wits: George Atherton and William Milnor.

Page 111. John Pursell, Nockamixon Twp. March 29, 1816. Proved April 15, 1816. George Wyker and John Williams, (son of Jeremiah), exrs. Wife Marsee. Mother. Bro. Brice Pursell. Sisters Elizabeth, Jane and Margaret ch. "both sons and daus."
Wits: Thomas Alexander, Reuben Lee, Jacob House. Contract for sale of lands with Peter Lees and Jacob Root.

Page 113. John M. Thomas, Warwick Twp. April 9, 1816. Proved April 17,

194

1816. Matthias Morris Esq. exr. Tombstones to be erected at Baptist Church of Montgomery, to the memory of "My Father Owen, my mother Susan and my two bros., Joseph and Azahel." $15.00 to said church and $1000 to new Britain Baptist Church, interest to be at the disposal of Dr. Silas Hough, (Pastor) and his wife during their lives, not to be considered as Salary. Charles Dungan $2500, he to immediately execute will disposing of same in default of issue.
Wits: John Pugh and Samuel Moore.

Page 114. Henry Wynkoop, Northampton Twp. Oct. 7, 1813. Codicil Jan. 9, 1816. Proved March 27, 1816. Son Jonathan and son-in-law Reading Beatty exrs. Daus. Christina Beatty, Ann Raquet, Margaret Lombaert and Mary H. Wirtz and Susanna Lefferts. Gddau. Claudine Raquet. Son Jonathan, Mansion House and 218 acres. 143 acres in tenure of Jacob Harding to be sold. Elizabeth Walton living with family $200. No wits. Proved by William Watts and Th. G. Kennedy.

Page 119. Jesse James, Bensalem Twp. 3-24-1816. Proved April 23, 1816. Sons Samuel and Jesse and Relative Ezra Townsend exrs. Wife Phebe. Daus. Elizabeth Comfort, Mary Knight, Joanna Gilbert, Phebe, Martha and Abi James. Eldest son Samuel land on Bustleton Road bought of --- Kelly adj. Samuel Cott and Abraham Staates. Youngest son Jesse balance of Real Estate.
Wits: Job P. Townsend and James Townsend.

Page 120. David Stockdale, Buckingham Twp., "Far advanced in years." May 8, 1811. Proved April 29, 1816. Isaac Chapman and David Warner exrs. And 2 acres in Buckinham to be sold. 5 ch. Robert Stockdale, Joyce Marcellus, John and William Stockdale and Sarah Skelton. Gdch. Elizabeth, Mary, Sarah and Jane, daus. of son Joseph Stockdale.
Wits: Mahlon Atkinson and John Lear.

Page 121. Robert Beatty, Middletown Twp. Feb. 12, 1813. Proved May 11, 1816. Son Samuel B. Beatty and Thomas Jenks exrs. Wife Rachel Plantation and Personal Estate for life. Land to sons Samuel and Robert at her death. "Have been at considerable expense in giving son John a good education" gives him $500. Daus. Ann, Sarah, Maria and Lydia each $500.
Wits: Joseph Harvey, Phineas Briggs and Joseph Richardson Junr.

Page 123. Samuel Winder, Senr., Falls Twp. 9-15-1814. Proved May 2, 1816. Giles Satterthwaite and Giles S. Winder exrs. Wife Sarah, sole legatee.
Wits: James Stradling and Giles Satterthwaite.

Page 123. Jacob Kulp, Hilltown Twp., yeoman. Nov. 1, 1806. Proved May 13, 1816. Sons Isaac and Jacob exrs. Wife Elizabeth, son Henry, part of

Plantation adj. Michael Kulp, Samuel Musselman, Daniel Rickert, Christian Rule, Henry Weisel, Samuel Moyer, Jacob Letherach and Martin Fretz. Son Tilman, balance thereof. Timber loand adj. Joseph Greer, John Licey and Daniel Rickert. Sons Isaac, Jacob, John, Abraham, Tilman and Henry. Daus. Gertrude, Elizabeth and Catharine.
Wits: Martin Fretz, Joseph Moyer, Henry Moyer.

Page 126. Stacy Hutchinson, late of N.J. but now Falls Twp. 4-6-1816. Proved May 20, 1816. Bro.-in-law Joseph Johnson exr. Nephew Joseph Johnson Junr., son of sister Ann, sole legatee.
Wits: James Ash Junr. and John W. Balderston.

Page 127. Elias Gilbert, Warwick Twp. Jan. 20, 1816. Proved May 27, 1816. Nephew Josiah Hart exr. Ch. of sisters Elizabeth, Rachel, Hannah and Edith. Jonathan Conard, son of my niece Elizabeth Croasdale. Trustees Pres. Church of Warwick $40. Mary dau. of John and Martha Jamison $50.
Wits: Henry Doughty and James McMinn.

Page 128. William Kitchin, Solebury Twp., Taylor. 9-13-1804. Proved June 19, 1816. Wife Ann and Bro.-in-law Moses Paxson exrs. Son William Kitchin and dau. Sarah Duer.
Wits: Watson Fell, John Comfort and Charles Fell.

Page 130. James Armitage, Solebury Twp., Farmer. 7-19-1811. Proved July 31, 1816. Sons John and Samuel and Bro. John Armitage exrs. Wife Martha. Son Samuel part of Plantation adj. John Armitage and Joseph White. Sons Henry, Charles and Amos, the two latter minors. Daus. Elizabeth Armitage, Hannah Walton and Letitia Hartley. Gddau. Evelina Walton.
Wits: Moses Paxson and Joshua Ely.

Page 131. Jane Kennedy, ---, "aged and infirm." March 10, 1807. Proved June 27, 1816. Barnet Manner and William Paulison exrs. "Barnet Manner, Robert Manner and Jean Manner, the two other ch. of said Barnet Manner" 50 acres part of 100 acres devised by will of husband Thomas Kennedy. Balance of same to William Paulison.
Wits: William Erwin and Fran. McHenry.

Page 132. Richard Arrison, Solebury Twp. June 19, 1816. [Proved?] June 28, 1816. Wife Martha extx. Dau. Eupheme Arrison "bed which I had before I married my present wife." Son Pearson Arrison. Ch. Letitia, Martha and William, all minors.
Wits: Joseph Hambleton, William Rice and Moses Eastburn.

Page 133. John Kelly, Bristol Boro. "Trader in Porter." Feb. 8, 1816. Wife Rebecca extx. Real Estate in N.J. belonging to first wife to be taken

possession of by bro. Aaron Kelly for use of my sons William and Aaron Kelly. Dau. Mary Kelly.
Wits: Amos Gregg, Abrm. Warner.

Page 134. Ebenezer James, New Britain Twp., yeoman. April 25, 1815. Proved Aug. 10, 1816. Bro. William James and John Riale of New Britain exrs. Sister Alice wife of Thomas Mathew. 5 ch. of late bro. Simon James, viz. John and Ebenezer and his 3 daus. Niece Naomi dau. of Bro. Morgan James. Ch. of Nephew Isaac James, son of bro. William James. Ch. of Benjamin James son of said William.
Wits: David Riale and Evan Riale.

Page 135. Smith Price, Plumstead Twp. July 4, 1812. Proved Oct. 25, 1816. Samuel Gillingham and Joseph Stradling exrs. Wife Hannah. Son John land adj. Jonathan Swain, Samuel Harris, Randal and Thomas Fenton purchased of Eleazer Fenton and Abraham Brown. Sons Jonathan, Joseph, Samuel, Smith and Burroughs. Dau. Mary, Asher Miner, Guard.
Wits: Samuel Pownall and George Burgess.

Page 137. Henry Rees, Springfield Twp., "Ancient and infirm." Aug. 29, 1816. Proved Oct. 26, 1816. Son Joseph Rese and William Haft exrs. (Letters to W. Keft.) "Beloved Widow . . ."
Wits: George Keft and Michael Keft. (Ch. not named.)

Page 138. Abraham Lewis, Northampton Twp. Aug. 24, 1816. Proved Oct. 26, 1816. John Road, weaver and John Tomlinson of Bensalem exrs. Wife ---. Eldest son William and other ch.
Wits: James Vanartsdalen, Samuel Dickson and Derrick K. Hogeland.

Page 139. John Moyer, Plumstead Twp., yeoman. Oct. 4, 1804. Proved Sept. 17, 1816. Sons Henry, Abraham and Christian exrs. Wife Mary. Daus. Mary and Ester and Charles, Edward and Elizabeth Dyer, ch. of dau. Barbara.
Wits: Henry Hockman, John Moyers, Ralph Stover.

Page 141. Daniel Headley, Bristol Twp., Farmer. June 24, 1815. Proved Nov. 7, 1816. Sons Samuel and John Headley and Amos Gregg exrs. Wife Grace frame house on Mill Creek and ½ of Profits of Farm for life. Daus. Christiana wife of William Patterson and Jane Headley.
Wits: William Headley and Samuel Lounsbury.

Page 143. Jacob Ratzel, Bedminster Twp., Farmer. Oct. 1, 1816. Proved Dec. 2, 1816. Sons Frederick and Joseph exrs. Daus. Margaret "who was mar. to Peter Henry," Catharine wife of Andrew Fatter and Madelina wife of George Melcher (her ch. George and Mary Melcher). Sons Frederick, Jacob, Joseph and George.

Wits: Frederick Lutz and William McNeeley.

Page 144. Barnet Driesbach, Lower Makefield Twp. June 1, 1807. Codicil dated March 11, 1813. Proved Dec. 14, 1815 and Aug. 26, 1816. Nearest neighbor John Miller and Joachim Richards of Falls Twp. exrs. (Richards d. before date of codicil, Mahlon Kirkbride substituted). Wife Catharine ½ of estate. The other ½ to only child Christiana Driesbach of Kraffshafft, Witgenstein, Germany.
Wits: Henry Clymer, Mary Clymer, Amos Howell and Ann Howell.

Page 145. Robert Margerum, Lower Makefield Twp. Nov. 12, 1816. Proved Dec. 20, 1816. Harvey Gillingham of Falls Twp. exr. Wife Phebe ⅓ of income of Plantation. Sons Jesse and Mahlon. Daus. Fanny Margerum, Sarah and Hannah.
Wits: Mahlon Milnor and Samuel Moore, Jr.

Page 146. William Worthington, Buckingham Twp., "advanced in age." 6-9-1815. Proved Dec. 21, 1816. Sons William and Jesse exrs. Wife Esther. Daus. Mary wife of Benjamin Smith, Esther wife of Thomas Spencer. Sons William, Benjamin, Jesse and Hiram. Land purchased of Bro. Isaac, Archibald McHatton and Kimble Hicks, adj. Ely Carver, William Kemble, Benjamin Smith and Watson Welding. Gdsn. William Worthington son of son William.
Wits: Abner Worthington and Anthony Worthington.

Page 148. Anna Poe, Buckingham Twp., "advanced in age." Nov. 16, 1816. Proved Dec. 28, 1816. Patrick Fenton exr. Note of Jonathan Doil, and apparel &c. to Margaret wife of Patrick Fenton.
Wits: Silas and Margaret Preston.

Page 149. Charles Echline, Durham Twp., yeoman. Sept. 18, 1813. Proved Jan. 7, 1817. Son John Eichline and John Jacoby Senr. exrs. 43 acres on which I live to be sold proceeds equally to all ch. except three sons, Andrew, John and Leon and to have £40 each.
Wits: Michael Fackenthall and Peter Long.

Page 150. William Barns, Warminster Twp. Dec. 18, 1816. Proved Jan. 3, 1817. Robert Ramsey and Samuel Hart exrs. Wife Edith $400 & income of residue for life. Edith Hagerman $20. Residue to dau. Elizabeth Moss and all her ch.
Wits: Samuel Croasdale and Robert Lukens.

Page 150. Margaret Bennet, Northampton Twp., "advanced in years." April 9, 1816. Proved Jan. 11, 1817. Son Isaac Bennet and John Corson Esq. exrs. Daus. Agnes Cornell, Jane Vansant and Margaret Bennet. Sons Isaac, William and Mathias Bennet.
Wits: George Edwards and John Corson Jr.

198

Page 151. William Vanhorn, Bristol Boro., Taylor. Dec. 17, 1816. Proved Jan. 15, 1817. Josiah Costele of Burlington, N.J. exr. Wife Mary Ann, all property. Sons Charles, Uriah and Israel, having property secured to them by my father.
Wits: Lewis P. Kinsy and Thomas Adams.

Page 152. Hannah Pearson, widow of Crispin Pearson, Solebury Twp. Jan. 25, 1814. Proved Feb. 17, 1817. Son Jonathan Pearson exr. Ch. Amy Scarborough, Jonathan, James, Crispin, Robert, Benjamin, Charles, Elijah, William and Hannah Pearson.
Wits: Joseph Wilkinson, William Rice, Isaac Wright.

Page 153. Joseph Hough, Warwick Twp. April 9, 1816. Proved Feb. 10, 1817. Septimus Hough and John Meredith exrs. Wife Eleanor. Niece Eleanor Hough, res. with me. Bros. Thomas and John Hough. Sisters Mary Walker and Charlotte Meredith.
Wits: George Burgess and Margaret Moore.

Page 154. Martin Overholt, Plumstead Twp., yeoman. Dec. 5, 1816. Proved Feb. 13, 1817. Son Jacob and son-in-law Valentine Crotz/Kratz exrs. Wife Elizabeth. Debts and Funeral Expenses to be paid out of Legacy coming to me from my bro.-in-law Christian Hundsbury and Magdalene his wife. Sons Jacob, William, Abraham and heirs of Joseph. Daus. Agnes, Mary, Elizabeth, Barbary, Magdalene, Anna and Sarah.
Wits: Joseph Nash and Isaac Overholt.

Page 155. Jacob Hering, Rockhill Twp., yeoman. Feb. 6, 1817. Proved Feb. 27, 1817. Sons Henry and Jacob exrs. Wife Magdalene furniture &c. and interest of £700. Six ch. George, John, Henry, Jacob, Samuel and Catharine. 3 Tracts of land, 100 acres in Montgomery Co. where son John lives; 100 acres partly in Montgomery Co. and 28 Acres in Rockhill Twp.
Wits: Abraham Cressman, John Driesbach and Isaac Cressman.

Page 156. William Bryan, Springfield Twp., yeoman. Feb. 10, 1807. Codicil dated Oct. 29, 1813. Proved Feb. 27, 1817. Sons James and Joseph exrs. Differences to be referred to Bro. James Bryan, John Stokes and James Chapman. (John Stokes, dec'd. at date of Codicil, and Shipley Lester and Peter Ashton substituted.) Wife Olivia ⅓ of Personal estate and £50 per year. Sons James and Joseph, Plantation, paying 1/6 of £2000 each to sons William and Samuel and Jesse and dau. Mary wife of John Bechtel exrs. to make Deed to son William for House and Lot in Berwick bought of William Dean and 400 acres or 5 miles from Berwick on Summerhill, bought of Jesse Smith and wife.
Wits: James Chapman, Peter Ashton, Abraham Reeser and Elizabeth Burk.

Page 159. Mary Gaddes, Plumstead Twp. Feb. 7, 1817. Proved March 18,

1817. Thomas Henry of Plumstead exr. Bro. William Gaddes. Sisters Margaret Slaught, Matha [sic], Elizabeth and Jane Geddes [sic]. Legacy from estate of Father George Gaddes and estate of Uncle Henry Gaddes.
Wits: Nicholas Swartz and Cortlin Lear.

Page 160. Margaret Walton, Warwick Twp., widow. 2-25-1809. Proved March 27, 1817. Son Job Walton exr. Sons Isaac and John 5 s. each. Residue to Job.
Wits: Samuel Hart and Nancy Starling.

Page 161. Eleanor Price, Solebury Twp., "somewhat advanced in age." May 23, 1809. Proved April 3, 1817. Gdsn. John Price and gddau. Martha Price exrs. Dau.-in-law Anne Price.
Wits: John Kitchin and Esther Kitchin. (Esther dec'd. before probate.)

Page 161. Lydia Brown, Newtown Twp., nuncupative, declared Feb. 5, 1817, the day previous to her death, before Laura Linton and Mary Feathersby. Proved March 15, 1817. Sister Minerva Cole to have all bonds, notes &c. Sister Mary Worthington's daus. "to have everything after a few things are reserved for Mary and Lydia." Letters C.T.A. to James Linton.

Page 162. Lorence Hoffert, Rockhill Twp., yoeman. Jan. 4, 1816. Proved March 17, 1817. Henry Ott, Taylor, of Haycock Twp. exrs. 25 Acres bounded by land of George Maugle and Paul Cover, to wife Eave [sic] for life, then to be sold. Six ch. Simeon, Henry, Joseph's Heirs, John, Martin and Barbara.
Wits: Jacob Kramer Junr. and John Kramer.

Page 164. John Knowles, Upper Makefield Twp. 3-23-1809. Codicil 9-30-1814. Proved April 5, 1817. Son Joseph and son-in-law Joseph Taylor exrs. Wife Mary. Six daus. Letitia, Mary, Mercy, Ann, Hannah and Rachel; sons Robert, Banner, Jacob and Joseph.
Wits: William Lownes, William Taylor and James Longshore.

Page 166. Mary Long, Moreland Twp., Montgomery Co., Pa. March 29, 1816. Proved April 5, 1817. Gideon Prior of Warminster Twp. exr. Residue to be invested and interest to be paid to son Adam Kerr, alias Hugh Long, during joint lives of him and his father Andrew Long, the principal to be paid to son on death of father. If son die first to sister Ann McEacham, her dau. Mary and other ch.
Wits: A. McClean and Lydia McClean.

Page 167. Melchior Weidemeir, Tinicum Twp. April 10, 1816. Proved April 10, 1817. Son Jacob and son-in-law David White exrs. Wife Mary. Son Jacob Plantation for life then to his son Jacob. Dau. Mary £50 in addition to what she rec'd. at mar. Dau. Elizabeth.

Wits: Abraham F. Stover and Henry Bissey.

Page 168. Abraham Miller, Hilltown Twp., "Aged." May 25, 1810. Proved April 14, 1817. Son-in-law William Safelcool and Friend Henry Hertzell exrs. Plantation 110 acres to be sold. Son Abraham 5£, ½ of residue to gdch. Henry Miller, Magdalena Benner, Elizabeth, Catharine and Susanna Miller and ½ to dau. Elizabeth and her heirs.
Wits: Jacob Stout, Abraham Stout and Abraham Stout Junr.

Page 169. Jane McGrandy, Warwick Twp., Spinster. April 14, 1817. Proved April 24, 1817. Andrew Long and John Hart (storekeeper) exrs. Sister Isabella and her ch. Wilson and Gaun. Bro. John, his ch. Jane, Elizabeth and Mary. Sister-in-law Phebe McGrandy. Bro. Thomas and his dau. Ellen.
Wits: John McGrady [sic] and Abner Richardson.

Page 170. Margaret Walker, Warrington Twp., single woman. Nov. 5, 1813. Proved April 26, 1817. Lawrence Emery and Samuel Weir exrs. Sister Elizabeth wife of Henry Finley, now or late of Virginia. Niece Margaret wife of Samuel Wier. Nefew [sic] Robert Wier. Henry, Ann and Martha Magee, ch. of James and Martha Magee. Interest in 140 acres adj. James Bradshaw and others, Held as tenant in common with sister Mary to be sold. Nephew James Finley.
Wits: William Emery and Elizabeth Valentine.

Page 172. Mary Wildman, Lower Makefield Twp., widow. 3-27-1817. Proved May 1, 1817. Father John Miller and Bro. John Miller exrs. Wearing apparel to sisters Elizabeth Fish and Sarah Heley. Residue to son John Wildman at age of 21.
Wits: Alexander Derbyshire and Rachel Miller.

Page 174. Warner Peters, Solebury Twp., yeoman. April 27, 1817. Proved May 20, 1817. Son-in-law William Large and John Buckman exr. Wife Mary all estate for life. Ch. Ann, Martha, Patience, Mary, Isaac, Juliann and Maranda.
Wits: Joseph Rice, John Helwig, John Walton Jr.

Page 173. Jonathan Carlile, "Now in Middletown Twp." 11-9-1810. Proved May 14, 1817. James Wildman of Middletown and son John Carlile of Montgomery Co. exrs. All property to be sold. Sons David and Jonathan. Ch. of son Benjamin dec'd., viz. Amos, David, Hannah and Sinah (or Linah). Daus. Hannah Brelsford and Elizabeth Wildman.
Wits: James Linton, Elizabeth Rich.

Page 175. Hannah Hellings, Northampton Twp. March 20, 1817. Proved June 3, 1817. John Cornell (son of John dec'd.) exr. Nieces Rachel and Elizabeth James, and Elizabeth Randal. John Hellings son of nephew

John Hellings dec'd. Abel Hellings son of nephew John Hellings of York Co. Thomas James son of niece Rachel James. Jesse Vanhorn son of Rachel Vanhorn.
Wits: John McNair and Henry Feaster.

Page 176. Sarah Thomas, Hilltown Twp., single woman. April 22, 1817. Proved June 5, 1817. Bro. Nathan Thomas exr. Sister Eleanor wife of Thomas Williams. Joseph and Ephraim, minor ch. of bro. Ephraim Thomas, dec'd. William H. Rowland, trustee for them. Cousin Tacey Milnor. Mother Sarah Thomas. Sarah Ann and Maria, daus. of sister Eleanor Williams.
Wits: Henry Beringer and George Beringer.

Page 177. Huldah Moore, Solebury Twp. 8-20-1814. Proved June 5, 1817. Thomas Hutchinson exr. Sister Ann Moore, sole legatee.
Wits: Mathias Hutchinson Jr., Mary Eastburn and Frances Eastburn.

Page 178. Jonathan Fell, Warwick Twp. 3-9-1816. Proved June 16, 1817. Son Jonathan exr. Gddau. Rebekah Ann Fell $500 when 21. Ann Wilkinson $40, residue to son Jonathan.
Wits: John Hough and Mary Hough Junr.

Page 178. Francis Murray Esq., Newtown. April 20, 1811. Codicil Nov. 17, 1816. Issue directed to Court of C.P. Dec. 2, 1816. Verdict June 16, 1817. Son-in-law Dr. Phineas Jenks and Jonathan Wynkoop exrs. Housekeeper Martha McIlhaney $20. 54 acres bought of Hannah Harris to exrs. in trust for use of Grdsn. Francis M. Wynkoop, minor child of dau. Fanny. 60 acres bought of exrs. John Harris to exrs. in trust for use of Gdsn. John Wynkoop son of dau. Fanny 120 acres bought of Moses Kelly, John Vanhorn, Commonwealth of Penna. and Mary Carey, in tenure of William Dudbridge and Abraham Black, to exrs. in trust for use of "Adopted son Francis Heaton Murray, otherwise called by his mother Patience Heaton,"Joseph" whom I have adopted and now give him the name of Francis H. Murray." 112 Acres bought of Joshua Carey to exrs. in trust for use of John Dormer Murray, reputed son of my son John, for life then to his ch. Sister Mary Tracey, Emily Murray, reputed dau. of son John. Niece Nancy Martin. Buckingham Harrold Farm to be sold and proceeds held in trust for ch. born and to be born of son William. Mansion House and Lot to Exrs. in trust for use of son William for life then to his ch. George, putative [sic] son of my son George W. Murray dec'd., and gdsn. of Sarah Gardner. Lenah Subers and her two ch. Ann and Charles Jolly.
Wits. to will: E. Morris, Is. Hicks and Asa Carey.
Wits. to Codicil: Asa Carey and Thomas G. Kennedy. Caveat filed by John Dormer Murray and letters, "Pendente lite" to Samuel Hart, Esq.

Page 189. John Kerr, Warwick Twp., yeoman. July 5, 1817. Proved July 15, 1817. Nephews William Kerr and James Kerr exrs. Wife Martha. All

goods she brought to me at mar. Nephew James Kerr, Farm bought of Isaiah Keith and lot purchased of Elias Gilbert paying $1000 each to my nieces Margaret Bready and Catharine Ramsey. Nephew John Kerr, Farm purchased of exrs. of Benjamin Hamilton, paying $500 each to nieces Fanny Major and Mary Kimble, and $1000 to ch. of niece of Elizabeth Major, dec'd. Nephew William Kerr to be guardian. Nephew Henry Kerr, fulling mill purchased of Adam Kerr. Nephew Abel Kerr. Cousin Jane Cochrane of Phila. John son of nephew John Kerr, Lot bought of Joseph Twining.
Wits: Samuel Hart and Isaac C. Snowden.

Page 190. Thomas Wood, Buckingham Twp., "Advanced in age." 2-2-1810. Proved Aug. 11, 1817. Sons Crispin and Robert exrs. Son Uriah 60 acres in Plumstead whereon he lives. Sons Chrispin and Robert balance of lands, whereon I live, partly in Buckingham and partly in Plumstead; 148 Acres. Wife Mary. Sons Joseph and Jesse (a minor) £350 each. Daus. Martha Wolverton and Mary Green. Gdch. Thomas, Mary and Elizabeth Wolverton, Elizabeth Martha and Mary Green.
Wits: John Gillingham Jr., George Burgess and John Skelton.

Page 192. John Carlile, Plumstead Twp., "Advanced in age." 9-8-1807. Proved Aug. 11, 1817. Sons Daniel and Benjamin exrs. Son Benjamin Plantation in Plumstead, subject to ground rent to heirs of Richard Hill dec'd. Son Amos £40. Abi Carlile widow of son Jonathan. Ch. of son Jonathan. Ch. Daniel, John, Elizabeth Rich, Sarah Shepherd, Amos, Benjamin, Rachel Burgess and Rebekah Carlile.
Wits: Jonathan Shaw and James Shaw Jr.

Page 194. John Beal, Buckingham Twp., "Advanced in age." 1-10-1817. Proved Aug. 18, 1817. Wife Jane and son-in-law John Breace [sic] exrs. Dau. Mary Breece 124 Acres whereon her husband John Breece lives adj. Thomas Watson. Son Joseph Beal. Jane and William Beal, ch. of son William dec'd. Daus. Elizabeth Davis, Jane Breece, Rebecca wife of William Oram and Anne Beal. Gdsn. John Beal son of son John. John Breece and John Melone, to hold Rebecca Oram's share in trust and at her decease pay same to her ch. my gddau. Letitia wife of Joseph Oram excepted.
Wits: Joseph Watson and Samuel Ely.

Page 196. Jacob Carrel, Northampton Twp., yeoman. Feb. 23, 1814. Proved Sept. 2, 1817. Sons Jesse and Joseph exrs. Wife Elizabeth. Sons James, Joseph, Jesse and Benjamin. Daus. Mary Bennett, Sarah Banes and Elizabeth Carrel.
Wits: John McNair and Daniel Dungan.

Page 198. Abraham Souders, Rockhill Twp., yeoman. June 27, 1817. Proved Sept. 3, 1817. Sons Christian and Isaac exrs. Wife Catharine. Ch.

John, Christian, Isaac, Susanna wife of Henry Moyer, Mary Catharine, Anna and Elizabeth.
Wits: Jno. Bergy and Martin Fretz.

Page 199. Michael Walter, Plumstead Twp. March 4, 1817. Proved Sept. 5, 1817. Son Andrew Walter and son-in-law George Walter exrs. Ch. Christiana wife of Abraham Fry, Catharine wife of George Walter, Mary wife of Abraham Gaines, Susanna, Michael, Andrew and Elizabeth Walter.
Wits: William Kealer Sr. and George Poe.

Page 200. Ulrich Drissel, Lower Milford Twp., yeoman. Jan. 30, 1806. Proved Sept. 8, 1817. Sons-in-law Philip Baum and Christian Ruch exrs. Wife Mary all personal estate for life. Son John Plantation. Sons-in-law Philip Baum intermar. with my dau. Margaret. Jacob Miller intermar. with dau. Ester. Christian Ruch intermar. with dau. Elizabeth and son-in-law John Herweak. Wits: David Spinner and John Stahr.

Page 203. Mary Trauger, Nockamixon Twp., widow. Jan. 20, 1814. Proved Sept. 10, 1817. Abraham Wyker exr. Sister Magdalene Swope and her ch. John, William, George, Catharine, Margaret (Trauger), Mary, Magdalen and Elizabeth. Catharine's share to be divided between her 4 ch. Samuel, Mary, Catharine and Elizabeth Wildonger.
Wits: John McCarty Jr. and Abraham Wyker.

Page 204. John Waltman, Richland Twp., yeoman. "Advanced in years." June 16, 1815. Proved Sept. 20, 1817. Wife Maricha and Benjamin Johnson exrs. Wife Maricha use of Plantation until son Jacob arrives of age, she to bring up and educate said son in a suitable manner. Have advanced son Henry his share already. Son Jacob Plantation of 106 Acres when 21, he paying son John £100 and £50 to Catharine a dau. of my wife. John Himmelwright Junr. guardian of Jacob during minority.
Wits: John Shaw Jr., Everard Foulke and William Shaw Jr.

Page 206. James Graham, New Britain Twp. Feb. 17, 1815. Proved Oct. 17, 1817. Thomas Stewart exr. William Kennedy $20. Elizabeth Stewart dau. of Thomas $20. William Johnson bed and wearing apparel. Residue to Doylestown Presbyterian Church.
Wits: Abraham Godshalk, Joseph Anglemoyer and William Godshalk.

Page 207. Jacob Walton, Buckingham Twp. 5-19-1817. Proved Oct. 23, 1817. Son Jacob exr. Wife Lydia interest of ½ of Real Estate for life. Son Thomas $242. Dau. Alice wife of John Armitage Jr. $800. Dau. Sarah wife of Henry Armitage $800. Real Estate to son Jacob (Release of legacies by John Armitage Jr. and Henry Armitage, entered on margin of record).
Wits: James Price and Amos Randal.

Page 208. Henry Jamison, Warwick Twp., Nuncupative. Proved Sept. 2,

1817. Bro. John Jamison and Samuel Hart exrs. Mother Martha Jamison $1000. Fanny Carr, Household Goods, Farming utensils and stock. Robert, John and James Jamison, each $1000. Grizelda Shaw $5000 for life then to her ch. Martha Bishop $3000. Martha Bready $2000. William Carr $3000. Mary Carr $3000. William Jamison, son of Matthew, $3000. Robert B. Belville $500. "$500 to roofing Neshaming Meeting House."
Wits: William Hart and William Hart Jr.

Page 209. Samuel Bayley, Lower Makefield Twp. June 30, 1817. Proved Oct. 25, 1817. Thomas K. Biles exr. Wife Rachel ⅓ of income of clear estate after first of April next, until then at rate of $140 per annum, agreeable to provision during separation from me. Daus. Anna, Atlethia, Rachel and Amelia, when 21. Sons Edward, Peter V. and Samuel H. Bayley.
Wits: Levi Bond and E. Morris (signed "Bailey".)

Page 210. Hans Yost Smith, Springfield Twp., yeoman. Aug. 13, 1817. Proved Oct. 25, 1817. Son Abraham and Andrew Bruner Senr. exrs. Wife Margaret. Sons John and Abraham. Susanna and John, ch. of dau. Margaret, dec'd., wife of John Osterstock. 3 ch. of dau. Catharine, dec'd. Signed Hans Yost Smith.
Wits: Henry Paxson Jr. and Moses Marsteller.

Page 211. Alice Phillips alias Bell, Milford Twp. Aug. 10, 1806. Proved Oct. 30, 1817. Everard Foulke Esq. and Nathan Ball exrs. Dau. Ann Phillips. Hannah Walton dau. of John Walton. Samuel Walton, natural son of Nephew Moses Walton.
Wits: Jacob Smith and Daniel Widimer.

Page 212. Hannah Jamison, "(widow of Robert)", Warwick Twp. April 14, 1815. Proved Nov. 8, 1817. Son James Jamison exr. Sons Robert and William Jamison and dau. Jane wife of Daniel Craig.
Wits: Robert Jamison and John Kerr.

Page 212. Oliver Paxson, Solebury Twp., yeoman. 5-9-1815. Proved Nov. 12, 1817. Sons-in-law Benjamin Parry and Hugh Ely exrs. Wife Ruth. Daus. Jane Parry and Ruth Ely. Niece Sarah Paxton. Cousin Hannah Kirkbride. Friends Benjamin White of Solebury, son of Joseph, dec'd. and Edward Hicks, son of Isaac Hicks of Newtown.
Wits: Oliver Hampton, Hannah Hampton and Merrick Reeder.

Page 213. Jacob Sterner, Springfield Twp., yeoman. April 1, 1817. Proved Nov. 14, 1817. Son John Sterner. Son-in-law John Strawsnider exrs. Wife Catharine. Son Adam Plantation called "Shuman Place" adj. Peter Ashton. Ch. George, Jacob, John, Abraham, Adam, Mary and Catharine (single).
Wits: Samuel Ashton and Israel Foulke.

Page 216. Barnard Vanhorn, Upper Makefield Twp. Nov. 2, 1817. Proved Nov. 20, 1817. Wife Mary, son Andrew and William Long exrs. Five ch. Sons William and Isaac minors.
Wits: Archibald Graham and Thomas Betts.

Page 217. Elizabeth Knight, Middletown Twp. 7-7-1814. Proved Dec. 3, 1817. Son-in-law George Atherton exr. Dau. Susanna wife of George Atherton. Gdch. Joseph Knight, Hulme, Susanna and Rebecca Hulme, ch. of William Hulme dec'd. John Hulme son of Samuel Hulme and Elizabeth Atherton dau. of George and Susanna.
Wits: John S. Mitchell and Joshua C. Canby.

Page 218. John Stouffer, Lower Milford Twp., yeoman. Jan. 13, 1808. Proved Dec. 3, 1817. Son Samuel exr. Wife Barbara. Ch. John, Jacob, Abraham, Samuel, Henry, Peter, Mary, Barbara, Susanna.
Wits: David Spinner and Jacob Musselman.

Page 219. Abraham Stevens, Northampton Twp. Sept. 18, 1817. Proved Dec. 2, 1817. Wife Maria and son-in-law John Roads exrs. Sons Daniel and Benjamin. Daus. Eicie Roads, Sarah, Elizabeth and Maria Stevens.
Wits: Jacob Engle, Abraham Hogeland and Derrick K. Hogeland.

Page 221. John Gallagar, Bensalem Twp., Taylor. June 11, 1816. Proved Dec. 3, 1817. Wife Rebecca extx. and sole legatee.
Wits: John Rodman and William Stackhouse.

Page 221. Letitia Linton, Newtown, widow. Feb. 15, 1817. Proved Dec. 5, 1817. James Linton and Joshua Anderson exrs. Elizabeth wife of Joseph Buckman "Bureau that was her father's, my late husband." William Linton dec'd. Sarah wife of Jonathan Ellicott of Md. $1000. Letitia Ellicott dau. of Andrew Ellicott of Lancaster $1000. Ch. of Mary, late wife of Richard Lawrence of N.J. $500. Sarah Linton Junr. and Laura Linton, daus. of Isaiah Linton $400. Hannah Yardley widow of Thomas Yardley £50. Rebecca dau. of Joseph Harvey $400. Mary, Pleasant, Letitia and Sarah, daus. of Enoch Harvey, $800. William Harvey, bro. of said Joseph and Enoch $200. Residue of estate to Letitia, wife of Joshua Anderson of Buckingham.
Wits: Th. G. Kennedy and James Ragnet.

Page 223. Isaiah Penrose, --- no date. Proved in C. P. Court Dec. 6, 1817. Bro. Robert Penrose, "wearing close." Ann Penrose £200. Residue to sisters Phebe, Mary and Martha. No wits. Letters c.t.a. to Robert Penrose. Abel Roberts was deft. in trial, no caveat on file.

Page 223. Abraham Kratz, New Britain Twp., yeoman. March 3, 1808. Proved Dec. 9, 1817. Son Valentine Kratz and son-in-law John Godshalk exrs. Wife Barbara. Son Valentine 110 acres out of Plantation whereon

I live adj. Benjamin Kelly, Josiah Lunn, William Jones and James Fulton. Son Abraham balance of same and woodland adj. David Worthington. Daus. Barbara, Fronica, Catharine and Susanna and heirs of dau. Elizabeth.
Wits: Joseph Anglemoyer and William Godshalk, Senr.

Page 226. Daniel Hogeland, Warminster Twp. Oct. 2, 1808. Proved Dec. 12, 1817. Wife Cornelia and Derrick Hogeland Esq. exrs. Wife Cornelia sole legatee.
No wits. Proved by Harman Vansant Esq. and Andrew Reed.

Page 227. Richard Wilgus, New Britain Twp., yeoman. April 20, 1815. Proved Dec. 13, 1817. Abraham Lapp exr. Wife Tacey. Son John. Dau. Mary wife of Abel Lewis. Ch. of dau. Sarah wife of George Siegfried. Dau. Martha wife of John Clymer. Son Richard.
Wits: Susan Evans Jr., James Evans and David Evans.

Page 228. Watson Welding, Wrightstown Twp. 9-21-1811. Proved Dec. 10, 1817. Son Amos Welding and Sons-in-law Silas Twining and Joseph Taylor exrs. John Watson's Mtge. to Pa. Hospital to be paid. Son Amos land he lives on. Son Watson land he lives on, including mill, water rights, &c. Ch. Ely Welding, Elizabeth Twining, Mary Worthington, Alice Taylor, John and Macajah Welding, Ruth Williams and Joseph Welding.
Wits: Joseph Burson, Thomas Martindell and Stephen Burson.

Page 231. Philip Kressler, Nockamixon. April 25, 1815. Proved Dec. 30, 1817. Wife Margaret and son-in-law Henry Overpeck exrs. Wife use of Real estate until son John is 21. 117 acres adj. Philip Leidigh, George Deemer and Henry Kressler, to son John, when of age. 3 daus. unm., Catharine, Margaret and Elizabeth. Dau. Mary wife of Henry Overpeck.
Wits: Henry Barnet and Henry Alshouse (twice recorded).

Page 235. William Jones, Sr., Hilltown Twp. Declared Dec. 27, 1817, dated Dec. 29, 1817. Proved Jan. 14, 1818 (Nuncupative). Sons Jonathan and William exrs. Son James "A helpless boy," James Jones trustee for him. Dau. Mary wife of Joseph Trisler, share to be held in trust by Joseph Mathias. Dau. Elizabeth.
Wits: Joseph Mathias and James Jones. Agreement of widow, Ann Jones, and above-named ch. on record with will.

Page 236. Daniel Miller, Lower Milford Twp., yeoman. Aug. 28, 1817. Proved Jan. 19, 1818. Sons Joseph and Henry and son-in-law Adam Bossert exrs. Wife Esther use of all estate durng life or widowhood. Ch. Susanna, Catharine, Elizabeth, Polly, Joseph, Henry, Sophia, Esther and Daniel.
Wits: Henry Mumbauer and Conrad Smith.

Page 238. Joseph Hough, Warwick Twp., "Advanced in years." Feb. 1, 1812. Proved Jan. 17, 1818. Sons John and Benjamin exrs. Sons Richard in Septimus Trustees. Daus. Lydia wife of Elias Anderson, Mary wife of Dennis Conrad and Charlotte Hough. James Carey Hough, Samuel Mary and Robert Hough, ch. of son Robert Hough late of city of Baltimore dec'd. Rebecca widow of son Joseph, dec'd. and her ch. Rebecca and Jonathan Hough. Gdch. Thomas son of Richard Hough, Charlotte dau. of Lydia Anderson, Hannah wife of David Williams, Joseph son of Benjamin Hough, Joseph son of Septimus Hough, Joseph son of Mary Conrad and his bros. and sisters. Woodland in Warwick adj. Jacob Haldiman and John Fitzinger.
Wits: John Grier and Nathl. Irwin. Both dec'd. Proved by John S. Grier and John Mann.

Page 241. Benjamin Foster, Warrington Twp. Jan. 19, 1818. Proved Jan. 31, 1818. Jacob Shade and Christian Stugner exrs. Will committed to care of Neal McHue. Wife Catharine all estate for life, then to all ch. Son Benjamin watch at 21.
Wits: Neal McHue and Thomas McCray.

Page 241. Rachel Rice, Buckingham Twp., "advanced in age." Aug. 28, 1816. Proved Feb. 12, 1818. Son James Rice and Amos Kirk exrs. Daus. Mary Kirk, Elizabeth Stirk, Hannah Hutchinson and Ann Bodine. Sons Edward, John and James Rice.
Wits: William Worthington, Joel Worthington and Jesse Worthington Junr.

Page 242. Cornelius Carver, Buckingham Twp. 1-27-1818. Proved Feb. 16, 1818. Benjamin Smith of Buckingham exr. Wife Mary interest of all estate until dau. Sarah arrive at age of 18, she to educate daus. Rebecca and Sarah.
Wits: William Worthington and John Melone.

Page 243. William Simpson, Solebury Twp., "advanced in age." May 29, 1810. Proved Feb. 18, 1818. Son John Simpson and William Neeley exrs. Son John Plantation whereon he lives in Buckingham. Son Mathew Plantation whereon I live. Dau. Ann wife of John Davis. Andrew, John, William and Thomas, ch. of son John. George, Robert and James, ch. of Mathew. Dau. Mary Simpson, and her dau. Emily Simpson.
Wits: Thomas Smith, Thomas M. Thompson and John Terry.

Page 245. Philip Parry, Buckingham Twp. 2-6-1818. Proved Feb. 18, 1818. Son Charles Parry and Charles Paxson exrs. Wife Mary. Daus. Sarah wife of Mahlon Beans, sons Samuel, Charles and Seneca, dau. Rachel Iden and son Philip.
Wits: John Watson Jr., Samuel Gillingham and William Gillingham.

Page 246. Ludwick Nuspickle, Springfield Twp., "Advanced in years." June 7, 1813. Proved March 5, 1818. Son John and Everard Foulke exrs. Son John 145 acres whereon I live and 46 acres in Haycock Twp. Abraham Taylor, Abraham Taylor Jr., Henry Pearson and Philip Pearson, trustees for son Ludwick, a lunatic from birth, and of dau. Elizabeth and her natural son Andrew. Daus. Mary wife of Henry Pearson, Anna wife of Casper Metsgar and Susanna Nuspickle. Elizabeth dau. of son Philip dec'd. Son Henry.
Wits: Joseph Meninger and Samuel Foulke.

Page 248. John Fries, Lower Milford Twp., yeoman. June 6, 1815. Proved March 9, 1818. Sons Solomon and John Fries exrs. Wife Margaret. Ch. Solomon, John, Daniel, Elizabeth, Sarah, Margaret and ch. of dau. Catharine, late wife of George Gable, viz. Samuel and two others. Jacob Loh, their Guardian.
Wits: William Getman and Morgan Custard.

Page 250. Joseph Hayhurst, Middletown Twp. 3-21-1814. Proved March 9, 1818. Jeremiah Croasdale exr. Wife Ann $1400. Sarah, widow of Joseph Jackson of Shrewsbury. Ann wife of David Butler. Catharine wife of George Scott. Joseph son of Samuel and Mary Eastburn. Mary Paxson dau. of James and Rachel Paxson. Letitia and Samuel Eastburn ch. of Robert and Rachel Eastburn. Abi, wife of Evan Townsend. Margery, wife of Nathan Baker. Robert Croasdale Senr. and Jonathan Croasdale.
Wits: John Blakey and Phineas Paxson Jr.

Page 251. John Holcombe, Solebury Twp., "Advanced in years." 12-18-1817. Proved March 10, 1818. "Son Samuel and Richard Holcombe" exrs. Wife Mary. Sons John, Samuel and Richard. Daus. Eleanor wife of Asher Ely, Sarah wife of Phineas Walker, Elizabeth and Margaret Holcombe.
Wits: John Worthington and Allen Holcombe.

Page 252. James Johnson, Upper Makefield Twp. Aug. 16, 1817. Proved March 13, 1818. Wife Mary exr. Dau. Ann $25 when 18. Wife all profit of estate until youngest son James is 14. Ch. Ann, Joseph, Mary, Rosanna, Jane and James.
Wits: John Keith and James Vance.

Page 254. William Fell, Buckingham Twp. 4-12-1817. Proved March 24, 1818. Wife Mary and Samuel Gillingham exrs. Ch. Phebe Fell and Joseph Gillingham Fell..
Wits: Charles Watson and John Beecks. Proved by Watson, John Beeks having gone out of this part of the Country.

Page 255. Sarah Kitchin, Solebury Twp. 5-5-1802. Proved March 30, 1818. Nephew Joshua Ely, Junr. exr. Dau. Rebecca Eastburn £140 in hands of step-son David Kitchin. Gdsns. Ely, Jonathan and John Kitchin. Niece

Hannah Dubree.
Wits: Oliver Hampton, Aaron Ely and Hannah Hampton.

Page 256. Aaron Phillips, Solebury Twp. 6-18-1816. Proved March 30, 1818. Son Thomas Phillips and Relation John Comfort exrs. Wife Mercy. Daus. Rebecca Hampton and Elizabeth wife of Jonathan Hampton. Gdch. Mary and Mercy Sams.
Wits: Oliver Hampton, Moses Phillips and Elizabeth Paxson.

Page 257. Phebe Tucker, Warwick Twp. Oct. 7, 1816. Proved March 31, 1818. Son-in-law Samuel Lovett exr. Daus. Phebe and Martha Twining and Sarah Lovett.
Wits: Freedom Chamberlin and Louisa Moland.

Page 258. Ann Hayhurst, Middletown, widow of Joseph Hayhurst lately dec'd. 3-10-1818. Proved April 13, 1818. John Blakey exr. Bro. Jacob Drake. Margery wife of Nathan Baker. Deborah Livezey. Rachel Croasdale dau. of Jonathan Croasdale. Joseph H. Croasdale son of Robert, David Cutler. Jonathan Croasdale, Robert Croasdale Senr., Larence Jackson. Sister Elizabeth Drake.
Wits: Jeremiah Croasdale and David Landis.

Page 259. Mary McKinstry, Warwick Twp., "advanced in life." June 4, 1817. Proved April 16, 1818. Dau. Jane McKinstry Trustee. Son James McKinstry "all he owes me." Tombstones to be erected at graves of dec'd. husband and self.
Wits: A. Chapman and Sarah Fell.

Page 259. John Shelmire, Warminster Twp., yeoman. March 17, 1818. Proved April 20, 1818. Son Jesse and son-in-law John Vanartsdalen exrs. Wife Catharine. Ch. of son John dec'd., his widow Jane, now Hogeland to have the interest during their minority. Ch. of Dau. Elizabeth Rutherford, dec'd. Son George and his heirs. Son Jesse. Dau. Ann Vanartsdalen. Sons Abraham and Daniel. Son Benjamin. Dau. Maria Shelmire. Charles Johnston of Watborough, Montgomery Co.
Wits: John Hart and Thomas B. Montayne, last signature proven by William Watts Esq. of Doylestown.

Page 261. Stephen Wilson, Buckingham Twp., yeoman. 3-3-1818. Proved April 29, 1818. Sons Samuel, Stephen and Oliver exrs. Wife Sarah. Daus. Martha, Rachel, Rebecca and Elizabeth have rec'd. "Outsettings at their marriages." Codocil 4-8-1818, wife dec'd., her legacies to daus.
Wits: John Wilson and Samuel Gillingham. (Codicil Robert Smith, Hannah Carey.)

Page 263. John Knight, Durham Twp., yeoman. Dec. 29, 1812. Proved May 6, 1818. Son John Knight and William Long Esq. of Durham exrs.

210

Wife Margaret. Daus. Margaret, Catharine, Susannah and Mary and Elizabeth wife of Jesse Serivener.
Wits: John Grube (removed to Western Country before probate), William Long Esq. (Signature proven by Uriah Dubois Esq.) and David Stem.

Page 265. Michael Wissel, Tinicum Twp. April 22, 1818. Proved May 12, 1818. Sons-in-law Jacob Busy of Tinicum and Nicholas Swartz of Plumstead exrs. Wife Mary. Ch. Elizabeth Smith, Magdalena Busy, Eve Schwartz, Michael and Daniel Wissel, Susanna Swartz, Catharine, Tobias and Samuel Wissel.
Wits: John Lewis and Henry Stover. N.B. Name for Eve Schwartz spelled differently from Susanna all through. (W.S.E.)

Page 266. Michael Worman, Tinicum Twp., yeoman. June 27, 1814. Proved May 12, 1818. Sons Henry and Abraham exrs. Wife Catharine. Son Isaac 100 acres whereon I live, joining Jacob Hoppock and Thomas Henry. Son Jacob 100 acres joining Henry Overholtz and Tohickon Creek. Son Emanuel 7 acres he lives on joining Henry Worman and Daniel Sollada. Ch. Ludwick, John, Henry, Abraham, Joseph, Emanuel, Isaac, Jacob, Elizabeth, Catharine, and Mary. Gdsn. Lidy Worman.
Wits: Henry Overholt and Joseph Nash.

Page 267. Catharine Herr, Rockhill Twp. March 31, 1818. Proved May 13, 1818. Bro's. son David Herr exr. Bro. John, his ch. David, George, Margaret wife of Samuel Barnett, Elizabeth and Polly Herr. Share of estate of bro. Jacob Herr's to bro. David, his ch. Jacob, Tobias, Samuel, David, Polly, Elizabeth and Hannah. Bro. John's ch. Trustees of Lutheran Church near Indian Creek.
Wits: Samuel Gehman and Michael Shoemaker.

Page 268. John Leedom, Southampton, yeoman. April 9, 1818. Proved May 19, 1818. Sons Joseph, Isaac and Lucius C. Leedom exrs. Daus. Mary Meredith and Ann Leedom. Ch. of son John dec'd. Ch. of Daus. Sarah Davis and Rachel Biles.
Wits: John McNair and James Anderson.

Page 269. Nanny Hockman, widow of Ulrick Hockman, late of Bedminster Twp., dec'd. Jacob Loux Senr. of Bedminister exr. Sons Jacob, Henry, Abraham, Ulrick. Daus. Barbara and Nancy.
Wits: William McNeeley and Margaret McNeeley (latter dec'd. before probate). Dated June 20, 1814. Proved May 20, 1818.

Page 270. John Shaw, New Britain Twp. April 11, 1818. Proved May 21, 1818. Neighbors George Burgess and John C. Ernst exrs. Wife ---. Ch. Joseph, John, Francis, William, Mary and Martha. Indentured boy Robert Boyers.
Wits: Benjamin Carlile and John Dyer.

Page 272. Samuel Stelle, Northampton Twp. June 3, 1815. Executed Feb. 21, 1818. Proved June 2, 1818. Friend Thomas Montanney, Bro. William F. Manning and son Edward T. Stelle exrs. Wife Hannah. Sons Isaac, Edward T., John A., William N., Joseph W., Charles and James Madison Stelle. Daus. Sarah McGinnis, Anna B. and Mary Stelle. Gddau. Hannah Stelle. Son-in-law Benjamin McGinnis.
Wits: Nathan Cornell and William Watts.

Page 274. John Hutchinson, Solebury Twp. Jan. 1, 1818. Proved June 3, 1818. Sons Isaac and John exrs. Wife Phebe $1000 and to live in the house with her two daus. Elizabeth and Sarah. Jonathan Pearson's three ch. Hannah, Cyrus and Adah.
Wits: David McCray and Joseph Carey.

Page 276. Agreement of Heirs of above John Hutchinson, viz: Isaac, John, Elizabeth, Sarah Stor and Joseph Hutchinson, for division of Estate.

Page 276. Thomas McGrandy/McGraudy?, Warwick Twp. May 29, 1818. Proved June 27, 1818. Robert Polk and James Horner exrs. Wife Martha. Son Samuel and other ch.
Wits: Samuel Hart and Andrew Long.

Pge 277. Daniel Anderson, Lower Makefield Twp. 9-24-1817. Proved Sept. 2, 1818. Son James Anderson and Mahlon Kirkbride exrs. Wife Huldah $2000. Son James 126 ½ acres with Mansion House, partly purchased of father part of Thomas Yardley. Son Thomas that part of same in Bristol Twp. and Lot in Williams Twp., Northampton Co. Son Jesse balance of Plantation in Bristol Twp. Son Elias 2 acres where son James lives purchased of Daniel Richardson and 50 acres adj. purchased of Robert Margerum, also 61 acres bought of Nathaniel Shewell Shff. Daus. Rachel, Elizabeth, Huldah, Ann and Mary Ann Anderson.
Wits: John Kinsey and Benjamin Cadwallader and Cyrus Cadwallader.

Page 279. John Roberts, Warwick Twp. Jan. 7, 1818. Proved July 17, 1818. Jonathan Roberts and William C. Rogers of Warwick exrs. Jonathan Roberts and Elizabeth Lovett ch. of bro. Jonathan, dec'd. John Roberts, son of Jonathan and Fanny of Warwick. David, Jonathan, John, Phebe, Hannah Livezey ch. of nephew David Lewsley. Sisters Pheby Roberts and Lydia Loosely. John Lovet son of Rodman. Rebecca Whiitingham [sic], widow of William dec'd. and her dau. Rebecca Coggins.
Wits: Benjamin Hough, Francis G. Lukens, Henry Stuckert.

Page 281. Philip Kratz, Plumstead Twp., "Advanced in age." June 2, 1807. Proved July 20, 1818. Wife Susanna, use of all lands for life and £100. Ch. Anna Fratz, John Kratz, (Philip and Mary Fretz to take the share of their mother Elizabeth) (Henry, John and Abraham Fretz to take the share of their mother Mary Fretz, dec'd.). Rachel Fretz, Susanna and Philip Kratz.

Dau. Anna Fratz, son John Kratz and son-in-law Abraham Fretz exrs.
Wits: George Burges and Martha White.

Page 282. John Pope, Springfield Twp., yeoman. July 3, 1813. Proved
Aug. 1, 1818. Wife Catharine and Jacob Fulmer exrs. Dau. Mary interest
of ⅓ of estate. Sons-in-law Abraham Diehl and Benjamin Jacoby and their
wives each ⅓ of estate.
Wits: Jacob Smith and Jacob Apple.

Page 284. Absalom Knight, Southampton Twp. Feb. 8, 1818. Proved Aug.
5, 1818. Sons Amos, Aaron, Benjamin, John and Moses exrs. Wife Ann
shall have Plantation whereon I live with that bought of Charles and
Samuel Biles and wood lot bought of John Cornell during widowhood.
Dau. Grace Knight Lot bought of Henry and Isaac Krewson. Son Amos
assisted some years ago to buy Farm on which he lives, he to pay his 4
bros. $200 each.
Wits: Abner Buckman and Isaac Harding.

Page 285. William Neeley, Solebury Twp. July 10, 1818. Proved Aug. 10,
1818. Wife Elizabeth, son Robert T. Neeley and Friend Thomas M.
Thompson exrs. Personal Estate and 25 acre Ross Lot to wife Elizabeth.
Canby Lot 25 ½ acres to ch. of gdsn. Daniel Poor.
Wits: Richard D. Corson and Mary Logan.

Page 286. John Rankin, Warminster Twp. 7-10-1818. Proved Aug. 12,
1818. Son James Rankin and Isaac Parry exrs. Wife Mary. Son James
Farm whereon I dwell and Lot in possession of Mary Rankin, 97 acres.
Sons John and Joseph each $400. Daus. Rebecca, Sarah, Elizabeth,
Hannah and Mary, $300 each.
Wits: Robert B. Belville and William Knight.

Page 287. Mary Winder, Newtown Twp. July 21, 1818. Proved Aug. 13,
1818. Thomas Jenks exr. Bro. Thomas Winder. Rachel Winder, dau. of
bro. Joseph. Elizabeth Beans pewter plates &c. Mary Moore of Phila.
worsted gowns &c. Rebecca Harvey $150. for kindness and attention to
me when sick. Mary Winder Howton, dau. of Benjamin Howton spoons
&c. Residue to sister Rebecca Winder.
Wits: Phs. Jenks, John Terry and Joseph Harvey.

Page 288. John Shipe, New Britain Twp., yeoman. Nov. 20, 1817. Proved
Aug. 15, 1818. Son George Shipe and George Wysel of Montgomery Twp.
& Co. exrs. Wife Catharine. Son George 100 acres whereon I live and 20
acres in Hilltown Twp. Ch. Elizabeth wife of Andrew Berndt, George,
Catharine, Margaret and Joseph. George unmar.
Wits: Isaac Hines and Jacob Cassel.

Page 291. Abraham DeCoursey, Buckingham Twp. April 12, 1818. Proved

Aug. 17, 1818. Wife Anna extx. All estate for rearing younger children.
Wits: Asher Miner and Jesse Jones.

Page 292. William Shaw, Richland Twp. No date. Proved Aug. 24, 1818.
Sons Jonathan and Samuel exrs. Wife ---. Dau. Mary to be cared for.
Daus. Hannah Foulke and Abigail ---, Eldest son Jonathan Plantation
whereon I reside and ½ of lot adj. Everard Foulke. Son Samuel Plantation
adj. Enoch Roberts and others and ½ of said lot.
Wits: Israel Shaw and William Griffith.

Page 294. Ruth Dixon, City of Phila., widow. June --, 1813. Proved Sept.
1, 1818. Thomas Story and nephew Joseph R. Jenks exrs. Joseph Dixon,
son of my late husband John Dixon, dec'd. Mary Richardson, wife of
nephew Joseph Richardson of Middletown. Cousin Elizabeth wife of Jesse
Waterman. Niece Ruth wife of said Joseph Dixon. Niece Ruth wife of
Robert Croasdale. Niece Mercy wife of Abraham Carlile. Niece Sarah wife
of William Allen. Niece Rebecca wife of Jonathan Fell. Sister Mary
Richardson and bro. William Richardson. Grace Stackhouse and Anna
Gillam to divide apparel. Dau. of bro. William, viz. Mercy Shoemaker,
Rachel Story, Ann Richardson, Elizabeth Reeve and Mary Watson. 5 dau.
of sister Rebecca Jenks and 4 dau. of bro. Joshua Richardson, Rachel wife
of Thomas Story, Mercy wife of Abraham Carlile, Rebecca wife of
Jonathan Fell, Mary Jenks, Ruth wife of Joseph Dixon, Sarah wife of
William Allen, Jane Richardson, Martha wife of Seth Chapman and Ruth
wife of Robert Croasdale.

Page 297. George Fulmer, Nockamixon Twp., Miller. May 22, 1816.
Proved Sept. 8, 1818. Friend Jacob Fulmer of Springfield and sons John
and George Fulmer exrs. Wife Mary. Son George Plantation whereon he
lives, partly in Bedminster Twp. and ½ of wood lot in Haycock. Son
Frederick Plantation whereon I live (60 Acres) partly in Bedminster Twp.
at £11 per acre. Sons George and Frederick Grist Mill in Haycock.
Residue to sons Jacob, John, George and Frederick and daus. Magdalena,
Catharine, Elizabeth, Susanna and Sarah.
Wits: Nicholas McCarty Senr. and Nicholas McCarty.

Page 299. Samuel Moyer, Hilltown, yeoman, "Aged." May 28, 1812. Proved
Sept. 2, 1818. Sons Isaac and Samuel exrs. Housekeeper Catharine
Moyer. Son Abraham Plantation 158 Acres on which I dwell, adj.
Benjamin Hendricks, Michael Snyder, Jacob Krotz and others. Paying out
to ch. Veronica, Isaac, Christian, Samuel, Jacob, Abraham, Tilman and
Henry.
Wits: Martin Fretz and Joseph Moyer.

Page 301. Rebecca Whittingham, Warwick Twp. Sept. 9, 1818. Proved
Sept. 24, 1818. Gddaus. Rebecca Jackson and Sarah Ann ---. Dau. Betzey
and other ch. $100 devised by John Roberts. Letters to William

Whittingham and William Coggins.
Wits: William C. Rogers, Elizabeth McGookin and Hannah Picker.

Page 302. Baker Phillips, Solebury Twp. July 31, 1818. Proved Oct. 16, 1818. Friends Aaron Phillips and Merrick Reeder exrs. Wife Rachel. Son John and dau. Rachel under 15.
Wits: Thomas Phillips, Thomas Philips Jr.

Page 302. Isaac Parsons, Falls Twp., "advanced in years." May 6, 1815. Proved Oct. 23, 1818. Codicil dated 4-14-1818. Wife Elizabeth. Son Abraham and dau. Rachel Bailey Plantation whereon son-in-law Israel Bailey lives 4 Acres joining Lydia Reshea and George Stokom. Daus. Mary Martin, Sarah Crozer. Son John 62 Acres in tenor of Israel Bailey and $2000. proceeds of land in Licoming Co. lately sold. Son Amos 123 Acres whereon he lives bought of George Stockom [sic]. Son Isaac 83 Acres whereon I live adj. Mark Balderston and woodland adj. John Councilman.
Wits: Abraham Harding, Mark Balderston and Samuel Allin.

Page 306. Casper Faubian Junr., Durham Twp., yeoman. Sept. 24, 1818. Proved Nov. 2, 1818. Wife Mary and Jacob Kooker exrs. Wife Plantation during lifetime of my Father and Mother, she maintaining minor ch., six sons, George, Henry, John, Michael, Samuel and Isaac. 4 Daus. Nancy, Sarah, Elizabeth and Rachel.
Wits: Christian Cressman and Jacob Cressman.

Page 308. John Addis, Northampton Twp., yeoman, "Advanced in years." July 3, 1816. Proved Nov. 5, 1818. John Corson Esq. and James Dungan, son of Elias, exrs. Wife Mary. Ch. Phebe Dungan, Elizabeth Levenster, Miles, Martha, Nancy, Rebecca and Joseph Addis. Land adj. Enoch Addis and George Edwards.
Wits: Benjamin Corson and Benjamin Corson Junr.

Page 310. Terringham Palmer, Bensalem Twp., Farmer. Feb. 21, 1816. Proved Sept. 26, 1818. Dau. Mary Palmer, son Henry and son-in-law William Whitesides exrs. Wife ---. Ch. Mary, George J., Henry, Agnes wife of William Whitesides and Elizabeth wife of Dr. Guy Bryan. "Expectations of inheritance from near relations in England."
Wits: Samuel Hibbs, John Guyon and John Thompson. Latter "Gone and now in Western Country."

Page 312. Moses Neeld, Lower Makefield Twp., yeoman. 8-17-1818. Proved Nov. 17, 1818. Son Phineas Neeld and William Palmer exrs. Wife Sarah. Daus. Hannah Stradling and Mary Neeld.
Wits: Joshua Knight and Robert Palmer.

Page 313. Alice Gray, New Britain Twp., widow, "Advanced in years." April 16, 1812. Proved Nov. 19, 1818. Son John James exrs. Son James

Gray dec'd. Gddau. Elizabeth and Maria Gray. Son John James Land in
Newbritain Twp. and in Northampton Co.
Wits: James, Margaret and David Evans.

Page 315. Joseph Shelly, Milford Twp., yeoman. Oct. 3, 1818. Proved Nov.
30, 1818. Sons Jacob and Joseph exrs. Wife Barbara. Son John. Land adj.
Frantz Shelly, Jacob Moyer, Abraham Clymer, Henry Shelly, Dorworths,
Christian Huber.
Wits: John Shelly, Joseph Shelly and Everard Foulke.

Page 316. Sarah Carver, Buckingham Twp. 2-7-1818. Proved Dec. 1, 1818.
Widow of William Carver. Son Joseph Carver exr. Sons Joseph and
William Carver. Daus. Elizabeth Bradshaw and Mary Kirk.
Wits: Samuel Ely and Joseph Watson.

Page 317. Mathew McNeeley, Hilltown Twp. Oct. 16, 1818. Proved Dec.
4, 1818. Friend William McNeeley Esq. exr. Bro. David McNeeley and
sister Nancy McNeeley.
Wits: Henry Shellenberger and Joseph Weisel.

Page 318. William Jenks, Middletown Twp., Miller. 10-26-1818. Proved
Dec. 16, 1818. Wife Mary and sons Joseph and Michael exrs. Wife $600
per year until youngest child is 21. Sons Joseph and Charles, Homestead
Tract and 20 Acres on Neshaminy in Northampton Twp. Sons Michael
Hutchinson Jenks and William Jenks, Farm now in possession of my
Father transferred to me as his Homestead Farm, subject to provisions
made by him for my step-mother. Daus. Hannah, Mary, Margaret Ann,
Elizabeth and Susan.
Wits: John Watson, E. Morris and William Flowers.

Page 320. Eli Hibbs, Bensalem Twp. 11-17-1818. Proved Dec. 30, 1818.
Ezra Townsend exr. Ch. Elizabeth Wilson, Seneca, Ely, William, Abner
and Mary Hibbs. Share in Byberry Library to said Library. Wife Mary.
Wits: Giles Knight and Nathan T. Knight.

Page 321. Jacob Renner, Milford Twp., Blacksmith. April 26, 1818. Proved
Jan. 5, 1819. Jacob Smith and Philip Singmaster exrs. Sons Benjamin,
Jacob, Henry and Adam and Dau. Susanna Renner.
Wits: John Heller and Abraham R. Smith.

Page 322. Mary Zellner, Haycock Twp., "advanced in years." Oct. 28, 1815.
Proved Jan. 9, 1819. Son-in-law Henry Burger of Haycock exr. Ch. John,
Charles, Daniel, Elizabeth, Catharine, Mary, Susanna and Magdalene.
Susanna's husband Phillip Herring.
Wits: Samuel Fluck and Frederick Saulener.

Page 323. John Ely, Buckingham Twp. 12-2-1817. Proved Jan. 26, 1819.

Sons Samuel and Thomas exrs. Wife Hannah. Son Thomas 120 Acres whereon I live, mathematical books &c. that belonged to his bro. James, dec'd. Son John two Lots purchased of Isaiah Jones, whereon a Tanyard is erected. Other lands to be sold. Ch. of Dau. Elizabeth E. Parry, dec'd. Ely, Letitia, Rachel, James, John and Seneca. Their father David Parry Guardian. Dau.-in-law Rachel Ely and Gddau. Letitia Ely.
Wits: William Large, Aaron Ely and Hugh B. Ely.

Page 325. Abraham Myers, Buckingham Twp,. yeoman. April 28, 1813. Proved Feb. 3, 1819. Gdsn. Abraham Myers and son-in-law Abraham Delp exrs. Wife Magdalena. Daus. Elizabeth wife of Abraham Lapp, Mary wife of Joseph Smith, and Hannah wife of George Delp. Thomas Walton Overseer.
Wits: William Watson and John Past Junr.

Page 326. Rebecca Thomas, Hilltown Twp., Widow. May 1, 1815. Proved Feb. 15, 1819, "advanced in age." Son Thomas Thomas exr. Dau. Ruth. Other ch. Thomas Thomas, Abia Thomas, Adah wife of Morgan Custard, Zilla widow of Eber Thomas, Mary wife of Owen Rowland and Ann wife of Isaachar Thomas.
Wits: George Leidy, sadler and Stephen Rowland.

Page 327. Mary Reese, New Britain Twp. June 14, 1811. Proved March 1, 1819. Gdsn. John Polk exr. Sons Evan and Levi Holt. Dau. Jean McLown, ch. of dau. Tacey.
Wits: William Hines and Thomas Harris.

Page 328. Joseph Carver, Solebury Twp., yeoman. 5-6-1818. Proved March 4, 1819. Son Joseph Carver and son-in-law Thomas Bye Junr. exrs. Wife Mary. Eldest sons Cornelius and Garret, estate devised them by their gdfather. Garret Vansant, sold to Moses Quinby. Son Garret 100 acres in Buckingham. Son Joel 183 Acres of Plantation whereon I live in Solebury adj. Jonas Jopson, Joseph Jopson and John Vanhorn. Son Joseph balance of said tract, 88 Acres. Dau. Mary wife of Thomas Bye Junr. and Martha Carver.
Wits: Robert Smith, Robert Smith Junr. and Mary Smith.

Page 332. Daniel Larrew, Middletown Twp. Jan. 14, 1819. Proved March 6, 1819. Friend Moses Larew exr. Wife Elizabeth extx. 189 Acres whereon I live with Tavern, for life. Elizabeth, wife of William Vanhorn. Peter States. Juliana States, Elizabeth Randall and Herbert Fenton each £5.
Wits: Henry Atherton, John Thompson and George Atherton.

Page 333. Sarah Moore, widow of Alexander Moore, late of Newtown, dec'd., but formerly of Hopewell Twp., Cumberland Co., N.J. Sept. 10, 1813. Codicil dated April 16, 1816. Proved Feb. 25, 1819. Whereas Alexander Moore and Sarah his wife, Feb. 5, 1790, conveyed to Rev.

James Boyd of Middletown and James Ewing of Trenton, Hunterdon Co., N.J., 2 lots in Middletown Twp. conveyed to them by Henry Wynkoop and Sarah his wife, but which were part of the estate of Anthony Teate dec'd. alloted to his dau. the said Sarah Moore, but by said deed to be held in trust for the use of said Sarah Moore for life, and devised by her at her death; she now devises same to her son Alexander Tate Moore. Sister Margareta Tate. Margaretta and Sarah Boyd daus. of sister Jane Boyd and sister Elizabeth Ewing. Bro. James Tate, dec'd. Bro.-in-law James Ewing and son Alexander T. Moore exrs.
Wits. to will: Joshua Newbold and John Sunderland. To codicil: Thomas Wimer Junr. and Charles Ewing.

Page 335. Hester Abernathy, Tinicum Twp. Feb. 23, 1819. Proved March 17, 1819. Son Samuel Abernath[y], Esq. Exr. oldest son John Abernathy, res. in Shearman's Valley, Tobian Twp., Cumberland Co. £300. Dau. Jane Carrel of Tinicum Twp. £900. Hester Williams, alias Wilson, $40. Missionary Societies of English Pres. Session and Dutch Calvinist Church, $20. Residue to son Samuel.
Wits: W. DuBois and James Wilson Junr.

Page 336. Joshua Wright, Bristol Twp. Sept. 22, 1818. Proved March 24, 1819. Sons James and Henry Mitchell Wright exrs. Wife Sarah use of house where I now live on Hibbs Farm &c. Son James, Middletown Farm. Son Joshua, Hibbs Farm. Daus. Ann wife of Daniel Bailey, Mary Titus, Louisa Headly, Elizabeth Cabeen and Charlotte Dungan. Israel and Matilda Wright, ch. of dau. Harriet Wright, dec'd.
Wits: Abraham Warner and John Phillips.

Page 338. David Johnson, Warwick Twp., yeoman. Dec. 28, 1814. Proved March 26, 1819. Nephew David Johnson and Friend Thomas Stephens exrs. Wife Elizabeth, nephew David Johnson, now res. in New Britain Twp. Plantation, 139 Acres if Warwick. Ground Rents in Phila. to wife for life, then to ch. of Bro. Robert Johnson dec'd. Wife's bro's. son Joseph Pool. Elizabeth wife of Thomas Lovett. Elizabeth wife of Paul Brummer, David son of Thomas Stephens, John Hough of Houghville, Overseer.
Wits: William Dennison, Juliann Maria Chapman and James Chapman.

Page 339. Isaiah Vansant, Lower Makefield Twp. March 26, 1819. Thomas Yardly exr. Wife Jane Plantation for life, subject to support and clothing her bro. George Harvey, and support of the ch. during minority. Agreement with Peter Crozer for Sale of Grist Mill and 5 Acres to be completed by exr. Daus. Sarah wife of Charles Howell, Alletare, Mary, Eliza and Ann Vansant. Dau. Amelia Vansant. Sons Samuel and Isaiah Vansant.
Wits: John Depuy and Joshua Vansant.

Page 340. John Vanhorn, Solebury Twp., yeoman, "advanced in age." 1814.

Proved March 4, 1819. Nephew Cornelius Vanhorn of Solebury and John Simpson of Buckingham exrs. Sarah wife of Joseph Campbell and Alice wife of Francis Campbell. Dau.-in-law Mary Vanhorn, widow of son of Cornelius. Gdch. Amos A. Vanhorn, natural son of dau. Sarah Campbell, Juliann Vanhorn, William Bennet Vanhorn, Catharine and Mary Vanhorn, ch. of son Cornelius, dec'd.
Wits: Robert Smith and Elias H. Smith. (Elias H. Smith, dec'd. at date of Probate, signature proven by Robert Smith, Jr.)

Page 341. Hannah Meredith, Warwick Twp., widow. July 15, 1818. Proved April 24, 1819. Son Morgan Meredith exr. Sons James, Joseph, Morgan, Hugh and Simon Meredith. Dau. Mary wife of Benjamin Williams. 3 sons and 1 dau. of Dau. Elizabeth Beans, dec'd.
Wits: John Kerns, Mary Kerns, David Evans.

Page 342. Michael Martin, Richland Twp., Advanced in years. Aug. 6, 1816. Proved May 5, 1819. Son Peter and son-in-law Ab'm. Beihn exrs. Son John, Dau. Catharine estate to all ch.
Wits: Everard Foulke and Susan Foulke.

Page 343. Adam Shaffer, Bedminster Twp. April 6, 1815. Proved May 17, 1819. Son William exr. Wife Catharine and Dau. Sarah use of House and Lot for life. Ch. Jacob, William and John Shaffer, Elizabeth Young, Margaret and Mary Shaffer.
Wits: Henry Meyer and James Ruckman.

Page 344. Leonard Beidelman, Haycock Twp. May 29, 1819. Proved July 9, 1819. Gdsn. John Climer of Haycock exr. Dau. Susanna Clymer [sic].
Wits: William Strokes. Handwriting proven by James Chapman Esq.

Page 345. Abel Mathew, New Britain Twp., yeoman. Feb. 8, 1819. Proved July 8, 1819. Bro. Simon Mathew of New Britain exr. Wife Elizabeth yearly income of whole estate for life. Ch. Jonathan, Thomas, John, Edward, Amos and Abel.
Wits: John Gillingham and Abner Morris.

Page 346. Martha Scott, late of City of Phila., now of Northampton Twp. April 14, 1818. Proved Aug. 2, 1819. Kinsman James Buckman exr. Nephew John Briggs, now or late of Maryland. Nephew Josiah Briggs, now or late of N.J. Abbot Chapman of Newtown Twp. Ellen Dungan, dau. of Joshua Dungan. Martha Briggs, dau. of Nephew Josiah Briggs.
Wits: Joshua Dungan Junr., Sackett Dungan, Thomas Dungan.

Page 346. John Folmer, Rockhill Twp., yeoman, "advanced in years." Sept. 29, 1818 Proved July 30, 1819. Son-in-law Michael Yost and Friend Jacob Stout exrs. Wife Barbara Plantation of 100 Acres sold May 31, 1815 to son-in-law John Groff. Daus. Catharine and Christina. Ch. of son John

dec'd.
Wits: Jno. Benner and Everard Foulke.

Page 348. Catharine Phillips, Hilltown Twp. Sept. 7, 1812. Proved July 31, 1819. Abel Mathias and Joseph Mathias exrs. Joseph Mathias "with whom I live" present Pastor of Baptist Church of Hilltown. Amos G., Anna and Eliza Mathias, ch. of Abel Mathias, yeoman of Hilltown. Mathias and William J.Morris, son of Isaac Morris. Mary Trimby wife of Daniel Trimby of Plumstead and their dau. Catharine. Catharine Hummel dau. of Jacob and Mary Hummel, late Mary Pierce. John Mathias of Chester Co. Elizabeth Harding of Hilltown. Mary wife of Stephen Rowland. Mary wife of Thomas Thomas, late Mary Mathias.
Wits: John Campbell, John Mathias, Joseph Mathias.

Page 350. Phineas Paxson, Southampton Twp. 2-1-1819. Proved Aug. 12, 1819. Codicil dated 7-7-1819. Son Joseph Paxson and his ch. Walter, Phineas and Mahlon Gregg Paxson, Susanna and Caroline Paxson. Son Charles Paxson and Ezra Townsend exrs. Deed to be made to Obediah Willett for my int. in land held in partnership with him.
Wits: Amos Martindell, Henry Carver. To Codicil Artemus Valerius Banes and Jesse Randall.

Page 351. Sarah Hamilton, Solebury Twp. 5-26-1819. Proved Aug. 20, 1819. John Armitage Junr. exr. Bro. Joseph Hamilton. Nephew Benjamin K. Hamilton and William Hamilton. Nieces Mary and Sarah Hamilton. Hannah wife of Jesse Dean. Letitia and Martha Arrison daus. of Richard and Martha Arrison. John Armitage Junr. and Alice his wife and their ch. Lydia, Hannah, James, Julia, Martha and Charles Armitage. Aaron Crook, apprentice lad to John Armitage, Jr. William Hamilton, Guardian for Arrison minors.
Wits: John Armitage Sr. and Joshua Ely.
Agreement of Heirs filed with will, signed "Hambleton." (Proper spelling.)

Page 353. William Preston, Buckingham Twp. May 12, 1818. Proved Aug. 21, 1819. Three sons-in-law, John Jones, John Rich and Josiah Rich exrs. Daus. Ann Gillingham, Elizabeth Jones, Mary Rich and Martha Rich. Natural gdsn. Samuel W. Preston. Lot bought of Peter Stewart in Plumstead.
Wits: John Price, Samuel Brown and Elizabeth Price.

Page 354. John Wier, Warrington Twp., yeoman. March 21, 1810. Proved Aug. 30, 1819. Edward Hay exr., in case of his death, William Long, Miller. Sister Mary Flack and her ch. James, Henry, Robert and John. Nieces Jane Kellso and Margaret wife of James Donally. 2 Messuages 1700 Acres bounded by lands of John Long and Nathaniel Irwin to Edward Hay and Hannah his wife, until their son John Wier Hay is 21, then to him, if he die in minority to Hannah's child unborn.

Wits: Robert Sims and Henry Wierman.

Page 355. Peter Gift, Upper Makefield Twp. Feb. --, 1818. Proved Sept. 1, 1819. John T. Neeley Exr. Wife Catharine use of all estate for life. Son Abraham's ch., to wit. Isaac, Catharine, Elizabeth and Hannah Gift. Son Isaac's ch. Susanna, Mary and Rachel Gift. Dau. Rachel's ch., viz. Abraham, Mary and James Service.
Wits: Samuel McNair and Ann Wynkoop.

Page 356. Eleanor Carey, New Britain Twp. (Doylestown Twp. at date of Probate) 2-25-1803. Proved Sept. 3, 1819. Cousin William son of Uncle William Preston. Uncle Henry Preston's surviving ch. Deborah, Ann and Euphemia Preston daus. of Uncle Paul Preston, Plantation whereon I dwell. Cousin Ann Preston extx.
Wits: Jonathan Doyle and John Claney.

Page 357. Daniel Strawhen, Haycock Twp. 4-4-1819. Proved Sept. 25, 1819. Son William and Everard Foulke exrs. Wife Sarah $104 yearly in lieu dower, exclusive of yearly Dower by her former husband. Land in Ohio. Sons William and John, each $200. "Have advanced to ch. of 2nd wife considerable sums." Daus. Christina wife of John Heacock, Mary wife of Samuel Jolly, Hannah wife of William Hawck. Ch. by 2nd wife, Isaiah, Jacob, Thomas, Daniel, Jesse, Abel, Christina, Mary, Hanna, Margaret, Elizabeth, Eleanor and ch. of dau. Ann.
Wits: Samuel Moffty and Jacob Taylor.

Page 359. Susanna Klein, Milford Twp. Aug. 27, 1819. Proved Sept. 25, 1819. Son Jacob Weigart exr. and sole legatee.
Wits: Abraham Shelly, Anna Shelly.

Page 360. John Landes, Rockhill Twp. Nov. 14, 1818. Proved Oct. 2, 1819. Wife Elizabeth and son Jacob exrs. Ch. Abraham, Jacob and Samuel Landes, Susanna wife of Henry Derstine and Catharine Landes. Son Samuel 21 on Jan. 7, 1822. Lands adj. John Kinsey, Jacob Stout, Abraham Wambold, George Derstine, Andrew Schlichter and Philip Hertzel.
Wits: Jacob Stout and Caleb Foulke.

Page 364. Charles Hinkle, Newtown Twp. March 3, 1819. Proved Oct. 5, 1819. Wife Ann and son Charles exrs. Ch. Mary, Charles, John, Ann, Eliza, Adalina and Theophilus.
Wits: Enos Yardley and Is. Hicks.

Page 365. Louis Bache, Bristol Boro. Sept. 5, 1819. Proved Oct. 23, 1819. Wife Esther and Dr. John Phillips exrs. and Trustees. Natural dau. Margaret Bache, dau. of Margaret Riley. Dr. John Phillips to be Guardian of two ch. by 1st wife and of their rights and property under care of their Great-Gdfather. John Swift, wife Esther plate marked with Bache crest.

Dau. Elizabeth plate marked with Franklin crest, also ring that was her mother's wedding ring, marked with her mother's name. Son William chain of his grandfather's watch and medal left by Dr. Franklin to his grandfather, which has descended to me by will. Nephews Franklin, Benjamin and Hartman Bache. Bro. Richard Bache prints La Hoyne, Bayard and Boyne, presented to my gdfather. by Benjamin West. Sister Elizabeth Harwood portrait of my mother. To her son Allen Harwood of U.S. Navy, Officer's fusee presented by Capt. Paul Jones to his Grandfather, which was taken on board a British vessel. Bro.-in-law William J. Daune and his wife Deborah, bedstead that her gdfather. purchased at his wedding and on which he died. Nephew William Bache, son of William Bache, scotch pebble sleeve buttons of Dr. Franklin, now is possession of his mother. Lodge No. 25 of Masons at Bristol, Masonic Book. Friends Edward Paxson and Robert Erwin. Thomas Sargent Esq.
Wits: John White and Isaac Pitcher.

Page 367. John Trumbore, Rockhill Twp. Oct. 6, 1819. Proved Oct. 27, 1819. Bro. Andrew Trumbore exr. Bros. Jacob, Andrew, Henry and heirs of bro. George Trumbore. Heirs of sister Sophia late wife of Peter Trollinger. Heirs of sister Catharine late wife of Jacob Mack.
Wits: Jacob Wambold and Benjamin Rosenberger.

Page 368. David Watson, Middletown Twp. Oct. 26, 1818. Proved Oct. 29, 1819. Sons Stacy and Ezra Watson exrs. Wife Tamar Mansion House and Two acres bounded by lands of Robert Drake, Henry Watson and Road leading from Attleboro to Trenton. Son Stacy $1000. Son Phineas Blacksmith shop and land adj. Charles Watson. Son Ezra Grist Mill and Mansion House at death of wife. Daus. Mercy wife of Samuel White and Alice wife of James Anderson. Sons Stacy, Phineas, Ezra, Israel, Edward and Aaron.
Wits: Henry Watson and Mahlon Gregg.

Page 369. Joseph Frey, Springfield Twp., yeoman. Sept. 29, 1814. Proved Nov. 1, 1819. Sons Jacob and Joseph Fry [sic] exrs. Wife Elizabeth. 8 ch. Jacob, Joseph, John, Conrad, Elizabeth, Magdalena, Susanna and Margareth.
Wits: Paul Apple and John Smith.

Page 371. Ezra Townsend, Bensalem Twp. 9-4-1818. Proved Nov. 8, 1819. Sons John P. and James Townsend exrs. Wife Elizabeth. Son John P. Townsend Grist Mill and 60 acres of land in Byberry on Poqussing Creek adj. John Carver, John Adams, Evan Townsend and Jesse Tomlinson, son James residue of Land chefly [sic] in Bensalem. Gddau. Elizabeth Thornton $1000 when 21. Daus. Susanna Walton and Sarah Cadwallader each $1600. Daus. Elizabeth and Tacey Townsend each $2100.
Wits: "None thought necessary, my own hand writing deemed sufficient." Proved by James Verree and Israel Walton.

Page 373. Lewis Olmstead, Phila. Co., "Soldier in 16th Reg. U.S. Infantry." April 24, 1814. Proved Nov. 12, 1819. Mary Landoz, widow of Francis Landoz of Bristol Twp., Bucks Co. extx. and sole legatee.
Wits: Louis Notnagel, Henry Hildewirth and Edward D. Carfield.

Page 374. Cornelius Shepherd, Buckingham Twp. "Advanced in age." Sept. 19, 1811. Proved Nov. 29, 1819. Son Joseph Shepherd and Meschach Michener, my son-in-law, exrs. Wife Phebe. Daus. Rachel Burgess, Margaret Michener, Mary Michener; sons Joseph and Jonathan Plantation of 110 Acres in Buckingham whereon I live. Gdsns. Cornelius and Moses Shepherd.
Wits: Benjamin Carlile and George Burgess.

Page 375. John Jones, Plumstead Twp., "Advanced in age." 7-22-1819. Proved Nov. 30, 1819. Sons Eleazer and John exrs. Sons Eleazer, John, Ephraim and Jesse. Daus. Hannah Price, Mary Kirkbride and Huldah Gilbert.
Wits: Joseph Stradling and James Shaw Junr.

Page 376. John Caulton, Solebury Twp. Nov. 15, 1809. Proved Dec. 2, 1819. Wife Hannah extx. (she renounces on account of "being aged and infirm.") Sons Isaac and Aaron 10 acres of land adj. George Grubham and Joseph Jopson, at death of wife.
Wits: Thomas Hutchinson and Isaac Scarborough. Letters granted to Isaac Caulton.

Page 377. John Wireman, Doylestown Twp. Dec. 1, 1819. Proved Dec. 9, 1819. John Godshalk and Jonathan Wood exrs. Personal Estate to sisters Mary and Nancy and sister Catharine Fitsinger. Real Estate to John Godshalk.
Wits: John Shrager and David Overholzer. Housekeeper Ann Flack.

Page 378. Joseph Brooks, Plumstead Twp. Jan. 2, 1819. Proved Dec. 11, 1819. Daniel Boileau and Anthony Fretz exrs. Wife Mary and son --- , a minor.
Wits: Joseph Nash, James Davison. Codicil mention [s] "Mother."

Page 379. William Craven, Warminster Twp., yeoman. April 20, 1819. Proved Jan. 10, 1820. Son William and bro's. son John Craven and bro. James exrs. Wife Cornelia. Sons Thomas, Wilhalmas, Giles and William; Dau. Elshe.
Wits: Adriana Cornell and James Craven Senr.

Page 380. Mary McGraudy, Warwick Twp., Spinster. Dec. 10, 1819. Proved Jan. 21, 1820. Dau. Isabella Opdike extx. and sole legatee.
Wits: William Lee, Samuel Lovet.

Page 381. Richard Mitchell, Middletown Twp. 11-1-1814. Proved Jan. 21, 1820. Bros. Samuel and Pierson Mitchell exrs. Daus. Elizabeth Mitchell, Margaret Wilson, Sarah Gregg and Ann Brown. Son Richard, have sold him Plantation and Mill on Neshaminy Creek for $1600 and he hath sold same to Jonathan Buckman at a profit of $2000. Son John L. Mitchell. Sons-in-law John Wilson and John Brown.
Wits: Joseph Hayhurst and Charles Goheen.

Page 383. Larrance Johnson, Bensalem Twp. Jan. 9, 1818. Proved Jan. 31, 1819. Jonathan Thomas and Daniel Knight exrs. Wife Hannah. Her "neffew Jonathan Jackson." My sister Rebecca Johnson.
Wits: Henry Jacoby and John Burke.

Page 384. Philip Mann, Springfield Twp., yeoman. Sept. 3, 1819. Proved Feb. 7, 1820. Jacob Fullmer and Abraham Mann exrs. Dau. Anna Maria Ruch. Elizabeth, wife of Henry Hess and dau. of John Mann, dec'd. Philip, son of bro. John Mann. Gddaus. Elizabeth Hess and Catharine Mills and Anna Maria Ruch.
Wits: Nicholas Mensch, P. L. and Nicholas Youngken.

Page 385. Amy Hambleton, Solebury Twp. 1-3-1820. Proved Feb. 28, 1820. Bro. Benjamin Hambleton exrs. Nieces Louise, Ann and Amy Ellen Hambleton. Sister-in-law Letitia Hambleton. Sister Rachel Pidcock. Mother Elizabeth Paxson.
Wits: Aaron Paxson, John Case and John K. Paxson.

Page 385. Barbara Moyer, Lower Milford Twp., Widow. Feb. 1, 1800. Proved March 1, 1820. Henry Landis of Richland, yeoman, exr. John, Daniel, Abraham, Elizabeth, Ann, Mary and Catharine Stouffer, "brothers and sisters" and Henry Strunck and Henry Landis, all estate.
Wits: John Drissel and Abraham Taylor.

Page 386. Mary Lederach, Hilltown Twp., widow. May 13, 1817. Proved March 1, 1820. Bro. Abraham Taylor and Friend Martin Fretz exrs. "Aged and infirm." Nieces Mary Shelly, Mary Funk, Mary Shliffer, Mary Pearsy. Sister Veronica dec'd., her ch. 1/5. Sister Susanna Shelly, 1/5. Ch. of sister Anna, dec'd. 1/5. Ch. of sister Elizabeth, dec'd., 1/5. Bro. Abraham Taylor 1/5. Niece Mary Funk, dec'd., her husband Jacob Funk to have her share. Nephew Henry Shelly, dec'd., his widow Mary to have his share.
Wits: Jacob Lederach and Jacob High.

Page 387. Christian Diley, Senr., Richland Twp. Nov. 15, 1819. Proved March 6, 1820. Sons Joseph and Christian exrs. Sons Joseph, Christian, Jacob and Philip. Dau. Catharine, wife of Samuel Pettit.
Wits: Joseph Weaver Senr., John Matts.

Page 388. Jacob Janney, Newtown Twp. 1-3-1820. Proved March 6, 1820.

224

Sons Thomas, Richard, Jacob and John exrs. Wife Frances. Sons William, Joseph, Mahlon and Stephen, all under 15. Daus. Martha and Sarah, minors. James Worth and Joseph Briggs, guardians. Land purchased of John Brown in Lower Makefield, adj. Joseph Taylor, to Richard and Jacob.
Wits: John Lee and John Linton Junr.

Page 390. Manus Yost, Haycock Twp., yeoman. May 19, 1814. Proved March 9, 1820. Son-in-law John Allum exr. Wife Elizabeth use of 50 acres for life. 5 ch. Margreth, Elizabeth, Catharine, Mary and Sarah. Sarah "not to receive her share until such time as her husband Jacob Keller forces her to leave his house and live apart from him." Her ch. Caroline and Levi.
Wits: George Taylor and Henry Ott.

Page 391. Mary Martin, Middletown Twp. Sept. 7, 1819. Proved March 20, 1820. Thomas L. Allen exr. Mother Agnes Martin interest of Bonds, Notes & Bank Stock for life; then to sisters Frances and Ann and bros. Thomas, Daniel and Charles.
Wits: Joseph Richardson and Jonathan Walton.

Page 392. Garret Dungan, Northampton Twp., yeoman. Aug. 1, 1819. Proved March 27, 1820. Friends Joshua Dungan and Isaac Chapman exrs. Wife Tacey Dungan use of plantation for life, then to be sold. Dau. Elizabeth Swan $40. Residue in five shares: 1 to ch. of son David dec'd. (first deducting £20 to be paid to heirs of Eleazer Doan, dec'd., money said Eleazer stood bound for to David when he left Penna.); 1 share to dau. Rachel Kimble; 1 to dau. Charity Pearcy; 1 to be invested for use of dau. Elizabeth Swan for life, then to her ch.; 1 to Townsend Campbell, son of Tacey Foster, dec'd. when he is 21.
Wits: Cornelius Cornell, John Cornell and John Hart. (Gdsn. Abner Ross.)

Page 393. Jacob Nicholas, Junr., Tinicum Twp. March 8, 1820. Proved March 29, 1820. Conrad Harpel of Bedminster exr. Wife Elizabeth and 3 ch. Joseph, Samuel and Jacob (minors.)
Wits: Philip Harpel and Jacob Weidemeyer.

Page 394. Henry Huston, New Britain Twp. March 22, 1820. Proved March 30, 1820. Sons David and Abraham exrs. Wife Catharine ⅓ of profit of plantation lately purchased until sold, and interest of $800 out of proceeds of sale of plantation whereon I live. 5 ch. John, David and Abraham Huston, Barbara Shelly and Elizabeth Fritz.
Wits: Abraham Herman and Isaac Morris.

Page 395. Matthew Gill, New Britain Twp. March 20, 1811. Proved March 31, 1820. John Blankenhorn and Jonathan Large exrs. Wife Asenath all estate for life. Wife's nephew Jonathan Large and his ch. Mathew and

Asenath Large. Mathew Gill, son of my bro. Isaac. Mathew Wooster, son of my sister Elizabeth Wooster. Esther Smith, dau. of said Elizabeth Wooster.
Wits: William Burgess, John Blankenhorn and George Burgess.

Page 397. Moses Church, Buckingham Twp. 12-16-1811. Proved April 1, 1820. Cousen [sic] Jonathan Fell and William Large exrs. Bro. Joseph wearing apparel. Niece Elizabeth Carlile £20. Niece Sarah Brannon 5£, residue to seven nieces Sarah, Elenor, Rachel, Elizabeth, Jane, Mary and Melicent Church, daus. of bro. Joseph Church.
Wits: John Shroger and Anne Wilkinson. ("Ann has left this part of the Country.")

Page 397. Phebe Cooper, Falls Twp., single woman. 3-28-1810. Proved April 15, 1820. John W. Balderston and Mark Balderston of Falls Twp. exrs. Cousin John W. Balderston with whom I live. His wife Elizabeth and sons John and William. Cousins Mark Balderstom (wife Elizabeth), Ann Baderston [sic] of Solebury and Merab Balderston. Aunt Sarah Cooper.
Wits: Reading Beatty and Ann Beatty.

Page 399. Peter Shumon, Tinicum Twp., yeoman. March 20, 1820. Proved April 26, 1820. Wife Elizabeth and Henry Burger of Haycock exrs. Ch. Jacob, Henry, Peter and Joseph. 108 Acres in Tinicum to Henry.
Wits: Conrad Harpel, Abraham Worman.

Page 400. William Stephens, Doylestown Twp. April 15, 1820. Proved April 28, 1820. Sons Thomas and Jesse Stephens exrs. Wife Sarah. Sons Thomas and Jesse 120 Acres whereon I live. Daus. Ann wife of Mason Kindle, Issabella wife of Simon Mathews, Mary wife of William Thomas and three ch. of Dau. Effe Kearn, dec'd.
Wits: William Hair, Jonathan Doyle and William Watts.

Page 401. Joseph Jenks, Middletown Twp. July 18, 1805. Proved May 9, 1820. Son William (exr.) "Homestead Tract of land and the Mills, Houses and lands where he now lives." Daus. Margaret Gillingham and Elizabeth Shinn. Wife Hannah.
Wits: Aaron Phillips, Amos Warner and Is. Hicks.

Page 402. Andrew Brunner, Springfield Twp.yeoman. March 21, 1820. Proved May 29, 1820. Codicil dated April 11, 1820. Sons Henry and Jacob exrs. Wife Christina. Sons Jacob, Andrew and John Plantation, adj. Jacob Myers and John Smith, George Hess and Philip Trevey. Daus. Elizabeth wife of Frederick More, Catharine, Eve, Susanna and Christine and Margaret. Gdch. Charles, Margret and Elizabeth Brunner.
Wits: John Smith and Moses Marstellar.

Page 405. Mary Kramer, Haycock Twp., widow. May 17, 1820. Proved

June 1, 1820. Jacob Kramer, son of Casper of Bedminster exr. Daus. Barbara wife of Adam Nunnermaker, Mary wife of John Hinkle, Margaret wife of Benjamin Solliday, Catharine wife of James Nunnermaker, Magdalene wife of John Fretz and Hannah wife of George Cressman. Sons Lawrence, John and Jacob. Gdch. Henry Kramer son of John; Henry son of Jacob; Mary wife of Henry Hinkle, dau. of Elizabeth; eldest dau. of Henry Nice, carpenter; Mary, Margaret, Elizabeth and Magdalene dau. of Elizabeth Cover, dec'd.
Wits: Jacob Ott and Samuel A. Smith.

Page 406. Achsah Hill, Solebury Twp. 2-14-1817. Proved June 6, 1820. John Walton exr. Dau. Frances A. Hill.
Wits: Jona. Pearson, William Rice.

Page 406. Ann Gilmore, Falls Twp. 9-25-1814. Proved June 30, 1820. John and Jesse Brown exrs. Dau. Latitia and her dau. Charlotte Parson.
Wits: John Brown and Rebecca Brown.

Page 407. Henry Frankenfield, Tinicum Twp. Nov. 23, 1819. Proved July 4, 1820. Son Adam and son-in-law John Barnte exrs. Daus. Margareth, Modlen and Catharine. Gdch. Margaret Wilson of Easton, formerly McElroy; Abraham Wyker; son Frederick's ch. Juliana and Lovina; son Philip's ch. Lewis, Sally, Franey, Andrew and an infant; sons, Henry and Adam.
Wits: Frederick Kulp and Samuel G. Bailey.

Page 408. John Hayhurst, Northampton Twp. 4-19-1820. Proved July 22, 1820. Nephew John Gregg and John Corson, Esq. exrs. Wife Susanna all estate.
Wits: Phineas Paxson and Israel Paxson.

Page 409. Peter Kern, Rockhill Twp., Joiner. July 29, 1816. Proved July 25, 1820. Codicil dated June 10, 1818. Sons Frederick and Peter exrs. Son John. Daus. Margaret wife of John Resener, Elizabeth wife of John Reagle, Catharine wife of John Selner, Susanna wife of Frederick Fosbenner, Magdalene wife of John Geris and Hannah wife of Abraham Heany.
Wits: Jacob Hartman and Michael Lutz.

Page 410. Mary Watson, Buckingham Twp. 9-30-1812. Proved July 28, 1820. Bro. James Verree exr. Sons Thomas and Robert Watson. Daus. Ann, Mary, Sarah and Elizabeth.
Wits: Israel Jones and Isaiah Jones. (Israel Jones dec'd. at date of probate.)

Page 411. Grace Headley, Bristol Twp., Widow of Daniel Headley. 1-31-1817. Proved Aug. 21, 1820. Sons Samuel and John Headley exrs. Daus.

Christiana Patterson and Jane Headley.
Wits: Reading Beatty and Amaziah Headley.

Page 412. Joseph Barwis, Falls Twp., weaver. 12-1-1809. Proved Aug. 2, 1820. Wife Sarah and William Harper of Fallsington exrs. Daus. Mary Richardson and Elizabeth Boyd, Lots adj. Mary Warner.
Wits: Reading Beatty and Joseph Bowman.

Page 413. Christopher Keller, Haycock Twp., yeoman. Sept. 22, 1819. Proved Aug. 21, 1820. Sons John, Henry and Michael exrs. Wife dec'd. Son Daniel a minor. Ch. John, Henry, Michael, Catharine, Samuel, Joseph, Daniel and Catharine, ch. of dau. Elizabeth. Dau. Catharine wife of Joseph Staley. Son John's ch. Elizabeth and son Henry's ch. Charles. Land sold to sons John and Henry adj. Jacob Myers. Do. bought of Samuel Zeigler, adj. Michael Keller and Jacob Fulmer. Do. adj. Valentine Roar.
Wits: George Sheets, Solomon Litzenburger.

Page 415. Joseph Thornton, Middletown, "upwards of seventy-nine years of age." May 23, 1816. Proved Aug. 28, 1820. Codicil dated Feb. 12, 1817. Son Samuel Yardley Thornton and John Blakey exrs. Gdsn. John T. Hallowell. Gdsn. Joseph Hallowell 7 his ch. Joseph and Elizabeth. Gddaus. Eliza and Jane, daus. of son Samuel Y. Thornton. Gdsns. Joseph and Jacob Thornton. Thackery Tract and ½ of Tract bought of Joseph Hayhurst to gdsn. Joseph Thornton.
Wits: Oliver Norton, Mahlon Briggs and Is. Hicks.

Page 416. William Wigton, New Britain Twp. Feb. 8, 1815. Proved Sept. 4, 1820. Ch. John, Mary Wigton, Pheby Morris, James Wigton, Elizabeth Henderson and William Wigton. Benjamin, Elizabeth and Salome, ch. of dau. Pheby Morris. William and Matilda Henderson, ch. dau. of Elizabeth. Son William and dau. Mary exrs. Codicil Aug. 21, 1820 removes son William as exr. on account of his removal "to a remote distance" since his appointment Thomas Stewart of New Britain and Gdsn. Benjamin Morris exrs.
Wits: Joseph Anglemoyer, Elizabeth Wigton, William Godshalk, Joseph Mathias.

Page 418. Thomas Craven, Carpenter, Warminster Twp. Aug. 18, 1820. Proved Sept. 16, 1820. John Craven, Storekeeper, exr. Sister Elshe Vandyke and Bros. Wilhelmus, Giles and William.
Wits: Isaac and James Craven.

Page 419. Jacob Landes, Plumstead Twp., Weaver. May 5, 1816. Proved Oct. 23, 1820. Bro. Henry Landes exr. 2 horses in possession of sister Sarah Groce and other effects to be sold, proceeds to Bros. and sisters and ch. of dec'd. bros. and sisters.

Wits: Henry Wismer and John Fretz.

Page 419. John Hedrick, Doylestown Twp. July 10, 1820. Proved Oct. 31, 1820. Wife Catharine extx. Daus. Maudlin, Margaret, Cathrin, Mary and Sarah Anna Hedrick.
Wits: Thomas Morris Junr. and David Evans.

Page 420. Leonard Wickhart, Rockhill Twp., yeoman. March 14, 1804. Proved Nov. 13, 1820. Wife Mary and sons Christian and John exrs. Son John Plantation purchased of Michael Kreamer (93 Acres) subject to Dower of Catharine Kreamer, widow of Lawrence Kramer [sic]. Sons Michael, Christian, John, Leonard and Abraham and daus. Barbara, Mary and Elizabeth.
Wits: Christian Fluck and Isaac Cassell.

Page 422. Jacob Reed, New Britain Twp, yeoman. "Far advanced in years." April 9, 1808. Proved Nov. 7, 1820. Son Philip and son-in-law Jacob Conwer exrs. Eldest son Philip, 2nd Jacob, youngest son Andrew. Eldest dau. Margaret wife of Jacob Redline, 2d Elizabeth wife of Jacob Conwer, 3d Catharine wife of William Lincy, 4th Magdaline wife of Josia Wilson, 5th Eve wife of Wendle Fisher.
Wits: John Shellenberger, Andrew Triewig and Frederick Repard.

Page 424. Casper Faubian, Senr., Durham Twp., yeoman. Sept. 24, 1818. Codicil dated May 8, 1820. Proved Nov. 27, 1820. Jacob Fulmer exr. Wife Mary. Ch. Casper and George Faubian and Catharine Groop. Codicil makes son George exr.
Wits: Christian Cressman, Jacob Cressman, Michael T. Calaw and Daniel S. Afflerbach.

Page 425. Peter Vansant, Lower Makefield Twp., 76 years of age. July 4, 1820. Proved Dec. 8, 1820. Son Joshua and Gdsn. Peter V. Bailey exrs. Wife Alethea. Gdsn. Curtis Vansant Bond I hold against him and all I have against his father's estate. Dau. Rachel Bayley, 120 Acres whereon I live adj. John Stockdale and Timothy Howell.
Wits: John Stockton and Joseph Stockton.

Page 426. Thomas Dremen, Middletown Twp., "old and infirm." March 30, 1813. Proved Nov. 28, 1820. John Linton of Newtown Twp. exr. Lydia Yardley, widow of Samuel Yardley dec'd. "for tender care during my indisposition whilst I resided there" £20. Her ch. Samuel, Benjamin and Charles Yardley, £30. Elizabeth Harvey, dau. of Joseph Harvey of Newtown 10£; Elizabeth wife of Joseph Buckman of Middletown, all residue of estate.
Wits: Jacob Janney and Cyrus Wiley; both dec'd. Proved by Joseph Wiley and Dr. Phineas Jenks.

Page 426. Margaret Routenbush, Rockhill Twp., widow. June 5, 1809. Codicil March 20, 1813. Proved Dec. 11, 1820. Son George Routenbush exr. 2 sons and 4 daus. Daus. Barbara, Charlot, Margaret and Catharin. Wits: Adam Gearhart, Samuel Sellers, Abraham Stout, (last two dec'd.), and Samuel and Mary Gehman. Translated from German.

Page 428. Jacob Weaver, Tinicum Twp., yeoman. April 18, 1820. Proved Jan. 4, 1821. Sons John, Moses and William exrs. Sons John, Moses, Isaac, William and Henry. Gdsn. Stephen Weaver, son of Henry. Gdsns. Harrison E. Weaver and Wilson Bergstresser. Daus. Diana wife of Samuel Cooper, Mary wife of Joseph Haney and Hannah wife of Jacob Vanderbelt.
Wits: George Snider and Henry Ridge.

Page 430. David Stover, Senr., Nockamixon Twp., yeoman. Nov. 1, 1814. Proved Jan. 4, 1821. Two younger sons, Joseph and Abraham exrs. Gdsns. John, Henry and Lydia Stover. Daus. Anna wife of John Fretz, Elizabeth wife of Jacob Geissinger of Upper Saucon and Susanna wife of Abraham Stover of Bedminster. Wife Lydya [sic]. Son John £1000. Son Henry residing in Haycock £1000. Residue to Joseph and Abraham.
Wits: Isaac Weaver and Jacob Buck.

Page 431. George Michener, Plumstead Twp., "Advanced in age." Feb. 20, 1818. Proved Jan. 6, 1821. Son Abraham and George Burgess exrs. Sons George and Abraham. Daus. Elizabeth Robinson and Grace Michener.
Wits: Peter Cadwallader and William Rich.

Page 432. Catharine Wynkoop, Lower Makefield Twp. Nov. 23, 1820. Proved Jan. 9, 1821. Thomas Yardley exr. Dau. Sarah Winder and gddaus. Mary and Rebecca Winder. Nephews Isaiah and John Suber. Niece Ann Jolly.
Wits: Joseph Yardley, Lamb Torbert and Aaron Winder.

Page 433. John White, Nockamixon. Nov. 29, 1820. Proved Dec. 19, 1820. George Snyder exr. Wife Catharine all estate "til youngest child gets to age" then to wife and ten ch. Dau. Anna.
Wits: Isaiah Cole and George Rapp.

Page 434. Joseph Kelly, Junr., Fallsington. 7-26-1820. Proved Nov. 27, 1820. Wife Mary and bro. Benjamin Kelly exrs. Ch. Jesse, Ann, Mary, Priscilla, Rachel, Joseph and John. House and Lot where I live, bought of Joshua Bunting.
Wits: John Counselman and John W. Balderston.

Page 435. John Brown, Falls Twp. 4-1-1820. Proved Jan. 15, 1820. Sons David, Abraham and Moses Brown exrs. Wife Martha. Son David 215 Acres on which he lives. Son Abraham residue of Plantation 213 acres.

230

Son Moses remainder of Plantation purchased of Samuel Allen, 180 Acres. Gdsn. John Brown Balderston. Debt due Delaney's estate to be paid.
Wits: Anthony Burton, John G. Burton and John W. Balderston.

Page 436. Garret Johnson , Upper Makefield Twp. Dec. 6, 1820. Proved Jan. 13, 1821. James Johnson and John Johnson exrs. Wife Huldah. Sons James, John and Charles. James Plantation whereon he lives. John and Charles Plantation whereon I live. Sons Joseph Amos, Ira and Garret B. Johnson. Daus. Joannah and Hulah [sic] Johnson.
Wits: Thomas Betts, Samuel Roberts Junr.

Page 438. Peter Raub, Durham Twp. Dec. 9, 1820. Proved Jan. 25, 1820. Bro. Jacob Raub of Williams Twp., Northampton Co., weaver, exr. Wife Hannah and minor ch.
Wits: Jacob Uhler and Jacob Raub.

Page 439. Hannah Simpson, Doylestown Twp. Oct. 2, 1820. Proved Jan. 27, 1821. Son-in-law Benjamin Hough exr. 3 ch. John Simpson, Hannah wife of Benjamin Hough and Anne wife of Jonathan Smith, Hannah wife of David Williams, Catharine wife of Robert Ditterline, Elizabeth Myers late consort of John Meyers [sic] dec'd.
Wits: George Walter and Joseph Hough Junr.

Page 439. Elizabeth Ely, widow of Hugh Ely, dec'd., Solebury Twp. 5-9-1817. Codicil dated 11-21-1820. Proved Jan. 10, 1821. Son John exr. 3 ch. viz: John Ely, Sarah Smith and Hannah Harrold. Hannah's share to be held in trust by son John.
Wits: Aaron Paxson, John Paxson Junr., Elias Carey and Joseph Duer.

Page 441. Harmon Fryling, Plumstead Twp. April 24, 1818. Proved Feb. 19, 1821. Christian Myers, Blacksmith, exr. Wife Margaret. Sons Elias and Leonard. Dau. Elizabeth.
Wits: --- and Christian Myers Junr.

Page 442. Thomas Warner, Wrightstown Twp. May 16, 1815. Proved March 3, 1821. Nephews Joseph Wiggins and Amos Warner exrs. Nieces Mary Warner and Elizabeth Taylor who live with me. Mahlon Miller, who lives with me. Amos Warner son of bro. Croasdale, 168 Acres bought of bro. Joseph Warner. Ch. of bro. John Warner, viz: John, Rachel, David, Isaiah, Jonathan, Simeon and Amos. Ch. of Elizabeth Flood. Bro. Joseph Warner and his ch. Cuthbert, Aseph and Silas. Ch. of bro. Croasdale Warner, dec'd. viz., Hannah, Aron [sic], Mary, Amos, Sarah, Croasdale, Agnes, Asa, John and Ann. Bro. Isaac Warner. Nephews Amos Warner and Joseph Wiggins, guardians agreeable to will of Elizabeth Warner to care of money left to her daus. Rachel Weber and Elizabeth Flood. Nephew James Wildman of Middletown. Sarah wife of John Clark.
Wits: Isaac Chapman and Sarah Taylor.

End of Book No. 9

Will Book No. 10.

Page 1. Martha Michener, Plumstead Twp., "Advanced in age." 8-6-1813. Proved March 10, 1821. Son John Michener and George Burgess exrs. Ch. Elizabeth Plumly, Joseph Michener, Mary Rich, Martha Stackhouse, Ann Hough, William Michener, John Michener, Jonathan Michener and Harman Michener.
Wits: John Rich Junr., Rachel Rich.

Page 2. Peter Shive, Bedminster Twp. Aug. 14, 1817. Proved March 12, 1821. Sons George and John exrs. Wife Susanna. Ch. Elizabeth, Jacob, Peter, George, Martin, John, Henry and Philip.
Wits: Robert Smith, Philip Haney and Christopher Bleam.

Page 4. John D. Rowland, Hilltown Twp. Feb. 7, 1821. Proved March 12, 1821. Bro.-in-law William H. Rowland. Bro-in-law Joel Evans and Robert Evans exrs. Wife Rachel sole legatee.
Wits: Griffith Owen, Aaron Jones and Robert Shannon.

Page 5. John Landes, Milford Twp., yeoman. Oct. 4, 1817. Proved March 19, 1821. Abraham Geissinger exr. Son Samuel sums that I am bound with him to Baltzer Wynberger. Son Henry Plantation whereon I live. "If the heirs of Baltzer Wynberger Senr., dec'd. Demand what I got with my wife, dau. of said Baltzer, Senr." Same to be paid out of Personal estate.
Wits: Christian Raab and ---.

Page 6. Hannah M. Cully, Newtown. 1-8-1819. Proved March 4, 1821. Son John M. Cully exr. Sons John M. Cully and Thomas M. Cully. Daus. Mary Johnson and Rebecca Plumly. Gddau. Hannah M. Cully. Lot on Front St. opposite Jolly Longshore's adj. Everard Bolton and David Bartin.
Wits: Francis Mahan and Sarah A. Hagerman.

Page 7. John Bradshaw, Buckingham Twp., Farmer. Dec. 14, 1820. Proved April 10, 1821. Sons John and Aaron exrs. Son John 100 Acres with Mansion House, off large Farm surveyed by George Burgess. Son Aaron 2 tracts 40 Acres 134 P[erches] and 21 Acres 74 P. Dau. Phebe Meredith 75 Acres bought at Sheriff's sale late of George Rapp and 200 Acres in Northampton Co. bought of John Dyer. Also lot of 5 Acres of Woodland bought of son Aaron adj. Samuel Gillingham. Son Moses two tracts out of Large Farm, 65 Acres. Mary Bradshaw, widow of son Jonas, dec'd. and Amos and Jane Bradshaw his ch.
Wits: Mary Miner and Asher Miner.

Page 8. George Stockham, "late of Falls Twp." Jan. 1, 1821. Proved April 11, 1821. Sons Thomas and John exrs. 6 daus. Elizabeth Leach, Anna

Chambers, Thomagina Wynkoop, Mary Smith, Charlotte Bates and Nancy Parsons, $500 each. Residue to sons Thomas and John Stockham.
Wits: Benjamin Marsh and John Hellings.

Page 9. John Gosline, Bristol Boro. Dated -- 1811. Proved April 17, 1821. No exrs. Letters to William Rodman and John Gosline. Wife Hannah. Newphew Peter Gosline of Ky. and Richard Gosline of Bristol sons of Bro. William dec'd. John and Thomas sons of Nephew Levy Gosline, dec'd. Hannah, late Gosline, James and William, sons of Nephew William Gosline, dec'd. Nieces Elizabeth Elwood, Abigail wife of Isaac Gale and Mary wife of Abner Johnson. Elisha Turner of Conn. son of sister Rebecca Turner, dec'd. Maria, Ann Eliza and Margaret Gosline, daus. of Nephew Jacob Gosline. William and Richard Flowers, ch. of Niece Rebecca Flowers. John Johnson, who now lives with me, son of niece Mary Johnson; and Abner Johnson, when he arrives of age. Mary Gale, who now lives with me dau. of my niece Abigail Gale and Isaac Gale. Elizabeth, Sarah, Rebecca and Hannah Gale, other daus. of same. Mary Stackhouse, late Gosline, widow of Nephew Levy Gosline. Bristol Preparative Meeting. Wits: ---. Proved by Strickland Foster, Dr. Amos Gregg, Samuel Hulme.

Page 11. William Bunting, Middletown Twp. 10-14-1829. Proved April 23, 1820. Sons Samuel and Jeremiah exrs. Wife ---. Son William. Daus. Hannah Yardley, Jane Knight, Margaret Bunting, Sarah Stapler, Abigail and Elizabeth Bunting.
Wits: Nathaniel Price and William Blakey Junr.

Page 12. William Ridge, Senr., Tinicum Twp. June 17, 1815. Codicil Aug. 30, 1820. Proved April 23, 1821. Sons Henry and William exrs. Real Estate to six sons Thomas, William Junr., Edward, Henry, Joseph and Moses. Daus. Elizabeth wife of Andrew Boid, Mary wife of John Nees, Catharine wife of Jonathan Wood, Grace and Rebecca Ridge.
Wits: Frederick Keeler and William Keeler Senr.

Page 14. George Richards, Warminster Twp., Weaver. March 20, 1821. Proved May 10, 1821. Harman Vansant of Warminster exr. George Walton, son of Isaac Walton of Moorland Twp. Silver watch. Residue to Margaret Mackey, late Richards, wife of Philip Mackey and her ch.
Wits: James Vansant, Hogeland Banes.

Page 15. John Balderston, Solebury Twp. 5-16-1818. Codicil 11-9-1820. Do. dated 1-17-1821. Proved May 16, 1821. Sons John and Mark exrs. Wife Elizabeth. Dau. Hannah, wife of John Michel of City of Baltimore. Plantation in Falls Twp. whereon son John lives to daus. Merab and Ann Balderston. Son Mark. Plantation whereon he lives in Falls Twp. John 162 Acres whereon I live. Also 133 Acres in Loyalstock Twp., Lycoming Co., bought of William Watson. Maryk 164 Acres 1 do. Patented Sept. 1796 and 107 Acres in Muncy Twp., Lycoming Co., surveyed 12-3-1794.

Obligation on account of estate of Margaret Langdale, dec'd., executed to Thomas Savoy.
Wits: Joseph and William Rice, Robert Smith.

Page --. Henry Kilmer, Tinicum Twp., Farmer. Feb. 16, 1819. Proved May 26, 1821. Sons Jacob and Samuel exrs. Wife Magdalena. Eldest son Henry. Eldest dau. Elizabeth Kilmer. Sons John, Jacob, Samuel and Anthony.
Wits: Henry Myers, George Lear and John Trauger.

Page 21. Jacob Lease, Rockhill Twp., yeoman. Dec. 8, 1815. Proved May 28, 1821. Wife Elizabeth and Philip Lingmaster exrs. Ch. Michael, Magdalena and Catharine. Gdsn. George Scheetz, son of dau. Catharine. Son-in-law William Getman, Gdsn. George Lease. Catharine's other four ch.
Wits: Morgan Custard and Henry Neae Long.

Page 23. Margaret James, New Britain Twp., widow. April 13, 1821. Proved May 29, 1821. Son Isaiah James exr. Sons Benjamin and Isaiah, 60 acres of Land on which I reside, paying out to Dau. Naomi James and two ch. of Dau. Lydia, dec'd., late wife of Nathan Thomas.
Wits: John Riale and Levi James.

Page 24. Daniel States, Southampton Twp,. yeoman. Sept. 22, 1817. Proved May 31, 1821. Son Abraham States and Langhorn Files (?) exrs. Sons Abraham and Peter. Daus. Elizabeth Vanartsdalen and Mary Randall.
Wits: John McNair and Samuel McNair.

Page 24. Mary Conner, Bristol Boro. May 10, 1820. Proved June 1, 1821. John Adams, Tailor, exr. Gddau. Mary Conner, late Fulmer, dau. of Gasper and Mary Fulmer, late Conner, my dau. Houshold [sic] Goods to Hannah, wife of Joseph Osmond, for services rendered. Sale made to Samuel Vanchuper (?).
Wits: Henry Tomlinson and Jonathan Adams.

Page 26. Susanna Walton, Warminster Twp., widow. 2-20-1814. Codicil dated 10-31-1820. Proved June 5, 1821. Isac [sic] Parry exr. Son Jonathan Walton. Daus. Agnes Worthington and Mary Harding. Gddaus. Martha and Agnes Walton; Susanna and Sarah Worthington; Mary and Sarah Harding. Money devised by will of mother Mary Kirk at death of bro. Joseph Kirk, still living.
Wits: Gideon and Elizabeth Prior.

Page 27. Henry Pfaff, Lower Makefield Twp., "advanced in age." April 27, 1819. Proved June 13, 1821. Sons John and William exrs. Wife Mary. Son John plantation in Upper Makefield whereon he lives. William plantation

whereon I live. Dau. Mary Slack. Gdsns. Henry P. Slack and Henry P. Layton.
Wits: Thomas Yardley and G. Yardley.

Page 28. Susan Blyler, Milford Twp., widow, "aged and infirm." March 6, 1813. Proved June 18, 1821. Kinsman Peter Blyler of Milford exr. Ch. of son Peter, dec'd.; sons Abraham, Jacob, Lazarus, Henry, ch. of son David, dec'd.; son John and daus. Mary and Hannah.
Wits: Everard Foulke and Baltzer Wynberger.

Page 30. Agnes ? Kelso, New Britain Twp,. widow. May 11, 1820. Proved June 30, 1821. James Findley and James Wier Junr. exrs. Niece Jane Kelso. Nephew Henry Kelso. Mary Nicholas, Jane, Margaret and Thomas Forsythe.
Wits: Thomas Weir and Moses Aaron.

Page 31. Robert Croasdale, Middletown Twp. 2-17-1821. Proved July 10, 1821. Wife Ruth, Benjamin Croasdale and son Jeremiah Croasdale exrs. Ch. Jeremiah, Margery, Mary, Joseph, Tacy and Morris; last 4 minors. Dau. Margery goods that were her mother's. Land adj. David Landes and John A. Mitchell to be sold.
Wits: Jeremiah Croasdale and Joseph Richardson.

Page 32. Deborah Ely, Solebury Twp. 4-7-1821. Proved July 11, 1821. Uncle Thomas Carey exr. Two daus. Louisa Matilda and Pamelia. Sons Henry, Jesse and John.
Wits: Robert Smith and Hannah Carey.

Page 33. Silas Carey, Newtown Twp. 7-16-1821. Proved July 25, 1821. Bro. Joseph Carey and Joshua Knight exrs. Bro. Joseph land adj. his. Balance of land to his son Silas Carey. Cousins Beulah and Mary Carey living with me. Silas Johnson son of Samuel, dec'd., and Silas Bond, son Abraham Bond.
Wits: Joseph Worstall Junr. and Silas Phillips.

Page 33. Joseph Moyer, New Britain Twp. July 14, 1821. Proved Aug. 6, 1821. No executor named. Letters granted to Abraham Moyer. Son Joseph Moyer all interest in Lot and Mills and carding Machine, and equal share with rest of heirs, in remainder.
Wits: Benjamin Mathew Junr., Samuel Delp.

Page 34. James Chapman, Buckingham Twp. Dec. 2, 1820. Proved Aug. 20, 1821. Son-in-law Samuel Iden exr. All estate after dec. of "Widow" to daus. Elizabeth Iden and Abigail Chapman and gddau. Julia Maria Chapman, who I have brought up and now living with me. Son John "advanced his full share."
Wits: John Moore and Abraham Chapman.

Page 35. Catharine Fox, Bedminster Twp. Jan. 26, 1816. Proved Aug. 22, 1821. Polly Engerd, "the girl that I raised" extx. and sole legatee.
Wits: William Kealer and William Kealer Senr. Letters to Mary Furnace, late Mary Engerd, the extx. named.

Page 36. Ann Morton, Falls Twp. Feb. 26, 1818. Proved Aug. 28, 1821. John Morton and Mark Balderston exrs. Son John Morton and gdch. Evan, Andrew, Ann, William, Mary and Sarah, ch. of William Morton, dec'd.
Wits: Benjamin Marsh, William Lovett and Henry Lovett.

Page 37. Joseph Vanzant, Bristol Boro., Chairmaker. Aug. 14, 1821. Proved Aug. 29, 1821. Wife Rebecca and Abraham Warner exrs. Ch. Garret, Elenor, Martha, Tacy and Ann Vanzant, minors.
Wits: William Vanzant and S. Foster.

Page 38. Peter Laubenstine, Bucks Co. May 7, 1821. Proved Aug. 30, 1821. Sons John Lobenstine and Isaac Lobenstein [sic] exrs. Ch. Christian, John, Isaac, Susan Labenstone [sic], Catharine and Mary. Ch. of son Abraham dec'd. and dau. Elizabeth dec'd. Land adj. Samuel Cooper and Peter Barntz.
Wits: William Erwin and Joseph Haney.

Page 40. Joseph Twining, Warwick Twp. Dec. 17, 1820. Proved Sept. 4, 1821. Sons James and Edward exrs. Wife Hannah. Son Joseph. Daus. Sarah Kirk, Elizabeth Tomlinson, Mary Scott, Rebecca Tomlinson, Rachel and Deborah Twining.
Wits: Francis Tomlinson, Silas Twining, William Worthington.

Page 41. David Kinsey, Solebury Twp. 10-30-1813. Proved Sept. 12, 1821. Nephew Samuel Kinsey exrs. and sole legatee.
Wits: Oliver Hampton and Benjamin Dennis.

Page 42. Benjamin Mathew, New Britain Twp., yeoman. Sept. 4, 1821. Proved Oct. 16, 1821. Sons Benjamin and Joseph exrs. Wife Rachel. Daus. Ann Hough, Rachel Morris, Mary McEwen, Dinah Mathias, Margaret Swarts and Lydia. Gdch. Charles Dungan, Burges, Oliver and John Morris, Elizabeth and Dinah Swarts.
Wits: Joseph Mathew Junr., Simon Mathew.

Page 44. Timothy Wright, Lower Makefield Twp. Aug. 6, 1821. Proved Oct. 23, 1821. William Satterthwaite Junr. exr. Wife Sarah. Dau. Ann wife of William Kelsey and her ch. Sarah and John Kelsey. Mitchell Wright.
Wits: Andrew Gilkyson and Phineas Jenks.

Page 45. Lavinia Thomas, Plumstead Twp. Oct. 7, 1821. Proved Oct. 29, 1821. John Moore exr. Sister Charlotte Moore and her ch. Violtta,

Laviania T. and Hamilton Moore. Aunt Sarah Thomas.
Wits: George Burges and Julia Ann Closson.

Page 46. George Fulmer, Haycock Twp., Blacksmith. March 5, 1820.
Proved Nov. 1, 1821. Bro. Jacob Fulmer and William Stokes exrs. Wife
Catharine. Ch. John, George, Daniel, Abraham, Catharine, Elizabeth,
Susanna, Mary and Sarah.
Wits: Enoch Strawn and William Strawn.

Page 48. David Heston, Falls Twp. 10-15-1821. Proved Nov. 2, 1821. Son
David exr. Wife Phebe. Daus. Tacey wife of Lewis Smedley, Rachel wife
of Robert Johnson, Elizabeth wife of Hugh Smith and Mary wife of Daniel
Lovett. Land purchased at Sheriff's sale adj. Robert Bethel, John Carlile
and Mark Balderston to son David.
Wits: John W. Balderston and Abraham Harding.

Page 50. William Kirk, Buckingham Twp. 1-18-1817. Proved Nov. 2, 1821.
Son Isaac and John Melone exrs. Wife Mary. Gdch. Amos, Isaac, Miranda,
Elizabeth, Jesse, Cynthia, Rachel and Levi Carver, ch. of late dau. Sarah
Carver. Dau. Cynthia Walton and her ch. Cynthia Carver dau. of son
William Kirk, dec'd. Son Isaac plantation purchased of John Tucker
whereon I live, and two acres purchased of John Watson. Gdsn. William
Kirk, son of son John Kirk, dec'd., land I rec'd. as my share of my father's
estate, land bought of my bro. Joseph Kirk and 15 acres pruchased of
Isaac Kirk all three tracts lying together; he to pay each of his bros. John,
Isaac and Stephen $133.33.
Wits: John Watson, Samuel Ely, Sarah Wilson, Rebecca Ely.

Page 52. Susanna Kratz, Plumstead Twp., Spinster. Oct. 17, 1821. Proved
Nov. 9, 1821. Bro. Philip Kratz exr. Mother all estate for life, then to
bros. John and Philip Kratz and sister Rachel Fretz, widow.
Wits: Valentine Kratz and Isaac Kratz.

Page 53. Morris Davis, Newtown Twp. 9-28-1821. Proved Nov. 14, 1821.
Bro. Seth Davis exr. Father Samuel Davis $125. Aunt Mary Davis my
watch. Amos Phillips $8. Abner Atkinson $8. Residue to bro. Seth Davis.
Wits: John Lea and Thomas Janney.

Page 54. Moses Smith, Newtown Twp. 10-23-1821. Proved Nov. 17, 1821.
Cousin Joseph Stradling the elder of Plumstead and his son Thomas
Stradling exrs. Cousin Joseph Stradling, the elder 114 acres whereon I
live. Cousin Thomas Stradling the elder of Lower Makefield $200. Cousin
Sarah Rhoads and Elizabeth Marshall £25 each. Cousin Sarah Michener
£25. Sisters Lydia Stanley, Mary Hough and Ann Votaw all my lands in
N.C., with all moneys due me in said state.
Wits: Jeremiah Bennett, Benjamin Taylor Junr. and David B. Taylor.

Page 55. Uriah Du Bois, Doylestown Twp., Minister of the Gospel. Dated - --. Proved Nov. 23, 1821. Wife Martha and son Charles Du Bois exrs. All estate to widow for maintenance of herself and ch.
Wits: ---. Proved by Asher Miner and Abraham Chapman of "Town of Doylestown."

Page 56. Peter Ott, Bedminster Twp., yeoman. Dated ---. Proved Dec. 8, 1821. Sons Frederick and Daniel and son-in-law George Rotzel [sic] exrs. Wife Catharine. Sons Daniel and George same outsetting that Frederic had when mar. Dau. Susanna wife of George Ratzel. Dau. Polly 9 Acres of land adj. Frederick Garis, Abram Bewickhouse and Peter Stout, son Frederick 100 acres of land adj. said lot paying unto my ch. Peter, Henry, Elizabeth's ch. and Catharine wife of Christopher. Plantation adj. William Fritz 100 acres, to son George. Plantatoin whereon I live to son Daniel. Sons John and Peter. Dau. Catharine. Dau. Elizabeth's ch.
Wits: John Dieterly and Christian Bewighouse. Caveat filed Oct. 16, 1820 by Daniel and George Ott. Letters Pendente lite granted Oct. 27, 1820 to Daniel Ott and issue directed to court of the C.P. to try validity of Will.

Page 58. Sarah Tomlinson, dau. of Henry Tomlinson, dec'd., Bensalem Twp. 9-28-1821. Proved 1-2-1822. Sister Jemima Tomlinson and Friend John Comly exrs. Friend Giles Knight son of Israel Knight dec'd. $500. Cousin Isaac Bolton of Drumore $300. Sarah, wife of Elisha Newbold, $200. Sarah and Elizabeth Tomlinson, daus. of John Tomlinson $200. Phebe wife of Thomas Tomlinson and her dau. Isabel $100 each. Cousin Sophia Homer $100. Cousin Joanna Davis $200. Friend Edward Hicks $100. Rebecca wife of John Clossin $40. Temperence Hudson $40. Rachel Paul, dau. of Giles Knight, dec'd. $40. Susanna Vandegrift, who lives with me $300. Mary Skinner and her dau. Martha Douglass each $20. Catharine wife of Abraham Vandegrift $20. Bro. Jesse's three ch. Jesse, Rhoda wife of Moses Knight and Charles monies due me by Bond and Note. Land which I and sister Jemima purchased of Lewis Rue to heirs of James Street Junr. and of John Pexton by Joseph Croasdale and James Townsend, to Susanna Vandegrift. Interest in Farm left to me and Sister Jemima by father to Bro. Jesse's ch. Sister Jemima to have use of same for life.
Wits: Asa Knight, Grace Knight and Joseph Knight.

Page 59. Elizabeth Mathias, Hilltown Twp., widow. Dec. 16, 1820. Proved Jan. 4, 1822. Son Joseph Mathias exr. Son Abel, his Bond to me dated May 1, 1800. Gdsn. Dr. Amasby Mathias. Gddaus. Anna wife of Thomas Mathias and Elizabeth wife of Edmund H. Heaton. Gdch. Sarah, Gainor and John ch. of son Abel Mathias. Gdsns. Mathias Morris and Ashbell Mathias, son of Thomas Mathias dec'd. Elizabeth and Lydia Ann daus. of son Joseph Mathias.
Wits: William T. Metler and William H. Rowland.

Page 61. John Wasser, Hilltown Twp., Carpenter. Oct. 12, 1821. Proved Jan. 7, 1822. Son Jacob Wasser and Henry Cope exrs. Wife Maria household goods and Winter grain in field adj. Lester Ritch. Dau. Anna Wasser, equal portion to that given other ch. as outsets.
Wits: John Crater, Henry Fuhrman and Henry Cope.

Page 62. Peter Beigler, Durham Twp., Farmer. Dec. 5, 1821. Proved Jan. 18, 1822. Son Daniel and John Fackenthall exr. Dau. Margaret and other ch. not named.
Wits: Michael Fackenthall and Peter Long.

Page 64. John Atkinson, Doylestown Twp., Blacksmith. Jan. 12, 1821. Proved Jan. 26, 1822. Father William Atkinson exr. Bros. William, Benjamin, Joseph and Asa Atkinson. Land in Buckingham adj. William Titus. Debt due John Bradshaw.
Wits: Moses Bradshaw and Amos Jones.

Page 64. Agnes Martin, alias Ann Martin, Middletown Twp. Oct. 25, 1821. Proved Feb. 2, 1822. William Richardson exr. Ch. Frances, Ann wife of Augustin Mitchell, Thomas, William, Daniel and Charles. Cousin Riselma Murry, gold mourning piece that was my dau. Mary's. House and lot in Atteborough where I live to be sold.
Wits: William Blakey Junr. and Mahlon Gregg.

Page 65. Samuel Henderson, Northampton Twp., yeoman. --- 1821. Proved Feb. 9, 1822. Wife Elizabeth. Thomas Henderson of Doylestown, Taylor. Nephew William Henderson, son of bro. Thomas and William Henderson, son of sister Margaret. Proved by Samuel Hart, Esq. and Robert Ramsey. Letters to Francis Baird and Henry L. Coryell. Will made latter part of June 1821.

Page 67. Catharine Barndt, widow of John Barndt of Rockhill Twp. Jan. 14, 1822. Proved Feb. 11, 1822. Son Peter Barndt exr. Ch. Peter, George and Susanna Barndt and Mary Gearhart, dau. of Mary Barndt.
Wits: George Roehler, John Weidemer and Isaac Cressman.

Page 67. Thomas Henry, Tinicum Twp., "advanced in age." July 3, 1816. Proved Feb. 14, 1822. Sons Frazer Henry and Richard Henry exrs. Wife Margaret. Sons Frazer, John and Richard. Daus. Martha wife of Robert McNeeley and Juliana. Son Thomas.
Wits: George Burgess and Ulyses Blaker.

Page 68. Jonathan Smith, Solebury Twp. Feb. 3, 1822. Proved Feb. 18, 1822. Elias Ely of New Hope exr. and trustee. Wife ---. Dau. Mary Ann plate owned by me before dec. of first wife. Son Louis.
Wits: Richard D. Corson, M.D. and Samuel D. Ingham.

Page 69. Michael Snyder, Hilltown Twp., yeoman. Jan. 12, 1822. Proved March 1, 1822. Bro. Conrad Snyder and Bro.-in-law Jacob High exrs. Wife Margaret Plantation, 96 acres adj. Abraham Gearhart, John Fretz and John Wertz and 15 Acres woodland adj. Phililp Swartley to Bro. Conrad Snyder, paying out to bro. Christian Snyder and Sisters Hanna wife of Frederick Shull and Catharine wife of Jacob Heigh.
Wits: Abraham Gearhart and Henry Cope.

Page 71. Sarah Wismer, wife of Abraham Wismer of Plumstead Twp., yeoman. April 3, 1821. Proved March 2, 1822. Nephew Abraham Overholt and Christian Gross exrs. Husband $400. 7 ch. of nephew Joseph Overhold [sic], dec'd. $800. To be paid out of first two installments due me out of estate of said dec'd. nephew. Friend Daniel Carrell $100. Sarah, wife of Michael Delp, $66. Residue to Bro. now living, three sisters living, ch. of dec'd. bro and ch. of two dec'd. sisters.
Wits: Henry Landes, John Gross and --- a German.

Page 72. Adam Shitz, Nockamixon Twp. July 10, 1819. Proved March 4, 1822. Son Michael Shitz and Christopher Drauger exrs. Wife Catharine interest of £400. Sons John Andrew ch. of son Adam, son Jacob, Michael, ch. of son Conrad, dau. Ann Margaret Allshouse in Va. and her son Henry Allshouse and the two ch. of Conrad Allshouse, which he left with his wife when he run off and left her. Michael and John and other 8 ch. of dau. Ann Catharine dec'd. late wife of Jacob Stone. Dau. Mary Catharine Pesner interest of her share only, unless she separated from her husband. Dau. Elizabeth. Deed to be made to son John for land sold to him as per Agreement.
Wits: Henry Miller and Michael Kohle.

Page 73. Joshua Woolston, Falls Twp. 12-20-1820. Proved March 4, 1822. Wife Lydia and son Stephen and Joshua exrs. Wife House and Lot whereon I live, purchased of Stephen Comfort, also Lot purchased of Anthony Taylor, during widowhood. Ch. Stephen Woolston, Elizabeth Canby, Rachel Paxson, Joshua Woolston, Ann Comfort, Lydia and Sarah Woolston.
Wits: Thomas Jenks and Joseph Brown.

Page 75. Rebecca Delost, Bensalem Twp., "Old." Oct. 23, 1820. Proved March 6, 1822. Neighbor William Simmons exr. Hannah Eammons, wife of Andrew Emmons [sic] and her ch., sole legatees.
Wits: Mary Nelson and Samuel Hulme. Mary Nelson's signature proved by Joshua C. Canby.

Page 75. Philip Sipler, Bensalem Twp. Nov. 20, 1819. Proved April 2, 1822. Sons Simon, Jacob and David exrs. Sons Simon, Jacob, Philip, David and Samuel and heirs of son George dec'd. Dau. Mary, wife of William McMullin. David Jackson, heir of dau. Elizabeth , dec'd. Heirs of dec'd.

dau. Sarah Thomas.
Wits: Philip Lipler, Elizabeth Clark, Sarah E. Banes and Josiah D. Banes.

Page 76. Henry Ridge, Northampton Twp. Feb. 21, 1821. Proved April 6, 1822. Sons Aaron and Mahlon exrs. Wife Elizabeth all estate for life. Son William money left him towards purchase of Farm he lives on in Muncy Creek Twp., Lycoming Co. Son Jesse Ridge and his wife Hannah farm on river Delaware bought of Samuel Hulme, for life then to their ch. Son Aaron Ridge Farm he lives on purchased of Seth Chapman, Esq. in Northampton Twp. Son Mahlon Farm he lives on in Bensalem Twp. and small tract adj. bought of Mary Roberts. Farm bought of Richard Lands in Bensalem in 5 shares: 1 to dau. Grace Searle, 1 to dau. Rebecca Hicks and her husband Mahlon Hicks for life, then to their ch. 1 to dau. Elizabeth and her husband George Fisher for life then to their ch. 1 to ch. of son Henry dec'd. and 1 to gdsn. Henry Ridge, son of son Jesse. Farm bought of John Gregg and Susanna Hayhurst to daus. Mary Walton and Lydia Scott.
Wits: Henry Atherton and Joseph Vanartsdalen.

Page 77. Maria Elizabeth Nice, Lower Milford Twp., widow. Jan. 4, 1821. Proved April 27, 1822. Philip Cope exr. and sole legatee.
Wits: Henry Schlichter, John Sellers and Henry Cope.

Page 78. Rebecca Margerum, widow of William Margerum, late of Lower Makefield. 2-13-1822. Proved May 7, 1822. John Kirkbride exr. Son William. Daus. Delilah and others.
Wits: John Mills and Stephen Comfort.

Page 79. Catharine Lassaman, Nockmaxin Twp., widow of Jacob Lassaman, late of same place. May 30, 1818. Proved May 13, 1822. Son Jacob sole legatee.
Wits: John Reagle and Henry Miller.

Page 80. Harman Titus, Bensalem Twp. July 30, 1814. Proved May 27, 1822. Son Tunis, son-in-law Isaac Johnson and Neighbor John Paxson exrs. Son Tunis and dau. Catharine Titus. Farm to be divided as per draft. Sons Jacob, Edmond and Harman. Daus. Minah, Susan, Elizabeth, Sarah and Ann.
Wits: Garret H. Vansant and Is. Hicks.

Page 81. Joseph Church, Buckingham Twp. Jan. 1, 1822. Proved June 5, 1822. Son-in-law Jonas Fell exr. Wife Mary. Ch. Sarah Fell, Elenor Bradshaw, Elizabeth Church, Rachel Moore, Jane Moore, Mary and Melison Church.
Wits: William Watson and Samuel Smith.

Page 81. Joseph Worthington, Buckingham Twp. May 14, 1820. Proved

June 18, 1822. Sons Abner, William and Jesse exrs. Wife Esther. Ch.
Abner, Joel, Elisha, Jesse, William, Sarah Tomlinson, Hannah Shaw,
Martha Carlile, Amy Thomas and Esther Worthington. Land bought of
John Kimble and Enoch Bayley.
Wits: William Worthington Senr., William Worthington Junr. and Spencer
Worthington.

Page 83. Mary Thompson, Lower Makefield. Oct. 10, 1821. Proved June
7, 1822. Dr. Phineas Jenks exr. Half-bro. Henry Thompson and Dau. Alice
Thompson.
Wits: John Kirkbride and Elizabeth Kirkbride.

Page 84. William Blakey, Middletown Twp. 4-4-1811. Codicil 12-26-1811.
2d Codicil 10-9-1821. Proved June 25, 1822. Wife Sarah and sons Thomas
and John exrs. Daus. Mary Wilson and Lydia Watson. Son Thomas land
bought of Jonathan Kirkbride; he to make no charge against his bro.
William for debts, and son John balance of Real Estate, he give up all
claim to Mill Tract he and his bro. Thomas bought between them.
Wits: Simon Gillam, William Gillam and Elizabeth Kirkbride Junr. Son
William and wife, both dec'd. at date of last codicil.

Page 85. Catharine Leatherman, Plumstead Twp. April 29, 1815. Proved
Aug. 5, 1822. Bro. Abraham Leatherman's son Philip exr. Bros. Jacob,
Abraham, Michael, Henry and John Leatherman. Sister Magdalena, wife
of Jacob High. Ulry and Hannah Hockman, ch. of Henry Hockman.
Wits: Abraham Overholt and William Kealer, Senr.

Page 87. Laurence Kremer, (so signed), Haycock Twp. Aug. 7, 1818.
Proved Aug. 9, 1822. Wife Susanna and bro. Jacob Kreamer exr. Real
estate for use of wife and four ch. Mother to live in house. 28 Acres in
Bedminster bought of Michael Wiesel.
Wits: Jesse Smith and Mary Kreamer.

Page 88. Hannah Goslin, Bristol Borough. Nov. 21, 1821. Proved Aug. 10,
1822. William Rodman and John Goslin exrs. Sisters Elenor Vanhorn and
Lydia Vanhorn. Andrew Vanhorn, Anna Amelia Oakum, Hannah Randal
and Alexandra (?) Vanhorn, ch. of sister Sarah Vanhorn. Bros. William,
Joseph and Andrew Mode. John Johnson, great nephew of late husband.
Elizabeth Ellwood, niece of do. Jacob Goslin, nephew of do. Mary
Andrews, great niece of do. Mary Harrison, Sarah Thompson and Hannah
Porter, late of Gosline, great nieces of do. Abigail Gale, niece of do.
Martha, wife of John Gosline of Newport. Esther Gosline great niece of
do. Anna Vanhorn who lives with me. William Gosline, son of William
Gosline, Hannah wife of Richard Appleton and her two ch. by her first
husband. Elizabeth Watson, late Flowers, great niece of late husband.
Richard, Levi and Eli Gosline, nephews of late husband.
Wits: John Patterson and Samuel Allen, Junr.

Page 89. Robert Love, Warrington. Aug. 7, 1822. Proved Aug. 17, 1822. Dau. Ann Love exrs. Wife ---.
Wits: William C. Rogers, William Walker.

Page 90. Henry Feaster, Northampton Twp. Sept. 3, 1807. Proved Aug. 26, 1822. Sons John and David exrs. Wife Margaret, all effects she brought me at mar. &c. Ch. John , Rachel, Mary, David, Henry and George. Granddau. Susanna Feaster dau. of son David. Gdsn. Henry Feaster son of son John.
Wits: John McNair and John Corson.

Page 91. Scipio Brown, Middletown Twp. 9-19-1810. Proved Aug. 26, 1822. James Wildman and John Watson exrs. Natural sons Aaron Brown, who was formerly held by John Hulme of Holmesburg. Dau. Hannah Brown, who lately lived with Samuel Henderson at the Cross Roads in Bucks Co.
Wits: Robert Croasdale and David Landes, both dec'd.   Handwriting proven by Jeremiah Croasdale and Henry Atherton Esq.
Letters to John Watson.

Page 92. Joseph Kelly, Falsington. 2-2-1816. Proved Sept. 9, 1822. Wife Phebe and son Benjamin exrs. Ch. Priscilla Kelly, Joseph, Naomi Bunting, Jesse, Phebe Harper, Isabella Kelly, Thomas, Benjamin, John and William.
Wits: John W. Balderston and John Counselman.

Page 93. Allivia Bryan, widow, Springfield Twp. Feb. 6, 1819. Proved Sept. 9, 1822. Sons James and Joseph Bryan exrs. Dau. Molly wife of John Bechtel and her son William Bechtel. Gdsn. William Bryan, son of James. "Four children."
Wits: Peter Smith and William Moyer.

Page 94. John Price, Bensalem Twp. 10-6-1821. Proved Oct. 2, 1822. Wife Phebe and Jonathan Thomas of Lower Dublin exrs. Two ch. Joseph and Rebecca.
Wits: Sidney Osmond and Andrew Singley.

Page 95. Amos Yardley, Newtown. March 16, 1819. Proved Aug. 27, 1822. Codicil dated Aug. 8, 1822. Bro. Enos Yardley exr. Bro. Joshua. Sister Sarah. Mother Hannah Yardley.
Wits: Abner Reeder, John B. Winder.

Page 96. Priscilla Irwin, Warrington Twp., widow. Nov. 28, 1821. Proved Sept. 10, 1822. Nephew James Weir and Friend Samuel Hart exrs. Sisters Hannah Watson, Mary Weir and Jane Watson and their ch. Bro. Samuel McKinstry's ch.
Wits: William Carr and James Kerr.

Page 97. John Blankenhorn, Doylestown Twp. 1-16-1821. Proved Sept. 10, 1822. Jonathan Large and Daniel Stradling exrs. Sister Mary Johnson $50. Sister Martha Blankenhorn $800. Joseph Stradling $50 for use of Preparative Meeting of Friends at Plumstead. Residue to John, son of William Burgess, John Stradling, son of Daniel. John Large, son of Jonathan and Mary Byerly, dau. of John Byerly.
Wits: A. Chapman and Wilhelmina Chapman.

Page 97. William Goucher, Solebury Twp., Mason. June 2, 1822. Proved Sept. 11, 1822. Joshua Ely of Solebury, yeoman, exr. Wife Hannah. Ch. Lewis, Elizabeth, John and Mary Ann.
Wits: John Helwig and David M. Cray.

Page 99. Walter Shewell, Doylestown Twp. Feb. 1, 1820. Proved Sept. 18, 1822. Nephew Nathaniel Shewell and son Joseph Shewell exrs. Wife Rachel. Gdch. Martha, Elizabeth and William Leppard, ch. of dau. Ann Leppard dec'd. Real estate to John Riale of Doylestown Twp. in trust for use of son Joseph for life, then to son Joseph's ch. , also residue of Personal estate. Dau. Elizabeth, widow of Day Bitting dec'd. Dau. Mary. Gdsn. Charles Shewell.
Wits: Jacob Kephart and Charles Shewell.

Page 101. Hannah Field, Lower Makefield Twp. 4-19-1810. Proved Dec. 10, 1822. Son Benjamin exr. Dau. Latitia Warner, gdch. William and Ann Warner, William, Hannah, Joseph, Elizabeth and Isaac Field, ch. of son Benjamin.
Wits: Joseph Taylor, Mercy Taylor and Sarah Taylor.

Page 103. Arthur Henderson, Springfield Twp. June 15, 1822. Proved Aug. 9, 1822. Jacob Fulmer of Springfield, exr. Wife Mary, all estate.
Wits: Nicholas McCarty and Nicholas Youngker ? Probably Youngken.

Page 103. John Loh, Rockhill Twp., "advanced in years." June 6, 1812. Proved Aug. 10, 1822. Son Jacob and son-in-law George Wonsidler exrs. 5 ch. John, Jacob, Margaret (who is dec'd.), Barbara and Catharine. Margaret's ch. Frederick, Elizabeth and Catharine.
Wits: John Reed and Morgan Custard (?).

Page 105. John Kephart, New Britain Twp., yeoman. March 30, 1817. Proved Sept. 18, 1822. Jacob Smitt/Smith (?), and sons Jacob and John Kephart exrs. Wife Elizabeth. 9 ch. Jacob, John, Abraham, Magdalena wife of John Bear, Catharine wife of John Gerhart, Susanna wife of David Hestout, Hannah wife of Joseph Yocum, Elizabeth and Ann.
Wits: Abraham Fretz, John Riale and Samuel Landis.

Page 106. Joseph Greer, Bedminster Twp., "advanced in age." Sept. 12, 1821. Proved Sept. 23, 1822. Neighbor William McNeily and son-in-law

Andrew Wilson exrs. Wife Susanna Farm bought of John Gill in Bedminster. Dau. Martha Wilson Farm bought of John Shaw, except part sold to Adam Hoffman for life then to her ch., her sons James, Joseph and Francis.
Wits: George Burges, Joseph Burrows.

Page 108. "--- ? We the subscribers were attending in the chamber of Jane McKinstry on the evening of the 20th of August last past a few days before her death." "Her brother Nathan should pay her debts and all James's debts out of her estate and that the remainder be equally divided between her two brothers Nathan and Jesse." Sept. 2, 1822. Phebe Miller, Catharine Frankenfield.
Wits. to signing: James S. Pool and Catharine Frankenfield Junr. Proved Sept. 28, 1822.

Page 108. John Shellenberger, New Britain Twp., yeoman. June --, 1820. Proved Oct. 5, 1822. Son Jacob and Michael Hartman, son-in-law, exrs. Wife Elizabeth. Oldest son John, already advanced. Other 5 ch. Elizabeth wife of Andrew Hetman (?), Jacob Shellenberger, Rachel wife of Michael Hetman (?). Samuel and Anna Shellenberger.
Wits: Andrew Trewig and Andrew Reed.

Page 111. Isabella Bailey, Tinicum Twp. Aug. 31, 1822. Proved Sept. 10, 1822. Sons John and Samuel S. Bailey, Joshua B. Colvin and Daniel Boileau exrs. Son Thomas C. Baley [sic], interest of $500 for life, then to his ch. Sons John, William and Samuel S. Bailey. Dau. Jane. Gddaus. Isabella and Eliza Kitchin. Gdsn. John Bailey.
Wits: Beltshazer Smith and Thomas B. Williams.

Page 112. Samuel Ely, Buckingham Twp. 8-7-1822. Proved Oct. 7, 1822. Bros. John and Thomas Ely exrs. Ch. Seneca, John and Sarah to be brought up by my sister-in-law Rachel Ely.
Wits: John Watson, Joseph Carey.

Page 113. Elizabeth Moor, wife of Alexander Moor, of Newtown Twp. Sept. 25, 1822. Proved Oct. 7, 1822. Aunt Rebecca Cook $100. Residue to husband Alexander T. Moore (?), being proceeds of Messuage and Lot at Second and Arch St. Phila. held in trust by Samuel Ewing and William Davidson.
Wits: John Fox and Lewis Willard.

Page 114. Henry Blyler, Milford Twp., yeoman. March 26, 1813. Caveat filed by A. Chapman, Atty. for Jacob Blyler, Oct. 7, 1822. Proved Dec. 9, 1822. Friend Peter Blyler exr. Mother. Bros. and sisters £3 each. Ch. of bros. Peter and David dec'd. £3. Sister Ellnor Mary wife of George Wise $1. Residue to sister Hannah and her dau. Motelina.
Wits: Everard Foulke and Samuel Shelly.

Page 115. Thomas Noble, Falls Twp. July 23, 1811. Proved Oct. 11, 1822. Harvey Gillingham of Falls exr. All estate for illegitimate dau. Elizabeth, wife of Benjamin Hambleton.
Wits: Mahlon Milnor, Phebe Milnor and Samuel Moon Junr.

Page 116. Daniel Martin, Middletown Twp. Aug. 1, 1822. Proved Oct. 18, 1822. William Richardson exr. Lot in Washington Village to be sold. Bro. Thomas Martin and sisters Frances Martin and Ann, wife of Augustine Mitchell.
Wits: Mahlon Gregg and Jonathan Walton.

Page 117. Elizabeth Johnson, Doylestown Twp., widow. Aug. 21, 1822. Proved Oct. 23, 1822. "Friends and Relatives David Johnson and Joseph Pool of Doylestown, exrs. Husband's nieces, Jane Peterson and Ann W. Clemens, Thomas Stephens, his wife Mary and ch. Mary Ann Stephens and William. Mary Ann, Matilda and Aaron, ch. of James Pool, dec'd. Elizabeth Pool who now lives with me. Susanna wife of David Johnson. Elizabeth wife of Paul Brooner (?). Martha Metlin. Nathan Cornell. Elizabeth wife of Samuel James. John Cornell. 4 daus. of George Seigfried. Mary wife of Abel Lewis. Elizabeth wife of Thomas Lovett. Martha Clymer. Abraham Myers to continue to pay interest on Bond, not to be sued or distressed.
Wits: Sophia P. Rogers and John Pugh.

Page 119. Joseph McDowell, Warminster Twp. Feb. 25, 1822. Proved Oct. 25, 1822. Lemon Banes exr. Wife Tacey all estate for bringing up ch., Mary Ann, Selina and George Davis McDowell. Land adj. Isaac Craven.
Wits: John Crawford and William Beans.

Page 120. Mary Weir, Warrington Twp., "Far advanced in life." Oct. 26, 1822. William Long, Miller, and Lawrence Emery exrs. Codicil removes Emery and appoints Benjamin Hough of Doylestown Twp. "the Elder" in his stead. ½ part of 140 acres "my father's estate" to be sold. Proceeds to Dau. Margaret wife of Samuel Weir for life, then to her son Robert Weir and other ch. Gdsn. John Weir.
Wits: James Kirk and Jacob Cassel. Codicil: Mary Cassel.

Page 122. Jacob Shade, Doylestown Twp. Oct. 11, 1822. Proved Oct. 31, 1822. Wife Christiana dau. of Ann Shade and Bro.-in-law Joseph Fitzwater exrs. 5 minor ch. Jacob, Eliza, Charles and Adelina. Daus. Ann, Amelia and Rebecca. Agreement with John Barclay Esq. and my sisters by which I was to keep my mother, now living with me for 4 years and 6 months, compensation therefor part of estate.
Wits: Obed Aaron and John Pugh.

Page 124. Elizabeth Murhley, Warrington Twp., widow. July 3, 1819. Proved Nov. 4, 1822. Jacob Cassel of Montgomery Twp. & Co. exr. 12 ch.

Isaac, Abraham, Jacob, Levi, Daniel, George, Henry, John, Joseph, Catharine, Sarah wife of John Garner and Elizabeth. Elizabeth, infant dau. of Dau. Sarah. Elizabeth and Ann daus. of son Abraham.
Wits: John Delp and George Walter.

Page 125. Mary Meredith, Doylestown, "Feeling infirmities of age." Jan. 31, 1822. Proved Nov. 5, 1822. Son-in-law Abraham Chapman Esq. and gdsns. Campbell Meredith and Henry Chapman exrs. Son Charles, his wife Isabella and daus. Mary and Susanna. Son Thomas N. Meredith, his wife Rachel and ch. Matilda, Sarah and Ann. Gddau. Wilhelmina Chapman.
Wits: Asher and Mary Miner. Campbel Meredith renounced, letters to Abraham Chapman only.

Page 126. William Long, Warrington Twp., Miller. Aug. 25, 1822. Proved Nov. 12, 1822. Sons William, Alexander and Lewis exrs. Wife Sarah "and all my ch.."
Wits: William Long Junr., "Farmer" and William H. Long.

Page 127. Hugh Ely, Solebury Twp. 5-11-1821. Proved May 15, 1822. Son-in-law Richard Randolph and son Elias Ely exrs. Wife Ruth $10,500 willed by her late father Oliver Paxson, dec'd.; and annuity of $400 to be paid her by my two ch. Elizabeth Randolph and Elias Ely. Dau. Elizabeth tracts of land bought of Samuel D. Ingham and Bro. John Ely and another tract bought of Thomas Paxson, adj. Josiah Shaw, Mordecai Pearson and others. Son Elias estate whereon I live purchased of Father-in-law Oliver Paxson and another tract adj. John Pidcock, Thomas Cooper and others, ½ interest in Land in Amwell, Hunterdon Co., N.J. purchased with William Maris, ½ part of tract of land in Pike Co., Pa. on or near Shakola Creek, purchased of Joshua Vansant in company with Lewis S. Coryell.
Wits: Benjamin, Daniel and Oliver Parry.

Page 129. Mary Hibbs, Southampton Twp. 8-11-1822. Proved Nov. 21, 1822. Jesse Tomlinson exr. Sons Seneca, William, Eli and Abner Hibbs. Dau. Mary Randal. Dau. Betsey's ch. Son Eli's wife and Rachel Hibbs. Eli and John Wilson and Mary Randal.
Wits: Stephen Croasdale, Evan Townsend Junr.

Page 130. Grace Johnson, Newtown Twp. 6-13-1822. Codicil 11-4-1822. Proved Dec. 2, 1822. Jeremiah Bennett and Jonathan Paxson exrs. Niece Ann Nicholas Lot in Upper Makefield for life, then to exrs. Residue of estate to Mary Bennett.
Wits: Robert Hillborne, William Ryan; To Codicil: David Harvey and Robert Harvey.

Page 131. Israel Anderson, Buckingham Twp. May 10, 1821. Proved Dec. 6, 1822. Isaiah Jones and John Watson of Buckingham exrs. Bro. James

Anderson apparel, sisters Hannah Brooke, Mary Ramsey, Sarah Vandyke and Elizabeth Robinson $800 each. Two daus. of bro. David , dec'd. "Names not recollected" $600. 3 ch. of John Denison, issue of my niece Mary Denison late Anderson, dec'd. $800. Bro. Joshua Anderson $1500 and his ch. Joseph $1500. Latitia and Cassandra Anderson $1500. $800 in trust for use of James son of bro. John dec'd., at his death principal to his daus. Mifflin and Decatur Anderson sons of said James. Julia, Matilda and Sarah his daus. Late wife Margaret Anderson.
Wits: John Ely, David White and Jesse Johnson.

Page 133. Ezra Jones, Buckingham Twp. 8-24-1821. Proved Dec. 6, 1822. Father Isaiah Jones exr. and sole legatee.
Wits: John Watson, Martha Watson.

Page 134. John Singley, Bensalem Twp. 8-21-1822. Proved Dec. 7, 1822. Wife Sarah Singley and John Comly exrs. Dau. Hannah.
Wits: Hannah Dubre and Sarah Mitchell.

Page 134. Mary Smith, Rockhill Twp. Sept. 25, 1819. Proved Dec. 9, 1822. Bro.-in-law William Long of Durham exr. Bro. Jesse to live on and receive profits of 83 Acres in Rockhill adj. Robert Smith, for life, then to his ch. Sisters Jane Long and Martha Rittenhouse. Cousin John McHenry. Bro. Jesse's son Charles Smith. Mother to be provided for. Sister Martha's 3 daus.
Wits: Francis B. Shaw and John Stoneback.

Page 136. Benjamin Mather, Middletown Twp. 5-16-1822. Proved Dec. 10, 1822. Sons Jonathan, Benjamin and Joseph T. Mather exrs. Son Jonathan 94 Acres in Cheltenham Twp. whereon he lives, paying therefrom $1250 to my dau. Sarah Thomas. Son Richard.
Wits: Thomas and Richard M. Shoemaker.

Page 137. Henry Fluke, Richland Twp. Nov. 9, 1822. Proved Dec. 11, 1822. Wife Catharine and Jacob - [illegible] Benner exrs. Wife use of Farm of 45 Acres whereon I reside, at her death to be sold, proceeds to three ch. Sophia, Samuel and Joseph.
Wits: Samuel Smith and Henry Freed.

Page 138. John Scott, Warminster Twp., yeoman. Aug. 12, 1820. Proved Dec. 24, 1822. Thomas Beans and John Scott, son of bro. Andrew, exrs. Bro. James D. Scott. John, Andrew, Joseph Samuel, Margaret and Elizabeth Scott and Rachel McCue ch. of bro. Andrew Scott. Mary Scott dau. of bro. William, dec'd. Mary and Susanna Scott, daus. of bro. Archibald, dec'd.
Wits: Gideon Pryor and Joshua Walton.

Page 139. John Shepherd, Northampton Twp., weaver. Jan. 4, 1803.

Proved Dec. 26, 1822. Son Henry exr. Son John and Dau. Elizabeth Huston.
Wits: John Fenton, Blacksmith and John Randall.

Page 140. Charles McMicken, Warwick Twp., yeoman. July 20, 1821. Proved Jan. 2, 1823. Elijah Opdyke exr. Sons Andrew and Charles McMicken. Dau. Elizabeth Randall's ch. and Dau. Naomi Car's ch.
Wits: Jacob Swartz and Samuel Hart.

Page 142. John Fretz, Tinicum Twp. Nov. 14, 1822. Proved Jan. 8, 1823. Neighbour John Myers Senr. exr. Wife Ann legacy coming from Estate of her bro. John Shaw, dec'd. Bro. Christian Fretz. Nephews Henry and John Fretz, Real Estate in Nockamixon adj. Jacob Wolling and Solomon Wolfinger. 9 ch. of bro. Christian, viz. Anna, Henry, Elizabeth, John, Christian, Mary, Joseph, Jacob and Susanna Fretz.
Wits: George Lear and George Hillpot Junr.

Page 144. George Rufe, Nockamixon Twp. Oct. 3, 1822. Proved Jan. 15, 1823. Sons Frederick and John exrs. Wife Sarah and Family to remain on Plantation until son Samuel is 21. Son Samuel part of Plantation (described) adj. Conrad Custard, Mary Ann Wison, James Smith and River Road; at valuation of $20 per Acre. Son John remainder of same at $16 per Acre. Ch. Jacob, Frederick, John, Samuel, Elizabeth, Sarah, Susanna and Catharine.
Wits: Henry Miller and Michel Lipecap.

Page 146. Joseph Wharton, Falls Twp., Farmer. Dec. 19, 1822. Proved Jan. 23, 1832. Stephen Woolston exr. Wife Susan all estate for life, then to ch. of Jesse, Joshua, Isaac and Rachel Wharton.
Wits: John Counselman and Daniel Burgess Junr.

Page 149. George Sheip ? [illegible], Senr., New Britain Twp. March 3, 1818. Proved Jan. 25, 1823. Wife Barbara and bro.-in-law George Urich exrs. Ch. John, Noe, Levinus, Elizabeth and Mary, all minors.
Wits: Isaac Hines, Griffith Owen.

Page 150. Peter Leefferts [sic], Northampton Twp., yeoman. Jan. 1, 1822. Proved Feb. 11, 1822. Sons Leffert Lefferts and Simon Lefferts exrs. Wife Lamentie. Son Peter; daus. Leytie Folwell, Elizabeth Carrell, Adriana and Mary Magdalena Lefferts. Gddau. Adriana Folwell.
Wits: Garret Vanartsdalen and John Courson.

Page 152. Thomas Richardson, Middletown Twp. May 9, 1822. Proved Feb. 21, 1823. Bro. William Richardson and Relative Michael H. Jenks exrs. Son John B. Richardson all estate; if he dies in minority to Bro. William, Sisters Rachel Story, Elizabeth Reeves, Anna Richardson and Mary Hulme. To sister Mercy Shoemaker interest for her sons Jonathan

and Jacob Shoemaker, and to ch. of bro. Joseph Richardson, dec'd. Niece Susanna M. Allen.
Wits: Henry Atherton and Joseph Jenks.

Page 153. Charity Courson, Northampton Twp. Feb. 17, 1823. Proved Feb. 20, 1823. Jacob Thomas and Henry Vanartsdalen exrs. Son James Courson. Elizabeth, wife of Derick Kruson. Gddaus. Catharine Vanartsdalen, Charity and Elizabeth Finne. Gdsn. Thomas J. Corson.
Wits: Derick Kruson and Amos Martindell.

Page 155. Joseph Shaw, Richland Twp., Farmer. 1-13-1823. Proved Feb. 27, 1823. Bro. Israel Shaw and Friend Jonathan Shaw exrs. Ch. Alevia, Ann, Gulielma, Israel and Rebecca, last three minors.
Wits: Enoch Walton and John Shaw.

Page 156. John Detweiler, Bedminster Twp., "advanced in age." July 1, 1817. Proved March 11, 1823. Sons John and Peter exrs. Wife Barbara. Ch. John Dettweiler [sic], Elizabeth Overholt, Susanna Wisner, Peter Dettweiler [sic] and Barbara Hockman.
Wits: Adam Bryan and Samuel Gayman.

Page 159. Joseph Kirk, Buckingham Twp., yeoman. Feb. 13, 1813. Codicil dated May 13, 1815. Proved March 12, 1823. Wife Patience and nephew Amos Kirk son of bro. Thomas exrs. (Wife d. before date of codicil.) Nephew Joseph Kirk, son of bro. Thomas $300. Plantation 130 Acres and Lot on Durham Rd. 9 miles from Newtown to Nephew Amos Kirk.
Wits: Thomas Chapman, William Trego and Samuel Tomlinson.

Page 161. Abraham Leatherman, Bedminster Twp. April 29, 1815. Proved April 8, 1823. Sons Philip and Abraham exrs. Wife Ann. Sons Philip, Abraham, Henry, John and Jacob. Daus. Anna Leatherman and Magdalena wife of Jacob Heavinger.
Wits: Abraham Overholt and William Keeler. Keeler's signature proven by Jacob Keeler.

Page 163. John Corson, Northampton Twp. Jan. 13, 1823. Proved April 28, 1823. Nephew Richard D. Corson, M.D. exr. Wife Charity all estate for life, except goods bought of son James, which I devise to Bro.-in-law Harman Vansant in trust for use of son James, together with $500 at death or mar. of wife, at his death to be paid to his son Thomas Jones Corson and his other ch. $600 to said Harman Vansant for use of son Benjamin. Dau. Mary wife of Charles Finney, lot of 5 ½ Acres bought of widow Price. Gddau. Catharine Vanartsdalen dau. of dec'd. dau. Jane Vanartsdalen. To said Harman Vansant, Farm of 50 Acres and lot of 8 Acres bought of Henry Drinker, in trust for use of legatees before mentioned.
Wits: Jacob Thomas and Jonathan Lefferts.

Page 166. Abraham Benner, Haycock Twp., Joiner. Oct. 16, 1821. Proved April 28, 1823. Martin Wack and Nicholas McCarty exrs. Wife Susanna. Ch. Sebastian, Jacob and Abraham Benner, Mary wife of Philip Shroyer and Nancy wife of Jacob Wonamaker. Gdch. Ester, dau. of son Sebastian by his first wife, now mar. to --- Crouse and Dau. Nancy's dau. by Samuel Landes, named Catharine Landes.
Wits: Adam Benner, Jacob Simms.

Page 168. David Twining, Warwick Twp., yeoman. --- 1819. Proved May 28, 1823. Son Eleazer Twining and Watson Welding exrs. Sons William, Eleazer, Isaac and Thomas. Daus. Phebe and Buelah E. Twining. Watson Twining son of Silas, Guardian of son John Twining. Wife Martha.
Wit: John Tucker and Joseph Tucker.

Page 169. Miles Strickland, Lower Makefield. Jan. 4, 1823. Proved April 24, 1823. Son Amos exr. Other ch. Sarah wife of John Bennett, Mary wife of John Addis and Joseph Strickland and Ann, wife of Garret Wynkoop.
Wits: Mahlon Gregg and Alexander Derbyshire.

Page 170. Mary Gillam, Lower Makefield Twp. Jan. 27, 1823. Proved April 29, 1823. Son Benjamin Vanhorn exr. Ch. Benjamin Vanhorn, Mary and Isaac Gillam.
Wits: John Depuy, William Aspy and Aaron Larew.

Page 171. Anna Rhor, widow of Jacob Rhor, late of New Britain Twp. May 11, 186. Proved May 1, 1823. Dau. Catharine and her husband John Frick exrs. and guardians of minor gdch. Dau. Elizabeth wife of Charles Selnor (?). Peter, John and Anna Frick, gdch. Land in Plumstead Twp. to be sold.
Wits: John Funk Junr., Cadwallader Foulke and ---.

Page 173. Jesse Dungan, Northampton Twp., "Advanced in years." May 9, 1814. Proved May 6, 1823. Codicil dated June 12, 1820. Nephew Daniel Dungan and Samuel Young and wife Sarah exrs. Wife Plantation for life, then to Samuel Young. Isaac Dungan son of bro. Thomas dec'd. and his son Jesse Dungan. Robert Parsons son of William Parsons. Elizabeth Caffee, dau. of Garret Krewsen. Christiana Dungan and Isaac Dungan ch. of nephew James Dungan. Isaac and Daniel Dungan ch. of bro. Thomas, dec'd.
Wits: John Corson Junr. and John Corson. Codicil: John Corson Esq. and John Hart, Shopkeeper exrs.
Wits: James Evans and Richard Clayton.

Page 176. Abraham Wisner, Plumstead Twp. Oct. 29, 1822. Proved May 7, 1823. Sons-in-law Henry Landes and Abraham Overholt exrs. Youngest dau. Mad--- [illegible], not able to maintain herself, left to care of 3 sons-

in-law Abraham Overholt, Henry Landes and Christian Gross. 1st dau. Margaret, 2d Elizabeth, 3d Hannah, 4th Barbara.
Wits: Abraham Nash and John Gross.

Page 177. William Marshall, Tinicum Twp. Sept. 3, 1821. Proved May 10, 1823. Neighbor George Smith exr. Nieces Elizabeth, Rebecca, Sarah and Ann Marshall, daus. of Martin Marshall dec'd. --- [illegible]. Rifle and Shot Gun to William, son of Moses Marshall. £100 owing me by Joseph Smith of Tinicum to Buckingham Mo. Meeting of Friends.
Wits: Joseph Heany (?), Elias Shull.

Page 178. Henry Hockman, Bedminster Twp. April 13, 1823. Proved May 22, 1823. Bro. Ullry (?) exr. and guardian of son Ullry (?) who is not capable of having his money. Ch. Ullry, Christian, Abraham, Anna, Mary, Barbara and Finna (?) Hockman. Bro. Jacob guardian of dau. Anna, though "over age." Bro.-in-law Martin Fretz guardian of son Christian, "underage."
Wits: David Kulp and Jacob Leatherman.

Page 179. Philip Drevey, Springfield Twp., yeoman. July 12, 1817. Proved May 30, 1823. Andrew Brunner Senr. exr. Wife Catharine sole legatee. Brunner being dec'd. letters were granted to Catharine.
Wits: Joseph Hess Junr. and Moses Marstellar.

Page 180. Peter Grub, Durham Twp. March 23, 1823. Proved May 30, 1823. Son George Grub and Jacob Deemer exrs. Sons George, Jacob, John, Anthony and Peter. Daus. Mary, Sarah and Elizabeth. Land in Bucks and Northampton Cos.
Wits: Jesse Canby, Christian Sterner and David Afflerbach.

Page 182. John Blyler, Lower Milford Twp., yeoman, "advanced in years." Oct. 19, 1822. Proved May 31, 1823. Nephew Peter Blyler and William Corner both of Milford Twp. exrs. Wife Gertrude. William Corner "a lad I brought up from infancy," to farm the plantation. Heirs of Bro. Henry Blyler dec'd. Bro. Michael Blyler. Sister Magdalena. Bros.-in-law John, Jacob, Henry and Philip Diffenderfer. Sister-in-law Elizabeth Sholl. Sarah Phillips now wife of Jacob Snouffer, 30 Acres of land for life then to her ch. Do. to William Corner. Jacob While the House and enclosed lot in his possession for life and to his wife Margaret for her lifetime. John Ehl, John Wentz, Gertrude Diffenderfer, Solomon Diffenderfer (son of Philip), Solomon Diffenderfer (son of Henry), David Trumbauer (?), John Cline, (Smith), John Corner and John Snouffer (?), each £9. Bro.-in-law George Dursaim (?). Reformed Calvinist Congregation formerly called Trumbauers' Church $200.
Wits: John Heist and Morgan Custard.

Page 184. William Wharton, Lower Makefield. 2-19-1823. Proved June 20,

1823. Sons William and Johnson Wharton exrs. Sons William, Phineas and Johnson . Daus. Anna and Phebe Wharton and Mary Palmer. Land adj. Daniel Lovett, Daniel Wharton, Anna Aukland.
Wits: John Miller Junr. and Moses Wharton.

Page 186. Peter Rhul (? probably Ruhl), signed by mark, Richland Twp. April 28, 1823. Proved June 20, 1823. Sons Jacob and Peter exrs. Wife Sarah. Six ch. Jacob, Mary, Catharine, Elizabeth, Peter and Christina. Gddau. Sarah wife of John Yost, dau. of dec'd. dau. Barbara, wife of Philip Fluck.
Wits: Benjamin Johnson, John Shaw.

Page 187. Peter Williamson, Falls Twp., yeoman. June 10, 1822. Proved June 30, 1823. Sons Jesse and Mahlon and son-in-law William Croasdale exrs. Daus. Letitia Burton, Mary Croasdale and Sarah Kelly.
Wits: Job Winner and Reading Beatty.

Page 188. Stephen Yerkes, Warminster Twp. March 30, 1822. Proved July 4, 1823. Natural son Edward Yerkes and Thomas B. Montanye exrs. Wife Alice. Ch. John, Molly and Stephen Yerkes. Bros. Harman and William Yerkes. Plantation on York Rd. and county line, subject to Dower of Rebecca Gilbert, to be sold.
Wits: Benjamin Gilbert and John Roberts.

Page 190. John Benner, Richland Twp. Aug. 8, 1822. Proved July 5, 1823. Son John and Henry Messemer exrs. Wife Elizabeth. Six ch. John, Abraham, Lewis, Jacob, Magdalena and Elizabeth.
Wits: Andrew Heller and Peter Zegenfuss.

Page 191. Christian Ruth, Tinicum Twp. June 12, 1823. Proved July 19, 1823. Son David Ruth and Jacob Nash exrs. Wife ---. Ch. Abraham, Elizabeth, Jacob, David and Anne. Abraham, Elizabeth and Jacob's shares to be reduced by amounts they received when mar.
Wits: Daniel Solladay and Daniel Boileau Esq.

Page 192. Letitia Ely, Buckingham Twp. 5-5-1823. Proved July 22, 1823. Mother Rachel Ely extx. Cousins Seneca, John and Sarah Ely, ch. of Samuel Ely, late of Buckingham , dec'd. Cousin Letitia Carey, dau. of Joseph Carey and her bros. and sisters.
Wits: John Wilson, Joseph Carey.

Page 193. Henry Calf, Tinicum Twp. April 7, 1823. Proved June 30, 1823. Son John Calf and son-in-law Joseph Lear exrs. Wife Eve. Son John, all lands, 174 Acres. Daus. Mary, wife of Jacob Rooker (?), Margaret wife of John Angel, Elizabeth wife of Samuel Keller, Sarah wife of Joseph Lear and Nancy.
Wits: George Wyker and Frederick Stone.

Page 196. Edward Dyer, Northampton Twp. Oct. 22, 1821. Proved Sept. 5, 1823. Son Joseph exr. Wife Elizabeth. Dau. Deborah Krewsen and Mary Vandegrift.
Wits: William Delaney, Jonathan Croasdale, John Shepherd.

Page 197. Thomas Fell, Buckingham Twp. 1-2-1823. Proved Sept. 14, 1823. Son Benjamin and Benjamin Smith exrs. Dau. Rachel wife of Francis Good, sons, Benjamin, Jesse, David and Thomas. Ch. of son Phineas.
Wits: George Fell, Joseph Carr.

Page 198. Sarah Groce, Plumstead Twp., widow of Daniel Groce. Aug. 1, 1821. Proved Sept. 6, 1823. Samuel Wisner exr. Sons Abraham, Isaac and Jacob. Dau. Magdalena wife of Jacob George, Fanny wife of Peter Beeler, Barbara wife of Andrew Shaddinger, Esther and Susanna Groce. Land bought of John Shattinger.
Wits: James Worthington and John Fretz.

Page 200. David Dungan, Doylestown Twp. Oct. 1, 1821. Proved Sept. 6, 1823. Jacob Myers of Byberry exr. Bro. John Dungan 20 s. residue to Martha Dungan dau. of Thomas Dugan late of Byberry, dec'd.
Wits: Jonathan Doyle and Thomas Stephens.

Page 201. Esther Schlifer, widow, Richland Twp. Jan. 18, 1823. Proved Sept. 9, 1823. Son John Schlifer exr. Ch. of son Daniel, dec'd. and of dau. Elizabeth Metz, dec'd. John's ch. Elizabeth, Mary, Joseph and John. Gdch. Elizabeth Metz.
Wits: John Engle and Joseph Schlifer.

Page 202. Mary Starkey, Middletown Twp. Sept. 7, 1823. Proved Sept. 12, 1823. John Buckman Junr. exr. Dau. Mercy Vanhorn and her ch. Henry and Mercy Elizabeth Vanhorn.
Wits: Jolly Longshore and Daniel Mahan.

Page 203. Joseph Harvey, Newtown Twp. Sept. 8, 1822. Proved Sept. 15, 1823. Thomas Jenks and son Samuel T. Y. Harvey exrs. Sons Thomas and Samuel T. Y. Harvey and daus. Letitia Whitacar, Martha Blaker, Elizabeth Houghton and Rebecca Hibbs. Gdch. Ann Harvey, dau. of Elizabeth Houghton, Joseph Harvey Whitacar and Joseph Harvey. Bound boy Daniel Perass.
Wits: John Terry, David Scattergood and Nathan Watson.

Page 204. Lydia Purssell, widow of Jonathan Purssell, late of Borough of Bristol. 8-14-1822. Proved Sept. 16, 1823. Joseph Warner (Miller) and Samuel Swain. (Farmer) exrs and trustees, all estate in trust for use of son Isaac Wilson for life, then to his ch.
Wits: Abraham Warner, William McIlhany.

Page 205. James Wilson, Tinicum Twp. March 2, 1822. Proved Sept. 20, 1823. Sons James and Robert Wilson exrs. Daus. Jane Horner, alias Wilson, Mary Long and Ann Carrell.
Wits: George Fabian, Casper Fabian.

Page 207. John Furman, Falls Twp. 8-30-1822. Proved Sept. 22, 1823. Sons Steward Furman and Stephen Woolston exrs. Son Steward, Farm in N.J. where I formerly resided and where he lives paying my dau. Sarah Furman $900. Elizabeth Furman widow of son William, dec'd. Income of Real estate where I reside, except Smith Shop and lot which I devise to William Furman son of my son William. His sisters Susanna, Deborah and Sarah.
Wits: John Comfort, Aaron Comfort and Aaron Irvins.

Page 209. Phebe Wells, Bristol Twp. --- 1823. Proved Sept. 22, 1823. Joseph Burton and nephew John Headley exrs. Sister Mary Wharton and nieces Rebecca, Hannah, Phebe and Sarah Headley.
Wits: Samuel Lovett, Ann Lovett.

Page 210. Charles Jenks, [no residence]. Aug. 3, 1823. Proved Sept. 23, 1823. Father-in-law John Newbold and Bros. Joseph and Richard Jenks exrs. Wife Mary Ann all estate for life.
Wits: Thomas Martin, William Flowers. Mathematical Book to bro. William.

Page 211. Robert Hillborn, Newtown Twp., yeoman. July 29, 1823. Proved Sept. 27 , 1823. Son Samuel and daus. Elizabeth Conard and Mary Hillborn exrs. Wife Mary. Mother Ruth Merrick the room she hath occupied &c. --- son Samuel Mansion House and 100 acres of Plantation. Two daus. Elizabeth Conard and Mary Hillborn, balance thereof.
Wits: William Ryan and Jonathan Paxson.

Page 213. George Deihl, Richland Twp., yeoman. Sept. 30, 1823. Proved Oct. 17, 1823. Son George and son-in-law David Strunck exrs. Wife Margaret. Dau. Catharine's share to be paid to her heirs when of age. $20 out of son Henry's share to be paid to dau. Elizabeth Eatmen (?). Son-in-law William Young $1.
Wits: Joseph Himmelwright and Abraham Deahl. [sic]

Page 214. John Shaffer, Haycock Twp., yeoman. Oct. 5, 1823. Proved Dec. 1, 1823. George Smith Senr. exr. Wife Margaret House and Lot now occupied by --- Funk, Goods &c. for life, then to ch. Catharine, Eliza, Hannah, Susanna, Henry and Michael.
Wits: George Scheetz and George Smith.

Page 215. Harman Vansant, Warminster Twp. Sept. 4, 1823. Proved Nov. 8, 1823. Wife Alice and son James exrs. Dau. Jane Shelmire, Farm in

Southampton Twp. whereon George Tomlonson resides. Dau. Alice Vansant part of Farm whereon I reside and Lots purchased of Isaac Longstreth and Robert Lewis. Son James balance of Farm. Dau. Ann Eliza Vansant Farm in Southampton whereon Jacob Harding resides. If ch. and legacies made them by Giles Craven, late of Warminster dec'd. same are to be deducted from their legacies herein.
Wits: Leman Banes and Derick Kruson.

Page 217. Christian Stauffer, Lower Milford Twp., yeoman. Jan. 7, 1817. Proved Nov. 13, 1823. Wife Catharine and John Gehman, son of Abraham Gehman exrs. Land in Bucks and Lehigh "where we now live." Land in Montgomery to be sold. Son Jacob £300 more than David and Anna.
Wits: Samuel Schultz and Daniel Cooper, signature of latter proven by Peter Cooper. "Land to be made to Burchers or Burcher."

Page 218. George Piper, Bedminster Twp. June 14, 1823. Proved Nov. 18, 1823. Frederick Piper Senr., Joseph Piper and Jacob Katchline [sic] exrs. Wife Eve. George and Margaret, ch. of son William dec'd. "Surviving heirs Joseph, Mary, Frederick, Tobias, Susannah and John." Daus. Mary Keichline and Susannah Duke.
Wits: Daniel Gross and Frederick Keeler.

Page 220. Charlotte Hough, Doylestown Twp. Nov. 17, 1823. Proved Nov. 25, 1823. Codicil Nov. 18, 1823. Bro. Benjamin Hough exr. Sisters Mary Conrad and Lydia Anderson. Hannah Hough, Ann Stuckert and John S. Hough, ch. of bro. Benjamin Hough. Esther Hough, dau. of bro. Richard Hough. Mary Hough, dau. of bro. John Hough. Mary and Charlotte Anderson, dau. of sister Lydia.
Wits: Joseph Hough, George Watsen.

Page 222. Moses Lax, Milford Twp., weaver. Nov. 21, 1823. Proved Dec. 15, 1823. Rudolph Schoch of Richland Twp. exr. Wife Elizabeth all estate for maintaining minor ch. borne, and one likely to be borne.
Wits: Peter Hager and Abraham Smith.

Page 223. Hannah Milnor. Nov. 15, 1822. Proved Dec. 16, 1823. Joshua C. Canby exr. Son John $125 out of Bond given by him and John Brown (his gdfather.) to Daniel Riley. Sons Nathan, Isaac and David. Son George and dau. Elizabeth.
Wits: George R. Grantham, Joshua Cranby and Theodosia Milnor.

Page 225. Elcie Hogeland, Southampton Twp., "advanced in years." Feb. 23, 1815. Proved Oct. 13, 1823. Daus. Elcie Vansant and Mary Stephens exrs. Son Derick Hogeland. Gdch. John Wynkoop Hogeland Alcie Hogeland and Elcie Roads.
Wits: Charity Corson and John Corson.

256

Page 226. Samuel Gilbert, Buckingham Twp. Oct. 6, 1823. Proved Oct. 18, 1823. Son Joshua and William Watson exrs. Wife Huldah. Ch. Joshua, Hannah, Charles, John, Hiel, Pearson, Samuel, Harrison and Maris. Wits: Samuel Iden and John Ely.

Page 227. Susanna Grier, Bedminster Twp., advanced in age. Aug. 4, 1823. Proved Nov. 14, 1823. William McNeeley and son-in-law Andrew Wilson exrs. Gdsns. James Y. Wilson, Joseph G. Wilson and John Grier Wilson, William Wilson, George --- [illegible] Wilson, Francis Armstrong Wilson; gddau. Susanna Grier Wilson. Dau. Martha wife of Andrew Wilson. Gddau. Martha Wilson. Wits: William Kennedy and Hamilton Roney.

Page 229. Baltzer Stoneback, Haycock Twp. Feb. 2, 1821. Proved Dec. 2, 1823. Son-in-law George Afflerbach and George Smith exrs. Wife Anna Maria. "Ch. and gdch. viz. My son Michael's ch., Catharine, Dorothy, my son Henry's ch. Elizabeth wife of Christian Gressman, Philip and Maria." Son Henry's widow. Wits: Samuel Keller and John Datesman.

Page 230. Thomas (?) Blakey, Middletown. 7-5-1823. Proved Oct. 4, 1823. Bro. John Blakey exr. and Guardian. Sons Thomas and Paxson. Daus. Ann and Sarah. Wits: Sarah Kirkbride and Jonathan Kirkbride Junr.

Page 231. Joshua Anderson, Buckingham Twp. July 17, 1823. Proved Nov. 7, 1823. Son Joseph exr. Wife Latitia. Son Joseph Plantation on which I lie purchased of William Bennett. Daus. Latitia wife of James K---- --- [illegible] Anderson. Latitia, Susan and Israel Dennison, ch. of dau. Mary Dennison dec'd. Wits: Elisha Wilkinson, Thomas Bradshaw, John Watson.

Page 233. Frederick Gares, Bedminster Twp., Farmer. May 25, 1820. Proved Oct. 8, 1823. Jacob Kramer Jr. exr. Wife Mary. Dau. Lenna (or Tenna or Jenna) to live with her step-mother. Ch. Elizabeth, Catharine, Madelina, Susanna, Mary, Samuel, John and Jenna. Wits: John Hart and William McNeeley.

Page 234. Henry Nase, Rockhill Twp. July 6, 1822. Proved Nov. 13, 1823. Wife Maria Elizabeth House where I live adj. Henry Derstine, John Gedman and Jacob Driesbach. Son Frederick and sons-in-law John Keil and Henry Gerber. Heirs to appoint exr. Letters to Frederick Nase. Wits: Jacob Hetrick and John Frank.

Page 235. Sarah Ely, Newtown Twp. 8-11-1819. Proved October 18, 1823. Sons George and William Ely exrs. Sons Mark, Mathias and Amasa Ely. Dau. Jane wife of Benjamin Paxson. Son Aaron Ely.

Wits: William Ryan and Benjamin Featherby.

Page 236. Amos Eastborn, Middletown Twp. 10-11-1823. Proved Nov. 11, 1823. Moses Eastburn, dau. Grace Eastburn and sons Jonathan and Aaron exrs.
Wits: Isaac Stackhouse and John Buckman Junr.

Page 237. Joseph Brown, Bristol Twp. 10-6-1823. Proved Nov. 17, 1823. Wife Mary, Mahlon Yardley and David and Abraham Brown exrs. Wife use of Farm of 200 Acres whereon I reside for life, subject to maintenance of dau. Mary while she remains unm. 3 sons and 2 daus. Mary and Rebecca. Son John.
Wits: Joseph Burton, Jacob Cox, Reading Beatty.

Page 238. Jesse Randall (?), Blacksmith, Southampton Twp. Nov. 25, 1823. Proved Dec. 18, 1823. Wife Pamale and nephew Jesse Randall exrs. Lots purchased of Charles Paxson and Abner Buckman adj. Land late of Langhorne Biles, Jack Rhoads, George Willet (nephew Jesse Randal [sic] now living with me).
Wits: John Vanartsdalen, Christopher Vanartsdalen and Abraham Buckman, Derick K. Hogeland.

Page 239. George Grubum, Falls Twp. 9-18-1823. Proved Oct. 6, 1823. Benjamin Lloyd and Samuel Comfort exrs. Wife Martha Grubum all estate for life. Son George Farm at death of his mother. Gdsn. Stephen Betts, Farm in Solebury paying his mother Elizabeth Paist $50 per year during life. If son George and Stephen Betts die, Farm to go Bros. Nicholas and John and sister Ann or Nancy, all in England.
Wits: Thomas Kelly and William Kelly.

Page 241. John Beatty, Solebury Twp. 10-7-1822. Proved Oct. 11, 1823. Oliver Hampton and David Simpson exrs. Wife Ester all estate for life. Ch. Margaret and John and Mary.
Wits: Thomas Lands and John Simpson Jr.

Page 242. John Stapler, Lower Makefield Twp. 8-1-1821. Proved Oct. 29, 1823. Son Thomas, bro. Thomas Stapler and Bro.-in-law Thomas Yardley exrs. Wife Hannah. Sons Thomas, John and Charles. Daus. Sarah, Rachel, Acsah, Ann, Esther, Mary, Hannah and Christanna.
Wits: John Yardley and Mahlon Yardley and Asa Carey.

Page 243. Catharine Swartzlander, Doylestown Twp. (nuncupative) Declared Sept. 19, 1823. Died on morning of 22nd at house of John Reiff, "where she was taken suddenly ill." Proved Nov. 24, 1823. Bros. Joseph and David Swartzlander. Mother Salome Swartzlander. Salome and Catharine, daus. of sister Margaret, bro. Jacob. Salome Stem. Catharine Swartzlander, dau. of bro. Joseph. Barbara wife of Bro. David.

Wits: John Reiff Junr. and Margaret Reiff.

Page 244. Deborah Titus, Buckingham Twp. Nov. 1, 1823. Proved Dec. 11, 1823. Dau. Deborah and Samuel Large exrs. Sons David and William. Son Seruch's and dau. Elizabeth's ch. Dau. Mary.
Wits: John Ely and David Fell.

Page 245. Elizabeth Goslin, Middletown Twp. Oct. 22, 1821. Proved Jan. 7, 1824. Son-in-law David Milnor and Henry Atherton exrs. Daus. Mary wife of Jonas Davis, Esther Goslin and Elizabeth wife of David Milnor. Land adj. Tunis Hellings and William Johnson.
Wits: Jesse Roberts and Hannah Atherton.

Page 246. Derick Kruson, Northampton Twp., yeoman. Dec. 19, 1823. Proved Jan. 17, 1824. Sons Charles and James and son-in-law Garret Carver exrs. Wife Elizabeth. Ch. Charles, James, Elizabeth, Charity and Jane. 2 daus. of dau. Mary Cornell, dec'd.
Wits: Jacob Kruson, Thomas Dungan and Garret Vanartsdale.

Page 247. Michael Barnet, Mason, Springfield Twp. Nov. 11, 1823. Proved Jan. 17, 1824. Bro.-in-law Peter Korts and Jacob Solliday exrs. Wife Magdalena. Ch. not named.
Wits: Moses Marsteller and --- Jamison Senr.

Page 248. Ludwick Roth, Bedminster Twp. Aug. 1, 1818. Proved Jan. 28, 1824. George Delp of Bedminster exr. Wife Elizabeth. Sons George and Mathias and ch. of son Christian.
Wits: Abraham F. Stover and Jacob Stout.

Page 250. Mary Worthington, Northampton Twp. July 2, 1823. Proved Jan. 31, 1824. Timothy McGinnis exr. Son Finas Walton. Sisters Ann Worthington and Elizabeth Evans. Hannah Miginnis. Mary dau. of Nathan Worthington. Sarah Lewis, Mary Ann Walton dau. of Amos Walton. Abel Walton. Money coming from Daniel States' estate. Timothy Miginnis's son Benjamin.
Wits: Jesse Brown and John Willard.

Page 251. Mathias Hutchinson, Buckingham Twp. Dec. 23, 1822. Proved Feb. 4, 1824. Son-in-law Samuel Johnson and gdsn. William H. Johnson exrs. Son Thomas. Land in Solebury on which gddau. Elizabeth Pickering and husband Jonathan Pickering live and woodland adj. Israel and James Anderson, to be sold. Dau. Martha Johnson. Gddau. Ann Paxson. Gdsn. --- [illegible] H. Johnson, Mathias Hutchinson.
Wits: Israel Lancaster, Charles Shaw, Joseph S. Pickering and R. Hutchinson.

Page 254. Jacob Deal (? Diehl), Milford Twp. Nov. 28, 1823. Proved Feb.

9, 1824. Jacob Clymer Esq. exr. Wife Molly. Ch. John, Hannah, David and Catharine. Wife's bro. David Deal. Dau. Catharine goods left her by her sister Elizabeth.
Wits: Abram Shelly and Jacob Clymer.

Page 256. William Ely, Buckingham Twp., yeoman. 11-5-1823. Proved Feb. 10, 1824. Sons Aaron and Edward exrs. Wife Cynthia bond given by Thomas Smith to Rachel Fell. Son Benjamin obligation I hold against him. Son Aaron end of my Farm next York Rd. Son Edward and dau. Elizabeth the other half. Money due from Isaiah Jones one of assignees of Jesse Ely.
Wits: William Large and John Ely.

Page 257. Robert Scott, Falls Twp., "Advanced in years." Feb. 12, 1822. Proved Feb. 17, 1824. Codicil dated Aug. 29, 1823. Wife Mary and son James R. Scott exrs. (Wife dec'd. at date of codicil and son Samuel and Thomas Quinton added as exrs.) "Five ch., three sons and two daus." Sons James R., Samuel and Robert. Daus. Eliza Scott and Achsah Quintin. Adopted dau. Sarah Campbell Scott. Sisters Margaret Maichin and Elizabeth Kowen. Niece Sarah Cowen. Son James's sons Robert and Reynolds. Stephen Woolston, "umpire."
Wits: Henry Disborough, S. Foster, Andrew Quinton and Aaron Ivins.

Page 261. Thomas Jones, Hilltown Twp. Jan. 5, 1824. Proved Feb. 17, 1824. Son Amos Jones and bro. James Jones exrs. Friend Griffith Jones Guardian and trustee of dau. Clarissa. 4 daus. Philadelphia, Mary, Clarissa and Levina, stock in Farmers Bank of Bucks Co. and share in Cave Bank Fishery. Son Amos Plantation on which I live excepting 12 acres surveyed off adj. John Gile, Mark Fretz and others and lot of 40 Acres purchased of Peter Vastine and wood lot adj. Nathaniel Jones, Rowland Mathias and others, first and last tracts being devised by my father. (Philadelphia and Clarissa are evidently mar., while the other two are single, Levinia being a minor.)
Wits: Levi D. Bodder, Joseph Mathias.

Page 263. Robert McConway, "Late of Glenderment Parish, Londonderry Co., Ireland. Oct. 28, 1823. Proved Feb. 18, 1824. Joseph D. Murray and Merrick Reeder exrs. Bros. John, Alexander, William. Sisters Hannah, Catharine, Margaret and Jane all of Glenderment Parish.
Wits: Joseph E. Reeder and James Appleton.

Page 266. James Craven, Warminster Twp. Jan. 2, 1824. Proved March 3, 1824. Sons Thomas and Isaac exrs. Wife Aerianna. Sons Thomas, James, William, John and Isaac. Daus. Leanah Cornell, Jane Cornell and Elizabeth Finney. Son-in-law Adrian Cornell.
Wits: Leman Banes, Isaac Craven.

Page 269. Abraham Overholt, Plumstead Twp., yeoman. Nov. 15, 1823. Proved March 18, 1824. Samuel Wismer and Philip Kratz of Plumstead exrs. Sons Jacob and John. Dau. Catharine wife of Martin Overholt. Daus. Hannah, Elizabeth and Susanna (single) Farm of 118 Acres adj. Samuel Wismer and Joseph Crout.
Wits: Abraham Michener, Joseph Leatherman.

Page 271. Mary Wigton, Doylestown, single woman. May 12, 1823. Proved March 22, 1824. Nephew William Wigton exr. Niece Mary Wigton, dau. of bro. John $20 to be paid by her father out of what he owes. Niece Mary Wigton, dau. of bro. William, to be paid by her father out of money he owes me. Sister Elizabeth Henderson $20 and apparel. Residue to sister-in-law Elizabeth Wigton and three of her ch. William, Ann and Mary. Matilda Henderson a bed.
Wits: Mathias Morris and John Pugh.

Page 272. Henry Disborough, Bristol Borough, Physician. Sept. 26, 1823. Proved Oct. 17, 1823. John Newbold, bro. John Disborough and Nephew James S. Nevis exrs. Wife Henrietta all estate I received from her in right of mar. 4 natural ch. Mary, Sarah, Henry and John Disborough. Bros. and ch. of my sister. No claim to be made for sums due me from my mother's estate.
Wits: William F. Swift and Jno. Sommer.

Page 273. Yost Artman or Ertman, Hilltown Twp. Aug. 18, 1823. Proved March 29, 1824. Conrad Snyder and George Leidy exrs. Wife Barbara. Solomon Reaser of Upper Milford, Lehigh Co., Guardian of son David, to hold his estate for life. Other ch. Andrew, Joseph, Samuel, Maria wife of Samuel Hunsberger, Isaac, Elizabeth wife of John Leister, Michael, Jacob and John Artman.
Wits: John Beringer, Henry Beringer and Philip Shriver.

Page 275. Rebecca Eastburn, widow of Joseph Eastburn, late of Solebury Twp., dec'd. 10-7-1815. Proved March 29, 1824. Oliver Hampton exr. Daus. Letitia, Sarah and Mary. Gdsn. Joseph E. Reeder.
Wits: Oliver Hampton, Hannah Hampton and John Kitchin.

Page 276. William Sutton, Falls Twp. March 15, 1823. Proved April 8, 1824. Son Thomas L. Sutton and Benjamin Albertson, both of Falls, exrs. Wife ---. Son Thomas L. 82 Acres in Falls Twp. purchased of John Larrew. Dau. Elizabeth Shelmire 13 Acres 114 Perches purchased of Joseph Howell for life then to her sons Thomas and Bedford Shelmire.
Wits: Benjamin Albertson, David Heston and Thomas L. Sutton.

Page 277. Benjamin Rosenberger, Rockhill Twp., yeoman. May 19, 1823. Proved April 24, 1824. Son Elias Rosenberger exr. Wife Margaretta. Son Abraham $1, other sons Elias, William, John, Jacob, Joseph and Benjamin.

Daus. Elizabeth wife of Henry Nunemaker, Rachel wife of Isaac Clemmer and Rebecca Rosenberger. Gdsn. Jack Rosenberger son of Eli. "Grist Mill, Oyle Mill and Karding Masheen" with 27 acres of land in Haycock, bought of John Penrose to be sold, (adj. Michael Deterly) - or rented during lifetime of widow of John Penrose.
Wits: Adam Nunnemaker, John Bergy and Henry Cope.

Page 279. Charles Hailstork, Bristol Boro. Dec. 17, 1823. Proved April 27, 1824. Wife Rebecca Hailstork interest of real and personal estate to bring up ch. Ch. Robert Carey Hailstork, Catharine Berry Hailstork, Caroline Amelia Hailstork, Charles and Rebecca Hailstork.
Wits: David Swain and S. Foster.

Page 280. Joseph White, Middletown Twp. March --, 1824. Proved April 29, 1824. Sons Joseph and Malachi exrs. Wife Sarah, son Jesse $800. Joseph, Sarah Ann, Martha, Eliza, William and Samuel Vanschryer, ch. of dau. Elizabeth Vanschryer, dec'd. Farm wheron son Jesse lives, purchased of Benjamin Swain to be sold. Sons Joseph and Malachi, Farm whereon I live and 25 Acres in Bristol Twp., considered part thereof.
Wits: Nathan Brelsford and Jesse L. Hibbs.

Page 283. William Mitchell, Solebury Twp. March 1, 1823. Codicil March 31, 1823. Proved May 5, 1824. Son Elijah and Daus. Hannah and Elizabeth Mitchell exrs. To be buried in burying ground at Sandy Ridge Meeting House, (N.J.) "Owing to base conduct of George Holcomb, John Gordon, Alburtis King, John Opdyke and Jonathan More, who have endeavored to swindle me out of about $9000" - it is necessary to dispose of part of estate to satisfy just demands" &c. Residue of Plantation in N.J. bought of --- [illegible] Armstrong to be sold. Tavern House with Land below York Road to be sold. Proceeds to wife and daus. Hannah and Elizabeth and Mary. Son Joseph, his wife and ch. Codicil: Having bought at Sheriff Sale Plantation in Kingwood Twp., Hunterdon Co., late of estate of John Mason, dec'd., sold to Daniel Custer, who failed to pay for same, directs it to be sold, and monies paid to John and Andrew Mason, Jane Potts, Hannah Wilson and Mary Heaton and Edward Mason, agreeable to will of said John Mason.
Wits: Henry Gluck (?), John Horn, Uriah Larrew.

Page 287. Samuel Thatcher, Middletown Twp. April 23, 1814. Proved May 4, 1824. William Richardson exr. Wife Sarah Ann all estate for life, then to ch. Farm bought of John Mitchell. Exr. to obtain settlement for money advanced on Farm and Tavern House in Moreland belonging to Daniel Parr.
Wits: Henry Atherton and Jonas Thatcher.

Page 288. Henry Rosenberger, Rockhill Twp., yeoman. Aug. 17, 1817. Proved May 15, 1824. Son Henry and son-in-law George Diehl exrs. Wife

Anna interest of Personal Estate for life &c. Sons John and Henry and Samuel Rosenberger heirs, of dec'd. son Daniel. Dau. Margaret wife of John Freed, Elizabeth wife of Samuel Stouffer, Mary wife of Jacob Hoffel, Nancy wife of Michael Dirstine and Catharine wife of George Diehl.
Wits: Abraham Biehn and Michael Headman.

Page 290. David Evans, Doylestown Twp., yeoman. Jan. 15, 1821. Proved May 17, 1824. Son James exr. Wife Susanna. Gdch. Richard, David, Evan and Nathan Riale and Susanna wife of David Johnson, ch. of dau. Rachel Riale, dec'd. Ch. of dau. Ann Hill dec'd., Thomas, David and James Hill. Susanna wife of Jacob Kern, Elizabeth and Mary Ann Hill. 2600 Acres in Ohio Co., State of Va.
Wits: Simon Callender, Elias Long and ---, a Dutchman.

Page 292. Anna Kratz, Hilltown Twp., widow, "Aged." March 27, 1824. Proved May 27, 1824. Son-in-law Abraham Fretz exr. Dau.-in-law Mary Kratz, Widow. Son Valentine and Daus. Anna and Magdalena.
Wits: Philip Kratz and Henry Licey.

Page 293. Abraham Hunsberger, Milltown Twp., yeoman, "Aged." Aug. 11, 1809. Proved May 22, 1824. Sons Henry and John exrs. Sons Henry and John land adj. Abraham Dirstine, Thomas Mathias, Henry Licey, alias Lacy, Joseph Wismer and Isaac Colb; and George Seiple. Sons Christian, Isaac, Abraham, Ulricks, Henry and John. Dau. Elizabeth.
Wits: Isaac Colb and Henry Myers.

Page 295. John McMullen, Bensalem Twp. Nov. 22, 1814. Proved May 27, 1824. Son-in-law Lawrence Johnson and John Thompson of Bensalem and Daniel Knight of Byberry exrs. Wife ---. Sons John, Abraham, Robert and Joseph, last two to be bound to trades until sixteen. Sons-in-law Lawrence Johnson and Jesse Johnson. Daus. Margaret and Ketty to be bound out until 18. Henry Tomlinson and John P. Hod of Bristol Twp. Overseers.
Wits: Abraham Vandegrift and Joseph Knight.

Page 297. Rachel Harrold, Solebury Twp. 10-17-1813. Proved June 18, 1824. Codicil dated 10-7-1817. Son Joseph Carver and son-in-law Joseph Gillingham exrs. Ch. John, Benjamin and Joseph Carver; David Harrold, Rachel Ely, Elizabeth Olden and Rebecca Gillingham. My 4 gdsns., sons of Thomas Carver, dec'd., viz.: Samuel, David, Henry and James Carver. If Samuel do not return and pay debt to Elizabeth Olden, his legacy to go to said Elizabeth.
Wits: Joseph Stradling, Thomas Carey.

Page 300. Sarah Knight, widow of Israel Knight, Bensalem Twp. 3-6-1824. Proved June 19, 1824. Son Giles Knight and John Comly exrs. Sons Abel, Isaac and George. Daus. Esther and Elizabeth Knight.
Wits: Evan Knight and Joseph P. Knight.

Page 301. Mathias Harvey, Upper Makefield Twp. 3-25-1823. Proved June 26, 1824. Wife Sarah. Sons Mathias and William. Dau. Jane Slack.
Wits: John J. Boyd and Phineas Trego.

Page 302. Joseph Roberts, Wrightstown Twp. Nov. 28, 1818. Proved July 3, 1824. Son Jonathan exr. Wife Jane. Son Jonathan 57 acres whereon I live. Sons Joseph, Israel, John and James; and Phineas. Daus. Sarah Roberts and Jane ---.
Wits: Hugh Thompson and Samuel Thompson.
Dr. Isaac Chapman testifies to his writing of the above Will.

Page 303. Mathew Hare, Buckingham Twp. May 5, 1824. Proved July 5, 1824. John Ely, Sanr. [sic] exr. Wife Abigail all estate for life, then to all ch. and issue of dec'd. ch. Daus. Elizabeth, Abigail and Sarah, beds they claim as their own.
Wits: Moses Dunlap, John Dyer.

Page 304. Joyce Buckman, Newtown Twp. 9-15-1814. Proved Aug. 12, 1824. Dau. Hannah Buckman extx. Daus. Hannah, Elizabeth and Rachel.
Wits: David Story and James Buckman.

Page 305. William Moode, Middletown Twp. Oct. 26, 1822. Proved Aug. 20, 1824. Son William Moode and son-in-law William Flowers exrs. Wife Mary. Daus. Martha wife of Henry Hough, Hannah wife of Richard Appleton. Ch. of dau. Mary, late wife of William Flowers. Sister Hannah Goslin.
Wits: Henry Atherton and Malachi White.

Page 306. Sarah Linton, Middletown Twp., "Advanced in years." 4-13-1817. Proved Aug. 20, 1824. Sons Thomas and James Linton exrs. Daus. Sarah and Laura Linton. Son William Linton. Bonds against Dr. Mahlon Gregg.
Wits: John Worstal and Noah Lambert.

Page 306. William Rodman, Bensalem Twp. Jan. 22, 1820. Proved Aug. 25, 1824. Wife Esther, brother Gilbert Rodman and Neighbor Anthony Taylor exrs. Wife use of Plantation for life or widowhood, then to all ch. Interest in Tract of Land in Warwick, held with bro. and ½ interest in 400 Acres in Virginia, devised by Will of Uncle Peter Reeve to Bro. and myself to be sold. Exrs. to convey land sold to Samuel Benezet. Son John.
Wits: Samuel Wright and Walter Mitchell. Money advanced to dau. Esther, son Thomas, "While in Tanning business at Mt. Bethel." To dau. Elizabeth and Esther for Household Goods, &c.

Page 308. Joseph Penrose, Richland Twp., yeoman. 12-8-1819. Proved Aug. 28, 1824. Son Joseph and step-son-in-law Everard Foulke exrs. Wife Eleanor use of Plantation and all estate for life. Then Farm to be

264

appraised by Benjamin Foulke, Isaiah Jamison and Nathan Penrose and divided between sons Israel and Joseph. Dau. Jane Penrose and her son James Penrose. Land adj. Adam Bartholomew.
Wits: Thomas Strawn, Samuel Foulke, Everard Foulke Junr.

Page 307. Sarah Vansant, Bristol Twp. Nov. 21, 1820. Proved April 26, 1824. Son Joseph Brelsford and son-in-law William Sisom exrs. Dau. Christiana £16 interest only during mar. state, principal when she becomes a widow. Dau. Amy wife of William Lisom. Sons Joseph, John and William Brelsford. Sarah and Martha Brelsford, daus. of son John.
Wits: William Sisom Junr., S. Foster, William Vansant.

Page 311. Ann Knight, Southampton Twp. 8-27-1824. Proved Sept. 3, 1824. Sons Amos, Aaron, Benjamin and John Knight exrs. Dau. Grace Paul. Gdch. Moses son of Aaron Knight, Ann Paul, Sarah, Ann Knight dau. of dec'd. son Moses and Ann Knight, dau. of son Amos.
Wits: Rebecca Winder, Mary Martindale and Clayton Knight.

Page 312. William Deal (?) (Diehl), Springfield Twp. Nov. 13, 1824. Proved Sept. 13, 1824 [sic]. Bro. Abraham Deal exr. Dower of Mother Catharine Deal, and all other estate to said bro.
Wits: Andrew Gruber and Peter Selner.

Page 313. Elizabeth Folwell, Southampton Twp. July 16, 1824. Proved Sept. 17, 1824. Dau. Ann Hart extx. Son William W. Folwell, Family Bible only, he "having had his full left him by his father." Daus. Ann Hart, Elizabeth Jones, Mary Purdy and Rachel Reeder. Baptist church of Southampton of which I am a member $100 for use of its poor. To be bur. in their Burying Ground.
Wits: Daniel McVaugh and Benjamin Bennett.

Page 314. John Bethell, Wrightstown Twp., yeoman. June 3, 1824. Proved Spet. 23, 1824. Isaac Chapman and Hugh Thompson exrs. Wife Rebecca Farm of 69 Acres until youngest dau. Sarah is 21. Then same to go to son Thomas B. Bethell and dau. Sarah Bethell. Sons James and John and dau. Margaret.
Wits: Thomas Percy and Gilbert Percy.

Page 315. Jane Wright, Falls Twp., "Far advanced in years." 9-6-1819. Proved Oct. 13, 1824. Sons Benjamin and Amos Wright exrs. Daus. Grace Headley, Mary Swift, Elizabeth McCracken and Jane Brown. 4 daus. of dec'd. dau. Ann Hutchinson. Four sons, Samuel, Benjamin, Stephen and Amos.
Wits: William Crozer and Samuel Allen.

Page 316. Israel Foulke, Richland Twp., "advanced in years." 3-7-1820. Sons Thomas, Hugh and Amos exrs. Wife Elizabeth. Sons Thomas, David,

Hugh and Amos. Dau. Phebe Foulke. Son David's son Israel.
Wits: Jesse Iden and George Custard.

Page 317. Abraham Taylor, Richland Twp., "Advanced in years." May 3,
1815. Proved Nov. 22, 1824. Bro.-in-law Christian Zetty and Benjamin
Johnson exrs. Wife Catharine. Son Henry land adj. William Shaw, Moses
Wilson, Jacob Clymer and Henry Strunk. Sons Abraham, Jacob, Samuel,
David and Joseph. Dau. Mary, wife of John Shelly.
Wits: Everard Foulke and Jacob Climer.

Page 320. Jacob Cope, Hilltown Twp., yeoman. Sept. 10, 1824. Proved
Oct. 26, 1824. Son-in-law Henry Leidy. Wife Catharine. Dau. Maria as
much Household Goods as I have given her sisters Elizabeth, Margaret
or Magdalena. Dau. Catharine. Elizabeth, wife of Abraham Leidy.
Wits: Samuel Detweiler, George Spinser, Henry Cope.

Page 322. Robert Walker, Buckingham Twp. 8-6-1822. Proved Oct. 15,
1824. Bro. Benjamin Walker and Nephew Charles Shaw exrs. Wife
Susannah. Bros. Phineas and Benjamin Plantation whereon I live, 115
Acres with Mill and appurtenances. Then to pay Adms. of Samuel Shaw,
late of Plumstead $800 to be divided among the heirs of said dec'd. $300
for sister Mary Townsend. 56 ½ Acres of Land that formerly belonged to
Samuel Hanin to be sold. Step-mother Asenath Walker.
Wits: John Shaw and John Ruckman.

Page 323. Michael Holstine, Richland Twp. Dec. 7, 1823. Proved Nov. 5,
1824. Son-in-law Peter Been exr. Wife Catharine. Dau. Magdaline. Step-
dau. wife of Jacob Deile.
Wits: Samuel Berger, Moses Marsteller.

Page 324. Adam Fowler, Hilltown Twp., "Advanced in age." Nov. 4, 1822.
Proved Dec. 13, 1824. Son Eleazer and son-in-law Jacob Ratzel exrs.
Samuel Detweiler and Andrew Reed trustees for dau. Sarah who is "non
compus mentis." Sons Abel, Enoch, J ohn and Eleazer. Daus. Hannah wife
of Jacob Ratzel, Martha wife of Jacob Wise.
Wits: Henry Leidy, George Leidy and William H. Rowland.

Page 326. William McElhany, Bristol Borough. June 8, 1820. Proved Dec.
2, 1824. Abraham Warner and Joseph Warner exrs. Aunt Sarah Jobs.
Esther Gosline, Chriatian and Sarah Thompson. Residue to Aunt Sarah
Jobs for life, then to her son David Johnson and his sons William
McElhany Johnson and Isaac Johnson.
Wits: Samuel Bankson and Samuel Allen.

Page 328. David Burson, Springfield Twp. July 20, 1822. Proved Dec. 13,
1824. Son Edward, son-in-law Simon L. Wetherill and Charles Stroud
exrs. Wife Lydia. Dau.-in-law Tacy Shoemaker, late wife of my dec'd. son

Isaac Burson. Fanny Overholt, dau. of Ann Overholt, born in my house in 1799. Ann Alexander formerly Ann Skinner, who once resided in my house as an apprentice. Daus. Sarah Wetherill and Ann Welding, Amos Welding of Wrightstown, Silas Twining Senr. of Warwick and bro. Joseph Burson, Trustees for Ann and her husband John Welding. Dau. Susan Stroud. Gddaus. Evelina Burson and Hannah Burson, daus. of son John W., dec'd.
Wits: Jacob Trichler, John Brock and Joseph Edminston.

Page 333. David Fell, Buckingham Twp., yeoman. March 5, 1824. Proved Dec. 14, 1824. Son Septimus exr. Wife Sarah. Daus. Leitita wife of George Furman, Lucinda widow of Jonathan White, Belinda Fell, Mary wife of Levi Beans, Sarah and Elizabeth Fell.
Wits: David Fell, Josiah Rich and John Ruckman.

Page 335. Augustine Willett, Bensalem Twp. Oct. 13, 1821. Proved Dec. 22, 1824. Wife Elizabeth, son Joseph, John Paxson of Bensalem and Charles Dyer of Moreland exrs. Wife use of 234 Acres of land for life. Son Joseph, Daus. Mary, Elizabeth and Sarah and their ch. Daus. Grace, Euphemia, Margaret and Lydia Willet [sic]. Real estate devised to each of latter described.
Wits: Benjamin Mather Junr. and Joseph T. Mather.

Page 338. Mary Krewsen or Davis, Southampton Twp., advanced in years. July 7, 1824. Proved Dec. 7, 1824. Sons John B. Krewsen and Francis Krewson [sic] exrs. Son John B. Krewson [sic]. Daus. Esther and Elizabeth Krewson [sic]. Son Leonard Krewson [sic] and dau. Rachel Hibbs. Gdch., ch. of Mary Aurhton, viz. Mariah and Jonathan Aurhton; ch. of dau. Rachel Hibbs, viz. William, Ann, Elizabeth, Charles and Rebecca Hibbs; ch. of dau. Bridget States.
Wits: Silas Roads, Eness [sic] Ervin and Derick K. Hogeland.

Page 340. John Cole, Nockamixon Twp., Laborer. March 13, 1824. Proved Dec. 27, 1824. Wife Anna all estate for bringing up "our ch." Samuel, Nelson, William, John Asea and Courtlin.
Wits: Lewis Algard and Jacob Rufe.

Page 341. Sebastian Horn, Richland Twp. July 17, 1824. Proved Dec. 23, 1824. Sons Sebastian and Abraham exrs. Wife Catharine. Ch. Sebastian, Joseph, Abraham, John, Elizabeth wife of Jacob Shive, Eve and Catharine. Bastian Horn, son of Barbary Charles.
Wits: John Matts, George Groman.

Page 343. Elizabeth Jackson, Bensalem Twp. 10-3-1823. Proved Dec. 31, 1824. Jesse James exrs. Son Washington Jackson. Daus. Ann wife of James Ogilby and Levinia Jackson. Gddau. Mary Ogilby. Bro. John Kelly.
Wits: Joshua LaRue and Samuel James.

Page 344. Alexander Forman, New Britain Twp., "Far advanced in years." 1-4-1824. Proved Jan. 15, 1825. Sons Alexander and John Forman exrs. Dau. Elizabeth privilege of occupying part of house while she remains single. Daughter Gainor.
Wits: Evan Jones, William McKinstry.

Page 346. Sebastian Horn, Haycock Twp. Jan. 1,1825. Proved Jan. 28, 1825. Wife Catharine and Benjamin Bartholomew exrs. Catharine Steer dau. of Joseph Steer, a cow. Residue to wife during life or widowhood, then $100 to Samuel, son of Benjamin Bartholomew.
Wits: John Moyer Senr. and Moses Marstellar.

Page 347. Staples Thompson, Bristol Twp., "far advanced in age." May 15, 1824. Proved Feb. 1, 1825. Sons John and David Thompson exrs. Sons John, Staples, David and William. Daus. Sarah wife of Andrew Vanhorn, Mary wife of William Scott.
Wits: John Goslin and Nathan Hellings.

Page 348. Mary Horn, Richland Twp., "Single woman." Oct. 27, 1821. Proved Feb. 4, 1825. Nephew John Kroman exr. Bros. Daniel and Sebastian Horn. Sisters Levillah wife of Michael Kroman and Elizabeth wife of Benjamin Bartholomew. Nephew Daniel Charles. John, Joseph, Elizabeth, Michael and Samuel Kroman, Eve Barrin and Hannah Hinkel, ch. of Michael Kroman. Samuel Zeuk.
Wits: John Matts and Sebastian Horn.

Page 350. Edith Barnes, Warminster Twp. Feb. 4, 1825. Proved Feb. 14, 1825. Dr. John H. Hill exr. Dau. Elizabeth Moss, 7 her ch. William Barnes, Edith, Thomas and Ann Moss. Esther Hagerman.
Wits: John C. Beans and Edwin Yerkes.

Page 352. John Hedrick, Rockhill Twp. Jan. 13, 1825. Proved March 4, 1825. Abraham Hertzel and Adam Cressman exrs. Wife Barbara all estate during widowhood ½ thereof in case of mar. Mary Welel, now wife of John Nase. Bro. Jacob Hedrick; Christian Hedrick. Ch. of Daniel Dillinger of Upper Milford Twp. Plantation and lot purchased of Jesse Heacock.
Wits: Abraham Smith and Michael ---.

INDEX

182, 183; Rachel, 183;
Rebecca, 182; Sarah, 182;
Tamala, 182
BALEY, Thomas C., 244
BALKER, Catherine, 128; John,
128; Sarah, 128
BALL, Aaron, 20, 37, 142;
Abraham, 1, 20, 101;
Catherin, 128; Elizabeth, 41;
Isaac, 41; Jesse, 64; John,
20, 41; Joseph, 20, 41;
Katherine, 20; Mary, 15;
Nathan, 20, 37, 60, 101, 204;
Rebecca, 20; Sarah, 41;
Thomas, 101
BALLANCE, John, 8
BANE, Christina, 42; Margaret,
42; Mary, 42
BANER, Elizabeth, 143; John,
143
BANES, Ann, 189; Artemus
Valerius, 219; Erwin, 18;
Evan, 18; Hogeland, 232;
Isaac, 16; James, 17, 18,
143, 189; Jesse, 124, 151;
Joseph, 18, 100, 143; Josiah
D., 189, 240; Leman, 255,
259; Lemmes, 189; Lemon, 245;
Mahlon, 189; Mathew, 9, 18;
Sarah, 9, 18, 202; Sarah E.,
240; Valerius, 189
BANGHAT, Elizabeth, 49
BANKS, Thomas, 28
BANKSON, Mary, 123; Samuel, 265
BANN, John, 30
BARBER, Jane, 69
BARBIN, Amos, 173; Elizabeth,
173; Mary, 173; Thomas, 173
BARCLAY, Hugh, 168; James, 39,
76, 116, 117, 127; Jane, 116,
117; John, 16, 39, 45, 76,
82, 87, 117, 127, 168, 245;
John Erwin, 168; Mary, 168
BARCROFT, Lee, 155
BAREM, Elizabeth, 44; Henry, 44
BARKAY, Isaac, 41
BARKER, Joshua, 191
BARKEY, John, 41
BARNARD, Frederick, 116
BARNDT (BANT), Catherine, 111,
238; Christina, 111;
Elizabeth, 111; George, 111,
238; Henry, 111; John, 110,
111, 238; Ludwig, 111;
Margaret, 111; Mary, 111,
238; Peter, 111, 161, 238;
Philip, 111; Susanna, 111,
238
BARNES, Catharina, 76; Earl,
24; Edith, 41, 267; Hannah,
56; Jacob, 76; Jesse, 24;

John, 24; Margaret, 24, 41;
Thomas, 24, 56; William, 24,
267
BARNET, Andrew, 40, 42;
Elizabeth, 186; Henry, 42,
206; Jacob, 76; John, 76;
Magdalena, 258; Mary, 76;
Michael, 76, 258; Peter, 76,
186; Philip, 76; Tobias, 76
BARNETT, Margaret, 210; Samuel,
210
BARNS, Edith, 197; Isaac, 129;
John, 97; Mary, 97; Rachel,
137; William, 197
BARNSLEY, Major, 42
BARNTE, John, 226
BARNTZ, Peter, 235
BARR, Adam, 52; Charity, 52;
James, 39; Mary, 39; Thomas,
42
BARREL, Edward, 153
BARRIN, Eve, 267
BARRINGTON, Jonathan, 85
BARRON, Elizabeth, 59; George,
59; Jacob, 59; John, 59;
Margaret, 59; Mary, 89;
Philip, 59
BARTHOLOMEW, Adam, 100, 264;
Benjamin, 267; Elizabeth,
162, 267; Jacob, 132; John,
37; Samuel, 267
BARTIN, David, 231
BARTLEY, Hugh, 38; James, 38;
John, 38; Margaret, 38;
Richard, 38
BARTON, Anthony, 100; Britta,
52; David, 22; Deborah, 100;
Eli, 81; Job, 52; John, 52,
81; Joseph, 36, 52, 81;
Kimber, 81; Levi, 36, 81;
Mary, 73, 81; Pleasant, 52;
Rebecca, 104; Silas, 52;
Thomas, 104, 112
BARTRAM, Alexander James, 188;
Ann, 188; Jane, 188
BARWIS, Joseph, 227; Sarah, 227
BASLER, Mary, 34; Ulrich, 34
BASTOW, John, 85; Nancy, 85
BATEMAN, Mary, 54, 55
BATES, Ann, 64; Charlotte, 232;
Mary, 64; Thomas, 64
BAUM, Margaret, 203; Philip,
203
BAUMAN, Catherine, 71; George,
71; Jacob, 71; Margaret, 71;
Nicholas, 71; Peter, 71;
Philip, 71
BAVINGTON, John, 106
BAXTER, George, 17; Martha, 17
BAYLEY, Amelia, 204; Ann, 105;
Anna, 204; Atlethia, 204;

243; Joseph, 59, 74, 141;
Mary, 69; Rachel, 202, 222;
William, 225, 243
BURGIN, Edith, 191
BURGRY, Magdalena, 8; Susanna,
8
BURGY, Jacob, 188
BURK, Christina, 113; Edward,
113; Elizabeth, 198
BURKE, John, 223; William
Edomond, 72
BURLEY, Absalom, 155; David,
78, 155; Elizabeth, 155;
Gane, 155; Hannah, 20, 74,
78, 155; Jane, 78, 155; John,
78, 155; Joshua, 78, 155;
Mary, 155; Phebe, 155; Pheby,
78; Polly, 78; Rachel, 78,
155; Sarah, 78, 155
BURR, Elizabeth, 100; Joseph,
41, 100
BURRELL, Jonathan, 188
BURROUGHS, Henry, 119; Jesse,
150; John, 118, 119; Samuel,
119; Susanna, 81
BURROWES, John, 151
BURROWS, Ann, 50, 137; Jane,
50; Joseph, 244; N., 161;
Stephen, 20
BURSON, David, 8, 13, 38, 136,
137, 265; Edward, 38, 184,
265; Eliza, 153; Elizabeth,
28, 153, 192; Evalina, 266;
Evelina, 184; Hannah, 184,
266; Isaac, 8, 38, 47, 56,
147, 153, 184, 266; James,
38, 153; Jane, 153; John,
153, 167, 266; John W., 153,
157, 184; Joseph, 38, 206,
266; Lydia, 136, 137, 265;
Mary, 167, 184; Pettit, 192;
Sarah, 38, 192; Stephen, 206;
William, 147, 153, 192
BURTON, Anthony, 33, 80, 84,
85, 113, 141, 157, 179, 230;
Benjamin, 58; John, 13, 33,
84, 85, 141, 157; John G.,
230; Jonathan, 85; Joseph,
254, 257; Letitia, 252; Mary,
84
BUSY, Jacob, 210; Magdalena,
210
BUTCHER, Caleb, 159
BUTLER, Abiah, 71; Ann, 208;
Benjamin, 71, 94, 161; David,
208; George, 94; John, 161,
189; Joseph, 189; Mary, 5;
Sarah, 70; Thomas, 189
BUTTON, John, 13
BUZBY, Thomas, 106
BUZZARD, Michael, 115, 171;

Mickel, 116
BYE, Abigail, 51; Deborah, 175;
Enoch, 26; Hezekiah, 26;
John, 26; Jonathan, 26;
Martha, 30, 97; Mary, 4, 26,
28, 216; Rebecca, 41; Samuel,
26; Sarah, 65; Thomas, 4, 35,
58, 154, 216
BYERLY, John, 243; Mary, 243
BYRNE, Martha, 72
BYSLEISH, Elizabeth, 106;
George, 106; Jacob, 106

-C-
CABE, Elias, 134; Elisha, 134;
Rebecca, 20; Thomas, 134
CABEEN, Elizabeth, 217
CADWALLADER, Benjamin, 59, 68,
211; Cyrus, 26, 97, 142, 185,
187, 211; Elizabeth, 31;
Hannah, 68; Isacc, 31; Jacob,
9, 26, 142, 187; John, 26,
142, 187; Peter, 229; Phebe,
26, 33, 142; Sarah, 31, 221;
Tyson, 31; Uree, 59
CAFFEE, Elizabeth, 250
CAFFEY, Samuel, 103
CAHILL, Daniel, 9; Edward, 9;
Elizabeth, 9; John, 9; Mary,
9
CAHOON, Aaron, 43
CALAW, Michael T., 228
CALBRAITH, M.R., 178
CALDWELL, David, 90; Robert, 54
CALF, Eve, 252; Henry, 252;
John, 252; Nancy, 252
CALLENDER, Jesse, 120; Simon,
120, 262
CAMMEL, James, 23
CAMMELL, George, 44; Sarah, 44
CAMPBELL, Alice, 169, 218;
Andrew, 78; Elizabeth, 162;
Francis, 218; George, 187;
Hannah, 187; Jane, 150; John,
219; Joseph, 162, 169, 218;
Margaret, 150; Nancy, 162;
Phebe, 162; Sarah, 4, 162,
169, 218; Tacey, 162;
Townsend, 224
CANBY, Benjamin, 4, 15, 18;
Elizabeth, 239; Hannameel,
80; Jesse, 251; Joshua, 181;
Joshua C., 181, 205, 239,
255; Mary, 96, 159
CANTLEY, Hester, 100; James,
100
CAPE (COPE?), Abraham, 77;
Adam, 77; Henry, 77; Jacob,
77; John, 77; Margaret, 77;
Paul, 77
CAR, Naomi, 248

278

CAREL, Benjamin, 54; Jacob, 54
CAREY, Ann, 38, 40; Asa, 107,
131, 201, 257; Beulah, 234;
Catherine, 41; Eleanor, 220;
Elias, 38, 40, 41, 49, 185,
230; Elizabeth, 38, 40, 49,
107, 167; Ellen, 49; Hannah,
38, 40, 209, 234; John, 38,
40, 49; Joseph, 167, 211,
234, 244, 252; Joshua, 167,
201; Letitia, 252; Margaret,
53, 107, 167; Mary, 38, 40,
53, 201, 234; Middleton, 107;
Phineas, 131; Rachel, 163;
Samson, 131; Samuel, 38, 40,
49, 107, 131, 167; Sarah,
131; Silas, 167, 234; Thomas,
38, 40, 45, 49, 56, 71, 73,
84, 98, 134, 234, 262
CARFIELD, Edward D., 222
CARL, Cuniande, 90; Jacob, 90;
Johannes, 90; John, 84, 90;
Ketrin, 84, 90; Mary, 90
CARLILE, Abi, 202; Abraham, 73,
213; Amos, 200, 202;
Benjamin, 50, 200, 202, 210,
222; Daniel, 68, 117, 134,
202; David, 36, 200;
Elizabeth, 166, 225; Hannah,
200; John, 11, 26, 200, 202,
236; Jonathan, 3, 4, 16, 36,
50, 65, 66, 73, 112, 200,
202; Martha, 241; Mary, 36;
Mercy, 73, 114, 131, 213;
Rebekah, 202; Sinah, 200
CARLILSE, Abraham, 73; Mercy,
73
CARLIN, Effe, 19; Grace, 19
CARLISLE, Jonathan, 73
CARMAN, Joshua, 141; Phebe, 188
CAROTHERS, John Thompson, 105
CARPENTER, Conrad, 154;
Elizabeth, 42; Joseph, 96;
Martha, 42; Samuel, 42, 96
CARR, Adam, 12, 16; Ann, 12;
Elizabeth, 16, 151, 158;
Fanny, 204; Isabella, 158;
Jane, 12, 158; Jean, 16;
John, 16, 24, 106, 117, 158,
177; Joseph, 16, 63, 151,
158, 253; Lot, 16; Maria,
158; Mary, 16, 151, 204;
Peter, 16; Priscilla, 158;
Rachel, 106; Robert, 23;
William, 12, 16, 151, 158,
204, 242
CARREL, Benjamin, 54, 103, 202;
Elizabeth, 202; Jacob, 202;
James, 202; Jane, 217; Jesse,
202; Joseph, 202; Marcey, 103
CARRELL, Ann, 99, 254; Barnard,

108; Cornelius, 108, 124,
174; Daniel, 99, 239;
Elizabeth, 170, 248; Hannah,
108; Isaac, 108, 165, 170;
James, 49, 99, 108, 140;
Jesse, 170; Joseph, 170;
Lucretia, 108; Rachel, 108
CARRIE, Eliza, 152
CARROLL, James, 152; Sarah, 152
CART(MCCARTY), Nicholas, 70
CARTER, Ann, 52; Ebenezer, 136;
Elen, 52; Fanny, 52; Frances,
136; Helena, 107; James, 6,
53; John, 6, 164; Joseph, 6,
53; Mary, 6; Rebecca, 6, 85;
Rebekah, 53; Robert, 60;
William, 5, 6, 53, 60
CARVER, Amos, 236; Ann, 191;
Anne, 45; Benjamin, 262;
Cornelius, 20, 207, 216;
Cynthia, 236; David, 96, 262;
Elizabeth, 58, 96, 236; Ely,
197; Garret, 114, 216, 258;
Hannah, 134, 191; Henry, 96,
185, 219, 262; Isaac, 236;
Jacob, 64; James, 96, 262;
Jane, 45; Jesse, 236; Joel,
64, 102, 128, 191, 216; John,
64, 65, 221, 262; Joseph, 19,
20, 58, 64, 95, 114, 185,
215, 216, 262; Levi, 236;
Mahlon, 147; Martha, 185;
191, 216; martha, 36; Mary,
65, 114, 207, 216; Miranda,
236; Rachel, 191, 236;
Rebecca, 207; Robert, 191;
Samuel, 96, 262; Sarah, 45,
95, 96, 207, 215, 236;
Thomas, 86, 262; William, 58,
64, 95, 215
CARY, Agnes, 25, 82; Beula, 82;
Joseph, 104; Joshua, 104;
Margaret, 16, 104; Samson,
15, 25, 57, 104; Samuel, 15,
16, 104; Silus, 104
CASE, John, 223
CASSEL, Isaac, 137; Jacob, 190,
212, 245; Mary, 245
CASSELL, Barbara, 48;
Elizabeth, 48; Hubert, 48;
Isaac, 48, 139, 228; Susanna,
48
CASTER, Hannah, 162; Samuel,
162
CATELL, Rebekah D., 163
CATTELL, Peter D., 9
CAUFFMAN, John, 99, 168
CAULTON, Aaron, 222; Hannah,
222; Isaac, 222; John, 222
CAUTHRON, John, 103
CAVENDER, John, 37

CAWLEY, John, 73
CELLY, Moses, 191; Sarah, 191
CEPPARD, Francis, 74
CHAMBERLIN, Freedom, 209
CHAMBERS, Anna, 231, 232;
George, 180; William, 8
CHAPMAN, A., 105, 113, 114,
131, 209, 243, 244; Aaron,
78, 148; Abbit, 124; Abbot,
218; Abigail, 100, 125, 130,
234; Abraham, 6, 26, 30, 63,
73, 98, 103, 109, 118, 145,
186, 234, 237, 246; Amos,
119; Ann, 26, 79, 105, 119,
144, 155, 158; Benjamin, 26,
58, 98, 102, 124, 148, 158;
Charles, 51, 63, 119; David,
148; Edward, 26, 34, 78, 82,
174; Eliza, 100, 102, 105,
130; Elizabeth, 51, 124, 147,
158, 186; Emma, 125; George,
148, 158, 191; george, 124;
Henry, 186, 246; Isaac, 26,
35, 48, 57, 59, 66, 73, 78,
82, 89, 102, 105, 106, 109,
110, 114, 124, 126, 129, 132,
144, 147, 148, 149, 152, 158,
160, 174, 175, 185, 192, 194,
224, 230, 264; isaac, 101;
Isaac, Dr., 263; Isaiah, 51;
James, 2, 35, 38, 63, 80, 86,
100, 102, 110, 119, 122, 125,
130, 162, 170, 177, 198, 217,
218, 234; Jane, 78, 148;
Jesse, 119; John, 2, 8, 9,
26, 78, 153, 234; John, Dr.,
26; Jonathan, 26; Joseph, 1,
2, 26, 34, 51, 57, 158;
Josiah, 78; Julia Maria, 234;
Juliann Maria, 217; Letitia,
51; Margery, 78; Martha, 82,
114, 119, 124; Mary, 6, 51,
63, 69, 124; Mary/Mercy, 78;
Mercy, 26, 51; Owen, 124,
191; Rachel, 57, 119, 174;
Rebecca, 38, 51, 78; Robert,
6, 63; Samuel, 26; Sarah, 26,
63, 66, 78, 158; Seth, 78,
82, 213, 240; Stephen, 51;
Susanna, 51, 63, 124; Thomas,
26, 66, 107, 110, 133, 144,
147, 181, 185, 192, 249;
Wilhelmina, 186, 243, 246;
William, 1, 26, 95, 148, 155
CHARLES, Barbary, 266;
Catherine, 162; Daniel, 267
CHILCOTT, Amos, 110; Ann, 110;
Martha, 110; Mary, 110;
Penana, 110
CHILD, Agnes, 40, 77;
Cadwallader, 188; Cephas, 40,

77, 85, 188; Israel, 128;
Joseph, 188; Naylor, 69, 188;
Richard, 188; William, 188
CHILDS, Martha, 91
CHOTNAGLE, Leopold, 188
CHRISTY, Mary, 91
CHURCH, Daniel, 50; Eleanor,
225; Elizabeth, 225, 240;
Jane, 225; John, 50; Joseph,
5, 50, 225, 240; Mary, 103,
225, 240; Melicent, 225;
Melison, 240; Moses, 225;
Rachel, 225; Samuel, 62, 183;
Sarah, 22, 32, 62, 225;
William, 62
CLANEY, John, 220
CLARK, Ann, 69, 105; Charles,
14, 31, 43, 63, 69, 100;
Elizabeth, 240; Ellen, 178;
Francis, 63; Franky, 14;
Hannah, 10; Jane, 10; John,
14, 42, 63, 230; Joseph, 7,
31; Margaret, 10, 42; Martha,
10; Mary, 10, 82, 100, 105;
Rachel, 31; Richard, 10, 69;
Sarah, 230; Thomas, 14, 63,
129; Wheeler, 1, 14, 31;
William, 69
CLARKE, Theodoshe, 69
CLATTER, Jesse, 187
CLAUSON, Sarah, 92
CLAYTON, Richard, 250
CLEMENS, Ann W., 245;
Catherine, 43; Christian,
101, 114; Elizabeth, 121;
Jacob, 92, 113; John, 43;
Margaret, 121; Mary, 114;
Rodger, 121
CLEMMER, Anna, 44; Christian,
44; Isaac, 261; Martin, 6;
Rachel, 261
CLIMER, Jacob, 170; John, 218
CLINE, John, 251
CLINGAN, Mary, 157
CLIRK, Jeremiah, 117
CLOSSIN, John, 237; Mary, 185;
Rebecca, 237; William, 185
CLOSSON, James, 147; John, 39;
Julia Ann, 236
CLUNN, Joseph, 62, 63, 87, 143,
188
CLYMER, Abraham, 215; Barbara,
122; Catherine, 259;
Christian, 84, 153; David,
153, 259; Elizabeth, 125,
259; Ester, 84; Gerhard, 153;
Hannah, 259; Henry, 84, 122,
179, 197; Isaac, 153; Jacob,
49, 58, 84, 122, 125, 144,
153, 179, 259, 265; John, 21,
28, 125, 153, 206, 259;

Margaret, 188; Martha, 206, 245; Mary, 153, 197; Molly, 259; Samuel, 153; Susanna, 218; Valentine, 148

COATE, Margret, 22; Mary, 113

COATES, Hannah, 62; Joseph, 62; Mary, 62, 165; Sarah, 62; Walter, 62; William, 62

COBE, Adam, 6

COBLEY, Stephen, 100

COCHERUN, Abraham, 78

COCHRANE, Jane, 202

COFFIN, Abigail, 37; Ann, 37; William, 37

COGART, Martin, 62

COGGINS, Rebecca, 211; William, 214

COLB, Isaac, 262

COLBERT, Elizabeth, 7

COLE, Anna, 266; Courtlin, 266; Isaiah, 229; John, 92, 266; John Asea, 266; Mary, 92; Michael, 192; Minerva, 199; Nelson, 266; Samuel, 266; William, 266

COLEMAN, Elizabeth, 150

COLES, Ann, 176; Benjamin, 176

COLLINS, Andrew, 66; Ann, 87; Isaac, 58, 159; Lee, 155; Robert, 87

COLLISON, Grace, 31

COLLLISON, Jane, 31

COLLONS, Andrew, 115; Letitia, 115

COLVIN, John, 11; Joshua, B.

COMBLE, Mary, 17

COMELY, Jonathan, 189; Joshua, 189

COMFORT, Aaron, 254; Alice, 158; Ann, 174, 193, 239; Elinor, 1; Elizabeth, 158, 189, 194; Ellenor, 103; Ezra, 158; Hannah, 103; John, 195, 209, 254; Mary, 174; Moses, 96, 100, 166, 175; Robert, 7, 46, 103; Samuel, 257; Stephen, 174, 239, 240

COMLY, Asenath, 30; John, 74, 125, 237, 247, 262; Joshua, 80, 124; Samuel W., 189

CONARD, Elizabeth, 254; Johnathan, 195

CONE, Abraham, 25

CONGLE, George, 69; Henry, 69; Maragret, 69; Rebecca, 60; Rebekah, 69

CONLEY, John, 81

CONNARD, John, 95, 131, 147

CONNER, Mary, 233

CONNOR, John, 143; Mary, 143

CONRAD, Dennis, 207; Ebenezer, 144, 146; Jacob, 146; John, 146; Joseph, 146, 207; Martha, 146; Mary, 207, 255; Michael, 40; William, 146

CONWER, Elizabeth, 228; Jacob, 228

COOBS, Benjamin, 183

COOK, John, 17; Rebecca, 244; William, 17

COOMBS, Benjamin, 183; Martha, 183

COOPER, Ann, 21, 124; Benjamin, 21, 108; Daniel, 34, 133, 169, 176, 255; David, 153; Diana, 229; Elizabeth, 21, 179, 189; Ester, 65; Grace, 31; Hannah, 11, 85, 118, 179; Henry, 28, 44, 102, 110; James, 85, 111, 164; Jane, 111; John, 44, 110, 175; Joseph, 21, 108, 111; Letitia, 21; Mahlon, 94; Martha, 91, 110; Mary, 106, 108, 124; Mercy, 17; Peter, 255; Phebe, 225; Phineas, 110; Samuel, 14, 108, 229, 235; Sarah, 110, 111, 225; Thomas, 108, 111, 160, 246; William, 42, 44, 48, 108, 111, 179

COPE, Abeaham, 25; Abraham, 27, 77; Adam, 41, 77; Catherine, 168, 265; David, 168; Elizabeth, 74, 168, 265; George, 168; Hannah, 168; Henry, 70, 77, 238, 239, 240, 261, 265; Isaac, 168; Jacob, 77, 168, 265; John, 77, 168; Magdalena, 265; Margaret, 77, 265; Maria, 265; Paul, 77; Philip, 240; Polly, 168; Rebecca, 168; Salome, 168

CORBET, Willliam, 187

CORDER, Sarah, 188

CORE, Henry, 60

CORELL, Adrian, 259; Jane, 259; Leanah, 259

CORNELL, Abraham, 3, 95, 101; Adrian, 3, 133, 135, 155, 191, 192; Adriana, 222; Agnes, 101, 197; Ann, 36; Charles, 162; Cornelia, 3, 101, 147, 148; Cornelius, 95, 98, 224; Else, 19; Gilliam, 3, 19, 95, 101, 135, 147; Isaac, 147, 148; Jacob, 147, 148; James, 135, 155, 192; John, 3, 19, 38, 95, 101, 135, 147, 200, 212, 224, 245; Lambert, 133, 135; Margaret, 3, 101; Maria, 3, 101; Mary,

95, 133, 258; Nathan, 211,
245; Phebe, 3, 95; Phineas,
162; Rachel, 133; Rem, 105,
135, 148; Wilhelm, 147
CORNELLL, Cornelius, 140
CORNER, John, 251; William, 251
CORNISH, Catherine, 13; John,
85
CORSON, Benjamin, 142, 214,
249; Charity, 249, 255;
Elizabeth, 102; James, 249;
John, 66, 96, 132, 142, 170,
197, 214, 226, 242, 249, 250,
255; Margaret, 19; Richard
D., 212, 238, 249; Thomas
Jones, 249
CORYELL, Elizabeth, 10; Henry
L., 238; Lewis S., 246
COSNER, Hannah, 1; Peter, 1
COSTELE, Josiah, 198
COSTNER, Margaret, 122
COTT, Samuel, 194
COTTRAL, Elizabeth, 192
COUGHLIN, Thomas, 152, 159
COUNCILMAN, John, 214
COUNSELMAN, John, 229, 242, 248
COUPT, Jacob, 171
COURSON, Amos, 152; Benjamin,
3, 152; Charity, 65, 249;
Cornelius, 48; Elizabeth,
152; James, 249; Jane, 152;
John, 105, 161, 248; Joseph,
152; Joshua, 152; Mary, 152;
Mary Ann, 48; Rachel, 152;
Richard, 152; Sarah, 3, 152;
Thomas, 152; Thomas J., 249
COURT, Thomas, 45
COVER, Elizabeth, 226;
Magdalene, 226; Margaret,
226; Mary, 226; Paul, 199
COWDRICK, John, 46; Joseph, 46;
Samuel, 46
COWELL, Joseph, 185, 186;
Matthias, 185
COWEN, Sarah, 259
COX, Aaron, 175; Jacob, 257;
Samuel, 111; Sarah, 190;
William, 100, 110, 182
COXE, John D., 38, 40; William,
103
CRAIG, Daniel, 12, 152, 168,
204; Elizabeth, 125; James,
44, 126; Jane, 204; John, 6,
12; Mary, 126; Thomas, 39,
95, 103, 121, 168; William,
80
CRAMER, Ann, 123; Barbara, 123;
George, 123, 171; Hannah,
123; Jacob, 123; John, 123;
Lawrence, 123; Magdalen, 123;
Mary, 123; Valentine, 123

CRANBY, Joshua, 255
CRATER, John, 238
CRAVEN, Aerianna, 259; Ann, 74,
132, 141; Catrin, 74;
Charles, 141; Christiana, 74;
Christina, 74; Cornelia, 19,
222; Edath, 74; Edith, 9;
Eleanor, 9; Elizabeth, 143;
Elshe, 222; Giles, 34, 68,
74, 103, 141, 222, 255;
Helena, 74; Isaac, 68, 74,
227, 245, 259; Issac, 9;
Jacobus, 74; James, 68, 74,
141, 161, 167, 222, 227, 259;
John, 68, 141, 222, 227, 259;
Kelena, 74; Leanna, 29; Lena,
7; Samuel, 141; Thomas, 7, 9,
29, 68, 74, 141, 177, 222,
227, 259; Wilhalmas, 222;
Wilhelmus, 227; William, 68,
74, 222, 227, 259
CRAWFORD, Alexander, 45;
Hannah, 116; Isabel, 45, 116;
Jane, 116; John, 95, 116,
192, 245; Mary, 116; Moses,
116; Samuel, 116; William,
116, 186, 188
CRAY, David M., 243
CREAMOR, Mary, 79; Mathias, 79
CREELY, Daniel, 56
CREESMAN, Jacob, 144
CREMER, Alce, 100
CREMOR, Andrew, 24; Christiana,
24; Daniel, 24; George, 24;
Henry, 24; John, 24; Paul, 24
CRESSMAN, Abraham, 111, 198;
Adam, 267; Anthony, 144;
Christian, 214, 228; George,
25, 226; Hannah, 226; Isaac,
198, 238; Jacob, 89, 91, 138,
214, 228
CROASDALE, Achsah, 46;
Benjamin, 46, 56, 234;
Elizabeth, 195; Ezra, 46;
Grace, 46; Hannah, 46, 183;
Jeremiah, 38, 56, 105, 112,
208, 209, 234, 242; Jonathan,
46, 56, 208, 209, 253;
Joseph, 46, 112, 143, 234,
237; Joseph H., 209; Margery,
234; Mary, 46, 234, 252;
Morris, 234; Rachel, 112,
209; Robert, 38, 155, 208,
209, 213, 234, 242; Ruth,
213, 234; Samuel, 197; Sarah,
46, 112; Stephen, 246; Tacy,
234; William, 252
CRONER, Frederick, 175
CRONIN, John, 65, 127; Stephen,
74
CROOK, Aaron, 219; Ann, 71

282

CROSE, James, 25; Mabath, 23;
　Margaret, 26
CROSIS, Casper, 41
CROSS, Margaret, 26, 42
CROSSDALE, Joseph, 53
CROTZ, Valentine, 198
CROUSE, Anna Barbara, 111;
　Barbara, 111; Jacob, 111;
　Ludwick, 111; Michael, 111
CROUT, Anne, 81; Barbara, 113;
　Catty, 148; Ester, 81; Henry,
　81, 148; Jacob, 50, 81;
　Joseph, 148, 260; Mary, 81,
　148; Susanna, 81
CROWMAN, Barbara, 135;
　Catherine, 135; Conrad, 135;
　Elizabeth, 135; Eve, 135;
　George, 135; Margaret, 135;
　Maria, 135; Michael, 135;
　Sevill, 162; Susanna, 135
CROWTHAMEL, Andrew, 157
CROZEN, Andrew, 182
CROZER, Andrew, 31; Jane, 31;
　John, 31; Joseph, 31; Mary,
　31; Peter, 217; Robert, 14,
　31; Sarah, 214; Thomas, 14,
　31, 178; William, 31, 91,
　176, 264
CROZIER, Phebe, 1
CULLAM, Mary, 53; Thomas, 53
CULLY, Hannah M., 231; John M.,
　231; Rachel M., 231; Thomas
　M., 231
CULP, Abraham, 11, 159; David,
　1, 11, 159; Henry, 11; Jacob,
　11; Mary, 11; Nancy, 11;
　Tielman, 11
CUMINGS, George, 87; Grizel,
　87; James, 87; Jean, 87;
　Margaret, 87; Robert, 87
CUMMINGS, David, 85; George,
　104; Jane, 164; Margaret,
　157; Nancy, 140; Robert, 164
CUMMINS, Jane, 55
CUNNINGHAM, Matthew, 121;
　Mattthew, 170; Robert, 23;
　Thomas, 121, 170
CUSTARD, Adah, 216; Amelia,
　121; Ann, 121; Conrad, 248;
　George, 121, 179, 265; John,
　88; Joseph, 121; Mary, 121;
　Morgan, 163, 208, 216, 233,
　243, 251; Nicholas, 29
CUSTER, Amelia, 60; Daniel,
　261; Joseph, 60
CUTLER, David, 209; Hannah, 36;
　John, 29
CUTTING, John Brown, 68, 69
CYPHERT, George, 111; John, 13,
　25

-D-

DALBY, Abel, 165; Abner, 60;
　Clarah, 165
DALLAS, Alexandria James, 172
DAMUTH, John, 188
DANA, Martha, 75
DANELY, Bethinie, 110; Edward,
　110
DANFORD, Samuel, 33
DANNEHOUER, Elizabeth, 66;
　John, 66
DARBYSHIRE, Mary, 14
DARRAH, Archibald, 9; William,
　148
DARROCH, Agnes, 75; Elizabeth,
　75; Mark, 75; Robert, 75;
　Susanna, 75; Susannah, 75;
　Thomas, 75
DARROTH, Robert, 64; Thomas, 64
DATESMAN, John, 256
DAUNE, Deborah, 221; William
　J., 221
DAVID, Ann, 207; Catherine, 71;
　John, 71, 94, 120, 207;
　Rachel, 71; Sarah, 71;
　Susanna, 71
DAVIDSON, William, 244
DAVIS, Catherine, 71; David, 8,
　158, 188; Deborah, 188;
　Eleanor, 128; Elizabeth, 202;
　Jane, 97; Joanna, 237; John,
　16, 37, 71, 97; Jonas, 258;
　Joseph, 178; Mary, 236;
　Morris, 158, 236; Rachel, 71;
　Samuel, 78, 236; Sarah, 71,
　210; Seth, 158, 236; Susanna,
　71; William, 62
DAVISON, James, 155, 222
DAWS, Alice, 16
DAWSON, Agnes, 12; R., 69
DAY, Benjamin, 28, 70;
　Christopher, 28, 31; Mary,
　70, 158; Sarah, 28
DE NORMANDIE, Amos, 62;
　Anthony, 62; Elizabeth, 62;
　James, 62; John, 62
DEAHL, Abraham, 254
DEAL, Abraham, 264; Catherine,
　264; David, 259; Frederick,
　178; Jacob, 258; Michael, 75,
　86; William, 264
DEAN, Alydia, 192; Amos Hughes,
　154; Benjamin, 65; Charity,
　192; Charles, 33, 82; Daniel,
　7; Elinor, 7; Eunice, 184;
　Frances, 137; Hannah, 65, 94,
　219; Hezekiah, 65; Jacob, 7,
　65; Jesse, 65, 219; John, 73;
　Jonathan, 192; Joseph, 65;
　Martha, 65, 184; Mary, 184;
　Samuel, 24; Sarah, 88;

Mahlon, 61; Mary, 61, 117,
136, 146; Nathan, 4; Rachel,
61; Samuel, 61, 120, 155;
Thomas, 61; William, 161
DOANE, Charles, 79
DOBEL, Elizabeth, 60; Lucy, 63;
Peter, 60, 63; Rachel, 60;
Ruth, 60, 63; Sarah, 60, 63;
William, 42, 60; William John
Benger, 60, 63
DOBELS, William, 55
DOBLE, Elizabeth, 128; John,
128, 166; Mary, 128
DOERT, Mariah, 163
DOIL, Jonathan, 197
DOKE, John, 127
DOLBY, Abel, 119, 130; Clara,
119; Nathan, 142
DOLLACHN, Daniel, 17
DONAHAVER, Elizabeth, 177;
Jacob, 177
DONALLY, James, 219
DONE, Deborah, 179; Mary, 179;
William, 179
DONELY, John, 54
DORAN, Margaret, 38, 40
DORRICK, Christian, 57
DORROCH, William, 6
DOSH, Abraham, 83; Mary, 83;
Philip, 80, 83
DOUGHERTY, David, 158; Mary,
19, 56; Robert, 56
DOUGHTY, Henry, 195
DOUGLAS, Andrew, 116
DOUGLASS, Martha, 237; William,
79
DOWD, Michael, 17
DOWLIN, David, 116; Eliza, 116;
Elizabeth, 116, 123; Esther,
116; Hannah, 116; Jane, 116;
John, 116; Joshua, 116;
Margaret, 116; Mary, 116;
Paul, 116, 123
DOWNING, Martha, 14; Samuel, 14
DOYL, Patrick, 23
DOYLE, Ann, 73; Jonathan, 122,
220, 225, 253; Mary, 122
DRAKE, Ann, 148, 167;
Elizabeth, 148, 167, 209;
Jacob, 148, 209; John, 148;
Mary, 148, 167; Rachel, 148;
Robert, 24, 47, 148, 221
DRAUGER, Christopher, 131, 239
DREICHLER, John, 70, 149
DREMEN, Thomas, 228
DREVEY, Catherine, 251; Philip,
251
DRIESBACH, Barnet, 197;
Catherine, 197; Christina,
197; Jacob, 256; John, 198
DRIEWEG, Andrew, 84; John Yost,

84; Margaret, 84; Philip, 84
DRINKER, Henry, 249
DRISSEL, John, 131, 203, 223;
Mary, 203; Ulrich, 203
DRUMBORE, Henry, 139
DRUMMOND, Mary, 61; Sarah, 61
DU BOIS, Abigail, 135; Charles,
237; Martha, 237; Uriah, 75,
237
DUBOIS, Abram, 108, 105; Ann,
108; Catherone, 108; Helena,
105, 108; Henry, 43, 108,
110, 105; Jonathan, 105;
Nicholas, 108, 105; Sarah,
108, 105; Susanna, 105;
Susannah, 108; Uriah, 210;
W., 217
DUBRE, Absalom, 123; Hannah,
138, 247
DUBREE, Hannah, 209
DUCHLER, John, 169
DUDBRIDGE, William, 201
DUER, Charlotte, 185; James,
178; Jane, 178; John, 7, 76,
107, 134, 178; Joseph, 230;
Josiah, 178; Mary, 65, 74;
Sarah, 195; William, 107,
178; William H., 76, 134
DUFFIELD, Elizabeth, 36; Mary,
36
DUKE, Susannah, 255
DUMONT, Nargaret, 95
DUNCAN, Rachel, 125; William,
125
DUNGAN, Amos, 3, 174; Ann, 6,
12; Benjamin, 66; Carnelius,
19; Charles, 194, 235;
Charlotte, 217; Christiana,
250; Clement, 17, 23, 29;
Cornelius, 39, 139, 140;
Daniel, 142, 170, 179, 202,
250; David, 3, 19, 39, 104,
132, 224, 253; Deborah, 142;
Elenor, 23; Elias, 17, 23,
95, 98, 214; Elizabeth, 3,
17, 23, 66, 95, 96; Ellen,
218; Ester, 66; Garret, 17,
39, 98, 104, 132, 140, 162,
224; Gilbert, 3; Isaac, 142,
179, 250; James, 17, 23, 96,
98, 142, 153, 169, 214, 250;
Jane, 17; Jean, 23; Jeremiah,
3, 23, 122, 139, 150; Jesse,
100, 142, 159, 250; John, 50,
66, 142, 179, 253; Jonathan,
66; Joseph, 3, 39, 43, 54,
62, 66, 101, 142; Joshua, 3,
17, 66, 104, 139, 162, 169,
218, 224; Levi, 39; Lewis,
142; Mahlon, 39; Martha, 3,
253; Mary, 3, 39, 66, 104,

FAUBIAN, Casper, 214, 228;
   Elizabeth, 214; George, 214,
   228; Henry, 214; Isaac, 214;
   John, 214; Mary, 214, 228;
   Michael, 214; Nancy, 214;
   Rachel, 214; Samuel, 214;
   Sarah, 214
FAULDER, John, 38
FEASTER, Aaron, 105, 133, 155;
   David, 133, 242; Elizabeth,
   133, 148, 155; George, 242;
   Henry, 201, 242; John, 133,
   242; Margaret, 242; Mary,
   242; Mattie, 135; Rachel,
   242; Sarah, 105; Susanna, 242
FEASTUR, Henry, 4
FEATHERBY, Benjamin, 257
FEATHERSBY, Mary, 199
FEFFERY, Flora, 27; Sarah, 27
FELL, Amos, 117; Ann, 91, 143;
   Belinda, 266; Benjamin, 253;
   Charles, 119, 173, 195;
   David, 84, 143, 171, 178,
   253, 258, 266; Deborah, 117;
   Edith, 166; Elias, 119;
   Elizabeth, 21, 27, 32, 51,
   54, 57, 117, 119, 158, 266;
   Ely, 101; Esther, 119; Ezra,
   158; Frances, 119; Francis,
   173; Ganas, 27; George, 54,
   56, 84, 101, 119, 253; Grace,
   101; Hannah, 54, 190; Hugh,
   118; Jane, 26, 117; Jesse,
   32, 101, 117, 118, 253; John,
   54, 84, 119, 143, 158; Jonas,
   54, 240; Jonathan, 27, 54,
   57, 69, 84, 95, 117, 118,
   126, 143, 158, 201, 213, 225;
   Joseph, 84, 118, 143; Joseph
   Gillingham, 208; Joyce, 27;
   Mahlon, 54; Martha, 101;
   Mary, 117, 208; Miriam, 54;
   Morris, 1; Phebe, 208;
   Phineas, 253; Rachel, 14, 32,
   54, 101, 142, 259; Rebecca,
   14, 114, 213; Rebekah, 131,
   143; Rebekah Ann, 201;
   Samuel, 117, 139, 150; Sarah,
   30, 51, 84, 101, 117, 119,
   209, 240, 266; Seneca, 54,
   101; Septimus, 266; Stacy,
   101; Thomas, 29, 32, 117,
   158, 253; Titus, 27; Watson,
   40, 88, 158, 162, 173, 195;
   William, 208; Zenas, 32
FELLMAN, Agnes, 67; Henry, 169;
   Jacob, 169; John, 67, 169;
   Matlina, 169
FENCE, Jacob, 60
FENTON, Benjamin, 38; Eleazer,
   118, 196; Elizabeth, 141;

Ephraim, 176; Herbert, 216;
   Jesse, 38; John, 38, 44, 118,
   248; Joseph, 17, 38; Josiah,
   4; Margaret, 118, 176, 197;
   Mary, 7, 38, 118, 141, 176;
   Patrick, 197; Randal, 196;
   Randle, 118; Richard, 38;
   Ruth, 160; Samuel, 4; Sarah,
   38; Thomas, 110, 141, 196
FERGUSON, Ann, 91, 183;
   Elizabeth, 91; Hugh, 73, 74;
   James, 73, 74, 75, 134, 145,
   150; John, 73, 74; Josiah,
   73, 77; Margaret, 74; Mary,
   77, 150; Nancy, 75
FETHERBY, Ann, 41; Mary, 17
FETTER, Henry, 28
FETTERS, Ann, 23
FIELD, Benjamin, 141, 171, 243;
   Elizabeth, 243; Hannah, 243;
   Isaac, 243; John, 43, 96;
   Joseph, 243; Newberry, 58;
   Pricilla, 183; William, 243
FILES, Langhorn, 233
FINCKMAN, Mathias, 19
FINDLEY, James, 148, 234
FINK, John, 125
FINLEY, Elizabeth, 200; Henry,
   200; James, 97, 200; Mary, 97
FINNE, Charity, 249; Elizabeth,
   249
FINNEY, Charles, 249;
   Elizabeth, 259; John, 135;
   Mary, 249
FISH, Elizabeth, 200
FISHER, Ann, 49; Barack, 5;
   Bosham, 30; Elizabeth, 57,
   104, 240; Eve, 57; George,
   240; John, 57; Joseph, 5;
   Mary, 30; Nicholas, 57;
   Robert, 5; Samuel, 5; Wendle,
   118
FITSINGER, Catherine, 222
FITZGEREL, James, 61
FITZINGER, John, 207
FITZJEREL, Mary, 61
FITZWATER, Joseph, 245;
   Matthew, 47
FLACK, Ann, 90, 222; Benjamin,
   90; Edith, 90; Henry, 181,
   219; James, 90, 181, 219;
   John, 90, 95, 219; Joseph,
   90, 95, 144; Mary, 89, 144,
   181, 219; Robert, 26, 89, 90,
   144, 181, 219; Samuel, 90,
   144; Thomas Wier, 89;
   William, 90, 181
FLANAGAN, Elizabeth, 180; Mary,
   180; Reuben, 178; Sarah, 180;
   Stacy, 180
FLEAT, Jasper, 110; Mary, 110

Maria, 126; Mary, 157, 223;
Peter, 149; Ralph, 157;
Sarah, 157
FURMAN, Deborah, 254;
Elizabeth, 254; George, 266;
John, 254; Letitia, 266;
Sarah, 254; Steward, 254;
Susanna, 254; William, 254
FURNACE, Mary, 235

-G-

GABLE, Catherine, 208; George,
208; Samuel, 208
GADDES, Elizabeth, 199; George,
199; Henry, 199; Jane, 199;
Martha, 199; Mary, 198;
William, 199
GADSHALK, Jacob, 172
GAIN, Sarah, 89; Thomas, 89
GAINE, Thomas, 60
GAINES, Abraham, 203; Mary, 203
GALE, Abigail, 153, 232, 241;
Elizabeth, 32, 232; Hannah,
232; Isaac, 32, 153, 232;
John, 32; Mary, 232; Rebecca,
232; Sarah, 232; William, 153
GALLAGAR, John, 205; Rebecca,
205
GALLAGHER, John, 46, 172
GALLOWAY, Elizabeth, 105;
Robert, 105
GAMEL, William, 89
GARDENER, Carswell, 102
GARDINER, John Smith, 62
GARDNER, Nathan, 46; Sarah, 201
GARES, Catherine, 256;
Elizabeth, 120, 256;
Frederick, 256; Jenna, 256;
John, 120, 256; Lenna, 256;
Madelina, 256; Mary, 256;
Samuel, 256; Susanna, 256
GAREY, Jacob, 122
GARGES, William, 158
GARIS, Frederick, 237; John,
159
GARNER, Elizabeth, 246; John,
246; Samuel, 45, 127; Sarah,
246
GARRET (NEGRO), 162
GARRISON, Charles, 52, 177;
Daniel, 52; Elizabeth, 52,
177
GARY, Ann, 192
GAYMAN, Abraham, 91, 159; Anna,
159; Barbara, 159; Benjamin,
159; Eve, 159; Jacob, 159;
Samuel, 249
GEARHART, Abraham, 239; Adam,
229; Mary, 238
GEDDES, George, 24, 30, 39, 41;
Henry, 30; Jane, 30; John,

30; Mary, 30; William, 30
GEDMAN, John, 256
GEHMAN, Abraham, 41, 82, 89,
133, 255; Benedict, 133;
Christian, 19; Jacob, 180;
John, 89, 255; Mary, 229;
Samuel, 89, 109, 210, 229
GEHRY, Ann, 70; Jacob, 70
GEIL, Abraham, 95
GEISSINGER, Elizabeth, 229;
Jacob, 229
GELEN, Sarah, 6
GEOHGHEGAN, Bartholomew, 72
GEORGE, Frederick, 83; Jacob,
253; Magdalena, 253
GERBER, Henry, 256
GERHART, Abraham, 6; Catherine,
243; Christina, 22; John, 243
GERIS, John, 226; Magdalene,
226
GERMAN, David, 13; Jacob, 180;
Richard, 72
GETMAN, Elizabeth, 127; George,
127; John, 127; Sarah, 127;
William, 127, 208, 233
GETTMAN, Elizabeth, 69; George,
83, 87; Johannes, 83; John,
69; Samuel, 87
GEYER, John, 178
GIBBS, Benjamin, 53; Elizabeth,
53; Eupheme, 46; Hannah, 53;
John, 53; Samuel, 9, 53, 176
GIBSON, Elizabeth, 18; James,
18; Jean, 18; John, 18, 162;
Moses, 18; Robert, 1, 18,
182; Thomas, 18
GIER, Elizabeth, 175; Ellis,
175; John, 175, 178; Juliann,
175; Mary, 175
GIESTE, Eve Catherine, 78;
Jacob, 78
GIFT, Abraham, 220; Catherine,
220; Elizabeth, 220; Hannah,
220; Isaac, 220; Mary, 220;
Peter, 220; Rachel, 220;
Susanna, 220
GILBERT, Ann, 38; Benjamin,
252; Charles, 256; Edith,
195; Elias, 68, 195;
Elizabeth, 9, 195; Ellis,
202; Ester, 68; Hannah, 195,
256; Hannameel, 131;
Harrison, 256; Hiel, 256;
Huldah, 222, 256; Joanna,
194; John, 256; Joshua, 256;
Maris, 256; Martha, 38;
Pearson, 256; Rachel, 195;
Rebecca, 29; Samuel, 256;
Silas, 9, 151; Susanna, 9;
Thomas, 9, 96; William, 9
GILE, John, 259

GILES, Abigail, 125; William,
125
GILKESON, Andrew, 168
GILKYSON, Andrew, 235;
Jame(sic), 137
GILL, Agnes, 30; Asenath, 225;
Isaac, 225; John, 244;
Mathew, 225; Matthew, 69,
224; Thomas, 30, 59; Uree, 30
GILLAM, Anna, 213; Isaac, 250;
Mary, 250; Sarah, 124; Simon,
31, 100, 148, 171, 241;
William, 100, 241
GILLESPIE, George, 41
GILLIAM, Simon, 11
GILLIGHAM, Joseph, 10
GILLINGHAM, Amos, 55; Ann, 219;
Benjamin, 55, 159; Bridget,
56; David, 55; Elizabeth, 53,
96; Esther, 55, 159; Harvey,
96, 197, 245; James, 14;
John, 14, 31, 55, 59, 70, 96,
102, 159, 202, 218; Joseph,
1, 11, 39, 47, 49, 55, 56,
63, 73, 96, 159, 262;
Margaret, 225; Mary, 47, 55,
134, 159; Moses, 56; Phebe,
47, 55; Rebecca, 96, 262;
Samuel, 14, 55, 59, 68, 107,
154, 159, 167, 174, 196, 207,
208, 209, 231; Sarah, 55;
Smuel, 59; Thomas, 96;
William, 96, 207; Yeamans,
12, 21, 56; Yeomans, 26
GILLUM, Luke, 174; Susannah,
174
GILMORE, Ann, 226; Latitia, 226
GLUCK, Henry, 261
GODSHALK, Abraham, 101, 203;
Elizabeth, 43; Isaac, 174;
Jacob, 178; John, 178, 205,
222; Samuel, 95; Susanna,
174; William, 131, 147, 174,
177, 178, 203, 206, 227
GOFORTH, Ann, 128; Elizabeth,
91, 128, 191; Isabel, 128;
Jacob Hibbs, 191; John, 91,
124, 128, 191; Nancy, 91;
Thomas, 91, 128; William, 91,
191
GOHEEN, Charles, 125, 223
GOOD, Edward, 163; Eleanor,
163; Francis, 26, 253; Jane,
163; John, 163; Jonathan,
163; Margaret, 26, 163; Mary,
163; Rachel, 253; Sarah, 26
GOODE, Francis, 11, 26, 29, 35;
Mary, 25; Sarah, 26; Thomas,
29, 31
GOODWIN, George, 126; John,
126; Jonathan, 126; Joseph,

126; Susannah, 126; William,
126
GORDON, Frances, 150; John,
261; Joseph, 150; Martha, 146
GORHAM, Nathaniel, 122
GOSLIN, Elizabeth, 258; Esther,
258; Hannah, 241, 263; Jacob,
241; John, 241, 267
GOSLINE, Ann Eliza, 232; Eli,
241; Esther, 241, 265;
Hannah, 232; Jacob, 32, 232;
James, 232; John, 42, 45,
153, 232, 241; Levi, 241;
Levy, 232; Margaret, 32, 232;
Maria, 232; Martha, 241;
Mary, 232; Peter, 232;
Richard, 232, 241; Thomas,
232; William, 49, 232, 241
GOTTSCALK, Jacob, 34
GOUCHER, Elizabeth, 243;
Hannah, 243; John, 94, 243;
Lewis, 243; Mary Ann, 243;
William, 243
GOURLEY, Samuel, 23, 29
GOUZNEL, Bela, 128
GRAHAM, Archibald, 81, 205;
James, 203
GRANT, George, 158; Jesse, 187;
Robert, 23; William, 187
GRANTHAM, George R., 255
GRAVER, Elizabeth, 67
GRAY, Alice, 214; Elizabeth,
94, 215; George, 94; Hannah,
32; James, 32, 49, 214, 215;
Jane, 32; Jeremiah, 94; John,
32; Margaret, 32; Maria, 215;
Mary, 32, 94
GREASER, Anthony, 73
GREASLEY, John, 13, 38, 57, 86
GREASON, Anthony, 43
GREEG, Joseph, 243
GREEN, Alce, 90; Alice, 58;
Ann, 10; Benjamin, 119, 125,
150, 177; Elizabeth, 10, 202;
Evan, 110, 177; Hannah, 119;
James, 10, 119, 150; Jane,
60, 119; John, 58, 91, 97,
150, 165; Joseph, 86, 110;
Magdalen Hollock, 58;
Magdalen K., 90; Margaret,
10; Martha, 10, 202; Mary,
86, 202; Rebecca, 151;
Richard, 63; Robert Morris,
58; Thomas, 10, 106, 110;
William, 38, 86, 119, 177
GREER, Joseph, 150, 195;
Susanna, 244
GREGG, Amos, 32, 63, 68, 75,
92, 96, 104, 108, 112, 123,
153, 186, 188, 196, 232; Ann,
123; Elizabeth, 15, 32;

HAIR, Elizabeth, 77; Ernest, 6;
George, 77; Isabel, 77;
Jacob, 6; Joseph, 77; Robert,
77; William, 77, 225
HAIST, George, 136
HALDEMAN, Jacob, 163
HALDIMAN, Jacob, 207
HALL, Alexander, 107; Isaac,
40; Jane, 78; John, 19, 107;
Joseph, 107; Sarah, 107;
Thomas, 62, 107
HALLOWELL, Elizabeth, 227;
John, 52; Joseph, 227; Sarah,
149
HALSEY, Enos, 49
HALTIMAN, James, 45
HAMBLETON, Aaron, 113; Amy, 94,
184, 223; Amy Ellen, 223;
Ann, 223; Aron, 165;
Benjamin, 94, 184, 223, 245;
Catherine, 185; Elizabeth,
74, 86, 94, 169, 184, 245;
Hannah, 113, 165; James, 14,
21, 45, 94, 113, 165; John,
113, 165; Jonas, 113, 165;
Joseph, 94, 113, 177, 184,
195; Latitia, 113; Letitia,
223; Louise, 223; Margaret,
184; Martha, 94, 154; Mary,
94, 184; Moses, 113, 165;
Rachel, 169; Sarah, 94, 184;
Stephen, 94, 113; Thomas, 22,
94, 184; William, 21, 94,
113, 165
HAMILTON, Benjamin, 202;
Benjamin K., 219; Joseph,
219; Mary, 219; Sarah, 219;
William, 219
HAMMELS, Thrand, 172
HAMPTON, Ann, 30; Benjamin,
150; David, 30; Elizabeth,
209; Hannah, 184, 204, 209,
260; John, 30; Jonathan, 30,
209; Joseph, 30, 34;
Margaret, 173; Mary, 34, 130;
Moses, 150; Oliver, 19, 150,
151, 176, 184, 204, 209, 235,
257, 260, 128; Rebecca, 209
HAMTON, Aaron, 25; Ann, 40;
Benjamin, 152; David, 25;
Hanna, 76; Hannah, 107, 138;
Joseph, 25, 158; Mary, 25;
Mercy, 25; Oliver, 74, 76,
107, 138, 145, 74; Rebekah,
25
HANE, William, 91
HANEY, Joseph, 229, 235; Mary,
229; Philip, 231
HANIN, Samuel, 59, 265
HANNA, James, 9, 38, 48; John
A., 38; William R., 180

HANNAWAY, Ann, 20
HAPENNY, Amos, 62; Fanny, 62;
Mark, 23, 62; Mr., 61;
Rachel, 62
HARD, William, 145
HARDEN, Phebe, 103; Rachel, 103
HARDIN, Abraham, 83
HARDING, Abraham, 133, 148,
214, 236; Elizabeth, 91, 219;
Henry, 36; Isaac, 44, 212;
Jacob, 39, 194, 255; Mary,
233; Sarah, 233
HARDY, Mark, 27
HARE, Abigail, 263; Ann, 172;
Elizabeth, 263; James, 172;
John, 172; Mathew, 263;
Rebekah, 164; Sarah, 263
HARKER, James, 31; Samuel, 31
HARLAND, Ezekiel, 187; Hannah,
187
HARLESHIMER, George, 24
HARMAN, Abraham, 190; David,
190; Joseph, 92; Margaret,
190; Susanna (Ruth), 190
HARMER, Hannah, 189; Joseph
Mitchell, 189; Mary, 189
HARPEL, Anna Maria, 91; Conrad,
91, 96, 115, 128, 224, 225;
Elizabeth, 91; Magdalen, 91;
Margaret, 91; Philip, 91,
224; White, 91; Wilthonger,
91
HARPER, Phebe, 242; William,
227
HARPLE, Conrad, 135; Philip, 33
HARRIS, Hannah, 48, 201; Henry,
8, 164; John, 8, 13, 127,
164, 201; Joseph, 150;
Martha, 8, 13; Samuel, 8, 13,
196; Sarah, 9; Thomas, 9,
164, 216
HARRISON, George, 140; James,
190; John, 16; Joseph, 190;
Martha, 134, 190; Mary, 241;
Miles, 29; Rachel, 21, 190;
Sarah, 29; Thomas, 53;
William, 190
HARROLD, David, 95, 262;
Elizabeth, 96, 154; Hannah,
96, 99, 230; James, 95; John,
95, 96; Joseph, 95, 96, 131;
Rachel, 95, 262; Samuel, 95,
96; William, 95, 96, 154
HARROW, Mary, 136
HARRY, John, 54; Tesey, 59
HARRYE, Abraham, 18; Elizabeth,
18; Moses, 18
HART, Andrew, 164; Ann, 114,
142, 149, 172, 264; Clarissa
Maria, 149; Eliza Ann, 149;
Elizabeth, 9, 16; Euphemia,

220; Sophia, 6; Susanna, 6
HERTZELL, Henry, 41, 200;
Michael, 41
HERWEAK, John, 203
HESS, Elizabeth, 184, 223;
George, 225; Henry, 184, 223;
Joseph, 139, 251
HESTON, Ann, 51, 110, 167;
Bathsheba, 3; Catherine, 90;
Charles, 90, 91; David, 8,
34, 176, 183, 236, 260; Eber,
51; Elizabeth, 34, 64, 96,
98; Issac, 3; Jacob, 3, 52,
64, 98; Jane, 166; Jesse,
166; John, 34; Joseph, 166;
Joshua, 34; Mary, 3, 38, 91;
Phebe, 86, 166, 236; Rachel,
8; Rebecca, 91; Samuel, 166;
Sarah, 91; Susan, 189; Tacy,
8; Thomas, 3; Titus, 47;
William, 34, 91; Zebulon, 34,
47
HESTOUT, David, 243; Susanna,
243
HETMAN, Andrew, 244; Elizabeth,
244; Michael, 244; Rachel,
244
HETRICK, Catherine, 27; Jacob,
256
HETZEL, Philip, 144
HEVENER, Abraham, 123; Barbara,
123; Elizabeth, 123; Jacob,
123; John, 123; Margaret,
123; Mary, 123; Melchor, 123
HEWLINGS, Diana, 20
HEWSON, Alce, 90; Thomas, 63;
Thomas Tickell, 90; William,
58, 90
HIBBS, Abner, 215, 246;
Abraham, 7; Amelia, 37; Ann,
124, 266; Benjamin, 7, 19,
32, 189, 190; Betsey, 246;
Charles, 266; Deborah, 124;
Eli, 215, 246; Elizabeth, 6,
37, 61, 266; Hannah, 7;
Hester, 19; Isaac, 19; James,
19, 189; Jesse, 118, 179;
Jesse L., 261; John, 65;
Jonathan, 32, 37, 118, 179;
Mary, 7, 37, 189, 215, 246;
Nehemiah, 19; Pheaby, 7;
Rachel, 246, 266; Rebecca,
253, 266; Samuel, 179, 191,
214; Sarah, 179, 190; Seneca,
215, 246; Susanna, 7, 32,
179; William, 19, 37, 189,
215, 246, 266
HICKMAN, Benjamin, 7
HICKS, Anne, 101; Edward, 190,
204, 237; George, 129, 141;
Isaac (Is.), 4, 25, 29, 39,

56, 60, 64, 85, 99, 105, 118,
128, 129, 141, 155, 161, 162,
201, 204, 220, 225, 240;
James, 54; Jesse, 70, 101,
141; John, 142; Joseph, 2, 7;
Kimble, 197; Mahlon, 240;
Mary, 101; Rebecca, 240;
Samuel, 142; Thomas, 58;
William, 10, 64, 141
HIESTAND, Anna, 44; Barbara,
44; Henry, 42; John, 44
HIGGS, James, 78
HIGH, Barbara, 152; David, 152;
Jacob, 223, 239, 241;
Johannes, 91; Magdalena, 89,
241; Philip, 88, 89
HILBERN, Martha, 117
HILBURN, Ruth, 155
HILDEWIRTH, Henry, 222
HILE, Elizabeth, 4; Henry, 4
HILL, Abraham, 40, 70, 114;
Achsah, 30, 226; Ann, 21,
262; Catherine, 181; David,
262; Deborah, 120; Elizabeth,
29, 70, 182, 262; Ezekiel,
73; Frances A., 226; Hannah,
115; Isaac, 70, 98; James,
262; John, 14, 181; John H.,
267; Liddia, 71; Margaret,
70; Mary, 182; Mary Ann, 262;
Patty, 182; Rabecca, 71;
Rebecca, 71; Richard, 70,
202; Sarah, 70; Thomas, 70,
120, 262; William, 70, 115,
120
HILLAPOT, Barnet, 186;
Frederick, 186; George, 186;
Henry, 186; John, 186
HILLBERN, Martha, 117
HILLBORN, Amos, 43; Ann, 2;
Elizabeth, 6; Fanny, 43;
Hannah, 2; Jane, 43; John,
25, 43, 63; Joseph, 57; Mary,
2, 254; Mercy, 43; Robert, 2,
43, 254; Ruth, 2; Samuel, 2,
254; Thomas, 43
HILLBORNE, Robert, 246
HILLBRANDT, Diana, 42;
Elizabeth, 42; Henry, 42;
John, 42; Mary, 42
HILLEGAS, Adam, 120; Anna, 70;
Elizabeth, 120; Frederick,
70; George, 120; Henry, 120;
Jacob, 120; John, 120; Mary,
14; Michael, 120; Susannah,
138
HILLINGS, John, 82
HILLPOT, Barbara, 179; George,
248; Leah, 179; Zipporah, 179
HILLRUN, John, 2
HILLTOWN, Eben, 177; Elias,

177; Elizabeth, 177; Ephraim, 177; Issachar, 177; John, 177; Nathan, 177; Thomas, 177; Walter, 177
HIMBLE, Anthony, 58; Christopher, 58; Cynthia, 58; John, 58; Sarah, 58; Tabitha, 58
HIMMELWRIGHT, John, 203; Joseph, 96, 113, 254
HINES, Elizabeth, 9, 13, 54; Isaac, 212, 248; Margaret, 54; Mary, 54; Matthew, 54; Patrick, 173; Samuel, 54; William, 9, 148, 181, 216
HINKEL, Hannah, 267; Philip, 84
HINKLE, Adalina, 220; Adam, 135, 146; Ann, 220; Charles, 113, 220; Eliza, 220; Elizabeth, 113; George, 146; Henry, 226; Jesse, 127; John, 146, 220, 226; Leonard, 129, 146; Mary, 113, 220, 226; Philip, 113, 127; Theophilus, 220
HIRTZELL, Henry, 45
HISE, John, 42; Sarah, 21
HIXON, Eleanor, 39
HOAFMAN, Anthony, 70; Mary Elizabeth, 70; Michael, 70
HOAGLAND, Alice, 20; Else, 20; John, 20
HOBER, Catherine, 84; Henry, 84
HOCH, Jacob, 17; John, 160; Magdalena, 17
HOCH (HIGH), John, 160
HOCKMAN, Abraham, 46, 251; Anna, 46, 251; Anne, 46; Barbara, 46, 210, 249, 251; Christian, 46, 139, 251; Elizabeth, 46, 121; Finna, 251; Hannah, 241; Henry, 46, 196, 210, 241, 251; Jacob, 46, 121, 210, 251; Mary, 46, 251; Nancy, 210; Nanny, 210; Ullry, 251; Ulrick, 46, 210; Ulry, 46, 241
HOD, John P., 262
HODDLE, Molly, 122; Peter, 119
HOFFEL, Jacob, 262; Mary, 262
HOFFERT, Barbara, 199; Eave, 199; Henry, 199; John, 199; Joseph, 199; Lorence, 199; Martin, 199; Simeon, 199
HOFFMAN, Adam, 244; Anthony, 15; Elizabeth, 15, 76; Eve Mary, 15; George, 168; John, 15, 76; Margaret, 69, 168; Mary Elizabeth, 15; Merrick, 1; Michael, 14; William, 69
HOFFORD, Henry, 54

HOGE, Ann, 28; Elizabeth, 28; Thomas, 28
HOGELAND, Abraham, 205; Alcie, 255; Cornelia, 177, 206; Daniel, 141, 147, 206; Derick, 255, 266; Derick K., 141, 257; Derrick, 18, 206; Derrick K., 196, 205; Dirck, 7; Elcie, 255; Elizabeth, 4; Iaah (Idah?), 7; Jane, 209; John Wynkoop, 255
HOKS, Peter, 39
HOLCOMB, George, 261
HOLCOMBE, Allen, 208; Elizabeth, 208; John, 208; Margaret, 208; Mary, 208; Richard, 208; Samuel, 208
HOLDEMAN, Jacob, 19
HOLLAND, John, 101; Sarah, 101
HOLLAS, Abraham, 3; Martha, 3
HOLLERIN, Elizabeth, 8
HOLLINGSHEAD, Alice, 36; Alse, 74; Elizabeth, 134; Hester, 134; Jane, 134; Peter, 134; William, 76, 134
HOLSTINE, Catherine, 265; Magdeline, 265; Michael, 265
HOLT, Evan, 216; Levi, 216
HOLTZ, Jacob, 58
HOMER, John, 24; Sophia, 237
HOOGEY, Nicholas, 38, 40
HOOT, John, 139, 161
HOOVER, Henry, 23
HOPER, William, 81
HOPKINS, Elizabeth, 37, 113, 180; William, 37
HOPPOCK, Jacob, 210
HORLACHER, Eve, 176; George, 176
HORLACKER, George, 94
HORN, Abraham, 266; Bastian, 266; Catherine, 266, 267; Daniel, 162, 267; Eve, 266; Jacob, 188; John, 261, 266; Joseph, 266; Mary, 162, 188, 267; Sebastian, 161, 162, 266, 267; Stephen, 8, 171
HORNE, Daniel, 193; Elizabeth, 193
HORNECKER, Jacob, 77
HORNER, James, 211; Jane, 254; John, 9
HORTWICK, Margaret, 189; Morris, 188
HOTTLE, Mary, 55; Michael, 55
HOUGH, Amy, 155; Ann, 231, 235; Benjamin, 101, 123, 168, 190, 207, 211, 230, 245, 255; Beulah, 110; Charlotte, 207, 255; Daniel, 3, 11; Edith, 9; Eleanor, 198; Elizabeth, 145;

215; Josiah, 120; Levi, 233;
Margaret, 233; Martha, 194;
Morgan, 196; Naomi, 196, 233;
Phebe, 194; Rachel, 200, 201;
Rebecca, 117; Rhoda, 120;
Robert, 189; Samuel, 100,
194, 245, 266; Simon, 119,
196; Thomas, 100, 201;
William, 196
JAMESON, Hugh, 77
JAMISON, ---, 258; George, 62;
Hannah, 152, 204; Henry, 203;
Hugh, 13, 81, 125; Isaiah,
142, 264; James, 152, 204;
John, 23, 127, 152, 195, 204;
Margaret, 142; Martha, 195,
204; Mary, 13, 195; Mathew
C., 129; Matthew, 204;
Rachel, 81; Robert, 14, 57,
81, 129, 152, 204; Sarah, 57,
81; William, 152, 204
JANNEY, Frances, 224; Jacob,
16, 129, 134, 141, 223, 228;
John, 224; Joseph, 224;
Mahlon, 224; Martha, 224;
Mary, 16; Richard, 224;
Sarah, 224; Stephen, 224;
Thomas, 16, 224, 236;
William, 224
JARRET, Jonathan, 23
JARRETT, David, 107, 186;
Jonathan, 26; Joseph, 187;
Rachel, 187; Rebecca, 26,
107, 142, 187; Richard, 187
JEANES, Isaiah, 145; Jacob,
145; Leah, 145
JEHLINE, Charles, 40
JENIPER, Henry, 10; Mary, 10
JENKS, Charles, 215, 254;
Elizabeth, 16, 215; Hannah,
215, 225; John, 23, 64;
Joseph, 64, 73, 215, 225,
249, 254; Joseph R., 131,
137, 213; Margaret, 16;
Margaret Ann, 215; Mary, 73,
114, 131, 213, 215; Mary Ann,
254; Michael, 215; Michael
H., 248; Michael Hutchinson,
215; Peter, 2; Phineas, 73,
103, 130, 131, 162, 201, 212,
228, 235, 241; Rabecca, 73;
Rebecca, 5, 73, 114, 213;
Rebekah, 130; Richard, 254;
Ruth, 73, 114, 131; Sarah,
78; Susan, 215; Thomas, 4, 5,
19, 32, 64, 73, 80, 130, 131,
188, 194, 212, 239, 253;
William, 16, 171, 182, 215,
225, 254; Zebiah, 2
JENNINGS, Richard, 88
JENNY, Jacob, 192

JICE, Elizabeth, 26
JOBES, Clarrisey, 90; George,
41, 90; Hannah, 90; Jenniser,
90; Juliana, 90; Mary, 90
JOBS, Sarah, 265
JODON, Francis, 79; Peter, 21,
79
JOHN, Samuel, 17
JOHNS, Abraham, 8
JOHNSON, Abigail, 109; Abner,
166, 232; Abraham, 67, 72,
124; Agnes, 88; Alice, 78;
Amos, 230; Ann, 20, 114, 195,
208; Armstrong, 114;
Benjamin, 20, 86, 109, 113,
150, 170, 173, 174, 203, 252,
265; Casper, 49, 86, 113,
170; Catherine, 20, 145, 159,
190; Charles, 140, 209, 230;
Clark, 124; David, 28, 77,
217, 245, 262, 265; Deborah,
100; Elizabeth, 20, 61, 67,
217, 245; Evan, 123; Fender
Carter, 114; Garret, 81, 129,
191, 230; Garret B., 230;
George, 61; Grace, 246; H.,
258; Hannah, 12, 54, 100,
150, 223; Henry, 61, 113,
150; Hugh, 67, 72; Hulah,
230; Huldah, 230; Ira, 230;
Isaac, 48, 52, 53, 61, 159,
240, 265; James, 54, 115,
124, 208, 230; Jane, 31, 72,
106, 208; Jesse, 61, 65, 83,
159, 175, 247, 262; Joannah,
230; Joel, 138, 140; John,
20, 26, 31, 48, 52, 72, 82,
88, 104, 230, 232, 241;
Jonathan, 223; Joseph, 42,
49, 65, 72, 75, 96, 113, 195,
208; Larrance, 223; Laurance,
30; Lawrance, 97; Lawrence,
82, 124, 262; Levy, 166;
Margaret, 65, 72, 74; Martha,
105, 258; Mary, 18, 20, 72,
88, 105, 113, 208, 231, 232,
243; Mercy, 28; Nancy, 42;
Nicholas, 48, 155; Patence,
143; Pennington, 114; Peter,
48; Philip, 61; Rachel, 236;
Rebecah, 72; Rebecca, 95,
223; Rebeka, 140; Rebekah,
72, 138; Richard, 61; Robert,
72, 88, 217, 236; Rosanna,
208; Samuel, 23, 46, 51, 61,
65, 70, 107, 114, 154, 171,
234, 258; Sarah, 30, 61, 72,
124, 134; Silas, 234;
Susanna, 31, 245, 262;
Theodosia, 166; William, 20,
61, 150, 203, 258; William

152, 252; Thomas, 242, 257;
William, 60, 196, 242, 257;
William Tomlinson, 166
KELMORE, Henry, 54
KELSEY, Ann, 235; John, 235;
Sarah, 235; William, 235
KELSO, Agnes, 234; Henry, 234;
Jane, 89, 234
KELSOE, Thomas, 1
KEMBLE, William, 197
KENDALL, Catherine, 152;
Elizabeth, 152; Jacob, 152;
John, 152; Joseph, 152;
Peter, 152; Susanna, 152;
William, 152
KENNEDY, James, 50; Jane, 195,
50; Robert, 131, 144, 177;
Th. G., 168; Thomas, 195, 50;
Thomas G., 187, 188, 194,
201, 205; William, 40, 203,
256
KEPHARD, John, 190
KEPHART, Abraham, 243; Ann,
243; Elizabeth, 243; Jacob,
243; John, 243
KEPLER, Bernardus, 137;
Christopher, 137; Elizabeth,
137; Eve, 182; Eve Catherine,
137; Jacob, 137, 182; John,
137, 182; Susanna, 137
KERBER, Jacob, 83
KERIN, I.F., 178
KERN, Adam, 22, 161; Ann, 98;
Anna, 174; Anthony, 174;
Catherine, 43, 174;
Christian, 37; Deborah, 43,
98; Elizabeth, 98; Frederick,
226; George, 43, 98, 103;
Jacob, 98, 103, 262; John,
98, 226; Peter, 226; Polly,
174; Susanna, 98, 262
KERNS, J. Daniel, 178; John,
218; Mary, 218
KERR, Abel, 202; Adam, 63, 181,
199, 202; Anne, 63;
Elizabeth, 72; Esther, 63;
Henry, 144, 202; Hester, 181;
Isabel, 63; James, 201, 202,
242; Jane, 63; John, 9, 12,
16, 49, 52, 53, 62, 86, 95,
120, 127, 152, 155, 181, 201,
202, 204; John D., 178;
Lydia, 63; Martha, 155, 201;
Mary, 63; William, 63, 201,
202
KESBER, Joseph, 23
KESSELMAN, Fred, 11
KESTER, Rachel, 113, 165
KETTLEMAN, Henry, 8
KICKLIN, John, 115
KIDD, Isaac, 38; John, 37, 181;

Theodosia, 38
KILMER, Anthony, 233;
Elizabeth, 233; Henry, 233;
Jacob, 233; John, 233;
Magdalena, 233; Samuel, 233
KIMBLE, Ann, 193; John, 241;
Mary, 202; Rachel, 224
KIMMENS, Robert, 148
KINDELL, William, 46
KINDLE, Ann, 225; Mason, 225
KING, Arbutis, 261
KINSEY, Alice, 116; Ann, 92,
98; Benjamin, 51, 116;
Charles, 71; David, 51, 235;
Deborah, 71; Edmund, 51;
Eliza, 98; Elizabeth, 51, 92;
George, 32, 98, 159; Harman
V., 92; Henry, 148; Ingham,
71; James, 71; John, 4, 32,
35, 51, 58, 66, 84, 98, 185,
211, 220; Jonas, 71;
Jonathan, 28, 136; Margaret,
113, 165; Mary, 66, 92, 149,
159; Patience, 66; Phebe, 32;
Rebecca, 92; Samuel, 32, 51,
176, 235; Sarah, 84, 98;
Thomas, 51; William, 143
KINSY, Lewis P., 198; Mary, 190
KINZELY, John, 127
KIPLE, Margaret, 186
KIRK, Amos, 98, 187, 207, 249;
Asee, 98; Frederick, 14;
Isaac, 1, 236; Isaak, 187;
James, 245; John, 95, 236;
Jonas, 111; Joseph, 233, 236,
249; Margaret, 14; Mary, 15,
86, 95, 140, 207, 215, 233,
236; Patience, 136, 249;
Phebe, 187; Rachel, 32;
Samuel, 8, 14, 66; Sarah, 1,
235; Stephen, 1, 236; Thomas,
86, 98, 249; William, 15,
115, 187, 236
KIRKBRIDE, Ann, 11, 30, 69;
Benjamin, 69; David, 69;
Elenor, 182; Elizabeth, 107;
241; Esther, 69; Hannah, 14,
65, 69, 158, 204; John, 102,
145, 240, 241; Jonathan, 22,
38, 56, 79, 241, 256; Joseph,
145; Letitia, 69; Mahlon,
102, 145, 197, 211; Mary, 69,
192, 222; Robert, 11, 31, 65,
69, 98, 192; Sarah, 69, 256
KIRKLANDE, Mahlon, 30
KIRKLINDE, Joseph, 1
KIRKPATRICK, William, 129
KISER, Permela, 98
KISER (KAISER?), Joseph, 89;
Leonard, 89; Margaret, 89;
Michael, 89; Philip, 89

LERRNT, ---, 63
LERUE, Catherine, 74
LESLY, Mary, 39
LESTER, Catharina, 110; Elijah,
110; Isaac, 13, 110; Jane,
86; John, 13, 38, 57, 60, 86,
110, 119, 130, 159; Joseph,
28; Mary, 170; Peter, 170;
Shipley, 86, 106, 130, 198;
Thomas, 60, 86
LETCHWORTH, William, 75
LETHAM, William, 98
LETHERACH, Jacob, 195
LETHERMAN, Ann, 81; Anne, 108;
Chriatian, 108; Christian,
81; Elizabeth, 108; Ester,
108; Henry, 108; Jacob, 108;
Mary, 108
LEVENSTER, Elizabeth, 214
LEVERNS, Joseph, 155
LEVES, Samuel, 183
LEVINGA, William, 37
LEVINSTON, Lawrence, 15; Peter,
15
LEVY, Adam, 176; Andrew, 113;
Eve, 176
LEWIS, Abel, 206, 245; Abraham,
196; Ann, 88; David, 9;
Elias, 177; Elizabeth, 17,
61, 163; Ellis, 177; Henry,
60, 69; Isaac, 60, 69, 70;
Isabella, 188; James, 1, 60,
69; John, 73, 75, 88, 126,
132, 145, 210; Jonathan, 17;
Joseph S., 172; Lewis, 134,
177; Lydia, 17; Margaret, 60,
69, 89, 122, 177; Mary, 1, 6,
206, 245; Nathan, 17;
Nathaniel, 17; Rebekah, 9;
Richard, 89; Robert, 97, 142,
255; Samuel, 17; Sarah, 88,
152, 258; Thomas, 17, 88,
152; William, 17, 60, 69,
196; Zachariah, 17, 152
LICEY, Henry, 262; John, 195
LIGHT, Mathew, 4
LIGHTWOOD, Jacob, 146
LILLY, Kitty, 72
LINCY, Catherine, 228; William,
228
LINGMASTER, Philip, 233
LINTER, Hannah, 13
LINTON, Aaron, 155; Benjamin,
73; Daniel, 51; Elizabeth,
15, 51; Esther, 182; Hannah,
73; Hezekiah, 25, 90; Isaiah,
51, 147, 205; James, 51, 112,
147, 176, 199, 200, 205, 263;
John, 19, 51, 87, 105, 192,
224, 228; Joshua, 5, 73;
Laura, 51, 147, 199, 205,

263; Letitia, 87, 205;
Mahlon, 5, 73; Mary, 51, 91;
Rabecca, 51; Rebekah, 147;
Sarah, 51, 147, 205, 263;
Sarah C., 155; Thomas, 51,
147, 263; William, 20, 26,
51, 73, 87, 105, 147, 205,
263
LIPECAP, Jacob, 83; Michel, 248
LIPLER, Philip, 240
LIPPENCUT, Allen, 81
LIPPINCOTT, Allen, 138
LISEY, Henry, 177
LISOM, Amy, 264; William, 134,
264
LITE, Pendente, Adm., 78
LITLE, Andrew, 13; David, 13;
Jane, 13; Margaret, 13; Mary,
13; Robert, 13; Sarah, 13;
Thomas, 13
LITTLE, Agnes, 105; Ann, 112;
James, 105
LITZENBERGER, Adam, 165; Anna
Mary, 165; Juliana, 165;
Mayri, 165; Peter, 165;
Solomon, 165
LITZENBURGER, Solomon, 227
LIVEZEY, Daniel, 29, 56; David,
211; Deborah, 56, 209; Ezra,
56; Hannah, 167, 211; Isaac,
56; John, 211; Jonathan, 56,
211; Lydia, 6; Margery, 56;
Phebe, 211; Robert, 56, 167,
193; Samuel, 56; Sarah, 56,
193; Thomas, 56
LIVINGSTON, Anne Home, 68;
Margaret Buckman, 68
LLOYD, Benjamin, 257; Esther,
91; John, 31; Jonathan, 23;
Mary, 31; Peter, 138; Thomas,
23, 31
LOBENSTEIN, Isaac, 235
LOBENSTINE, John, 235
LOGAN, Elizabeth, 187; George,
187; John, 5; Mary, 212
LOH, Barbara, 243; Catherine,
243; Jacob, 208, 243;
Johannes, 22; John, 243;
Margaret, 243
LOLLER, Mary, 127; Robert, 7,
12, 97, 127
LOMBAERT, Margaret, 194
LONG, Adam Kerr, 63; Alexander,
45, 246; Andrew, 32, 45, 49,
63, 152, 164, 199, 200, 211;
Elias, 262; Elizabeth, 45,
132; George, 106; Henry Neae,
233; Hugh, 45, 49, 199;
James, 115; Jane, 247; John,
45, 158, 164, 219; Lavinah,
115; Lewis, 246; Ludwick, 29;

107; Jason, 63, 68; John, 43;
Joseph, 100; Martha, 28;
Mary, 100; Phebe, 43;
Priscilla, 1, 166; Rachel,
10; Robert, 28, 68; Ruth,
254; Samuel, 166; Thomas,
106; William, 68
MESSEMER, Henry, 252
MESSER, Lawrence, 138
MESSIMER, Henry, 127
METLER, William T., 237
METLIN, Martha, 245
METSGAR, Casper, 208
METTLEN, John, 77
METTLIN, Patrick, 43; Sarah, 43
METZ, Elizabeth, 253
METZGER, Andrew, 72; Anna, 72;
Casper, 72;
Christina-Catarina, 72;
Christina-Caterina, 72; John,
72; Jones, 72; Maria, 72;
Mary-Elizabeth, 72; Susana,
72; Susanna, 72
MEYER, ---, 62; Anna, 135;
Barbara, 135; Catherine, 135;
Christal, 135; Eve, 180;
Henry, 135, 218; Jacob, 126;
John, 154; Joseph, 126; Mary,
135; Peter, 135; Samuel, 24;
William, 135
MICHEL, Hannah, 232; John, 232
MICHENER, Abraham, 229, 260;
Ann, 33; Barak, 5; Benjamin,
104; Daniel, 97, 104; David,
94; Esther, 117; George, 229;
Grace, 229; Harman, 231;
Isaac, 176; Isaiah, 185;
John, 231; Jonathan, 231;
Joseph, 1, 231; Margaret,
222; Martha, 31, 97, 231;
Mary, 222; Meschach, 222;
Meshack, 101; Rebecca, 176;
Robert, 118; Sarah, 5, 28,
45, 236; William, 231
MICKLEROY, George, 29
MIDDLETON, Anna, 120;
Elizabeth, 120
MIGINNIS, Hannah, 258
MILCHEL, Richard, 20
MILES, Catherine, 96; Griffith,
149, 179; Samuel, 142, 172;
William, 172
MILL, Jacob, 81
MILLER, Abel, 177; Abraham, 27,
193, 200; Alexander, 39;
Catherine, 43, 184, 200, 206;
Charles, 43; Christian, 45,
62, 80; Daniel, 80, 139, 206;
Elizabeth, 200, 206; Ester,
203; Esther, 45, 206; George,
184; Henry, 12, 45, 54, 99,

106, 115, 200, 206, 239, 240,
248; Henry L., 70; Hugh, 58;
Isaac, 130; Jacob, 45, 203;
James, 37; Jane, 110; John,
45, 46, 64, 143, 163, 165,
175, 197, 200, 252; Joseph,
20, 99, 124, 130, 206;
Mahlon, 99, 230; Margaret,
60, 69, 97, 168; Martha, 12;
Mary, 12, 97, 139, 189;
Phebe, 244; Philip, 60, 69,
71, 94, 163; Polly, 206;
Rachel, 130, 200; Robert, 12,
130; Samuel, 130; Sarah, 189;
Sophia, 206; Susanna, 165,
200, 206; Thomas Craig, 168;
Tirzah, 70; William, 12, 168
MILLS, Catherine, 223; Elinor,
47; John, 67, 240; Solomon,
61
MILNER, John, 61
MILNOR, Catherine, 14; David,
1, 255, 258; Elizabeth, 255,
258; George, 255; Hannah,
255; Isaac, 14, 255; John,
14, 255; Jonathan, 1; Joseph,
14; M., 166; Mahlon, 14, 43,
81, 132, 197, 245; Marsha, 1;
Nathan, 255; Phebe, 14, 245;
Phoebe, 43; Rachel, 1;
Stephen, 1; Tacey, 201;
Theodosia, 255; William, 1,
85, 132, 193
MINCHINGER, Joseph, 70
MINER, Asher, 166, 186, 196,
213, 231, 237, 246;
Elizabeth, 130; John, 130;
Mary, 231, 246
MININSER, Joseph, 173
MINNICH, Joseph P., 45
MINNICK, Joseph P., 58, 61
MINSTER, Anthony, 85; John, 85,
95; Martha, 85; Mary, 85;
William, 85
MIRE, Michael, 88
MIRES, John, 40
MITCHEL, Carlile, 83; Daniel,
83; Elizabeth, 83; Esther,
83; George, 70; Hannah, 15;
Henry, 20; John, 83; Mahlon,
83; Martha, 20; Mary, 83;
Richard, 83; Sarah, 15, 83
MITCHELL, Amos, 20; Ann, 107,
238, 245; Augustin, 238;
Augustine, 245; Daniel, 127;
Elijah, 261; Elizabeth, 223,
261; Esther, 121; Gabnill,
102; George, 1, 60; Gove,
187; Hannah, 22, 85, 261;
Henry, 20, 22, 142; Hester,
74; Isaiah, 65; Jane, 37;

179
OVERHOLT, Abraham, 19, 75, 89,
129, 162, 198, 239, 241, 249,
250, 251, 260; Agnes, 198;
Ann, 266; Anna, 198; Barbara,
159; Barbary, 198; Catherine,
260; Christian, 19;
Elizabeth, 159, 198, 249,
260; Ester, 86, 159; Fanny,
266; Hannah, 260; Henry, 11,
19, 22, 89, 155, 162; Hester,
83; Isaac, 162, 198; Jacob,
11, 19, 22, 86, 89, 129, 159,
162, 186, 198, 260; John, 1,
19, 260; Joseph, 134, 198;
Madlin, 162; Magdalena, 159;
Magdalene, 198; Martin, 198,
260; Mary, 129, 198; Samuel,
19; Sarah, 19, 198; William,
198
OVERHOLTS, Abraham, 70; Ann,
70; Catherine, 70; Elizabeth,
70; Mark, 70; Mary, 70;
Susanna, 70
OVERHOLTZ, Abraham, 135; Henry,
210
OVERHOLTZER, Anna, 143; Henry,
83, 143
OVERHOLZER, David, 222
OVERPECK, Andrew, 68, 157, 181;
Anna, 68; Anna Maria, 68;
Anne, 181; Catherine, 68;
Conrad, 68; George, 67, 68;
Henry, 68, 206; Jacob, 181;
John, 68; Magdalena, 68;
Margaret, 68; Mary, 181, 206;
Philip, 170, 181; Rebecca,
68; Sarah, 68, 181
OVERPEEK, Andrew, 56
OWEN, Griffith, 67, 70, 77, 89,
110, 163, 175, 231, 248;
Jane, 77
OWENS, Bety, 122; Catherine,
122; Ebenezer, 122; Margaret,
122; Owen, 122; Rachel, 122;
Sarah, 122
OZMAN, Elizabeth, 181
OZMOND, Jonathan, 183

-P-
PAIST, Elizabeth, 257
PALMER, ---, 85; Amos, 186;
Ann, 140; Benjamin, 81, 92,
137; Beulah, 144; Elizabeth,
13, 20; George J., 214;
Henry, 214; Jesse, 92, 105;
John, 15, 16, 137; Joice, 13;
Lewis, 51; Martha, 78; Mary,
13, 214, 252; Richard, 137;
Robert, 137, 214; Tacy, 138;
Tamar, 144; Terringham, 214;

Thomas, 137; Tyrringham, 140;
William, 72, 137, 214
PALTIN, Thomas, 8
PANCOAST, Samuel, 180
PARK, James, 157, 158; Mary,
157
PARKER, Mary, 40, 72;
Nathaniel, 91; William, 72
PARR, Daniel, 261
PARRY, Benjamin, 80, 176, 204,
246; Charles, 207; Daniel,
246; David, 23, 36, 52, 187,
216; Eli, 216; Elizabeth,
187; Elizabeth E., 216;
Isaac, 107, 151, 187, 212;
Isabel, 52; Isac, 233; Jacob,
107; James, 216; Jane, 204;
John, 31, 136, 175, 216;
Letitia, 55, 216; Mary, 207;
Oliver, 246; Philip, 55, 136,
207; Rachel, 175, 216;
Rebecca, 74; Samuel, 207;
Sarah, 107, 216; Seneca, 207, 216;
Thomas, 107
PARSON, Charlotte, 226
PARSONS, Abigail, 19; Abraham,
214; Amos, 214; Elizabeth,
214; Isaac, 214; John, 214;
Margaret, 29; Nancy, 232;
Robert, 250; William, 250
PARTRIDGE, Mary, 53
PAST, John, 216
PASTE, John, 82; Jolly, 82;
Jonathan, 159; Robert, 182
PATTERSON, Christina, 196;
John, 241; Rebecca, 74;
Robert, 42, 61; William, 123,
196
PATTISON, Anthony, 30;
Elizabeth, 30; Jane, 30
PATTON, Jane, 48
PAUL, Ann, 264; Caleb, 28; Evan
T., 74; Grace, 264; Hannah,
117; James, 28, 74; Jesse,
74; John, 28; Jonathan, 28,
92, 155; Joseph, 28; Joshua,
103, 117; Rachel, 74, 237;
Susanna, 74; Thomas, 28
PAULISON, William, 195
PAXSON, Aaron, 25, 44, 71, 86,
88, 99, 102, 113, 119, 127,
149, 162, 185, 223, 230;
Abraham, 18, 88, 113, 184,
193; Ahaz, 155; Ann, 258;
Aron, 165, 166; Asher, 162;
Benjamin, 12, 25, 45, 71, 94,
111, 127, 175, 183, 192, 256;
Betsy, 63; Caroline, 182,
219; Catherine, 128; Charles,
166, 167, 173, 175, 207, 219,
257; Daniel, 29; Deborah, 63;

219; Hannah, 196, 222; James,
35, 47, 98, 203; Jane, 102;
John, 2, 85, 102, 167, 196,
199, 219, 242; Jonathan, 196;
Joseph, 102, 196, 242;
Martha, 199, 64; Mary, 196;
Nathaniel, 15, 73, 232;
Phebe, 242; Rebecca, 242;
Samuel, 196; Sarah, 2, 98;
Smith, 17, 196; Stephen, 22;
Thomas, 22, 68; Timothy, 186;
Widow, 249
PRINGLE, Elizabeth, 169; John,
169
PRIOR, Charles, 2; Elizabeth,
233; Gideon, 63, 152, 199,
233; Huldah, 2; Joseph, 2
PRONG, Barbara, 162
PRUTZMAN, Margaret, 109;
Nicholas, 109
PRYOR, Gideon, 247; Joseph, 96
PUFF, Henry, 90, 124; Joseph,
90; Mary, 90, 124
PUGH, Abram, 47; Ann, 60;
Daniel, 27, 171, 177;
Elizabeth, 122; Ellis, 77,
163; John, 27, 66, 69, 70,
71, 108, 115, 116, 118, 122,
154, 171, 190, 194, 245, 260;
Rebecca, 27, 171; Sarah, 171
PURDY, Mary, 172, 264; William,
149, 172
PURSEL, Jonathan, 183
PURSELL, Brice, 138, 193;
Elizabeth, 193; Jane, 193;
John, 193; Jonathan, 108,
136, 145, 151; Margaret, 193;
Marsee, 193
PURSLEY, Ann, 104; Brice, 104;
Dennis, 104; Elizabeth, 104;
Jane, 104; John, 104;
Margaret, 104; Ruth, 104;
Thomas, 104
PURSSELL, Ann, 5; John, 5;
Jonathan, 5, 72, 191, 253;
Lydia, 191, 253; Mahlon, 5;
Mary, 5
PYSHER, Adam, 47

-Q-

QUEEN, David, 91
QUINBY, Hannah, 163; Jane, 158;
Lydia, 40; Moses, 158, 216
QUINTON, Achsah, 259;
Alexander, 178; Andrew, 259;
Thomas, 259

-R-

RAAB, Christian, 231
RACENER, John, 117
RAGNET, James, 205

RAILE, David, 196; Evan, 196;
John, 98; Joshua, 98; Mary,
98; Nathan, 98; Richard, 98
RAISNER, John, 192
RAMPSON, Ann, 193; George, 193
RAMSEY, Ann, 50, 175;
Catherine, 202; David, 50;
Eleanor, 14; Elizabeth, 167,
175; Hugh, 14; Jane, 50;
Janet, 14; John, 14, 50, 53,
62, 149, 167, 175; Maria,
167; Mary, 50, 247; Robert,
14, 32, 50, 158, 167, 175,
197, 238; Samuel, 50; Thomas,
50; William, 14, 50, 57, 68,
81, 91, 167, 174, 175
RAMSON, Jacob, 190
RANDAL, Amos, 203; Eliza, 193;
Elizabeth, 200; George, 129,
143; Hannah, 241; Jacob, 193;
Jesse, 183, 193; Jonathan,
193; Mary, 193, 246
RANDALL, Elizabeth, 124, 216,
248; George, 143; Jesse, 219,
257; John, 143, 248; Mary,
233; Pamale, 257; Rebecca,
173; Thomas, 173; William,
173
RANDLE, Elizabeth, 178; John,
78, 178; Joseph, 178;
Margaret, 178; Rebecca, 178;
Sarah, 178; Thomas, 178;
William, 178
RANDOLPH, Elizabeth, 246; Jane,
149; Richard, 246
RANKIN, Catherine, 39;
Elizabeth, 39, 212; Hannah,
212; James, 33, 39, 173, 212;
John, 33, 39, 173, 212;
Joseph, 212; Mary, 173, 212;
Rebecca, 212; William, 39,
173
RANSOM, George, 65; Jacob, 65;
Mary, 65; Sarah, 65
RAPART, Peter, 66
RAPP, Elizabeth, 76, 151;
George, 186, 229, 231;
george, 151; Jacob, 76, 151;
John, 151; Michael, 151;
Philip, 48, 58, 63, 111, 117,
184; Phillip, 81; Samuel,
151; Sarah, 151; Susannah,
151
RAQUET, Ann, 194; Claudine,
194; James, 145
RASENBERG, Christian, 81;
Elizabeth, 81
RATCLIFF, Isaiah, 33; James,
33; Jean, 82; John, 33;
Jonathan, 33; Joseph, 33
RATZAL, Joseph, 190

RATZEL, Frederick, 196; George, 172, 196, 237; Hannah, 265; Jacob, 196, 265; John, 139; Joseph, 196; Susanna, 237
RAUB, Hannah, 230; Jacob, 230; Peter, 230
RAUGHT, Catherine, 111; John, 111; Michael, 111
RAWLINGS, Ann, 60, 80; Jane, 60; Joseph, 60, 80; Margaret, 60; Samuel, 60; Thomas, 60
RAY, Ann, 30; Dolly, 11
READER, Elizabeth, 138; Rachel, 172; William, 26
READHEFFER, Rachel, 167
REAGLE, Elizabeth, 226; John, 226, 240
REASER, Solomon, 260
REASONER, Barbara, 43; Catherine, 43; John, 43; Joseph, 43
REASOR, Abraham, 35; Anna, 35; Mary, 35; Susanna, 35
REBBART, Peter, 91
REDLINE, Christian, 163; Elizabeth, 163; Jacob, 163, 228; John, 163; Margaret, 228; Michael, 162
REDLION, Michael, 71
REED, Abijah, 129; Andrew, 116, 175, 206, 228, 244, 265; Elizabeth, 177; Esther, 29; Jacob, 228; John, 151, 243; Mary, 29, 168; Obijah, 71; Philip, 176, 228; Sarah, 29; Thomas Craig, 168
REEDER, Abner, 242; Abraham, 87, 101; Andrew, 17; Benjamin, 101; Charles, 50, 101; David, 50, 87, 101, 110; David K., 183; Eleanor, 101; Jesse, 101; John, 101; Joseph, 101; Joseph E., 259, 260; Joseph Eastburn, 183; Mark, 204; Merrick, 101, 102, 155, 214, 259; Priscilla, 36, 74, 82; Rachel, 264; William, 26
REES, David, 9, 34, 127; Henry, 196; John, 18; Joseph, 181; Mary, 46, 127, 158; Rebecca, 9; Thomas, 85
REESE, Mary, 216; Tacey, 216
REESER, Abraham, 198; Philip, 161
REEVE, Elizabeth, 171, 213; Josiah, 171; Peter, 46, 263
REEVES, Elizabeth, 248
REIFE, George, 71
REIFF, Benjamin, 180; John, 257, 258; Margaret, 258

REILEY, Elizabeth, 70; Nathan, 70
REILY, John, 142; Richard, 11
REIMER, Mary, 142
RELING, Catherine, 31; Jost, 31
RENNER, Adam, 215; Benjamin, 215; Henry, 215; Jacob, 215; Susanna, 215
RENSIMER, Jacob, 157
REPARD, Frederick, 228
REPPARD, Frederick, 103; Jacob, 103; Margaret, 103; Mary, 103; Peter, 77, 103; Susanna, 77
RESCH, Christina, 78; Henry, 78; Jacob, 78; John, 78; Nicholas, 78; Peter, 78; Polly, 78
RESE, Anna Margaretha, 36; Elizabeth, 36; Henry, 36; Joseph, 36, 196; Susanna, 36
RESENER, John, 226; Margaret, 226
RESHEA, Lydia, 214
RETHERFORD, Elizabeth, 124; Isaac, 124; John, 124; Joseph, 124; Mary, 124
REWIN, Scott R., 179
REYERSON, Hendrick, 4; Margaret, 4
RHOADS, Isaac, 146; Jack, 257; Jacob, 146, 159, 160; Margaret, 160; Peter, 109; Samuel, 85; Sarah, 236
RHOAR, Ann, 97; Barbara, 97; Barbary, 97; Christian, 97; Elizabeth, 97; Freaney, 97; Jacob, 97
RHOR, Anna, 250; Jacob, 250
RHUL, Catherine, 252; Christina, 252; Elizabeth, 252; Jacob, 252; Mary, 252; Peter, 252; Sarah, 252
RIALE, David, 262; Evan, 262; John, 119, 167, 196, 233, 243; Nathan, 262; Rachel, 262; Richard, 262
RICE, Ann, 59; Edward, 86, 177, 207; Ellener, 59; George, 76, 177, 182; Hannah, 86; James, 86, 96, 177, 207; John, 86, 177, 207; Joseph, 128, 177, 200, 233; Letitia, 128; Mary, 149, 177, 185; Nancy, 86; Peter, 171; Rachel, 86, 207; Thomas, 177; William, 128, 177, 195, 198, 226, 233
RICH, Alexander, 163; Ann, 28; Benjamin, 95, 159; Elizabeth, 200, 202; James S., 163; John, 219, 231; Jonathan,

163; Josiah, 219, 266;
Martha, 219; Mary, 136, 219,
231; Phebe, 125; Rachel, 231;
Sarah, 159; William, 229
RICHARD, Adam, 163; Elizabeth,
163; Margaret, 163; Maria,
179
RICHARDS, Alice, 64; Ann, 126;
Elizabeth, 34; George, 232;
Joachim, 197; John, 126;
Margaret, 232; Thomas, 158;
William, 34
RICHARDSON, Abner, 200; Amos,
1, 47, 60, 64, 128, 136, 148;
Ann, 128, 171, 213; Anna, 13,
248; Bersheba, 132; Clayton,
182; Clement, 82, 132;
Daniel, 16, 102, 211; David,
132; Elizabeth, 64, 182;
Hannah, 182; Hezekiah, 128;
Jane, 82, 102, 114, 128, 213;
Jeremiah, 132; John, 128;
John B., 248; Joseph, 5, 31,
73, 82, 85, 114, 132, 134,
170, 171, 178, 181, 188, 194,
213, 224, 234, 249; Joshua,
5, 82, 213; Malachi, 132;
Martha, 5, 128; Mary, 5, 65,
82, 113, 132, 182, 213, 227;
Rachel, 104; Rebecca, 182;
Rebekah, 128; Ruth, 5, 46,
82; Samuel, 66, 82, 132;
Sarah, 128; Susanna, 182;
Thomas, 170, 248; Thomasine,
178; William, 5, 20, 24, 72,
82, 170, 181, 182, 213, 238,
245, 248, 261
RICHE, Ann, 41; Lydia, 41;
Philip, 41; Thomas, 1, 40
RICHEY, Agnes, 3; Ann, 3, 29,
117; Ann Mary, 117; David, 3;
Elizabeth, 117; Hannah, 117;
Henry, 29, 117; Isaac, 117;
Jacob, 117; John, 3, 121;
Margaret, 117; Moses, 117;
Thomas, 3; William, 3
RICKERT, Daniel, 195
RICKEY, Alexander, 30; Ann, 30;
John, 14, 79, 81; Keirl, 14;
Mahlon, 81; Samuel, 14;
Sarah, 14
RIDGE, Aaron, 240; Amos, 125;
Edward, 232; Elizabeth, 240;
George, 125; Grace, 232;
Hannah, 240; Henry, 31, 125,
179, 185, 229, 232, 240;
Jesse, 240; Joseph, 232;
Mahlon, 125, 240; Mary, 31;
Moses, 232; Rachel, 125, 151;
Rebecca, 232; Thomas, 31,
146, 232; William, 31, 125,

130, 232, 240
RIEGEL, Daniel, 66; Elizabeth,
66; George, 66; Henry, 66;
Jacob, 66; John, 66;
Margaret, 66; Michael, 66;
Nicholas, 66; Peter, 66
RIFE, George, 41
RIGBY, Ann, 8; Mary, 8; Sarah,
8
RIGHT, Joel, 166; Joseph, 166;
Phebe, 166
RIGHT (WRIGHT), Martha, 11
RILEY, Daniel, 255; Magaret,
220
RING, Elizabeth, 193; Grace,
193; Jacob, 193; Jonathan,
193; Rebecca, 193; Sarah, 193
RINKER, Catherine, 21; Isaac,
21; Molly, 131
RISE, Sananah, 23
RISLER, Jacob, 61
RITCH, Lester, 238
RITTENHOUSE, Martha, 247;
Michael, 66
RITTER, Ann, 137; Jacob, 137
ROAD, Ann, 95; John, 196
ROADS, Eicie, 205; Elcie, 255;
John, 205; Silas, 266
ROAR, Nancy, 95; Valentine, 227
ROBERTS, Abagail, 129; Abel, 6,
13, 108, 119, 129, 205;
Abigail, 119, 183; Abraham,
183; Amos, 119; Amos Hughes,
154; Ann, 9, 86, 106, 142,
189; Benjamin, 163; Brakey,
19; Catherine, 183; Daniel,
106; David, 3, 6, 60, 108,
119; Edward, 60, 64, 80, 86,
103, 106, 119; Eleanor, 183;
Elizabeth, 3, 163, 170;
Enoch, 213; Evan, 119, 129;
Everard, 6, 8, 86, 106, 113,
119, 187; Fanny, 211; Grace,
163; Henry, 3, 163; Henry
Lymbacker, 42; Isaiah, 183;
Israel, 9, 60, 263; Issac, 9;
James, 103, 111; Jane, 3, 6,
263; Jesse, 47, 258; John, 6,
10, 19, 20, 60, 86, 102, 103,
105, 106, 108, 119, 129, 142,
163, 211, 213, 252, 263;
Jonathan, 6, 142, 163, 211,
263; Joseph, 3, 23, 26, 38,
88, 114, 148, 163, 263;
Judah, 183; Letitia, 9, 105;
Levi, 183; Lewis, 38; Loseph,
60; Lydia, 142; Margaret, 6;
Margery, 3; Martha, 119;
Mary, 3, 6, 38, 60, 103, 142,
163, 182, 240; Mercy, 70;
Miriam, 183; Nathan, 6, 108,

Jacob, 155; James, 21, 111;
Joseph, 111; Joshua, 111;
Lewis, 37, 155, 237; Martin,
155; Mary, 155; Mathew, 83,
111; Matthew, 155; Rebecca,
20, 111; Richard, 111, 155;
Ruth, 49; Samuel, 111
RUFE, Catherine, 248;
Elizabeth, 248; Frederick,
248; George, 248; Jacob, 193,
248, 266; John, 248; Samuel,
248; Sarah, 248; Susanna, 248
RUFF, Christian, 28; Elizabeth,
28; Frederick, 28, 99;
George, 28, 76; Henry, 28;
Jacob, 28
RULE, Christian, 195
RUSH, Andrew, 2; George, 13;
Jacob, 29, 67; Susanna, 190
RUSSELL, Jemima, 183; Thomas,
183
RUTE, Henry, 140; James, 140;
Peter, 159
RUTENANER, Ann Mary, 62;
Christian, 62; Christopher,
62; Elizabeth, 62; Eva, 62;
George, 62; Henry, 62; John,
62; John Adam, 62; Samuel,
62; Susannah, 62
RUTH, Abraham, 252; Ann, 124;
Anne, 252; Christian, 252;
David, 97, 124, 157, 252;
Elizabeth, 140, 252; George,
184; Henry, 124; Isaac, 140;
Jacob, 252; John, 124, 158,
179; Mary, 95
RUTHERFORD, Elizabeth, 209
RYAN, Daniel, 59; Elizabeth,
59; Isaac, 59, 85, 183;
Modake, 59; William, 59, 246,
254, 257
RYER, Abraham, 109
RYMOND, Anna Margaretta, 126;
Catharina, 126; Elizabeth,
126; Jacob, 124, 126, 184;
John, 126; Margarette, 126;
Michael, 126; Paul, 126
RYNEAL, Elizabeth, 142

-S-
SACKETT, Clauche, 66;
Elizabeth, 66; Joseph, 66,
114; Rachel, 66; Rebecca, 66;
Sarah, 66; Simon, 66
SACKS, Adam, 94; Christopher,
10; Elizabeth, 94; Martin, 94
SAFELCOOL, William, 200
SAGER, John, 141
SAMPLE, Ann, 98; James, 10;
John, 10; Margaret, 10;
Robert, 10, 67; William, 67

SAMS, Mary, 209; Mercy, 209
SAMSEL, Anne Mary, 2; Theobald,
2
SAMSELL, Abraham, 76; Hannah,
76; Paul, 76
SANDERS, Elizabeth, 30
SANDHAM, Mathias, 162; Rebecca,
162; Rebekah, 166
SANDS, John, 65; Thomas, 182
SARGENT, Thomas, 221
SATTERTHWAITE, Giles, 182, 194;
Mary, 74; Michael, 73;
Pleasant, 15; William, 15,
21, 41, 54, 56, 71, 73, 74,
92, 235
SAUCERMAN, Catherine, 92;
Jacob, 92
SAULENER, Frederick, 215
SAVECOOL, Isaac, 77
SAVERY, Thomas, 143
SAVITZ, George, 13
SAVOY, Thomas, 233
SAX, Elizabeth, 35; Martin, 35;
Mary, 35; Stophel, 35
SAXTON, Daniel, 146
SCARBOROUGH, Amy, 198; Ann, 74,
86; Enos, 182; Isaac, 173,
222; Jane, 21, 44; John, 173;
Joseph, 173; Rachel, 174;
Robert, 173
SCATTERGOOD, David, 253
SCHAEFER, Daniel, 89
SCHAEN, Casper, 89
SCHEETZ, George, 254
SCHLEIFFER, Abraham, 177; Ann,
177; Jacob, 7
SCHLICHTER, Andrew, 22, 77,
220; Henry, 161, 240
SCHLIFER, Daniel, 253;
Elizabeth, 253; Esther, 253;
John, 253; Joseph, 253; Mary,
253
SCHLOCK, Mary, 51
SCHNEIDER, Catherine, 115;
Christian, 115; Conrad, 115;
Hannah, 115; Jacob, 115;
Mary, 115; Michael, 115;
Rebecka, 115
SCHNIDER, Adam, 62
SCHOCH, Rudolph, 255
SCHOEN, Casper, 121, 125
SCHOFIELD, Ann, 33; Benjamin,
33, 60, 86; David, 33; Edith,
33; John, 33, 86; Jonathan,
33, 37, 189; Martha, 143;
Phebe, 86; Rebecca, 86;
Samuel, 33, 86, 166; Thomas,
33
SCHOLL, George, 141
SCHONTZ, Abraham, 55
SCHOOLEY, Azaliah, 174

Mathias, 25; Peter, 8, 22
SHNIDER, Ann, 80
SHNYDER, George, 66
SHOCK, Rudolph, 100
SHOEMAKER, Conrad, 157; Isaac,
151; Jacob, 54, 170, 249;
Jonathan, 248, 249; Mercy,
170, 213, 248; Michael, 45,
89, 182, 210; Richard M.,
247; Samuel, 29; Tacy, 265;
Thomas, 42, 247
SHOLL, Elizabeth, 83, 251;
Michael, 83; Peter, 83
SHOOP, Jacob, 77
SHOPP, John, 139
SHOUT (STOUT?), Abraham, 17
SHOWALTER, Jacob, 47
SHRAGER, John, 222
SHREIGLY, Mary, 59
SHRINER, Adam, 6
SHRISON, Elijah, 16
SHRIVER, Philip, 260
SHROGER, John, 143, 225
SHROYER, Mary, 250; Philip, 250
SHRYER, Philip, 15
SHUCK, Jacob, 76
SHULER, Elizabeth, 43
SHULL, Barbara, 76; Catherine,
48; Elias, 48, 251;
Frederick, 239; George, 120;
Hanna, 239; Peter, 76
SHUMAN, Arnold, 29; Peter, 180
SHUMON, Elizabeth, 225; Henry,
225; Jacob, 225; Joseph, 225;
Peter, 225
SHURE, Amy, 176
SICKLE, John, 130
SIEGFRIED, George, 94, 206;
Sarah, 94, 206
SILBY, Joseph, 72
SILFUSE (TILFUSE?), Abraham, 70
SILVER, David, 34
SILVERS, Catherine, 39; James,
39
SILVERTHORN, Thomas, 122
SILVEUES, Henry, 79; John, 79;
Mary, 79
SILVIUS, Abraham, 89;
Catherine, 89; Henry, 89;
Isaac, 89; Jacob, 89; John,
89; Joseph, 89; William, 89
SIMMONS, Henry, 119, 120; John,
120, 146; Joseph, 120; Mary,
28; Mordecai, 120; Sarah,
119, 120; Thomas, 120;
William, 119, 120, 190, 239
SIMMS, Jacob, 250
SIMPSON, Agnes, 185; Andrew,
207; Ann, 52; Anna, 42;
Brita, 42; Britta, 52; David,
155, 183, 257; Elizabeth, 42,

47, 52, 91; Emily, 207;
George, 207; Hannah, 148,
230; Isabel, 47; James, 4,
155, 175, 207; Jane, 47;
John, 47, 52, 95, 103, 151,
155, 207, 218, 230, 257;
Martha, 42; Mary, 46, 47,
148, 207; Mathew, 207;
Rebecca, 148; Robert, 103,
207; Samuel, 148; Sarah, 47,
148; Thomas, 47, 207;
William, 47, 95, 207
SIMS, Robert, 220; Walter, 58
SINFRAS, William, 9
SINGE, Ann Mary, 165; Caty,
165; John, 165; Juliana, 165;
Solomon, 165; William, 165;
Willimina, 165
SINGLEY, Agnes, 181; Andrew,
181, 242; Hannah, 247;
Jemima, 181; John, 181, 247;
Joseph, 181; Mary, 181;
Sarah, 247
SINGMASTER, Adam, 169;
Christina, 169; Daniel, 169;
Elizabeth, 169; George, 169;
Jacob, 169; Molly, 169;
Philip, 169, 215
SIPLE, George, 101
SIPLER, David, 239; George,
239; Jacob, 239; Philip, 239;
Samuel, 239; Simon, 239
SIRLOCK, James, 49
SIRRELL, Deborah, 100
SISEM, Jane, 49
SISOM, Jane, 72; John, 72;
Joseph, 72; Martha, 72; Mary,
72; William, 72, 83, 128,
166, 264
SITZMAN, Susanna, 24
SKELTON, John, 45, 58, 59, 102,
202; Joseph, 35, 83, 145;
Mary, 49; Robert, 59; Sarah,
58, 194; William, 59
SKILLMAN, Rachel, 94
SKINNER, Ann, 266; Elizabeth,
52, 136; Mary, 237; Rulin,
136
SLACK, Abraham, 91, 172; Alice,
172; Cornelius, 2, 82, 91,
104, 191; Henry P., 234;
James, 91, 172; Jane, 263;
John, 2, 155, 173; Joseph, 2,
178; Martha, 32, 91, 191;
Mary, 234; Noah, 2; Philip,
2; Thomas, 2; Timothy, 2;
William, 178
SLAUGHT, Margaret, 199
SLAUGHTER, Christian, 115
SLEIFFER, Jacob, 126, 159
SLIFER, John, 140

Sarah, 179; William, 179
SOLADAY, Benjamin, 57
SOLADY, Elizabeth, 146; John, 146
SOLLADA, Daniel, 210
SOLLADAY, Daniel, 252; Peter, 172
SOLLIDAY, Benjamin, 226; Catherine, 103; Henry, 103; Jacob, 258; Margaret, 226
SOMMER, John, 260
SOMP, Henry, 40; John, 40
SORVER, David, 109, 116, 182; John, 101, 168
SOTCHER, Hannah, 48; John, 20, 21, 32, 42, 49, 85
SOUDER, Christian, 19; Mary, 19
SOUDERS, Abraham, 202; Anna, 203; Catherine, 202; Christian, 202, 203; Elizabeth, 203; Issac, 202, 203; John, 203; Mary Catherine, 203
SOUTH, Thomas, 121
SOUX, Andrew, 89
SPANKENBERG, John, 28
SPARVENBERG, John, 15
SPEAKMAN, Catherine, 64; Esther, 128; Joseph, 96; Phebe, 33; Rachel, 143; William, 97
SPEAR, Elizabeth, 50
SPENCER, Amos, 149; Esther, 197; Hellena, 103; James, 20; Jane, 100; John, 62, 90, 159; Mahlon, 5; Margaret, 62; Mary, 149; Samuel, 14, 16, 17, 62; Sarah, 5; Thomas, 20, 23, 62, 149, 197; William, 149
SPINNER, Catherine, 176; David, 25, 70, 94, 120, 132, 134, 149, 151, 155, 164, 176, 185, 203, 205
SPINSER, George, 265
STAATES, Abraham, 194
STACKHOUSE, Benjamin, 32; Cassandra, 179; Charles, 69, 145; Daniel, 145; David, 12; Elizabeth, 145; Grace, 123, 213; Hannah, 100; Isaac, 20, 38, 123, 257; Job, 100, 143; John, 38, 87, 123; Jonathan, 38, 123; Letitia, 145; Marcy, 123; Martha, 82, 87, 231; Mary, 87, 232; Moses, 100; Rachel, 87; Rebecca, 145; Rebekah, 49; Samuel, 134, 145; Sarah, 32, 87, 92, 112, 145; Thomas, 38, 145, 187; William, 49, 145, 205

STAGNER, Christian, 190; Elias, 190; Henry, 190; Lewis, 190; Louise, 190; Mary, 190
STAHLNECKER, Andrew, 159
STAHR, John, 203
STALEY, Catherine, 227; Joseph, 227
STALFORD, Thomas, 7
STALL, Christian, 8
STAM, Margid, 109
STANBURY, Abraham Ogier, 91; Martha, 91
STANLEY, Lydia, 236
STAPLER, Acsah, 257; Charles, 143, 257; Christiana, 257; Esther, 143, 257; Hannah, 257; John, 15, 18, 97, 142, 143, 181, 257; Joseph, 189; Mary, 189, 257; Rachel, 257; Sarah, 143, 232, 257; Stephen, 143; Thomas, 143, 257; William, 143
STAR, Andrew, 175; John, 82; Mary, 82
STARKEY, Mary, 253
STARKY, Thomas, 107
STARLING, Nancy, 199
STARNER, Jacob, 182
STARR, Anna, 149; Conrad, 51, 149; Elizabeth, 51, 149; Hannah, 149; Jacob, 149; John, 51, 149; Mary, 149; Samuel, 149; Susanna, 51, 149
STATES, Abraham, 233; Bridget, 266; Daniel, 233, 258; Juliana, 216; Peter, 216, 233
STATS, Andrew, 51; Issac, 51; James, 51; Mary, 51; Peter, 52
STAUFFER, Anna, 255; Catherine, 255; Christian, 255; David, 255
STEEL, Elizabeth, 77; James, 32; John, 77
STEER, Andrew, 44; Catherine, 267; Christiana, 45; Eve, 44; Joseph, 267; Margaret, 45; Nicholas, 44; Sebastian, 44
STEGNER, Lewis, 190
STEIN, Christian, 33; Maria Catherina, 33; Philip, 33
STELLE, Anna B., 211; Charles, 211; Edward T., 211; Isaac, 211; James Madison, 211; John A., 211; Joseph W., 211; Mary, 211; Samuel, 211; William N., 211
STEM, David, 210; Salome, 257
STEPHENS, Ann, 170; Benjamin, 122; David, 122, 217; Garret, 170; Isaac, 122; Jane, 170;

SWARTZ, Andrew, 132; Catherine, 132; Christian, 143, 163; Elizabeth, 143; Eve, 210; Jacob, 103, 132, 248; James, 86; Jannakey, 87; Joseph, 132; Margaret, 103; Michael, 132; Nicholas, 132, 192, 199, 210; Sophia, 132; Susanna, 132, 210; Thomas, 132
SWARTZLANDER, Catherine, 177, 257; David, 257; Jacob, 114, 257; Joseph, 257; Margaret, 257; Salome, 257
SWEETMAN, Kesiah, 21
SWENKER, George, 27
SWIFT, Charles, 40, 41, 172; John, 37, 120, 220; Magdalena, 41; Mary, 41, 172, 186, 264; Robert E. G., 172; Sarah, 41; Thomas Riche, 41; William F., 260
SWINKER, George, 126
SWINNEY, James, 67; Rebecca, 67
SWISE, John, 139; Margaret, 139
SWITZER, Adam, 71; Anna, 114; Barbara, 114; Conrad, 114; Henry, 114; Lewis, 114; Ludwick, 7; Simon, 114; Valentine, 114
SWOPE, Catherine, 203; Elizabeth, 203; George, 203; John, 48, 203; Magdalen, 203; Magdalene, 48, 203; Margaret, 203; Mary, 203; William, 203

-T-

TAGGART, David, 100, 133; Helena, 105, 108
TATE, Anthony, 37; Elizabeth, 168; James, 168, 217; Jane, 168; Margareta, 217; Margaretta, 168
TAYLOR, Abraham, 7, 21, 28, 44, 51, 64, 133, 149, 160, 173, 208, 223, 265; Alice, 206; Ann, 86, 91; Anna, 223; Anthony, 141, 239, 263; Banner, 18; Barnard, 21, 22; Benjamin, 5, 22, 27, 63, 109, 119, 236; Bernard, 18, 21, 22; Catherine, 265; David, 265; David B., 236; Elizabeth, 30, 43, 119, 170, 223, 230; George, 224; Hannah, 5, 18, 21; Henry, 265; Jacob, 220, 265; James, 174; Jemima, 18; John, 18, 21; Joseph, 15, 18, 21, 63, 82, 130, 141, 178, 199, 206, 224, 243, 265; Letitia, 22; Lewis, 91; Mahlon, 22, 141;

Mary, 21, 22, 141; Mercey, 243; Mercy, 18, 21; Mercy (Mary?), 18; Peter, 18, 21; Samuel, 265; Sarah, 18, 21, 91, 230, 243; Thomas, 144; Timothy, 22; Veronica, 223; William, 18, 21, 97, 173, 181, 191, 199
TEATE, Anthony, 217; Sarah, 217
TEATERLY, Michael, 1
TEICHLER, Jacob, 184
TEMPLE, Rachel, 41
TEMPLETON, Elizabeth, 117; James, 104
TENNIS, Rebekah, 131; William, 131
TERRY, Benjamin, 109; Charles, 25, 152, 165; Daniel, 109; David, 109; Elizabeth, 109; Esther, 109; Grace, 109; Jane, 109; Jasper, 109, 110; John, 2, 5, 8, 20, 25, 33, 58, 95, 99, 109, 115, 126, 207, 212, 253, 64; Joseph, 25, 109; Joshua, 33; Levi, 33; Lucy, 109; Martha, 109; Mary, 25; Rachel, 25, 109; Ralph, 109; Ruth, 64; Sarah, 25; Susanna, 109; Thomas, 109; William, 25
TERY, Susanna, 81
TETHRO, Catherine, 118; Elizabeth, 118; Zachariah, 118
THACKERAY, Amos, 66; Sarah, 66
THACKERY, Phineas, 55; Sarah, 82
THACKRAY, Amos, 50, 155; Ezer, 155; Isaac, 155; James, 50; Joseph, 155; Joshua, 50, 155; Phin, 137; Phineas, 50, 155; Rebecca, 155; Ruth, 155; Sarah, 155
THANY, Philip, 11
THATCHER, Jonas, 261; Samuel, 261; Sarah Ann, 261
THAWMAN, Martha, 69
THERRY, Elizabeth, 72
THICK, Michael, 68
THILLUSSON, Peter, 72
THOMAS, Abel, 43; Abia, 216; Abner, 154, 192; Absalom, 110; Alice, 125; Amos, 25, 27, 43, 192; Amy, 241; Ann, 216; Anna, 43; Arthur, 91, 183; Asa, 43, 60; Azael, 73; Benjamin, 6, 12, 57; Catherine, 183; Daniel, 110, 145; David, 6, 12, 13, 17, 62, 71, 94, 101, 160; Dinah, 89; Eber, 88, 216; Edward,

ULMER, Peter, 48
UNDERCUFLER, Magdalena, 18
UPDEGRAVE, Edward, 147
URICH, George, 248
URINNER (WINNER?), Rebecca, 21
URIR, Ann, 2; Hendrey, 2; Jean,
2; Jeane, 2; Margaret, 2;
Robert, 2; Samuel, 2

-V-
VALENTINE, Elizabeth, 200
VAN BOORSKIRK, Mahlon, 39
VAN ETTER, Johannes, 2
VAN HORN, Isaac, 16; Mary, 16;
Rebecca, 16
VAN HORNE, Isaac, 55; Isaiah,
48; Peter, 49; William, 7
VAN KIRK, Barnit, 54
VAN PELT, Sarah, 59; Susanna, 3
VANADA, Mary, 3; Thomas, 3
VANARSDALE, Jacob, 102; Simon,
105
VANARSDALEN, Christopher, 170;
Else, 4; Nicholas, 12, 20;
Phebe, 170; Rebecca, 82;
Rebekah, 191; Simon, 20
VANARTSDALEN, Ann, 209;
Catherine, 249; Christopher,
105, 257; Derrick, 141; Elce,
141; Elizabeth, 233; Garret,
161, 248, 258; Henry, 249;
Jacob, 141; James, 196; Jane,
170, 249; Jean, 135; John,
141, 209, 257; Joseph, 240;
Simon, 96, 135, 141
VANCE, Agnes, 63; Elizabeth,
63; James, 208
VANCHUPER, Samuel, 233
VANDEGRIFT, Aaron, 16; Abraham,
4, 16, 52, 80, 237, 262;
Amos, 16; Anna, 155; Anne,
53; Barnard, 42; Benjamin,
53; Bernard, 106; Bernard,
Catherine, 176, 237; Charity,
16; Cornelia, 141; Cornelius,
4; David, 80, 106; Eleanor,
176; Elinor, 4; Elizabeth,
53, 167; Folkard, 53;
Folkert, 167; Fulkhart, 4;
George, 4; Harman, 4; Henry,
52; Jacob, 16, 53, 80, 106,
167; John, 4, 23, 42, 80,
106, 155, 160, 189; Jonathan,
23; Joseph, 16; Joshua, 53;
Josiah, 16; Leonard, 16, 52,
53; Mary, 53, 253; Rachel,
52; Rebecca, 16; Sarah, 80;
Susanna, 237; Thomas, 16;
William, 80, 106, 187
VANDERBELT, Aaron, 164; Aron,
48; Cherity (sic), 164;

Egnes, 164; Hannah, 229;
Jacob, 164, 229; Peter, 164
VANDUREN, Barnard, 29; Jacob,
30; Susanna, 30
VANDYCKE, John, 160
VANDYKE, Abraham, 168; Elshe,
227; John, 168; Jonathan,
152; Joseph, 151; Lambert,
151; Mary, 168; Sarah, 247
VANFASSEN, Elizabeth, 24; John,
24
VANHART, Adam, 78; Elizabeth,
78; Jacob, 78, 92, 186;
James, 78, 87; Jane, 78;
Michael, 145; Pamela, 145;
Sarah, 87
VANHORN, Aaron, 191; Abraham,
41, 191; Alexandra, 241;
Amasa, 169; Amos A., 218;
Andrew, 164, 205, 241, 267;
Ann, 86; Anna, 100, 241;
Barnard, 41, 87; Barnet, 24,
86, 135, 164, 169; Benjamin,
250; Bernard, 205; Catherine,
41, 174, 218; Charles, 198;
Cornelius, 154, 169, 174,
218; David, 39, 83, 191;
Elenor, 241; Elizabeth, 78,
191, 216; Gabriel, 20;
Garret, 86, 128; Henry, 31,
253; Isaac, 24, 41, 55, 69,
90, 94, 133, 169, 205;
Israel, 20, 198; Jacob, 20,
38; Jemima, 86; Jesse, 201;
John, 20, 41, 55, 86, 128,
201, 216, 217; Jonathan, 71;
Joseph, 39, 83; Joshua, 20,
128; Juliann, 174, 218;
Lydia, 241; Margaret, 170;
Martha, 20, 174; Mary, 94,
128, 164, 174, 190, 191, 205,
218; Mary Ann, 198; Mercy,
253; Mercy Elizabeth, 253;
Peter, 20, 33, 128; Rachel,
24, 201; Rebecca, 94; Robert,
191; Sarah, 241, 267;
Susanna, 31; Uriah, 198;
William, 24, 41, 191, 198,
205, 216; William Bennet,
174, 218
VANKIRK, Agnes, 59; Elizabeth,
124; John, 62
VANORTSDALEN, Christopher, 110;
James, 110; John, 110;
Nicholas, 110; Rebecca, 110;
Simon, 110
VANOSTIN, Rachel, 168
VANPELT, Charity, 7; Daniel,
114; Elizabeth, 114; Richard,
7
VANSANAT, Amelia, 162; John,

Rachel, 18; Ruth, 83; Samuel, 221; Sarah, 83, 85, 134, 186, 261; William, 31, 35, 39, 164
WHITEACRE, Robert, 27
WHITEHEAD, R., 52
WHITESIDES, Agnes, 214; William, 214
WHITSON, David, 174; Mary, 174; Sarah, 174
WHITTINGHAM, Betzey, 213; Rebecca, 213; William, 121, 153, 168, 213, 214
WHITTON, Elizabeth, 42
WICKART, Abraham, 228; Barbara, 228; Christian, 228; Elizabeth, 228; John, 228; Leonard, 228; Mary, 228; Michael, 228
WIDIMER, Daniel, 204
WIDNER, Adehit, 70
WIER, Ann, 89; James, 234; John, 89, 181, 219; Margaret, 200; Mary, 89; Robert, 89, 200; Thomas, 181
WIERBACK, Jacob, 184
WIERMAN, Henry, 89, 220
WIERNER, Philip, 164
WIESEL, Michael, 241
WIGDON, Elizabeth, 77; Jane, 77; Samuel, 77
WIGGINS, Agnes, 99; Benjamin, 35, 47, 136, 155, 185; Bezaleel, 47; Cuthbert, 47; Hannah, 165; Isaac, 34, 47; Joseph, 155, 185, 230; Phebe, 34; Rachel, 99; Sarah, 37, 99, 185
WIGTON, Ann, 260; Christopher, 163; Elizabeth, 163, 227, 260; James, 227; John, 227, 260; Margaret, 163; Mary, 163, 227, 260; Nancy, 163; Samuel, 19, 67, 163, 183; William, 227, 260
WIKER, Rachel, 99
WILAON, Benjamin, 136
WILARD, Margaret, 170
WILCOX, Margaret, 191
WILCOXE, John, 60; Jonathan, 60; Margaret, 82; Sarah, 60
WILDMAN, Abigail, 137, 146; Ann, 146; Elias, 175; Elizabeth, 137, 141, 200; Hannah, 31; James, 47, 73, 75, 82, 100, 200, 230, 242; John, 47, 137, 147, 175, 200; Joseph, 137, 146; Margaret, 167; Martin, 47, 137, 143, 146; Mary, 99, 147, 200; Rachel, 75, 137; Sarah, 104, 167; Solomon, 105, 137, 146;

Thomas, 137, 146, 147; William, 137, 146, 175
WILDONGER, Catherine, 203; Elizabeth, 203; Jacob, 128; Mary, 203; Samuel, 203
WILES, Aaron, 106
WILEY, Cyrus, 228; David, 161; Joseph, 228; Margaret, 47; Susanna, 161
WILFINGER, Frederick, 110
WILGUS, John, 206; Richard, 25, 180, 206; Tacey, 206
WILHELM, Ave, 70; Catherine, 70; Henry, 70
WILKELM, Catheren, 15; Eve, 15
WILKINSON, Abraham, 85, 192; Ann, 2, 8, 35, 98, 201; Anne, 225; Eleanor, 192; Elisha, 2, 8, 35, 126, 256; Elizabeth, 2, 71; Hannah, 2, 8, 35; Ichabod, 26; Jane, 192; John, 30, 192; John C., 192; Jonathan, 66, 71; Joseph, 2, 21, 66, 86, 198; Martha, 2, 8, 35; Mary, 2, 85, 192; Samuel T., 192; Sarah, 2, 26, 74, 86; Stephen, 2, 8; Tamer, 2; William, 71
WILLARD, Hetty, 191; Isaac, 191; Jacob, 146; John, 258; Joseph, 187; Lewis, 244; Sarah, 187; Susan, 124; William, 191
WILLAUER (WILLANER?), Christian, 32
WILLET, Augustine, 40, 41; Elizabeth, 41; Euphemia, 41; George, 183, 257; Gilbert, 183; Horatio Gates, 41; Jonathan, 6; Margaret, 41; Martha, 182; Mary, 39; Phineas, 183; Sarah, 41; Thomas, 183; Walter, 183
WILLETT, Augustine, 11, 266; Deborah, 107; Elizabeth, 266; Euphemia, 266; Grace, 266; John, 107; Jonathan, 107; Joseph, 266; Lydia, 266; Margaret, 266; Mary, 266; Obadiah, 107; Obediah, 219; Samuel, 107; Sarah, 266; Walter, 107
WILLIAMS, Ann, 123; Anne, 136; Anthony, 3, 187; Barbara, 106; Benjamin, 101, 104, 120, 131, 136, 137, 218; Charles, 138; Christina, 106; David, 123, 207, 230; Eleanor, 154, 192, 201; Elenor, 120; Elizabeth, 43, 106, 131; Em., 5; Enoch, 32; Ester, 106;

338

Frederick, 136; Hannah, 207,
230; Hester, 217; Isaac, 36,
43, 101, 131; Jane, 123;
Jeremiah, 28, 137, 193; John,
123, 126, 131, 136, 193;
Joseph, 3, 123, 131; Luke,
21; Margaret, 36, 59; Maria,
201; Marsa, 3; Martha, 21;
Mary, 3, 28, 91, 123, 136,
218; Nathan, 3; Rachel, 106,
123; Ruth, 206; Samuel, 136,
137; Sarah, 123, 154; Sarah
Ann, 201; Susanna, 123;
Thomas, 131, 201; Thomas B.,
244; William, 66, 83, 106,
123, 131, 136, 137
WILLIAMSON, Elizabeth, 141;
Jesse, 252; Mahlon, 85, 252;
Peter, 65, 85, 252
WILLIARD, Elizabeth, 44;
Jonathan, 44
WILMINGTON, Katherine, 30
WILSON, Agnes, 95; Alexander,
39; Amos, 105; Andrew, 32,
185, 244, 256; Ann, 8, 80;
Asa, 121; Benjamin, 4, 95;
Betsy, 151; David, 14, 27,
32, 95, 121, 138, 158; Dr.,
145; Edward, 15, 88; Eli,
246; Elizabeth, 39, 105, 158,
209, 215; Francis, 27, 32,
185, 244; Francis A., 185;
Francis Armstrong, 256;
George, 256; Hampton, 103,
183; Hamton, 1; Hannah, 49,
121, 261; Henry, 116; Hester,
217; Isaac, 14, 79, 88, 108,
153, 253; Jacob, 121; James,
39, 185, 217, 244, 254; James
Y., 256; Jane, 27, 80, 86,
151; Jesse, 105; John, 14,
15, 27, 32, 67, 75, 78, 92,
95, 103, 105, 115, 122, 138,
151, 154, 158, 174, 185, 209,
223, 246, 252; John Grier,
256; Jonathan, 121; Joseph,
4, 95, 105, 244; Joseph G.,
256; Joshua, 121; Josia, 228;
Judith, 32; Juliann, 185;
Magdaline, 228; Margaret, 4,
20, 95, 138, 223, 226;
Martha, 27, 32, 91, 95, 209,
244, 256; Mary, 27, 32, 77,
151, 185, 241; Mary Ann, 27,
32, 185, 248; Mercy, 136;
Moses, 86, 125, 265; Naomi,
32; Oliver, 14, 209; Polly,
151; Rachel, 105, 121, 209;
Ralph, 32; Rebecca, 27, 209;
Rebekah, 15, 91; Robert, 32,
254; Sally, 151; Samuel, 14,

27, 32, 175, 209; Sarah, 14,
15, 20, 30, 91, 121, 137,
158, 209, 236; Stephen, 14,
91, 154, 209; Susanna Grier,
256; Tacy, 80; Thomas, 3, 14,
20, 50, 94, 95, 105, 121,
138; William, 32, 39, 77,
185, 256
WIMER, Henry, 71; Thomas, 217
WIMMER, Philip, 135
WINDER, Aaron, 4, 15, 229;
Elizabeth, 4, 80; Giles S.,
194; James, 15; John, 15;
John B., 242; Joseph, 4, 212;
Mary, 4, 212, 229; Moses, 15;
Rachel, 212; Rebecca, 4, 15,
212, 229, 264; Samuel, 194;
Sarah, 194, 229; Thomas, 2,
4, 212
WINEBERGER, John, 170
WINER (URINER?), Abraham, 92
WINNER, Abraham, 80; David, 33;
Job, 252; John, 33, 65;
Joseph, 104; Joshua, 33;
Maricha, 127; Mary, 33;
Samuel, 33; Stephen, 127
WIREBACK, Anna, 109; Elizabeth,
188; Henry, 109; Isaac, 109;
Jacob, 109; Peter, 109
WIREMAN, Catherine, 95;
Christian, 96; John, 95, 222;
Mary, 222; Nancy, 222
WIRTZ, Mary H., 194
WISE, Anna Mary, 151; Ellnor
Mary, 244; George, 151, 244;
Jacob, 265; Martha, 265
WISEL, George, 91; Jacob, 91;
Joseph, 91; Mary, 91; Peter,
91; Sarah, 91
WISELL, George, 56; Henry, 56;
Michael, 56
WISEMER, Jacob, 179; Joseph,
179
WISENER, Mary, 98
WISER, Elizabeth, 187; Joshua,
187; Sarah, 187
WISHART, Ann, 123; Thomas, 123;
William, 123
WISME, Henry, 24
WISMER, Abraham, 1, 90, 140,
174, 239; Barbara, 140;
Henry, 6, 80, 84, 140, 162,
228; Jacob, 1, 140; John,
140; Joseph, 262; Margaret,
1; Mary, 115; Nancy, 140;
Samuel, 140, 260; Sarah, 239
WISNER, Abraham, 250; Barbara,
251; Deborah, 76; Elizabeth,
251; George, 76; Hannah, 251;
Henry, 2, 132; Isaac, 76;
Mad..., 250; Margaret, 251;

340

217; Mitchell, 235; Moses,
105; Nathan, 160; Rachel, 70,
161; Robert, 79; Samuel, 32,
33, 136, 141, 263, 264;
Sarah, 161, 217, 235; Seth,
176; Sidney, 160, 161;
Solomon, 70, 160, 161;
Stephen, 141, 264; Thomas,
28; Timothy, 235
WRIGTON, John, 116
WYKER, Abraham, 131, 159, 203;
Anthony, 159; Antony, 131;
Catharina, 131; Dina, 131;
Elizabeth, 131; George, 111,
126, 131, 158, 159, 193, 252;
Henry, 126, 131, 159; Mary,
131; Nicholas, 131, 159;
Susanna, 159; Susannah, 131
WYLER, George, 124
WYNBERGER, Baltzer, 231, 234
WYNKOOP, Ann, 174, 220, 250;
Catherine, 161, 229; David,
105, 108, 133, 161; Fanny,
201; Francis M., 201; Garret,
161, 250; Gerardus, 4, 31,
42, 100, 161; Henry, 17, 31,
43, 100, 105, 108, 133, 160,
194, 217; Isaac, 161; James,
161; John, 8, 105, 161, 201;
Jonathan, 105, 133, 160, 194,
201; Matthew, 161; Sarah,
143, 217; Thomagina, 232;
William, 161
WYREBACK, Henry, 184
WYSEL, George, 212

-Y-
YARDLEY, Amos, 242; Benjamin,
228; Charles, 228; Elizabeth,
87; Enos, 220, 242; G., 234;
Hannah, 105, 205, 232, 242;
John, 87, 257; Joseph, 24,
109, 229; Joshua, 242; Lucy,
24; Lydia, 228; Mahlon, 257;
Rachel, 75; Richard, 75;
Saeah, 242; Samuel, 24, 109,
228; Samuel T., 109; Thomas,
96, 205, 211, 229, 234, 257
YARDLY, John, 170; Mahlon, 170;
Thomas, 170, 217; William,
170
YARDNELL, Ellis, 123
YEARKES, Sarah, 61
YEARLING, Jacob, 77; Magdalena,
77; Susanna, 77
YELLERS, Henry, 174
YERKERS, Harman, 29
YERKES, Alice, 252; Andrew,
164; Edward, 252; Edwin, 267;
Harman, 3, 152, 164, 252;
John, 252; Josiah, 50;

Letitia, 164; Margaret, 164;
Mary, 3; Molly, 252; Stephen,
252; William, 164, 252
YHOST, Catherine, 66; John, 66
YILLINGHAM, John, 45
YOCUM, Hannah, 243; Joseph, 243
YODDER, Jacob, 19
YODER, Abraham, 26, 44, 49,
159, 182; Barbara, 182;
David, 182; Henry, 182;
Jacob, 7; John, 89, 182;
Mary, 89, 182; Samuel, 182
YOLLR(?), Abraham, 44
YOST, Catherine, 224;
Elizabeth, 224; Han, 11;
Hanus, 110; John, 252; Manus,
224; Margreth, 224; Mary,
224; Michael, 170, 218;
Sarah, 224, 252
YOTHER, Jacob, 103
YOUNG, Anna, 1; Elizabeth, 218;
Jacob, 68; Johannes, 27;
John, 28; Kathren, 125;
Margaret, 73; Mary, 38;
Michael, 125, 153; Samuel,
179, 250; William, 1, 14, 254
YOUNGKEN, Abraham, 131;
Catherine, 12; Elizabeth, 12,
121, 131; Frederick, 12;
Henry, 12; Jacob, 12; John,
12, 68; Mary, 131; Nicholas,
223; P. L., 223; Rudolf, 12;
Rudolph, 121
YOUNGKIN, Abraham, 16; Daniel,
16; Eve, 16; George, 16;
Gillion, 16; Harman, 16;
John, 16

-Z-
ZEAGENFUSE, Henry, 184; Nancy,
184
ZEARFOSS, John, 161
ZEBY, Abraham, 43; Anna, 43;
Christian, 44; Hanna, 44;
Peter, 43
ZEGAFOOSE, George, 67; Mattin,
67
ZEGENFUSS, Peter, 252
ZEIGENFUS, John, 148
ZEIGENFUSS, Catherine, 88, 127;
Henry, 88; Peter, 127
ZEIGINFUSS, Abraham, 121; Adam,
121; Catherine, 121;
Christina, 121; Elizabeth,
121; George, 121; Henry, 121;
John, 121; Margaret, 121;
Mary, 121; Mathias, 121;
Peter, 121
ZEIGLER, Samuel, 227
ZELLEFONT, Catherine, 168
ZELLNER, Catherine, 215;